History of Computing
William Aspray and Thomas J. Misa, editors

IBM

The Rise and Fall and Reinvention
of a Global Icon

JAMES W. CORTADA

The MIT Press
Cambridge, Massachusetts
London, England

First MIT Press paperback edition, 2023

© 2019 Massachusetts Institute of Technology

This book was set in Adobe Garamond Pro and Berthold Akzidenz Grotesk by Westchester Publishing Services. Printed and bound in the United States of America.

Library of Congress Cataloging-in-Publication Data

Names: Cortada, James W., author.
Title: IBM : the rise and fall and reinvention of a global icon / James W. Cortada.
Description: Cambridge, MA : The MIT Press, [2019] | Series: History of computing |
    Includes bibliographical references and index.
Identifiers: LCCN 2018023090 | ISBN 9780262039444 (hardcover : alk. paper)
ISBN 9780262547826 (paperback : alk. paper)
Subjects: LCSH: International Business Machines Corporation—History. | Computer
    industry—United States—History.
Classification: LCC HD9696.2.U6 C67 2019 | DDC 338.7/61004—dc23
LC record available at https://lccn.loc.gov/2018023090

10 9 8 7 6 5 4 3 2

To IBMers, customers, and historians
who taught me what I know about IBM

Contents

Preface

Nobody ever lost their job for recommending the purchase of
IBM products.

—COMPUTER INDUSTRY FOLK WISDOM

MORE THAN ANY other company since World War II, IBM has shaped the
way the modern world goes about its business. Large corporations and
governments began to use IBM's products before 1900. Its computers
served as global computing gearboxes for decades before the public "discovered" the Internet in the 1990s. Many of IBM's computers had been
part of the Internet since the early 1970s and part of even older networks
since the 1960s. The U.S. census of 1890 was the first in the world to be
done using automation tools—the punch card—and that too came from
what would come to be IBM. For a long time, the company has been at the
center of much of what makes a modern society function.

By working in conference rooms and data centers for over a century,
IBM made this achievement possible. For that reason, few people outside those two places knew what it did, or how. They just knew that it was
big, important, and usually well run. What they understood was largely
the product of a century-long marketing and public relations campaign
by IBM to manage carefully what we imagine when thinking about the
firm. Its influence proved so powerful for so long that whenever there were
problems at IBM—and there always seemed to be—the information technology world was affected, including the operation of large enterprises and

government agencies, stock markets, and even how national governments armed themselves for global wars.

So what? We live in an increasingly dangerous world, profoundly influenced by computing, so understanding the role of one of the world's most important providers of such technologies is crucial and urgent. We face three problems: ongoing acts of terrorism; a cyberwar involving the United States, Russia, and China but also affecting other countries caught in the crossfire, evidenced by cyberattacks on German elections, Chinese hacking of companies, and Russian influence on the U.S. presidential election in 2016, for example; and a global political and economic environment that is becoming increasingly uncertain as nations flirt with trade restrictions and efforts to keep jobs from migrating to other countries. In the thick of all these conditions, information processing plays a profound role, and in the middle of that role stands a few technology companies, notably IBM. Which would be more important for the security of a nation under a cyber-attack, IBM or Netflix, IBM or Apple? For decades, commercial enterprises and government agencies in the United States and in other nations considered IBM a national treasure.

When the West needed computing for national defense, it turned to IBM. In World War II, IBM provided the Allies with machines to organize national economies for the war effort; in the Cold War, it implemented a national air defense system, assisted in making space travel possible, and did intelligence work. IBM has nearly a century of experience dealing with Russian counterintelligence operations—today's hacking and intelligence operations are not new to it.

We again face a time when many countries need the skills long evident at IBM. Nevertheless, it is a company that has suffered chronic problems, a malaise that while it tries to shake it off leaves open questions about its long-term viability. Understanding what this company is capable of doing begins by appreciating its history. Such insight helps employees, citizens, companies, and entire industries and nations understand what they can do to ensure that IBM is there when they need it. The company is too important to do otherwise. That is what led me to write this book.

IBM is a company that has a century-long history of not being gener-ous in explaining how it interacts with the world. Like most large multi-national corporations, it works to control what the public knows about it, including its global practices. Why, for example, several years ago, was IBM willing to share with China the guts of some of its critical soft-ware in exchange for being allowed to sell in that country? Why does it have a history of also doing confidential work for the U.S. intelligence and military communities? During World War II, when it was a tiny company, the Allies and the Axis used its products. Is IBM as American a company as it was 30 or 50 years ago? With an estimated 75 percent of its workforce now located outside the United States, some tough questions have to be asked. Such national security interests are addressed in this book and head-on in the last chapter, because this company may be one of those too critical to allow to fail.

Business historians, economists, and business management professors have their own concerns as well. Scholars and journalists have studied IBM for decades. Historians are interested in how large corporations func-tion, why they exist for decades, their effects on national economies, and how they influence their own industries. A crucial question raised by IBM's experience is how it became an iconic company yet also experienced periods of severe business crises that nearly killed it. Across all of IBM's history, nearly lethal troubles accompanied its successes. How could that be? What lessons for other firms can IBM's story teach? What can be learned that scholars and managers can apply in their explorations of how other firms flourished, failed, or are floundering? Answering such questions is central to this book.

IBM's influence on our lives is significant, but the company remains little appreciated. Occasionally we hear about it, such as when its stock goes up or down, in the 1980s when it introduced the world to the term "personal computer" and in the process made it now "O.K." for corpo-rations, not just geeks and commercial artists, to use PCs. Did you know that selling computers is now the tiniest piece of IBM's business? Did you know that it is the world's largest software firm, or that it operates in 178 countries? Did you know that it almost went out of business several times, including as recently as 1993? Or that as this book was being written in 2017, observers thought IBM was on a slow march to extinction while still generating billions of dollars in profits each year? It is time to pull aside the veil to see how this fascinating and powerful company was able to thrive for over a century while being both respected and disliked, and to understand what essentially has been its positive impact on the world while at the same time it demonstrated toughness against its enemies and in its constant battle to survive and thrive.

Today IBM functions under ugly storm clouds, but let a blogger friendly to it describe what I mean: "International Business Machines might be the most iconic company in the entire multitrillion-dollar tech industry. For decades, its name was synonymous with technology, to the point where 'IBM' was all but shorthand for computing hardware. Its century-plus history might even make it the oldest tech company in a world where tech titans rise and fall every few years. It's also one of the world's largest tech companies, trailing only a handful of others in the global market-cap rankings." Here is the clincher: "But it's probably bound to be the worst-performing tech stock on the *Dow Jones Industrial Average* for the foreseeable future. High performance isn't a requirement to remain in the Dow, but if IBM can't do something about its flatlining revenue, it might eventually force the Dow's handlers to do the unthinkable and replace it with a more appropriate company."[1] What is going on?

One of the important, little understood findings presented in this book is the profound influence of prior events on what the company does today. Some of its long-serving senior executives are aware, for example, that our grandparents received Social Security payments because of IBM, since nobody else at the time could calculate and print checks quickly enough, or in the millions needed, permanently assisting millions of older Americans out of poverty. Many are aware that IBM could radically define and then build computers that do what one expected of them, thanks to a "bet your company" life-threatening decision in the 1960s that led the majority of the world's large organizations to finally start using computers. IBM employees wrote software and managed its implementation so that humans could go to the moon for the first time and be brought safely back to earth. They are aware that it was IBM's introduction of the PC in 1981, not Apple's introduction of the Macintosh, that led the world to finally embrace this technology by the hundreds of millions. It is a company taking the half-century promise of artificial intelligence and turning it into actions that smartly do things humans cannot do, such as advise a doctor based on all human knowledge of a medical condition or calculate more precise weather forecasts. This is happening now, and IBM is making millions of dollars providing such capabilities. We do not know whether IBM is going to be around in 20 or 100 years, but we do know that it is a large, technologically muscular company in the thick of what is going on with computing. Generations of managers, economists, and professionals, and tens of millions of customers, knew about the role of this company during the twentieth century. Now the rest of us should, too.

The purpose of this book is to introduce a new generation to IBM's role by telling the story of its long history, its culture and values, and, most important, explain how it helped to shape the world in which we live, a process still unfolding. I argue that it is essential to understand its corporate culture, one that academics and reporters found difficult to describe but that they recognized was essential to describe. Published accounts of IBM offer insufficient insights. IBM is also a multinational company operating around the world, so we need to understand its role in international disputes. Is it an American corporation or is it so globalized that only its senior leaders are U.S. citizens? What are the implications for Russia, China, Germany, the United States, the Netherlands, Saudi Arabia, Taiwan, Australia, and so many other countries?

What made IBM iconic included technological prowess, enormous business success, massive visibility, and hundreds of thousands of aggressive, smart, ambitious men and women used to success and always fearful of failure. It was the "IBM Way." For over a half century, it was said no worker ever lost their job for recommending that their firm acquire IBM's products, because those products normally worked. IBMers would make them work, and "everyone" seemed to think IBM was one of the best-run firms in the world. They joked about IBMers as too serious, focused, polished in their presentations, and facile in dealing with all manner of technology. Competitors feared and hated them; customers accepted them as the safe bet.

IBM's iconic role thus left IBMers, their customers, and the public in dozens of countries ill prepared for its near-death experience in the early 1990s. A fired CEO, John F. Akers, almost went into hiding; he never spoke publicly of IBM for the rest of his life. His successor, Louis V. Gerstner Jr., observed the IBM culture as a customer and now had to face a depressed yet combative workforce. He had worked at Nabisco as a turn-around leader and came into IBM as the butt of cookie jokes but with the hope that he could save the firm. He brought the company back to iconic status. Afterward he reported that the biggest problem he faced was IBM's culture, invented by Thomas Watson Sr. and his son Thomas Watson Jr., remade partly by Charlie Chaplin's character the "Little Tramp," and bat-tered by hundreds of competitors, including Steve Jobs at Apple. To any IBM employee, the company always felt small, because it was a firm filled with characters, more a collection of fantastic personalities than a faceless corporation, an ecosystem with its own culture.

IBM's corporate culture is central in understanding much about "Big Blue." That is also a clue for answering a central question about IBM: How is it that a company viewed as so stable and reliable for decades had so many ups and downs over the course of its 130-year history? The com-pany's history from its origins in the 1880s to the 1970s was essentially a story of repeated successes, despite enormous difficulties. By the end of the 1970s, however, the company had entered a new era in which it was now large, difficult to run, and slow to make decisions and to take timely actions, and so its subsequent history took on a very different tone. It continued to grow, shrink, reconfigure itself, grow again, and spin off vast sums of profitable revenue while laying off tens of thousands of employees almost without the public hearing about it. How could that be? Observers had been predicting its demise since the mid-1960s, loudly in the early 1990s, and again after 2012. Yet there it stood as this book was being published: bloodied, anemic, slow to move, and grey around the cultural temples but also vigorous, employing vast numbers of young employees around the world while having shed tens of thousands of older ones, financially sound, and still a major player in one of the world's most important industries. Again, how could that be? Our purpose is to answer that question.

OVERVIEW OF THE BOOK

I provide a history of IBM from its origins to the present. I discuss its sales, marketing, product development, and manufacturing, and its evolution from its U.S. origins into a global enterprise. IBM's history represents a departure from prior accounts of the firm in several ways. Although IBM thrived in most periods, the story I tell is one of intense uncertainty about its success. It always faced competitors, changing technologies, government lawsuits, national economic policies, wars, and those hostile to "big business." This is a tale of constant stress and tension. IBM's future was never certain, its long-term survival a surprise, never inevitable. My history places into broader context topics such as product innovation and managerial practices. It tells the story of individuals who made dramatic contributions to the successes and failures of the firm, its industry, and its customers. I demonstrate that IBM was not some anonymous monolithic entity. It was and is an ecosystem made up of communities, much like a midsize city has neighborhoods and political and social factions. IBM's CEOs were often like mayors: they had to persuade internal factions to do their bidding. They could also be authoritarian and were always demanding. While historians have retreated from earlier notions that individuals profoundly affected affairs—the idea of the great man on horseback—this book demonstrates that they may have gone too far. At IBM, individuals made a difference, authoritarian CEOs (in particular) but also others situated in circumstances that leveraged their experiences, authority, and influence to affect how the company and its customers performed. I also engage in the growing interest in how large firms operate as ecosystems, as communities.

I argue that IBM's presence, prestige, successes, troubles, and failures reflected the behavior of large twentieth-century enterprises that emerged in the United States and Western Europe. IBM became an iconic example of how these enterprises developed and evolved with a heavy American stamp but were also international. Since historians, journalists, and economists have paid inadequate attention to the influence of corporate culture on the evolution of IBM, I describe the firm and its business practices worldwide. I contend that one reason for IBM's importance is that it quickly became a hub for a large ecosystem of business activities. IBM engaged with tens of thousands of companies and hundreds of government agencies for over 13 decades. Its (our) data processing ecosystem included the exchange of information, employees, and business practices. This book gives IBM's customers and government officials a larger role than in previous accounts, because IBM's evolution and accomplishments were shaped by how they interacted with the firm. It succeeded and failed in public, despite the company's wish to keep its operations opaque.

I focus on the roles of management, strategy, and business issues. I include discussions about technologies and products. Scholars, economists, and journalists have insufficiently explored IBM's sales and marketing practices; I do not neglect these practices or the profound role customers played in the success of the firm. I view the combination of various parts of IBM, customers, government officials, and the media as constituting the large, indeed massive, business ecosystem enveloping IBM. This approach promises to transform how we view the role of large enterprises. I end with a discussion of the implications of IBM's current worldwide status.

In solid IBM tradition, this is a book filled with personalities from clock makers in upstate New York to 19-year-old programmers in India, from the first female executive to people with names like "Buck" and "T. V.," and from some geniuses who won Nobel Prizes to others who quickly put the first PCs together, which then dominated their market for years. It discusses how they lived and worked, from not drinking alcohol to a few employees bribing officials in Latin America, from 100-hour workweeks to beautifully executed vacations for the top 1 percent performers. It is the story of over a million employees.

The adjective *iconic* in the title of this book is purposeful. Although the word is used far too loosely, the highly respected editor Harold Evans recently reminded readers that iconic "came to mean a representation of a model of virtue."[2] It is how I mean the word to be read, as IBM was considered a well-run, ethical company. As both a historian and a retired 38-year employee of the company, I argue that IBM's iconic role goes far in explaining its long-lived success, but I also demonstrate that iconic status does not guarantee never-ending success.

SOME ESSENTIAL FINDINGS

IBM was and is in many ways similar to other large globalized corporations, so there are lessons learned by looking at this company's history. Here, briefly, are several.

First and foremost, then and now, corporate culture determines the success and failure of an enterprise. The single most important reason IBM survived for over a century, and usually successfully, was because of a corporate culture that motivated employees to give their all to the success of the firm and to its customers. Once you have a culture, you must nurture, protect, and improve it as the central tool kit containing the guiding principles of management and employee behavior. When IBMers deviated from theirs, they stumbled.

Second, at least in IBM's case, when it honored and nurtured its sales force and its sales culture, it was productive and successful. That statement may sound incredibly obvious. When their values prevailed, IBM did well. But beginning shortly after the new millennium, they did not always prevail. IBM, like many other corporations, in recent years has relied increasingly on what came to be known as "financial engineering" to improve performance. It was never enough to ensure success.

Third, remember the customer pays the bills and determines a company's future. Almost from the beginning at IBM, the customer was king. That did not mean they received whatever they wanted; rather, they obtained whatever they needed. IBMers demonstrated they could fanatically support customers and generate a great deal of revenue for IBM, actually over one trillion dollars over the life of the firm.

Fourth, "shareholder value," the current buzzword, is turning out to be a cancer. Companies succeed when they sell products customers want, when their employees are nurtured, encouraged, and prosper, and when the firm contributes to the overall welfare of society. All three elements must be in play.

Fifth, and perhaps more important than the first four lessons, IBM did well, even fantastically well, when it had its employees' backs. They generated the value of a corporation even more than investors did, so they, too, needed a seat at the table. Employees need to be honored, protected, nourished, paid fairly, and not be treated, to use an ugly, fashionable term, as "resources." They are the company.

Sixth, and crucially for the future of the world, IBM learned how to succeed, indeed coexist, in a globalized economy fraught with political, military, and economic dangers. Its ability to use a common corporate culture tailored to meet local conditions made it relevant to scores of countries, and its use of corporate culture has much to teach other international firms.

These are the six most important lessons learned from exploring the history of IBM and, by extension, the behavior of other successful firms. This book incorporates what a large number of people learned over 130 years.

HOW TO READ THIS BOOK

Since this book is intended for multiple audiences, I purposely wrote it with them in mind. You do not have to read it cover to cover; it can be read in chunks, which is why I organized it into four parts. It is a big book but can also be a small one—you decide. The chapters within a part are integrated, so if you read a chapter, I recommend that you read the others in the same part to get a full picture of what was going on. One audience will be IBMers and industry watchers who want to know what happened recently at IBM and what is happening today. These readers should start with the three chapters in part 4, but for perspective I also recommend reading part 3. Those chapters are analytical and are oriented toward business management. For readers interested in modern business history and how IBM became such a major computer company, part 2 covers that and can be read without starting earlier or going into part 3. Finally, for the serious business, economics, and information technology student, part 1 discusses IBM's origins, the development of its corporate culture, its role in World War II, and so forth. I wrote the book so that one can also read it cover to cover, building on events, ideas, and even language I introduced in earlier chapters as I moved along. The company's history is remarkable, and aspects of a long-ago past still silently influence events inside the company today.

On purpose, I wrote the text using the vocabulary and tone more familiar to business professionals than to scholars, but I engage in issues of interest to both. For business and technology historians, I offer two features. First, as a lifelong employee of the company, I address issues that were of concern to employees, their customers, and their industry in the manner in which IBM employees would but in the way a professional historian could, too. A thesis unfolds that one could apply to the study of other long-lived enterprises: that corporate cultures influence events, social and political dynamics govern decisions and events within a firm, and information ecosystems are useful analytical tools, which have been the subject of a number of other books I have written. What you read in this preface, see throughout the book, and then encounter again in the last chapter present a perspective on the history of this large, multinational corporation.

THE GENESIS OF THIS BOOK

I became an employee of IBM in 1974 and quickly realized that I had joined an iconic enterprise; IBM was constantly ranked as the most or second most highly respected firm at that time. It was the Google or Apple Computer of its day. Over the years, I had access to IBM's archives, which I used in writing earlier books on the history of computing. I incorporate in this book what I learned from that prior research. I also consulted other archival materials held in various academic libraries. The Charles Flint Papers at the New York Public Library, the massive files at the Charles Babbage Institute at the University of Minnesota, and the U.S. National Archives and Records Administration provided answers to thorny questions.

This book represents a journey of discovery about IBM's history that took four decades. I accumulated many debts, but a number are so important that they must be acknowledged. Saul Englebourg wrote the first history of IBM, in 1954. Bob Sobel, who wrote the second modern history of IBM, published in 1981, and Emerson Pugh, who wrote the third, in 1995, shared insights over a long period of time. Before writing my first book that incorporated a major account of the history of IBM, *Before the Computer*, in 1993, Bob walked me through many of the issues he thought I needed to explore. After Emerson wrote his book, I read everything he had written before and asked him questions about technology at IBM. In 2011, Jeff Yost assembled an anthology of historically significant materials on IBM that reminded me of the rich legacy of memoirs and other publications about this company. All three have been friends, colleagues, and influential in shaping my views about IBM. The late Al Chandler and the very much alive Walter Friedman—both historians at the Harvard Business School—spent hours helping me understand how to view business history and then invested years supporting my efforts and answering my questions. Three book editors over the years forced me to defend the importance of IBM: Jack Repcheck at Princeton University Press, and Herb Addison and the late Terry Vaughn, both at Oxford University Press. They taught me how to share my fascination with this company with a large audience.

While colleagues and retirees at IBM encouraged me to write this book over the years, I was particularly moved by the practical advice followed by materials from longtime retired IBMers, including those of two 100-plus-year-old executives, Luis A. Lamassonne, who worked in Latin America, and another, who preferred to remain anonymous. Retired senior vice president Chuck McKittrick, a second-generation IBM executive, just about ordered me to write this book, followed up by sending me materials he and his father had accumulated over a half century, and then patiently answered my many questions. For over four decades, IBM's corporate archivists generously allowed me to study the company's records. In particular, I want to thank Robert E. Pokorak, Paul Lasewicz, and Jamie Martin, and their staffs.

Credit Al Chandler for shaping my initial intellectual worldview about how a business book should be written. British historian Martin Campbell-Kelly sparked my original interest in the business history of computing by writing a corporate biography of ICL, Britain's great computer company, and then a slew of other histories. He provided the intellectual bridge from the grand strategy and big book mantra of an Al Chandler opus to the more tactical question of what a computing business history book should look like. Since the 1980s, Bill Aspray, a prolific author about information technology, has encouraged my work and routinely challenged my first drafts. I am a better historian for what he did. Tom Misa, who I think of as a hardcore historian of technology and steadfast supporter of a rigorous approach to any kind of history, did not destroy my desire to write a less academic history of IBM but instead insisted that my logic and evidence link tightly together. He read every line of this book, rarely leaving a sentence untouched.

Four other students of IBM's history influenced my views about IBM. Lars Heide transformed how historians think about the use of punch card technology in the pre–World War II period, reminding us how difficult and competitive a market that was for IBM and its rivals. Geoffrey D. Austrian, an IBM media expert and longtime editor of the company's internal magazine, *THINK*, wrote the standard book on the life of Herman Hollerith, an early critical protagonist in IBM's history, calling him the "forgotten giant of information processing." His view of Hollerith influenced my view of him to a large extent, while journalist Kevin Maney's magisterial biography of Thomas Watson Sr., ultimately the primary thorn in Hollerith's side, shaped my perspectives on the most important early leaders of IBM. Maney has never received credit for the sheer number of hours of research he had to invest to put that book together. Steven W. Usselman wrote several articles on crucial managerial issues facing IBM in the mid-twentieth century that I relied on to inform me on how to interpret the considerations facing the company's management in those middle years of the 1950s and 1960s. To all four authors, I owe a profound debt of gratitude.

A new generation of historians interested in IBM's role taught me about new issues, reminding me of the continuing interest scholars and others have about IBM. In this category, I thank Petri Paju, who has been mining the company's archives for insights about its role in Europe for over a decade. Gerardo Con Diaz, a young historian who is shedding much new light on the legal issues confronting IBM in the post–World War II period, has influenced my work. Peter E. Greulich, a retired IBMer who is not a historian but is gifted in analyzing IBM's financial performance, educated me on the company's recent performance, grounding me in the harsh realities of modern management practices that might otherwise have been overlooked by financial analysts, business management professors, historians, and me. I owe a broader general thanks to many scores of IBMers who preferred to remain anonymous yet shared their insights, information, and support for this project. Three anonymous reviewers went over and above in their duties to critique the manuscript and suggest improvements. I am deeply grateful to them for a job well done, and even more for what was clearly their solid commitment to help me make this the best book I could write. I want to thank the Charlie Chaplin Estate for permitting us to reproduce the IBM PC advertisement, and also Billy Scudder, the actor who played the role of Charlie Chaplin's "Little Tramp" in IBM's advertisements.

The book's dedication is not gratuitous. I believe it was informed with an insight that could not be extracted from documents and publications but had to come from being in the arena of the daily affairs of IBM and its customers. Unknown to them, but that I appreciated, is that they taught me much about the company. For their advice and support, I am profoundly grateful. The publishing team at MIT Press did much to make this book possible, from my editor, Katie Helke, to Deborah Grahame-Smith in production. I also want to thank the marketing team at MIT.

The views expressed in this book are my own and do not necessarily reflect those of my publisher or IBM. This book was not sponsored or supported by IBM, another quirk of its culture being that when you stop being an employee, the door shuts behind you if you are writing a book, no matter how good your ties were before within the company. A central figure of this book, Thomas J. Watson Jr., experienced the same when he was writing his book. I am in good company, and the company was none the worse for its practice.

JAMES W. CORTADA

Part I

FROM BIRTH TO IDENTITY: IBM IN ITS EARLY YEARS, 1880s–1945

1 ORIGINS, 1880s–1914

> The last three decades of the nineteenth century were the glory years of
> the self-employed American entrepreneur/inventor … to start one's own
> business—that is, to be an entrepreneur was a badge of success.
> —ROBERT J. GORDON[1]

A HISTORY OF a company is like a biography. Biographers tell the reader
something about their subject's parents and where their families came from,
and identify values and customs in which they were raised. This chapter is
about a number of little companies that grew up to form one called C-T-R.
In time, it evolved into IBM. Because we are discussing the biography of
an important corporation, it is necessary to understand its long heritage.
IBM was an American company, not only a global enterprise. Established in
New York State, it remained an East Coast corporation. Its headquarters
is in Armonk, New York; many of its corporate executives live in nearby
Connecticut. They carry in their corporate genes practices and attitudes
that emerged out of those three (one could argue four) tiny companies, and
from IBM's creator, also a New Yorker, Thomas J. Watson Sr. (1874–1956).

More than a century later, these small companies might seem irrelevant
to the history of the mighty International Business Machines Corporation.
Historians have not ignored them, although it has not always been clear
to them, to generations of businesspeople, or to IBM employees how
these firms shaped the global behemoth. Nevertheless, some employees
of these tiny companies worked at IBM into the 1940s. The basis for
what became IBM began with these people before "*The* International

Business Machines Corporation," as it was known for nearly a century. The word *the* is purposeful, used universally by company executives and employees since the 1920s, so the heritage from the little firms warranted a chapter of its own.

To understand IBM's origins, this chapter briefly describes the economic and innovative climate of the late nineteenth and early twentieth centuries, because while familiar to historians of business and economics, that environment is less appreciated by today's business managers and IBM employees. The economy of the United States made a profound shift from agricultural to industrial between the 1870s and the 1940s, making it possible for IBM to exist. This chapter also explores the history of each firm that emerged out of this economic environment, which merged into the holding company eventually known as IBM.

Historians normally bundle IBM's history into three chronological periods: first, the1880s to 1914, the period discussed in this chapter; second, the years when Thomas J. Watson Sr. ran the firm, 1914 to 1956, with some scholars opting for a new period beginning after World War II, when IBM switched to computers and away from punch card tabulation data processing; and then finally a third period, from the early 1980s and the arrival of the personal computer through roughly the end of the century. Because this book extends IBM's history to the present, a fourth period is introduced, which began roughly at the dawn of the twenty-first century, as IBM evolved into a software and combined technical-business managerial consulting services enterprise. When historians discuss the pre-Watson period, they focus on one of the three companies that made up IBM, that run by Herman Hollerith for punch cards, because it was the piece of the business that became the core of IBM.

I question that construct of IBM's early history because, as argued in this book, understanding the origins of IBM's corporate culture is central for understanding how it did so well for so long. I linger longer with those firms than prior historians have done. The experiences of these firms support the argument that IBM was successful because of the combination of products in demand in industrializing economies, managerial practices that aligned well with serving this demand, and a corporate culture that affected how management, innovation, technology, and day-to-day operations shaped IBM. I take a step in the direction of addressing the need for organizational theory, which Mairi Maclean, Charles Harvey, and Stewart R. Clegg argue for in such a compelling way.[2]

Historians have done much to flush out the story of Herman Hollerith's punch card business, focusing on his technical achievements and early efforts to persuade governments and large businesses to use his equipment.[3] They discuss in detail the acerbic relationship that existed between Hollerith and Watson Sr. from the latter's arrival at C-T-R until the end of the 1920s. Described almost as an irritant to the latter, their relationship could not be ignored, so beginning in the 1980s, historians looked at Hollerith in more depth, beginning with Geoffrey D. Austrian and continuing with Robert Sobel, Emerson Pugh, Rowena Olegario, and, most recently, Kevin Maney, in his rich biography of Watson Sr.[4] Historians have not prepared full histories of the other firms. Rather, these are either largely ignored in favor of discussing the punch card business or receive cursory treatment in which their influence on the future of IBM is presented as being limited. However, a closer examination of their role in this chapter and the next suggests a different story. Senior executives of these other firms populated IBM's early boards of directors, their facilities were used as retail outlets and manufacturing sites, and their engineers and employees were deployed among the various organizations, although not enough to increase productivity as one would expect from the synergies of shared information and assets.[5]

Features of a company's history manifest themselves through institutional behaviors and the role of individuals. Companies are collections of people, so while historians sway back and forth between telling the story of key players, such as CEOs, and corporations or divisions, I strive for balance. Institutional history blends with activities of individuals throughout this book. A few pages from now, we encounter Charles R. Flint, the entrepreneur who put together the initial company that eventually became IBM, and Herman Hollerith, the inventor of the punch card tabulating technologies. Both were archetypes of economic actors of their time: Flint the stock market promoter, Hollerith the inventor-entrepreneur. But, as historian Alfred D. Chandler Jr. explained, there was also the professional manager, who emerged between 1870 and 1930 and mitigated between the two archetypes, and one of the most visible of these new participants was Watson Sr., who ran IBM for over 40 years.[6] In this chapter, Flint is central to the birth of IBM. Hollerith plays a secondary role and, because he only became part of the new firm in the final stages of the history of Flint's creation, he is purposely introduced late in the chapter. Watson is barely mentioned, in the final pages. In the chapter 2, Watson is the archetypal Chandlerian manager pitted against Flint and the amateurish executives running the firms Flint had put together. Their stage is made up of the three firms, a setting that was rapidly transforming. As Robert J. Gordon recently argued, not since the period between 1870 and 1940 has the world enjoyed such a remarkable era of prosperity and innovations in products, science, technologies, and quality of human life.[7] That was the world into which IBM was born.

A MAGICAL TIME IN AMERICAN HISTORY

Inventions and economic growth transformed the United States from the 1870s into the 1930s as entrepreneurs and inventors, even children, applied for patents. Just in the United States, the U.S. government issued nearly 13,000 patents in 1880, almost 42,000 in 1900, and over 86,000 in 1920. Even during the Great Depression of the 1930s, people kept inventing. In 1930, over 93,000 people applied for a patent. In 1941, 41,000 received them.[8] Innovations remained the underlying engine of progress and increased economic productivity.[9]

Inventing was the magic of its day. With inventions came businesses to commercialize them—the genius of a capitalist economy. In that half century, many basic inventions emerged that define how we live today, most notably electricity, electric lights, the internal combustion engine, and the automobile. Other advances included the telephone, radio, and refrigerator. On the information-handling front as well, there were hundreds of inventions, including the typewriter, desktop calculator, adding machine, punch card tabulator, and billing machine. File cabinets, three-ring binders, and even the humble 3 × 5 index card made possible modern accounting practices, flexible record keeping, and greater accumulation and use of information. People increasingly used numbers rather than adjectives to measure and describe all manner of phenomena, from the weather to profits, and scientific practices and engineering displaced lingering folk wisdom. One went to the store and the butcher weighed a purchase and calculated "down to the penny" the cost per pound; merchants sliced cheese in more precise amounts to optimize prices and profits.

The combination of the telegraph and all manner of office equipment made it possible for large companies to function. Management could communicate with employees scattered across the nation; collect data on financial and operational performance in a coordinated and timely fashion; synchronize advertising nationwide; and, to use the late James Beniger's term, *control* ever-larger organizations, which he defined as purposeful "influence toward a predetermined goal."[10] Railroads crisscrossing the nation became the largest enterprises of their day. In the steel and automotive industries, massive enterprises emerged, controlled by entrepreneurs with names such as Rockefeller and Ford. Henry Ford took the internal combustion engine and applied it to the growing fashion of the "horseless carriage" using mass production methods. Now, members of the middle class could own an automobile. Banking, insurance, and later retail expanded, resulting in what historian Olivier Zunz argued was the stitching of "regional networks together to create a national market," increasing economies of scale and opportunities for sales and profits.[11] Whole industries consolidated into a few powerful firms, called trusts, creating monopolies, although many failed to survive because of organizational challenges unique to their industries and later because they were outlawed for constricting competition.[12] One of the consolidators, Charles Ranlett Flint (1850–1934), the king of rubber and chewing gum, founded two companies and bought a third, which became the fundamental building blocks of IBM.

Flint, little known today, was a member of the same business world as John D. Rockefeller and J. P. Morgan, lived in the same era, and also lived in New York. He was smart, eccentric, and full of panache. In his day, he was well known to the financial and business community in New

Figure 1.1
Charles Flint was highly creative in forming new stock-holding companies, including C-T-R, the core of the future International Business Machines Corporation. Photo courtesy of IBM Corporate Archives.

York for his enormous breadth of accomplishments, which most modern business tycoons would find difficult to equal. Flint was a small-town boy, born along the coast of Maine. He was an adult at the time when businessmen were creating mighty enterprises. Their behavior was so egregious that Congress eventually passed legislation to block creation of monopolies and crafted other laws to protect workers from horrible working conditions. That was Flint's world. He worked when a new form of business came into existence: the modern corporation capitalized by stocks, led by salaried professional managers, and employing thousands of workers. By the time he was mature and wise in the ways of the world, he had created C-T-R— and it had not been his first business endeavor.

Flint was small but fit, with sharp features, dressed impeccably, and was a bit formal but fashionably adorned with muttonchop whiskers. He loved to run and swim, raced yachts, and became an early owner of an automobile, yet another form of sporting. A founding member of the Automobile Club of America, he promoted competitive auto racing. He flew airplanes, a risky endeavor at the time, providing a window into his character and style of working. He enjoyed hunting and fishing, as did his contemporary Teddy Roosevelt. He was aggressive, energetic, and imaginative, the quintessential entrepreneur of pre–World War I America. Like Watson, he was constantly on the go, traveling to different places around the world, nurturing various business deals. At any one time, he had a dozen major projects under development; C-T-R was one of them.[13]

If Flint had created a résumé, it would have included early years in international trade as a commission agent in Latin America, dealing in guano (bird and bat droppings used as fertilizer), nitrates, other raw materials, and arms in the region. He learned to work with senior political figures there and subsequently in other countries, including in New York State. He sold ships to Japan in 1895 for its war against China and ten years later to Russia for its failed war against Japan, later sold airplanes to European armies, and even advised the German kaiser on how they should be used in war.

However, such activities were the least of Flint's achievements, because of more important ones in the United States. Known as the "father of trusts," he combined companies under an umbrella firm—the business model of the trust—then let others manage them as he went on to the next project. His profits came from owning stock in these firms. He argued that they enhanced economies of scale, made possible large infusions of capital needed to mass-produce products, and created sufficient scale to compete on the world market.[14] Rockefeller and others would have agreed with him. Stockholders were king, and managers had to bow to their wishes. Another of Flint's basic beliefs was that customers and employees were second in line, so, long before IBM executives in the current century announced their priorities of stockholders' wishes for immediate returns at the expense of employees, customers, and possibly the future health of the firm, here was Flint espousing a similar philosophy. For example, in 1892 he created the United States Rubber Company, which dominated its market from day one. He went on to help establish American Chicle out of six companies then known as the "chewing gum trust." He capitalized the new firm at $9 million, although it was worth only $500,000. He argued that its value lay in its trademarks, which he judged to be worth $14 million. Was it a scam? Of course, and it was legal and typical smart business in an opportune era.

With every new innovation came waves of small companies that in time became larger ones, with the lion's share of the new ones emerging between 1870 and the Great Depression. The story of how IBM became a behemoth reflects that pattern of evolution, with earlier companies dropping by the wayside as IBM focused correctly on one of the real prizes of the twentieth century: management of information using data processing machines. Many other small office equipment vendors new to the period also consolidated, notably Remington Rand, Burroughs Corporation, and the National Cash Register Company (NCR), but not as part of Flint's C-T-R. Burroughs and NCR were well established by the time Flint began creating C-T-R, making him a late arrival to the office machines business.

To pull off extraordinary success at IBM and other companies in their own industries, such as General Electric, Kodak, Ford, and General Motors, required three actions. First, inventors developed products that solved old problems or offered new conveniences. Cash registers, invented in the 1870s and 1880s, helped prevent sales clerks from pilfering cash from money boxes, electricity made possible movies and many new household appliances, and electric water pumps meant farm wives no longer had to carry heavy buckets of water to their kitchens. Second, entrepreneurs converted their inventions into commercially successful products. Sometimes the inventor and entrepreneur were the same person, such as Thomas Edison, but in many cases they were two different types of people, because one could see and solve a problem, whereas the other knew how to create a business and sell products. For example, Ohio saloon owner James Ritty (1836–1918) invented the cash register and first used it in his saloon in the

1870s, but it took John H. Patterson (1844–1922) to create a great corporation, NCR. His corporate sales culture introduced many practices embraced by companies in the next century, including IBM for over a half century, through the efforts of Watson Sr., one of Patterson's protégés. Executives in other companies admired Patterson's innovations in running sales offices in a uniform manner, requiring salesmen to dress like their customers and use a sales pitch developed by the corporation, and applying statistical analysis to a wide range of company activities, including sales.[15]

Third, to scale up in order to drive down the costs of building and selling an invention required either a creative and often ruthless entrepreneur or what Alfred D. Chandler called the new mandarins of American business: professional managers. These men often did not create the firm but went on to run it, like Watson. They were employees in corporations owned by stockholders. When all three types of people—inventors, entrepreneurs, and professional managers—coordinated their activities, great businesses emerged. The least relevant of the three in creating successful firms was usually the inventor; the two others proved more essential. Entrepreneurs created companies, while managers grew and sustained them. Each brought unique skills required to make firms thrive. The 1870s to 1920s saw the birth of the companies that eventually became IBM. In its case, all three types of actors were present and kept appearing over the next century.

New York State became an intense hotspot of entrepreneurial activity, particularly in its center, in small towns such as Endicott, Painted Post, and Johnson City, and cities such as Rochester. New classes of high-tech companies began operations in this region, including Corning Glass, Kodak, and the International Time Recording Company. Solid American Protestant values merged with the strong work ethics of newly arrived European immigrants with mechanical abilities.[16] In the midst of these communities, the first seeds took root in what would grow into IBM. To this day, IBM remains largely a New York State–centered company, with corporate headquarters in Armonk, just outside of New York City, a presence in Endicott (which used to be *the* home base, site of Factory No. 1), and for nearly a century facilities up and down the Mid-Hudson Valley.[17] Each of the three entities comprising IBM has a unique history, and we turn to them now.

BUNDY MANUFACTURING COMPANY

Most histories of IBM, while overlooking this little company, occasionally acknowledge that its owners held stock in what eventually became C-T-R, a point made most thoroughly by historian Robert Sobel. Its founder invented a device used to "clock in" and "clock out" of work, making it possible for employers to know how many hours each employee had to be paid for. Copies of the original invention shipped to customers as late as 1949, some 60 years after its introduction. Time recorders spread the practice of "punching in" to work.[18] Bundy Manufacturing experienced intense family rivalries and patent disputes, with patent issues afflicting IBM in the 1920s and 1930s and family issues from the 1930s through the 1960s. These family disputes were between Thomas Watson Sr. and his son Thomas Watson Jr. from the 1930s to the 1950s and later between Thomas Watson Jr. and his younger brother, Arthur, in the 1950s and 1960s.[19]

Willard Legrand Bundy (1845–1907) was born in Otego, New York, grew up in Auburn, and became a local jeweler familiar with clock machinery. For most of his adult life, he tinkered with similar devices and continually obtained patents. Of his many creations, the one of interest to us is a mechanical time clock he built in 1888. His younger brother, Harlow E. Bundy (1856–1916), demonstrated a more entrepreneurial nature. Harlow suggested they go into business to sell the time clock. The following year (1889), they incorporated the Bundy Manufacturing Company in Binghamton, New York. Harlow's business talent, Willard's inventive ability, and growing demand by factories to convert time into salary payments brought them success. By the end of the century, their firm had over 100 employees and had sales offices around the United States. By then, they had manufactured over 9,000 Bundy Time Recorders.[20] In 1900, they sold the firm to Flint, who formed another company, the International Time Recorder Company (ITR), in Endicott. He moved Bundy Manufacturing to Endicott. In time, Bundy became one of the three parts comprising C-T-R. The merger facilitated Bundy's sale of time recording equipment in other countries, too, thanks to a small overseas operation ITR launched. The presence of foreign sales became useful to C-T-R in the 1910s and 1920s, when Watson sought to expand international sales.

Just as the Watson family dominated IBM's affairs from 1914 to 1971, the Bundys dominated the little firm. There were seemingly trivial and also confusing rivalries within that family as would occur later at IBM under Watson Sr. Early executives at C-T-R were familiar with the Bundy brothers, and undoubtedly their behavior affected how the three major parts of C-T-R interacted. Willard L. Bundy left Bundy Manufacturing and ITR in 1903 because of his deteriorating relations with his brother Harlow, with whom he had cofounded the company. The problems between the brothers began when Harlow forced out the inventor's son, Willard H. Bundy, in 1900. Willard L. moved to Syracuse, where he and his son established the Bundy Time Recording Company, so now there were two Bundy product lines and companies with similar names: one from father and son, the other from the original Bundy firm, now part of ITR.

Fighting began over the actions of Willard L. and his son in what appeared to Harlow and ITR to be an obvious usurpation of the original Bundy patent. Inventor Willard denied that, arguing he had a new device. Next came a flurry of lawsuits filed by both Bundy Manufacturing and ITR against Bundy Time Recorder Company between 1903 and 1907. These ran the full gamut of accusations regarding patent rights of Bundy Time Recorders, disputes over Willard L.'s contract with the original firm of 1889, and, of course, use of the Bundy name in the sale of time recording equipment. Inventor Willard L. died on January 19, 1907, making it easier to clear away some of the pending cases while reinforcing ITR's control over the patents on time recording equipment. Subsequent products reduced the patent influence of the Bundy clan. Harlow remained at ITR and became a vice president at C-T-R in 1911. Willard H. Bundy formed the W. H. Bundy Time Card Printing Company in 1910 and engaged in other entrepreneurial activities for the rest of his life.

INTERNATIONAL TIME RECORDING COMPANY (ITR)

ITR was Flint's brainchild, the initial core of his creation he unimaginatively named C-T-R, with each letter representing the first names of the three companies he bound loosely together. Flint considered C-T-R just another of his usual business wheelings and dealings, perhaps scams, to create and profit from a stock offering that had a lot of air between its value and asking price, but he lived long enough to see his little creation evolve into a respectable IBM by the time of his death in 1934. He inched toward C-T-R and IBM in a way he would not have suspected at the time. After creating the chewing gum trust, the next year he worked on the International Time Recording Company (ITR), creating its initial parts out of the Bundy operation. He later added other firms to it. ITR dominated its market, shipping at least 2,000 time recording clocks to customers by the end of World War I, and during World War II, it shipped over 3,000 of them each year, by then as IBM products.[21] Flint expanded operations outside the United States and bought out almost all its competitors, creating a minimonopoly, adding more products to ITR's suite of offerings. The company generated $1 million in sales in 1910, not a bad little enterprise. By 1916, it had sold several thousand machines and had a small sales force specializing in the sale and maintenance of time recorders.

COMPUTING SCALE COMPANY OF AMERICA

Flint bought another small firm a year after ITR, Computing Scale Company. Two Dayton, Ohio, businessmen, Edward Canby and Orange O. Ozias, had acquired patents for a newly designed commercial scale, formed their company, and began manufacturing. Their tabletop scale made it easy for a clerk to calculate costs. Its primary market lay in Midwest grocery stores and in cheese and butcher shops. The firm later added cheese slicers and other retail scales, which so famously appeared in IBM advertisements. The small company was marginally profitable. However, Flint saw it as another piece of a puzzle he was putting together around the theme of data handling by mechanical means.

Flint kept Computing Scale Company a separate business during the first decade of the new century, despite its mediocre business performance. He wanted to fold it into several others to create a new venture to profit off a stock offering. It was vintage Flint strategy. At first blush, it may seem odd since the two firms—Computing Scale Company and ITR—were a thousand miles apart and in different markets, one selling to stores, the other to factories. However, Flint saw the opportunity for capital gains. Evidence for his thinking came from the Computing Scale Company itself, which technically was a holding company organized to own other little firms. These consisted of the original Computing Scale Company of Dayton, Ohio, the Moneyweight Scale Company in Chicago, the W. F. Simpson Company, located in Detroit, and the Stimpson Computing Scale Company, established in Elkhart, Indiana, all of them small firms. Flint was on his way to building a miniature trust, but his attention soon turned to a larger prize that surfaced out of the magic of innovation and weak management, taking us to the story of the Tabulating Machine Company, the third leg of his new stool.

TABULATING MACHINE COMPANY

Born in 1860, ten years after Flint, Herman Hollerith was raised by his German immigrant parents in Buffalo, New York. He studied mining engineering, graduating from Columbia University in 1879 at the tender age of 19. He remained one of the nearly forgotten geniuses of data processing, the inventor of punch card tabulating equipment (see figure 1.2), an ancestor to computing, until rescued by historian Robert Sobel in his history of IBM and by Hollerith's biographer, Geoffrey D. Austrian, both works being published in 1982. Since then, no account of early IBM or business equipment has ignored him.[22] The heart of his system was a card with holes punched in it to represent data and equipment with which to make those holes and then store and read the data that each hole represented, such as a number. This equipment sorted cards by topic, later "processing" the data, such as adding up totals from many cards by column, with each column being a topic. While the number of potential columns on a card varied over the years, by the end of the 1920s it had standardized on a card with 80 columns, which famously became known as the "IBM card." By then, results could also be printed on cards or as paper reports. Before Hollerith's machines arrived, all these activities had been done by hand: recording information on paper and manually tabulating

Figure 1.2
Tabulating machine. Herman Hollerith's machines were used by U.S. and European census takers and companies in the 1890s and early 1900s. They were considered the most sophisticated data processing equipment of their day. Photo courtesy of IBM Corporate Archives.

results.[23] His equipment sped up "data entry" and tabulating by more than one order of magnitude. His machines later used electricity to improve calculating speed, and their engineering was continuously improved.

It would be difficult to overestimate the importance of this invention for large enterprises and government agencies saddled with great amounts of numerical data that required analysis and storage. Use of that information took far too much time and cost, problems mitigated by Hollerith's invention. Daniel Boorstin, a historian of American cultural and economic life, explained the significance of Hollerith's invention: "Now it was as easy to tabulate the number of married carpenters 40 to 45 years of age as to tabulate the total number of persons 40 to 45 years of age."[24] James Beniger observed that it became easier to manage large bureaucracies and complex accounting and statistical systems, recognizing "in its processing of information as material flows something akin to their function of organizing their employees into processing, decision, and control structures."[25]

To further understand the impact of Hollerith's invention, consider the U.S. census taken in 1880. The nation was growing, and that year it had a population of just over 50 million people. Nose counters had to track over five sets of information about each person, add up the results, and write detailed reports on trends, totals, and implications. They did it all by hand and took eight years to report the results to the nation. Before they completed their work, they knew the 1890 count would be bigger, because Congress had already asked that more information be collected in exchange for the census budget appropriation. Meanwhile, the nation's population kept growing; only later did officials learn it was over 63 million souls in 1890, a whopping 26 percent increase over 1880's count. Hollerith worked on the 1880 census and thus understood both the required data handling tasks and the time they took. The director of that census and the next one, John Shaw Billings (1838–1913), an army colonel, librarian, and medical doctor, explored options for automating some of that processing.[26] Staff had already turned to a young engineer—Herman Hollerith—and to others to find ways to automate some of the data collection, sorting, and calculating.

Over dinner one night, Billings approached Hollerith with the challenge that somehow there ought to be a way to automate some of the census work by using machines. After all, adding machines, calculators, cash registers, and other devices were being used to collect and manipulate other data, so why not census numbers and facts? Obliquely, according to Hollerith, it was Billings who suggested that somehow a description of a person could be recorded by notching a card of some sort. Other accounts agree that Billings and Hollerith talked about the issue.[27] Hollerith gave much thought to the problem. He knew that punch cards had been used in weaving cloth since the eighteenth century. He struck upon the idea of punching a card in predesignated places by observing a train conductor punching his ticket, known as a "punch photograph." To prevent train passengers from cheating the railroad on rates offered for long trips by buying tickets for a short trip, at the time of purchase a conductor would punch holes next to various types of descriptions of the person, such as that the passenger was a man, had a mustache, dark or light hair, color of his eyes, and so forth, along with punching out where the ticket was purchased or the passenger's destination. Other conductors then could see if the passenger flashing a ticket matched the description of where he or she was going or was the original purchaser.

Hollerith had "connected the dots" by realizing the same could be done for everyone counted by census takers and that this data could be sorted by state, gender, age, and so forth, using needles to search for the holes in cards by topic. By organizing the array of needles searching for holes in the right spot on a card, one could sort for males between certain ages or of a certain race or profession, for example. Hollerith focused on his idea and worked part-time in various jobs while perfecting his invention. Others were busy at work on the same problem, such as Charles Pidgin and William Hunt, so there was a footrace under way to come up with a patentable system that could be used by large organizations, not just the U.S. government. Hollerith obtained his first patent in 1884 and moved quickly to commercialize his advantage, winning the business to provide equipment for a census in Baltimore and to tabulate mortality data for New York and New Jersey. Thus, before the 1890 census, he had a working system before his rivals did. More patents in 1889 solidified his position, and he won the contract to do the census processing work in 1890.

For the 1890 census, Hollerith's equipment made it possible to shave two years off the total job of completing the census, from eight years to six, but more spectacularly, within 18 months, the nation received preliminary counts and data on the size of its population. The media, Congress, and other government officials praised the job done. Hollerith became a celebrity around town. One consequence of his success was the establishment of the Census Bureau as a permanent agency, no longer the ad hoc grouping thrown together every decade. Now, as a permanent bureau, it received many requests to conduct other counts, such as in agriculture, medicine, and for the U.S. Army. From then up to the present, in both the United States and around the world, all census activities were conducted using Hollerith's technology, that of competitors, and eventually computers.[28]

Hollerith's invention is why we are interested in him. In 1882, he had gone to work at the relatively new Massachusetts Institute of Technology (MIT) to teach mechanical engineering while continuing his studies toward an advanced degree. He completed his PhD at Columbia University in 1890, such a degree being unusual at that time, signaling that here was a bright engineer. He moonlighted and tinkered with various inventions, hoping to find a moneymaker. In those days, he was still thin, sported a huge, bushy mustache, was fun loving and humorous with friends and family, but was rather formal and uptight in his business dealings. In the 1890s and early the next decade, he successfully rented his machines to governments and

Figure 1.3
Herman Hollerith, inventor of the tabulating equipment used by governments and corporations for half a century. Photo courtesy of IBM Corporate Archives.

corporations, creating for himself a niche market for complex data collection and analysis. After his success with the U.S. census of 1890, he won contracts to do similar work from Austria (1890), Canada (1891), and later Italy, among others. Hollerith outsourced construction of his equipment but personally persuaded organizations to rent his equipment and buy his cards. He became wealthy, famous, and enjoyed life in Washington, D.C.

Hollerith's machines were fast and accurate. They were expensive, yet their speed and accuracy outweighed their cost, just as those same two features of computers justified what were pricey technologies. Hollerith improved his technology as new uses surfaced from his own thinking or from his customers. He also enhanced and redesigned his cards. A card could only be used once, so his customers had to constantly buy vast quantities of them, which Hollerith supplied and insisted be his, arguing that their quality ensured that the equipment worked properly. By the mid-1920s, IBM derived over 4 percent of its revenue from selling cards. That source of revenue was like Kodak making its cameras available but generating greater profits from selling film, or Gillette profiting from its safety razor by supplying blades. Like film and blades, Hollerith's cards were more profitable than rental income from hardware. Card revenue came in immediately, whereas lease revenue accrued over many years. This meant that, as business grew, Hollerith's firm, later C-T-R/IBM, constantly had to scramble for capital to fund the manufacture of more equipment, because some or all of the cost of building a machine was expended at the moment of manufacture, not amortized over the leasing life of the device. Revenue from cards was collected at almost the same time as IBM paid to manufacture them, providing additional capital and cash flow.

By the time Hollerith's firm became part of the predecessor to IBM (C-T-R, with the "T" being his piece) in 1911, people encountered a man with a temper whose feelings were easily hurt and who had a knack for turning off colleagues and customers. His negatives presented a problem whenever someone wanted to suggest improvements to his equipment or changes in how he ran his operations. His behavior became especially problematic when he butted heads with Flint and later Thomas J. Watson Sr., the new general manager at C-T-R, who joined the firm in 1914 and with whom Hollerith had to contend for the rest of his life. The strong-willed Hollerith and Flint tussled alone from 1911 until 1914, when the strong-willed Watson entered the ring. Not until Hollerith's death in 1929 was the far more determined, opinionated Watson free of his influence, ensuring that all through the 1910s and early 1920s these three men shaped the foundations of IBM. This is an important observation, because most historians and IBMers almost make it sound like Watson dominated the firm from the moment he came onboard, and that clearly was not the case. He had to wrest control from Flint and Hollerith, a task made particularly urgent since he quickly realized that the crown jewel of Flint's creation was Hollerith's business. That realization shaped the trajectory of the company.

Hollerith was jealous and protective of his inventions, and resolved in how to run his company by the early 1890s. But by early the following decade, a rival had emerged out of the Census Bureau, James Powers (1871–1929), who dogged him into the 1920s, and a succession of firms competed with IBM until the late 1950s.[29] Powers was a university-educated Russian immigrant who came to the United States in 1889 and competed against Hollerith, beginning about 1907, for business at the U.S. Census Bureau and elsewhere. Powers enjoyed some success, such as in 1910, when the Census Bureau decided to use his equipment, which was cheaper and technologically more advanced than Hollerith's. Their two firms spent nearly 30 years dueling over patents and business at a time when Powers, Hollerith, and Watson were pushing the technology forward as customers kept demanding faster processing, printing capabilities for partial results and outputs, and other functions. Their rivalries and disputes, both legal and internal (in the case of Hollerith versus Watson), contributed much stress to all their lives.[30]

It did not help Hollerith that his employees and customers disliked him, although all acknowledged that he was bright. However, Hollerith's only fundamental creative accomplishment was his development of a tabulating system of cards and equipment, and a process for using them. Although comfortable with mechanical and electrical devices, he paid little attention to other problems and opportunities, even at home. The story was told that on one occasion his car broke down and instead of trying to figure out how to fix it, he left it on the side of the road for anyone who wanted it to haul it away. His business grew, and he incorporated it in 1896. After it became part of C-T-R, he was expected to expand his business and report to the board of directors of the new company. That circumstance did not sit well with him. Watson added his strong personality into the mix, with a high level of energy. His relentless and effective selling acumen also helped set the stage for fireworks.

Watson knew that C-T-R's future lay in expanding adoption of Hollerith's services. He accepted the strategy of renting equipment and understood the wisdom of selling cards, but he thought Hollerith was a poor salesman. Watson pushed on this last point, and over time he took over that function, hiring salesmen in the United States and later in Europe and Latin America to expand sales. The two men clashed, but eventually

Figure 1.4
Thomas J. Watson Sr. in his 40s, when he had taken over C-T-R to shape it into IBM. Photo courtesy of IBM Corporate Archives.

Watson shunted Hollerith aside, reducing him to serving as an adviser. By the mid-1920s, Watson had won undisputed control over all of C-T-R, including the all-important tabulating piece of the business. The cheese slicers were still in the company's product line, but would not be for long. Watson had seized control over Hollerith's technology and had brought in engineers from NCR and elsewhere to modify the equipment to meet the changing needs of his customers. These engineers were loyal to him, not to Hollerith. For the rest of his life, Watson invested in sales and technological innovations of this equipment. Powers and others competed against Watson, but unlike Hollerith, Watson knew how to run the business well. That is why Geoffrey D. Austrian, Hollerith's biographer, correctly summed up Hollerith's legacy as the "forgotten giant of information processing."[31]

THE CORPORATE GRANDFATHER OF IBM: C-T-R

Between 1901 and 1911, Flint's companies were little. ITR dominated its niche market, growing to where it reported $1 million in revenue in 1910. Scales and slicers was a bleak business by 1910. In an attempt to improve its prospects, Flint considered linking it to ITR, arguing years later that such a merger made sense. But with the two businesses in different markets separated by nearly a thousand miles, his argument that they both measured things proved a weak one. He was too smart to believe that. Instead, he probably wanted to put the businesses together to enjoy a capital gains transaction through the sale of stock.

While mulling over what to do that year, Flint met Hollerith, but how remains unclear. Hollerith had insufficient funds with which to run his own company, while Flint probably saw in the Tabulating Machine Company an opportunity to expand it with an infusion of capital. So Flint bought Hollerith's company for $2.3 million, paid for with 5,138 outstanding shares in the company. Flint allocated $1.2 million to Hollerith for his personal purchase of nearly 2,700 shares. Hollerith agreed to put $100,000 into the newly issued C-T-R stock. The deal was vintage Flint. Sobel speculated that perhaps Flint could apply profits from ITR to fund Hollerith's company's growth, and even use ITR's salesmen to assist in selling tabulating equipment, since both firms called on the same kinds of companies.[32] Flint's scheme turned out to be not only one of his last but also one of his biggest failures, for it struggled over the next three years. Flint brought all three firms into one holding company that displayed no sense of synergies, even giving it the boring and uninspiring name of Computing-Tabulating-Recording Company, which in turn was part of Flint & Company in the beginning. Each continued to function independently. Flint could issue stock at inflated prices to pocket a handsome profit while feeding additional funds to Hollerith's slow-moving business. The C part of his company, small and ineffective, could face its destiny without damaging Flint or C-T-R as a whole. ITR would remain prosperous. C-T-R started with facilities in Ohio, in New York and with agents in the United States and Europe (recording), and Hollerith's office/factory in Washington, D.C. C-T-R employed 1,200 people; its board was populated largely by senior management from ITR.

Hollerith was only allowed to be the dominant engineer, and only within his piece of the new company, and could not hold any managerial positions. Flint named him a consulting engineer and paid him $20,000 a year until 1924, the year C-T-R's board of directors then renamed the old company IBM. As part of Flint's arrangement, Hollerith had veto power over changes in the tabulating product line. After 1914, this particular power created problems for Watson, who wanted to make changes in the product line, which Hollerith frequently contested. Even worse, Hollerith's contract with C-T-R stated that he would not be "subject to orders of any officer or other person connected with the company."[33] The leadership at ITR was eager to harvest profits, not focus on growing the business. Meanwhile, Flint went about his usual practice of putting together other stock deals.

C-T-R demonstrated Flint's genius for pulling off scams—yes, *scams* is the correct term to use—in an age when doing so was more widely practiced than was possible later. Leave aside the obvious mismatch of these businesses and look at the numbers. Flint valued C-T-R's total assets at $17.5 million, of which only a million dollars was assigned to revenue, the other $16.5 million being the paper worth of the companies. The owners of the three companies were given $10.5 million in face value of C-T-R stock, with Flint increasing the value to that amount by some $6 million. In other words, the old stock of the prior firms might have been worth $4 million, making the $6+ million the "water," or fake capitalization. The new company had assets of $35,000 in cash and $200,000 in treasury bonds. This sum served as collateral for short-term loans to keep the businesses going. Flint funded this deal by going to the Guaranty Trust Company, which he had used for earlier ventures, convincing it to buy a $7 million gold issue to mature in 30 years with a sinking fund that started two years later, in 1913.[34] The purpose of this transaction was to establish (secure) a lien with an interest rate of 6 percent, nearly usurious for the day. The deal reeked, even by the standards of the time.

While our discussion about finances seems arcane, it is important to understand, because all companies of consequence and size have underpinning them both a financial strategy that helps provide the economic wherewithal to run the business and another for generating revenues from sales and service. The latter usually is easily explained by historians, the former less so, and yet for senior executives it is often the financial aspect that most shapes their behavior. Throughout IBM's history, we run into this issue, either because the company needed additional funds to build machines and to pay for people or because its sales and profits were inadequate to prop up the value of its stock. As sorry as Flint's financial behavior was, financial strategies were an essential part of making it possible for a company to thrive so, periodically, we must pay attention to them. In Flint's case, such strategies began almost immediately, because with his inflated stock issue for C-T-R came the problem of how to run what really looked like a sickly three-legged horse of a company in a dynamic economy that could rapidly heat and cool.

TRYING TO RACE A THREE-LEGGED HORSE, 1911–1914

So, C-T-R began as a troubled business. Flint loaded it with debt. The company was literally all over the map from Detroit and Dayton to Endicott to New York and Washington, D.C., with no hopes of leveraging economies of scale and not enough customers. The Census Bureau did not need cheese slicers. Managers and employees at each firm functioned independently, hardly collaborating, and sometimes irritating one another. At Hollerith's company, customers had long been treated contemptuously, because he thought they should feel privileged to use his clever machines. Morale among his employees remained low, as before the sale to Flint, thanks to Hollerith's foul temper and arrogance. It did not help that his health was deteriorating, too, because of rich food, smoking too many cigars, and lack of exercise. His nemesis, James Powers, meanwhile was expanding his business.

C-T-R's board and the leaders of the three businesses did not grow the overall company as aggressively as they might have or even seem willing to do so, nor did they demonstrate much creativity. However, ITR's ongoing profits on flat revenue sustained C-T-R. The board used its profits to reduce C-T-R's debt, a proper action. In 1912, ITR generated $541,000 in net profits, which rose to $635,000 the following year. That incremental growth in profits came largely from Tabulating Machine, with the rest from ITR. In 1913, C-T-R paid its first dividends.[35] Such steps were probably designed to project an image of managerial respectability while promoting the stock as a good investment. By late 1913, however, Flint had quietly started recruiting a general manager for C-T-R. That year, the United States experienced an economic slump that softened demand for C-T-R's products, probably suggesting to Flint that he needed to improve operations. His private papers did not reveal his thinking on the matter.[36]

Nobody could have predicted how successful Flint would be in finding a general manager. With a little probing, a potential candidate for the job might have uncovered the heavy debt load, the inflated price of C-T-R's stock, the desire of board members to extract profits, their inattention to investing in innovative products, the company's poor treatment of its customers and probably also its employees, mismatches in lines of business across the three parts of C-T-R, lack of collaboration by the three lines of business, and the clash of personalities that inevitably came with such situations. However, in one of those flukes of history, Flint ended up hiring Thomas J. Watson Sr. as general manager, who in time would be recognized as one of the most effective senior executives in twentieth-century America. How that happened and why Watson was willing to work for this holding company launches the next chapter.

2 THOMAS J. WATSON SR. AND THE CREATION OF IBM, 1914–1924

There is a future for every man in this building.
—THOMAS J. WATSON SR., 1920S

BETWEEN 1914 AND 1924, C-T-R evolved into IBM. The three little firms acquired a new culture, team of executives, and updated products that put it on its path to becoming an iconic American company. IBM's experience demonstrates that small companies sometimes transform slowly in response to changing economic conditions because they are fraught with internal politics and buffeted by complex market circumstances. It was not clear in 1914 what IBM's transformation should look like. George W. Fairchild and other managers across C-T-R resisted changes. Similar battles occurred throughout IBM's history, too.

Transitions represent an important theme in IBM's history and serve as measures of how the company was able to operate for a long time. IBM's ability to change, while not always as effective as one might want, was sufficient to sustain the firm. Thus, we must understand the nature of its transitions, and the first one is the subject of this chapter. Each transition took at least a decade to accomplish. In the process, careers were made and broken, and new product lines were created and discarded, while customers encouraged the firm to change. As IBM became larger and its customers more dependent on its products, its transitions became public affairs, drawing the attention of government regulators and even other nations and their political leaders. Each of these transitions occurred when senior executives saw the need for change. Until that happened, it seemed that most

employees and stockholders viewed these changes as potentially dangerous for themselves and left well enough alone. Each transformation also
affected the next one. The evolution from C-T-R to IBM remained in the
firm's memory well into the 1950s.

As the twenty-first century approached, interest in how companies survived for over a century attracted considerable attention among business
executives.[1] Managers learned that changes in corporate cultures affected
the survivability and success of firms. Historians like Ken Lipartito suggest
that survival was often made possible by an existing group of employees
who already embraced a shared set of new values and practices.[2] However,
that was not the case for the first transformation into IBM. In 1914, C-T-R
did not have a unified culture.

The first person to see the need for change at C-T-R was Charles Flint,
and the second was Thomas J. Watson Sr. Flint took a cautious view; he
wanted a general manager to improve the productivity of the firm. C-T-R's
president, George Fairchild, wanted that too, but also dividends more than
growth. Watson proved bolder, because he wanted to build a large business. Flint understood enough about what C-T-R needed for him to support incremental changes, while Watson presided over a far more aggressive
transformation than any of the senior leaders of C-T-R had anticipated.
Both Flint and Watson experienced enormous stress-filled challenges, while
Herman Hollerith and Fairchild were marginalized as support for Watson
grew. The emergence of IBM is the story of Watson Sr. taking control of
C-T-R and infusing it with new ways.

We proceed through this unfolding story by explaining Flint's immediate tactical problem of finding a general manager. We next meet Watson Sr. and introduce his view of managerial practices. Unlike founders of
many start-up firms, he came to C-T-R with a fully developed view on how
a business should operate, which was just what one would expect from an
experienced executive, and he immediately put those beliefs to work. The
central discussion of this chapter is a description of what he did, and it
argues that he introduced new strategies, changed organizations, and hired
and fired executives and managers. He implanted the sales culture that had
served him well at NCR. His sales management reforms remained intact

for nearly a century. In this chapter, we see the earliest foundations of what came to be known as IBM. Chapter 3 will explore how IBM took shape, explaining the implications of Watson's accomplishments as they unfolded in the 1920s and 1930s.

BUT FIRST, FLINT SOLVES C-T-R'S PROBLEM

Flint's problems were minor in comparison to those faced by future generations of IBM managers, but had they not been solved there would have been no IBM. Watson would have turned up at some other company.

Recall that when Flint created C-T-R with its sketchy financial underpinnings, he needed to give it a patina of credibility. One of his first steps had been to recruit George W. Fairchild (1854–1924) as C-T-R's president, later chairman of the board. Fairchild presented a good image of C-T-R to the financial community. He was a one-time newspaper editor in his hometown of Oneonta, New York, had been a member of several corporate boards in the New York area, and had been an early and successful president of International Time. He was handsome, well connected, and "vigorous" at 57 years old.[3] In 1911, he was experienced in business matters. He had served on and off for six terms as a Republican congressman from 1907 through 1918, which distracted him from the day-to-day operations of C-T-R. President William Howard Taft appointed Fairchild special minister to Mexico in 1910 for an assignment that literally kept him out of the United States.

Flint intended that Fairchild would be only a figurehead to appease bankers and stockholders. Flint still needed a hands-on manager. In 1912, he selected Frank N. Kondolf (1863–1944), who had served as the chief operating officer at ITR, and elevated Fairchild to board chair. Kondolf, although amiable, proved insufficiently forceful or clever to improve operations. Flint was not impressed with him, but Fairchild was and had recommended him for the role. Flint's disappointment with Kondolf became an early wedge between himself and Fairchild, which expanded. Neither Fairchild nor Kondolf demonstrated leadership in developing new products, in aggressively adding customers, or in promoting sales of Hollerith's tabulators.

They did nothing to integrate the three firms, eliminate redundant operations, or improve productivity, but ITR generated sufficient profits to keep the firm above water.[4] The inactions of both Fairchild and Kondolf help to explain why the board could pay out dividends in 1913 instead of investing in the future of the business. That state of affairs worried Flint enough that he sought out a new leader, and when he found Watson in 1914, he let Kondolf go. Kondolf went on to become president of the Remington Typewriter Company in 1915, serving in that capacity until 1922, when he was elected chairman of the board.

INTRODUCING THOMAS J. WATSON SR., THIRD FOUNDER OF IBM, AND HIS COMPANY CULTURE

Following Flint and Hollerith, Thomas J. Watson Sr. was the third founder of IBM. Watson did more to create IBM than any other individual did, although his son—arguably a fourth founder—ran a very close second. Born in Campbell, New York, in 1874, near the Finger Lakes region in the northern part of the state, he grew up on his parents' farm. His father also ran a lumberyard. Watson dabbled with the two businesses and disliked both. As with so many of his generation, he was educated locally but never attended college. As a young man, he found bookkeeping uninteresting and soon after took a job as a traveling salesman, selling pianos and organs off the back of a wagon. Watson joined the National Cash Register Company (NCR) in 1895. He rapidly moved up the organization, becoming its senior sales manager before World War I. Watson was at NCR when it was developing the paradigm of professional sales operations.

Because Watson's experience at NCR played an enormous role in shaping IBM, it is worth understanding his role at "the Cash," as it was known. NCR had a forceful leader, John H. Patterson (1844–1922), who hired and fired at will but also commanded loyalty and generously rewarded successful employees. For example, he gave Watson a house in Dayton, Ohio. In the late nineteenth century, Patterson was considered one of the country's most imaginative and effective executives. He trained dozens of others who went on to run companies in his mold, including Watson. He was also

Figure 2.1
John H. Patterson was the creator of NCR and had a reputation for being an innovative and successful executive. Photo courtesy of IBM Corporate Archives.

impatient, intolerant of poor performance, and put everyone under pressure to do well. He dressed conservatively and expected his executives to do the same, to be lean and energetic, and to live respectable personal lives. He started his business by buying the rights to a cash register and from there grew NCR into the largest manufacturer of this technology.[5]

Watson joined the company in 1895 at age 21, already an experienced salesman and, like Patterson, disciplined in his work and private life. He did well in central New York, coming to Patterson's attention. In 1899, Patterson appointed Watson manager of a branch office in Rochester, New

York, a region yet to be saturated with NCR's products. There, Watson faced competition from the Hallwood Company, but he quickly turned things to NCR's favor through aggressive and creative selling efforts.

In 1903, Patterson had Watson set up a company to sell secondhand cash registers at low enough prices to put rivals out of business. Nobody was to know that the operation was being underwritten by NCR. Watson set up stores next to competitors, hired their salesmen, and underpriced products in places such as Philadelphia and Chicago. He successfully competed against NCR's rivals for four years. It is not clear whether Watson knew that this kind of activity was illegal. In 1907, NCR announced that Watson was now in charge of all secondhand sales, working out of Dayton and therefore able to learn how corporate headquarters functioned and the role Patterson played. Watson was only 36 years old when in 1910 he began to run into major problems.

The American Cash Register Company, the second-largest company in the business, accused NCR of violating the Sherman Antitrust Act. Two years later, the U.S. Department of Justice joined in the legal case against NCR. Most of the company's top executives were charged with violating the Sherman Act, were tried in federal court in Cincinnati, and were found guilty on February 13, 1913. The case turned on the testimony of Hugh Chalmers (1873–1932), the NCR executive to whom Watson reported while running his secret operation. Watson and Patterson were fined $5,000 and sentenced to one year in jail, the maximum sentence the judge could hand out. Meanwhile, Watson had become engaged to marry Jeanette M. Kittredge (1883–1966), the daughter of a prominent local businessman.

Then, Mother Nature came to the rescue. In late March, Dayton experienced a massive flood, leaving 90,000 people homeless. Patterson quickly ordered his entire local workforce to help the citizens. They built boats in the factory to rescue people, fed them, and allowed them to shelter in NCR's buildings, located on high ground. The company helped thousands of people. The press lionized Patterson as a national hero. Pressure mounted on President Woodrow Wilson to pardon NCR's executives because of their humanitarian work. Patterson made it clear that he wanted simply to be cleared of wrongdoing by an appeals court. In 1915, that court ruled the original case defective and ordered the U.S. Department of Justice to retry it. The government prosecutors never did. Watson denied having done anything wrong, saying, "I do not consider myself a criminal" and "my conscience is clear."[6] Was he guilty? Probably, but he spent the rest of his life avoiding even the hint of impropriety. Before the case ended, in April 1914, Patterson fired Watson over a minor disagreement about sales strategy. Watson was 40 years old. He walked out the door as much an NCR employee as any the firm had groomed. Everything Watson knew about how to run a business he had learned at NCR.

What kind of person was he? He was alert, energetic, clear thinking, enormously confident, and always decisive. Watson had a sense of humor he rarely revealed; by nature, he was serious, with business always on his mind. Unlike Flint, and more like Hollerith, he had no interest in exercise or sports. He feared airplanes and was not personally adventuresome. He insisted that his buildings be conservative, too. For decades, their interiors were painted in two tones of green, darker below chair rail height, lime green above it to the ceiling. His son found him ill-tempered and formal, even with his family. Known for decades at IBM as "the Old Man," he insisted that everyone call each other by their last name, such as "Mr. Jones."[7] By the 1960s, it had become more customary to call one another by their first names. "Mr. Watson" wore starched collars, and his son recalled that his father came out of his bedroom every morning wearing a suit, white shirt, and tie, even for breakfast.[8] The Old Man prohibited consumption of alcohol on IBM property or with customers—a rule that remained company policy until the late 1980s.

One IBMer who worked on Watson Sr.'s personal staff in the early 1950s, Bryson H. Ainsley (b.1928), observed that Watson was critical of anyone who used the word "small" when identifying a strategy or action; he wanted "big." Ainsley recalled that Watson was a simple-talking man who never used large words; texts of his speeches confirm that observation. Watson was autocratic, confident, and sensitive. He could be harsh and demanding but was always optimistic. His picture hung on the walls of offices, conference rooms, and lobbies of IBM's buildings around the world. If Watson heard that an employee suffered a personal tragedy, he responded immediately with assistance, a well-phrased little note, or flowers. IBM was all about outstanding people properly trained as members of the "IBM Family" and with a clear understanding that much was expected of each.

Watson learned at NCR that clarity of purpose was essential. At NCR, he observed the power of frequent communications about goals and purposes and the effectiveness of having specific numeric measures of performance, such as establishing sales quotas and measuring performance against them. He brought these practices to IBM, making them central to its culture. It seemed to employees that "everything" was measured with targets compared to results achieved in sales, expenses, and production of machines. This feature is discussed in more detail later.

Watson had some of his own ideas, too. The most important involved his attitude toward failure, which he usually tolerated if lessons could be drawn from the experience and applied in a positive way. Unlike Patterson, Watson avoided firing people who made mistakes, although it was not uncommon to put someone who had failed into the "penalty box." That person either did not receive promotions or had them delayed. Ainsley witnessed Watson saying that IBM's success was because of people, not some elegant business strategy. He heard Watson frequently make the points that "people make the difference" and that "people make things happen," and Watson admonished IBMers in speeches and in meetings that "you make the difference."[9]

For decades, stories circulated about Watson's views on failure and on how he dealt with them. These included not firing someone who lost a large piece of business, because that person and IBM had just learned a lesson equal in value to the amount of revenue of the lost opportunity. So why not take advantage of that training some poor salesman just received? As in a hockey game, all employees could see the player in the penalty box. A young executive on his way up the organization might suddenly be pulled from his job and be assigned to a lateral or slightly less attractive position, have his job change posted on bulletin boards, and then six months to a year later be assigned to a more attractive role, also announced on bulletin boards, signaling that he could play again. This practice continued until the 1990s. Patterson, by contrast, was simply cruel. He was famous for cleaning out someone's office and putting a new name on the door without informing the executive that he had been fired. One fired executive found his desk on fire on the front lawn of corporate headquarters. That was not Watson's style.

IBM corporate mythology held that Watson established the company as the brilliant young sales executive brought over from NCR in 1914. Watson did not establish IBM; rather, he molded it out of the conglomeration of the three firms. So large was his influence inside the company that for nearly a half century tens of thousands of IBMers knew little about the origins of the company other than the story that Watson single-handedly turned the three firms of C-T-R into IBM. They heard nothing about the fact that it took him and a close coterie of long-serving handpicked executives nearly two decades to do that—or that he nearly failed.

Watson inherited a mess when he became C-T-R's general manager. Let us recall the situation he faced. The individual parts of C, T, and R were limping and hardly collaborated. In investigating whether to join the firm, Watson would have easily uncovered these facts. He must have scratched his head about how one could expand sales of meat scales, although time recording equipment fit with the basic function of collecting data. The tabulating machine business resembled cash registers that collected information of value to large organizations. Hollerith was difficult to deal with, proved less successful in selling his services, and took suggestions poorly. Years earlier, Watson had seen Hollerith's machines work at Eastman Kodak while visiting its headquarters in Rochester, New York. Kodak employees showed him how they used this equipment to track sales activities and explained the benefits obtained. At NCR, Watson reached out to Hollerith to do the same at his company. Watson began to track what his district managers were doing.[10]

Probably not anticipated by Flint was how Fairchild would work within C-T-R. He was supposed to be a figurehead to please the company's bankers and stockholders in ITR. Fairchild expressed most interest in enhancing the stock's value, reducing debt, and paying dividends. Watson wanted to plow profits back into expanding the business. Part of the dynamics of the relationships at the top of the business resulted from Flint's decision to bring Watson in as a general manager rather than as president. Recall that in 1914 Watson was a convicted federal felon, his case pending appeal. Flint, the board, and Watson struck a deal that if Watson were cleared of charges he would be named president, which happened the following year, shortly after his conviction was dismissed. Watson and Flint had already negotiated salary and profit-sharing terms. Because his original contract with C-T-R included provisions for sharing profits—not just stock and salary—when IBM became a large firm, he became one of the richest men in America.

Watson's experiences in sales and his basic optimism influenced his priorities and ways of working. The best salesmen and sales managers share a sense of optimism, the ability to envision a field of apple trees where others only see a field of grass. That was Watson's attitude. Watson had various options available to him when looking for a job. There were many executives John Patterson had fired for becoming too influential, who then scattered across many companies. But Watson also wanted a share of the profits, and that he wrangled out of Flint.

C-T-R's businesses held possibilities, with Hollerith's business desperately needing a professional sales force and new machines, too. Watson tapped other engineers besides Hollerith to develop them. Watson had learned at NCR how to develop a sales force and how high-tech machines were developed. ITR seemed poorly managed, but its products were in demand, and it had facilities outside the United States. Watson concluded that the scale business should be left alone for the time being. What made C-T-R attractive to Watson was the combination of applying his sales experience to an existing market and the opportunity to create personal wealth. His decision to join C-T-R turned out to be one of the best he made in his life, for it put him on the path to developing one of the iconic firms of the twentieth century and in the process made him a wealthy and highly respected businessman. That C-T-R had serious operational problems, while not to be ignored, represented *challenges* to overcome. Watson's fundamental problem was to generate sufficient sales to keep the business going, and when he realized that two parts of C-T-R, ITR and Tabulating Machines, made data processing equipment, he had to create new products attractive to the market. Hollerith was not effective in fighting competitors, most notably James Powers (1871–1927) and his company, Powers Accounting Machines. Powers never went away; his efforts became part of Remington Rand in 1927.[11]

When Watson decided to prioritize the tabulating equipment market, he shifted resources to Hollerith's side of the business, brought in new people to develop tabulating equipment, created an effective professional sales force, and expanded placement of tabulating equipment worldwide. Watson began to implement the NCR culture. Already a stern, self-disciplined, sober man, he projected his personal values and behaviors on C-T-R more thoroughly than Patterson had at NCR, because he had a fully formed view of the business world. It is an important point to make, because the cultural evolution of a firm usually takes time and yet it happened so quickly at C-T-R/IBM. The speed with which this happened can be explained by a combination of Watson's preexisting practices and beliefs and his determined will and confidence.

Later in this chapter, I describe the wholesale adoption of NCR's approach to sales operations. Watson injected NCR's approach to sales by bringing in new salesmen and teaching them NCR's way of doing business. Watson often quipped that he enjoyed "collecting salesmen," and he continued to do so at C-T-R. For decades, it was common for an unsuspecting IBM branch manager to get a phone call from New York headquarters telling him that Watson had hired a salesman in that manager's city who would soon be showing up to work. That manager quickly had to figure how to fund his salary, get him trained, and carve out a territory for him, all unplanned, of course.

Watson reshaped budgets and personnel practices into NCR's model. To create synergies across the three divisions, he implemented a Quarter Century Club to celebrate the twenty-fifth anniversary of an employee's tenure at C-T-R, posting pictures of these people together, regardless of which part of the business they came from. Salesmen from each division underwent common training. Watson Sr. personally ran the first of what famously became known as "Sales School," a training program that continues to the present, where one learned about IBM's values, selling techniques, internal operational procedures, and products.[12] A salesman was not allowed to "manage" a sales territory without having "graduated" from Sales School. It took several years to implement these selling and sales management techniques. There seemed to be no significant exceptions to Watson's wholesale borrowing. NCR's sales culture became IBM's, tailored to sell the more complicated tabulating products. In the process, IBM's corporate culture also became a sales culture.

Watson made other appropriations from NCR's engineering and product development, hiring engineers from his old employer, notably for punch card tabulating. To improve efficiencies, he situated product developers and manufacturing staff in the same buildings. They could borrow talent from one part of a plant site to help out on problems and designs. IBM honed collaboration among designers and manufacturing staff, such that it was able to nearly mass-produce tabulating and, later, computer products.[13] IBM's production methods brought yet another form of NCR's discipline to the company. Extensive training of *customers* in how to use IBM's products took place at factory sites, giving engineers opportunities to receive feedback and ideas from users of their creations.[14]

Just as important as operational improvements were the values Watson implemented, again over many years but so thoughtfully that for many decades they remained core to any understanding of how IBM functioned. A new CEO, Louis V. Gerstner Jr., when faced with a "mess" of his own in the early 1990s, found that he could not change the firm's values and culture as much as he wanted. Watson had brought to the company a philosophy, an ethos almost spiritual in form, which had helped to guide decisions and ethical practices of IBM's employees for generations. By the 1930s, employees had embraced the opinion that if everyone shared common beliefs and practices, individuals could make decisions and take actions confident they were doing the right thing. When IBM became large, this feature of its culture increased in importance. IBM had over 400,000 employees by the 1980s; over 1 million people had worked for IBM during its century of existence, in some 170 countries, so they could not run to management every time they faced a conundrum. Too often, they had to make their own decisions. That is where a shared system of values and practices proved its worth.[15] It would be difficult to exaggerate the importance of the worldview Watson implanted in IBM.[16]

Of course, there were countercurrents. Managers wanted to control activities. That impetus for control and management of potential risks led to the rise of bureaucracy, characterized by highly defined processes. Generations of executives micromanaged people all the way down the organization while fighting the growth of paperwork and "signoffs." Such behavior also originated with Watson Sr., who exhibited such contradictory behavior. A vast number of decisions came to him, so many that when his son Tom took over the business in the mid-1950s, one of the first things he did was reorganize IBM to move decision making out of headquarters and into the broader organization.

Yet, simultaneously, the Old Man admonished employees to take individual responsibility for running their "piece of the business," a phrase used frequently by executives with their staffs. Reflecting back on his first ten years at IBM in 1924, Watson Sr. told a class of the company's executives that, "It is our policy not to burden any one man, or any group of men, with the responsibility of running this business."[17] He gave thousands of talks to employees extolling these themes and a positive philosophy about IBM sales. By the early 1920s, this eternal optimist had begun telling salesmen that only 5 percent of all business information was handled by data processing, leaving 95 percent yet to be seized, a magnificent sales opportunity. He spent more time talking to his employees around the world than most future CEOs at IBM would. He met continuously with customers and public officials, far less so with the media.

FROM C-T-R TO IBM: WATSON'S EARLY ACTIONS

With the federal charges behind him and the board having named him president, Watson moved forward with authority. His biographer Kevin Maney argued that Watson "had to prove to the world that he was a moral and straight-shooting businessman. To do that, Watson needed to build C-T-R into a great and admired company, instilled with the high moral values of an orthodox religion."[18] In other words, he wanted to do better than Patterson. He dove into C-T-R's operations with energy, leaning on his executives for improved performance and information about their business. Soon after his arrival, World War I sharply reduced U.S. exports and demand for his equipment in Europe. Not until the United States entered the war in April 1917 would that situation turn around.

One of Watson's first priorities was to scour C-T-R to see where in-house talent lay. He also recruited executives from NCR. He recalled years later that C-T-R's three lines of business "were not disorganized—they were unorganized. There were plenty of ideas lying around, but many of them seemed too big for the organization to handle."[19] He needed managers who could integrate these operations. An early recruit to his management team, Otto Braitmayer, helped him navigate through C-T-R. Described by associates as loveable, chubby, thoughtful, and smiley, he had worked for Hollerith since age 15. He emerged as one of Watson's favorite employees, serving as his secretary. As Watson became more serious and autocratic, Braitmayer remained approachable and likeable. Watson assigned him responsibility for improving engineering operations and later for opening offices outside the United States. In the early 1930s, he joined the board of directors of IBM. From Computing Scale, Watson found a second ally, Samuel Hastings, an older, highly skilled businessman. At ITR, Watson discovered A. Ward Ford, who had helped Flint find Watson and sat on C-T-R's board. He became a confidant and friend of Watson's.

Watson preferred to recruit his managers from within the firm, a practice brought over from NCR, but in the beginning of his tenure in 1914–1916, he sometimes had to reach out. He brought in Fred Nichol, his assistant/secretary when he served as general sales manager at NCR, to fill the same role: secretary, adviser, and "go-to" manager for ad hoc projects and crisis management. Maney described Nichol "as indispensable to Watson as Oxygen."[20] He brought discipline and order to operations around Watson as the new president became involved in all facets of the company's operations. Some recruits did not work out, while board members often sided with Fairchild.

Watson also had to run the business, not just recruit executives and fight his board. Ford wrested engineering away from Hollerith, despite

Fairchild's hostility to an expensive R&D operation. Almost from the beginning, and increasingly as the years passed, Watson made it clear to anyone who would listen, or had to, that Hollerith's side of the business represented the growth opportunity, to the consternation of management in the two other divisions.

ITR's management never felt that Watson took them seriously enough, although they were profitable, and so sometimes they worked behind his back. Until Watson arrived at C-T-R, ITR was the flagship of the company. While Watson devoted less attention to ITR, its management dominated the board of directors, so they could challenge his requests to invest more in tabulating sales and manufacturing. Watson successfully cultivated Flint as an ally, especially after two bad years for C-T-R at the start of the 1920s. Remember, Watson had yet to become the absolute ruler at C-T-R. Flint backed Watson, having concluded that Watson's energy and attitudes could improve business and that Watson would run a "clean operation." Flint sided with him on funding for an R&D laboratory in 1916, an extra budget to train salesmen, sharing part of ITR's factory space in Endicott to make tabulating equipment, and blocking payment of dividends so that Watson could invest in the firm. No dividends were paid in 1914 and 1915.

After Watson became president in 1915, he instructed engineering to develop new tabulators, time recording devices, and printers, pushing them harder at the end of World War I, when he anticipated expanding demand to continue. He wanted Computing Scale to generate profits to feed the rest of the business, wanted ITR to improve its performance, and began shifting resources to Tabulating Machine.

In the late 1910s, Watson increased the number of managers and replaced others to strengthen C-T-R's capabilities. For example, Watson hired Joseph Rogers as the general manager of ITR, since Fairchild—its head—was spending much of his time in Washington, D.C. Watson and Rogers were the same age, had experienced the NCR lawsuit together, left NCR at about the same time, and shared a vision of how businesses should be run. Rogers played a crucial role in implementing Watson's worldview, style of management, and corporate culture. Over in R&D, Ford brought in Clair Lake and Fred Carroll, two young draftsmen who went on to develop many tabulating products in Endicott. In the beginning, they acquired Powers equipment, taking them apart and coming up with their own versions with slight modifications or improvements. It was a quick way to develop competitive products. Once Watson was able to wrest funds from his board, his engineers began designing new products from scratch to gain technological leadership. Watson kept building up his capability to sell these new products. With new offerings, C-T-R could lease machines that were technologically competitive, priced lower than Powers's, and could be offered on more attractive terms. The strategy worked.

Watson's first national sales campaign came in the summer of 1915. Already he had imposed enough of the NCR way to push for increased sales, especially for tabulators. World War I created demand for C-T-R's products, so his timing was good for improved sales operations and new products. It is difficult to tell if he knew how bad things had been at tabulating sales, as he received much of his information from Hollerith, but we have the memoirs of a tabulating salesman of the period, Walter D. Jones. He had joined Hollerith's operations in 1912 as a salesman in Cincinnati, and other than for a short stint outside the firm between 1918 and 1922, he worked at IBM until he retired.[21] He spent the bulk of his successful career in sales and exhibited good powers of observation. In Hollerith's organization, he had already spent two years selling before Watson showed up. His perspective reflected Watson's: "At the time when Mr. Watson took over the management of CTR in 1914, it is safe to say that every member of the sales force of the CTR thought that The Company was on the upswing of an unending period of growth," Jones reflected. But Jones also recalled an ugly story that confirmed Watson's negative suspicions about Hollerith's inability to sell. Jones told the story of a potential customer he was calling on around 1912 who pulled "out of his desk a four- or five-line letter from Dr. Hollerith" that no salesman would ever want to see go out to a prospect:

> To answer your letter of today relative to the use of our tabulating machines for our business: I can say only that your company's scope and activity is not sufficiently large enough to warrant an installation of our machines.

Yet Jones reported in his memoirs that at the time he and all his colleagues thought the current pre-Watson product line could be sold to such customers, that they "would do the trick."[22]

Sales in 1914 reached $4.1 million, but by the end of 1917, Watson had pushed them to $8.3 million. Earnings (profits) quadrupled, from $400,000 to $1.6 million, with all three divisions prospering. Even Computing Scale did well, because its products were adapted to new purposes, such as weighing nuts and bolts in shipyards and factories. ITR's products were in greater demand because of increased wartime manufacturing. In 1917, ITR opened a factory and a sales office in Toronto, Canada.

But the big news came out of Tabulating Machines. By the end of 1917, it had 1,400 tabulators and 1,100 card sorters on lease with some 650 customers. Almost every large U.S. insurance company, many federal and state agencies, and numerous railroads used Hollerith's machines. Tabulating Machines moved into ITR's facility in Toronto to extend its reach into Canada. The card business was booming, too, with the Washington, D.C., plant producing 80 million per month, with even more from Computing Scale's factory in Dayton, Ohio. The following year, production grew to 110 million cards per month. Historian Robert Sobel pointed out, however, that success was less the result of great salesmanship and more a result of Powers's crippling inability to produce enough of its machines during the war. C-T-R simply seized the day.[23] Part of C-T-R's success was made possible by the war's high equipment demand, which Watson and his senior managers expected would shrink with peacetime unless additional customers could be found, especially for tabulating products.

In 1918, Watson brought together under single management all three sales forces reporting directly to him in order to increase his ability to quickly shift salesmen to specific opportunities. Inventory would be coming back from expired leases. To lease this equipment again, he needed continued economic prosperity in North America and elsewhere. In 1919, C-T-R introduced a new printer-lister that printed data from tabulators and sorters. It was an important product because until then one could not see totals and printed reports. For years, auditors and accountants had requested C-T-R build such a machine. Watson priced it below Powers's equivalent product. This machine signaled that Watson's engineers, largely Ford, Lake, and Carroll, were on their way to building a new post-Hollerith generation of equipment. By 1923, C-T-R's products dominated the market for punch card equipment with competitively priced offerings. Demand for the printer-lister exceeded forecasts, and both North American and European markets were expanding. Watson increased production and research at Endicott. To give a sense of the firm's prosperity, in 1919 net sales and lease revenues had reached $13 million and profits (earnings) exceeded $2.1 million.

But all was not perfect. Available cash for expansion became a serious problem in 1920 as the nation entered a recession. That year, the business spun off barely enough earnings to finance Watson's investment in manufacturing, product development, and staffing, but the Tabulating and ITR divisions were sustaining demand. European sales rose. Watson and most others in the company were optimistic as they worked their way through 1921, but they were wrong.

The following year, revenue fell by nearly a third and profits by 40 percent. Computing Scale became a colossal mess with shrinking revenue, which forced it to shutter a subsidiary at a cost of $216,000. Meanwhile Fairchild and other board members wanted dividends, while Watson still advocated investing in the business. He lost that argument. Dividends cost a half million dollars, which plunged C-T-R into an operating budget deficit of $100,000 that year. Watson had no choice but to start trimming costs. For the first time in the company's history, he laid off workers and "furloughed" some salesmen. His R&D operations shrank to almost nothing; wages were slashed by 10 percent for everyone, including himself. He even had to stop manufacturing printer-listers, despite demand, to keep C-T-R solvent. So the early 1920s were hardly a period of healthy recovery. Watson's quick retrenchment of costs and operations saved the firm, as did his ability to persuade creditors to delay debt payments. Flint's old bank, Guaranty Trust, which had bankrolled C-T-R in 1911, allowed Watson to refinance the company's debt, while Tabulating Machines kept coming through with sales and hence cash. Senior management in 1921 and 1922 had thought customers would pull back purchases during the U.S. recession, the main cause for retrenchment at C-T-R, but for the second time they were wrong, because this time customers were coming out of the recession.

Customers wanted equipment to control their own expenses as they, too, struggled through the recession. In hindsight, reducing production of the printer-lister had been a mistake. Even during 1922, when Watson restarted production of this and other equipment, ITR's performance remained flat because of layoffs. Watson decided not to supply it or Computing Scale with an investment budget. Available funds had to be plowed into the successful tabulating business, regardless of what the two other divisions or the board wanted. Fortunately for Watson, his position within the firm was sufficiently strong to ward off critics, buttressed by his positive performance prior to 1922.

But Watson learned some lessons that stayed with him for the rest of his life. Never again would he allow the company's supply of cash to drop below what the firm needed. He paid low dividends but always paid them. By the standards of his day, he maintained relatively high cash reserves, and always closely monitored all expenses, both capital and operating, even in boom periods. Future generations of IBM executives did the same.[24]

BIRTH OF A SALES CULTURE

The purpose of a sales force is to bring a company's value proposition—its "deal"—to customers. That value proposition results in the development of a company's "go-to-market" strategy, how it will implement that plan. Central to that activity can be a direct sales force, people who meet face-to-face with customers, a typical approach with complex and expensive equipment. For simple products, a catalog or store can suffice, and today even a simple website will do. In 1914, ITR's and Hollerith's products were complicated, and so one had to make a clear case about why customers should buy them.

There was considerable consistency across the decades about IBM's value proposition.[25] Watson explained to a new batch of executives that, "We are furnishing merchants, manufacturers and other businessmen with highly efficient machines which save them money." For the larger IBM community, he followed with, "That is why we are going to make more money for this business."[26] He spoke about how IBM created value. By 1920, Watson was preaching that the way to accomplish C-T-R's goals was "to serve better industry's vital requirements—the need to conserve time, motions and money."[27] He introduced a signature for IBM sales literature, too, that delivered a sound-bite value proposition used for decades:

"Speed,
Accuracy, and
Flexibility."

Watson established the first company-wide view at C-T-R, which continued to solidify after it became IBM. At its heart was what employees should believe, and what motivated them was their sales culture, even in such seemingly faraway places as the factory floor, development lab, or some administrative office. Watson implemented measures of performance, along with financial and career incentives aligned with objectives of the firm and its beliefs, a collection that remained remarkably intact for decades.[28] Although difficult to explain to someone who has not worked at IBM, its culture could nevertheless be seen by looking at its values, already briefly introduced. They are worth expanding on, specifically the incentives and expectations placed on sales and, effectively, on the entire company. They shaped IBM's information ecosystem, reinforced through its symbols and rituals. Between 1914 and 1924, many of the elements of IBM's culture were solidly in place. In the first decade of Watson's rule, it was unclear to customers and to other observers what C-T-R's business was all about. Undoubtedly, its employees wondered, too, particularly as Watson went about the task of remaking the firm. But not Watson; he had a clear and confident view of what he was attempting to do. By the 1930s, executives in other companies were marveling at how quickly this strategy had occurred at IBM and how effective it seemed to be. Watson's creation of C-T-R's sales culture represented a giant step forward in making IBM an iconic company.

After barely six months at C-T-R, Watson was telling employees that the "factory force backs salesmen in spirit and in fact." He encouraged cross-divisional collaboration to "be familiar with your own and similar lines" of products and procedures. "Cooperation" was key to success.[29] Watson was already touting the importance of individual motivation, preaching that "every man works for the same thing—success." He delivered these homilies thousands of times over the next 40 years.

The firm had the makings of a working viewpoint to underpin collaboration among product developers, manufacturing, and sales, discussed earlier in this chapter. The numerous company-wide slogans, beginning in the 1910s, captured the essence of much of the sales thinking of both NCR and IBM: "Time lost is time gone forever," "We must never feel satisfied," and the most pervasive, "THINK." Watson had used the last one with his sales force at NCR and transferred it to C-T-R nearly the day he arrived at his office at 50 Broad Street in Lower Manhattan, but he also said "Act." He valued the good citizen salesman who was sincere, always exhibited absolute integrity, was loyal to the firm, and looked out for the best interests of the company's customers. Watson spoke in slogans, a way of talking that pervaded many of his speeches: "We sell and deliver services," and the often used, "A company is known by the men it keeps." He paid particular attention to instilling his worldview among salesmen: "When practicing the art of selling use all your talents," and "Put everything you have into your efforts; above all, put your personality into them."[30]

To today's readers and historians, these missives seem so obvious and simplistic, and THINK is seen as innovative. However, in Watson's day, with a less educated workforce and with a limited body of codified best practices such as managers have today, his sound bites set expectations for performance that he considered essential for the success of the firm. These reflected his thinking, his "philosophy," and he was not shy about spreading these messages.[31]

A closely related idea was his urging people to collaborate—today we call it teamwork. If a salesman ran into a problem with one of his customers, he was expected to go to his management or colleagues to collectively figure out how to resolve the issue. Failure to bring forward a problem that the salesman could not solve himself was a mortal sin to Watson and to generations of sales managers and executives; not being able to solve it individually was seen as less of a problem. Many of the issues a sales "rep" faced were complicated, such as how to use a tabulator in a specific accounting operation that perhaps someone else had already resolved in another account, or how to persuade a customer to pay a long overdue bill. Collaboration made sense. To collect information from salesmen and their customers, management brought them to Endicott to sit down with design engineers and manufacturing employees, a practice still occurring today. The need to work long hours in an increasingly cerebral business as products became more complex required commitment and loyalty to the firm on the part of large swaths of the company, from factory floor to corporate headquarters.

So, how was all this done? Following the practice of the day, Watson opened small sales offices around the United States, increasing their number to dozens over his first decade at C-T-R/IBM. He did the same in Europe, Latin America, Asia, and finally in Africa. These were called "branch offices" (figure 2.2), a term still used. They were small, often with less than a half dozen salesmen and a "branch manager." Those in large cities like New York and Chicago grew to dozens of employees. Branches reported to district managers, who had geographic territories, and those also increased in number over the decades. In the period from 1914 to the late 1930s, all sales functions reported directly to Watson Sr., who managed them much as he had done at NCR. Every regional manager, then every branch manager, and then every salesman was assigned a "quota," which when all rolled up equaled or slightly exceeded targets set by Watson for the company's performance as a whole.

It is important to understand Watson's quota system because it remained in use at IBM for over half a century. Unlike at most firms, quotas were not expressed in dollars (revenue). Watson's measure of revenue was one point for every dollar of rent that came in each month. For example, if a machine rented for $200 per month, it was worth 200 points to a salesman. He was expected to keep that 200 points installed, and if it was replaced, it would ideally be with a machine that rented for more than $200 per month, or more than 200 points, because his quota was set in points that he was to add to the "install base" of points. If the salesman was assigned a quota of

Figure 2.2
An early branch office (1927), this one located in Washington, D.C., with its staff. These offices were a combination retail outlet and training center. Photo courtesy of IBM Corporate Archives.

200 points, and what was already installed was 1,000 points, he would be expected in the course of the year to "grow the account" by 200 points so that at the end of the year his customer was spending $1,200 per month, and he now had an "installed base" of 1,200 points. If some installed equipment went away because of a competitor's good work, or was swapped out for newer IBM equipment, the salesman had to make up the loss, in our example ending the year with 1,200 points installed. He was paid a salary, commissions per point installed, plus bonuses if he sold specific items the company was promoting or exceeded his targets. IBM was emphasizing bonuses at any particular moment or for exceeding the salesman's objectives. Watson's point system kept a salesman focused on simple numbers and on building up his installed base. It worked.

It also worked at another level. Watson knew that to sell tabulating equipment, his sales staff needed to invest time in an account to deeply understand a business function. That meant maintaining relations with customers based on collaboration focused on improving a customer's operations. As long as equipment was leased, the salesman's success was tied to that of his customer and the point system, which debited equipment that left a client's data center. The point system also focused the salesman's attention on the specific increase in revenue at the exact spot of its creation (a specific machine, for example).

When a salesman, sales manager, branch manager, or district manager "made their numbers," meaning "made quota," achieved their targets, in our example the 200 points or more, he (decades later, she, too) joined the "100 Percent Club." At NCR, it had been the "100 Point Club." Over the decades, it became a crucial measure of how successful sales personnel were: the more clubs one had earned, the more prestige they experienced, and as the company grew in size, an essential set of targets was required for promotion. In Watson's day, he would bring all the 100 Percent Club members together for a spring or early summer celebratory meeting. That gathering consisted of about 80 percent of the sales force, a percentage that remained fairly constant for decades. In the United States, in the C-T-R days, they came to a hotel, as they numbered around 20, which increased to a couple of hundred in the 1920s and to over 800 by the end of the 1930s.

Later, American salesmen came to "Tent City" at Endicott, New York, lived in military-styled white tents, ate in a larger one, and endured motivational speeches by Watson and other executives in humid June, all wearing suits. Plant personnel made presentations about new products and ideas, and Watson brought in famous speakers, too. Ainsley recalled that Watson liked his rustic tents; life was easier in the earlier 100 Percent Clubs. Watson and his wife stayed in a house on the IBM site, called the Homestead. When Ainsley attended Sales School in Endicott, he lived in a tent for eight weeks and later came back to the same tents for his 100 Percent Club meetings.[32] The walkways between rows of tents were given names such as "Customer Circle," "Prospect Road," and "Demonstration Thoroughfare."

A bugle woke up the camp, and everyone was then given a glass of warm water.

But points, quotas, and 100 Percent Clubs were not enough to ensure success. Watson had learned at NCR that careful training of salesmen was crucial to their success. Because the company's products were so essential to the operations of large enterprises, at C-T-R/IBM it likewise was necessary that his sales force know what they were doing. Failure to recommend and then implement equipment properly could put a customer at risk of severely damaging their own operations and shutting off future sales.[33]

Watson published a sales manual that used NCR's as a model, which grew in size as the product line evolved. NCR's manual had almost 200 pages by the time Watson joined C-T-R.[34] These were loose-leaf binders that contained descriptions of every product, their technical specifications (such as how fast they processed cards and the amount of floor space they required), cost in points, and leasing terms and conditions. Updated pages were constantly mailed to salesmen, which they placed in their binders, throwing away earlier pages. A parallel group of workers, field engineers, had a similar set of materials, which included instructions on how to install and repair equipment. They worked closely with salesmen. Field engineers from around the world learned to set up and repair equipment in Endicott. Their binders, embossed with their names, served as their bibles.

Watson required salesmen to meet every Friday to review that week's results, to discuss issues they faced, to learn about changes in company policy, to work out what they planned to do the following week, and to forecast how much additional business they were going to bring in; that is to say, what they were going "to close." By the 1930s, they sang songs about IBM and how wonderful Watson and other executives were to the firm. Branch managers reported sales results, their information moving up the chain of command until landing on Watson's desk in the form of consolidated reports by region and product, sometimes presented as low in the organization as at the branch level. By the early 1920s, salesmen were required to report in writing how many sales calls they made and the results, which Watson's staff combined with forecasts and revenue gained, using punched cards to collate the data to inform senior management about sales activity. Watson read these reports with enormous interest, demonstrating to his district managers that he often knew as much about their business as they did. That information was shared with product development and marketing as well, adding another link to tightly connect field operations (sales and services) to other parts of the firm. Today this is a routine operation in any corporation, but in the 1910s or 1920s, only the most operationally advanced firms had begun to build this kind of information ecosystem.

Watson introduced a third practice that he had used both as a new salesman and later in his various sales management positions at NCR: the salesman's "territory." A salesman would be assigned a "patch," consisting of one or more "accounts," which constituted *his* territory. He was the lord and master over that "patch," the "gatekeeper." No other IBM salesman could "sell into" or "poach" in another's territory. Many IBM people might come in and out of an account (defined as a company or entire agency, not an individual) to help a salesman, but only the assigned "rep" was paid commission on what was sold in that territory. The same applied to branch offices, which had territories comprised of the sum of those assigned to their salesmen.[35]

Watson added various measures, creating a culture of measuring everything. Some of his favorite measures included size of accounts, quotas and whether they were being attained, budgets, expenditures, number of employees, trends in sales, losses to competitors, and "wins," the latter either the acquisition of a new customer or new large orders within an existing account. In the 1920s, branch office reviews began, a practice that quickly became routine. These reviews conformed to Watson's style of management and how sales reviews were handled at NCR. Middle managers and executives listened to formal presentations made by branch management and salesmen about their account plans, activities, results, forecasts, and needs. We come back to these in later chapters because such reviews became major events in "the field."[36]

Central to "growing" sales was expanding the reach of branch offices, because salesmen had to live in the same communities as their customers, belong to the same country clubs, civic organizations, and churches, and be members of the local social and political elite. That is largely why Watson insisted on conservative dress and behavior. To draw in entire families of IBM employees from across the company, not just the sales force, to be loyal to the firm, he instituted the practice of hosting Family Dinners all over the world. A branch manager would arrange, at the largest, fanciest hotel in his city, the dinner for wives and husbands, at which Watson and his wife, Jeanette, or a senior executive and his spouse, would attend as hosts, give a pep talk about the company, and thank the wives for being supportive of their husbands. These were elegant, dressy events with formal written invitations and elegant meals. In cities like New York and Paris, it was not uncommon for live music to be played and for many hundreds of IBM employees and their wives to attend. Local newspapers covered these dinners in their society pages.

At plant sites such as Endicott, there soon developed the additional practice of IBM hosting family picnics with children, held at Easter time, in the summer, and even as Christmas parties with presents for the little ones. Beginning in the 1920s, plant sites ran IBM country clubs where local employees could join for $1.[37] Many practices came from NCR, where an extensive paternalistic approach toward employees and their families had gained the company much national acclaim. NCR and IBM fit squarely into the model of welfare capitalism described by Andrea Tone, for example.[38] Watson understood very well what was required to offer such amenities and the benefits that accrued to the company by doing so.[39]

In trying to link together the three legs of C-T-R, recall that Watson devised the Quarter Century Club to recognize employees who had worked for the various divisions for a quarter century. He would send an employee a congratulatory letter, thanking him or her for their service, and welcome them to membership in the Quarter Century Club. In time, that milestone would be accompanied by a certificate and lapel pin, and after World War II by a Quarter Century Club logo on their calling cards. Later, an employee would also receive a gift. As early as the 1910s, when an employee reached this milestone, local management hosted a luncheon for the employee, spouse, a few old C-T-R friends, and relatives. Small speeches honored the individual's contributions to the firm.

These various activities reinforced a common view of the firm's objectives and culture around the world, with hundreds of small groups of IBMers. To foster a view of the business that was shared worldwide, from the earliest days, Watson and his senior executives spent the majority of their time speaking to groups of IBMers and meeting with customers and local public officials around the world. That helped to project a consistent image of IBM while ensuring that Watson's messages reached the IBM community. Sales School classes, Family Dinners, and 100 Percent Club events were some of the most widely used occasions for Watson to spout his philosophy, including the quotations cited earlier. Sometimes his speeches were long and boring, but his wife would slip him a note to "sit down." Nobody in IBM could ever say that to the Old Man, but Jeanette could do so. In his early years, Watson communicated frequently to individual IBMers and through mass mailing of messages. Newsletters came and went, but by the 1930s, plant general managers began publishing division or "site" newsletters, too.

IBM added layers of additional features and events onto Watson's original system of incentives and rituals. By the start of 1924, Watson had laid down much of the groundwork for the sales and corporate culture that would endure for most of the twentieth century. By that time, manufacturing, development, and sales talked to each other, while employees understood much of the mission and goals of the company. The rudiments of the Basic Beliefs were emerging, along with how to implement them through the hiring of quality people, good and timely training, and a focus on customers and selling solutions rather than machines, which required a solution-minded selling process. Aligning organizational structures, incentives, and marketing in support of this strategy had been pretty much set on its trajectory by 1924. Much had been accomplished. Just a few months earlier, Watson had spouted that "everybody was a salesman." Much remained to be done, of course, but future CEOs ignored these perspectives at their peril.

Did Watson's innovations at C-T-R work? To what extent had he transformed the business to leverage synergies across the enterprise and improve productivity, two concerns Flint had when searching for a general manager in 1914? Besides measuring revenues and profits for results, another concern was situating branch offices. They needed to be near potential customers in fashionable business centers. IBM had to rent office space, fill it with equipment, have desk space for salesmen and storage space for parts, and everything had to look attractive. IBM had to build a staff and pay them, so their cost had to be offset by the prospect of gaining more business than if they did not have a local office. For example, in Nashville, Tennessee, IBM salesmen had been coming to the city from other locations to sell tabulating equipment to the state government and had started to do the same with local banks and insurance companies since the early 1920s. Business kept growing, creating a need for locally resident repair personnel and sales representatives, so in 1935 IBM opened a branch office in the city.[40] While some branch offices later closed or were consolidated, IBM retained its presence in Nashville into the twenty-first century. A branch office therefore reflected a certain level of business already achieved before opening its doors and served as an optimistic statement of future prospects. They were expensive, because they had to look sharp and modern as part of the selling of IBM's image, much like Apple stores today. Watson opened the first ones in large cities, such as New York, London, and Chicago, often personally selecting their sites and managers.[41] By 1924, over one hundred operated worldwide, some as wholly owned subsidiaries or franchises. Almost all displayed the C-T-R or IBM logo. Figure 2.3 documents the expansion of branch offices during Watson's first decade at IBM.

ON THE VERGE OF A TRANSFORMED COMPANY

By the end of 1923, Watson had finally gained control over a company with a bright future. Fairchild had lost much influence by staying so focused on his congressional and diplomatic career, and he died at the end of the next year. Flint was still vigorous at 73 years of age and solidly a Watson ally, and an ailing 63-year-old Hollerith had been sidelined, no longer influencing decisions and the direction of the company. Watson had his own handpicked team running sales, R&D, and manufacturing, and he was rapidly building a sales culture. He assumed the position of chief executive officer, the position of chairman of the board having been abolished. No one told him what to do

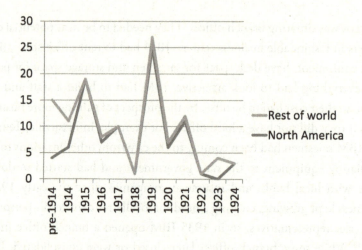

Figure 2.3

Number of C-T-R branch openings, 1914–1924.

but himself and his wife. Watson was 50 years old, vigorous, in great health, and in charge of an exciting company. The company's financial picture was improving, too. In 1922, gross income had been a flat $9 million, just as in the previous year, but in 1923, the company turned in a solid performance, with income of $11 million. More crucial for the health of the business, net earnings doubled from $1 million in 1922 to $2 million in 1923. In both years, C-T-R employed over 3,000 people, hundreds of them new to the firm. A third of the total worked outside the United States. Table 2.1 summarizes the results of Watson's first decade at the helm of IBM.

The number and diversity of IBM's customers increased throughout the decade, as did the variety of new products. The 1910s and early 1920s were all about table setting: the unglamorous work of fighting competition and board members with conflicting agendas, and shaping a culture and purpose. In 1914, C-T-R was adrift and Watson was unemployed, but the world was rapidly embracing the mantra of information as a mechanism for running big organizations. If only someone could harness that energy underlying the expansion of so many "office appliance" firms and their customers, going beyond desktop calculators, adding machines, cash registers, and the humble typewriter. America was booming; Europe hoped to be soon.

Table 2.1

C-T-R/IBM revenue, net earnings, and number of employees, 1914–1924, select years
(revenue and earnings in millions of dollars)

Year	Revenue	Net earnings	Number of employees
1914	4	1	1,346
1916	6	1	2,529
1918	8	1	3,127
1920	14	2	2,731
1922	9	1	3,043
1924	11	2	3,384

Amounts rounded.

Source: Emerson W. Pugh, *Building IBM: Shaping an Industry and Its Technology* (Cambridge, MA: MIT Press, 1995), 323.

Watson's in-house inventors were busy, as we will see in chapter 3.[42] Powers remained a thorn in Watson's side—a point overlooked by many observers. Hollerith still showed up to work. Yet the future "Old Man" was clever and calculating. None of his contemporaries doubted that, and neither did his biographers.

On the matter of business strategy—always the darling of business historians and managers—one normally begins by turning to Alfred D. Chandler Jr. for insights.[43] He found that successful firms invested heavily in product development, manufacturing, and distribution; that is, they scaled up to meet market demands. However, our narrative suggests that C-T-R did not have a cohesive strategy before 1914. But within a year of Watson's appearance, he had a "game plan." He took many of the same methodical steps commonly evident in large enterprises after management and business historians had discovered the existence of strategy.[44] Watson behaved like a Chandlerian manager. His plan involved creating a professional sales force, focusing on tabulating equipment, introducing new tab products, too, and expanding the set of customers he wished to sell to by focusing on large enterprises and government agencies in a dozen countries.

Anticipating our discussion in chapter 3, the 1920s and 1930s saw a solidified IBM emerging as an up-and-coming American enterprise. Its culture jelled; Watson found his voice. In the 1920s, Watson had cast aside "the impossible and absurd project of rendering ourselves universally agreeable," to use Adam Smith's description of a well-formed adult.[45] Corporate culture proved important in the early years and even more so in the decades that followed, reinforcing arguments made by business historians such as Scranton, Fridenson, and Zeitlin that successful corporations were social institutions as much as economic ones.[46] Watson did not precisely understand the concept of "corporate culture," but he appreciated the need for shared values and rituals as mechanisms to impose order in how his company operated and dealt with the world. His tabulating machines extended the accountant's penchant for numeric and operational structure, predictability, and rational views of their entire enterprise.

Business historians have long debated the nexus of strategy and management. Often the debate seemed to turn on pro-Chandlerian versus anti-Chandlerian perspectives. Watson's early efforts at C-T-R/IBM suggest that all historians have a place at the table. Watson would have agreed with Chandler that the organization should be professionally run, focused on specific strategies, and operate with sufficient investments in product development, marketing and sales (what Chandler called distribution), and post-sale services and support of customers, but Watson also knew, as did Chandler's critics, that a company was a social ecosystem.[47] We follow both perspectives throughout this book.

Other historians argue that large enterprises were subject to "path dependencies," meaning they followed preexisting technological, social, economic, and cultural paths.[48] In Watson's early years at C-T-R, such path dependency was less secure, as he was shaping a new way in emerging markets, but to secure our chronology, this alternative collection of interpretations, often contrary to Chandler's, increasingly applied to Watson's organization. Shaping IBM was a continual process of solidifying Watson's view of how a great company should function. In subsequent chapters, we will see practices that lent themselves to historical interpretations of how large U.S. companies blossomed along alternative paths, such as path dependencies, or that viewed enterprises as ecosystems made up of many subcommunities but also not incompatible with Chandler's focus on strategy, its implementation, and the role of well-informed professional managers. Indeed, a sociological view of IBM's evolution makes perfect sense, along with doses of path dependency.[49]

All subsequent chapters will demonstrate that the various schools of thought regarding evolution of different-sized organizations have much to offer, and here I find value in combining them. To be clear about what I mean, first, I accept that Chandler was absolutely correct in saying that successful businesses had a strategy for implementing what they wanted to do and how and that they built organizations for the purpose of carrying out that strategy. Second, as Scranton and others have argued, both small and large enterprises were social constructs, and the behavior and evidence they offered in their own studies are reinforced and further demonstrated in this history of IBM. In other words, there is no pro or contrarian view of Chandlerian history. Both schools of thought are compatible and coexist, and this history of IBM offers evidence of how that occurred. Third, I demonstrate that IBM was an information ecosystem in which both information and a combination of employees, customers, and regulators interacted. The notion of an information ecosystem is relatively new to business historians and warrants more inclusion when studying the history of small and large enterprises, as the patterns evident in either are manifest. Thus, considering the combination of strategy, structure, social constructs and behaviors, and information flows offers a rich set of perspectives for understanding the life of a company.[50]

C-T-R's early history offers an example of small firms thriving in an age when large enterprises seemingly dominated. Watson's case reflected the successful effects of innovation and strategy combined.[51] A few economic historians argue that economic performance is better understood within the context of culture, values, and innovation, behaviors evident at C-T-R as a result of Watson's pivotal role.[52]

IBM thrived through the Roaring 20s and survived the Great Depression. At the height of the Depression, it seemed that many firms were shrinking or going out of business, but not IBM, despite the fact that 25 percent of the U.S. workforce was out of work. Watson saw opportunity, and enough IBMers believed him to make him right. IBM's customers confirmed his vision by signing leases, while his board and competitors questioned his optimism, even as IBM ran on razor-thin margins. Time took its toll, as Watson read the obituaries of Patterson, Fairchild, Hollerith, Powers, and Flint. By then, he owned much IBM stock and had complete control of a prosperous business. The time seemed propitious for the change that came in February 1924—renaming the company—and we turn to that decision in chapter 3.

3 THE EMERGENCE OF IBM AND THE CULTURE OF THINK

> This business has a future for your sons and your grandsons and your great-grandsons, because it is going on forever. Nothing in the world will ever stop it.
> —THOMAS J. WATSON, 1926[1]

ON FEBRUARY 15, 1924, the *Wall Street Journal* published a small article, buried on page 3, announcing that the "International Business Machines Corp. has been incorporated under the laws of New York to take over business and assets of Computing-Tabulating-Recording Co. Capitalization is the same as for Computing-Tabulating-Recording Co. and shares will be exchangeable." The article went on to explain that the name change "has been made because of increasing growth of the company business and the development of additional lines of business devices. No change is involved in the names of the subsidiary companies, the Tabulating Machine Co., International Time Recording Co. of New York and Dayton Scale Co."[2] That is how the world learned about the existence of IBM, unless they worked in Canada, where employees had known their employer as IBM since 1917.

When Watson was remaking C-T-R, he already thought the company's name was awkward and uninspiring, but changing it was the last thing he had on his mind; too many other issues required his urgent attention. Why he decided to rename the firm adds to our understanding of IBM's early evolution. On February 13, 1924, Watson wrote a letter addressed to all employees to announce the change, explaining: "Our new name is particularly adaptable and suitable to our business, in view of the fact of our increasing growth, the consistent development of additions to our line, and our products covering such a wide range in the field of business machinery." He concluded, "We are confident that this change in name will be beneficial to the business, and that the members of our field organization will find it of direct value in introducing our company and the products which we manufacture and distribute."[3]

The event was also important to C-T-R's customers and vendors. They may not have read the press announcement but received a letter announcing the change, and their salesmen rushed forward to explain how wonderful it would be. Then there was this little story in the *Wall Street Journal* three months after IBM's incorporation that may not have been true but hints that everything comes down to execution. The article began by stating that some people were confused by the change in the old name, which it called "unwieldy," and maybe this really did happen:

> The other day an uptown merchant called up a friend in Wall Street and inquired if he had ever heard of a new concern called the International Business Machines Corp.

> "We have a big order from them," he said, "and I am trying to check up on their credit rating. My partner has just gone downtown to demand a balance sheet from them." "Well," said the broker, "in their last balance sheet they showed $800,000 cash and about $8,000,000 current assets. Their position seems pretty good. How big was the order?"

> "About $100," said the merchant. "Wait a minute, I want to head off my partner."[4]

Implicit in that story was the real business problem of retaining the positive reputation of C-T-R among customers, investors, employees, and the media while leveraging its new name to build business momentum. Watson and his colleagues spent the 1920s and 1930s creating a brand image that reflected their positive view and plans for the future but that also translated into transactions, profits, growth, and prestige. They battled ignorance of what their products could do, invented new ones, hired people, expanded operations, overcame the worldwide economic tragedy of the Great Depression, and endured an antitrust challenge, the first of several that would threaten to scar IBM. As historian Robert Fitzgerald has pointed out, American firms were early adopters of various marketing and market segmentation practices, many of which were in evidence at IBM. The company did not go after mass markets—its products were too specialized—but the IBM case demonstrates that practices used by large manufacturing and distribution firms were common at IBM, such as market segmentation, use of advertising, and education of customers.[5]

The name change ultimately signaled a larger transformation under way. While it occurred halfway through the years discussed in this chapter, it had been a long time coming, as the Canadian example suggested. Whether the firm should have had a different new name than IBM was less important than that Thomas Watson felt it was time to declare a grander purpose for the company. The tone of his comments, the nature of the company's communications, and the way its staff interacted with the media and with customers evolved almost as a step change after the adoption of the new name. He was declaring that IBM wanted to become a major player in both the office appliance industry and as a major corporation.

There was a great deal going on at IBM besides a change in name, which makes it possible to view the announcement as a signal to the company's employees and its market. In chapter 2, we focused largely on Watson the leader and what he did during his first decade at C-T-R. In this chapter, we continue to discuss his role but with additional emphasis on the actions of the firm at large. This chapter begins to tell the wider story of IBM as an institution, although Watson continued to dominate the further formulation of its ways of operating. We focus on developments in the 1920s, but because many developments and trends continued through the 1930s, they are explained here, such as the arc of technological and product development, which is best understood as a whole over the entire period. Chapter 4 takes up events of the Great Depression of the 1930s, a time that threatened the existence of so many corporations. That IBM came out of it financially stronger, which was a unique experience for an American company, was part of a broader pattern that historian Mira Wilkins neatly termed "the conquest of markets."[6]

This chapter begins with a discussion of the transition from C-T-R to IBM, a case of marrying desired image to corporate strategy. Changing the name of a company is never straightforward, being rare and fraught with complications, so IBM's experience needs consideration. We discuss the unfolding of IBM's strategy and business operations in the 1920s, continuing a discussion begun in chapter 2. We identify the effects of Watson's sales culture at work. Since he tied strong sales operations to technological innovations, we examine the evolution of IBM's products. Finally, we add a fuller account of the role of customers, because part of Watson's way of doing things was to nurture a tripartite interaction of customers, sales, and product development. As chapter 5, on the World War II years, demonstrates, the combination of strong sales, a modern product line, and a data processing ecosystem facilitated IBM's substantial expansion during the war years.

HOW C-T-R BECAME IBM

As Watson expanded the business outside the United States, he set up independent companies owned by C-T-R, as required by local laws. He established one in Great Britain, another in Germany, still others in France and Italy, and so forth. He experimented with different names, even using his own family name, but usually with the concept of the International Business Machines Corporation. To use the word of Watson biographer Kevin Maney, that name had "heft," on par with names such as General Motors and United States Steel.[7] In 1917, Watson used the IBM name when he set up Canadian operations and when the company moved into Latin America. It fit nicely with his worldview.[8]

Despite some resistance from board members, and of course from Charles Flint, the board gave Watson permission to move forward and so, on February 5, 1924, he filed the necessary paperwork to change the company's name. He then expended considerable energy selling the idea to employees with speeches, a new company newsletter, and other correspondence. Managers began taking down C-T-R signs in front of their branch offices, replacing them with IBM ones. As part of his branding initiatives,

Figure 3.1

C-T-R/IBM had only two logos until the end of the 1940s. The IBM logo did not become a highly recognized image until the late 1940s, although it was respected earlier by its customers. Photo courtesy of IBM Corporate Archives.

Watson introduced a new logo. Figure 3.1 shows one of the old C-T-R logos alongside the new IBM one. The new world logo remained in use until 1947, when a plain "IBM" replaced the global image. The 1924 logo captured the essence of Watson's business being big and global. Using black for the logo connoted that IBM was serious, yet fashionably modern. It would be decades before IBM would become known as "Big Blue."

IBM'S STRATEGY FOR GROWTH IN THE ROARING 1920S

IBM grew in terms of bricks and mortar, number of people, and products built, transported to customers, and leased. IBM's growth was physical, yet the company grew as fast as many digital companies of the early twenty-first century. Executives of many companies, and business professors, have long been fascinated with IBM because of its ability to grow profitably, normally thinking only of the mainframe computer years, but the 1920s and 1930s provide an even more remarkable story of growth and prosperity. The numbers tell an outstanding story, suggesting the complexity of the issues IBM faced, which demonstrated the results of sound execution.

In 1923, the year before Watson changed the company's name, C-T-R generated $11 million in revenue, and by 1939 that had tripled to $38 million; profits had quadrupled. The company began 1924 with 3,161 employees, nearly a third outside the United States. In 1939, IBM employed over 11,000 people, still with a third outside the United States (see table 3.1). It therefore remained very much an American company, but one that paid attention to expanding its business worldwide. The salient fact is that its workforce had grown in size by three and a half times in just 16 years! Almost as impressive as any of these numbers is that IBM dominated its chosen markets. Eighty percent of all tabulating machines around the world came from IBM, as did nearly all the cards these machines consumed, both providing a continuous, safe revenue flow to the company.[9]

There was plenty of credit to go around for this success. Dominating all major decisions was Watson himself. His engineers executed well, too, as we will see later, while his sales force grew and matured over time. Luck helped in the 1920s, when the economies of the industrialized world expanded; bad luck followed in the 1930s, when they shrank; but more good fortune came when Watson refused to let the Great Depression slow him down

Table 3.1

IBM's revenue, earnings, and employee population, 1914–1940, select years (revenue and earnings in millions of dollars)

Year	Revenue	Net earnings	Worldwide employee population
1914	4	1	1,346
1918	9	1	3,127
1923	11	2	3,161
1928	15	5	5,102
1933	17	6	8,202
1938	34	9	11,046
1940	45	9	12,656

Source: Emerson W. Pugh, *Building IBM: Shaping an Industry and Its Technology* (Cambridge, MA: MIT Press, 1995), 323.

and the U.S. government launched Social Security and other economic and welfare programs.

For the kinds of products IBM sold, it needed a healthy economy, especially in the United States. The start of the 1920s was terrible, but the economy shifted to prosperity, increasing GDP and per capita income by 30 percent during that decade. New industries emerged and rapidly expanded. These included radio, movies, automobiles, appliances, construction, electricity, and chemicals, a long list. The 1920 U.S. census reported for the first time that more people lived in cities than in the countryside. New and old companies needed office appliances, including everything IBM was selling except more cheese slicers. IBM rode the wave, with revenue rising from $10.2 million in 1922 to $20.3 million in 1931. Because profits also grew, making Watson a wealthy man, while his senior executives profited handsomely from their IBM stock. Another generation of management would enjoy the same experience in the 1960s, but in the 1920s, as in the 1960s, it was not a free ride; results had to be earned.

IBM had its rivals to contend with, such as Burroughs, NCR, and Powers (later as Remington Rand), which also enjoyed expanding demand for their products, although not to the same extent as IBM. Often ignored by historians was Underwood Elliott Fisher, created in 1927 to sell typewriters and business machines.[10] It had an excellent sales force, comparable to IBM's, and a popular product line. The Powers Accounting Machine Corporation was folded into Remington Rand that year as part of another merger effort like Flint's of 1911. NCR did marginally well, but by the second half of the 1920s it was not diversifying sufficiently beyond the cash register business.

IBM made a few acquisitions to strengthen its technology portfolio and to keep potential rivals at bay. IBM retained the business model of leasing hardware, selling the cards needed to feed these machines, and offering tailored terms. The sales force designed accounting processes for their customers that used equipment to lower operating costs and improve efficiencies. Throughout the 1920s, Watson and his sales executives kept telling everyone at IBM that they had barely tapped the opportunity. Leasing and card revenues were sufficient to fund the manufacture of more equipment, support R&D, and pay dividends.

Card sales became increasingly important as a cash cow for IBM. By the mid-1930s, it sold over 4 billion cards annually at $1.05 for a box of 1,000. This was such a lucrative business that IBM's first two antitrust lawsuits with the U.S. government focused largely on these pieces of stiff paper. ITR's customers also used cards, as every worker needed to punch in and out daily, each using one card per week. Card sales also strongly supported ITR's financial performance. Between ITR and Tabulating Machines, demand for cards kept growing, only slowing a tad during the Depression years. Cards were also more profitable than leasing equipment. By the late 1930s, card sales made up 15 percent of the company's revenue.

To turn over every rock to look for revenue, IBM expanded its services business, offering smaller enterprises the chance to do their accounting work at an IBM data center. That offering introduced smaller enterprises to data processing in an almost ad hoc manner and in the process introduced them to IBM's technology, so that when they eventually leased their own equipment they understood and were already dependent on IBM's equipment and procedures. That expanding IBM ecosystem rested on its technology. For new and smaller users, the spread of IBM's equipment became more formularized through its Business Services Department, established in 1925 and put under the control of Frederick W. Nichol (1892–1955). Pushing hardware and services were twin features of IBM's strategy that reinforced the ecosystem. In 1932, IBM reorganized its services business into the Tabulating Machine Services Bureau, better known as the IBM Service Bureau Division, the organization used to expand services in the United States and later worldwide.[11] This business can be viewed as quintessential IT outsourcing, today known as cloud computing. IBM's decision to expand service bureau work during the Great Depression proved prescient, because some customers could not afford to set up or expand their existing data processing operations but wanted to save on their own operating costs by using tabulating equipment. IBM's offering became a convenient option. Government and commercial users took advantage of IBM's data centers, located in major cities. Uses were as diverse as in one's own data centers: accounting, inventory control, human resource management and record keeping, marketing surveys, and sales management.[12]

As IBM increased its focus on the tabulating market, its interest in scales and cheese slicers waned. Those products were sold with no follow-on sales for supplies, so there was no ongoing sales opportunity. In 1923, Watson sold Dayton Scale to Hobart Manufacturing, a solidly performing company, in exchange for 100,000 shares of common stock. These shares would spin off between $125,000 and $150,000 in revenue each year. This transaction took off the table a troubled business that had absorbed too much of management's attention over the years, although IBM kept making some scales for industry, a business tucked into a new organization within the firm, International Industrial Scales and Counting Devices. IBM acquired other small rivals in this industrial market in the 1920s and 1930s. By the end of the 1930s, the experiment was over; IBM had become the world's largest supplier of punch card tabulating equipment.

One feature of life at IBM was its seemingly constant reorganizations to align and optimize products, people, and customers. After its return to prosperity in the early 1920s, IBM reorganized the old Hollerith business with a broader scope, renaming it International Electric Tabulating and Accounting Machines. Fortunately, C-T-R's tabulating equipment had originally been electric, whereas Powers did not make the transition away from manual machines until the 1920s. Electrification made C-T-R's, and later IBM's, equipment easier to use and usually faster, and it appeared more modern, more advanced. Even more product innovations arrived during the Great Depression.

Senior managers paid considerable attention to innovations or, to use economic historian Deirdre Nansen McCloskey's more precise term for such matters, *betterment*, which speaks more to the purpose of changes in a technology or product while thinking tactically about the matter.[13] In October 1927, for example, Watson called all his senior executives into a conference room in New York, including Otto Braitmayer, James W. Bryce, Frederick W. Nichol, and others, "to talk about the future." Analyzing IBM's current circumstances, he wrote off the scale division as nearly useless, and opined that ITR was properly managed and doing fine, though its opportunities seemed limited. But now Tabulating was increasingly becoming the company's major source of cash and profits. Watson wanted his machines to dominate their market, not simply do well. He told his senior managers that this could be done by controlling all patents related to tabulating, regardless of whether they were held by IBM or others, and that is why IBM was willing to buy out other companies. It was essential that IBM have the most effective, uniquely designed, and patented cards in the business—IBM's with square holes, Powers's with round ones—so that rivals could not displace its equipment. IBM would need to expand manufacturing. Watson wanted IBM to have the best R&D and sales operations in the office appliance industry. None of these messages was new to the men assembled in that room.

What seemed new, however, was the intensity of IBM's growing commitment to this strategy and to the message that the others embrace it as enthusiastically as Watson did. It was vintage Watson: "There isn't any limit for the tabulating business for many years to come."[14] After a great year in 1927, in which IBM brought in $4 million in profit and was set to increase that by an additional $1 million in 1928, Watson again brought his close associates into the same conference room. This time he lashed out at them for not having done even better. He wanted everyone to push harder, to "never feel satisfied."[15]

So IBM in the 1920s was all about growth, opening more offices, and reaching out to new markets in Europe, Latin America, and even Asia. It was also about Watson being completely in charge of "his" company. Everyone of any consequence in the firm reported to him. In the late 1920s, 13 companies made up IBM, and Watson had regional and division executives, the R&D community, and manufacturing reporting to him. Watson biographer Kevin Maney looked at an early organization chart of the 13 companies, which included the IBM holding firm, and saw a list of 14 executives who also worked across the 13 subsidiaries, plus the board of directors, now made up of handpicked men. Maney calculated that there were nearly 200 people reporting to Watson. He called it "a web, with Watson as the spider."[16] Watson was behaving very much like a company founder who, by growing up with the company as it expanded, kept up with what so many other people were doing and, like many start-up founders, had difficulty surrendering authority to his direct subordinates. Nevertheless, he expected them to take initiatives to fulfill his vision. The two staff meetings just discussed were typical.[17] In fairness to Watson, while unable to surrender authority, he generously shared praise and credit for successes. Many of his speeches were devoted to praising "the men of The IBM."

His views became IBM's policies. Management overwhelmingly did not like unions, so they provided enough benefits to keep workers in Endicott, and later elsewhere, from organizing. Watson fed his vanity through speechmaking and communicating with his employees, but his management team also knew they had to keep their employees content because they were crucial to the expansion of IBM. Especially in Endicott, management did not want them trying to get jobs at the other big firm in town, the Endicott Johnson Shoe Company, run by George F. Johnson (1857–1948), a highly progressive entrepreneur who Watson came to admire and learn from, which usually had better benefits. IBM raised salaries, built employees a golf course, and introduced two weeks of paid vacation, all in the mid-1930s at the height of the Great Depression. Watson believed IBM could afford to construct a large training building in Endicott to educate factory workers, engineers, salesmen, managers, and customers. His optimism was not fully shared by the company's board of directors, but he built the facility anyway.[18] His benevolence mirrored policies implemented by other U.S. corporations.[19]

IBM's strategy involved creating a corporate culture that kept everyone informed about the company's intentions, values, expected behaviors, objectives (targets) individuals and their organizations were expected to achieve, and employees' actions outside the walls of IBM. That goes far in explaining the many presentations Watson and various levels of managers made to groups of employees, and why Watson spoke to every sales training class held in Endicott and to other classes and groups of customers. In 1934, IBM published an 886-page anthology packed with hundreds of Watson's missives, adding to IBM's information ecosystem.[20] Each division had its own processes to inform employees, distribute executive memoranda, host departmental or division-wide meetings, and publish newsletters. In

1924, Corporate launched a company-wide internal publication, *Business Machines,* which became IBM's primary channel for printed communications to all employees. It reported on Watson's talks, new products, employees, personnel practices, events in the company, and market conditions.

IBM's information ecosystem was designed to reinforce its culture of THINK, one based on the use of data and practical thoughtfulness. Recall, too, that by the early 1920s, field engineers and salesmen were relying on their own manuals for product information. The company added weekly reports on sales up the chain of command and did similarly at the factories. Each country had its own board of directors, which was expected to communicate quarterly with New York headquarters in a prescribed manner. Country general managers spoke increasingly with headquarters staff and more frequently wrote reports addressed to New York about daily operations. Executives were expected to be active in this information ecosystem. By the mid-1920s, there had emerged an information ecosystem involving employees and customers and an effective corporate culture supporting that community. The company's culture facilitated the functioning of the ecosystem, with many activities supporting this community, reflecting company values and desired behaviors. The interlacing of IBM's "world"— ecosystem—and its culture is a theme that has permeated the history of IBM.

The 1920s became a good time for Watson to build his company, its collection of customers, and its culture. Businessmen were considered "hot," fashionable. In January 1925, President Calvin Coolidge famously said, "The chief business of the American people is business." American companies basked in this glow. IBMers were caught up in it, too. Engineers came up with new equipment, and salesmen found new customers and new uses for IBM's machines. A biographer said Watson still "loved coming up with data processing ideas, which he then dropped like hand grenades onto his beloved engineering teams," who had to respond by trying to implement them.[21] His ideas ranged from coming up with machines for use by bank tellers to developing a heating lamp to keep his machines from breaking down during humid weather.

No history of IBM's culture would be complete without discussing "Songs of The IBM." By the mid-1920s and extending deep into the 1940s, even the 1950s in some parts of the company, IBMers sang songs about Watson, other executives, and IBM. Harry Evans, a spunky, short, high-energy executive with a sense of humor, wrote many of them. In 1925, he published the first *IBM Songbook,* and after that, his creations were sung at sales conventions, branch offices, and factory gatherings, often as tributes to Watson on the occasion of one of his visits. All relied on existing melodies, such as *Over There* and *Auld Lang Syne.* If the company had an anthem, it was *Ever Onward,* with a chorus that shouted out "Ever Onward—Ever Onward! That's the spirit that has brought us fame!"[22] Other companies sang songs as part of how they linked to their employees. Other methods IBM and others deployed included softball teams, picnics, and even a company band at Endicott that lasted for decades.[23]

IBM'S TECHNOLOGICAL EVOLUTION

No customer of high-tech industrial equipment will long tolerate products that fail to help reduce operating costs or improve productivity. Customers aggressively pressured vendors to continuously introduce new information-handling tools that were cheaper, faster, and more reliable. Underlying a great deal of that innovative process, usually hidden in the shadows, was a century-long guerrilla war involving the unexciting, yet important, topic of patents. Many of IBM's customers accepted the company's combination of "leading edge" developments but also its habit of lagging other innovators. Both patterns existed in pre–World War II IBM. Watson drove his engineers and lawyers hard, without which other vendors could have bypassed IBM because customers always had options for what kind of tabulating equipment to use or to use other types of data processing equipment, neither of which required IBM's punch cards. These included calculators that were increasingly sophisticated, adding machines, billing equipment, and electric typewriters.

IBM's legacy of lagging and innovating characterized its behavior from Hollerith's day to the present but became a purposeful intertwined strategy during the 1920s. The strategy turned on two issues: when an innovation had matured enough to be converted into a product or new feature that could be protected by patents and when the market was ready to accept an innovation. IBM's engineers did not hesitate to patent myriad innovations, but not all of them surfaced as new features and products. IBM vigorously collected patents and dueled with rivals over control of innovations. Historians of IBM's early history devoted considerable attention to this issue, focusing more on the actions of the company to protect its innovations with patents than on the timing of new product introductions, the latter always coming along after an innovation first existed.[24]

Inside IBM, not all heroes were executives and salesmen. Engineers, representing the development and manufacture of products, and salesmen, with their requests for new products reflecting market timing, needed to collaborate. Engineers developed products that enabled corporations and government agencies to grow, function, and leverage data. In the 1920s and 1930s, IBM's engineers made up a small group, fewer than several dozen souls, but they were productive. Speaking to the 100 Percent Club in January 1928, Watson recalled how quickly engineers had developed new products in months rather than the more customary years, citing events that year and ending with, "I cannot say enough for our engineers and for the wonderful work they have done in producing these machines in such a short time."[25] In a speech delivered at Princeton University that October, he made the critical point that "eighty percent of the business of our company today is done on products that have been developed since 1914."[26]

Watson's praise was not hype. Less than a dozen engineers fundamentally transformed IBM's product line. They worked on the second generation of punch card equipment, which replaced Hollerith's original creations. The first generation served IBM's customers from the late 1880s to the start of the 1920s. They were due for replacement, and Watson and his technical managers assembled a remarkable new team to do that, bringing together talented engineers already in the firm and hiring others. Hollerith hired one of the first who Watson liked, Eugene A. Ford (1866–1948). Ford began his career as an inventor of typewriters, bringing to the company experience with keyboards. He developed a numerical keypunch machine for the Tabulating Machine Company in 1899 and became an employee of the company in 1905. In 1914, Watson put him in charge of a development center located on Sixth Avenue in Manhattan. His small team electrified parts of the tabulating product line. They developed a verifier, used to confirm that cards had the same data punched in them as those typed by a keypunch operator, as an aid to improve data accuracy.

Watson hired Clair D. Lake (1888–1958), who had worked in the automotive industry. He had only attended school through the eighth grade and later a two-year industrial training program but had demonstrated a masterful understanding of engineering principles. A third member of the team, also brought in by Watson, was Fred M. Carroll (1869–1961), who had worked as an inventor at NCR. Watson asked the three to invent a card printer. Meanwhile, when Ford left the company for a while, Lake took charge of tabulator development. In 1917, C-T-R brought on a fourth engineer, James Wares Bryce (1880–1949). Bryce started out as a draftsman and designer at the turn of the century, studied mechanical engineering at New York City College for three years, and then moved to Endicott in the Time Recording Division.

Lake went to work on improving the tabulator product line, simplifying machine operation and reliability. Just after World War I, he introduced the concept of plug boards, similar to those that already existed in the telephone industry, to simplify maintenance. Benjamin M. Durfree (1897–1980), who joined CTR in 1917 to do tabulator maintenance and repair, worked with him to make such improvements. All their efforts came together with the introduction of the Type I printing tabulator in 1921, which customers had wanted for years. It worked so well that in 1924 Durfree went to Europe to promote and install these machines. Meanwhile, Lake began recruiting a new generation of engineers. In 1917, he brought in Ralph E. Page (1896–1991), making him the chief draftsman working on the new tabulator.[27] George F. Daly (1903–1983) came in 1920, also as a draftsman working with Lake. Meanwhile Watson promoted Lake to Endicott's superintendent of tabulating machines.

IBM accumulated relevant patents largely by acquiring companies and their employees. An important acquisition was J. Royden Pierce (1877–1933), a highly regarded inventor in the office appliance industry, and his little engineering company in New York City. Pierce brought along at least two employees. He had completed his degree in engineering at the Stevens Institute of Technology in Hoboken, New Jersey, making him the first worker at IBM to have achieved that distinction. Pierce joined C-T-R in 1922 as an employee, signing over his patents to the company, patents he had developed while he built a tabulator for use in the life insurance industry. Later he developed test-scoring equipment, another that could subtract numbers, and yet another to do multiplication.

So now IBM had two development centers: one in Manhattan with Bryce, Pierce, and a few other employees, and a second in Endicott with Lake and Carroll. Lake worked on tabulators, while Carroll improved the machinery needed to manufacture cards better and more quickly. In 1923, Ford returned to IBM and worked on a new sorter, introduced in 1925 as the Type 80 Sorter. It was also known as the "horizontal sorter," because all the card pockets were of the same height. The machine was faster, easier to use, and incrementally improved Hollerith's original design. This was a critical innovation, because sorting subtotals of accounting information was crucial, requiring that cards be tabulated in the correct order. Tabulators in the 1920s and 1930s were also equipped with "accumulators," which held subtotals. The company introduced incremental changes in its product lineup throughout the 1920s and 1930s. One, for example, was a "summary punch" that made it possible to print subtotals, crucial in competing against mechanical bookkeeping systems from companies like Burroughs and more specialized office appliance firms. That product became possible because of the dialogue that took place between sales and engineering, with the needs of IBM's sales staff and customers driving engineering's R&D agenda. These kinds of collaborations became fodder for Watson to use in speeches when opining on the virtues of THINK.

An important development involving the cards themselves came from this small team. All during the 1920s, customers had asked IBM to find a way to put more data on its cards. Lake and Bryce thought that with some changes to the equipment they could squeeze more and narrower columns on a card by punching square holes rather than round ones. They had to develop a card that had more than the 45 columns available at that time.

They created a stronger card with 80 columns, which IBM immediately patented and introduced. IBM's engineers modified all its equipment to handle the new cards. Over time, that new card became known as the "IBM Card," and it remained in use for the next half century. IBM's main card rival—Remington Rand—also had a 45-column card, and it responded with a new card that had two rows of 45 columns. Customers loved IBM's card, and so it became *the* standard for the industry and the continuing source of much revenue for IBM. The basic changes that appeared in so many products in the 1930s grew out of the work engineers initiated in the 1920s. While the story of IBM's innovations of the 1930s might later seem to make sense to tell, they were a logical outcome of earlier work.

Recall how IBM introduced innovations in its products but often slowly. How does one explain this apparent contradiction? IBM's behavior was purposeful, as it chose a lower-risk strategy. The alternative ran the risk of introducing a product that failed; IBM would experience that in the 1980s with minicomputers and some models of the Personal Computer. For most of its history, IBM reacted to requests by customers for new functions rather than these functions being the brainchild of an employee. Innovations were incremental but numerous and were rarely revolutionary. Even the 80-column card grew out of experiences with cards over the previous quarter century. Innovations relied on existing engineering principles. Innovations often took years to develop, but because they arrived continuously, IBM and its customers enjoyed the fruits of new features and functions, and learned from each of them to inform future developments. Incremental introduction of innovations built up momentum, going far toward explaining why so many products came out in the 1930s and not in the 1920s, when a great deal of R&D and patent collecting went on.

In the 1930s, IBM completed its conversion of the entire tabulator product line to 80-column cards while introducing a continuous flow of new devices that could perform more accounting functions, such as alphabetical accounting, and a multiplying punch (later called the Type 600), both introduced in 1931 in the middle of the Great Depression. The Type 600 was replaced two years later with the Type 601, to provide what accountants called "footing" and "cross-footing," used to sum tables of numbers by column and row. Now users could subtract and add, making possible even more accounting functions than before.

Improvements out of the two engineering shops made it possible to sell more tabulating applications, so the two U.S. engineering centers merged into a new building in Endicott in 1933, with the Manhattan workshop being closed down. Known as the North Street Laboratory, the Endicott facility housed seven engineers, including Ford, Lake, and Carroll, a number of draftsmen, one patent attorney, various other people to run the office, space to handle special machinery, one metallurgist, and an industrial designer. The building included a blueprint room, a machine shop, and storage for parts. Now all could collaborate more frequently and work faster—essential in order to respond to market demands in the 1930s and 1940s and to meet the immediate needs that soon emerged from the U.S. Social Security Administration and other U.S. and state government agencies.

So, what products could a customer obtain from IBM by the early to mid-1930s? An IBM system included three groups of leased devices. First there was the punch, also known as a keypunch, which looked like a typewriter and was used to punch holes in cards fed to the keyboard. Second was the sorter, used to shuffle decks by columns, alphabetically, or from one number to another. The cards would fall into a bin in the order sorted. Then there was the processor itself, known as the tabulator and, increasingly in the 1930s, as an accounting machine. That machine printed reports or documents (such as checks) and performed basic mathematics (adding, subtracting, multiplying). In larger installations, one might also have a verifier attached to keypunch machines to ensure that cards punched were accurate. Since inputting—punching cards—was labor intensive and involved a great deal of information, it was normal to have many keypunch machines and staff (largely women) to type all those little square holes into cards.

Keypunch machines could be located all over a company or agency, sending boxes of punched cards to other keypunch operators for processing using verifiers, after which they would be sorted. These bigger machines were housed at a central site, often called the "IBM Room," later a data processing center. That practice of having operating equipment in their own center served as the model for data processing centers after the arrival of digital computing. Many of these centers continued to use keypunch machines for decades, while all other tabulating functions became embedded in computers.

Responding to customers' suggestions became crucial to IBM's success. By the late 1920s, some customers had been using tabulating equipment for over a quarter century, so they were both dependent on it and deeply knowledgeable about what they needed next. In 1940, a young engineer, John C. McPherson (1908–1999), became head of a new organization, the Future Demands Department. A graduate of Princeton University (class of '29), he joined IBM in 1930 as an engineer and later served as a salesman in the railroad industry for three years. Being both an engineer and a salesman, he brought to his new assignment a perfect match of technology/engineering and sales/customer knowledge. The timing of his new assignment was propitious, because as the number of customers increased, their needs became more diverse, often clustering around industry-specific requirements. For example, banks needed accounting tools that differed from those used in, say, inventory management processing in railroads or manufacturing. McPherson's appointment reflected the culmination of a process long under development at IBM.

Product requirements had to be defined, coordinated, and worked on by the growing engineering community. Customers wanted to reduce the amount of "setup" time needed to run different sets of calculations (known as applications) on their equipment, which called for using removable plug boards. Table 3.2 lists many of the improvements made during the interwar period in response to their requirements. Market needs had to be collected by the sales branch offices and then transmitted to the engineering community. In the 1920s, this was often done in an ad hoc manner, in the form of letters requesting changes, but by 1940 a more formal manner had finally been adopted. It was not enough to write to the "Old Man" for help. IBM and McPherson created a product development process that proved effective for decades. Formalizing that and linking it to market and customer intelligence gathering, although not unique to IBM, was still novel in the 1930s. GE, Burroughs, and a few other major firms had moved in that

Table 3.2

Tabulating technology evolution, 1920s–1930s

C-T-R

Six hardware products in 1920
  Automatic sorting machine
  Two keypunch machines
  Quick set gang punch
  Hand set gang punch
  Tabulators
45-column cards

IBM

32 hardware products in 1933
  Seventeen keypunch machines and one verifier (several models for various sizes of cards)
  Five sorters (several models for various sizes of cards)
  Nine tabulators (in addition to several models within each type)
45-column cards
80-column cards

IBM's Technological Innovations

1930	Numeric interpreter to print on cards
1931	Automatic multiplying punch and duplicating summary punch
1932	Alphabetic printing tabulating device; verifier with automatic feed and eject
1933	Alphabetic keypunch (Type 3) and reproducing punch
1934	Automatic carriage for printing tabulator
1936	Alphabetic verifier, alphabetic interpreter, collator
1938	Transfer posting machine, reproducing gang summary punch
1939	Mark sensing equipment

Remington Rand, IBM's leading rival in this market, and Powers-Samas in Europe introduced an equal number of innovations in this period. See James W. Cortada, *Before the Computer: IBM, NCR, Burroughs, and Remington Rand and the Industry They Created, 1865–1956* (Princeton, NJ: Princeton University Press, 1993), 111.

direction in the 1920s, but since most slowed product development in the 1930s, IBM's lunge forward during the Great Depression proved fortuitous.

IBM's crowning technological achievement came in 1934, when its salesmen were able to sell the Type 405 accounting machine (figure 3.2). One group of IBM engineers later wrote that it was "an outstanding success" that "remained the flagship of IBM's product line until after World War II."[28] It could perform many accounting functions electronically and led IBM to rename its tabulating business the Electric Accounting Machine (EAM) Division.

In the process of introducing so many new machines and making hundreds of incremental changes, IBM dominated the world's patent portfolio for tabulating equipment. Bryce, Carroll, Ford, Lake, and Pierce accumulated over 500 patents in their lifetimes; Bryce personally had 244. But they were not alone. C-T-R/IBM cumulatively acquired over 1,200 patents between 1911 and 1940, and another 900 by 1950.[29] The bulk of IBM's

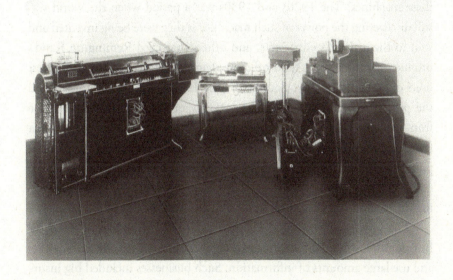

Figure 3.2
The IBM Type 405 was sold as a "system," not as one product, and was introduced just as IBM's customers' volume and complexity of work expanded dramatically. Photo courtesy of IBM Corporate Archives.

patents came between 1926 and 1940, when 969 were granted, but it took a long time for ideas and then patents to emerge as products, a process that Watson and his executive team understood. Hollerith and the executives in ITR and the Scales Division did not fully appreciate that reality, which helps explain why C-T-R obtained only 11 patents between 1911 and 1915. In the next five years, the company garnered 65 patents, adding 143 more between 1921 and the end of 1925.[30] Comparing that performance to the products listed in table 3.2, we see the results of Watson's faith in the future of the data processing market. Add in the constant feedback from the field and customers, and one can see why IBM's investments were not as bold or irrational as many thought in the 1930s. Rather, IBMers were listening to the market, responding prudently in thoughtful ways.

CUSTOMERS AND HOW THEY USED IBM'S EQUIPMENT

Who were IBM's customers in the 1920s, and what were they doing with these machines? The 1920s and 1930s was a period when the world was still discovering the power of such machines as they were being invented and sold to them. IBM's customers, and others that used Remington Rand's products and those of various office appliance vendors, became the earliest users of computers. Why? Because, by the 1950s, they already understood the power of data processing. The majority of IBM's business still came from the United States, but it had expanded across Western Europe and to a lesser extent into Latin America and Asia. Because their heritage was largely punch card equipment, knowing what they did about this technology in the half century preceding the arrival of the computer is crucial in understanding the relationship customers had with IBM over the rest of the century.

The process of becoming a customer of IBM, Remington Rand, or Burroughs was not simple. First, an organization had to collect, analyze, and use large amounts of information. Such businesses included big insurance companies, banks, railroads, and large data collecting agencies, for example a census bureau or a national pension department. It helped if one had thousands (or millions) of people to track, such as an automotive manufacturer or an army. Second, that largeness meant that without using

IBM's expensive and complicated equipment, one had to collect and use information manually or rely on simple desktop calculators. Either option often proved more expensive than deploying IBM's machines. For scientific applications, calculating by hand might be too tedious, slow, or impossible, such as in defining rotations of planets. Third, the equipment had to perform functions that made sense to a customer, which is why accounting, census taking, and inventory control attracted early users.[31]

Fourth, a customer had to have a capable staff. These included key-punch operators, others who could use peripheral equipment and "program" tabulators to do their bidding, and still others to manage the flow of cards coming in and out of a data processing center and to deliver reports to where they were needed according to some fixed schedule. Such managerial requirements meant accounts had to employ one or more managers able to work with IBM to acquire equipment, help shape how it would be used, and decide who would be responsible for day-to-day interactions with salesmen, maintenance people, and those collecting bills for IBM. If a customer did not have one or more of these prerequisites, IBM still had an answer for them: its services bureau.

In the 1920s, dozens of companies and government agencies that were C-T-R's customers before 1924 grew into hundreds of organizations, and by the late 1940s several thousand.[32] As a corporation became big by the standards of its day, an IBM salesman would show up, in the beginning more as an expert on routine accounting and the machines but later also knowledgeable about the data processing needs unique to an industry. While census taking and accounting were the first wave of applications fairly regularized across organizations, every customer was nonetheless unique, so IBMers tailored use of their equipment to their user's operations. That took months of study, design, and negotiation, so acquiring a new account, or a new user within an existing account, took time, sometimes more than a year or two. This also meant customers were reluctant to swap out office machine vendors.

When the installation of IBM equipment was completed and the equipment was functioning as needed, customers became dependent on IBM's products for decades, binding them to their supplier for equipment and cards. Over time, IBMers sought new ways for customers to use their equipment and, as IBM's revenues demonstrate, customers did more data processing, evolving into information-intensive enterprises. They learned from each other and from IBMers how best to use this equipment. How IBM did something therefore often became how their customers did it, too, whether in processing data in accounting, inventory control, or sales. Through individual adoptions of data processing, IBMers influenced how companies and agencies worked. Watson captured the essence of that influence in 1930 when he said, "But as fast as one company after another demonstrated that the tabulating machine was a success, it became possible to apply the same use throughout a whole industry."[33]

Arming accounts with more information was not the only by-product of IBM's activities. At least as important was the expansion in the number of people working in offices, particularly women, as typists, clerks, secretaries, and keypunch operators. Women who entered this world began as keypunch operators, a job almost as easy to learn as using a typewriter, which they had been doing since the 1880s. Some keypunch operators moved on to operate IBM's data processing machines. IBM was willing to train a customer's personnel to operate its equipment at no cost, in the process creating a small army of workers who knew how to use only IBM products. They could be counted on to favor these products over those of an unfamiliar competitor. By the end of the 1930s, one could even see in business such formal titles as the "IBM Department" or "IBM operators," much like the term "xeroxing" meant photocopying in the 1970s. IBM intentionally promoted the branding of professions after its name.

Users of IBM's equipment clearly understood what they were doing. Saving on operating costs proved important, as one user reaffirmed: "Tabulating our labor costs by hand would, of course, be impractical as it would require at least six more people," while the IBM machine was "paying for itself every week."[34] Others focused on efficiency, keeping "a running check on exactly where they stand and to maintain a more nearly continuous contact with customers and prospects by frequent dunning and soliciting."[35] Data accuracy was always critical, described by one observer as "the elimination of errors," because IBM's machine "saves confusion and time wasted in checking besides promoting better organization and efficient management."[36] Users appropriated new functions as they became available, such as using tabulators to do payroll accounting and printing paychecks, tracking these transactions, reducing errors, and resolving disputes with workers. A typical example is Ford Motor using the equipment to pay its thousands of workers.

Over time, scientists and engineers began to use IBM's products. In the 1930s, it became possible to use these machines for complex mathematical calculations, such as in astronomy or in mechanized testing and grading. Watson personally led the development of a strong relationship with nearby Columbia University, a tie that lasted for decades. The Statistical Bureau at Columbia pioneered uses of punch cards in science and mathematics, providing IBM with positive press and goodwill among academics and engineers. One astronomer in particular, Wallace John Eckert (1902–1971), was an effective evangelist. During the 1930s, he persuaded Watson to donate equipment to his laboratory, donations that IBM's leader concluded would burnish his company's reputation while creating new demand for his machines. By 1937, Eckert had established the Thomas J. Watson Astronomical Computing Bureau, involving Columbia University, IBM, and the American Astronomical Society.[37] Working with scientists, IBM's engineers, other scientists and engineers, and customers learned how to calculate statistics using tabulators, an application of increasing importance to government agencies.

Scientific applications were different from commercial ones, requiring different thinking and uses. Commercial applications were relatively simple to perform but required processing of a great amount of data, such as millions of social security or inventory records. Scientific and engineering applications required calculations more complex than the four basic mathematical functions and far less data. For the former, handling volumes proved important, while for the latter it was speed of calculation.[38]

Becoming a new customer and staying with IBM seemed easy because of the study IBM would conduct to determine how best to use its equipment and because it would help do the financial analysis to justify its cost. IBM's practice continued throughout the century, but it was always the hardest step for both sides to take. In addition, by leasing equipment, customers did not need to risk precious capital on some new technology, and machines could be replaced whenever IBM brought out a more attractive product. By the end of the 1920s, there existed a growing pool of workers experienced in using IBM equipment. Both customers and IBM shared a stable cash flow, for customers as a budgeted expense and for IBM as predictable income. Best practices and the use of experienced, trained personnel spread from one account to another, creating the IBM-centric ecosystem that proved so successful that some 80 percent of all tabulating users in the world knew it.

IBM used its growing presence to branch out into other office appliances, most notably electric typewriters. IBM's engineers knew a great deal about keyboards and electricity, two technologies central to IBM's products for decades. IBM's senior management appreciated the strategic business nature of the two linked together. When contemplating new opportunities in the 1920s and 1930s, they explored developing specialized banking systems, developing test equipment for education, and bringing out their own line of typewriters. To add to IBM's ability to produce electronic keyboards for its tabulating systems, in 1933 the firm acquired Electromatic Typewriters, located in Rochester, New York. It was rare among the many typewriter firms in that it produced electrical machines and held patents on them. While electric typewriters had existed since around 1900, secretaries preferred manual ones, and ultimately they, not data processing managers, were the customers for such machines. Unfortunately, however, Electromatic's machines cost about $250 each, roughly twice that of a manual typewriter, and so they did not sell well, even after becoming part of IBM. At only about 6,000 units a year, its sales accounted for only 5 percent of the market for typewriters.[39] Its real asset was the keyboard technology, which IBM's engineers appropriated for their keypunch machines. Expertise in keyboards made it possible to produce typewriters and other accounting machine keyboards for decades. Engineers even toyed with the idea of connecting typewriter-like devices to telephone lines to create a teletype tool that a half century later we called e-mail. Because of technological and patent issues, they set aside this idea.

IBM introduced its first commercially successful electric typewriter in 1935. By the end of World War II, its salesmen had gained significant momentum in that market at the expense of Underwood (the largest vendor), Royal, and Remington Rand. In addition to selling well, IBM's machines proved superior and highly reliable, leading a generation of users to remain loyal to it and subsequent products.[40] IBM developed a sales force specializing in selling typewriters. Within IBM they were considered the best individual salesmen in "pitching" a product. For decades, they cultivated typists and secretaries, making it both highly successful and useful to place the IBM logo in so many visible corners of a customer's enterprise beyond the data processing center, such as immediately outside a manager's or executive's office door, where his secretary sat.

TABULATING THE EVOLUTION OF IBM AND THE CULTURE OF THINK

For decades, the central challenge for C-T-R and then for IBM was not just efficient management to improve productivity—Flint's primary reason for bringing in Watson—or to improve the product line and the quality of sales operations, although both were essential to the company's long-term prosperity. The central challenge for the company was to create a broader market for its products than envisioned by Hollerith. That effort required IBM to educate potential customers *and* salesmen about its products and how best to apply them at the individual account level. Watson never quite explained it bluntly, but he hinted at it when he repeatedly argued that only a tiny percentage of the world used tabulating equipment. The closest he got to the central issue was when he used the term "data processing," which he combined with exhortations to "think," "learn," and "take action."

A considerable amount of economic activity involves persuading people to take action to buy something, what one scholar called "sweet talking."[41] As products and activities became more complex or expensive, persuasion as an economic activity became more sophisticated. Selling industrial equipment clearly falls into this category. IBM's selling efforts—persuasion—exemplified that activity, extending the scope and sophistication of such actions far beyond what Hollerith had, and what ITR or the scale business needed. IBM's customers had to be persuaded what to do. The importance of that function in an economy, or for IBM, accounts for the enormous investment of effort, time, and thought in the development and use of IBM's sales organization.

IBM had to wrap all its actions and successful "sweet talking" into a set of contractual terms and support services that made it possible for new users to embrace punch card equipment. Even those who had already taken the plunge still needed to learn about new uses of the equipment and how to properly adapt the equipment to their needs. Then IBM's challenge was to keep them committed to using its products. Watson instinctively understood that the way his company could prosper and grow was to lead in the development of the market for IBM's machines. As that happened, it was the sales organization that was present at the creation of demand for products at the individual account level. IBM essentially had few rivals. Powers had to do the same thing for this tiny niche market, but it did not do so as effectively as IBM. IBM expanded its market at approximately the rate that it could increase manufacturing, sales, and services.

That ability to keep market size and capacity synchronized resulted in two consequences. First, IBM overwhelmingly continued to dominate a larger market. It did this so well that in the 1910s it already "owned" over 90 percent of the market, and as it expanded, thanks to Powers (later Remington Rand) and a French company called Machines Bull in the 1930s, it actually *lost* market share, which dropped to nearly 80 percent, where it remained until the end of the punch card era, but in a market far larger than the one inaugurated by Hollerith. The British Empire market represented an exception. BTM and Powers shared a great deal of the market, but IBM split it in half with those two rivals. By controlling the market's growth, IBM dominated it, executing normal sales, services, and product development and manufacturing.

Second, because IBM was de facto the only supplier of this class of technology for most companies and governments, it became the hub, the center of the tabulating data processing ecosystem, the "go to" place for goods and information, and, later, management practices, for organizations automating their largest information processing activities. Other office appliance vendors did not enjoy that level of influence (they thought of it as *control*) over their clients, because customers could swap out calculators, billing machines, adding machines, cash registers, and typewriters at will. There were many suppliers and users that also had a half century of experience with these technologies. Customers never became as dependent on one vendor as they did when it came to large data processing projects. Tabulating equipment made larger enterprises possible.

Being able to persuade customers to concur with IBM's suggested actions and proposals remained a high priority within the firm's corporate culture. THINK as an idea was about forming an opinion about an issue in a rational manner and being able to persuade others of a point of view. It came back to the notion of "sweet talking," which makes sense if the rationale is persuasive both to IBM's colleagues and its customers. The act of persuasion and the desired decision by IBMers and customers to take action became the key economic task of the company. All else followed: product development, advertising, training, installation, maintenance, and use.[42]

That symbiosis of growing the market as quickly as the company could serve it and becoming the center of that market (its ecosystem) made it possible for IBM to grow and prosper. When computers came along, a new generation of IBM executives understood the need to hop onto the new technology that otherwise would replace their tabulating machines. To his credit, Thomas J. Watson Sr. created the data processing ecosystem that made it possible for IBM to do well in a relatively tiny but lucrative market. In each decade between 1910 and 1940, there were only a few hundred accounts, a few thousand machines, and only a few tens of millions of dollars, but IBM learned how to optimize all these moving parts to make the business profitable. When demand for data processing surged during World War II, IBM essentially had to ride the wave, running its operations as they had evolved them in the 1930s. Not until after World War II did a new generation of managers confront different circumstances that made Watson's older generation, his inner circle, and now aging tabulating engineers outmoded and in need of replacement.

While most of the world suffered during a nearly decade-long economic depression, IBM had a different experience, one that led it to become what Watson envisioned back in 1914. How that happened is the story told next.

4 IBM AND THE GREAT DEPRESSION

We have all the things necessary for greater success.
—THOMAS J. WATSON, 1931[1]

THE GREAT DEPRESSION was a scary time around the world. In the United States, IBMers going to work in Manhattan walked past large crowds of unemployed men waiting in "soup lines." Just four years into the economic crisis, the economy had shrunk by half of 1929's, with 16 million unemployed people having few prospects of finding work. Americans and Europeans entertained radical political ideas; even socialism wafted in the air in the United States. Fascism—a relative of socialism—was already a fact in Europe. Stock values had dropped by 80 percent. The strain intensified in the first half of the 1930s. In the United States, divorces increased, people lost their homes, the great Dust Bowl disrupted the lives of over 2 million families, young men hit the road, but most aggravating was the sense that the Depression would never end. The nation's problems dragged on until the end of the decade. A child born in 1927 would be 12 years old before he or she experienced a time when poverty was not a way of life. An unemployed teacher in Texas caught the mood just right for millions when she sighed, "If, with all the advantages I've had, I can't make a living, I'm just no good, I guess."[2]

Against that somber background, IBMers had to survive, too, to take care of their families. Many remembered that IBM laid off employees during the recession of 1920–1921. Would the same president of the company who reigned then do the same now when there was a larger economic crisis?

Would enough business come in to keep the company going? In a sales culture where shame and risk of a career ruined was sure to follow someone who could not make their quota, what was one to do? Customers were firing their workers. If failure was inevitable, why exert oneself for the Greater IBM? Here was IBM's president running around saying everything was going to be fine, that "the sun never sets on IBM products. We are serving the whole world." Newspapers carried articles about how much he made as president—more than any other American—and he was being decorated with medals and wearing fancy suits and top hats to meetings of the International Chamber of Commerce. The problem, of course, was that IBMers took to heart "THINK" and wondered how long they could stare at those signs before the hammer came down on them.

But IBMers also had access to a secret weapon that most did not know about: a corporate culture resilient enough to help them along, everyone from Watson to the newest employee on the shop floor. Great business leaders understand the power of "can do" and, to quote another CEO facing a crisis of confidence and potential failure at IBM six decades later, Louis V. Gerstner Jr., IBMers had "mo-men-tum"—momentum. But all of IBM's CEOs and executives relied on similar thinking to such an extent that we can consider that attitude part of IBM's values. Watson hammered on a similar point, cementing it permanently into the company: "If we do not take advantage of our opportunity, it is our own fault."[3] That struck at the soul of IBM's culture. Historians describe Watson's aphorisms with some derision, attributing them to some egotistical behavior. Perhaps they are right; nonetheless, he had a real problem on his hands. IBM's stock was declining in value by double digits; early in the Depression, sales were dropping, too. In some countries, the Depression was less severe, such as Germany, where IBM was opening new sales offices. Watson had to cheer the troops on, to give them reason to use their skills and resources. The option of giving up was not a good one for any IBMer, let alone their customers. Watson had no choice but to speak in the language of the day to motivate his employees relentlessly, every day, worldwide.[4] IBM had to fight back. It worked. Add in some spectacular luck, and that is how IBM navigated through the Great Depression.

The Great Depression represented IBM's first massive existential threat that could have crushed the company. Thousands of other firms failed in the 1930s, although larger enterprises fared better than smaller ones. The threat to IBM came in two forms: economic and political/legal. Global trade and national economies shrank, which translated into lower demand for IBM's goods and services. Political and regulatory problems escalated. As economic stresses exacerbated, political tensions complicated IBM's relations with government agencies in Europe and in the United States. Governments were both customers and regulators. If chapter 3 focused on what IBM did internally to expand its business, being more in charge of its destiny than responding to the economy in the 1920s, during the 1930s IBM responded to circumstances largely out of its control. Watson was not yet done creating the company he wanted, so he pushed forward, driven by his optimism that the Depression would soon end. A major proactive strategy he pursued involved expanding business outside of the United States. Employees turned over every rock that they could find worldwide, looking for business. This chapter describes IBM's activities in the 1930s. What emerges is a picture of a company that refused to seek cover while the storm of the Depression blew over it; it fought back. By the end of the decade, IBM had survived, indeed thrived, but then faced a world where the Great Depression had been replaced with a greater calamity: World War II.

HOW IBM DEALT WITH THE GREAT DEPRESSION

It is rare to find specific events that so change circumstances. The assassination of President Abraham Lincoln in April 1865 led the North to turn harshly on the Confederacy, the Japanese attack on Pearl Harbor in December 1941 brought the United States into World War II the next day, and the 9/11 attack in 2001, which ushered in a war against Islamic extremists and embroiled the United States in conflicts from Kabul to Iraq, come to mind. But one event that qualified for a nearly similar level of change occurred in October 1929, when the U.S. stock market sold off shares, diminishing private fortunes and the equity of many small investors to the tune of some $30 billion, which was followed by the onset of the global

Great Depression. Economies on both sides of the Atlantic did not recover for a long time: the United States did not recover until it engaged in World War II. Europe went directly from depression into such a destructive world war that it did not achieve economic prosperity again until the early 1950s. It was not uncommon for U.S. corporations to see sales collapse or, if they were lucky, only shrink by a third or more. The world's economy shrank to what it had been in 1913. IBM was not immune to the shock.

Back in 1929, during the greatest boom year of the decade, IBM was having another good year. IBM stock could be had in 1927 for $54 a share; in the fall of 1929, it topped $240 the month before the Crash—important to keep in mind, because IBM's executives were heavily invested in the company's stock, often having purchased it on margin. In November, less than two months later, IBM stock traded at $129 a share. The nation had gotten hooked on investing in stocks, from the wealthiest folks to those working in the mailroom; it seemed everyone was involved, and that was part of the problem. With the value of stocks rising so fast, people borrowed money to buy more shares, so when the market collapsed they had to pay for those they bought "on margin" or lose them. Many individuals went bankrupt. IBM was still making money, but the old-fashioned way, by generating business and profits in that first nine months of 1929. That year, IBM had six factories working full-time in North America and Europe.

The crisis had started a tad earlier when on Thursday, October 24, investors began selling in the belief that stocks were overvalued. The run quickly became irrational. Although the market temporarily calmed down over the next two days, the following week it headed down again. Disaster struck on Tuesday, October 29, in New York, when a great panic broke out, as it seemed "everyone" wanted to sell stocks. By the end of the day, people had traded over 16.4 million shares. That number traded in one day would not be matched again until 1968. Tens of billions of dollars in value evaporated that day. IBM's stock sank, too, and within days it had lost half its value. Meanwhile, Watson and his senior executives were on their way to Endicott by train for a meeting that day and did not learn about the catastrophe until they arrived. Most of the nation learned the magnitude of the financial disaster from their newspapers the next day.

Instead of panicking, Watson assured everyone and the local press that the economy was sound and that businesses would survive. He was speaking out of the experience IBM had been enjoying all year of expanding business and, of course, from his natural optimism. But, as with so many other executives across America and Europe, he got it wrong. The world had changed overnight. For the next three weeks, Watson was forced to spend a great deal of time assuring his executives whose IBM stock had shrunk in value not to panic. He loaned some of them money to cover debts they had incurred investing. Everyone worried, from executives, to factory workers, to salesmen and customers.

At a staff meeting on November 18, Watson acknowledged that business would slow but that IBMers had to persevere in finding ways to grow the business. He ordered sales to sell to companies one would not have thought needed IBM's equipment and to expand sales in Europe, Latin America, and Asia. He did not want to wait for the economy to turn around. He wanted IBMers to take action now. He instructed engineering to come up with new products and instructed manufacturing to hold down costs and increase productivity. Watson called on finance to work with sales to collect outstanding receipts from slow-paying customers. Every part of the company was going to have to chip in to overcome the crisis; being scared or fighting each other was not going to be tolerated. Watson declared, "The thing upon which we must rely is the organization. That is the biggest asset of the IBM. As members of the organization, we are all stronger men in this business today than ever before and better prepared to take care of the future of IBM."[5] He returned to his optimistic view: "The IBM spirit is one of ever looking ahead. Our goal is a bigger and better IBM."[6] "Ever Onward," the name of IBM's anthem, entered the company's lexicon for a generation.

Watson believed what he said in the face of a rapidly deteriorating business climate and took actions in support of his optimism. It worked. IBM came out of the Great Depression a stronger, wealthier, nearly iconic company. Watson's only misstep was perhaps being more optimistic than circumstances warranted. Many of his employees thought he was too optimistic, that he believed in his own hubris.

There were some business realities Watson and his employees could not ignore. It is important to understand these larger business issues, because Watson's response proved fortuitous in hindsight, propelling the company closer to its near-legendary status. Getting these right provided strategic insights for the next generation of managers, who led IBM into the computer business. If one sat in Watson's chair at the end of 1929, or during 1930–1931, a vision and a plan for dealing with unfolding problems were good to have, even if the company almost went out of business as it committed almost too much to the vision and the plan. Only careful modulation of how resources were deployed, notably cash and people, and perhaps the greatest piece of dumb luck ever to fall into the lap of a company, saved IBM from shrinking back to a small niche firm.

IBM's customers and the economies of the United States and Europe continued to deteriorate rapidly. The U.S. economy shrank by 8 percent in 1930 and by another 7 percent the following year. Hundreds of thousands of people were initially laid off, eventually 12 million; some 3,000 banks failed. Trade worldwide shrank, resulting in IBM's manufacturing customers laying off more people, closing plants, and initially returning some equipment. Firms in banking and insurance wanted to delay acquiring more tabulators or time clocks. By the end of 1930, demand for all manner of office appliances had shrunk by 50 percent, and it kept dropping. IBM's revenue peaked in 1931, at $20.3 million, driven by a relentless push by the sales organization to uncover every possible piece of business. However, IBM's business shrank in 1932 and 1933, with the firm reporting revenue of $17.6 million for 1932. Watson paid his salesmen a salary to hold onto as many of them as possible, although hiring by branch offices essentially stopped.

Company mythology holds that Watson single-handedly made the decision to keep running the entire business—sales, R&D, factories—in anticipation of an upturn in demand, and he filled up warehouses with new machines to be ready for it. The historical record shows that indeed this is what he did. Although it was a bet on the future, it was not so risky. IBM had cash reserves to fund payroll and manufacturing, and while demand dipped, it proved less than that experienced by such competitors as Burroughs, NCR, and Remington Rand. The Depression did not end quickly, however. This one just kept lingering. While historians of IBM's early history made it appear that Watson was unique in expanding production, which he was within the office appliance industry, other firms in other industries invested in the future, a finding Mira Wilkins pointed out as early as 1970.[7] Technological innovations proceeded in many industries, too, so IBM was not unique in its actions. Watson and his executives were talking to peers in other industries, picking up lessons along the way.

Then IBM got a break—the greatest one in its history. It began with the election of Franklin D. Roosevelt and his Democratic Party, ushering in the sweeping reforms of the New Deal in 1933. Elected to fix the job market and to end the Depression, the Roosevelt administration moved rapidly to increase the engagement of the federal government in the nation's economy. Initially, it sought to cut supplies of manufactured goods and agricultural production to stabilize prices. It established new agencies to improve labor conditions and farm productivity, protect banks from closing, and block wild stock speculation. Many of the laws and agencies needed to carry out its program were created in the first 100 days of the administration, during spring and early summer of 1933. In hindsight, we know that the depressed economy lingered until the start of World War II.

Roosevelt's initiatives rescued IBM in two ways. First, his agencies needed more information to determine how best to improve the economy. They experimented with new public policies that also needed to be measured for results. Second, these activities caused businesses to collect more data either to respond to the government (e.g., Social Security, other labor reporting) or because the economy in their industry was recovering. Both developments were only partially anticipated by IBM's management and sales organization. True, Watson was almost alone in his optimism. Although he had argued early on to prepare for the surge in demand that would come when the Depression ended, as the hard times continued, getting ready was rapidly depleting his cash reserves, causing board members to wonder if he should be replaced with someone prepared to cut expenses, as it seemed everyone else was doing. His competitors were doing that, and their CEOs were asking Watson why he was not doing so as well.

The problems his critics saw were visible. Between 1929 and the end of 1932, Watson increased IBM's manufacturing capacity by a third. Cash reserves could only carry IBM to the end of 1933; then it would have to slash production and other expenses. As the months ticked by, the company's senior management team urged a pullback, even though disagreeing with Watson required courage because IBMers were reluctant to cross him.

Sales stalled in 1933 and 1934—not shrinking but slowing—meaning money from leases still came in, making it possible to manage cash flows. The value of IBM's stock fell back to levels not seen since the last recession, in 1921. Watson kept arguing that the good times would return soon. Meanwhile, he continued to do some hiring, although his executives thought he hired too much, to build up manufacturing capacity and to expand in different markets and geographies. In 1930, IBM had 6,346 employees; it ended 1934 with 7,613, an increase of some 20 percent. Recall that to ease things a bit, in 1934 Watson sold the scales division to Hobart Manufacturing, although a year earlier he had acquired the Electromatic Typewriter Company. These moves involving hiring workers, expanding production, and purchasing a company were actions normally done in boom times, not during a depression. Watson seemed headed for failure, and he came close to disaster as his cash on hand and credit options diminished. Nevertheless, 1935 was also the year he launched *Think* magazine, aimed at employees and customers, as a slick, high-end, expensive trade publication, publishing articles by famous authors and personalities. That is when the great miracle occurred, the most essential piece of good fortune in IBM's history.

Experienced sales professionals argue that lucky breaks are usually earned, because of prior relations that had been built, a deep understanding of what a customer needed (or wanted), and salesmen who were present as an opportunity surfaced so they could seize it with knowledge and good timing. In short, good things did not happen by accident. For IBM, the lucky part was President Roosevelt being elected and implementing the New Deal, which launched a more activist involvement by officials in the nation's economy. Crucially for IBM, the New Deal led to massive increases in the use of information, and the company knew how to respond to that circumstance.

On August 14, 1935, President Roosevelt signed the Social Security Act, creating a national insurance program for the aged, a pension program that eventually expanded to include an economic social safety net for other groups, such as orphans and widows. But the initial legislation, similar to programs already in existence in parts of Europe, called on employers and employees to contribute a portion of all employees' salaries to a fund maintained by the U.S. government to pay recipients. When an individual reached retirement age, they would qualify for a pension. In the mid-1930s, the central requirement relevant to IBM was that the law mandated that employers track the hours, wages, and dollars paid to the Social Security Administration (SSA) for the vast majority of private sector employees in the United States. This data had to be sent to the SSA, which in turn calculated payments and then transmitted the information to the U.S. Treasury Department, which then sent monthly checks to qualified recipients. These actions involved thousands of businesses and millions of individuals.

Congress stipulated that the SSA set up and start running rapidly, as its funds had to be distributed as part of the larger campaign to stimulate the economy and to deal with a dire financial crisis among the elderly. The government set up the new agency between the summer of 1935 and the following spring, opening up hundreds of field offices all over the nation. The SSA developed the concept of social security numbers issued to every individual. By April 1937, over 25 million people had a social security number. Several million more did by the end of the decade. The SSA put out bids for office equipment to handle all the necessary processing.

What clearly was now the largest accounting project in the history of the nation was up for grabs. To make a long story short, IBM won the business to provide the necessary equipment for three reasons. First, as was normal IBM practice, IBMers worked with the SSA to design a system for how the agency could use IBM's products. IBM engineers included proposed changes in the machines wanted by the SSA, quickly implementing desired modifications so there was a system that SSA and IBM believed

Figure 4.1
The U.S. government became a massive user of IBM punch cards beginning in the 1930s in support of the Social Security Act. Photo courtesy of IBM Corporate Archives.

would work, and it did. Second, IBM priced its proposal competitively, since cost was a criterion for selecting the winning bid.

Third, and most important as it turned out, was IBM's ability to respond quickly in providing equipment. Remember all those machines Watson was storing in anticipation of a rebound in the economy? This was it for IBM. IBM could also make more machines, parts, and cards (figure 4.1), because it had fully staffed manufacturing organizations, unlike those vendors that had trimmed their sails. IBM was ready to go. In addition to SSA's needs were those of all the companies that had to collect information for the SSA. They, too, needed punch cards, sorters, and tabulators. IBM proved successful in supplying the SSA and so many other businesses, which in turn led other federal agencies to sign on with IBM to process their information needs. IBM had proven it could successfully handle very large projects.

It is difficult to exaggerate the importance of the Social Security win to the evolution of IBM. That one piece of business, along with its effects on other agencies and businesses, wiped out the Great Depression for IBM. That transaction handed IBM a potential market of 20,000 other companies that would need to process social security data. When the books were closed on IBM's business in 1937, revenue had increased by 48 percent over 1935's, and by the end of 1939, by 81 percent over 1935's.[8] In 1935, with minimal impact from the law but with some business coming in from the federal government, IBM's revenue climbed by $2 million over 1934's, to $21 million from all sources, not just the U.S. government. The first big revenue year for the SSA project was 1936, when IBM generated $25 million in total revenue. The following year, IBM brought in $31 million. By 1937, the SSA had installed more than 400 IBM accounting machines and over 1,200 keypunch machines. Other agencies even discarded their equipment from NCR, Burroughs, Remington Rand, and others to become IBM-compatible, so the effect on IBM's balance sheet was immediately measurable and permanent.

Historians and IBMers traditionally explain the Social Security win as a single dramatic event, even though that agency only accounted for approximately 2 percent of IBM's revenue.[9] As a single event, its importance would clearly have been exaggerated, particularly inside IBM, but it is best understood as a catalyst. Within several years, its success stimulated such significant increases in IBM's revenues from other U.S. government agencies that these agencies contributed approximately 10 percent of the company's total. But recall that meeting the reporting requirements of the SSA led other U.S. companies to acquire IBM's equipment, so when the SSA project is considered in its totality—SSA, government sales, private sector conformance to SSA reporting—that original order and the ongoing project as a whole was one of the most significant chapters in IBM's history. Most IBM sales offices in the United States felt the consequences, and many hundreds of IBM employees personally did, too. Most observers of IBM's history concluded that this win and others related to it gave IBM dominance over the data processing business in the United States until the 1980s.[10] No other company in the office appliance industry so dominated its market for as long as IBM did. If Watson wanted to build a greater company than Patterson at NCR, he now had done so.

To get an even greater sense of his victory, look at the profits, as they were greater than the percentage increase in revenue growth. By 1939, IBM was harvesting nearly 25 percent in profits out of its rapidly increasing revenue. That year, IBM's profits amounted to $9.1 million on $39.5 million in revenue, whereas the profits of its top three rivals—Burroughs, NCR, and Remington Rand—combined totaled only $7.6 million. Remington Rand produced more revenue ($43.4 million versus IBM's $39.5 million), but that included sales of office furniture.[11]

Watson had no idea how successful IBM's recovery would be. Neither did Congress or the SSA understand what a burdensome effort they imposed on corporate America, let alone the government. But Watson needs to be given credit for being ready across all fronts for an economic revival: he had a sales organization in place in both Washington, D.C., and around the country, a fully operating manufacturing organization with skilled workers and the components they needed, and an adequate supply of modern data processing products that could be shipped in days to the SSA. That agency located its operations in Baltimore, where it could find enough space quickly enough in an old Coca-Cola facility (the Candler Building). IBM trucks could roll in from Endicott, a trip that took less than a day door-to-door.[12] Kevin Maney, a leading biographer of Watson, cleverly, but accurately, summed up Watson's role: "Watson borrowed a common recipe for stunning success: one part madness, one part luck, and one part hard work to be ready when luck kicked in."[13]

We need to probe deeper into the "hard work" piece of this story, because, without it, all the luck in the world would not have been of any use, as IBM's rivals learned to their regret. Not until the massive information demands of World War II, which even highly successful IBM could not meet by itself, did other rivals regain momentum and prosperity.

RELATIONS WITH GOVERNMENTS AND THE CREATION
OF A CORPORATE IMAGE

During the 1920s, Watson established relations with senior U.S. and European political leaders to expand IBM's presence and prestige. By the end of the decade, he had met and communicated with U.S. presidents, including Herbert Hoover, a staunch advocate of fact-based decision making since serving as U.S. Secretary of Commerce in the early 1920s. In the 1930s, Watson expanded IBM's worldwide contacts with public officials. He and his executives were quick to endorse activities of the Roosevelt administration, breaking from many other business-oriented Republicans, who viewed Democrats with suspicion. Watson made it a personal mission to cultivate Roosevelt, which he had begun to do when FDR was governor of New York, because IBM had more employees in New York State than anywhere else in the world. He continued that initiative in Washington, D.C. Watson communicated frequently with Roosevelt, thinking of himself as an influential member of the president's inner circle, which was an inflated view of his own importance. But he supported FDR in speeches, defending the New Deal in business circles, particularly in the New York City area, and within IBM.

For example, when the president announced an employee redeployment program in July 1933, Watson fired off a telegram to the White House: "International Business Machines Corporation endorses your program and has taken steps to put it into effect. Congratulations on your splendid address."[14] In a speech to employees on September 7, 1933, Watson praised the administration's National Recovery Act (NRA) program, stating, "I have been interested in keeping our people employed" and "we were reaching a point in the affairs of this nation where something different had to be done." He added, "The National Recovery Act, to me, is one of the fairest and squarest propositions that has ever been presented, because it not only takes care of employees, but it also looks after stockholders."[15] And so it went through the 1930s. In the 1920s, Watson had promoted free trade and commerce worldwide, too. U.S. presidents appreciated his support, as he had cultivated a visible profile by the late 1920s. He used his growing celebrity to defend public policies. His ties to

Roosevelt were the most intimate he had with any U.S. president, flowering at a time when FDR was being criticized by many CEOs, such as Henry Ford. At one point, President Roosevelt wrote to Watson, "You go back and tell them [business executives] that I have to think about millions of people, that my concern is to take care of them and if I am successful, I'll automatically take care of the rest of you."[16]

Despite his support for the New Deal, often more out of idealism than for business reasons, and winning the Social Security contract, IBM's dealings with the federal government were seriously troubled. Patent issues in combination with growing market share created difficult relations with the U.S. Department of Justice, while at the same time IBM was selling increasing amounts of its products to federal agencies and Watson was cultivating the White House. Such problems had dogged IBM from its earliest days and continued almost to the end of the twentieth century. Though often overlooked in earlier histories of IBM, the events of the 1930s were not lost on the company's senior leadership, beginning with Thomas Watson Sr. but later also by his son Tom Jr. in the 1950s and then again by the same son when he faced antitrust litigation near the end of his term as CEO in the early 1970s.

IBM's patent problems originated when Hollerith obtained patents for his tabulating equipment in the 1880s. When James Powers started making his own machines in 1914 in his own firm, the Powers Accounting Machine Company needed to license some of Hollerith's patents now owned by C-T-R. Just before Watson arrived at C-T-R, the firm had agreed to license them but also fixed minimum prices James Powers could charge his customers and limited what technologies he could use. This agreement violated the Sherman Antitrust Act of 1890 and the Clayton Act of 1914. C-T-R also had insisted on harsh terms, forcing James Powers to fork over 20 percent of all his revenue. Over the years, the U.S. Department of Justice had observed that C-T-R, then IBM, dominated the punch card business.

The terms with Powers Accounting were renegotiated in 1922 and again in 1931 with Remington Rand (which now owned Powers Accounting). This last time they cross-licensed each other's patents and settled various disputes over fees. In 1932, the Justice Department filed suits against both IBM and Remington Rand, accusing them of restraining commerce through this patent pool. The government's lawyers challenged the practice by both firms of leasing, never allowing purchase of machines; of forcing users to buy only their cards; and refusing to sell cards to anyone who did not use their machines. The U.S. Government Printing Office (GPO) had earlier concluded that it could have saved considerable sums if it had been allowed to manufacture cards without paying IBM a fee. The case was litigated between 1935 and 1937.

Here was a case where, as one historian put it, the government was the "prosecutor, litigant, and customer."[17] It had to defend the antitrust laws yet simultaneously leased machines and consumed millions of cards each year. The case reflected the multifaceted relations IBM had with national governments. Such contacts demonstrated that national governments consisted of ecosystems comprised of multiple agencies and departments often working at mixed purposes. As a result, IBM faced conflicting tensions—litigation and, simultaneously, close political and business relations. Remington Rand faced a similar set of circumstances but immediately agreed to a settlement to get the case behind it. Watson had to decide what to do about the charges that he was operating a cartel and restricting trade in the sale of cards. As part of the discovery process, IBM turned over to the Justice Department a large body of records. They showed that IBM, and C-T-R before it, was a rough player in the marketplace, aggressive in wanting to dominate sales of its equipment and in constraining competition. Watson was a secretive person and therefore disliked letting out that kind of information.

He had cause to worry, because IBM dominated 80 percent of the market, and any change to IBM's terms and conditions posed a potentially huge loss of revenue to the company. It took years for government lawyers to see the unfolding IBM dominance and the role Remington Rand played, too, especially as the federal government became increasingly dependent on their technologies. The government was forced to pay a fee for cards produced by the GPO, irritating to officials concerned with rising costs for hundreds of millions of cards at a time when tax revenues were declining because of the Great Depression. The GPO had been pushing for litigation since the late 1920s, so it was a long-festering issue.

Federal prosecutors maintained that IBM prevented its customers from acquiring products from other possible suppliers, especially cards. The discovery information obtained from IBM demonstrated that profits from card sales were huge and that the company did not tolerate competition. In 1936, the U.S. Supreme Court sided with the Justice Department on the issue of card sales. It noted that IBM had intended "to prevent competition and to create a monopoly in the production and sale of tabulating cards," recording that IBM made 3 million cards annually, "81 percent of the total," and that IBM collected 10 percent of its revenue from card sales. The justices concluded that this behavior "tends to create monopoly, and has in fact been an important and effective step in the creation of monopoly."[18] The U.S. Supreme Court ordered IBM to stop prohibiting its customers from using non-IBM cards. Meanwhile, Remington Rand and IBM nullified their patent cross-licensing agreements, thereby eliminating the first of the two charges against them. IBM lowered the cost of its cards to the government, while no competitors came forward to sell similar ones.

By the time the Supreme Court rendered its decision, IBM was well on its way to selling vast quantities of cards. It continued to dominate both the tabulating machine and card markets. While the lawsuit had no appreciable effect on IBM's business, as sales continued to grow from federal and commercial users in the United States, it was Watson's second bout with the Justice Department, the first having been his conviction back in the NCR days. Every time the U.S. Department of Justice raised a concern with IBM's behavior, Watson's stubborn streak showed. He would not give in lightly to lawyers and judges. Disturbing to him was a fundamental disagreement with the government that never went away: if a company became big enough to dominate a market, thanks to being a successful business, it should not become subject to antitrust litigation. That the government pursued other firms in a similar situation, such as Standard Oil, American Tobacco, and DuPont, made no difference to Watson and his executives. To Watson, it was just wrong.

Patent protections did not play a role in this trial, making it possible for IBM to continue collecting and protecting its patents. The one cloudy issue in patent litigation was the original Hollerith-Powers agreement of 1914, which had become the basis for the government's accusation that both firms had formed a cartel. Watson and his executives remained mum about the case, a sign that they had been nervous about the lawsuits and settlements. They turned their attention to getting business and promoting the greater IBM. IBM linked relations with officials to what it did with the press, increasingly recognizing that both constituencies affected one another.

Watson & Company had made it a point to engage with the press all through the 1920s and 1930s, having the IBM president's speeches reported on hundreds of times each year and putting out press releases. Slowly during the 1920s and increasingly in the 1930s, both the business community in the United States and the public came to learn more about this successful company and its celebrity CEO. They had already learned that he was the best-paid executive during the Great Depression, making more than any other famous person, including movie stars. The company was successful, and many people knew that fact. The Great Depression did not press down IBM. As IBM went from one success to another, Watson the man and Watson the company fused into one. He was IBM. Biographers spoke of his expanding ego as his sense of self-importance grew, but for him it was all about promoting "The IBM Company," of constantly pushing his employees and the world to make greater use of data processing and increasingly to embrace his idea of World Peace through World Trade.

The economic boosterism of the period was not unique to Watson, just exaggerated in his case. As president of the International Chamber of Commerce in 1937, he found an even larger platform to promote trade and, in the process, IBM. He had the logo "World Peace through World Trade" painted on the side of IBM's new corporate headquarters in midtown Manhattan.

IBM AND THE 1939 WORLD'S FAIR

Nothing seemed to capture Watson's growing sense of the importance of both himself and IBM more than the World's Fair in New York City held at the end of the decade (figure 4.2). Of the more than a dozen such fairs held in the United States during Watson's lifetime, this was the most

Figure 4.2
The IBM exhibit at the New York World's Fair, 1939–1940. Photo courtesy of
IBM Corporate Archives.

extravagant. Major corporations built pavilions the size of a square city
block. Every exhibitor hawked the future. General Motors installed an
elevated pathway to guide visitors through its vision of the future urban
America. RCA installed television sets—something Americans saw for the
first time. A kitchen filled with new appliances gave families something to
dream about, including dishwashers and robots. Life was going to be fantastic. The Great Depression had been beaten. Pavilions built by nations
promoted peace while Adolf Hitler occupied Czechoslovakia.

Watson quickly signed on to help with the fair, donating money and
then renting space in a pavilion, even though IBM was still a relatively
small company compared to some of the behemoths that were its customers. He convinced the organizers to declare an IBM Day two years in a
row to promote his company as if it were as large and important as GM,
Ford, or RCA. May 4, 1939, was the first IBM Day, set on the twenty-fifth

anniversary to the day when Watson showed up to work at C-T-R. IBM took out a full-page advertisement in the *New York Times*. Watson invited 4,000 guests to IBM Day, which included IBMers, executives, customers, luminaries, and political figures. Seventeen mounted riders led a parade up to the building, along with the IBM band and a car with Watson in it. Inside the pavilion, Watson had IBM's products on exhibit. On the walls hung paintings from the 79 countries where IBM had a presence. Pomp, ceremony, and speechmaking fit his style. Watson delivered a message of economic success and world peace at a time when the clouds of war were rolling over Europe and Asia.[19] In the heat of the moment, he reminded his thousands of guests that IBM's future accomplishments would exceed those of the previous 25 years, arguing that IBM was not so much a business "as a great world institution."[20] The IBM staff gave him a portrait of himself to celebrate his quarter century with the company.

The next year on IBM Day, May 13, 1940, events unfolded differently but also provided a window into the culture and practices of the company. Watson had invited thousands of IBMers and their spouses to the fair; some ten thousand committed to arriving from all over the United States, Canada, and even a few from other countries, the Americans largely on 12 trains chartered for that purpose. As in the previous year, his staff launched a media campaign to let Americans learn about the ten thousand showing up. It cost IBM just over 10 percent of its annual profits to fund this event. The day before the event, IBM offices and factories in the United States closed as employees and families headed off to New York. It all seemed so exciting. While rounding a curve at Port Jervis, New York, the fourth IBM train crashed into the third IBM train. Some 400 people suffered cuts and bruises, 35 people required hospitalization, but nobody died. Watson soon received a phone call at his home about the accident, immediately rallied his family and executives to help, and ordered IBM's media people to keep the story out of the newspapers. Soon enough, the press picked it up, but the point of this story is that Watson thought of his employees as an extension of his family. Kevin Maney, his leading biographer, captured Watson's thinking: "Just as he expected unerring loyalty and extraordinary deeds, he reciprocated, giving his complete loyalty and nearly all of his energy."[21]

Watson took charge of this crisis out of instinct. He arrived at Port Jervis, by which time the injured had been moved to nearby hospitals. He and his wife talked with IBMers at the site, while his secretary, Fred Nichol, in New York sent doctors to Port Jervis. Although he arrived home late that night, the next day Watson showed up at the World's Fair for IBM Day. Four months later, the fair closed, a resounding success. Forty-four million people had visited the fair. IBM garnered a great deal of positive exposure, but the world had already plunged into global war. For IBM, its employees, and hundreds of millions of people around the world, World War II upended everything.

IBM GOING GLOBAL

One reason IBM thrived in the 1930s was because of its expanding global business. While Watson had taken steps in the 1920s to expand overseas operations, the urgency to do so increased in the 1930s. Not all countries were in the depth of a depression, notably Germany, which had an economy more suited to IBM products than many other countries did. The benefits enjoyed from the Social Security Act came late in the decade and were unanticipated by IBMers. Meanwhile, the company called for finding business all over the world. IBM's non-U.S. and Canadian operations accounted for a third of the company's revenue, or over $8 million in both 1938—the last full year of peace—and 1939, the first year of the world war in Europe. That expansion had started with little C-T-R as Watson came into the company, and it kept growing until World War II.

IBM's foreign experience raises a number of practical questions relevant to any history of an international corporation. How does one expand an American company into so many different cultures? How did IBM's employees implement their business culture elsewhere, or should they have? How does a multinational corporation handle the different national business and tax laws? Answers were not obvious in 1914, much more so by the early 1930s at IBM, and even more so to historians today. The New Deal themes discussed earlier applied to two-thirds of the company's business and obviously to what went on in IBM's headquarters in New York, but much of what occurred in the rest of the world, while linked to events in the United States, also had their own features. These non-U.S. themes attracted a great deal of attention at IBM.

For one thing, IBMers sought out business opportunities, which led Watson to travel frequently to Europe during the interwar years. In 1927, he told U.S. IBMers that every time he went to Europe he found "limitless possibilities, tremendous opportunities and a great future" for IBM.[22] For another, he imposed the values and practices of the American company everywhere and upon meeting European IBMers "found them imbued with the same spirit which actuates the members of our organization over here," or at least wishing to be.[23] That year, IBM's products were in good use in Great Britain, and the firm had just opened factories in France and Germany, meaning that IBM had a local presence in Europe's three most advanced economies. IBM operated in 54 countries, and it would expand into 25 more by the start of World War II. Watson and his executives hired agents in a new country and, as business expanded, established a local company with sales (branch) offices. The boards of directors of these firms were populated with influential local elites, and branches were staffed with citizens of the country, trained in the same way as Americans and equipped largely with the same products, leasing terms, and IBM's corporate culture and procedures. Watson continuously visited his growing empire to reinforce IBM's way of doing things and to inspect what was going on. IBM's expansion into markets outside the United States mimicked many of the same practices of its large customers, which also extended their businesses outside their home U.S. market.

In 1933, Watson closed the C-T-R holding company and transferred the firms it owned to IBM, some now as divisions. That transfer involved the old Hollerith Tabulating Machine Company, the International Time Recording Company, Dayton Scale Company, International Scale Company, and the Ticketograph Company. Watson's move was logical, as it made reporting lines and accounting easier to manage as the company expanded. Table 4.1 chronicles IBM's expansion in the 1930s. Clearly the company was expanding rapidly, even in difficult times. Between 1930 and the end of 1939, IBM opened 32 facilities in North America, 22 in

Table 4.1
Chronology of IBM's global expansion, 1930s

1930	Opened a sales office in Lima, Peru
1930	Established a direct subsidiary in Rome, Italy
1931	Opened a sales office in Bogota, Colombia
1931	Opened a sales office in Manila, Philippines
1932	Started opening sales offices in various cities in France, having already been in Paris since 1919
1933	Established direct subsidiary in Austria, replacing agent Furth & Company
1930s	Established a direct subsidiary in Norway
1930s	Established a direct subsidiary in Yugoslavia, called Yugoslav Watson AG
1932	Established a direct subsidiary in Morocco
1933	Established a branch office in Shanghai, China; previously had an agent
1933	IBM and its German subsidiary begin opening sales offices and factories in various cities in Germany
1933	Established a direct subsidiary in Czechoslovakia; established card plant in 1935
1934	Established a direct subsidiary in Poland to replace the Block-Brun agency
1934	Established a branch office in Sao Paulo, Brazil
1935	Moved its European headquarters to Geneva, Switzerland
1935	Established a sales office in Bermuda
1935	Established an office in Goteborg, Sweden
1935	Opened a sales office in Ankara, Turkey
1935	Opened a sales office in Athens, Greece
1936	Expanded its French operations, which dated from 1919, by establishing Compagnie Electro-Comptable de France (CEC)
1936	Established a card printing plant in the Netherlands
1936	Opened a sales office in Calcutta, India
1937	Established a direct subsidiary in Yokohama, Japan, called Nihon Watson Tokei Kaikei Kikai (known also as Watson Japan), and a card plant
1938	Opened a sales office in Malmö, Sweden
1938	Established a sales office in Johannesburg, South Africa
1938	Established a direct subsidiary in Romania, the Compania Electrocontabila Watson

This list is not complete, as in many countries multiple offices were opened in the 1930s, such as in Great Britain, Germany, and France, while other obvious candidates had started operations in the 1920s, such as Mexico City in 1927. Operations had started even earlier in Brazil (1917) and Canada (1914).

Source: IBM Corporate Archives, "Frequently Asked Questions," April 10, 2007.

Europe, 8 in Latin America, 5 in the Middle East and Africa, and 5 in Asia, most as directly owned subsidiaries.

Looking back on the 1930s from the perspective of the early twenty-first century, we probably understand events better than Watson did. Fascism and the harsh brand of National Socialism (Nazis) were spreading over Europe in the 1920s and 1930s, the Japanese Empire was rapidly militarizing, and Adolf Hitler came to power with an agenda to fundamentally change the course of Europe's destiny. One can ask, how much did Watson understand? In November 1933, the year Adolf Hitler became German Reich Chancellor and the Nazis came to power, Watson reported in IBM's *Business Machines* that on his recent trip to Germany he found the German IBMers "intensely proud of the fact that for the first nine months of 1933 they were leading all countries of the world in percentage of quota, and are determined to keep their lead." He had just opened a factory in Germany that would "contribute greatly to [IBM's] future success there and throughout Central Europe."[24] Had he not noticed the changes under way in Germany? If so, he did not share them in public. Over the next several years, several German branch offices opened.

When a national economy industrialized or formed large commercial enterprises and government agencies, these organizations became the kinds that could most benefit from IBM's products. IBM would establish a presence by forming an alliance with a local agent. This approach worked reasonably well. One in particular, however, complicated life for IBM. Back in 1910, Willy Heidinger, a tough, strong-willed entrepreneur, had established a firm, Deutsche Hollerith Maschinen Gesellschaft mbH (better known as Dehomag), as an agent to sell Hollerith equipment in Germany. The Americans had a similar arrangement in Great Britain to sell punch card equipment through the British Tabulating Machine Company (known as BTM). The German firm sold all over Europe, whereas BTM sold only in Great Britain and the British Empire. By 1914, the Germans had 44 accounts, Powers no less than 4, while BTM probably had closer to 55 by the end of World War I. The German and British firms survived the war and thrived during the 1920s and 1930s, even investing in local R&D. After the war, Watson posted long-time Bundy Manufacturing employee

Andrew Jennings to Paris to expand European operations. Jennings was an aggressive entrepreneur, quickly setting up operations all over Western Europe. Dehomag became the largest of this collection of companies and agencies, pursuing the kinds of customers C-T-R and IBM had in the United States: banks, railroads, large insurance companies, government agencies, and manufacturing firms. When business resumed after the Christmas holidays of 1924, BTM had 100 customers, while the Germans had a larger installed base of 115 tabulators and 100 sorters. Powers had fewer accounts.[25]

However, the German relationship became problematic. In the early 1920s, Germany experienced horrible inflation that required people to use baskets full of paper currency to buy a loaf of bread. Dehomag at one point was unable to pay royalties to C-T-R, so Heidinger agreed to turn over half ownership of his company to Watson, who quickly expanded that to 90 percent ownership. The German had no choice but to settle for 10 percent ownership to wipe out his debt to C-T-R. Heidinger hated Watson for trapping him this way and never forgave him. The takeover was a logical move for Watson to make, albeit harshly done, as he consolidated control over his markets around the world. What he could not realize was that during the Nazi period he would face serious problems as a result of Heidinger still being at the helm of the German operation.

Watson, Jennings, and others never trusted Heidinger, who enjoyed legal and mental combat with customers and IBM as much as he thrived on business. In the process, Heidinger held back information from IBM's auditors, one of whom called him "a very selfish man,"[26] but he ran the business well. The newly installed Nazi regime wanted to use punch card equipment to work with massive quantities of new data, which brought more business to the German subsidiary. Because of Heidinger's success across Europe, Watson tolerated his rebellious behavior, something he never did with U.S. executives. When Germany went to war with the United States in 1941, Watson had a huge problem on his hands thanks to Dehomag's success and close ties to the Third Reich, discussed further later.

Meanwhile, overall, European business grew and, like Watson, Jennings remained optimistic about the future. He opined, "The European business will exceed that done in the United States of America."[27] The overall business for tabulating equipment was still small, however, generating income of $1.6 million in the peak year before the Great Depression, not a great deal when compared to IBM's overall net income of $7 million.[28] In addition to the existing British, German, and French operations, IBM-owned operations opened in Finland, Norway, Belgium, Portugal, Yugoslavia, Poland, Hungary, Turkey, Bulgaria, Japan, Mexico, Brazil, and Argentina, among other markets.

IBM compelled its subsidiaries to sell and service the same products, with minor exceptions, largely to control costs. Manufacturing overseas for the European market depended on whether it was less expensive to do so, say in France, than in Endicott. Dehomag had manufacturing in Germany and outsourced manufacturing, too, making it possible for the firm to go from less than five hundred tabulating machine installations in 1930 to more than twice that many by the end of the decade.[29] European customers embraced these products for the same reasons as the Americans. By the start of World War II, IBM had become a global enterprise. Table 4.2 shows the breadth of IBM's growth from 1914 through 1940, closing out the company's prebehemoth phase.

As the company improved its performance, Watson aspired to leverage this celebrity status to help IBM, but biographers also think he personally wanted to do more, perhaps out of ego. He hosted senior public officials and national leaders at IBM events and used his presidency of the

Table 4.2
IBM's growth, 1914–1940, select years (revenue in millions of dollars)

Year	Revenue	Number of employees
1914	4	1,346
1924	11	3,384
1934	19	7,613
1936	25	9,142
1938	34	11,046
1940	45	12,656

Source: Emerson W. Pugh, *Building IBM: Shaping an Industry and Its Technology* (Cambridge, MA: MIT Press, 1995), 322.

positively regarded International Chamber of Commerce (ICC) as a platform to influence world events. Unfortunately in hindsight, Watson, after many years of membership in the ICC, was elected its president in 1937. He knew little about international politics when he became president, as global politics were turning ugly. Benito Mussolini was running Italy. Adolf Hitler was jailing dissidents and ethnic and religious minorities, and was beginning to implement plans for dominating Central Europe. Spain was in the midst of a bloody civil war, with Hitler supporting the Nationalists, and Josef Stalin, another dictator, the Republican side. Japan was in the midst of war, expanding its empire in Asia. The Great Depression still lingered.

Germany became a problem. The 1936 Olympics in Berlin introduced to the world a disturbing picture of a militarizing society. IBM and other U.S. firms, including such iconic companies as Standard Oil, Quaker Oil, three U.S. automotive companies (Chrysler, General Motors, and Ford), and General Electric, were selling to the Germans. Their CEOs knew each other and Watson; all were IBM's customers. None wanted to pull out of Germany, since they believed Germany would dominate Europe, and so to pull out of that market was to walk away from much of Europe.[30] It is not certain whether Watson subscribed to this view, but he probably did, since U.S. CEOs shared similar views on many issues. In 1937, the ICC held its annual conference in Berlin, which Watson hosted as its president. While there, he met Hitler and accepted a medal from the Nazi regime for his international business leadership in the ICC. Watson believed he could talk Hitler and others out of reverting back to world war and achieve "world peace through world trade." The Nazis hailed him as a business leader.

Watson was pleased with his German award, not yet realizing it would prove to be a mistake to have accepted it. He left Berlin to visit 11 other countries, touting his message of peace through trade. In 1937, Hitler's most heinous activities had not yet started, although Americans and Western Europeans were already nervous about his intentions. Watson's peers in other companies believed they could still do business with Germany. Four more years would pass before Germany declared war on the United States. Henry Ford received a more prestigious award than Watson's from the Germans as late as July 1938, after Germany had annexed Austria, while earlier

U.S. corporate executives had feted the German ambassador to the United States in New York with both Nazi German and U.S. flags on display. Watson began writing to the Germans, cautiously urging them not to persecute religious minorities, as doing that would hurt business. With the U.S. entry into World War II, it became obvious how naive Watson had been in his dealings with the Germans, an issue discussed further in chapter 5.

IBM AT THE END OF THE GREAT DEPRESSION

Many observers have written about how Watson became increasingly arrogant, overconfident in his ideas and actions, and in his own mind even essential to the world's prosperity. This behavior helps to explain why his optimistic and relentless pressure on everyone around him made it possible for IBM to perform the way it did. One could not execute poorly—that was just not tolerated. Watson obsessed over this issue for decades. Almost every speech he gave spoke about personal commitment and proper execution. One example of that attitude regarding the work of his employees was how they ran an "IBM Family Dinner."

Recall that Watson spent the majority of his working life on the road, visiting customers, employees, and political figures, giving speeches, receiving awards, and hosting an endless number of Family Dinners all over the world. Other than the train wreck on the way to the World's Fair, one would be hard pressed to find any event in which he participated that was not run properly as planned; the IBM culture would not tolerate less. The poor branch manager in Nashville or Madrid who learned from headquarters that the "Old Man" and Jeanette, his wife, were coming to host a Family Dinner in two or three months had his work cut out for him. His career would be on the line. He would spend enormous amounts of time booking a hotel ballroom; negotiating terms and a menu for the meal; preparing, printing, and sending out formal invitations to every IBMer and spouse within a hundred or more miles; tracking R.S.V.P.s; arranging logistics to pick up the Watsons and their entourage of executives and staff at the train station; ensuring they had hotel rooms; and flooding everyone with accurate, up-to-date itineraries. There might be music to include in the evening's events, never alcoholic beverages, and if an IBM glee club was to be used, it had better be well rehearsed. There were sales calls on the local mayor or governor and certainly on several presidents of the branch's accounts, all carefully choreographed, with both sides properly briefed on issues and responses to questions. For the branch manager, such events demonstrated his managerial prowess and access to the senior executives of his accounts.

Now consider the hundreds of managers around the world doing the same thing for over 40 years. Their activities were so ubiquitous, so routine, that rarely did IBMers writing their memoirs mention them, yet they were obviously so important that invariably photographs of Family Dinners with them posing with Watson and his wife appeared in their publications. That style of staff work for Watson spilled over into how the company's executives were handled. While they might seem like a waste of time and talent, these events taught young IBMers what completed staff work looked like and how certain events important in the company's culture should be handled. It might be that in one's long career at IBM they would attend only three or four Family Dinners, but each would have been prepared meticulously.

Field inspections by Watson also had a common feel to them, a tradition in managerial practice that is still in evidence at IBM. New York set the agenda and called for the event, but local IBMers were expected to pull it off flawlessly. That this behavior was well in place by the start of the 1930s adds evidence demonstrating that IBM's corporate culture of THINK existed back then, hardwired into every corner of the company, even extending into organizations of its customers worldwide. By World War II, IBM had become well known and its CEO a celebrity, joining the likes of Henry Ford and Thomas Edison. The press kept IBM in front of the public more in the 1930s than in the 1920s and no longer buried on page 3, as had happened with the announcement of C-T-R's formation in 1911. But did IBM's image have a discernible impact on the world yet?

A salesman, and IBM's management, would argue yes, because their customers were willing to spend millions of dollars leasing equipment and buying hundreds of millions of punch cards. Its image and the relevance of its products were central to the company's success. Proof came during the Great Depression, when IBM's customers did not return leased equipment as extensively as they did products from other vendors, although they used them less. IBMers worked to ensure that leases continued, although card sales declined. Revenue continued to arrive at a steady rate for accounting equipment and sorters, while the number of keypunch machines increased. Lease revenue dipped from $11.5 million in 1931 to $10.5 million the next year but then rose to $12.2 million in 1934 and subsequently shot up to $29.6 million in 1939. Sales of punch cards reached $3.4 million in 1932, dropped to $2.8 million for each of the next two years, and then returned to their 1931 level in 1934. Revenues for time clocks and scales shrank immediately, but IBM's overall income remained flat, thanks to the Tabulating Machine piece of the business.[31]

After implementation of the U.S. Social Security Act, U.S. firms had no choice but to use IBM's equipment, since it was compatible with SSA's. Both used the same formats and cards. So did the U.S. Treasury Department. Government agencies in Europe with similar applications argued that use of punch cards made a difference in their work. IBM's equipment contributed to a new *style* of management of large organizations, which relied increasingly on large bodies of data to inform decisions and on the timely preparation of accounting and financial reports. Manufacturing floor operations, billing, and other uses were often conducted using smaller, less sophisticated office equipment, such as billing machines and desktop calculators. In the interwar years, management teams learned about the possibilities of data processing, experiencing enough benefits to offset the cost of using IBM's products.

Did Watson's high profile influence the role of other executives in various industries and countries, or was he an uber-example of a larger trend in business? He had become a celebrity.[32] Unknown to the public were his communications with President Roosevelt, dispensing all kinds of advice regarding business matters, most of which FDR ignored. But Watson made so many speeches to groups of hundreds and thousands of people, often reported in the press, that he seemed to be an emerging voice of the business community, especially in the United States and within the International Chamber of Commerce. It did not hurt that IBM had expanded across Europe and Latin America and had thrived while other firms suffered. Many of the social and business elite where IBM had a presence knew something about this company by the end of the 1930s. They understood it was successful and well run. They had been exposed to a smattering of IBM's unique culture of optimism. They increasingly heard that its employees sang songs celebrating Watson but also that IBM was introducing the world to "thinking machines."[33]

We are still left with a question: Was Watson a unique celebrity CEO or just another version of a U.S. business leader? In hindsight, he was probably both—a relentless promoter of IBM but also now filled with a bolder ambition to use his celebrity status and success to play the role of statesman with some of the most dangerous people in European history. In that game, he played the amateur, but as a business leader, he and his company made the prosperity they enjoyed in the 1930s seem like child's play. However, he needed a stage, a platform, on which to perform. William Lazonick reminds us that American managerial practices affected executives at all levels.[34] Watson was a part of his own IBM ecosystem. World War II hurried the company to a new destiny that could not have been imagined by a novelist. That is the story we turn to next.

5 IBM IN WORLD WAR II, 1939–1945

> We, too, are proud of our service man, and glad too that he was employed
> by a company whose understanding and policies make it possible for him to
> do his duty with no worries about those at home.
> —WIFE OF AN IBM SOLDIER, 1944[1]

EUROPE BLEW ITSELF up in 1914 and never resolved its issues in the 1920s
and 1930s, so it collapsed into another continent-wide civil war in 1939,
which spread worldwide. The damage caused by the two wars is difficult
to fathom. In World War I, some18 million people died, many more were
injured, and almost every government in the industrialized world collapsed.
But all that was paltry when compared to World War II, during which an
estimated 80 million people died, or 3 percent of the world's population.
The Soviet Union lost 26.5 million lives and Germany over 5 million.
Europe's colonial system disintegrated. Europe's economy never achieved
the robustness it had enjoyed before 1914. The United States came out of
World War I as the world's largest and healthiest economy, positions it kept
throughout the twentieth century. Because World War I saw the marshal-
ing of much information, C-T-R was able to ride that wave of opportunity,
doubling its tiny revenue. C-T-R increased its employee count by 2.5 times,
a big change for a small company in such a short time. Like everything else
in World War II, events were bigger, more dramatic. IBM's revenue grew
explosively from $38 million in 1939 to $138 million in 1945. Its number
of employees rose from just over 11,000 in 1939 to over 18,000 in 1945,
and exceeded 22,000 the next year, many of them returning veterans.[2] In

the United States alone, one out of every four IBM employees went into the military.

IBM made it easy for them to do so. Once the United States entered the war, Watson announced that any employee serving in the U.S. military would receive 25 percent of their prewar salary every month that they were in uniform, paid to their families (or if unmarried to the soldier or sailor directly). Watson had already established a separate subsidiary to manufacture war-related goods, such as weapons, capping profits on those military contracts at 1.5 percent, which IBM set aside in a fund to support IBM widows and orphans. Every employee in uniform received gifts of food and toiletries from IBM during holidays and received *Business Machines* so that they could stay in touch with the company. Soldiers appreciated the packages—a practice IBM continued deep into the twentieth century. In the lobby of IBM's new world headquarters at 590 Madison Avenue in New York City, built in the late 1930s, nine panels listed every U.S. IBMer in the military.

The number of IBMers in uniform, others working in the plants, and the revenue and profits gained signaled far greater changes at IBM than during World War I. Information played a greater role during World War II than ever before. IBM's involvement proved more crucial to the war effort, especially in the United States. IBM came out of World War II large, muscular, and critical to the nations now engaged on both sides of the Cold War, from the United States to the far reaches of the Soviet Union, even to badly damaged Japan. Nobody at IBM could have foreseen in 1939 the wild ride they would take or the complexity of the issues they would face, many of which could have crippled the company. Instead, IBM grew. The U.S. Social Security project may have involved a large dose of luck, but successfully navigating an event the size of World War II required more than a lucky break.

Historians, journalists, and others writing about IBM during World War II have focused largely on the company's American experience, emphasizing the company's support of the Allied cause and its role in developing war-relevant technologies.[3] Others concentrated on IBM's early encounters with computers, notably the Mark I.[4] Shortly after the start of the new millennium, a book appeared accusing IBM of collaborating with Nazi Germany in implementing the Holocaust.[5] None of these publications, however, looked at IBM's managerial issues and operations during the war the way a senior- or division-level executive would have. By putting together the various elements, we can contribute to the broader discussion of how U.S. firms transformed and grew as a result of this war. In the process, we can contribute insights surrounding the contentious issue of what role U.S. and European companies played in Germany's wartime activities, including the Holocaust. IBM's story contributes evidence in support of Louis Galambos's contention that even though the U.S. government did much to control the economy, large firms were "creative and successful" in supporting the nation's war effort and in finding ways to flourish themselves.[6]

To demonstrate that IBM's experience was far more complicated and the issues it confronted more nuanced than is often acknowledged, including by me in an earlier account of IBM's role in World War II, we proceed as follows.[7] We begin by describing IBM's American activities and many of the managerial challenges faced by "Corporate" (the company's top-level management, based at IBM headquarters), followed by a discussion of IBM's earliest encounters with computers, situating that experience within the context of the war. We then discuss how IBMers individually, and as a community, experienced the war, including members of the Watson family. With the Allied side of the story told, we turn to IBM and its role in Nazi Germany, clarifying what for many has been a polemical issue, offering a more detailed account of how the German government used information technology in its attack on Jews and enemies of the state. We end with a summary of how IBM changed during the war.

IBM SUPPLIES EVERYONE'S WAR MACHINE BUT MOSTLY THE AMERICAN ONE

After Japan attacked Pearl Harbor on December 7, 1941, reaction was nearly instantaneous and uniform across the United States. The next day, the U.S. Congress declared war on Japan. Barely a week later, the country was also at war with Germany. The war in Europe had been under way since Germany invaded Poland in September 1939. Between then and December 1941, the U.S. government increased its support to the British against the Germans and expanded U.S. industrial and military capacity. That preparation extended to the office appliance industry in the form of increased demand for its products, including IBM's.[8] Once the war was "official," Thomas J. Watson Sr. did not hesitate to align with the Allies. He wrote to President Roosevelt pledging his support and, if needed, to turn over his factories to the war effort. Watson's speeches and communications to his employees made it clear that he backed the American side in the war. He preached patriotism and support of the Allied cause until the end of the war but then quickly reverted to his "world peace through world trade" slogan. In October 1945, when the Allies were sorting out what the postwar world would look like, he argued that "complete victory depends upon international political policies that will give all nations the independent right to determine their own form of government and also international economic agreements that will give all nations an opportunity to buy and sell in world markets on a basis fair to every country, regardless of size or power."[9]

Before Pearl Harbor, IBM was already responding to events in Europe. In early 1941, Watson established the Munitions Manufacturing Corporation to produce goods for the U.S. military. Much of the work done by this division took place in Poughkeepsie, New York, where the cost of new facilities could be charged to the war effort. Watson kept his personal remuneration at 1939's level. IBM donated financially to war-related projects in the United States.

Watson and the rest of IBM's U.S. operations went about the routine of making and selling equipment and punch cards. Far more quickly and more thoroughly than during World War I, the U.S. government created agencies to control the use of raw materials and what products could be manufactured. Nearly everything was rationed during the war, not just food. Automobile manufacturers were not allowed to introduce new models unless they were tanks, jeeps, airplanes, and other military equipment. NCR stopped making cash registers, as its metal had to be used for the war effort. If a firm wanted to acquire office equipment, it applied for a permit to do so, and IBM and others could not supply them until authorized. Roughly 10 percent of IBM's U.S. revenue came from the new Munitions Manufacturing Corporation, another 10 percent from other war-related products, and the remaining 80 percent from government demands and from companies now bursting with orders from the U.S. military. IBM kept prices the same as before the war.

Business during the war was superb. Revenue had come in at $49.5 million in 1939 and climbed to nearly $63 million in 1941. Then the takeoff occurred. Revenue in 1942 reached $90.7 million and climbed to over $143 million in 1944, at the height of the ramp-up in war demand. Earnings jumped from $79 million in 1939 to over $136 million in 1944, before dipping by $2 million the following year. A wartime excess profit tax kept that performance from tripling, with flat earnings in the $9.1 to $9.2 million range being maintained through 1944 and earnings rising only to $10.9 million in 1945. In other ways, however, IBM did extremely well: its net assets grew from $79 million to over $134 million, which included buildings, parts, and inventories. Its accumulated cash and other liquid assets amounted to $6.5 million in 1939 but by the end of 1945 totaled $23.5 million. IBM's U.S. plants were now completely modern.[10]

Given constraints on supplies of components and raw materials, and government controls over production quotas, IBM and its rivals never fully met the needs of their customers. IBM and Remington Rand combined shipped over 9,000 tabulators in 1943 and nearly 10,200 the following year, at the height of war demand, while open orders for these machines over and above what they sent to customers exceeded 2,000 in 1943 and were over 5,000 the following year![11] IBM set up an office in Washington, D.C., just to handle the paperwork for permissions.

What were U.S. agencies and corporations doing with all that IBM equipment? Routine accounting, inventory management, and manufacturing applications continued as before. There were war-specific uses, too. Aircraft manufacturers performed calculations to design military aircraft. Computerized wing design became an early use of computers in the next decade, building on the experience gained during World War II with punch card equipment and other office machines. Wage controls required extensive calculations by companies and agencies, too. New uses appeared in most industries. Over 16 million Americans were in uniform. Accounting for all their weapons, uniforms, food, vehicles, bullets, aircraft, and medical supplies was managed using tabulating equipment, over 80 percent of which came from IBM. Every person in uniform required a set of 80-column cards to track their personnel history, training, and assignments from the time they were sworn in until they were discharged. Their health and death records appeared on punch cards. Cards were used to track those missing in action and to provide every military unit with payroll records and records about where personnel were assigned. Surveys of bombing targets and statistics ended up on cards, too. Equipment from IBM and NCR also proved useful in breaking the enemy's coded messages.[12]

Tabulating machines and other office appliances went to war. One IBMer in the U.S. Army landed three days after D-Day at Normandy, France, as part of a data processing contingent trying to keep up with the U.S. invasion of Europe. Army Lieutenant Arthur K. "Dick" Watson, younger son of Thomas J. Watson Sr. and serving in the U.S. Army Signal Corps, was credited with the idea of creating portable data processing centers that could move with the military, initially using IBM Electric Accounting Machines (EAMs). Called Mobile Machine Records Units (MRUs), they consisted of various office appliances, including IBM's, set up in trucks, tents, ships, and other makeshift facilities to provide a fighting force with information about supplies, materiel, whether members of the force were wounded or available for duty, lists of the dead, and what medals were needed and awarded. They gathered and analyzed field intelligence and combat reports in nearly real time. These units proved highly successful, adding to their duties the gathering of information about bombing results, number and types of prisoners captured, and even about displaced persons. Communicating this kind of data through electronic means—largely telephony—became an important part of their work. Reports each morning for General Dwight D. Eisenhower, supreme Allied commander in charge of Normandy and the invasion of France, came from the MRUs. Staffers from IBM, AT&T, and office appliance manufacturers who were now in the military served in these units. As one IBMer serving in an MRU in France recalled, "We knew within a two week accuracy where all our troops were around the world."[13] Robert P. Patterson, secretary of war in 1946, recalled that these IBM units "went everywhere our fighting men went. They landed on the beaches ... they operated in the jungles and snow-covered huts of the Arctic."[14]

IBM ENCOUNTERS COMPUTING

While the majority of IBM's attention was focused on expanding its traditional business, its scientific and technological innovations were spectacular. During World War II, the ability to now mass-produce penicillin led to quick application that controlled battlefield infections, saving countless lives. Scientists, engineers, and thousands of other people worked in secret on the Manhattan Project, developing atomic bombs. Innovations in data processing and electronics proceeded, such as the development of radar. Drawn into advanced electronics, IBM's engineers acquired experiences that helped make it possible for IBM to enter the computer business. Becoming involved, however, required participation by the "Old Man," who was keen on learning about new developments and willing to invest in them if they appeared advantageous to IBM. Nevertheless, Watson, and therefore IBM, bumped into early computing mostly "for prestige and philanthropic motives [rather] than for commercial ones," according to his son Tom Jr., who would lead IBM into the center of the computer industry and dominate it almost as fully as his father had dominated the tabulating business.

Engineers, mathematicians, and military and intelligence organizations during the 1930s and World War II took many steps toward computers. Watson and the technical staff in Endicott already had excellent relations with Columbia University. Watson next sought to establish similar ties to Harvard University. In 1937, Howard Aiken (1900–1973), a bright young physicist at Harvard, had proposed building a machine to his university, which rejected it because of its anticipated great expense. In 1939, IBM executive John G. Phillips (1888–1964), a future president of IBM, established the initial connections. He soon met with Aiken. Aiken was creative, arrogant, and difficult to work with. He told Phillips that he could construct a high-speed machine using IBM equipment with some modifications. Watson saw the project as a way to establish links he wanted with Harvard and therefore authorized a budget to build the machine at Endicott, from which it could then be moved to Aiken's campus.

It was essentially a large punch card device, not a computer such as those soon to be built, using advanced electronics of the day. The aging Clair Lake, still in Endicott, would work with Aiken as the experienced IBM engineering manager, protecting the company's patent rights. IBM engineers worked on the machine when they had time, as their priority during the war shifted to military projects and to their R&D priorities, of which advanced electronics was not one of them. However, John McPherson (1908–1999), in charge of engineering, advocated that work be done on vacuum tube circuits for future business machines. He saw Aiken's project as being useful for that purpose. Aiken provided the high-level early design, and IBM engineers did the engineering and construction of the machine. In early 1943, they completed the task. Aiken named the machine the Automatic Sequence Controlled Calculator Mark I, better known as the ASCC/Mark I but within IBM just the Mark I (figure 5.1). It cost $300,000 and many hundreds of hours of IBM engineering to build. So far, everything seemed to be going well. Then came the problems that so attracted the attention of every historian of IBM.

Watson wanted to use the machine for public relations. He had it repackaged into a slick art deco frame 8 feet high and 51 feet long. It weighed 5 tons and used 530 miles of wire. One IBM engineer wrote that "it was the largest electromechanical calculator ever built."[15] It could perform numerous mathematical operations in a sequence defined by instructions using punched paper tape. It looked big, modern, and high-tech, with lots of knobs at one end. The system relied on current input and output equipment, including a card feeder, card puncher, and two typewriters. In January 1943, it began solving mathematical problems in Endicott. Meanwhile, Aiken and the IBM engineers haggled over credit for building the machine and who would retain patent rights. Watson refused to let the machine be moved to Harvard until these issues were resolved to his satisfaction. By mid-1944, installation of the machine at Harvard had been completed.

Figure 5.1

IBM Mark I. This system gave IBM engineers exposure to the possibilities of advanced electronics. It was the largest calculator built in the United States before the arrival of the computer. Photo courtesy of IBM Corporate Archives.

Watson and his wife, Jeanette, came to Cambridge on a rainy Sunday, August 6, for the machine's unveiling the next day. No one from Harvard met him at the train station, a snub not lost on him or other IBMers. Instead, the local sales branch manager, Frank McCabe, took the Watsons to their hotel in his personal Chevrolet, not in a limousine as was more customary in such situations. Watson blamed Harvard for that slight. One biographer said Watson "seethed" at the way Harvard treated him, but what really got to Watson was when McCabe gave Watson that morning's newspaper in the car, in which a story on page 1 covered the Mark I, crediting Aiken and Harvard for all the work, a story told to them by Harvard's media folks. The *Boston Post* spoke of it as an "Automatic Brain for Harvard," saying Aiken had invented the "World's Greatest Calculator," with IBM cited once as a minor player. Harvard had not reviewed the press release with anyone at IBM.

Watson's rage in that car knew no bounds. In his hotel room at the Copley, he picked up the phone and let the folks at Harvard experience his wrath. Watson did not want to attend the opening ceremonies the next day, so Aiken and a dean rushed to his hotel to apologize. After calming down, he changed his mind and attended the launch, which was followed by letters from Harvard to smooth over the problem. Watson called on Jim Bryce and Clair Lake to build a new machine better than the Mark I. As one biographer put it, "IBM got into electronics as an act of vengeance."[16] In the late 1940s, IBM engineers converted this work into advanced electronic products that inched IBM into the world of computing.

Meanwhile, IBMers were exposed to other computational projects, notably the ENIAC at the University of Pennsylvania, for the Army. Its inventors later went on to build the UNIVAC computer, which competed against IBM in the early 1950s. Tom Jr. went to see the machine at the end of the war and was impressed that its developers, Presper Eckert and John Mauchly, had incorporated electronic circuits into the system instead of the electromechanical relays used in the Mark I and by IBM in its current accounting machines. The ENIAC was being used to calculate ballistic tables. Eckert and Mauchly thought their machine would supersede IBM's in a few years. At the time, Tom Jr. was not impressed with it, saying, "I couldn't see this gigantic, costly, unreliable device as a piece of business equipment." In hindsight, he recalled, "I never stopped to think what would happen if the speed of electronic circuits could be harnessed for commercial use."[17]

A few weeks later, Tom Jr. did, when he saw a small device using radio tubes that had been built by an IBM engineer and could perform multiplications to do payroll calculations much more quickly than IBM's current equipment. His machine spent nine-tenths of its operating time waiting for IBM's equipment to punch cards to feed it for processing. "That impressed me as though somebody had hit me on the head with a hammer," Tom Jr. said.[18] That September, the device was introduced as the IBM 603 Electronic Multiplier. It calculated at electronic speeds but was still slow, since it relied on mechanically punched cards. It was not a computer, but it was a step forward. It did well with customers, who acquired hundreds of them,

Figure 5.2
IBM 604. The success of the IBM 604 convinced many executives that advanced electronics was the wave of the future, including Thomas Watson Jr., who would lead the charge into computing. Photo courtesy of IBM Corporate Archives.

eager to speed up calculations. The next version of the machine could also divide, a task far too expensive to do with mechanical machines, leading to the introduction of the IBM 604 (figure 5.2). The sales force sold thousands of them. IBM had gone from a "gimmick," as Tom Jr. called the IBM 603, to a real, "truly useful" calculator. Just as important as support from customers was that now Tom Jr. understood the potential of electronics, setting him on the path to embracing computing at IBM. His experience with the 604 was his eureka moment.

A third leg—following the Mark I and the IBM 604—in creating the base for entering the computer business, but tied closely to the company's wartime work, involved cryptanalysis, breaking enemy codes used to mask communications. It was the successful use of computers by the British at Bletchley Park, involving a machine called the COLOSSUS, kept secret from the public until the 1970s, that ensured a strong commitment by military officials on both sides of the Atlantic to advanced electronics and computing in the postwar period. The U.S. military turned to NCR, IBM, and others for assistance in using office appliances to help break enemy codes. The Americans, French, Polish, and Germans had used mechanical cryptanalysis since World War I. All had worked on refinements in the interwar years. In the United States, the navy and army experimented, periodically working with IBM's engineers in Endicott. These early links to the military years later made it possible for IBM and the U.S. military to work closely together. During the war, such projects seemed minor to IBMers, who were more focused on immediate needs.

IBMers GO TO WAR, INCLUDING THE WATSON BOYS

IBM's presence in Endicott grew slowly over the decades, with the biggest surge occurring in the early 1930s, with construction of two buildings, one in which to train employees and customers and the other to house its laboratory and product development. Across the street was the factory or, we should say, factories. As the war continued, more buildings went up to produce products and to house many new employees. The war came home and quickly became personal. In 1940, IBM employed 4,130 people in Endicott, adding 320 more the following year. Construction along North Street kept the area crowded as IBM added 700,000 square feet of space. In 1943, the employee population nearly doubled to over 9,000 and then expanded to over 10,500 the following year. It became difficult to maintain a workforce of that size, however, because so many IBMers were entering the military. By 1943, some 1,600 Endicott IBMers were in uniform, increasing to more than 2,000 the following year. Nearby, the shoe factory was producing hundreds of thousands of boots and therefore was also hiring everyone it could get, and it, too, saw employees go off to war. In time, that region of New York began to mourn its dead and care for the wounded as the ugliness of war hit home.

The plant in Poughkeepsie was situated on the banks of the Hudson River. Built in 1941, funding from the U.S. government made further modernization possible, and the plant expanded to manufacture Browning automatic rifles, 30-caliber carbines, pistols, munitions, 20-millimeter aircraft cannons, electric typewriters, keypunch machines, and aircraft parts. The plant began in 1941 with only 250 employees but employed nearly 10,000 by the mid-1940s. By the end of the war, this factory had manufactured nearly $200 million in products for the U.S. military. Even the sleepy town of Poughkeepsie had become part of the bustling wartime economy.

The war involved every family in some way. As an employee, either you were in uniform or making and selling machines and cards for use by the government and its commercial suppliers. All over the nation, IBM families planted victory gardens in their backyards. Their children collected old rubber tires and scrap metal. Families on both sides of the Atlantic were limited in what goods they could purchase and lived under the rule of food ration cards. Even the mighty Watson family was subjected to the realities of war.

Nowhere could one see this more dramatically than with Watson Sr.'s two sons. The Watsons had four children—two boys and two girls—born between 1914 and 1919: Thomas J. Watson Jr. (1914–1993), then two daughters, Jane and Helene, and finally Arthur K. "Dick" Watson (1919–1974). All historians of IBM discussed the tumultuous role of the two sons, particularly during the 1940s and 1950s, when they grew to adulthood, dealt with the fact that their father ran IBM and was as much a giant at home as in the company, and then worked through the issues of what roles they would play at IBM. The story is one of ferocious fights and rivalries between Tom Jr. and his father, with Arthur trying to please his father. The girls grew up essentially outside the influence of the company, one marrying a lawyer and the other marrying a financier who did have dealings with IBM, but the girls were peripheral to the company's story. The biographers of Watson Sr. described the high drama of what happened within the family before the war, tensions masked from employees who were exposed only to him and his wife at public events, and once in a while to the children on a plant tour with their father. Tom Jr. recalled that his first tour took place when he was five. Observers and employees assumed the oldest son, and perhaps Arthur, would someday inherit the leadership of IBM. That was not predestined, as they first had to grow up, and that meant living through World War II.

In many ways, Tom Jr. differed from his father. The elder Watson was physically cautious, even disliking flying in airplanes, but Tom Jr. was adventuresome—flying became his lifelong hobby. His father was prudent in his private life, whereas Tom Jr. liked to party hard while a student at Brown University and later as a young man working at IBM before the war. Tom Jr. liked sports, whereas his father was never athletic. IBM, rather than his family, was the center of Watson Sr.'s world, while Tom Jr. was ambivalent about IBM until he was in his early 30s. Watson Sr.'s children grew up in the IBM orbit, visiting plants and branch offices yearly, hearing shoptalk at home, and meeting many IBMers. As with so many father-son relationships, Tom Jr. wanted to compete against the Old Man but also meet with his approval, calling for a test of wills that continued to play out after World War II. Upon graduating from Brown University in 1937, and after considering alternative career paths, Tom Jr. joined IBM in sales. His father was delighted. Watson Sr.'s friends saw the move into IBM by Tom Jr. as inevitable, while the young man harbored mixed feelings. In October 1937, Tom Jr. headed up to Endicott to attend Sales School. He was not a stellar student there; he needed remedial coaching to get through some of the more technical aspects of the training program. In this class and afterward, IBMers were, in the words of one historian, "in a tizzy" about how to deal with him because he was the son of the Old Man.[19]

Then one of the most uncomfortable events in Tom Jr.'s life happened: he made quota too quickly. Assigned to a branch office in Manhattan, he told this story:

> On the first business day of 1940, I became the company's top salesman when U.S. Steel Products, an account that had been thrown into my territory to make me look good, came across with a huge order. With one day's "work" I filled my quota for the entire year.[20]

IBM media people touted his wonderful achievement and fellow salesmen in his office smirked behind his back—and he knew that—while some poor marketing rep who had spent time cultivating that order was cut out of his achievement and bonus that the boss's little rich kid got. In his memoirs, Tom Jr. wrote, "I felt demeaned."[21] Furthermore, "Everybody knew that I was the old man's son," and so people went out of their way to give him sales opportunities to curry favor with his father. When he actually closed a deal on his own, his father did not compliment him. In those prewar years, he was peddling while living at home with his parents. By 1940, the young man was not being as diligent in his IBM duties as expected, and employees in the branch had to cover for him or ignore his poor attention to his responsibilities. In 1939, he met his future wife, Olive Cowley, who during and after the war helped shape him into a serious husband and responsible man. But before she got to do that, there was the war intervening.

Tom Jr. was eager to enter it. He wanted to take advantage of his more than 1,000 hours of flying experience gained over the previous seven years. In 1940, he was 26 years old. He joined the National Guard, where he could qualify as a pilot, and soon was Second Lieutenant Watson. The Guard was mobilized later that year, so now the new pilot entered the war, apart from IBM. He could now succeed or fail on his own, as his father was out of the picture. He remained in the Army until the end of 1945. Historian Richard S. Tedlow summarized how Tom Jr. changed during the war: "When he joined the service, he was twenty-six years old, unmarried, depressed, drinking too much, and suffering from low esteem. When he was mustered out, he was a few days short of thirty-two years old. He was married and had fathered two children." The result was that "he left the service full of self-confidence bordering on bravado."[22] He spent the war years flying aircraft over Africa, Asia, and the Middle East and shuttled military and government officials back and forth to Moscow. He experienced some personal dangers, which must have made his family nervous just as in so many other IBM households. Upon the end of the war, Tom Jr. contemplated becoming a commercial pilot until his last commanding officer thought that odd and commented, "Really? I always thought you'd go back and run the IBM company."[23] Within a day, Tom Jr. called his father and asked if he could rejoin IBM. The Old Man proudly replied, "I'd be delighted, son," and Tom Jr. returned to the company in January 1946.

For him, the war had been the transformative experience he needed to do well at IBM.

Every account of IBM either ignores Tom Jr.'s brother, Arthur, or minimizes his role. The truth proved different, for Arthur got along with his father better than Tom did in the interwar years, also served in the Army, and in time ran all of IBM's operations outside the United States, performing as well as his brother. He became an effective executive who worked in the shadow of his father and later his brother. IBMers writing about the company avoided the sad end to his IBM career and his post-IBM professional life, terminated largely by the effects of alcoholism. His virtual anonymity in the company's history can also be laid at the feet of those writing about IBM who poorly served the non-U.S. story of the company, favoring the U.S. side of its history. While Arthur's success and decline in postwar IBM is the story for a later chapter, back in the 1930s he played a minor role at IBM. Like his brother, he went to private schools, grew up a rich man's son, followed his father on many of his rounds to IBM offices in the United States and Europe, and attended Yale University, with an interruption for service in the Army but graduating just after the war. He joined IBM in February 1947.

Arthur, the younger of the two boys, had a wonderful sense of humor, could tell a joke, and like his brother was not the best of students. However, he had an outstanding facility with foreign languages. In time, he learned French, Spanish, Italian, and German, all of which came into good use when he ran IBM's World Trade operations, and he could imitate almost any accent. On demand, he yodeled. As with so many other younger children, he worshiped his older brother. He had been a moody child and rarely fought back when his father criticized his behavior. He was less healthy than his older brother, as he had asthma, which could be serious at times. Arthur craved his father's approval and did not push back against IBM as a child and young man as Tom Jr. did. On one of his summer breaks from college, he worked in the machine shop at IBM Endicott. Tom Jr. dressed slovenly before entering the Army; Arthur was always a dapper dresser.

When war broke out, Arthur was in his third year at Yale and immediately dropped out to join the Army. Soon assigned to the Army's ordnance

Figure 5.3
Arthur Watson in uniform. Arthur is the lesser known of the Watson boys. It was during his military service that he, like his brother, matured before assuming significant responsibilities at IBM. Photo courtesy of IBM Corporate Archives.

corps, he excelled, and by the end of the war, he had risen to the rank of major. He was 28 years old, had a girlfriend, and was ready to join IBM. The Watson family was blessed that their two sons had not been wounded or killed. Fifty-seven other U.S. IBM families were not so fortunate. Both Watson brothers left home as boys and came back as men willing to make their way in the Old Man's company. Their father could not have been prouder. To other IBMers, Tom Jr. and Arthur were veterans who surely had important futures ahead of them in their father's company.

GERMAN NAZIS, EUROPE, AND WARTIME IBM

Back in New York, Thomas J. Watson Sr. faced other difficult problems. In Germany, where IBM's wholly owned subsidiary, Dehomag, had built or expanded factories and branch offices in the 1930s, it also stretched to meet requirements of the German war effort.[24] It saw employees march off to war, some never to return, and others become part of the restored German IBM operation in West Germany after the war. In every European country where IBM had a presence, operations continued, or sometimes collapsed after equipment was confiscated by the Axis or co-opted for their war effort. Employees were drafted into the armies and navies of over a dozen nations. During the war, IBM Corporate had little or no control over operations in many of its European and Asian subsidiaries. The experience with Germany demonstrated the challenges faced by IBM and other large U.S. corporations. That history exposed the limits U.S. companies had in influencing their war zone subsidiaries.

The role of companies headquartered outside Germany but operating within the Nazi zones has been the subject of growing attention by historians.[25] Germany tolerated foreign companies operating in territory it controlled, provided they did not resist national policies, such as elimination of Jewish employees, resulting in what historian Geoffrey Jones called their "complex, but often ethically ambiguous, relationship" with the Nazi regime.[26] European, German, and American firms had to work out how to survive and to what degree they had to conform. Many management teams walked a fine line between being taken over, shut down by the Germans, and staying alive.[27] In the pages ahead, we add to the growing evidence that IBM, too, walked that fine line. IBM's case illustrates the managerial requirement to stay in business, the struggle with how best to do that, and how to square its activities with the company's values. Its response to wartime realities was not monolithic but rather varied from one country (or war zone) to another as Corporate's authority over its subsidiaries diminished and as country managers reacted to the realities their employees faced. The observation Jones made about companies in general applied to IBM as well.

As German armies rolled over Europe between 1939 and the end of 1942, they occupied large swaths of France, imposing dictatorial rule over the remaining Vichy France to the south, the Benelux countries, Poland, all of Central Europe, Denmark, and Norway. Wherever they went, the Germans usually left in place existing corporations but dictated the use of their products, prioritizing resources for the Third Reich.[28] While recently it has been argued that some firms "deliberately under-produced" as their way of resisting the Nazis, Dehomag did not hold back; it expanded its business, given the pro-Nazi political feelings of its local senior management.[29] Government agencies and manufacturing plants used IBM equipment. By 1945, Dehomag had some 300 customers in Germany, leasing 2,000 Hollerith-type machines. It employed nearly 10,000 people, some 8,000 located in the Berlin metropolitan area. The company dominated its market, crushing Powers and Siemens-Halske.[30] Critical to IBM's welfare was the fact that the Germans blocked the transfer of foreign exchange out of any country. Thus, for IBM as an example, profits made in French currency had to remain in France, and the same was true in Germany. As in the United States, the Germans imposed windfall profit taxes on all firms. After the United States entered the war, Germany confiscated U.S. assets. In occupied countries, industrial goods were sometimes moved to Germany, including IBM tabulating gear from Poland, France, and Central Europe. When Germany conquered a country, Watson had his accountants carry the local company on IBM's books for only $1. So, IBM operations limped along. Not until after the war could IBMers in New York try to sort out how best to recover machines and profits, attempting to track them through their office in Geneva.

Of interest to historians and others looking at IBM's relations with Nazi Germany is the fundamental question about Watson's role. He faced the uncertain and dynamic situation of his markets, assets, and operations being disrupted as Hitler advanced, the complete loss of IBM's assets in Asia, even the ability to communicate with, let alone control, operations in these regions. He had the natural inclination, and duty, to attempt to continue operations, collect revenue, and extract profits, however futile it might be. If Dehomag did not obey Nazi requests, the German government had the options of setting up a new company to make IBM-like products or nationalizing his firm, in which, recall, IBM had 90 percent ownership. It was still being run by Watson's old nemesis, Willy Heidinger, who, for political and personal reasons, was now a member of the Nazi Party.[31] As a manager, Watson had to track what was happening with his business interests and then make the best of a bad situation. These were the practical day-to-day managerial realities Watson contended with.

Then there were the personal, ethical ones that could not be ignored. Recall that Watson had received a medal from the Nazis in 1937, followed by his attempts to gently persuade them to temper their policies. He clearly miscalculated their intent, having no sense of their determination to pursue policies contrary to his own beliefs or of the magnitude of their plans. They were going to exterminate Jews, Slavs, gays, the mentally handicapped, political dissidents, the military leadership in Poland and Russia, and even Gypsies. They aimed to dominate Central Europe. Watson thought his influence could change what little he knew of their intentions. Watson's assessment proved so wrong. As events unfolded between 1938 and 1940, his Nazi medal made him look like an appeaser. He returned it to Hitler in June 1940 with a strong letter of criticism, and he made sure the media knew what he had done. Employees, customers, and others wrote to him saying he did the right thing in returning it, but the gesture seemed late. Returning the medal infuriated Dehomag's leadership, particularly Heidinger, and Hitler, too. Local Dehomag management now feared for the safety of their company, themselves, and their families.

Watson did not collaborate with the Germans, but he did not use his self-perceived influence aggressively with them to complain more assertively rather than gently prior to 1942. He failed to push back, even though he personally helped individual Jews leave Germany and Austria. Watson's biographer got it right when he concluded that he "had misjudged the power of commerce, misread the Nazis, and missed an opportunity to make a difference. They were the biggest mistakes of his life."[32] There remains some question whether Watson realistically had an opportunity to make a difference, but at least he should have tried aggressively. He did not.

A problem bigger than this lapse in Watson's ethics, and that blew up into a momentary international controversy, occurred when a book appeared in 2001 accusing IBM of collaborating with the Nazis in the Holocaust.[33] The charge posed was that IBM had provided the Nazis with tabulating equipment to pinpoint who was Jewish in Germany and to track their roundup and extermination. It argued that without such equipment extermination of the Jews would not have been possible. IBM's German operations made census equipment used all over Europe, a heritage of the old Hollerith days, and in 1933 Germany conducted a census. Actually, Germany had long used multiple card systems to track its citizens and business operations, not just Hollerith punch cards. The German government used multiple overlapping card systems, think 3×5 card-styled systems, which were typed or handwritten.

The Nazi Party's paramilitary organization, the SS (*Schutzstaffel*), required all Germans to register their home addresses per the Reich Compulsory Registration Decree of January 6, 1938. These files were standardized nationally as the *Volkskartei*. However, this file did not contain information about a citizen's religious affiliation; that was added in 1939. For both files, the Germans did not use IBM punch cards. They recorded data by hand, cross-referencing national identity cards with others kept by local police on religious preferences. In other words, the Germans used traditional data collection methods, not data processing machines, techniques similar, as one historian put it, to those American doctors used with their colored tags to alphabetize records.[34] Copies of the files used in the 1930s confirmed that the Germans did not use IBM equipment.[35]

Application of punch card equipment in statistical work for their war-related efforts did come slowly to government agencies, not beginning until late 1942 or early 1943.[36] As part of the armament industry's labor-planning efforts, concentration camps began collecting information about their prisoners in late 1942 to early 1943 at the earliest, a decade after the Nazis came to power. The primary center for implementing extermination practices, the SS Race and Settlement Office, obtained its first Hollerith equipment in 1943.[37] Extant historical evidence demonstrates that use of punch card equipment in a few camps did not begin until the middle of 1944, after the Allies had already landed at Normandy and were pushing the Axis into defeat. As one historian concluded, "Traditional means of records-keeping more than sufficed for the destruction of the European Jews."[38]

While IBMers in Dehomag undoubtedly knew where most if not all machines were being used, down to the serial numbers of each, probably even during the chaos of the late war years, no credible evidence has surfaced that Watson or his senior managers in New York or Geneva authorized use of their equipment to facilitate extermination of Jews. The height of collaboration by U.S. companies with German customers and occupation forces occurred between 1940 and 1942; after that, these firms had little control over events, especially in occupied territories such as France, Poland, and the Netherlands.[39] Nor did IBM New York have sway over the events in Germany and Nazi-controlled Europe. The Nazis themselves were frustrated with foreign manufacturing companies because these companies were not collaborating with them as much as they desired.[40] Lack of raw materials and components slowed or stopped production, just as in the United States at NCR in the manufacture of cash registers or in the introduction of new models of cars by Ford and General Motors.

Given the chaos and lack of control over operations, local IBM employees in a country were on their own. They began the war doing business as usual, and as the occupations and fighting spread, they adapted. Anecdotal "war stories" came to light after the war. In Bulgaria, for example, the tiny organization managed to stay in business by having IBMers repair bicycles instead of tabulating equipment. They made enough money to keep IBM families fed until they could rebuild the tabulating business after the war.[41] Stories such as these emerged from other Eastern European countries. The key objective of branch and country managers was to keep together as many of their employees as possible in anticipation of restoring normal business when the fighting ended. IBMers in the U.S. Army ran into IBMers in other armies or still working as civilians during the occupation. These were occasions to celebrate a return to normalcy, to catch up on events at IBM, and to facilitate reconnecting.[42]

Then there was Japan, where the first IBM machines were installed in 1925 and a subsidiary was established in 1937 as the Watson Business Machine Company. On December 8, 1941, the government arrested IBM's local manager, Ko Mizushina, and his bookkeeper, and seized the company "as an enemy property." In 1943, the Japanese designated tabulating equipment as being permitted to be manufactured, assigning responsibility for IBM and Powers machinery to the Kobe Steel Works. Whether any such equipment was produced is lost to history. IBM was not officially reestablished in Japan until 1949, following two years of negotiations with the local government.[43]

When the war ended, IBM Corporate picked up the pieces. That meant attempting to identify, locate, and recover assets and gathering together those employees who were still alive and able to work back into offices and factories.[44] As part of that process, management in New York rethought how best to organize the company's worldwide operations.

HOW THE WORLD CHANGED FOR IBM

The war forced IBM, other multinational firms, and national governments to deal with what by the late 1940s was being called the "political economy." National governments imposed their will on economic activities during World War I, less so during the 1920s, but increasingly in the 1930s in response to global economic depression and rising military tensions. The days of Watson Sr. running his business with minimal interference by public officials ended during World War II. Corporate and country managers had to do more than curry the favor of public officials; they also had to learn how to navigate a growing complex of governmental rules (such as gaining permission to sell goods) and how to shape political views on economic policies. As IBM expanded, these skills became important and needed to be performed with rigor, careful planning, and in alignment with the company's business strategies. "Government relations," IBM's polite term for its lobbying activities, increased. A larger number of senior executives in many companies engaged in such activities as normal duties. Almost every senior IBM executive discussed in subsequent chapters was involved, too.

James W. Birkenstock (1912–2005), who we encounter later in this book negotiating with the Japanese government, even though he is remembered for his work as an American sales executive, serves as a convenient path into IBM's postwar activities. He benefited from IBM's growth from the time he joined the company as a salesman in 1935 in sales offices in St. Louis and Kansas City. He rose to corporate vice president in 1958 and then served as a director of IBM World Trade Corporation in 1966. Smart, a good communicator, hard working, and a great golfer, he quickly caught the eye of management. He gained a reputation as a problem solver. He also came to the attention of Thomas Watson Sr. During World War II, Birkenstock remained in sales but periodically helped out with army contracts, troubleshooting projects. In January 1946, Watson Sr. convened a class for branch managers in Endicott on the current product line and about where IBM was going now that the war was over. Many had just come out of the military, so they needed a refresher on IBM. Tom Watson Jr. attended this class. Although not a branch manager, he, too, needed to catch up. Birkenstock was assisting in the class and ended up making a presentation on behalf of the original presenter, who had to duck out to take care of a problem. While Birkenstock was doing so, Watson Sr. slipped into a chair in the back of the room to listen. That is when Birkenstock's future changed.

Birkenstock was lecturing on why IBM needed "to double the number of IBM branch offices to maximize sales potential." After listening to this 36-year-old salesman, Watson got up, walked to the podium, interrupting the presentation by his movement, and announced to the class that "he had just discovered his postwar general sales manager." As Birkenstock recalled years later, "With that he announced my appointment as IBM general sales manager, filling a six-month vacancy."[45] He was to figure out what IBM should do in the postwar period and convince the sales organization to implement his recommendations. He argued that IBM would have to "retool" marketing and restaff for a civilian market that everyone expected to grow rapidly as a result of massive pent-up demand. Competition would increase for the same reasons. The current product line was "tired" and needed refurbishing. Watson brought Birkenstock to New York and did not hesitate to push him to get things moving. Watson was impatient for progress in a rapidly changing business environment.

Birkenstock presided over another spurt of IBM expansion. In his words, "Meeting market demand for IBM systems from government, industry and academia drove the company to a phenomenal expansion of branch offices—from 85 to 135 in a single year."[46] Each of those 50 new branches required branch managers; salesmen had to be hired, trained, and assigned territories; offices had to be found, rented, and decked out in IBM style with the company name on the front and sample products to demonstrate; and customer engineers had to be recruited and trained. Regional sales managers led the charge, but ultimately it seemed that everyone in the "field" had to help recruit and set up an expanded sales organization. Watson Sr. personally traveled up and down the East Coast looking for rental space. IBM's need to expand led to its transformation from a wartime to a civilian market that included adding updated products such as, soon after, computers. These were Birkenstock's challenges.

Because Watson Sr. acted as his own general sales manager during the Roaring '20s, he knew what it meant to shift from wartime to peacetime selling, introduce new products, expand rapidly worldwide, and do so before rivals filled the breach. The 1940s would not be the last time IBMers faced similar challenges, some of which they met well, whereas others they stumbled over. But the schooling of the postwar generation of managers took place right after World War II. They had to develop and then dominate the computer business. In the process, they turned IBM into a behemoth, an unquestioned international company, guiding it through its Golden Age. Birkenstock and his generation rode a fabulous wave. That is the subject of the next several chapters, beginning with how IBM entered the computer game.

Part II

IBM THE COMPUTER BEHEMOTH, 1945–1985

6 IBM GETS INTO THE COMPUTER BUSINESS, 1945–1964

> The new equipment combines for the first time in one machine the great
> memory capacity and flexibility of cathode-ray tubes, magnetic drums, and
> magnetic tapes, as well as employing the use of punched cards.
> —THOMAS J. WATSON SR., 1952[1]

IBM BECAME A dominant player in one of the most important industries
of the twentieth century at the moment when its technology and industry
came into existence. How was it able to do that? How did IBM hold its
lead for decades? Answering these questions is key to understanding how
IBM entered a remarkable Golden Age that changed the way large companies and government agencies worked. When IBM's Golden Age ended, it
seemed that the only thing the company shared with Thomas Watson Sr.'s
punch card firm was its name, although it acquired a nickname—Big Blue.
At the same time, rumbling underneath IBM's seemingly bright future
were forces at work that would upend its customers' comfort zones and
IBM's products, and cause IBM's senior managers to reshape the company
again. When it was over, the Watsons were gone and so were most of the
employees who had ushered in IBM's Golden Age, but before that happened, IBM's revenue climbed from $116 million in 1946 to nearly $69
billion in 1990.[2] It took two generations of IBMers and customers to usher
in all that prosperity.

Employees and observers generally divide this golden period into
two halves.[3] During the first, from the late 1940s to 1964, IBM entered
the computer business, growing up with the new computer industry. Its

employees hustled to keep up with the new market, which nearly got away from them. The second era extended from the introduction of one of the world's most successful transformative products—the IBM System 360 family of computers—in 1964 to the end of the 1980s. In this period, IBM dominated computer technologies, how they were used, and the markets for mainframes. Both periods were fraught with dangers and opportunities, competition, antitrust suits, customers deeply knowledgeable about data processing and impatient for more technology, and accelerating technological transformations emanating from outside of IBM. Increase by at least one order of magnitude the challenges IBM faced compared to those encountered by Watson Sr.'s generation, increase the number of employees by two orders of magnitude, and more than double the number of countries where IBM did business, and we begin to sense the magnitude of the tectonic events IBM faced. Size, success, and influence made IBM well known, but that status carried with it more than revenue and prestige; it included grave risks and consequences. IBM's experience is introduced in this chapter.

In this chapter and chapters 7 and 8, we navigate the arc of this Golden Age, focusing on the role of IBMers in ushering the company into the world of computers. More than on any previous period in IBM's history, historians, observers, economists, and IBM have commented about events reviewed in these three chapters, so for many familiar with the company's history it may seem familiar. However, the majority of the discussion on the pre–System 360 history of computing at IBM emphasized technological innovations, placing engineers at the center of the company's history in the 1950s and early 1960s.[4] That emphasis discounted the work of the vast majority of IBMers going about their business of making other products and servicing customers, so we need to bring balance to that perspective. IBM's customers and observers of the technological and business scene also influenced the company's actions, and to recognize their role, chapter 7 is devoted to discussing their activities. In both this chapter and chapter 7, the number of participants in the narrative expands. Readers familiar with the emergence of IBM computers encounter new players and are exposed to rivalries and disagreements about how the company should evolve. Understanding these interactions contributes insights on how large U.S. corporations functioned. By exploring IBM's entry into computing as the confluence of activities by various internal constituencies, customers, and members of the emerging computer ecosystem, we can appreciate the story of success with the IBM System 360. Part of the history of the System 360 was IBM's ability to scale up to the opportunity it presented and supply the required resources. That is why we explore events of the 1950s and early 1960s in two chapters.

More than in any previous chapter, we engage in issues at the core of what business historians study. We will encounter Paul A. David's path dependency issues, adding evidence that innovation was also shaped by prior skills and technological platforms.[5] Structural inertia also exists, despite all the change described here, driven as much by the emergence of new organizations and personalities within the firm as by innovations in the base technologies needed for computing,[6] so Birger Wernerfelt's emphasis on resource-based views of firms is borne out in IBM's case.[7] But what so many historians find crucial is that the hunt for organizational theory and strategy as practice have influenced how the history discussed in this chapter and chapters 7 and 8 was shaped.[8] However, this portion of the book does not promise a Bourdieusian social/anthropological theory, as our view of IBM's events is presented as a highly descriptive narrative in order to understand both the events and their motivations.[9] However, these chapters pay homage to the importance of IBM's corporate culture, relying more on Paul DiMaggio's approach of how key people shape an organization, such as the Watsons and other executives at IBM.[10]

This chapter describes IBM's entry into advanced electronics and the first computing products. We situate IBM in broader issues presented by the Cold War, which proved essential in guiding IBM toward computers and a commercial market that proved a larger magnet to IBM than military customers did. While it would be novel to argue that military contracts diverted IBM's attention away from the larger commercial markets, that view is only possible in hindsight.[11] As Steven W. Usselman argued, IBM's ability and willingness to enter the computer business "involved a massive mobilization of private capital in support of a project aimed overwhelmingly at commercial users."[12] Sitting in conference rooms inside IBM in the late 1940s and through most of the 1950s, one would have faced a different world of technological uncertainties and risks that until resolved made the reach into commercial computing less certain, especially by a company that took cautious, prudent steps into any new technology or market. When it did, it was the combination of Cold War government support and the insistence of customers that propelled IBM into its Golden Age.

IBM'S MOVE INTO ELECTRONICS AND COMPUTING

Thinking ahead about a postwar era, Watson Sr. knew he had a problem: what to do with all his new manufacturing space and all those veterans expecting to return to their jobs at IBM, as he had promised them. How was he going to generate civilian demand for IBM's products and services to replace the lost military business? He concluded that part of the answer involved developing new products. In June 1943, he gathered together his senior engineering managers to discuss that: "Everybody who makes any progress in business is going to work along different lines than they have ever worked before. The people who did not change in time are going to be sitting on the curbstone waiting for the parade to come by."[13] His solution in the 1910s and 1920s, and again in the 1930s, was the same: push forward technological change. That month's debate was about what to press on with. Watson Sr. and his managers settled on a new printer and expanding sales of electric typewriters, both of which could quickly bring in additional revenue. Watson Sr. wanted developments that could be rapidly converted into products, which explains his uncharacteristically modest initiatives. Further down the organization, some engineers wanted to press R&D into advanced electronics, which he ruled would be a secondary priority. But he did want more electronics in existing products. He ordered engineering to hire college graduates and other experts coming out of the military to apply this expanding area of knowledge. During the late 1940s and 1950s, that happened, leading to new products.[14]

Moving from one technology to another is tricky business, some of the most difficult work any management team confronts. The central challenge is to do so without reducing sales or profits, which stockholders, banks holding a company's loans, and employees depend on for their welfare and so have little patience for slow or failed transitions. It helps to replace old products as quickly as the market is capable of receiving or requiring new ones and slightly ahead of competitors. Few high-tech firms get this right, so IBM's experience presents a remarkable case to study. How did IBM's product transition happen? Its older product lines were healthy and while many organizations were either inventing or figuring out what to do with computers, it seemed that Watson had the time and resources to transform his products and employees. The commercial computer business began quickly at the start of the 1950s. IBM managed the transition relatively smoothly on the surface but with debates and struggles inside the firm. Never again was it able to pull off such a change so neatly, so understanding what happened between 1946 and the start of the 1960s teaches us about IBM's longevity and its influence.[15]

The boldest thinkers about the new electronics did not work for IBM. Some were in universities, some were engineers in the military, and others were in other businesses. For a possible alliance, Watson turned to Columbia University, where Wallace Eckert had been using IBM machines for years. Watson offered him a job at IBM to build scientific calculators. In March 1945, Eckert became an IBMer. Watson wanted a bigger, faster machine than the Mark I. The first was the IBM 603 Electronic Multiplier, the first commercial electronic calculator, but the real prize was a super calculator. Note that it was not to be a supercomputer. Watson Sr. forbade use of the word *computer,* fearing the word would offend people who thought it replaced workers,[16] so IBM's computers of the 1940s and early 1950s had *calculator* in their names. The first example was the SSEC (Selective Sequence Electronic Calculator), dedicated in January 1948. Endicott built it, assisted by new employees familiar with the novel electronics, such as Eckert and Robert R. "Rex" Seeber (chief architect on the project). The SSEC had a memory and calculated 250 times faster than the Mark I. With an eye toward practical implications, the engineers secured a number of patents that served them well with future machines.

Engineering management used the project to train staff in what eventually would be called programming. These included John Backus (1924–2007),

who soon after created the first widely used programming language, FOR-
TRAN, and Edgar F. "Ted" Codd (1923–2003), who years later developed
some of the earliest relational database management software. Eckert kept
his ties to Columbia while working at IBM, continuing to run his Columbia laboratory. In 1945, Watson funded the facility, renamed the Watson
Scientific Computing Laboratory, better known as the Watson Lab, to conduct research on pure science, something Watson had originally envisioned
might have been done with Harvard.

The big developments in computing were occurring outside of IBM,
stimulated by the U.S. government, which began to fund R&D on a variety of computer-like devices. By the late 1940s, agencies were supporting
over a dozen, spending millions of dollars. IBM either had to become part
of that new world or be marginalized, sitting on the "curbstone" to watch
the computer parade pass by. Corporate management knew that Remington Rand, its longest-running competitor, had yet to get into the computer
game but probably would soon. Engineering manager John McPherson
(1908–1999) had relations with federal officials and understood the R&D
they were funding. Another important computer scientist of the postwar
period, Herb Grosch (1918–2010), who knew McPherson, recalled that
"he was the door through which almost all the IBM inventors and engineers, and us scientific types, reached TJ."[17]

By the fall of 1946, McPherson had become nervous, and Eckert
agreed that the company's pace of innovation remained "inadequate," so
they cosigned a letter to Watson Sr. raising the alarm, warning that companies would be hired to do the work officials were funding. "Whereas before
the war IBM was the only organization able and willing to carry on large
scale development of calculators, such development is now taking place on
a large scale," they wrote, although stating that what to do about it was "not
obvious since questions of basic policy are involved."[18] It is inconceivable
today that someone would write the CEO with such a message for change
and then have that executive take action based on it, but that was how
things were done at IBM.

The biggest threat came from the developers of the U.S. Army's
ENIAC system, John W. Mauchly (1907–1980) and J. Presper Eckert Jr.

(1919–1995), because not only was their machine advanced but, more importantly, they left the University of Pennsylvania to set up their own company, eventually building the UNIVAC I. Other engineers were rallying around the architectural design for computers described by mathematician and early pioneer in game theory John von Neumann (1903–1957), which he wrote in June 1945. The following summer, engineers interested in all manner of computing gathered at ENIAC's old home at the Moore School at the University of Pennsylvania to share information about the state of computing projects. Many organizations working on computers in the United States were there: the Office of Naval Research and the Army Ordnance Department—two big funders—Columbia University, Harvard University, the Institute for Advanced Study in Princeton, New Jersey, Massachusetts Institute of Technology (MIT), AT&T, Kodak, General Electric, the National Bureau of Standards, and others. IBM did not receive an invitation to attend since it was not working on a computing project sponsored by the U.S. government. IBM simply was not in that milieu.

Mauchly and Eckert (no relation to the Columbia University one) were off creating their commercial enterprise, a potential threat to IBM. By February 1950, they had run out of money to build the machine so they sold their firm to Remington Rand in exchange for continued support. In June 1951, they unveiled the UNIVAC built for the U.S. Bureau of the Census. Things got personal quickly. Both Watson Sr. and Tom Jr. exploded. Census had been C-T-R's first customer. As far back as 1946–1948, internal debates had centered on whether and how fast to get into computing. These discussions included whether to use more or less electronics in IBM's products or continue relying on tried and proven electromechanical machines fast enough for most business applications, although not for the tiny demand for scientific uses. Historians normally portray the engineering community in Endicott as hostile to change and the young bucks hired in Poughkeepsie as pro-electronics. That characterization is not quite accurate. James W. Bryce, still at Endicott and by then a 30-year veteran of IBM, liked the idea of using the new electronics, such as vacuum tubes, rather than remaining wedded to technologies that he had done so much to improve during his career, but in March 1949 he died of a cerebral hemorrhage at the age of 68. However, a new champion had already stepped forward: Tom Jr.

When Tom Jr. rejoined IBM in January 1946, his father made him assistant to Charles A. Kirk (1905–1947), executive vice president for manufacturing operations and close confidant of the Old Man. At 41, Kirk was young for that role, but he knew how the company worked. It was now his job to bring Tom Jr. up to speed. Tom Jr. went along with this approach despite his and probably Tom Sr.'s concern that Kirk might later compete against Tom Jr. for the top job at IBM. Tom Jr. learned quickly, and his father pushed him along, too, appointing him vice president in June and to the board of directors that October, all while Tom Jr. was still only 32 years old. In June 1947, Kirk died of a heart attack while traveling in France with Watson Sr. In September, Tom's father promoted Tom Jr. to executive vice president.

As all these rapid changes were unfolding in Tom Jr.'s life, he embraced electronics as IBM's future and devoted his energies in the late 1940s to incorporating these technologies into products. By assuming that responsibility, he freed up the still vigorous Watson Sr. to focus on the bread-and-butter IBM products of calculators, punch cards, and his new interest, electric typewriter sales. Watson Sr. also wanted to expand IBM's overseas business, particularly in Europe, but many arguments occurred between father and son as the son competed for his place in the IBM world and his father tried to sustain the business essentially the way it had worked in the past and seemed still to be working. Over the next few decades, their battles filled many pages of histories of IBM, making for high drama.[19] The two Watsons argued largely over the rate and extent of transformation from the old to the new, not over the need to transform. They argued about policies, implementation of programs, and personnel matters. Watson Sr. knew from his trusted advisers—James Bryce and John McPherson—that moving to the new electronics would be good for IBM in the long term, and since he did not understand these new technologies, he was happy that his son was pursuing them.

Watson Sr. had already begun building critical mass in electronics in Poughkeepsie, relying not on government financing but rather on retained earnings and rental cash flows. When U.S. Navy veteran Ralph Palmer (1909–2005) returned to IBM in 1946, he and Kirk decided to establish an R&D laboratory in Poughkeepsie. Palmer moved quickly, launching studies around electronic mathematics and storage devices while hiring engineers. Unlike at Endicott, where engineers tended to operate in secrecy from each other, Palmer cultivated a more collaborative culture. He believed it was essential to recombine and integrate emerging knowledge about electronics to create new products, and soon he had results. In late 1948, IBM shipped the first of many 604 Electronic Calculating Punchs (not a computer, per Watson Sr.'s edict), a transitional product from the old to the new, renting at a competitive $600 per month.[20] It turned into an outstanding business success. At the product's peak production cycle, IBM annually manufactured more than 1,000 for a total of 5,600 before retiring it a decade later. Poughkeepsie consumed over 1.5 million vacuum tubes each year to put into this product. Watson Sr. had found work for his war veterans, while new engineers were learning how to develop and manufacture computers cost-effectively. The 604 machine reduced the amount of card handling and could perform scientific and engineering computations, which made it attractive to large manufacturing and defense firms. A new version, called the IBM Card-programmed Electronic Calculator (CPC), came out in May 1949. The story of computer development over the next 30 years was essentially of incrementally applying new methods and components to make machines operate faster and more reliably, be easier to operate, and be able to perform a greater variety of functions.

Customers helped, such as Northrop Aircraft, Inc., which in the late 1940s advised IBM on changes it sought. In this instance, its data processing staff wanted to move data electronically from one machine to another by using cables but without going through the intermediate step of outputting to cards and then inputting them back into another device. That collaboration led to the CPC. Introduced in 1949, a year before UNIVAC I came out, government agencies and defense contractors embraced it as a state-of-the-art machine. IBM shipped nearly 700 of these systems before the mid-1950s; UNIVAC shipped only 14 systems in the same period.[21] Even the Census Bureau took a CPC. Tom Jr. was proving to his father and peers that he could succeed at IBM. The firm "was rapidly creating an infrastructure of knowledgeable customers, salesmen, and servicemen for electronic computers."[22] That know-how led to IBM having "the fastest start in the market for electronic computing capability,"[23] but the looming UNIVAC remained threatening.

It was one thing to sell computers to the tiny scientific market but quite another to displace IBM's large installed base of tabulating equipment for business applications. That was the direction in which UNIVAC and other rivals were headed. The emerging technological battlefield included tape versus cards. By the early 1950s, it had become possible to record and retrieve data on magnetic tape that otherwise would be on cards, saving time and space. One school of thought held that with cards a user had the security of a physical object, which could be read by the human eye. One could not do that with tape. To get to a piece of information on tape, one would have to read everything before the desired data. But tape proponents argued that information could be rearranged at high speed, saving enormous amounts of time and labor costs. UNIVAC's proponents favored tape, as did many IBM engineers. IBM sales and many customers resisted tape or opted for a combination of both. IBM overcame concerns by developing a small army of salesmen who could sell computers. Tape proponents won within IBM and among customers. Tabulating salesmen were now retired, trained on the new products and ways of processing data, or replaced with college graduates sporting degrees in engineering and the physical sciences.

IBM's senior management decided to rely on some federal funding in the early 1950s for large computer projects, a first for the company. Inventing new computers involved too much expense and risk for any one company to take on alone, so it made sense to change strategy. The head of IBM's office in Washington, D.C., Louis H. "Red" LaMotte (1896–1984), enjoyed enormous respect from both Watsons. He had joined IBM as a sales trainee in 1922 and in 1952 became vice president of sales. He held various senior positions, including simultaneously running sales and engineering in the 1950s. LaMotte aligned with the pro-computer faction when he learned of the many large computer projects the government was funding.

He feared IBM might miss a huge emerging market. He became a crucial ally of Tom Jr. The old strategy was too slow and too limited for LaMotte in the wake of a rising tsunami of technological developments. Tom Jr. gave him the go-ahead to delve into government computing. The first project, a computer for the U.S. Navy, called NORC (Naval Ordnance Research Calculator), at the start of the new decade taught IBM how to estimate the cost of R&D for computers. Just as important, IBMers in engineering, sales, and at Corporate learned how to deal with government contracts for such projects. IBM funded most of its own computer development, even borrowing money, rather than fully relying on government support.[24]

Tom Jr. still had to strengthen his internal operations, remove those resisting change, and bring in new talent. Albert L. "Al" Williams (1911–1982), a long-time Watson Sr. era executive, who joined IBM in sales in 1936 and served as the company's controller and treasurer in the 1940s and as president from 1961 to 1966, pointed out that IBM's rivals and other high-tech companies spent about 3 percent of their gross income on research, whereas IBM spent less. That kind of analysis convinced senior management to allocate more funding to computing. In May 1950, Tom Jr. gave W. Wallace McDowell (1906–1985) responsibility for driving R&D. McDowell had a degree in engineering from MIT, had joined IBM in 1930, and had worked on various projects, so he knew his way around the company's politics. He embraced electronics while working at the Endicott lab. McDowell took over an organization of 1,000 people and within five years had 4,000 employees, 60 percent of whom were engineers. To put those numbers in perspective, in the same five years, IBM's total employment nearly doubled, while McDowell's staff quadrupled. McDowell is best remembered as the father of the IBM 701 computer. Tom Jr. focused Jim Birkenstock on future needs, which suited him even better than serving as the general sales manager. Birkenstock was one of the first senior IBMers to understand the advantages of tape over cards, and he began to promote the change.

To complete his management team, in 1949 Tom Jr. hired Cuthbert Hurd (1911–1996), a mathematics PhD who demonstrated ability in developing computational equipment. Before joining IBM, he had worked at the U.S. Atomic Energy Commission in Oak Ridge, Tennessee, and moved in the federal scientific computing world, which IBM wanted to join. In time, he developed the popular IBM 650 computer.[25]

With McDowell, Birkenstock, and Hurd in position to facilitate IBM's transformation to computers, Tom Jr. had become serious about winning the race into the new business. His actions illustrated how often change is effected in a large organization where conflicting constituencies vied against one another for noble or parochial reasons. His behavior demonstrated that an IBM executive had to cultivate the personal loyalty of a cadre of managers and then had to persuade layers of employees to embrace a vision. Ordering or intimidating them rarely worked at IBM; the company's culture would not tolerate it. Tom Watson Jr. successfully carried out his campaign to convert IBM into a computer vendor. Many opportunities helped, including a new war.

When the Korean War broke out in June 1950, Watson Sr. wrote to President Harry S. Truman, offering the services of his company for the nation's defense. Birkenstock quickly established a military products division. Hurd and Birkenstock visited 18 potential customers for computing to learn what they needed. These needs were similar to those for World War II, such as cryptanalysis, but there were new ones, too, such as weather forecasting, designing jet engines, and strategic planning. The IBMers made these meetings (called "sales calls" in IBM parlance) without attracting attention to themselves within IBM's sales community, because Tom Jr. had cautioned them that sales was not enthusiastic about engineering resources being diverted from the development of more punch card equipment, which was still in great demand. The sales force still had the ear of the Old Man; remember, Tom Jr. was not yet IBM's leader.[26] IBM's engineers drafted specifications for a computer to meet these new requirements, which came to be known as the Defense Calculator, so named to appeal to the patriotic sentiments of Watson Sr. and the sales community. Tom Jr. tasked Ralph Palmer to build it. Shifting from commercial equipment to a defense-related computing project made sense, because of technological risks, uncertain development costs, and an unknown market for computers.

The Defense Calculator evolved into the IBM 701. For the first time, a computer system did not consist of some long, massive device, like the

Mark I or the SSEC. Rather, it consisted of a group of machines that individually fit into a service elevator, could be built and tested at IBM, and could be installed in days instead of months. IBM retained patents for all the 700 class computers, including the Defense Calculator, because IBM had funded their development. As one engineer on the project reflected, "It got IBM into a new business."[27]

Future mainframes across the industry would be constructed in the same way, as collections of modular metal cabinets that looked like large industrial refrigerators. They connected to each other with cables, through which data moved from one to another. They included an analytical control unit, electrostatic storage unit, punch card reader, alphabetical printer, punch card recorder, magnetic-tape reader and recorder, and magnetic-drum reader and recorder. The electrical power supply had its own "units." For the next 40 years, computer systems consisted of these kinds of configurations: control units, memory devices (tape and, later, disk), printers, card input-output (I/O) units, and telecommunications devices. In theory, everything could be delivered right through the front door. In practice, many salesmen had to order a crane to shoehorn at least the mainframe through a busted-out window to a second- or third-story data center if there was no service elevator.[28]

The epigraph starting this chapter was Watson Sr.'s introduction of the IBM 701. New engineers and salesmen were hired to go up against Remington Rand's highly publicized UNIVAC and the machine of another rival, Engineering Research Associates (ERA). These two competitors staffed their sales organizations with engineers more than IBM had done, the latter choosing a more educationally diverse sales organization. IBM aimed the 701 at scientific and engineering customers, so the sales force complained that they could not easily offer it to commercial customers. Remington Rand was talking to IBM's customers, raising the specter of massive displacements of tabulating equipment. Customers told their IBM salesmen, visiting engineers, and Tom Jr. that IBM needed to enter the commercial computing business. In September 1953, Corporate responded with the IBM 702 Electronic Data Processing Machine (EDPM), inching closer to using the word *computer*. Commercial customers liked both the 702 and the UNIVAC system.

IBM 702 users represented an impressive collection of companies and agencies in the "military-industrial complex" that President Dwight D. Eisenhower would warn about. This collection of suppliers to the military attracted all computer vendors. The 19 702s installed included machines at IBM (installed at its headquarters in New York to show off), Lockheed Aircraft, Douglas Aircraft, General Electric, Convair, United Aircraft, North American Aviation, RAND Corporation, Boeing, and General Motors. Among the federal agencies having 702s were the National Security Agency, U.S. Navy, Los Alamos Laboratory in New Mexico, the Livermore Laboratory in California, and the U.S. Weather Bureau.[29]

Nevertheless, their technical staffs still worried about losing data or unseen information on tape drives. Customers and IBMers fretted over having enough adequately skilled personnel to operate and maintain these new machines. For most organizations, it was their first encounter with computers, although not with tabulating and other simpler office equipment. Watson Jr. turned to T. Vincent Learson (1912–1996) to help provide products and support to ease customers' appropriation of IBM computers. A future CEO of IBM from 1971 to 1973, Learson was a tall, physically imposing man who came up in IBM sales, having joined the company in 1935. He had majored in mathematics at Harvard, led the sales division from 1949 to 1953, and at the time was general sales manager. Tom Jr. made him director of Electronic Data Processing Machines six months after the introduction of the 702, giving him the task of coordinating all of IBM's computing activities. An executive who moved very quickly and with an intimidating, results-oriented, no-nonsense approach, Learson developed a library of software for customers and developed tools salesmen used to assess potential applications for their accounts. He limited sales of the 701 to 50, and installed only 14, because he wanted a better machine, which he got with the IBM 704 (figure 6.1).

Learson pressed engineers for more reliability, spawning new computer memory technologies, starting a practice of incrementally replacing components being built or already installed. New models kept coming out in the 1950s, evolving into the 7000 series when transistors replaced vacuum tubes.[30] Remington Rand's early momentum had slowed by mid-decade.

Figure 6.1
The IBM 704 computer established IBM as a serious supplier of digital computing for commercial users, suggesting that business uses would expand. Photo courtesy of IBM Corporate Archives.

Tom Jr. reflected later that IBM had "conclusively asserted its leadership" in data processing. At the high end of computing, IBM was on its way to dominance, even in the face of increasing competition, but there was more to come.

Tom Jr. later admitted "an almost near miss" in uncovering the emerging market for federally funded computer projects. He needed to institutionalize the process by which IBM identified new markets early enough to determine how best to deal with them and to persuade constituencies within IBM to commit to new directions. The company was now so big that factions worked at cross purposes that needed to be controlled but not suppressed, such as sales supporting more punch card equipment, while engineers were enthralled with developing digital computers.

Tom Jr. resolved the issue in such an effective way that for the next half century IBM used his solution. He asked Birkenstock to develop a process to avoid future strategic errors. Birkenstock recommended creating two departments within Corporate, called Product Planning and Market Analysis, staffed with ambitious IBMers and outside experts. Watson put Birkenstock in charge of both. In Birkenstock's own words, "From 1953 to 1956, the Product Planning and Market Analysis departments shifted IBM product and systems development emphasis toward Electronic Data Processing Systems and away from Electromechanical Punch Card Accounting Machine Systems."[31] These departments identified markets, such as for electric typewriters, of small and large customers. Henceforth, engineering developed technologies to solve specific customer problems. Birkenstock noted that "what had been a feeble voice in the past now became a loud and persistent cry with full management support."[32] His approach, however, did not eliminate the contentious system that had long existed. In the coming decades, various constituencies and divisions would disagree for honest or political/personal reasons, while collaboration across the growing ecosystem comprising IBM and its customers ebbed and flowed as part of the process of defining solutions for customer problems and needs. But now there existed a more disciplined process for controlling diverse intentions, with disagreements being ultimately resolved by Corporate's management committee. It was a better system for a large company than Watson Sr.'s decision-making approach. Tom Jr.'s management style differed from his father's, and this way of determining what products to develop exemplified the changes under way in the way IBM governed itself.

In Endicott, ancestral home of the punch card faction at IBM, electrical engineers were working on computing projects, too. When Watson Sr. said he wanted a better machine than the Mark I, Frank E. Hamilton (1898–1972), an engineer at the laboratory, received the assignment, in 1948. Hamilton was an interesting choice for an engineering project manager. He had joined C-T-R as a draftsman in 1923, so he came up in the world of punch card technology. By the time management tapped him to develop the 650 Magnetic Drum Calculator, he had two decades of experience developing products.

Hamilton designed a computer for small customers, not for the hulking aviation firms supported by the 700s. He initially thought of developing a machine aimed at scientific users, and he was supported in that line of thinking by his manager, John C. McPherson. However, Hamilton's proposed machine cost too much for the market analysis folks, $1,600 per month instead of an ideal $400 per month. Hamilton soldiered on into the early 1950s, as competition challenged the 604 and CPC. Remington Rand's Type 400-2 calculator ran faster, had more capacity, and rented for less. This was only one of seven small stored-program computers in the market going after IBM by 1952. IBM's two products were becoming, in sales parlance, "tired." Cuthbert Hurd, responsible for selling computers to scientific and engineering users, now found Hamilton's project attractive and directed more resources to him. With Tom Jr.'s approval, he dramatically expanded Hamilton's staff, from 4 to 50.

Their efforts resulted in the announcement of the IBM 650 Magnetic Drum Calculator (figure 6.2) on July 14, 1953. IBM's press release nicely situated the 650 computer, still called a calculator, in the market:

> International Business Machines Corp. announced today the introduction of a new commercial electronic decimal calculator designed to meet the vast accounting and computing requirements in areas between those now served by its "giant brains" and the widely-used smaller machines such as the 604 Electronic Calculating Punch and the Card-programmed Calculator.[33]

IBM rented it for $3,250 per month, one-fourth the amount for an IBM 701 but also four times as much as originally envisioned. Marketed initially to scientific users, commercial customers saw it as a useful system for business applications. It quickly became the most popular computer of the 1950s, often referred to as the "workhorse" or "Model T" of commercial computing. Its input-output accepted data from cards, so it could use the massive quantity of card records customers already had.

John Hancock Mutual Life Insurance Company took delivery of the first 650 in December 1954. It fit into Hancock's existing EAM operations and operated faster than IBM's rivals from NCR, ElectroData Corporation, and Underwood. By the time IBM stopped making 650s in 1962,

Figure 6.2
IBM's 650 computer was its most successful data processing product of the late 1950s. Mass-produced and widely accepted by customers, it solidified IBM's lead in the computer industry. Photo courtesy of IBM Corporate Archives.

nearly 2,000 had been installed around the world.[34] Often overlooked is the fact that this system introduced hundreds of companies and departments within large corporations to computers, expanding IBM's set of business customers, which became crucial users of future IBM computers. The 650 made it possible for universities to embrace computing as a discipline. Donald Knuth, later a leading computer scientist, explained: "Computing courses got started in universities largely because IBM donated about 100 'free' computers during the 1950s, with the stipulation that programming courses must be taught. This strategy made it possible for computing to get its foot in the academic door."[35] IBM engineers and manufacturing staffs mastered how to mass-produce computers. To facilitate that learning, optimize the redesign of manufacturing processes to build in volume, and reward work done well, in 1954 Hamilton took over management of the Endicott laboratory.

THE COLD WAR AND NEW TECHNOLOGIES

In late summer 1949, the Soviet Union entered the atomic age by detonating its first atomic bomb. In the early 1950s, it built ballistic missiles, and in 1957 it launched the world's first satellite, *Sputnik*, which led the American public and many in government to fear that the United States was losing "the space race." The U.S. military had already responded in 1949 with a strategy to build a national air-defense network to warn of a Soviet attack. Visions of another Pearl Harbor attack haunted military and political leaders. While salesmen were busy expanding the number of installed IBM computers in the early to mid-1950s, the company did not ignore the ongoing requirements of the U.S. government and the intensification of the Cold War.

One military project in particular endowed IBM with the reputation of being the most sophisticated producer of computers, capable of taking on the most complex data processing assignments. In the late 1950s and early 1960s, this military project did for IBM in a new era what Social Security had accomplished in the 1930s: it generated a great deal of business, enhanced its prestige, and spurred its market dominance. It spun off more patents and stimulated R&D research that assisted IBM in producing the most important computer in the history of the industry. This military project differed in one important respect from the Social Security one in that this time luck played no role. IBM's participation in the growing network of computer developers and the military, relations nurtured over the previous 15 years, positioned the company to take on a complex, risky project. There was an old IBM salesman's saying passed down over generations that applied here: "Ninety percent of a sale is about showing up." That is what IBM did; it bid on the project and won. After its completion, it became natural to turn to IBM to manage computing projects that put men on the moon, help build the Federal Aviation Agency's national flight control system, provide computing for ballistic missiles, and feed growing requirements for computing by U.S. intelligence agencies.

To protect the nation from attacks by the Soviets using bomber aircraft, the U.S. Department of Defense moved to evaluate what kinds of computers could manage a complex radar early-warning network to sound the alarm in seconds if Soviet aircraft were headed toward North America. It selected for the system a large computer under development at MIT, begun in 1944, called Whirlwind. Initially the U.S. Navy and then the U.S. Air Force funded it. The plan called for a series of command and control centers, each equipped with two computers, making it possible to manage a radar network at electronic speed. By the fall of 1953, MIT had a working system using various new components, such as more reliable parts making up its memory (ferrite cores), but already engineers at MIT began to face the problem of how to manufacture, install, and maintain systems scattered across the northern United States.

That is where McPherson, who had been cultivating relations with the government and other computer builders, entered the picture. MIT wanted to put construction of the system out to bid, and McPherson let it be known that IBM was interested. Tom Jr. wanted to win this deal, as it would establish IBM as the "go-to" firm for big computing projects. Raytheon and Remington Rand were also eager to obtain this contract. IBM won the business because, as one MIT project manager put it, "In the IBM organization we observed a much higher degree of purposefulness, integration, and esprit de corps than we found in the Remington Rand organization." MIT's engineering management found "evidence of much closer ties between research, factory, and field maintenance in IBM."[36]

Munro K. "Mike" Haynes (1923–1957) became IBM's project leader. He had come to IBM in 1950 with a PhD in electrical engineering from the University of Illinois. He was an expert on magnetic core memories, a technology critical to IBM's success. IBM's first contract as a supplier for the MIT system came in October 1952, to build the hardware while Remington Rand would write the necessary software. IBM quickly assembled a team to work on the project in Poughkeepsie and a year later won the contract to build two prototypes of the new system, which MIT and IBM installed in Massachusetts, called the Cape Cod System.[37] They ran successfully. That achievement led to the Whirlwind project. In June 1956, IBM shipped the first system to McGuire Air Force Base in New Jersey. In 1957, Watson established the Federal Systems Division (FSD) to concentrate resources on the project and to focus on pursuing other government business. FSD proved successful, even if profits on government projects were less than for commercial clients. It sold its services to the Department of Defense, Department of the Treasury, all the national laboratories, the Internal Revenue Service, the Social Security Administration, the National Aeronautics and Space Administration, and others.

Meanwhile, back in 1954, the system had been named Semi-Automatic Ground Environment, better known as SAGE. Unlike on the Harvard computer project a decade earlier, this time IBM and MIT shared the spotlight. An engineering executive at IBM observed that "the size and scope of SAGE was almost unbelievable. When fully deployed in 1963, there were twenty-three direction centers distributed near the northern boundary and the east and west coasts of the United States. Each of these contained an AN/FQ-7 computer system having almost 55,000 vacuum tubes, weighing 250 tons, occupying an acre of floor space, and using up to 3 million watts of electric power."[38] For backup, each location had two AN/FQ-7s. RAND ended up writing the bulk of the software for the system. Most important, SAGE worked.

SAGE deterred the Soviets and allowed the U.S. military to learn how to conduct simulated attacks and to train officers in potential Cold War warfare. The computer industry obtained new computer memories, software, online real-time processing, transmission protocols using telephone lines, and terminals, among other things. Emerson Pugh, the IBM engineering executive quoted earlier, pointed out that the most significant accomplishment of SAGE was that it served as "the first geographically distributed, on-line, real-time system implemented with digital computers."[39] Between 1952 and 1955, SAGE generated shy of 4 percent of IBM's total revenue, which accounted for some 80 percent of all the company's revenue from computers. SAGE represented a big piece of business that signaled to all governments, IBM's computer rivals, and corporations that computing was becoming more sophisticated and that IBM was in the thick of it all. Watson Jr. got what he needed from SAGE. Remington Rand lost the lead in computing, if it ever had it, never to regain it again. Over 7,000 IBMers learned a great deal about computing.

Paul Edwards, studying the role of defense computing during the Cold War, concluded that SAGE provided IBM with more than profits. Benefits "included access to technical developments at MIT and the know-how to mass-produce magnetic core memory—the major form of random access storage in computers from the mid-1950s until well into the 1970s—and printed circuit boards," essentially arriving at conclusions similar to Pugh's.[40] IBM's SABRE airline reservation system was a descendant of SAGE. Kenneth Flamm, an early student of the U.S. computing industry, went further, arguing that IBM's decision to participate in the development of SAGE was one of the most important business decisions the company ever made.[41] The evidence that this project did wonders for IBM became clearer as it learned much about computing and how to develop and manufacture these systems.[42] The effort enhanced its reputation as a developer of complex systems, which translated into commercial success, while military contracts took the risk out of investing in R&D.

Poughkeepsie continued to expand during the SAGE project, adding R&D space and engineering staff. A new engineering culture emerged that would serve IBM well with computing. At Endicott, the old tabulating-era culture lingered. Groups collaborated less willingly in Endicott or elsewhere in IBM, a concern that bothered IBM's engineering executives when they considered how to help develop SAGE. That project required far more collaboration internally than when the company developed tabulating machines. That behavior had to change. In part, that meant expanding the Poughkeepsie facility, but because so many new electrical engineers did not want to live in what they perceived to be a small, isolated town, IBM set up a new research lab ("site" in IBM parlance) in San Jose, California, in 1952 at a punch card manufacturing site it had used since the 1940s.

Reynold B. Johnson (1908–1998), who had been hired by Watson Sr. in 1934 to develop test scoring equipment and had established a record of effective engineering leadership, proved to be a good choice to lead the

SAGE project. Johnson insisted that his engineers be familiar with every other project at the San Jose laboratory and collaborate across projects. In addition to helping each other, calling that one's "most important assignment," he declared that "the second most important assignment is that of carrying on the project to which you are assigned."[43] Johnson is best remembered, however, for developing the first disk drive, the IBM 305 RAMAC (figure 6.3), introduced in 1956, which changed how people used computers. His transformation of the engineering culture at IBM turned out to be of more value internally, but first we need to understand his RAMAC achievement and others that followed.

Two developments proved significant: the invention of disk storage and the controversial Project Stretch. Customers had complained that when they used computers for inventory control, they could not directly look up discrete pieces of information using tape or card files, both of

Figure 6.3
The IBM 305 Disk Storage Unit made it possible for data processing users to access data directly, making online systems possible in the 1960s. The device was also known as RAMAC. Photo courtesy of IBM Corporate Archives.

which were also error-prone. In the early 1950s, engineers in San Jose developed a direct access data storage device that allowed a computer operator to go directly to the spot on a disk drive to get the desired piece of information instead of reading all the information on a tape before what one wanted or dealing with massive quantities of cards. The new process was similar to how you select a song you want to play on a vinyl record or CD. In May 1955, IBM unveiled its technological development, and over the next two decades it introduced dozens of new disk drives, as they were called, with storage that could access ever-increasing amounts of data ever faster and at lower cost. In June 1956, IBM made available 14 IBM 305 RAMACs (Random Access Memory Accounting Machines) with the new storage device, called the IBM 350 Disk Storage Unit. It forever transformed how computing would be done.[44]

By itself, this enormously important development would not have been enough to push IBM further toward dominance of the computer market or even toward SAGE. That market presence took more than outstanding engineering and manufacturing. A combination of coordinated activities and capabilities made the difference.[45] Tom Watson Jr. made a similar point in his memoirs:

> The importance of a tradition of technical innovation; expertise in electromechanical manufacturing; a high-quality sales force; well-developed service operations; a tradition of employee and customer training; electronic know-how; and experience with integrated data-processing installations. Although IBM may not have been the absolute best company in each of these areas, it did well in all of them.[46]

But give the engineers their due: their inventions led to a decline in batch processing methods and to direct access uses of computers. Paul Ceruzzi, a leading expert on the history of computing technology, observed that people processed information differently: direct access to data "spelled the end of the batch method of processing, on which IBM had built its financial strength ever since the tabulator days."[47] That transformation took both IBM and its customers more than a decade to digest. In the meantime, magnetic tape became the most widely used format for storing data, while use of cards declined.

Tom Watson Jr. sensed many of these developments. We will see how his understanding of the way business circumstances were changing influenced his reaction to an antitrust suit as the world of cards shifted within IBM's technological world. In 1954, Tom Jr. wanted to develop a plan to retain IBM's technological leadership. Called Project Stretch, it has come down in history as a failed project, but was it?[48] Reacting to recent successes by Remington Rand with its UNIVAC, Tom Jr. wanted a newer, bigger supercomputer that could be sold to government agencies, possibly producing as many as eight or so. Initially, the focus was on designing a machine based on vacuum tubes, but that technology died before machines could be rolled out, superseded by technological developments. One seemingly unlucky engineering manager, Stephen W. "Steve" Dunwell (1913–1994), got the assignment to run the project. To fund it, he won a proposal for such a machine from the U.S. Atomic Energy Commission (AEC). His staff grew from less than 50 in 1955 to some 200, where it remained until 1959, when it further expanded to build the new computer. While that never happened as originally planned, engineers developed new, faster operating computer memory and learned to use transistors. They began to insert these innovations into other computers, including a sequel to the 700s called the IBM 7090 Data Processing System, a Stretch computer that IBM started to ship to customers in November 1959.[49]

The earliest member of the family, the IBM 7030, ran 200 times faster than a 701 and 7 times faster than a 7090. It was IBM's first transistorized large computer, often called a supercomputer. For a year, it was the fastest computer on earth, but not as fast as originally promised to the AEC and a few other customers, so Tom Jr. lowered the rental price.[50] He also concluded that IBM could not make a profit on it. Only eight customers obtained one, while IBM kept one for its own use. We now know that Stretch was not a failure, although at the time Tom Jr. thought so. IBMers gained experience with solid-state technologies and, more importantly, insights on computer architecture that influenced their design of the System 360—IBM's most successful product ever.[51]

For a few years after the Stretch project ended, the engineering community avoided controversial projects for fear of failing and suffering the wrath of Tom Jr., even while Control Data Corporation (CDC) moved forward with high-end computing. Watson recognized that he probably encouraged that caution among his engineers and that perhaps he had been too quick to declare Stretch a failure. In 1966, after several years of seeing Stretch lessons incorporated into the System 360, at an awards dinner for Steve Dunwell, who had been badly maligned, Tom Jr., the event's main speaker, got about as close as any Watson ever did to publicly apologizing to an engineer. He acknowledged that things had not always gone as well "as they might" for Dunwell and that he had not always been treated in a "fair" manner, adding, "I just thought I would take the opportunity of publicly trying to correct the record."[52]

Watson Jr. had already learned that a major asset needed to achieve IBM's dominance in computing was his engineers. One could see it in the numbers. In 1950, some 600 employees, or 3 percent of IBM's workforce, worked in R&D. By the end of 1954, that population had grown to 3,000, or 9 percent of the workforce. Poughkeepsie's engineering community expanded from 200 to over 1,400 in the same period. W. Wallace "Wally" McDowell, their director, drove much of that expansion, and in recognition of that, in July 1954 Tom Jr. promoted him to vice president. McDowell promoted other engineering managers to executive positions to give his constituency greater influence at Corporate. In the 1950s, research and development increasingly separated to intensify attention on their differing objectives. In 1956, IBM hired as director of research Emanuel R. Piore (1908–2000), a Lithuanian by birth whose family immigrated to the United States when he was 9. He later earned a PhD in physics at the University of Wisconsin. He was another World War II veteran and had worked in the Office of Naval Research. Piore brought to IBM a solid sense of strategic know-how and a deep appreciation of organizational politics. He convinced Tom Jr. to let him move his researchers to a new facility, and in 1963 his organization became the Research Division, giving it a status that made it easier for its presidents to influence company-wide product strategies.[53]

IBM's engineering community kept busy in the late 1950s and early 1960s, moving from one success to another in the rapidly evolving technology landscape. To clarify, by then there were several lines of computers emerging: the 700s, which evolved into the 7000s; the highly popular 650;

and the transistor-based 1401, first shipped in 1960. Like the 650, the latter opened up the world of computing to many smaller enterprises than the 700s to 7000s and could be used for bread-and-butter computing, including at IBM's service bureaus. Software for the 1401 was some of the best at the time: a simple operating system, utility software tools, and several programming languages, such as Assembler, FORTRAN (for engineering/scientific uses), COBOL (useful for business applications), and a simple-to-use programming tool called RPG.[54] The 1401 system proved far more popular than the 650, selling some 10,000 units, more than all the other computers in the world introduced in 1959. Just as the 700s and the 650 assured IBM's status as the world's leading computer vendor, the 1401s encouraged many companies around the world to become avid users of computers. The world's dependence on computers was increasing as much through IBM's success in convincing them to enter that world as from their own desires.

ON TECHNOLOGICAL INNOVATION AND BUSINESS CAPABILITIES

In the early 1990s, historian Steven W. Usselman pondered the dynamics of technological innovation and the role of bureaucratic organizations, with IBM in mind. He picked a good case study, because IBM had an expanding technological prowess but was also becoming increasingly bureaucratic, two features that intensified in the 1960s and 1970s. From the late 1940s through the early 1960s, its technology and bureaucracy were already formidable, however, and even typical of what also existed at such peer firms as AT&T, RCA, and GE. Usselman concluded that IBM "succeeded because the hothouse of the Cold War computer industry rewarded it for what it already was; GE and RCA stumbled because their established strengths mattered less in that environment."[55] He carried his argument further, contending that "IBM was an organization whose business had naturally fostered these qualities: salesmanship that required close attention both to technology and to the particular requirements of each customer, regular exchange of information between the field and the plant, flexibility in production, and a willingness to compromise. In my view, these qualities put IBM in an excellent position to adapt to the electronic computer and the solid-state revolution."[56]

The story told in this chapter reinforces his assessment but with one caveat reinforced in subsequent work by other historians. In large organizations, various constituencies existed whose influence rose and fell because of the vagaries of corporate politics and culture, ensuring that outcomes were less predictable than protagonists might have wanted. Individuals shaped events, whether Tom Jr.'s impatience to enter the computer business or the eagerness of engineers in Poughkeepsie to do the same, and, as we will see in chapters 7 and 8, these views were not always supported by the sales side of the business. The new insight building on Usselman's is that corporate culture needs to be given more due.

The evidence in this and earlier chapters suggests that what Usselman spoke of as bureaucracy can also be seen as a form of what I characterize as a cultural path dependency reinforced by circumstances that played to IBM's existing strengths and inclinations. IBM could get into advanced electronics; Watson Jr. was inclined to enter the computer business. It is also why the products produced by Endicott's engineers returned to the corporation more revenue and profits than Poughkeepsie's early computers had. But this is not destiny, because as Robert Freeland demonstrated in studying another iconic U.S. corporation, General Motors, the shape of a large firm and its destiny were achieved through debate and discourse, not just by technology and bureaucracy.[57] Bureaucratic practices also shaped IBM's culture, by providing context for its evolution. I would add that debate and discourse were also necessary but not determinative. Usselman, Freeland, and my suggested consideration of corporate culture in combination help explain what happened at IBM between 1945 and the early 1960s more effectively than the analysis of earlier students of IBM's emergence as a behemoth in the computer industry. Because it was part of a larger computing ecosystem, it is important to understand other participants affecting its work. To complete that description of IBM's world, we turn to other aspects that shaped its activities.

7 HOW CUSTOMERS, IBM, AND A NEW INDUSTRY EVOLVED, 1945–1964

> [T]he computer was a blazing white-hot nova in the marketing heavens and the once ubiquitous accounting machine was a fading red giant destined to grow dimmer by the year.
> —WILLIAM W. SIMMONS[1]

FOR OVER FOUR decades, historians discussed whether IBM was early or late to the computer market. The epigraph by an IBM sales executive, William W. Simmons (1912–1997), was immediately followed by another observation: "But in 1958 this understanding and acceptance by IBM management was still several years in the future."[2] Thomas Watson Jr. admitted as much when reflecting back on the quality of IBM's computers during the last few years of his father's reign and the early period of his own during the 1950s:

> Technology turned out to be less important than sales and distribution methods. Starting with UNIVAC, we consistently outsold people who had better technology because we knew how to put the story before the customers, how to install the machines successfully, and how to hang on to the customers once we had them.[3]

Others could introduce a new product, and if it took off, IBM played a fast game of catch-up. If it was too slow, it missed the bulk of a new market, but it usually could catch up and exceed the competition, just as it did with the printer-lister. More insightful was that Tom Jr.'s comment about the UNIVAC could as easily have been made about IBM's performance in 1917–1922, and even in the 2010s, as when the company again played catch-up, this time with cloud computing. Ultimately, the argument seems esoteric, because historians agree that IBM proved enormously successful and that it dominated the computer market with shares of between 40 percent and 80 percent in one country after another.

The critical issue is, how did it do that? How did IBM become the largest, most important computer firm? The answers to these questions are crucial for a number of reasons. First, private enterprises are in business to generate revenue and profits, and, to protect them, they expand their market share. Second, other firms not yet behemoths in their industries are eager to learn how others did it before them. Third, in a world in which economies are managed as much by public officials influenced by the thinking of economists and business school professors as by laws, knowing how a company prospers is more important than whether a firm was early or late to market. By the end of this chapter, it should be clear that IBM was well on its way to becoming an enormously successful vendor of computer equipment. Subsequent chapters lay out the case for how that happened, a presentation begun in chapter 6 and broadened in this one.

The seeds of IBM's success came from two sources. Steven W. Usselman's observation that IBM was constructed out of the right skills and organization needed to enter this industry—a point we can apply to its tabulating equipment phase, as early as the 1910s—suggests the first one. A second source is the sales and corporate culture that made it possible for IBM not to be shy about engaging with new technologies and circumstances. As the company became larger and affected operations of an increasing number of customers, the complexity of the explanation for IBM's success did also. In this chapter, we demonstrate that reality by examining three topics: the role of customers in IBM's early computer business, IBM's participation in the creation of this new market (the computer industry), and finally, as in earlier chapters, the company's performance, which we assess by looking at its business results. Permeating the narrative is the extension of more forms of coordination and collaboration within the company and across its market ecosystem.

These questions and the supporting organization of this chapter leave open the question that often attracts students of the company: the role of the Watsons. Rowena Olegario is typical in giving the two Watsons enormous credit for the success of IBM, and indeed this book does, too.[4] It also took many people, numerous strategies, and multiple product innovations to make the story of IBM, in the words of historian Thomas K. McCraw, "epic in the business history of the United States," strong words from a sober scholar. Yet McCraw also gave much credit to Watson Sr.[5] Here, we tell a far more complex story that makes clear that the Watsons, while a necessary component of IBM's success, were not the whole of it. Because they were present, we cannot imagine the company having succeeded the way it did without them.

CUSTOMERS AND NEW COMPUTERS

By 1956, barely a half decade into the computer business, IBM had 87 computer installations and another 190 systems on order. IBM's rivals combined had 41 installed and another 40 on order.[6] Those statistics did not include several thousand tabulating machine users scattered around the world, all of which Corporate saw as potential future customers for computers. By 1960–1961, the world had 6,000 systems installed, over half of them from IBM. Customers rapidly demonstrated interest in these "giant brains" and talked among themselves, often one data processing manager to another, leveraging introductions to each other by vendors and through industry organizations, such as SHARE, discussed further here.

These customers articulated to IBM and other vendors what they wanted. Conversations began among engineers and scientists inside and outside of IBM. Initially, IBMers did not initiate these discussions; however, they increasingly became involved either as individuals or as representatives of IBM. Recall the Moore School lectures after World War II. Academics established journals, such as the *Mathematical Tables and Other Aids to Computation* (established 1943), *Digital Computer Newsletter* (1948), *Computers and Automation* (1951), and the *Association for Computing Machinery Journal* (1954). Commercial publications appeared also, such as the respected and well-distributed *Datamation* (1957) and IBM's *IBM Journal of Research and Development* (1957) and *Computer Journal* (1958). Noncomputing trade press and business magazines explored the role of computers on both sides of the Atlantic in the 1950s and worldwide in the 1960s. Industry trade journals carried articles inspired by vendors or on early user experiences with computers. No industry seemed exempt from the exercise.

During the 1950s, accounting, manufacturing, process, public sector, and other industry organizations published hundreds of articles describing how people used computers and the benefits gained, a number that would expand to tens of thousands in the following decade. These associations hosted seminars and other training events at national and regional meetings. Computing was a "hot" new business topic, while accounting auditors fretted about whether they could track transactions on computers, where the only paper trail was what entered or came out of a computer, not what was going on inside one. Cuthbert Hurd observed that one of the biggest selling problems IBM faced in the 1950s was educating potential customers about using computers.[7] Salesmen and their managers also had to go through the same learning curve.[8] To be clear about the matter, business managers needed the education that Hurd referenced, as did data processing managers engaging with computers for the first time. The closer a potential customer was to the technology, the more likely they were reading technical literature and discussing issues with peers.

As the number of users of tabulating and computing machinery expanded, a community of several thousand managers developed to deal with electronic data processing in the United States and roughly half as many more in Western Europe. In the United States, they did what other professions had long done: they organized themselves into "user communities," mostly aligned by computer vendor, and gathered at annual conventions to present to each other their experiences using specific computers. They bragged about their successes and met with vendors to inform them of problems and opportunities, much the way automotive or motorcycle clubs do today. These were important opportunities for IBM technologists to discuss their projects and to collect insights on the performance and needs of their systems.

Of these groups, one of the most important was SHARE, meaning the word *share,* as in sharing information about IBM products. Users of IBM 701s in the Los Angeles area established the group in 1955. By the mid-1960s, it had become the most important of these user groups, made essential by all the technological changes occurring. Run by volunteers, not IBMers, it set the agenda for meetings. The group discussed every form of IBM technology: computers, peripheral equipment, operating systems, programming languages, other utility programs, database management tools, and other software. SHARE published reports, hosted conventions, and expanded. By the early years of the new millennium, it had over 20,000 members working in 2,300 organizations, all of them IBM customers.

There were other organizations, more broadly based, that included users of equipment from vendors other than IBM. Of these, the most important was the Data Processing Management Association (better known as DPMA). Founded in 1949, its members focused on managerial issues, while SHARE focused largely on technical considerations. Both shared information. DPMA still exists as the Association of Information Technology Professionals (AITP). DPMA was where data processing managers most frequently made presentations about their use of this technology. Manufacturers were particularly active from its earliest days, with members publishing case studies in annual DPMA proceedings and in their own trade publications. David R. Clarke was typical of his generation. A vice president at Johnson & Johnson, he presented a paper at APICS (American Production and Inventory Control Society, founded in 1957), a major manufacturing trade group keenly interested in using computers, about production planning in his company, in which he described how he used computing. That was in 1964, looking back on over a decade of experience with computers.[9] As early as 1954, others were commenting on computerized production planning in industry trade journals, such as *Electrical Manufacturing*.[10] Cases and presentations became a flood of publications by the early 1960s.

While IBM sales reps always talked to customers, factory workers, with the exception of those who were literally constructing machines, also interacted with customers who toured factories and wanted to chat with employees. It became routine for visitors to pose for photographs next to the computer being constructed for them, accompanied by the actual workers involved. A sign hung from the ceiling with the name of the company or agency for which a particular machine was being assembled. Employees shared information, insights, and opinions with customers in offices, conference rooms, and in visits to customers' plants and classrooms.

Such discussions proved helpful, if sometimes contentious. Recall the case of whether to use cards or magnetic tape in the 1950s. Customers embraced tape before IBMers did, seeing its advantages in storage, reduced space, speed of operation, and reduction of manual operations. A million binary digits stored on tape took up one cubic inch of space, compared to 500 cubic inches on IBM cards, using 3,000 cards.[11] As early as 1948, Jim Madden, vice president responsible for computing at Metropolitan Life Insurance Company, told Tom Watson Jr., "Tom, you're going to lose your business with us because we already have three floors of this building filled with punch cards and it's getting worse. We just can't afford to pay for that kind of storage space. I'm told we can put our records on magnetic tape." Tom Jr. recalled that Roy Larsen, the president of Time Inc., said the same thing: "We have a whole building full of your gear. We're swamped. If you can't promise us something new, we're going to have to start moving some other way."[12] Metropolitan Life used both Univac and IBM computers. Madden was the typically knowledgeable customer who since the 1890s had routinely influenced what products IBM had introduced. Tom Jr. learned as much from customers as from IBMers, saying, "You've got to feel what's going on in the world and then make the move yourself."[13] By the mid-1950s, customers were confident, empowered, and made sure IBM understood their needs.

A NEW IBM AND THE EMERGENCE OF A COMPUTER INDUSTRY

On June 19, 1956, IBM's world stopped turning for a moment. Thomas J. Watson Sr. died. The word spread quickly through all of IBM's facilities around the world, the press reported the news, and even customers were stunned: An IBM without Watson Sr.? It seemed momentarily inconceivable. Watson had been the "Old Man" for so long that hardly anyone remembered what he looked like as a young man. He had run IBM for decades. He was never going to die, but when he did, the *New York Times* published the longest obituary it had ever written. It called him "the world's greatest salesman" and noted that "to a great extent, the International Business Machines Corporation is a reflection of the character of the man who led it to a position of eminence among the business machines manufacturers of the world." Equally obvious to many at the time, the piece continued, "From the slogans that adorn its walls in eighty nations ... by which it introduces recruits to what may be called the I.B.M. way of life, the company is the creature of the man who commanded it for forty-two years." Watson took a small group of companies "to a position so akin to a monopoly that competitors and Government antitrust officials hauled it into court." The newspaper captured the essential element of his thinking, that "habitually he saw nothing but the best of days ahead."[14] He was a force of nature. In the process, he changed how companies and government agencies went about their work. On his watch, IBM entered the computer business.

Historians looked at him with a more critical eye, although their view was not fundamentally at odds with the accomplishments celebrated by the *New York Times*. In a survey of business historians published in 1971, they ranked him ninth in importance, in the company of the likes of Henry Ford (#1), Alexander Graham Bell (#2), and Thomas Edison (#3), and just before George Eastman (#10). Thirty years later, in another survey of business historians, he ranked eleventh, while the top three were Henry Ford (#1), Bill Gates (#2), and John D. Rockefeller (#3).[15] Such lists suggest the value placed on managerial acumen and entrepreneurial results, two areas of considerable interest to historians in recent decades. Watson's biographer Kevin Maney emphasized his intense desire for respectability, personally and for IBM.[16] Watson was a superb salesman who intensely went about his work. He was so optimistic that, as Richard Tedlow suggested, his activities entailed risks, such as when he put the fate of the firm on the line in developing new products at the start of the Great Depression.[17] As Tedlow and I have independently argued, luck, too, played a crucial role in his career. Historian Steven W. Usselman reminds us that "the key question raised by the entire genre of business biography" centers on one fundamental question: "How do the personalities of business leaders influence the firms they lead?" In the case of Watson Sr. and IBM, the answer is a great deal for a long time. In future chapters, we will see his shadow cast over IBM for well over two decades after his death, propelled by the culture he created and his use of nepotism to keep Watsons at the helm. But it, too, faded over time, as Usselman explained, because "the links between personality and enterprise grow much more muddled and complicated, however, as the size of the firm increases and its range of activities expands."[18] Whatever one wants to think about Watson Sr., he left the company in good shape.

When IBM's accountants closed the books on 1956, they reported the corporation had booked $892 million in revenue; the following year, the company jumped over the $1 billion mark in revenue, growing business by an additional $300 million. When Watson Sr. died, 51,000 employees in the United States and an additional 21,000 scattered throughout the world, their families, and customers paused to mark his passing. *Think* magazine, which still carried articles about IBM, devoted the entire Fall issue to his life. The whole company seemed in mourning. And to think that when Watson Sr. came to C-T-R in 1914, the company only had 1,346 employees and had generated $4 million in revenue and $1 million in profits. The year he died, IBM reported $87 million in profits (see figure 7.1).

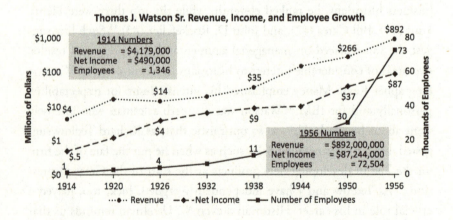

Figure 7.1

A summary of IBM's business performance and growth while led by Thomas J. Watson Sr. Courtesy of Peter E. Greulich, copyright © 2017 MBI Concepts Corporation.

It is routine in histories and memoirs of IBM to see 1956 as a transition date because of Watson's death, but it was not a significant date in the daily affairs of IBM. IBM had already stepped into a new era of business coming from computers, different from the one the Old Man ran. Since the return of his two sons from the military, Watson Sr. had been slowly letting loose his reins of power. Kirk and Phillips had been running much of the day-to-day operations since the late 1940s, while Tom Jr. embraced computing as his ticket to success. In 1952, Watson Sr. made him president of the company, and while the two men disagreed over policies and decisions, the father gave in to his son, grudgingly if strategically appropriate at first but by the mid-1950s by necessity caused by old age and the growing evidence that Tom Jr. was up to the task of leading "his" company. It is why IBMers could pause to pay tribute to Watson Sr. and then keep growing. The year after Watson Sr. died, IBM hired another 11,000 employees and brought in $110 million in profits on revenue of $1.2 billion.[19]

ANOTHER ROUND OF ANTITRUST ACTIVITY

But Tom Jr. had to earn the right to lead the transition. Historians and IBM memoirists are in agreement that during the transition from father to son, the key switch unfolded as the two dealt with a new bout of antitrust litigation. It is a case that is quickly described by most historians before moving on to other topics.[20] However, it cast a long shadow over IBM's U.S. operations for years. New employees showing up for work in the United States in the late 1950s and 1960s went to Endicott for initial training about IBM, its role, and its products. Their welcome packet contained a map of Endicott, a directory of churches, a flyer about the IBM Country Club, and booklets about IBM's Suggestion Program, its products, and Chamber of Commerce literature.[21] But also included was the text of the "Final Judgment" of "Civil Action No. 73-344," better known as *United States of America v. International Business Machines Corporation,* filed and entered on January 25, 1956. This 36-page booklet spelled out in legal language what came to be known as the IBM consent decree of 1956. In particular, salesmen in the United States were admonished to live by its terms, and a small army of IBM lawyers and "business practices" staff patrolled their activities. By the 1970s, new hires and those attending Sales School heard a lecture on its terms, delivered by an IBM lawyer.

H. Graham Morison, the U.S. assistant attorney general running the Anti-Trust Division in the early 1950s, was on a roll, successfully prosecuting cases against large corporations. Looking at IBM's dominance in the punch card and tabulating markets, he considered Watson Sr. "a robber baron" who had been "getting away with it for years."

Tom Jr. was president of the company when government lawyers came calling, and he took the lead in defending IBM. Events revealed IBM's view of the market. On Monday morning, January 22, 1952, at 8:11 P.M., Charles E. McKittrick, an IBM manager in St. Louis, received a telegram from Western Union, signed by Tom Watson Jr., as did sales managers and executives all over the country: "Late this afternoon the Department of Justice announced to the press that it was commencing a civil suit against IBM charging monopoly. The investigation that resulted in this action started about 7 years ago. We have gone into the matter exhaustively and feel our position is unassailable. A letter containing details is being mailed to your office at once. This letter will give you information with which to answer detailed questions. Meanwhile we want you to know that the company's position is strong."[22] Since the 1920s, senior management had quickly informed "the field" of unfolding major events in the belief that IBM's employees and customers would discuss them. To maintain a unified voice, it was essential to create a narrative, a point of view, on an issue. The telegram demonstrated how IBM did this. The government's press announcement was no surprise to Corporate.

The day before the promised letters (there were two separate ones) to the field had been completed, Tom Jr. instructed all IBM managers and district managers "to hold a meeting at the earliest possible time to read and discuss the enclosure with all personnel. Questions are to be encouraged and the fullest possible explanations given so that every IBM man and woman will understand the Company's position." When queried by customers, salesmen could "illustrate IBM's competitive position" by reminding them of all the other vendors, machines, and methods that they and other customers used and that their "personal opinion is the major determining factor in the choice of the type of machine used on each application in each company," not some monopolistic action by IBM. To the public, IBM declared it was not a monopoly, saying, "We deny the charge." Watson Jr. wrote to his managers: "The complaint filed by the Department of Justice appears to be based on their idea that the punched card field is a separate field from that of other business machines designed to perform accounting and record keeping work, and that, since we have a major portion of the punched card business, we are, therefore, a monopoly. We know, of course, that punched card machines do not occupy a separate field in accounting and record keeping work, but rather that they constitute one of the many machine methods being used today by American business." He ended with, "No one better understands just how competitive our market is than you men in the field."[23]

Two single-spaced typed pages of statistics on market shares of IBM and its dozen largest rivals were attached to these communications to demonstrate that the market consisted of $932 million in sales, of which $215 million (23.1 percent) was IBM's, and that its definition was understated, because revenues for four major competitors (Elliott, Friden, Powers, and Victor) were unpublished. All 16 listed companies sold products used for "personnel records, payroll, sales accounting, billing, accounts receivable, accounts payable, cost accounting, inventory and material, property records, financial control, corporate records, and operating records."[24]

Both Watsons called on Morison in 1952 to explain that IBM did not dominate the office appliance industry and that the tabulating portion of that market was small. The assistant attorney general did not buy the argument. His problems with IBM arose from their forcing customers to use only IBM-made cards so other firms could not enter that market; that IBM killed off competition by buying patents; that by only leasing machines rather than selling them IBM prevented the emergence of a secondary market in used IBM machines and parts; and that this practice made it impossible for others to compete with IBM to provide service for its machines. Morison said he could have filed a criminal case, but he opted for a civil suit.[25]

Watson Sr. must have had a rush of bad memories of the criminal case at NCR and the civil suit against IBM in the 1930s. Now here was a third one, just as he was ending his career at IBM. There was truth in everything Morison said. IBM had collected patents, hired rivals, invested in patentable R&D, and maintained leasing and card sale practices, despite the antitrust actions of the 1930s. IBM had always been aggressive, combative, and competitive in dealing with rivals. Now again the U.S. government wanted to punish Watson for doing what he believed was such an American thing—running a successful, growing business—within the cultural norms of the day.

His ethics challenged, Watson Sr. refused to give in to a consent decree. He wanted to fight Morison. Tom Jr. saw IBM's future in areas that were not part of the case, specifically its growing computer business. The case seemed a leftover from before World War II. IBM's legal counsel said the company could be sued because it had monopolistic power under the Sherman Antitrust Act. Tom Jr. wanted to settle and get past it, but his father stubbornly resisted. They debated, argued, and Tom Jr. even shouted at him over it. The case dragged on with endless rounds of meetings within IBM and with the Justice Department. Tom Jr. was president of IBM but could not put an end to it without his father's permission, as Tom Sr. was the chairman of the board. Tom Jr. believed IBM would have lost the case because it had sharply dominated its chosen market.

Then, in late 1955, it all came to a head. Tom Jr. was just leaving his office at 590 Madison Avenue and ran into his father in the hallway. When his father asked where he was off to, Tom Jr. said he was going to see the judge. His father exploded, saying he was wrong to do that, and when Tom Jr. asked if his father wanted him not to go to the meeting, Watson Sr. said go but don't make any decisions. Tom went off to see the judge, and while he was at that meeting, an IBM secretary slipped into the room and handed him a note from his father:

100%
Confidence
Appreciation
Admiration
Love
Dad

Everyone who has reported on the event drew the same conclusion, confirmed by Tom Jr. in his own memoirs, that his father at that moment had truly turned over IBM to his son and that Tom Jr. realized it while in the judge's conference room.

Tom Jr. moved quickly, and on January 25, 1956, he signed a consent decree with the U.S. Department of Justice. IBM agreed to offer machines for purchase or lease at comparable total cost; it would allow others to sell punch cards to IBM's customers; and it would license some of its patents, among other terms. The actual settlement was pretty benign, largely about shrinking markets as IBM moved into tape-based computer sales. Watson Sr. ordered employees to adhere "100%" to the terms of the agreement, which is why a new employee showing up at Endicott received the 1956 consent decree to study.[26]

TOM JR. TAKES FULL CHARGE OF IBM

Some consequences of the consent decree were less visible: Watson Sr. turned over daily operations to his son, spent more time helping Arthur Watson with business in Europe, and began to address some of his own ailments. He was 82 years old, frail, and losing weight. On May 8, he politely and with dignity asked Tom Jr. to assume the role of chief executive in addition to his role as president. Watson Sr. retained the title of chairman, and his aging sidekick George Phillips would serve as figurehead vice chairman until the latter's impending retirement. Tom Jr. had proven to his father that he was ready to take over leadership of the company. It was an ideal transition and widely expected by IBMers, customers, and observers. It was clear to the elder Watson that a different IBM was emerging, with a new generation of competent executives and IBMers eager to get into the computer business. His work was done. On June 17, his heart began to fail and his family gathered around him at Roosevelt Hospital in New York. On June 19, his heart stopped, he took his last breath, and gently passed into history. The court case had been his last battle.

As Tom Jr. expanded his influence, he imposed his style of management, best seen by his first reorganization. His managerial problem was straightforward to describe but difficult to fix: IBM was getting too big for one or a few people to manage. Multiple computer products, each with their own R&D issues, exemplified one aspect of the problem. The tabulating machine business generated the lion's share of IBM's revenues. While that market experienced less change, the sales force defended it in the face of what Tom Jr. saw as the future: computers. The move into computing promised larger revenues, but also increased costs for R&D, infrastructure, and marketing. In the 1950s, IBM faced a growing list of well-financed, creative competitors for computers, a good half dozen in the United States alone. Outside the United States, IBM had to expand into new cities and industries, all of them expensive and requiring localized attention and more hiring. That expansion called for increased coordination. As the computer market heated up, IBM and others introduced new products. IBMers had to do something with older computers and tabulating equipment, deciding to sell them into less developed, less competitive markets, such as Asia. All these various activities were sufficiently different from one another, each with its own organizational and staffing requirements, expense structure, and profits, that Corporate could not manage and coordinate them as it had in earlier times.

Tom Jr. had seen in the army how a large organization operated, while he also observed how companies bigger than IBM made decisions. His answer to the problem was to distribute decision making and responsibility for results. Here was a clear break from his father's centralized administrative style. They had different styles of management, but fortunately for IBM, their styles matched the needs of their times: Watson Sr.'s authoritarian hand in shaping the original company, his son's more collegial and inclusive style for a diverse business ecosystem. The Old Man did not tolerate objections. Tom Jr. welcomed them and indeed insisted on being exposed to differing opinions. However, both men expected absolute obedience in implementing a decision once it had been made.

Tom Jr.'s ability to successfully launch a process for reorganizing IBM's assets and employees made him the fourth founder of IBM after Flint, Hollerith, and Watson Sr. When he was done, IBM was substantially larger than Watson Sr.'s company, and with the help of his brother, Arthur, had become a global behemoth. It had exited the tabulating business that had sustained it for a half century, making itself totally a computer vendor, led by a generation of executives and middle managers able to use Watson Sr.'s sales culture but also reflecting Tom Jr.'s style of management. In addition to the incremental changes Tom Jr. implemented in the first half of the 1950s was his all-important meeting held in Williamsburg, Virginia, in 1956.

In his memoirs, Tom Jr. argued that he feared not being able to run the huge business on his own, so he needed others to participate. He brought together 110 IBM executives to distribute power and responsibility. He succeeded, or to put it in his words, "In three days we transformed IBM so completely that almost nobody left that meeting with the same job he had when he arrived."[27] They came to the meeting after many changes at IBM that year: Tom Jr.'s promotion to chief executive officer, settlement of the antitrust suit, and the death of Watson Sr. It was the first gathering of senior executives in a meeting without the Old Man. They were now on their own. It was exciting and a bit unnerving. The only holdover present from Watson Sr.'s reign was George Phillips, who was due to retire later that year. Everyone else was new and from a generation after Watson Sr. At only 42 years old, Tom Jr. was typical.

So what did Tom Jr. do? He relied on preliminary planning by a Harvard MBA, Richard H. "Dick" Bullen (1919–2005). Bullen had entered IBM's sales force in 1945 after serving in the U.S. Army and stayed at IBM for 27 years, retiring as a senior vice president. He was compatible with Tom Jr. In Tom Jr.'s words, "We took the product divisions that we'd already established, tightened them up so that each executive had clearly defined tasks, and then turned the units loose to operate with considerable flexibility. These were IBM's arms and legs, so to speak." At the top of the management pyramid, the group created a corporate management committee, an innovation that continued to operate under various names up to the present. This committee, initially with only about six members, oversaw plans and important decisions. The initial group included Tom Jr., his brother, Arthur, running World Trade, Williams, LaMotte, and Learson. Each assumed responsibility for a "piece of IBM," with Tom Jr. roaming across the entire corporation.

The attendees at Williamsburg also created a corporate staff with specialists in finance, manufacturing, personnel, and communications (later marketing) that essentially characterized Corporate staffs over the next half century. Their job was to coordinate so that one did not have multiple divisions unwittingly duplicating activities or simultaneously bidding for business. It was a noble attempt to break up political competition but worked only partially, because divisions still competed against each other for influence and resources for decades. The work done in Williamsburg paralleled what many other large corporations had already done in creating a "line-and-staff structure," which Tom Jr. acknowledged was "modeled on military organizations." His description of the approach could just as easily be read as a history of IBM's managerial culture for decades to come:

> Line managers are like field commanders—their duties are to hit production targets, beat sales quotas, and capture market share. Meanwhile the staff is equivalent of generals' aides—they give advice to their superiors, transmit policy from headquarters to the organization, handle the intricacies of planning and coordination, and check to make sure that the divisions attack the right objectives.[28]

Most participants at the meeting grew up in sales and knew how to get things done. The challenge was to figure out what to get done. They had to become more strategic, not just good operationally. Tom Jr. told the assembled executives, "Now we must learn to call on staff and rely on their ability to think out answers to many of our complex problems."[29] That style of management remained for the next 60 years.

Watson Sr.'s "yes men" were gone. Tom Jr. did not bring in outsiders except when specific technical skills were needed, as in law and science. The company could always hire consultants to advise it on specific issues as needed. At the meeting, new assignments were handed out. Al Williams assumed the role of chief of staff, ensuring that a highly admired field executive would attract respect for these staff from the product and sales divisions. According to Tom Jr., "The great strength of the Williamsburg plan was that it provided our executives with the clearest possible goals. Each operating man was judged strictly on his unit's results."[30] All major decisions were subjected to financial analysis so their impact on IBM could be understood. Others would look at the public relations component to make sure decisions enhanced IBM's reputation. Still others would make sure manufacturing could turn in the highest levels of quality and productivity. Watson was thrilled with the results of the conference, saying, "There was no doubt that IBM had been totally transformed."[31] He soon published one of the first widely distributed organization charts in IBM's history.

In the months that followed, Williams filled new staff positions, division presidents reorganized in a similar staff-and-line manner, and managers began writing strategy and operational papers. Thinking strategically and expressing themselves in writing became important components of a manager's tool kit. It became increasingly impossible to sustain a career at IBM without being able to be thoughtful about the nature of its business. Employees had to be effective in performing the day-to-day job. In subsequent decades, one's normal career path involved a back-and-forth rotation between line management (running something like a sales office or manufacturing operation) and staff, all the way to the top of the firm.[32] Tom Jr. and his management team now had an organization in which decision making projected out and down into all divisions worldwide in a structured way. Divisions held the authority to execute with the help of corporate staff. Arthur remained head of World Trade, although he was now a member of the corporate management committee. He reported directly to his brother.

After the Williamsburg meeting, the United States remained the center of IBM's market through the 1980s. It also proved to be the most competitive one. In 1956, there were 756 computers installed in the United States, representing a sharp rise from approximately 20 at the end of the 1940s. Computers in 1956 were commercial products, not one-of-a-kind devices. Commercial enterprises used most of the business-oriented smaller systems, scientists and engineers the bulk of the larger ones, and government agencies a combination of small, medium, and large computers. To build on the Williamsburg reorganization, in 1959 IBM implemented yet another restructuring, dividing the company into two parts, essentially aligning products and customers based on whether they spent more or less than $10,000 per month in rental fees. For smaller customers, the General Products Division (GPD) would develop and manufacture products. GPD took responsibility for the RAMAC and 650. A second division, the Data Systems Division (DSD), took over the 700s and other large systems.[33] Each developed its own sales force.

The reorganization was not perfect, because sometimes a large customer might also want small computers and therefore receive the attention of two divisions competing for sales, but the new structure worked in creating a focus on different emerging markets. Other things did not go so smoothly. GDP gained responsibility for the 1410, whereas it really should have gone to DSD. Multiple operating systems began to proliferate when engineers did not anticipate the problems that would cause for the firm. Success led to more diversity, with eight solid-state computers in 1960 alone, from the 7070 at the high end to smaller systems such as the 1400s and 1410. Two years later, the 1440 came out, with disk storage, and in 1963, the 1460 was introduced, with faster printing and memory. Each system used different peripheral equipment, adding to the plethora of products.

In 1964, the year IBM introduced the System 360, the focus of chapter 8, 19,200 computers were installed in the United States. Big, boxy mainframes accounted for about 87 percent of all systems in 1964, the rest being smaller devices, many of them sold by vendors other than IBM. In the late 1950s and early 1960s, the U.S. economy absorbed about 500 big systems a year. IBM's market share for large mainframes hovered at 80 percent all through the period. The market was expanding so fast that IBM's rivals also initially did well. These included RCA, NCR, Remington Rand, and Honeywell at the high end, CDC with its supercomputers, and Digital Equipment Corporation (DEC) and SDS with small systems. Most were large enterprises that had ample financial resources to take on IBM.[34]

COMPUTERS COME TO WORLD TRADE

Outside the United States, IBM also had a rapidly developing market for its computers. The computer industry quickly became a global industry, although historians of IBM have focused more attention on events in the

United States. That situation is changing, however. Martin Campbell-Kelly and Daniel D. Garcia-Swartz, in their history of the computer industry, covered international developments as thoroughly as those in the United States.[35] In an earlier study I conducted on the worldwide diffusion of computers, it became obvious that earlier historians had underestimated the extent of computing in many countries but that IBM had not.[36] Discussing IBM's international computer sales as though they had begun in the 1960s, as had been the custom since the days of Robert Sobel's useful account of IBM, is being displaced by a greater realization that all vendors were affected by international events, from embracing technical standards to conforming to local business practices across Western Europe, Japan, and Latin America in this crucial era of the 1950s through the early 1960s, when American companies expanded outside the U.S. market.[37]

Recall that after World War II Watson Sr. had to find homes for both his sons in IBM, admittedly a blatant act of nepotism reminiscent of similar practices by other firms, such as at the Ford Motor Company. He decided that he would groom Tom Jr. for the opportunity to run the company. As Tom Jr. moved up the corporate ladder, he demonstrated his ability to perform new responsibilities. Then there was Arthur to place. Watson Sr. solved the problem of Arthur's career trajectory and also how to manage foreign business. Remember that in 1946 Europe had a destroyed economy, a third of its physical infrastructure needed rebuilding, and there were even people starving. Watson Sr.'s assorted collections of prewar companies needed to be restarted, reorganized, and rationalized into a coherent form. The major markets for tabulating equipment, and soon for computers, were the same as before—Great Britain, France, West Germany, and Japan—with a second tier of smaller but attractive economies, such as the Netherlands, all the Nordic countries outside the Soviet bloc, Italy, and Spain. A number of countries in Latin America also presented opportunities, primarily Mexico, Brazil, Argentina, and Peru, but also a second, smaller group, which included Cuba, Venezuela, and Uruguay, among others. In a third category, smaller than the first two, were colonial outposts of the European states of old. These were often in Africa and Asia, where the customers were local extensions of European organizations.

In 1949, Watson Sr. created a subsidiary called IBM World Trade Corporation (WTC) and put his son Arthur in charge of it. Its results were reported in the company's annual report as a separate line item. Country-level companies were established as wholly owned components of the WTC. That is why, for example, some countries published annual reports of their own, such as France, while World Trade reported its financials, too. Corporate in New York eliminated various odd naming conventions. Now each national company was called IBM and the name of the country, such as IBM Spain or IBM Japan, both in English and in their local language.

While IBM's global performance is discussed in more detail in chapter 11, in the 1950s demand for IBM's products was so great that World Trade grew faster than the domestic company. It experienced less competition and growing demand for IBM's products, although the number of computers installed lagged that of the United States. However, rivals were similar: office appliance firms (such as British Tabulating Machines), electrical supply firms (such as Ferranti and English Electric in the British market, Siemens and SEI in West Germany), and start-up computer vendors (such as Leo Computers in Britain, Zuse in West Germany, and SEA in France). IBM was constrained by the U.S. government and the Soviets regarding how it could operate behind the Iron Curtain, which enveloped Europe from the eastern end of Berlin to the Chinese border. China was engaged in a civil war that resulted in the Communists taking control in 1949; they, too, blocked U.S. businesses. IBM World Trade operated similarly to IBM's domestic business: it built factories and a sales force, and it imposed consistent managerial practices worldwide. Overall, it was not uncommon for Europeans to double the number of installed computers from all sources year over year, while the Americans, with their larger base, grew at a slower pace. In 1955, Europe had 27 computers, whereas the United States had 240; in 1960, Europe had 1,000 systems, the United States 5,400; and in 1964, Europe had 6,000, the United States 19,300.[38]

By the late 1960s in most countries, between 60 percent and 80 percent of all systems came from IBM World Trade, despite efforts by local governments to support indigenous suppliers.[39] Already in the 1950s, worldwide, IBM had more computing capabilities than any other company, including

European challengers. To quote Campbell-Kelly and Garcia-Swartz, "IBM was more daring in its attempt to grapple with the challenge posed by digital computers," both in the United States and in Europe. "IBM was always one step ahead relative to its European peers, both in incorporating electronics into traditional data processing equipment and in exploring the possibilities of digital computers," they added.[40] That situation remained through the 1980s. While World Trade experienced less competition, European businesses and agencies proved slower to embrace computing than their American counterparts had been.

WHY DID IBM SUCCEED IN THE COMPUTER BUSINESS?

We need to ask this same question for each period, because the answer is key to understanding how IBM became iconic. Historians are increasingly reaching a consensus on the answer for the 1950s through the 1970s, centering on the combination of effective sales, excellent services, training of IBMers and customers, growing knowledge about electronics, and preexisting customers being well known to IBM. Jeffrey Yost argued that the firm's ability to acquire necessary scientific and technological expertise in the construction of computers proved crucial.[41] Others contended that IBM mimicked its competitors, citing its late arrival into the market. But in time, the tables turned, as rivals mimicked IBM's approach, particularly in the 1960s. Tom Watson Jr. attributed the transition's success to his superior workforce's selling approach. Anticipated end results always remained uncertain, as the technologies proved risky and unstable, evolving rapidly in form and function, while being expensive to develop and use. It was urgent to bring these technologies to market, as over a dozen rivals in the United States alone were engaged in doing the same by the early 1960s. In four books, Emerson Pugh, who spent his IBM years in R&D, described the risks while calling out the uncertainties and difficulties of developing and selling this new class of products.[42] Historian Alfred D. Chandler Jr. and IBM memoirists made the point of the importance of coordinated action, even though uncertainty hovered over IBM's initial forays into the computer market.[43] That is why the initiative at Williamsburg proved so important. It reinforced specialization in those skills and know-how essential to the emerging markets in combination with organized collaboration and control.

When analyzing the early history of the computer industry, Campbell-Kelly and Garcia-Swartz spoke of IBM's capabilities as "phenomenal" while acknowledging that IBM did not always have the best, most advanced computers. This admission was made also by Tom Jr.—"It offered the best systems—the best *bundles* of processors, peripherals, software, and services." Many rivals had good computers but poor-quality peripherals (such as tape drives or printers), or software but not hardware, and so forth. The key was bundling, which is why I highlight the word *bundles,* one for each mainframe computer, a concept Watson Sr. and even Hollerith before him had used in putting together (configuring) systems (groups of machines working together). IBM's ability to put together the whole package—product, training, sales, and services—proved especially attractive to customers acquiring computers for the first time, which for them involved "dealing with the uncertainty of adopting an unproven technology."[44]

Another historian, Usselman, well versed in the interaction between IBM's strategy and how it organized itself, offered another view consistent with the bundles idea. He reminded us that the IBMers in Poughkeepsie pursued the high-end scientific computing needs so often funded by the federal government, while others in Endicott converted IBM's traditional electromechanical products into all-electronic ones that, when combined with what was going on in Poughkeepsie, made it possible for IBM to produce data processing systems. But each remained sufficiently distinct to appeal to specific audiences. Government managers requested proposals to meet specific computing needs. IBM's engineers and salesmen responded best when asked to devise a solution to a customer's problems—the way they sold tabulators. They fared poorly when bidding based on price. The government's procurement process created a competitive market with opportunities to compete that included GE, RCA, and others. To respond to a problem-oriented bid, a successful bidder would need to coordinate solid sales execution, maintenance, and both software and hardware. That is how IBM naturally operated. Each win introduced IBM to new customers, as happened with SAGE. That project alone catapulted IBM squarely into the middle of military computing, which grew massively as the Cold War unfolded over the next three decades.[45]

Usselman also offered an interesting twist to the story: the notion that IBM was humble. Hubris among technologists working on new computing machines was rife, but not at IBM. IBMers did not claim a monopoly on computing know-how. IBM bought components, just as in the tabulator days. Employees listened to customers about how to resolve an operational or design problem, as happened with the Social Security Administration in the 1930s and with Northrop in the 1940s, the first with punch cards, the second with early IBM computers. So IBM occupied a middle ground of sorts, becoming a gearbox, an information center for its customers. IBM did not lean into a customer with tales of fancy engineering, unlike ERA and Univac salesmen, but instead led with business considerations. It all worked.

By the mid-1950s, IBM dominated the four existing market segments: large commercial systems (such as those served by Univac); large scientific and engineering installations; systems that did real-time processing, such as SAGE; and small companies just getting into data processing. For these four segments, IBMers led with the 700s, SAGE, and the 650, and later the 1401s. That collection of machines and markets gave IBM's senior management insights that made development of the System 360 possible, which is why Tom Watson Jr. and his executives could take remarkably bold steps in the 1960s that further transformed the company. Watson understood what was happening and had a far greater tolerance for the turbulence and ambiguity inevitable with emerging technologies and markets. That is why decentralizing authority made it possible to leverage—to coordinate—much insight and knowledge within the firm.

Then there was "the field," the matrix of sales offices set up all over the world, staffed with well-trained salesman who went out every day to do IBM's work. Recall that since the 1920s IBM had tracked sales calls made on customers, which is why, in 1952, Tom Watson Jr. could tell his sales management that "for every new account we sell, our salesmen make 135 prospect calls" and that "of the 100,000 larger business establishments in the United States, 94,000 accomplish all their accounting and record keeping work without IBM accounting machines. Fewer than 6,000 are IBM punched card customers," evidence of the company's early and long-lasting large-account focus. Tom Jr. added that of the largest 7,000 enterprises and government organizations in the United States, "only 7 percent of the total accounting cost is spent for IBM machines and operators." Over half also used other vendors' equipment, leaving management to conclude that their market was competitive in all industries. Watson Jr. stated, "Our selling efforts in the past have been directed toward fixing the buyer's opinion in favor of our products. We intend to continue those efforts. That is the American way of doing business."[46]

IBM's momentum in the early 1950s may also be attributable to Watson Jr. becoming more confident in his abilities, although a reading of his memoirs suggests that ambiguity and complexity made him nervous. Like his father before him, he was being recognized as a success. In this company's case, nepotism helped, too. A small, telling piece of publicity must have pleased him enormously, because his father was still alive and certainly would have seen it. The March 28, 1955, issue of *Time* magazine carried a picture of the younger Tom Watson on its cover. He looked distinguished with his greying hair, serious, and confident. The lengthy, laudatory article placed IBM at the center of the new computer era. In a cover note accompanying a reprint of the article sent to IBMers, Watson Jr., the new president, commented, "My father and I realize that it is only through the efforts of every employee of the IBM Company that the type of reputation reflected in the TIME article can be brought about."[47]

An opinion survey conducted in the U.S. field organization in 1960 offered evidence that the good feelings extended out from Corporate. Ninety-five percent of the 16,000 employees who completed the survey reported that they were enthusiastic about working for IBM. Ninety-seven percent were bullish about the company's future prospects. They liked the type of work they did (92 percent positive), the kinds of colleagues they worked with (93 percent positive), the company's benefits, and IBM's reputation. They reported that job security and opportunity for advancement were excellent. Of course, they groused about not being paid enough, that one's immediate managers did not communicate sufficiently, the existence of some favoritism, and growing work pressures. These were the kinds of pluses and minuses employees reported in other surveys between the 1950s and 1980s. Write-in comments, coming from salespeople working with customers, provided additional evidence of IBM's growing influence:

> "There is a definite amount of prestige in being able to say you work for IBM."
> "The name IBM is … respected and admired throughout the business world."
> "Impeccable reputation and outstanding ethics in business matters."
> "Pride in being with a company that is a leader in its field and enjoys the respect of the majority of people I come into contact with."
> "The company name is well known and opens doors."[48]

The last point would have pleased Watson Sr. the most, because he had worked for decades on establishing IBM's status precisely to "open doors" to IBM business. IBM in the late 1950s and early 1960s had entered its Golden Age.

KEEPING SCORE ON THE 1950s AND EARLY 1960s

A few numbers help to describe how the company changed. In 1946, IBM generated $116 million in revenue and from that $10 million in net earnings (profits). Volumes increased all through the 1950s and early 1960s. In 1964, the last year before IBM began shipping System 360s to customers, it generated $3.2 billion in revenue worldwide, of which $2.2 billion came from leasing computers, and $431 million in net earnings. Roughly a third of all revenue came from outside the United States, from IBM World Trade.[49]

IBM enjoyed positive blips in its revenue, too. For example, it began earning money from the SAGE project in 1952, when it received $1 million, a sum that crept up slowly until 1955, when it drew in $47 million. Revenue then climbed each year to $122 million in 1957, slipped to $100 million the following year, then began to decline as installations were completed, but was still $100 million in 1958 and another $97 million in 1959. That last year, 8,000 IBMers worked on the project. The company kept drawing revenue from SAGE through 1964, for a grand total of over a half billion dollars between 1952 and 1964.[50]

Other U.S. military contracts brought in additional revenue north of $700 million. Commercial computers in IBM USA began contributing to the revenue stream in the early 1950s, making the double-digit jump in 1956 to $49 million from the prior year's $12 million. In 1957, commercial computer revenues in the United States tripled to $124 million and then kept growing. In 1963, IBM generated just over $1 billion in revenue from computer equipment and supplies in the United States and increased that number the following year by over $250 million, for a grand total of $1.3 billion.[51] None of these revenues included the substantial contributions made by World Trade, discussed later.

Another way to look at IBM is by how many employees it had. In 1946, a total of 22,591 people worked at IBM, of which 16,556 lived in the United States. As with revenue, this population increased explosively over the period in the United States and worldwide. By the end of 1964, 149,834 people worked at IBM, of which 96,532 resided in the United States; sales expanded 15-fold and profits even faster, nearly twice that rate. But look more closely at the employees, who increased not only in number but also in type, with more engineers, college graduates, and staff in Europe, Latin America, and Asia. The numbers hide the fact that hiring was even greater than one might suspect as older IBMers retired, to be replaced with new people. Using statistics of year-end numbers of employees (called "headcount" in IBM language), the population increased sevenfold.[52]

While Watson Sr. turned in impressive growth numbers for revenue and number of employees, his two sons combined did a far better job in growing the business while simultaneously shifting from one technology base, electromechanical tabulators, to another, digital computers—all while continuing to increase business and profitability. The leadership for making that happen came largely from Watson Jr. and a new generation of executives and middle managers, most of whom were only in their 30s and 40s and ranging from less than 10 years to over 20 years at IBM. But their success came at a frightful price, the possibility of IBM crashing to death over their attempt to sustain its growth and solve myriad technical problems that many different types of computers imposed on IBM, its customers, and the computer industry as a whole. Their success also brought on the longest antitrust suit in U.S. history. How they began dealing with all these problems is the subject to which we turn next. It is the story of the System 360.

8 SYSTEM 360: ONE OF THE GREATEST PRODUCTS IN HISTORY?

> Today we are making the most significant product announcement in IBM history—the System/360. ... The day so many of you have worked so hard for has now arrived.
> —THOMAS J. WATSON JR., APRIL 7, 1964[1]

IBM'S SYSTEM 360 was one of the most important products introduced by a U.S. corporation in the twentieth century, and it nearly broke IBM. A short list of the most transformative products of the past century would include it, competing with electricity and the light bulb and with Ford's Model T car. IBM's System 360 changed its industry and helped the world transform how it worked, making new tasks possible, and enhancing the productivity of companies and governments. But that was all in the future. In the early 1960s, System 360 was one of the scariest dramas in American business history. It took a nearly fanatical commitment—consensus—at all levels of IBM to bring forth this remarkable collection of machines and software.[2] In hindsight, it seemed a sloppy and ill-advised endeavor, chaotic in execution yet brilliantly successful. Tom Watson's father had made "bet your company" decisions, such as his commitment to tabulating equipment and to keep expanding through the Great Depression, and now it was the son's turn. IBM could take on the System 360 because built into its culture was the knowledge that such gambles had to be made from time to time, and it was able to do so. Large bets on a company's future were never welcome events. IBM's CEOs preferred to ride waves of existing successful strategies, introducing incremental changes. The success of a bet depended on how quickly it was placed and how well it was implemented, in order for it to be cost-effective and timely to market. Executives understood their market realities and the strengths and weaknesses of IBM's problems, strategies, and capabilities. Most got it right, or at least right enough.[3]

The story was about an old issue that kept coming up. In the 1920s and 1930s, there were internal disagreements about such bets, and the 1960s proved no different. While IBM CEOs solicited advice from all around them, had staff scurrying to collect market data, and sought consensus within their inner circle of advisers, ultimately everyone around a conference table looked to the CEO to say "let's go with it." Consequences of that decision were dealt with by thousands of employees committed to the decision or ordered to execute it, from dealing with the media to facing antitrust lawyers, from customers needing to be persuaded to embrace the System 360 to manufacturing the machines, writing software for them, and installing and maintaining them. Each of IBM's CEOs faced the gaze of their senior executives waiting for the decision. Those were some of the loneliest moments in the life of any CEO, but they were also some of the most important ones.

It would be difficult to find any historian who would challenge the importance of the System 360.[4] This one part of IBM's long history has led to so much commentary that it is easy to lose sight of the forest because of the many trees. We can clarify our understanding about System 360 by limiting the discussion to this one chapter, because it is essential that we appreciate the transformative nature of this product on IBM and the computer industry at large. To keep from being mired in the details or having System 360 dominate the company's larger history, several key messages need highlighting. First, this was an important product and chapter in IBM's history. Second, in contrast to what historians of technology claim, while the technological innovations were important, how they were created and deployed bordered on disaster. We live in an age that celebrates innovation, so understanding how that is done remains a high priority for scholars in many disciplines. As William Lazonick puts it, "What makes a firm innovative? How have the characteristics of innovative firms changed over time?"[5]

Third, IBM's experience presented here is of people clashing and collaborating in a rapidly growing company with unstable, and in some instances unknown, technologies. Keith Pavitt calls this behavior "tribal warfare," and a growing number of scholars would agree with his notion that corporations can either innovate or become rigid. We understand the features of either behavior, thanks to Alfred D. Chandler Jr.'s typology and notions of "paths of learning."[6] His notion of the role of professional management, clearly evident in this chapter, extended to engineering and manufacturing.[7] IBM illustrates that internal warfare was not just a behavior of one company versus another but can be better understood as occurring within any large enterprise. For example, we saw similar behavior between IBM's engineering communities located in Endicott and in Poughkeepsie, and between sales and Poughkeepsie's management in the 1950s and early 1960s. That behavior continued during the development and diffusion of the System 360 as uncertainty and ambiguity dogged the footsteps of all the protagonists in this drama. This chapter, however, departs from a recent trend in business history in that it does not discuss the S/360 through some broad interdisciplinary lens, with one possible exception: I present the story through the eyes of management, departing purposely, if partially, from the technological focus that engineers took when studying the S/360.[8] Nevertheless, the chapter describes how IBM relied on its own employees to develop and service this new product line.[9]

It may seem that major actions were undertaken almost oblivious to external events, which is only true at some tactical level in the organization, but it is also misleading since IBM's development of the S/360 was in response to customer demands and with an observant eye cast toward what its competitors were doing or might do.[10] IBM's experience demonstrated that its engineers operated within the confines of the firm, because IBM was big and diverse enough in talent, staffing, financing, and materiel while at the same time cognizant of external realities. IBM succeeded with the S/360 because in an almost entrepreneurial fashion it took advantage of emerging technologies about which it had knowledge, no matter where they were located within the enterprise. That experience contributes another case to a growing list that historian Geoffrey Jones argues function regardless of geographic roots, being based more on its capabilities.[11] The one qualification to his thesis is that in IBM's case all its leaders involved with System 360 worked in the United States.

We deal with six related issues. We need to understand the business and technical problems customers and IBM faced that motivated the company to develop the System 360. Second, once development had begun, the engineering and technological events unfolded as much as politics as they did as technical issues. Third, contrary to IBM mythology and many reports long after the fact, when this family of computers was introduced, customers took a cautionary "wait-and-see" attitude toward them. Fourth, I describe how IBM responded to myriad problems faced by the firm and its customers after initial deliveries, because those problems also, not just those that surfaced during the rush to develop new machines and software, nearly sank the company. I summarize the consequences of this product, which justifies the accolades it received from two generations of business managers and academics. As in earlier chapters, we end with an assessment of business results.

IBM'S BIG PROBLEM

By the end of the 1950s, computer users faced a problem that had never been seen before. Until it appeared in the data centers of large companies and government agencies, it was merely theoretical, hardly anticipated, not real. Nevertheless, it was such an intractable problem that if not solved it could have prevented computers from becoming widespread. It might have led IBM and its competitors to grow slowly, probably at 1–2 percent a year instead of by an order of magnitude or two over the next decade. It seemed that all other computer-related problems could be traced to this one. If it were not solved, thoughts of living in an Information Age would have been fiction. So, what was this key problem?

Customers acquired computers from vendors in great numbers in the late 1950s, turning the corner on automating many of the old punch card processes and doing more with data processing. The popularity of the IBM 1401 illustrates the rapid adoption of computing. Introduced in 1959 and sold until 1971, by the time it was over, IBM had installed over 12,000 of these systems. By 1961, one-fourth of all installed computers in the United States were 1400s (2,000 of them), and over 10,000 had been installed by the mid-1960s. Between 1960 and 1966, the company shipped four-fifths of the value of all computers. IBM's profits tripled thanks to these systems, so any problems with the 1401 were serious. One of them was that 1401s, like their rivals, were too small.

Users found these machines so useful that they kept piling more work on them, reaching their system's capacity. In some cases, data centers acquired an additional one or more, which they parked near their first one or in another data center. Thousands of customers in that situation had several options: move to a bigger system, such as an IBM 7000, install a competitor's system, or acquire more 1401s. They had the same problem with all vendors' equipment. None of these options was attractive. To change systems to get more computing power required rewriting software, since what they had would not work on a different type of machine. The cost of rewriting could easily exceed the financial benefits of moving to a bigger machine. Such a change also called for retraining or hiring new staff familiar with the new system. The alternative of adding more units of the same system was equally unattractive because each required duplicate staff, equipment, and maintenance of hardware and software.

None offered the benefits of a bigger system. For example, if a company had a customer file of names and addresses used by two or more applications, such as order taking and billing, that file could not be shared across both uses of computers. If the two applications sat in two different machines, staff needed to create and maintain two sets of customer files, ensuring errors caused by redundant data and uncoordinated updates to the records. It was not uncommon for data processing personnel costs to consume 80 percent of a data center's budget, with rental of equipment making up most of the rest. Customers wanted systems that were "upgradable" or "compatible"; that is, computers of different sizes such that as the customer's needs grew, they could bring in larger machines and run the same software and peripheral equipment as with their smaller processor. In the 1950s and early 1960s, it was a wish, and for vendors an aspiration.

IBM had worse problems than its customers did. The 1401s were proving so popular that engineering in Endicott, which had developed the system, resisted attempts by Poughkeepsie to build large-end computers, leading to growing rivalry between the two organizations. One engineer recalled that "so intense was it that sometimes it seemed to exceed the rivalry with external competitors."[12] Systems made by Poughkeepsie would not run programs written for the 1400s, the fastest-growing part of IBM's product line, most frequently replacing old tabulating systems. Customers wanted to move to the more expensive Poughkeepsie machines without having to go through conversions from the less-extensive small 1400s. They put increasing pressure on IBM sales, executives, and IBMers visiting SHARE meetings to provide compatibility. Senior management faced the prospect of trying to reorder their half dozen different incompatible systems. Besides the internal political and economic costs of Endicott and Poughkeepsie competing against each other were the R&D expenses of multiple product lines and the burden of training IBMers to sell and maintain so many systems. These internal struggles were not unique to IBM, as they existed in many large enterprises and in governments, such as army versus navy.

IBM needed to get down to one system to lower its costs and be more competitive against a growing array of rivals. IBM required only one to establish dominance—a monopoly—in the market for computers. That last aspiration, better known as "lock in," meant getting customers to use one system, so when they needed more horsepower they could swap out one computer, or type of peripheral equipment, for another from the same vendor. When this goal was finally achieved, IBM's customers traded out machines over a weekend. IBM wanted scalability to simplify production and to reduce the cost of R&D. Competitive pressures weighed on the divisions. If a customer had to upgrade in the early 1960s, they could just as easily move to a competitor's machine, since they would have to rewrite their software anyway. Attractive alternatives existed that sometimes were cheaper, faster, or better, such as machines from GE, Honeywell, and Sperry Rand.

In addition to these concerns, all intimately familiar to Watson Jr. and thousands of employees, he had another. He recalled in his memoirs that "paradoxically, there also was a feeling in the early '60s that IBM had reached a plateau. We were still expanding, but less quickly than before—in the year Kennedy beat Nixon, for example [1960], we only grew nine percent. As we reached the two-billion-dollars-a-year mark people began to speculate that we'd gotten so big that naturally our growth rate had to fall." Watson thought "that seemed illogical." The two divisions he created to compete against each other raised up an ugly side effect: "Our product line became wildly disorganized," he said, with eight computers by late 1960, plus the older tabulating products.[13] How to solve IBM's problems was not obvious, but many people in the company thought they could fix it. Consensus grew that the problem involved finding a way to make multiple systems compatible with each other so that a program running on one could operate on another with little or no modifications. Once the decision to proceed had been made, the central challenge for IBM's management was, to use historian Steven W. Usselman's words, "massing the resources."[14]

THE DIFFICULT PATH TO APRIL 7, 1964

The power of compatibility was demonstrated in the fall of 1960, when IBM introduced the more powerful 1410 to replace the 1401. Software and peripheral equipment for the 1401 worked with the 1410. Customers and IBM sales loved that fact. Poughkeepsie's engineers were close to completing work on a set of four computers that were also "upwardly compatible," two for scientists and engineers and two for business users, all known as the 8000 series, to replace the 7000s. Compatibility of peripheral equipment between the 1401 and the 1410 suggested the path IBM would have to take.

Engineers already had nearly a decade of experience developing new computers. They knew that roughly half of any increased ability of a computer to process work resulted from advances in electronics, the rest by modifying computer designs to rebalance a combination of software and basic pieces of hardware. Did these tricks work? Between 1953 and 1965, IBM's computers increased performance by 50 percent *each year*.[15] Such improvements drove up IBM's profits. Engineers were confident that a path forward existed, but internal politics got in the way of good engineering.

T. Vincent "Vin" (also known as "T. V.") Learson (1912–1996), then in charge of future product development as the vice president of manufacturing and development, had to move quickly. Learson was a gifted problem solver. Watson described what happened: "He saw that it was time to break down the rivalry between the two divisions, and he did it by applying a management technique called 'abrasive interaction.' This means forcing people to swap sides: taking the top engineer from the small-computer division and making him boss of the best development team in the large-computer division. A lot of people thought this made about as much sense as electing Khrushchev president."[16] He replaced the Poughkeepsie manager in charge of the 8000 project with Bob O. "Boe" Evans (1927–2004). Evans had served as the engineering manager for the 1401 and 1410 in Endicott. Earlier, Evans had made it clear that he favored compatibility across all future products. In 90 days, Evans came back to Learson, recommending that work on the 8000s be stopped and that both sites should begin working "to develop a total cohesive product line."[17] To block competitors, since such a change in strategy would delay announcements of new computers, Evans recommended some upgrades to existing equipment. He also boldly proposed a new base technology for all future systems, Solid Logic Technology (SLT), to make IBM's machines more competitive.

Frederick P. Brooks Jr. (b. 1931), who led the design team for the 8000, fought back. The two men (Evans and Brooks) were formidable opponents. Both were engineers, each with years of experience running engineering and product development activities at IBM, articulate, and highly respected by their staffs and senior management. Brooks was not as high ranking as Evans, so to constrain the former, Learson brought in as Brooks's manager Jerrier A. Haddad (b. 1922). Learson knew Haddad because Haddad had spent the previous two years in charge of the Advanced Engineering Development Division. Learson asked him to study the proposed approaches of Evans and Brooks. Haddad recommended going with Evans's ideas. Learson accepted his suggestion and killed the 8000 project in May 1961. Bob Evans had won. He immediately asked Brooks to develop the plan for a compatible family of computers. Brooks recalled, "To my utter amazement, Bob asked me to take charge of that job after we had been fighting for six months."[18] Brooks accepted the invitation and with that both engineering communities stopped feuding and began collaborating. There were still opponents in the company, but no matter, the trajectory toward a common system had been set.

Using a tactic similar to Evans bringing Brooks into the fold, Learson next turned his attention to John W. Haanstra (1926–1967), president of the General Products Division, which produced the 1400s. Haanstra wanted to continue riding that wave of attractive products. Learson wanted to further cement collaboration across IBM's management, so he assigned Haanstra to chair a task force called SPREAD (Systems Programming, Research, Engineering, and Development), with Evans as vice chair. Brooks joined later as one of 11 other members. In December 1961, the task force presented its technical recommendations, the basis of which eventually became the System 360. Their report called for five compatible computers, labeled *processors* (defined as the computer, its memory, and channels to connect to peripheral equipment). Software and peripherals on one processor were to work with all other processors, a collection of machines that had a 2,000 range of speed and volume of performance using SLT circuits and myriad other innovations. Most of the recommendations were on the hardware side, less so on the software side, specifically regarding operating systems. The hardware-software systems had to be competitive in the market, not just benchmarked against existing IBM machines. The plan called for using standard hardware and software interfaces between computers and peripherals, such as between disk and tape drives connecting to computers, so these did not have to be swapped out when a new processor was installed.[19]

Because so much would be new, these processors would not be compatible with IBM's existing products. That was an enormously important point. Customers moving to the new IBM machines would have to rewrite existing software, but only once, after getting on the path of the new system. Sales teams would find incompatibility with existing products an enormous risk because customers would naturally also consider machines offered by other vendors. IBM expected competitors to have systems competitive with its current product line by 1963, which made everyone nervous. In fact, in December 1963, Honeywell introduced its inexpensive H-200 to go after the 1401 and be compatible with it, meaning software on the IBM machine would supposedly run on Honeywell's computer and its future systems. IBM's salesmen reported that within two months of the announcement Honeywell had received 196 orders for the H-200.[20] Evans urged not responding with an improved 1401 because then the 7000's engineers would want to do the same for their system, slowing or stopping progress toward one unified system. The situation looked bad.

Then, "Almost miraculously his [Evans's] vision of the new product line was saved by a last-minute technical accomplishment. In mid-1963 engineers in the Poughkeepsie and Endicott laboratories had begun exploring the possibility of adding special microcode to the control stores of computers to improve their performance *when simulating earlier IBM computers.*"[21] I italicized part of the quotation from an IBM engineer to emphasize the lucky break. Microcode improved simulation of software from earlier computers so well that it became the silver bullet IBM needed, and even led to wide use of the word *emulator*. This function allowed software working on a 1401 to do so in the two smaller models of the proposed new system, emulating 1401 computing. To a user, it was the same as running actual 1401 software on the new machines. Pugh understood the attraction that salesmen would find in this lucky break: "It was a salesman's dream come true. The new product line now offered computers that would execute a customer's current programs faster than his present computer and that provided a path into the new world of compatible computers, capable of applications not possible with older equipment."[22] Sales now got on board, and its executives began pressuring R&D and manufacturing management for early introduction of the new processors.[23]

Watson recognized the gravity of what was at stake:

> From the beginning we faced two risks, either of which was enough to keep us awake at night. First there was the task of coordinating the hardware and software design work for the new line. We had engineering teams all over America and Europe working simultaneously on six new processors and dozens of new peripherals ... but in the end all of this hardware would have to plug together. The software was a bigger hurdle still. In order for System/360 to have a common personality, hundreds of programmers had to write millions of lines of computer code. Nobody had ever tackled that complex a programming job, and the engineers were under great pressure to get it done.[24]

A second set of problems involved IBM manufacturing its own electronic components for the new systems. The electronics industry was about to start making integrated circuits—computer chips—and the new computers were going to be filled with these components, which were new to everyone. To be independent and not rely on others, IBM had to make its own. As Al Williams told Watson, "If we are going to stay in the computer business, we'd better learn how to make these things ourselves."[25] It proved to be an expensive proposition. In those days, a computer factory cost about $40 per square foot to build, and a dust-free integrated circuit factory cost over $150 per square foot. Once the project started, the board of directors began giving Watson a hard time, much as it did to his father in the 1930s when he invested in new products. Eventually, the corporate management committee, including Watson and the board of directors, sucked in a deep breath and approved the SPREAD recommendations. Watson made the final decision on March 18. IBM was off to the races in the wildest ride of its history. The easy part was telling the world what was going on, but that, too, was high drama.

THE BIG DAY AND HOW CUSTOMERS RESPONDED

IBM could not hide what was going on. New employees flocked to Endicott, Poughkeepsie, and other labs and plants. IBM labs on both sides of the Atlantic were abuzz. Customers heard rumors, salesmen were spreading them too, the computer press was speculating, and executives at GE, Honeywell, Sperry Univac, and elsewhere were trying to anticipate what IBM would do and how they would react to it. At IBM, nobody seemed comfortable with progress on the new system, and April 7, 1964, the day the world would meet the System 360, had not even arrived yet. Engineering, manufacturing, sales, and Corporate were still debating, literally losing sleep, in many cases working 100-hour weeks to make the deadline. Engineers moved cots into their offices. One engineer yelled at Watson, who stopped in to see how programming was going, telling him to get out of his office so he could work. The chairman of IBM beat a hasty retreat.

It all became public at noon eastern time in the United States on April 7, 1964. In the United States, over 100,000 customers, reporters, and technologists met at the same time in 165 cities, while others gathered around the world over the next few days to hear the same news. Watson must have felt elation and relief that he could stand up and declare the obvious, that this was "the most important product announcement in the company's history." In the years it took to get to that announcement and in the several following it, he wondered whether the company could pull it off: make the equipment work, and deliver it when promised to customers. Years later, when asked whether IBM would ever engage in such a massive project again, one executive barked out, "Hell no, never again."[26] Watson tilted toward a similar reaction, commenting in 1966 that, "At our size, we can't go 100 percent with anything new again," meaning anything that big. He opined privately to his managers that, "There is no question that we cannot go through another announcement like 360 where we obsolete virtually our entire installed revenue base at one time and where we commit a very substantial portion of our total production to a new technology." He made it a policy "never to announce a new technology which will require us to devote more than 25% of our production to that technology."[27] The generation that brought out the S/360 remained unique in the company, a special clan, bonded ferociously to IBM. While their experience was not entirely a positive one, it generated an endless supply of memories and company lore.

On April 7, 1964, IBM introduced a combination of six computers; dozens of items of peripheral equipment, such as tape drives, disk drives, printers, and control units, among others; and a promise to provide the software necessary to make everything work together—a mindboggling total of 150 products. The breadth of the announcement is hard to imagine today. Then as now, a computer company introduced one or a few products at a time, such as Apple does when it brings out a new generation of 3 or 4 compatible smartphones. IBM's press packet was an inch thick, the internal announcement materials—known as Blue Letters—the thickest ever, and manuals describing all the machines, components, software, and their installation and operation filled more than 50 linear feet of bookshelves.

New technologies in the machines, in combination with existing ones, sped up processing, made it possible to handle larger volumes of information, and handled more complex business and scientific applications. The new architecture was significantly different from what had existed before. An analogy suggests the nature of that difference. Think of an architecture that might differentiate a Victorian house of 1890 from a split-level ranch in suburbia of the 1960s. Like the ranch house, the Victorian involved new building materials, rooms laid out differently, and included electricity and water heaters, and that made it possible for owners to experience different lifestyles than their grandparents had. The IBM announcement promised a 50-fold range in performance from the smallest processor to the largest, a commitment IBM was able to deliver. While this might sound less dramatic than the jump from one to another achieved by earlier systems, System 360's capacities were much larger than those of earlier systems, and the performance range from one system to another was even greater within this family. Forty-four peripheral devices could attach to these computers. Historians sometimes confuse how many processors were introduced so, to be specific, the computers were System 360 Models 30, 40, 50, 60, 62, and 70, for a total of six. Before IBM delivered Models 60, 62, and 70, the better-performing Models 65 and 75 had replaced them.

The central feature of the System 360 was its compatibility with other models. A growing data center could install a small System 360 computer and when it needed more computing power upgrade to a larger one without rewriting software or replacing peripheral equipment. Once familiar with the System 360, its peripherals, and its software, one did not have to learn a great deal more to handle an upgrade to a new model. The name 360 was chosen to suggest an analogy with the idea of 360 degrees, covering everything; it had nothing to do with the decade of the 1960s. IBM published fisheye photographs (figure 8.1) of the new system to reinforce the point of comprehensiveness. The first deliveries of the smaller machines were promised for the third quarter of 1965 and deliveries of the larger ones in the first quarter of 1966. All could be purchased or leased; much software continued to be bundled as part of the hardware, although private software developers could sell or lease software that ran on these IBM systems.

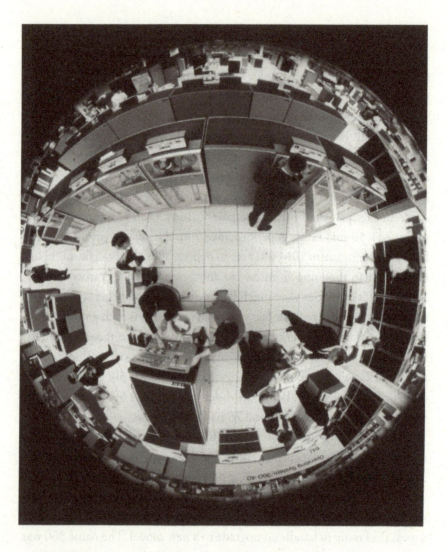

Figure 8.1
This image of the System 360—known as the fisheye 360—was widely used in IBM's advertising and marketing materials. Photo courtesy of IBM Corporate Archives.

As was normal practice, the sales force was briefed on the announcement the day before it was made public. Salesmen for large systems, housed in the Data Processing Division (DPD), heard that the S/360 was "one system" for "all customers." They were told that, "Whatever your customer's data handling requirements are, whatever they will be in the foreseeable future, the System/360 can be custom-fitted to perform his job. In fact, this amazing new system makes possible, for the first time in the industry, a truly long-range growth plan for all customers." They were briefed about the system's flexibility and numerous choices of configurations. They were promised that additional information would arrive in their offices that week and that they would receive training about the "one system in many sizes," which could be customized and open up new markets, creating "new customers" while expanding "existing applications." They were urged to "reach out for new and additional applications to be integrated with current ones for a System/360 total operating system. For everyone."[28] This was all sweet music to a salesman.

Users knew they had a potential game changer on their hands. It was the combination of compatibility and modularity that drew their attention. As one economist touting IBM's new system put it, "The 360 system will be modular; and accordingly could be expanded, or contracted, without need for reprogramming," adding, "The system will also be compatible with 'most' programs of the 1401 system—now IBM's most popular computer."[29] Users quickly understood the significance of the product, but they prudently took a wait-and-see attitude until IBM delivered on its promised shipping dates, while all of IBM's competitors went home to figure out how to respond. In a single stroke, IBM had wiped out demand for its current product line and ultimately that of most of its rivals. For a while, competitors sold their existing computers using the old sales trick of FUD, sowing *F*ear, *U*ncertainty, and *D*oubt among their customers. They had little choice, because they needed to introduce upward-compatible systems of their own and price them competitively with IBM's. The computer industry had changed.

Initial press coverage of the System 360's release offered muted reaction but nonetheless confirmed something big had happened. "The internal IBM reaction could be characterized as quiet, smug elation." One competitor was quoted as saying, "The 360 looks like a clean machine and it took a great deal of courage for IBM to break with its past product line," because the courage involved "opening the door to that chamber of expense horrors, reprogramming." *Datamation,* the leading computer magazine of the day, argued that when IBM makes an announcement it "creates an automatic bandwagon effect." The magazine reported a range of reactions from delight to criticism, with concerns about reprogramming in the air as more than a whiff, despite the attraction of compatibility. The economics seemed to work on announcement day, however. One customer said that the "rental cuts of 50 percent … will force [me] down the 360 route." An economist explained, "The crucial advantage of the System/360 is that it will offer more computer power per dollar than any system now available. This advantage derives from IBM's success in achieving low-cost mass production of its logic circuits and its memory cores," with "the cost advantage" backed "by IBM's reputation, by its superb sales and service organization—more important to IBM even than its innovating capabilities—by its library of programs available, without additional charge, to users of its computer systems."[30] The announcement was an early example of IBM's "total cost of computing" justification to customers for moving to a new product.[31] Everyone wanted more information, of course, despite the fact that IBM's marketing announcements were excellent. "They touched all the bases" while buying themselves up to two years to make good on promises and knock competitors back on their heels.[32]

IBMers did not know at the time of the announcement, or in the next two to three years, how extensively their products would change the world, but we do today.[33] What they knew was that careers had been made and broken, personal lives and marriages disheveled. They understood that they had to overcome monumental technological problems ranging from mechanical and electronic issues to development of frightfully complex software. Customers had to be persuaded to abandon the comfort of known technologies. The company had spent vast sums, in excess of what it made in any one year, in developing this system. Then, after the system's release, they spent several more years fixing software, spending more billions of dollars so that it would work as advertised. For "I.B.M.'s $5,000,000,000 Gamble," it spent every penny it could get its hands on or borrow.[34] Failure meant the death of IBM, and every IBMer believed it.[35] Some historians thought the fear was exaggerated, but that did not matter, because the IBMers engaged in System 360's history acted on that belief.[36]

IBMers got more than an inkling of the consequences of their work when "first day orders" started coming in. In this industry, a company would announce that it would start shipping a product on a certain date, such as six to nine months later for peripheral equipment, 18 to 24 months for mainframes. That delay between announcement and shipping date gave customers and suppliers time to determine which models made sense to acquire, get them approved and budgeted, allowed time for the physical planning on where to house them, make changes to air conditioners in data centers, train staff, complete software remediation, and so forth. The pre-release announcement served as a clever way to shut off competitors or, as with the S/360, pressure them to respond with their own products.[37] Placing a tentative order at announcement time reserved machines, since IBM followed the practice of shipping computers to customers in the sequence in which they received orders.

In the first month following the S/360 announcement, customers worldwide ordered over 100,000 systems![38] These were "positional orders"; that is, to get in line for such systems should they need them when their IBM salesman came around 9 to 18 months later to "confirm" their order. Most initial orders were submitted configured with more memory and with a greater number of peripherals than IBM's sales force had forecast. To put that set of orders in perspective, in that same year in the United Kingdom, all of Western Europe, the United States, and Japan, there were slightly more than 20,000 computers installed. IBM's first orders were five times that number. Not all would be installed, of course, but by the end of 1966, IBM had shipped some 7,700. In 1965, it had shipped 668, and it would ship more in the early 1970s.[39]

For now, IBM had to navigate from April 7 to when it started delivering machines to customers. That is when the company entered the most dangerous, intense, and challenging era of its history up to that time. It is also when Arthur Watson was thrust into the middle of the S/360.

HOW IBM FIXED ITS PROBLEMS

IBM rushed to announcement day to fend off competition and rumors when only some of the hardware had been built, let alone tested. On April 7, to quote Watson, "Not all of the equipment on display was real; some units were just mockups made of wood. We explained that to our guests, so there was no deception. But it was a dangerous cutting of corners—not the way I think business ought to be done—and an uncomfortable reminder to me of how far we had to go before we could call the program a success."[40] Learson had gotten the S/360 to announcement day. Watson then assigned his brother, Arthur, responsibility for managing the project going forward as a way to reintegrate him into mainstream IBM and position him to someday take over the company. He would be responsible for both engineering and manufacturing. Learson would run sales for the new system, "twisting the tails of our salesmen," as the skilled and aggressive sales leader that he was. Tom Watson Jr. thought Learson had the more difficult task, since the engineering community had momentum on the S/360. The risk of customers converting to someone else's machines rather than to the S/360 greatly concerned Watson.

Almost immediately, software problems slowed development. Throwing more programmers at the project did not help. Brooks famously observed years later that "the bearing of a child takes nine months, no matter how many women are assigned."[41] Based on the S/360 experience, Brooks went on to write one of the most widely read books on computing still studied today.[42] Battles and concerns also existed regarding components. Palmer, McDowell, and others wanted to lead the industry in components, so IBM entered the chip manufacturing business. While developing SLTs, IBM engineers learned how to make them. Developments in digital memory and storage progressed. Individual hardware problems kept emerging, which engineers resolved.

As the number of orders for all S/360 processors and peripherals kept increasing, manufacturing became nervous, especially in 1965, when they were asked to increase production by a factor of two. One production manager said it could not be done, refused to do so, and was replaced. As one engineer recalled, "The result was a near disaster." Quality declined and, by the end of the year, the Quality Control Department had impounded 25 percent of all SLT modules, bringing production to a halt. In 1965, some 36 million were made. Problems were solved, and manufacturing proceeded in 1966, resulting in 90 million produced. A new plant just south of Poughkeepsie at East Fishkill made more semiconductor devices than all other manufacturers worldwide combined. Production expanded to new facilities in Burlington, Vermont, and Essonnes, France. Problems in manufacturing ferrite-core memories were resolved. In 1965, IBM set up a plant in Boulder, Colorado, to work on these components also, but it took the handwork of workers in Japan to get production of memories up to required amounts and quality.

Manufacturing became a worldwide effort, causing new problems in coordinating activities and fabricating machines. Arthur Watson had some experience managing IBM's small factories outside of IBM USA but none with resolving engineering problems, let alone massively large global problems in development and manufacturing. He could do little to break through the mounting engineering and manufacturing problems. He was out of his league, as his heritage was sales and general management. His brother increasingly challenged him to resolve these problems. Meanwhile, Learson and his sales teams wanted additional improvements to the product line. Relations between Learson and Arthur completely deteriorated. Then, in October 1964, IBM had to announce significant delays in shipping products.

Tom took his brother out of his job and turned over his responsibilities to Learson, who in turn quickly brought in four engineering managers to punch through the problems. Nicknamed the "four horsemen," they had full authority worldwide for getting the S/360 manufactured and to customers. Their collection of problems, one noted later, was "an absolute nightmare," "a gray blur of twenty-four hour days, seven days a week—never being home."[43] In five months, they had worked out enough of the problems to start meeting delivery dates. In January 1966, Learson became president of IBM. Al Williams retired, as he and Watson had long planned. When Tom took Arthur out of his job, the latter was shunted into the role of vice chairman. Arthur's career was broken, and he retired in 1970.

Tom Watson Jr. left a record of the sad decline of his brother's career. "I went after my brother in the same way I'd have gone after anybody else," he said, and they argued over progress, or rather the lack thereof. "I castigated him" and told "him he'd better make sure the 360 wasn't going to be obsolete before it was even delivered."[44] Some of Arthur's managers were not collaborating. Al Williams was becoming frantic because of the increasing costs of production, forcing him to borrow money and to spend every penny IBM had on the S/360. Some $150 million in parts were moving from one plant to another as part of the production process, with accounting for their costs and whereabouts out of control. To fix that problem, John Opel (1925–2011), a young executive in the Data Products Division, was brought in. He started in sales but acquired manufacturing experience and had a fine analytical mind. In the 1980s, he became CEO of IBM. Meanwhile, back in 1965–1966, IBM sold $370 million in stock to raise cash.

Tom Watson Jr. admitted to being in a nearly continuous panic from 1964 to 1966. He was also beginning to see what was happening to his family: "By now [1964–1965] I knew that my plan for bringing him [Arthur] into the domestic company had been a horrible blunder, bad for Dick's career and for our personal relationship." Instead of giving him an opportunity to shine, Tom had "handed him a stacked deck. He couldn't hold his own against the demands put on him by Learson."[45] Meanwhile, "everybody was scared" that the whole S/360 initiative was going to crash.[46] Tom admitted that his father's standards and expectations played with his mind. Nevertheless, machines shipped, and field engineering somehow kept them functioning. Tom confessed how he closed out Arthur's involvement in the S/360: "I felt nothing but shame and frustrations at the way I'd treated him." He should have left him in World Trade. Tom added,

"As it was, we remade the computer industry with the System/360, and objectively it was the greatest triumph of my business career. But whenever I look back on it, I think about my brother I injured."[47]

Intractable software problems in 1964, 1965, and 1966 kept IBMers frenetically busy. As one engineering manager described the problem, "Of all the challenges presented by the System/360 announcement, none was more difficult to accomplish than providing the promised software support."[48] Without software, especially the operating system, nothing worked. The operating system had many problems, especially in its ability to multiprocess—that is, run more than one job at a time—so essential to making the S/360 fast and productive. Other software problems surfaced with telecommunications, and even with application programs. Programming support became another contentious issue. It seemed that every aspect of software had problems, with the software development staff often described as being in "disarray" as early as 1963. But Evans and others worked out the elements of the new operating system, called OS/360, and began writing software before, during, and after its introduction on April 7, 1964. "The magnitude of the task of developing the proposed operating system was grossly underestimated," recalled Emerson Pugh.[49] Fred Brooks volunteered to help, and IBM added 1,000 people to the operating system project, costing IBM more for software in one year than had been planned for the entire development of the S/360 system. The software would take years to complete, but at last it worked well enough to keep the shipping delay to one month.

It would be safe to say that almost every initial customer and their sales team encountered problems. By then, however, branch offices had been hiring "systems engineers" (SEs) to help. These were college graduates, usually with technical degrees, systems engineers who knew about software and how to "debug" their problems. They became the technical sales arm of the "account reps," serving in that capacity for the next several decades. SEs were the employees IBM had started to hire in 1962 to assist the sales force in selling and supporting computers. They now heroically tackled S/360's software problems. Field engineers, who installed equipment, fixed hardware problems. Salesmen calmed their customers, while branch managers worked to keep their staffs motivated and focused. S/360s were worth a couple of thousand points, and a normal complement of peripheral equipment added thousands more, so there was much to protect and so much to sell. The only good news it seemed was that sales commissions were great, bonuses increased across IBM, and stock values rose. Nearly every account of what happened with the hardware and software between 1962–1963 and the end of 1966 cites the *Fortune* magazine article that carried the headline "IBM's $5,000,000,000 Gamble," published in September 1966.[50] The gamble *Fortune* wrote about proved to be far greater than executives originally considered.

Tom Watson Jr. told a different version: "The expense of the project was indeed staggering. We spent three-quarters of a billion just on engineering. Then we invested another four and a half billion on factories, equipment, and the rental machines themselves. We hired more than sixty thousand new employees and opened five major new plants. It was the biggest privately financed commercial project ever undertaken."[51] The number of new hires exceeded 70,000. A business strategist looking back at the history of the project may have gotten it more right than reporters or Watson did when he argued, "The monumental project was launched with less planning than a typical company payroll system would get."[52] While harsh, it was a fair judgment, which resulted from IBMers moving into unknown technological territory. Watson later confessed that some of the products announced in April 1964 should have been introduced two years later. Bob Evans referred to the S/360 project as a "you bet your company" one but "with less risk than it would have been to do anything else, or to do nothing at all."[53] The amount spent was comparable to the total revenue IBM earned in 1967, some $5.3 billion ($38 billion in today's dollars). William Rogers, an early historian of IBM, concluded that by sticking with the project "IBM could keep most of the market to itself."[54]

Despite the costs and anxiety, in 1965—the first year IBM had committed to shipping systems to customers—it managed "by some miracle" (Watson's words) to ship hundreds of medium-sized S/360s. Their quality did not always match the original design specifications. Shortages of parts, others that did not work, and software filled with "bugs" (problems) spread to the field and many countries. Watson was amazed, because despite these problems, "customers were still ordering 360s faster than we could build them," forcing delivery dates out as much as three years. That delay created an opening for rivals, which worried IBM's sales executives and branch offices.[55]

IBM CONQUERS THE MAINFRAME MARKET

One would expect that with the churn inside IBM it would face severe problems in the marketplace. While it did, success with the S/360 papered over enough of them to give customers confidence in acquiring System 360s. By the end of 1966, customers had taken delivery of nine models of the S/360 for a total of 5,261 systems in the United States, an enormous increase in volume for any IBM system, equaling 13 percent of all computers in the United States. IBM's backlog of unfulfilled orders accounted for 57 percent of all machines on order from all manufacturers. IBM's dominance was immediate and obvious.[56] Its competitors responded. Honeywell, Burroughs, GE, NCR, and Sperry Rand, operating largely in the United States, CII in France, and ICT (later ICI) in Great Britain introduced systems compatible with each other, much as IBM had done, but they were not compatible with IBM's. A second, smaller group chose to manufacture machines compatible with IBM's, including RCA and others in Europe and Japan, relying on RCA's licenses. This second set of firms grew in importance in the 1970s when they, IBM, and their customers were acquiring post-S/360s—the S/370. A third response involved niche players not competing against the S/360s, such as for specialized uses or supercomputers.

All vendors combined in the 1960s and 1970s were often called Snow White and the Seven Dwarfs. It was a pejorative term irritating to IBM's competitors, but it came at a time when other nicknames were being used also, such as "Big Blue" for IBM, after the color of many of the company's machines. IBM (a.k.a. Snow White) was followed into the compatibles market by most of its rivals, which held smaller market shares but were nonetheless capable of competing for a while against Big Blue. They included Burroughs, Control Data, GE, Honeywell, NCR, RCA, and Sperry Rand.

All sold large mainframes. As of 1964, they controlled 30 percent of the computer industry. The industry was valued at about $10 billion, so they owned just over $3 billion of it, IBM the rest. IBM's S/360 proved so successful that five years later, IBM's worldwide inventory had grown to $24 billion, with that of the Dwarfs growing to $9 billion.[57]

IBM's product single-handedly grew overall demand for computing so massively that it raised all boats, its own as well as those of old and new rivals. The industry's annual compound growth in the second half of the 1960s was in double digits year over year, so many thousands of organizations expanded their use of computers in those five years. Thanks to the 1400s and systems from other vendors, in that first decade, big and medium-sized companies across the industrialized world now used computers. S/360 was the turning point. This growth proved so massive that the volumes of machines and users of the 1950s seemed small in comparison by the end of the 1960s and tiny by the end of the 1970s. Usselman made the salient observation that this system "introduced a useful measure of stability into computing at a time when the industry might have suffocated under a staggering array of independent approaches," spurring that demand.[58]

In the long run, another group of companies produced plug-compatible machines that fit into IBM's S/360 technological ecosystem. They did the same to some rivals of IBM. Plug-compatible companies comprised a new segment of the industry. These included Memorex and Telex on the hardware side and for software Informatics and ADR, among others. A different class of rivals included service bureaus, notably ADP and Ross Perot's EDS, and even time-sharing firms, such as Comshare and Tymeshare. Because of the IBM consent decree of 1956, third-party leasing companies proved successful in financing new and secondhand S/360s and, later, S/370s, largely in the United States. Leasco and Greyhound were the biggest players, but many dozens of small participants, even one-person operations, also thrived. European governments entered the arena with their "national champions." The European initiatives failed to slow IBM's relentless dominance of their computer markets, discussed in a later chapter.[59]

GE had its 400, 600, and 100 series in the mid- to late 1960s but exited the mainframe market in the 1970s. IBM's old nemesis Sperry

Rand promoted its UNIVAC 1108 and 1106, later the 9000 series. It acquired RCA's customers and machines. Honeywell brought out the 500 series and the Century 100 and 200, and when GE got out of the business, acquired its customers. The earliest producer of compatibles, RCA, dropped out of the market in the 1970s. By then, the big threat to IBM came from Amdahl, formed by Gene Amdahl (1922–2015), a highly gifted IBM engineering manager who had played a pivotal role in the design of the System 360. When IBM refused to innovate beyond the S/360 to the extent he wanted, Amdahl formed his own company, which produced S/370-like machines that competed effectively against IBM in the 1970s. Key niche players in the 1960s and 1970s included SDS, CDC, and DEC.[60]

Throughout the 1960s and 1970s, peripherals also grew as a business, covering all manner of equipment, such as tape drives, disk drives, printers, control units, point-of-sale terminals, remote job entry (RJE) terminals, and even cash registers. According to Campbell-Kelly and Garcia-Swartz, "By the late 1960s, IBM derived more revenues from peripherals (60 percent of the total) than from the processors themselves. IBM's peripherals also accounted for between 75 and 80 percent of all peripheral-related revenues in the United States at that time."[61] So, it had become an important new battleground for IBM, one where fighting increased in the 1970s. These rivals displaced about 14 percent of IBM's tape drives and nearly 5 percent of its disk drives in the United States by 1970, enough to catch the attention of IBM's sales force.[62] At the time, the United States had the most competitive market in the world. The number of salesmen from IBM and other vendors increased by the thousands worldwide, with large organizations often having to deal with dozens of them constantly visiting data processing managers. Battles were fought over every computer a customer contemplated acquiring, and over peripherals and software, too. Normal sales tactics were applied by all: leading with discussions about "feeds and speeds"—that is, technical features—largely everyone's line; IBM's cost justification and financial presentations, RCA's and the leasing company's 15 to 20 percent lower prices; and so forth.

But once in a while a threat called for particular attention. In IBM's case, that meant Control Data Corporation (CDC), a company based in

Minneapolis, Minnesota, which produced systems for the scientific and engineering communities. Formed in 1957 by former employees of Sperry Rand, by the early 1970s it accounted for some 5 percent of the value of all computers installed around the world. It also sported an outstanding team of executives and engineers. William Norris (1911–2006), a World War II Navy cryptanalyst and founder of Engineering Research Associates (ERA), a formidable postwar computer start-up targeting scientific users, which Remington Rand bought in 1952, launched CDC. Seymour Cray (1925–1996), one of the most important designers of supercomputers, led the charge in developing computers at CDC and in 1972 formed his own supercomputer company, Cray Research. In 1964, CDC introduced the 6000 series, a highly successful family of supercomputers. Watson and his management team wanted to blunt CDC's initiatives and therefore pressed their engineers for a new high-end machine, named the System/360 Model 90, to be enhanced with new technologies. The machine was announced, and the sales force was sent off to sell it. CDC considered IBM's actions predatory and filed an antitrust suit against it in December 1968. The two firms settled out of court, but it was one of many court cases that erupted as a result of IBM's S/360 and later S/370, about which we devote an entire chapter. It seemed to some that "if you couldn't compete against IBM, sue them and maybe make money that way." For others, IBM was simply a ruthless, predatory rival.

A SUMMARY OF RESULTS

IBM was growing the size of the computer industry and its own business. In the process, it constrained its rivals, although they continued to increase in size and number simply because the entire market expanded so rapidly. Pent-up demand for computing was released by technological innovations brought forth by IBM but also by users who accumulated enough experience with computers to understand their value in driving down operating costs through automation of clerical functions, better inventory control, more effective management of complex manufacturing operations, and by performing new functions in engineering, science, and early uses of online distributed computing.

Because the S/360 was the heart of much computing by the end of the 1960s, its users constituted a world of their own. Thousands of programmers only knew how to use software that ran on S/360s. Additional thousands of data processing personnel had only worked with IBM equipment, from keypunch machines, such as the popular IBM 029, to printers, tape drives, and disk drives, and, most important, its software, which in many instances took years to master. IBM continued cultivating middle and senior management in their accounts, not just heads of data processing, to discuss business uses and costs of computing. They proved so effective in cultivating relations that it became almost a throwaway line that "nobody was fired for recommending IBM." That bit of folk wisdom floated around until the late 1980s. User groups like SHARE grew in size and importance, such that by the early 1970s the computing space was largely an IBM world on both sides of the Atlantic, most assuredly in the emerging markets in Latin America, and Japan. IBM's computing vernacular, approaches to computer uses, and ways of doing business seeped into other organizations to a greater extent than in Watson Sr.'s day.

It is worth revisiting the company's numbers. From IBM's revenue in 1964 of $3.2 billion, the firm grew to post revenues of $8.2 billion in 1971. It hired thousands of people to feed the hungry R&D and manufacturing IBM needed to get S/360 going. In 1962, IBM had 127,000 employees worldwide, a figure that increased by some 10,000 each year until 1965, when they started shipping S/360 systems to customers. In 1965, IBM hired an additional 22,000 people, another 25,000 the next year, and ended 1971 with 265,493 employees. In other words, in the decade since 1962, the company doubled in size.[63] Few of those hires remembered Watson Sr. Women came into IBM in droves, especially into manufacturing. Not since World War II had so many entered IBM. While a flood of veterans joined IBM in the late 1940s, by the early 1960s new hires were largely college graduates, especially those in engineering and sales. The employee population worldwide was now younger. IBM had quickly entered a new reality. A generation of engineers, executives, and salesmen were wiped out in the transition to the S/370. Arthur Watson was only one casualty. Tom Watson Jr. suffered a serious heart attack in November 1970, leading him to step down as chief executive officer in June 1971. At that time, Learson, president since 1966, replaced Watson at the age of 58, as an interim head before placing the planned heir, Frank T. Cary (1920–2006), who was slotted to take over in 1974 if Watson made it to the mandatory retirement age of 60. Learson made it to retirement, at which time Cary took over, in January 1973, a story for another chapter.

Did the S/360 cause Tom Watson Jr.'s heart attack? It is hard to say, although photographs of him taken in the 1960s showed a fit man. In his memoirs, he repeatedly spoke of "fear of failure" as "the most powerful force in in my life," especially of not living up to his father's standards. It probably did not help that on January 17, 1969, at the height of his career, the U.S. Department of Justice filed an antitrust suit against IBM. The antitrust case must have weighed on him, because this one concerned IBM's current core business, computers. This litigation consumed Frank Cary and IBM's senior management for 13 years. During the presidency of Richard Nixon (1969–1974), a recession in the United States and the first global computer industry depression erupted; IBM's stock dropped in value by 50 percent.

Watson had been an outstanding leader in the most difficult of times for his company, his industry, and computing technology more generally,

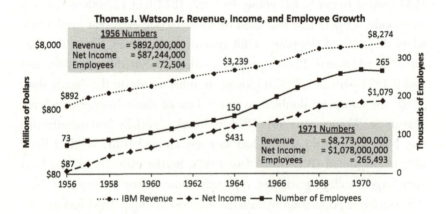

Figure 8.2

Revenue, income, and employee growth under Thomas J. Watson Jr. Courtesy of Peter E. Greulich, copyright © 2017 MBI Concepts Corporation.

and his financial record demonstrated his achievements (figure 8.2). For his reputation, it seemed fortuitous that Watson left IBM when he did, because the company entered a period of even more intense competition, accelerating technological changes, the antitrust case, and a global economy experiencing severe recessions in waves in the 1970s and 1980s. One observer might have gotten things just right in assessing the end of Tom Jr.'s career: "In a macabre sense, his father's terminal illness and his own brush with death were beneficial to the company in that they forced timely transitions of the top executive. Almost every other major computer firm would be less fortunate."[64] All the same, his accomplishments proved so great and lasting that we can consider Tom Jr. the fourth founder of IBM.

Watson & Co.'s greatest legacy was the world in which IBM's products and its users operated, the form the company assumed in its Golden Age as the world's dominant provider of computing, and in setting or reinforcing a style of managerial behavior among so many of its customers in the 1970s and 1980s. It was a magical period but dogged by disastrous stagflation in the U.S. economy and many innovations that nearly crushed the company to death when its Golden Age ended. Before that event, much happened. That is what we turn to over the next several chapters.

9 "THE IBM WAY": HOW IT WORKED, 1964–1993

> I attribute our success in the main to the power of IBM's beliefs.
> —THOMAS J. WATSON JR.[1]

FOLLOWING THE INTRODUCTION of the S/360 in 1964, IBMers walked the hallways of almost every large organization in the industrial world. IBM came to dominate about 60 percent of the U.S. mainframe computer market and up to 70–80 percent elsewhere. Everywhere executives, political leaders, and regulators felt the influence of IBMers who behind the scenes quietly shaped computing events around the world. Some loved that role, while others resented IBM's influence and market dominance.

Inside IBM, its corporate culture, also referred to as "business culture" by historians, was known as the IBM Basic Beliefs—while outsiders called it "The IBM Way." For sentimental retirees, IBM was always about the people and the way they worked with each other. IBM's culture reflected the soul of this company; that is how IBM became iconic. As one senior executive put it in the 1980s, "There really is an IBM way of marketing and managing. ... IBM's approach to business, technology and people has nothing clever or slick about it. How it functions, and why, has more to do with IBM's success than what it does."[2] Earlier, Tom Watson Jr. explained, "The real difference between success and failure in a corporation can very often be traced to the question of how well the organization brings out the great energies and talents of its people. What does it do to help these people find common cause with each other? How does it keep them pointed in the right direction despite the many rivalries and differences which may exist among them?"[3] This chapter and chapters 10 and 11 explain the essence of IBM's massive growth into an iconic firm. Midway, in the 1970s, customers, the media, regulators, historians, and the public worldwide thought of IBM as *the* computer company. When this paradigm changed in the 1980s and 1990s, the resulting crisis nearly destroyed the firm.

Business historians and other academics focused on business management practices have paid great attention to corporate cultures since the 1990s. While Alfred D. Chandler Jr. focused on strategy and structure, other historians began to work through the issues of a more sociological, values-driven approach to the history of corporations and disciplines. As Kenneth Lipartito observed, corporations had both effective and ineffective cultures that directly affected the performance of the firm. Lipartito may well have started the current trend in studying corporate cultures by rethinking "the relationship between business and culture."[4] As he described it, the study of corporate culture "starts from the position that all experience is mediated through some symbolic or linguistic system," since employees (and customers) needed "some framework of meaning," such as the "IBM Way."[5] Historians are increasingly looking at how actors in a company navigated in a defined culture, taking into account their own self-interests.[6] This chapter and those that follow continue to engage in the issues that Lipartito and others have served up.

One finding presented here is that not all was rosy within IBM's corporate culture, despite that culture's positive effects on the life of the corporation. IBM's slow response to changed circumstances suggests limits to the value of a strong corporate culture. One reason it faced tremendous challenges after the 1970s was precisely because its way of doing things aligned so well with the realities of selling, the needs of its customers, and its ability to coordinate and control most of the technological, and hence economic, impacts of these changes as they existed before the changes in technology and markets. The IBM Basic Beliefs were codified into the daily operations of the firm. Next, this chapter shows how the company's culture revolved around selling practices. Finally, we see that much of the cultural glue that held the company together was its personnel practices. In short, the Basic Beliefs provided a shared view of the world, its sales operations converted beliefs into revenue, and how employees were deployed and how they managed the "nuts-and-bolts" encouraged alignment with the corporate mission across the entire company. These three elements of IBM's operations underscore historian Alfred D. Chandler Jr.'s observation that once a company had a strategy, it made the necessary investments to produce, distribute, and service its products in order to remain successful.[7]

CORPORATE CULTURE AS A WAY TO VIEW HOW COMPANIES OPERATED

Earlier chapters showed that IBM had its own style of work, which evolved into a complex social ecosystem. IBM's engineers, sales force, and finance and planning (F&P) staff might follow their own practices, but those were not incompatible with IBM's overall values and procedures. The same held for IBM's expanding international activities. While French, American, and Japanese IBMers behaved somewhat differently, they were linked together by shared practices. English as the corporate language, as part of the "similarity of approach," emerged from shared values, viewpoints, and practices so carefully nurtured by IBM.[8]

Today, we understand that corporate culture begins with top management's beliefs, values, and actions, as they are communicated in a consistent way over time. These can be embraced intensely and create a company-wide consensus. Management can enforce these values with salaries and bonuses, promotions, public recognition, and approvals, often with rituals (e.g., IBM's 100 Percent Club), all codified to sustain the company's norms.[9] As two experts phrased it, corporate culture for large enterprises was (and remains) "the ultimate strategic asset," and that is why it is so important in explaining IBM's successes, later its troubles, and always its behavior.[10] Companies with strong corporate cultures pay careful attention to who they hire and extensively train them, two practices evident at IBM for many decades.[11]

IBM'S BASIC BELIEFS AND WAY OF WORKING

Every keen observer of IBM speaks of its culture as its secret hot sauce. Was it still Watson Sr.'s American values and idiosyncratic admonitions, Family Dinners, and singing songs? Did those white shirts and blue suits constitute the "IBM Way?" Did IBM transform its culture when it grew fourfold from 1960 to 1985, from fewer than 100,000 employees to 405,000, a community the size of Oklahoma City in the United States and twice as large as either Bordeaux or Brussels?

Earlier chapters touched on several features of IBM's corporate culture that shaped how its employees went about their work, such as Thomas Watson Sr.'s persisting values. His son Tom Jr. codified these into the three Basic Beliefs: respecting the individual, offering the best customer service, and working in a "superior fashion." His codification was part of a broader pattern of formalizing work practices and beliefs. Watson Jr. directed that managers at all levels spend a "major" portion of their time sustaining the Basic Beliefs. From these emerged practices first developed during Watson Sr.'s time that survived until the late 1980s. These culture-shaping practices included IBM's famous policy of "full employment." Employees, even during economic downturns, would be retrained, not fired. Another practice was the Open Door: anyone who felt they had been mistreated by their manager could write to the chairman's office (or to any other executive) to have their grievance investigated and fixed if warranted. Instituted in the 1920s by Watson Sr., it was soon taken seriously at all levels of the corporation. All employees were put on a salary; Watson Sr. had considered either piecework or hourly pay as undignified. Salaries meant no distinction between blue collar and white collar IBMers, since each achieved solidly middle-class standards of living. After Watson Sr.'s time, there developed a tradition of using first names everywhere, with one exception: CEOs continued to be called "Mr." and in the third person as "the Chairman." A factory worker could call Bob Evans "Bob."

The second Basic Belief of customer service set the corporation on a trajectory to become fundamentally sales and services oriented. This was critical when for decades IBM leased equipment, because the company owned the equipment and so its customers could swap these out if they were disappointed with IBM's support. That support called for collaboration across IBM, meeting expectations, and honoring commitments: "We found that good service to the customer requires the cooperation of all parts of the business."[12] This belief helps explain why IBM was selective in who they hired, how they were trained, and how their compensation and benefits reinforced the priorities of service and company-wide collaboration.

These actions facilitated the third Basic Belief regarding doing work well, about holding everyone to high standards of performance. It explains IBM's long-standing practice of "completed staff work"; that is, thoughtful and thorough analysis of issues, such as the work of the Stretch and Future Systems task forces. That requirement of excellence made it possible to aim—IBM used the term *stretch*—for high objectives: creation of S/360, overachieving to meet seemingly impossible sales goals. Watson Jr. described the pursuit of excellence as "a blend of optimism, enthusiasm, excitement, and pace. The company was always on the move, constantly changing, always striving for something better."[13]

All three beliefs underpinned IBM's culture throughout its Golden Age, as Watson Jr. put it, "because they fit together and support one another." He noted further, "If you hire good people and treat them well, they will try to do a good job. They will stimulate one another by their vigor and example. They will set a fast pace for themselves."[14] Any ambitious IBMer feared failure, and when it occurred, it was studied, because the real danger was accepting as habit something less than excellent performance.[15]

The memoirs of dozens of IBM employees, great or modest, illustrate how these ideals played out. Most observers of IBM's culture speak about the outward manifestations in 100 Percent Clubs, Golden Circle trips, Family Dinners, white shirts and blue suits and black wingtip shoes, the Open Door, and IBM language. People could move around the company and find a familiar world. For decades, IBM jokingly stood for "I've Been Moved." As one progressed through their career, many did move, especially as they rose into executive ranks, but all were constantly working on new things with new managers. The culture helped everyone work together. During IBM's Golden Age, and despite the challenges of bringing out the S/360s and S/370s, fighting lawsuits, and battling competition, IBM was successful; employees felt the company had a Midas touch, which reinforced the value of its culture. People could not afford to "screw up," and perhaps became overly cautious.

IBM's style of working helps explain the thorough staff work presented for decades in the form of flip chart presentations, then in large slide decks called "foils," and more recently PowerPoint presentations. Louis Gerstner, CEO in the 1990s, complained that his executives had difficulty discussing business issues without a stack of slides. It was not uncommon for an executive presenting to the corporate management committee for 30 minutes to prepare two dozen slides, with 250 others in reserve in case a question required additional detail.

Throughout these decades, IBM consisted of the U.S. half of the business, called "Domestic," and the rest, called "World Trade." While both halves shared the Basic Beliefs, measuring business in points, and the same budget and accounting methods, each operated differently. Domestic was a tightly managed monolithic structure. World Trade was a mosaic of different countries and cultures (as it is today). Domestic imposed its culture on everyone else, what one could call "corporate colonialism." Its domineering mode of operating created tensions and even conflicted loyalties during World War II. Does a U.S. Army pilot who worked at IBM before the war bomb a German IBM manufacturing plant, surely killing fellow IBMers? Should IBM run a national company with Americans or use locals? In the Golden Age, management understood that national cultural styles varied.[16]

There was a third sphere of IBM—Corporate—with its satellite group and division headquarters located in the middle of New York's Hudson Valley. The stories of Corporate operating in its own world were legion and were sufficiently believed that senior executives forced colleagues progressing up the organization to spend time working in the Domestic and global sides of the business before bidding for top jobs in Armonk. It was said that senior management and their staffs in Corporate believed executives who reported to Armonk's Corporate executives were responsible for "their own business," not the CEO. In reality, of course, no major divisional or group decision was made without the blessings of the chairman. Possibly a leftover from Watson Sr.'s days, it was more realistically the need to develop and coordinate worldwide strategies for product development, manufacturing, and distribution. The sorts of debates that occurred during the development of IBM's early computer business and the S/360 continued through the rest of the century.

One student of the Golden Age, Nancy Foy, explained that, "IBM recruits people who value learning, change, and group achievement."[17] Change and flexibility were needed when technologies and markets evolved quickly, while frequent rewards for achievements reinforced the desired behaviors. Foy added, "Every time people transfer within the company, the IBM ethic as well as the technology goes with them, so the organization retains a cohesiveness, and internal unity that is self-grown, relatively undisturbed by outside forces."[18] This was true through the 1970s. As long as IBMers were guaranteed a job and played by IBM's cultural rules, their employment proved secure and interesting.

This culture was fabulously expensive, requiring sustained financial success. Sales, consulting, and factory managers believed the company was run by a powerful financial community, the "F&P crowd" (finance and planning), always whispering into an executive's ear, "No you can't do that as we cannot afford it," or offering up creative "financial engineering" strategies. Through the early 1980s, the F&P staff seemed less of an irritation, but in the late 1980s, sales managers thought them harsh and counterproductive when business began to deteriorate.[19] Finance proved crucial to the effectiveness of IBM's culture and operations. For example, during its decades of leasing, IBM paid up front for the development and manufacture of its products and only recovered these heavy costs over 48 months at best, or even 64 months. As sales branches leased more machines, the company had to borrow heavily to fund their manufacture. In the cash-starved Watson Sr. years, the company developed financial management into a fine art. IBM controlled growth, curtailing it to what could be delivered. Sales targets were set and managed to provide the company with a predictable annual rate of growth, typically 12 to 15 percent.

IBM noticed a pinch in the 1960s when third parties could buy an IBM machine and pay for it outright. These firms then leased equipment to a customer for less than IBM charged, amortizing the lease over 10 years, while IBM did it over 4 years in anticipation of replacing leased machines with a new generation. Changing IBM's depreciation schedule from 48 months to 56 months in 1970 was a good example of financial strategy at work in support of corporate sales objectives. National tax laws and regulated accounting practices, most notably depreciation, affected IBM's strategies. When consulting firms, such as Gartner, IDG, and Forrester, described IBM's financial strategies, customers became more impressed with IBM's managerial practices, while competitors feared and hated the firm even more.

IBM tied financial strategies to how it structured organizations and managed budgets. During the 1950s to 1980s, Corporate constantly introduced reorganizations from "groups" that consisted of divisions to sales branch offices. A neophyte staring at a bulletin board at work might have been forgiven for wondering what was happening. It seemed that the same executives and managers kept popping up in these announcements, taking on different responsibilities, almost as if playing a game of musical chairs every 18 months. IBMers became students of the organization in order to figure out where they fit and to nurture contacts to get things done, such as optimize their ability to solve problems, bring experts to their customers, leverage contacts to obtain exceptions to rules, and recruit resources to meet changing market conditions.

IBM developed a culture of cross-reporting, consensus-building conversations at each level of IBM to vet issues, which then got kicked "upstairs" to the next level, where another round of "concurs" or "non-concurs" took place. The process was often slow, frustrating an impatient workforce. However, once an issue came to the top of the company, a decision could be made quickly and, just as important, be executed rapidly, because much of the thinking about how something could be done had been worked out at lower levels. "Defining the problem" was the slow part, "executing" the strategy for addressing it the quick one. Basic Beliefs motivated many a mighty fight, such as about what computers to develop or with personnel practices, sometimes taking on the tone of a theological debate. However, in IBM's world, once the relevant manager made a decision, no further complaining or debating occurred. Experts, such as sales or F&P, informed the decision-making process and execution.

It seemed everyone lived in a world of matrices, yet, regardless of organizational changes, employees knew what they had to do. As one veteran of the process described it, "I've never seen this in any other company," but "with all those dotted lines and multiple bosses, everybody's on the same side."[20] Recall that matrices first emerged when scores of executives and organizations reporting directly to Watson Sr. and codified into divisions had to coordinate their activities within the larger IBM of the 1950s and 1960s. The use of matrices proved useful in an environment of constant reorganizations. Jay R. Galbraith, a European business professor, opined, "It is probably the most complex organization that I have seen."[21] IBM "uses matrix designs throughout its structure to make key linkages."[22]

But how did financial planning engage with how IBMers managed organizations? Watson Sr. developed the process. He had a sign in his office: "Businesses are built on net profits." Net profits are earned and reported within one year, translated into earnings per share. Management at IBM always wanted earnings per share to increase at a steady, predictable pace over the years, an objective facilitated by leasing equipment in a growing market. The challenge, of course, was to maintain that gentle growth rate in earnings and have sufficient profits to reinvest in products and staffing in support of future net profits. It was a delicate balance, as illustrated by the problems of the early 1920s and 1930s, and again in 1952, when gross profit rose to 18 percent. Why was 18 percent a problem? Spending had grown just as much, hence there was no increase in net profits. Watson Jr. pointedly asked, "Where's the control?" Before then, and subsequently, CEOs wanted to decide what the year-end numbers should be. A process of managing "the numbers" monthly developed, including the ritual of the chief financial officer going to the CEO in the fall to offer several scenarios for year-end numbers to choose from. F&P refined planning in the mid-twentieth century. Often their influence at all levels seemed to be micromanagement, such as occurred when an edict came out of Corporate canceling "nonessential" travel or employee education during the difficult years since the 1980s.

Organizations were given two types of targets: budgets (capital and operating) and year-end headcount. The first was about *how much* money an organization could spend. Management immediately above a subsidiary organization decided *how* it would be spent, such as on buildings, people, and travel. Management determined how many people any subsidiary organization could have by the end of the year. This approach resulted in every organization having an "admin," F&P "staffee," or manager to track—"control" (in IBMese)—the "numbers." Nobody tolerated surprises involving their fiscal and headcount plans.

How did the numbers roll up, especially revenue? The lower one operated in an organization, the larger their target as a percentage of the quota, so that when "actuals" (results) were consolidated, they were sufficient to make each level's targets up through Corporate. A hypothetical example from sales illustrates the practice. Suppose a sales VP at the division level receives a point target of 10 million and has ten districts. He might assign to the districts 10,100,000 points in total, spread across the ten districts. A district might then take its target of 1.1 million points and assign each of its ten branch offices roughly 120,000 points. Each branch manager might then assign to his sales managers a total of, say, 125,000 points. Not everyone was going to achieve their targets, so the delta (difference) between one's targets and what one assigned was often calculated to account for the historic gap between target and actual achievement. The sales organization at each level provided guidance as to how much flexibility in assigning quotas was possible, because a higher quota could hurt the chances of someone making or exceeding their targets, which could have a direct impact on their commissions and bonuses. Organizations would meet their objectives or possibly "underperform" or "overachieve." Overachievers low in the organization made up for underachievers. The larger the business unit, the less variation from targets occurred. This rollup occurred across all countries.

The clever part of the process was that IBM kept two sets of books. One, expressed in local currencies, conformed to local national laws around the world, as done by corporations worldwide. A second set was kept by every country organization reporting forecasts and actuals in *points*, not currency. Recall that one point equaled one dollar or "x" amount in pesos, francs, and so forth. Everyone was using points as the firm's internal currency. Salesmen spoke in terms of points in their quotas and achievements. Product divisions did the same when forecasting pricing for new machines and software. Employees subconsciously converted currencies into points and points into currencies within a month of joining the company. Inflation, deflation, or other currency fluctuations could be accounted for using the points system. While country headquarters management kept accounting books in local currency, they internally spoke of points and only at the highest levels converted them back to revenue, profits, and expenses, all in dollars. Points were IBM's version of a multicountry currency, like the Euro in Western Europe. The system worked and was used until IBM abandoned leasing in the early 1980s, at which time it switched to currency measures.

Other processes underpinned these activities involving setting of budgets and quotas, and financial management. The first and second linked the current year's targets with a preliminary glance toward the next year or, in the case of manufacturing and product development, sometimes three years out. Financial planning involved the delicate dance of income versus expenditures. The entire company participated in annual time-consuming "Fall Planning," a process that began in July or August and extended in iterative give-and-take manner until November, when objectives for the following year were locked down. By the mid-1980s, volatility in the marketplace had led to an additional "Spring Planning." Both planning cycles occurred at all levels, with every account, product, and organization examined to see what costs and revenues and their scheduled occurrence were anticipated. It was both a top-down and a bottom-up process. Everyone around the world used the same forms and had similar agendas and deadlines. F&P imposed measures of performance, often as ranges, such as to expect 16–18 percent of IBM's revenues in the first quarter, 21–22 percent in the second quarter, and so forth, so that if anything went awry, such as during an economic downturn, management knew instantly, across the company and within organizations, where performance gaps existed and probably how to fix them.

HOW IBM SOLD

It seemed everyone at IBM, and most supporters and critics, believed that IBM's sales force was superb. Many of Watson Sr.'s sales processes persisted for decades with only minor modifications. Articles and books were written about them, Harvard professors taught about IBM strategies, competitors constantly raided IBM's sales staff for employees, and customers mimicked the "IBM Way." "Buck" Rodgers, a popular and dynamic sales executive, published a best-selling book about them, *The IBM Way*, in the 1980s.[23] The most widely sold business book of the decade, *In Search of Excellence*, by Tom Peters and Robert Waterman, celebrated IBM's customer service ethos. Such publications appeared in multiple languages.[24]

Since the 1950s, IBM's salesmen have evolved, too. One change noted earlier was the replacement of tabulating salesmen with others more suited to selling computer systems. Worldwide, they were still young hires, usually under the age of 26, and all college graduates. So, they could be molded into IBM's way without prior experiences causing them to qualify their adoption of the company's practices. They continued to wear dark suits, white shirts, and regimental ties. Women and ethnic minorities entered sales in the 1960s and 1970s and also began working their way into other jobs at IBM. A sales background remained the fastest way to reach the largest number of managerial and executive positions in the company.

Sales School evolved, too. By the end of the 1960s, sales personnel went through a series of classes about how computers worked, IBM's products, and even a bit of programming to teach them concepts of how software and hardware worked together. They took a one-week course on how to make sales calls. Some seminars explored telecommunications, others specific industries. Sales trainees, as they were known, shadowed a salesman for several months to learn what went on in an account. Finally, a trainee attended Sales School, armed with a case study of a customer from their branch office that they used to navigate through a half dozen mock sales calls with instructors playing the role of customers, culminating in a final presentation. Sales School was still the gate through which they passed to qualify as a "rep" into the 1990s.

Salesmen still worked in branch offices. Beginning in 1962, systems engineers (SEs) began appearing in branch offices. They knew in more detail than a salesperson how software and hardware worked but were also trained in many of the same topics as salesmen, including how to make sales calls. They solved software problems ("debugging" in IBM language), installed programs, and did technical analysis to see how much computing a customer needed. More women worked as SEs than in sales roles.[25] SEs were largely paid a salary, while a salesman received a paycheck amounting to between 70 and 85 percent of their "assigned earnings," the rest of which they were expected to make up by achieving their quota, which spun off monthly commission and bonus checks. Overachieving their quota was one way to pick up substantial bonuses useful to young peddlers buying their first home.

By the early 1970s, it was not uncommon for branch offices to have two to six marketing managers, each with seven to ten salespeople, one to three systems engineering managers, each also having seven to ten SEs, and an office-wide administrative manager to provide back office order processing, F&P services, and accounting. Field engineers (FEs), and by the end of the 1980s customer engineers (CEs), had a similar organization within separate branch offices managed within their field engineering division.

Branch offices had a "branch manager," still a coveted position, an essential career milestone for those eager to enter the executive ranks. Through the 1960s, branch managers were quite independent, but in the 1970s they received more direction from regional and divisional management. By then, they were increasingly being told the types of sales and support people to have and what percentage of their attainment to achieve by product type and market niche. Nonetheless, it remained a coveted position. Career branch managers who ran large branches for a decade or more, as in Chicago, New York, and Paris, were famous inside IBM and took little guff from a young regional manager or divisional vice president. When any branch manager telephoned an executive, their call went through. A call from the "field" to a staff or headquarters employee was a priority to deal with.

By the end of the 1960s, there existed two computer sales divisions: DPD and GSD, later renamed the National Accounts Division (NAD) and the National Marketing Division (NMD). Office products, largely electric typewriters, had their own division, called the Office Products Division (OPD). OPD was the last bastion of the "tab salesmen" and home to some of IBM's most consummate peddlers, who could charm a secretary into telling her boss that she could only work with an IBM Selectric typewriter, and were frequently able to "sell ice cubes to an Eskimo." Branch offices reported to geographic regional offices. As these grew in size, they aligned by industry, particularly in DPD.

Watson Sr. opened the Nashville, Tennessee, branch in the 1930s, long before DPD, GSD, or OPD existed. Its experience was broadly typical. A half dozen accounts supported this office, consisting of the state government, local banks, insurance companies, and Vanderbilt University. By the 1960s, some of its salesmen specialized in government (public sector), others in banking and insurance. They knew what computers were used by those industries and introduced their customers' data processing managers to others in their industries to share information. In the 1970s, the sales branch office split into DPD, GSD, and OPD, and FE. By the early 1980s, the DPD (now NAD) branch had a sales unit devoted to banks and insurance, another for manufacturing and process accounts, and a third for state and local government, elementary and secondary schools, and higher education.[26]

In 1983, a 32-year-old branch manager, Buzz Waterhouse, successfully managed these "territories," propelling him into IBM's executive ranks. In addition to himself, his branch had a mixture of young and permanently stationed older salesmen and a young and ambitious set of first-line managers. Dave Condeni, a new salesman in 1983, became a divisional executive in sales, while a salesman from the 1950s, P. E. "Bud" Cook, served as DPD's vice president of marketing operations. All the first-line managers went on to successful careers at IBM after their tours in Nashville. The same could be said of many branch offices around the world. It was a continuation of Watson Sr.'s ideal.

Each region had a half dozen or more branch offices in the 1960s and 1970s, and in some countries these reported to "areas" with several dozen branches or directly to a division vice president. Regional and area managers were usually stars on their way up, typically in their 30s in the 1960s, often older by the mid-1980s. Divisional vice presidents were also in their late 30s to early 40s. DPD had a practice in the 1960s and 1970s that its president had to be under the age of 40 so that he would still have enough time (*runway*) to get through that assignment (usually two to three years) and move on up to compete for the role of CEO. In those decades, IBM had ten layers of management.[27] In small countries, the organizations had less structure, although large countries such as Great Britain, Germany, France, and Japan supported considerably larger organizations. Each regional, divisional, group, and corporate organization had accountants, F&P staff, lawyers, "marketing practices managers," and personnel managers (human resources, better known as HR). Divisional, group, and corporate staffs had marketing people to do product support for the branches, "media relations" (PR and press relations) people, and "competitive analysis" people with sales experience tracking competitors and educating sales staffs about their activities and offerings.

One student of the company's operations aptly explained the behavior of IBM's salesmen: "They embody the combination of arrogance, image, pretentiousness and service that gives IBM its present eminence," another manifestation of the company's culture.[28] These employees and their regions and areas kept lists of customers they needed to work with, including companies yet to become customers. They tracked their computing activities, firm by firm, agency by agency, and country by country. Over the decades, these lists acquired different names, such as "key accounts" (1960s and 1970s), "target accounts" (1980s), or "Top 100" (post-2000), with "large accounts" always the most important. Multiple levels of IBM interacted with these organizations, and if an important sale was at risk, senior management would swoop in to talk with customer executives. IBM divisions paid close attention to customer needs, ran task forces, and conducted studies to understand and address customer issues.

For enterprises such as multinational corporations with many locations and multiple salesmen, IBM sales established two programs, called "Selected National Accounts" (SNA) and "Selected International Accounts" (SIA), the former for a customer within one country, the latter for global accounts. Participants included General Motors, Shell, British Petroleum, and Canadian Bell, among others. One branch office would be responsible for ensuring all others working with that account coordinated support and sales. Large corporations with many offices and factories around the world appreciated this feature of IBM because no other vendor provided that level of coordination. The headquarters branch office received duplicate points for all sales made by SNA and SIA branches. It also carried a higher quota to account for those extra points. If a problem developed, IBM's response time was lightning fast, with SNA headquarters staff arriving on the scene within hours or, if they had to travel across the world, within a day or two, if needed. Problems leading to such actions included major competitive threats, large accounts receivable problems in one location that might affect others, changes in national regulations (such as de Gaulle encouraging French companies to consider buying French computers before IBM's), or a customer's business downturn compelling budget cuts.

Customers admired, feared, and sometimes disliked their sales support. Data processing managers did not like the intimidation they experienced if it appeared they were going to make a non-IBM product acquisition. If they were not one of IBM's top customers, they sometimes felt unloved, "remote," and spied on with the efficiency of a national intelligence agency. In fact, most, if not all, salesmen kept detailed written files on every account. If a large account was not an SNA or SIA customer, by the 1960s these accounts endured multiple sales divisions of IBM calling on them, often competing against each other for the same business with different IBM products. The SNA/SIA program was intended to address that problem and proved relatively successful.

IBMers were maniacal competitors, but they had their limits, delimited by corporate ethics. Beginning in the 1960s, every year, all who worked with customers had to read and sign a document saying they had read the booklet *Marketing Guidelines*. A by-product of the 1956 consent decree, reinforced by a desire to be both ethical and in conformance with national trade laws, it was influenced also by the extended series of lawsuits in the 1960s and 1970s. Over time, IBM established written rules to follow. Failure to do so frequently led to IBMers being fired, often within days or weeks of a violation. These rules were meant to keep IBM out of court and to prevent it from being accused of "predatory marketing." The rules were simple: Thou shalt not disparage a competitor, only compare features of IBM's products to those of a rival in a factual manner. Thou shalt not "unhook," meaning cause an account to cancel an order with a competitor. Thou shalt not bribe a customer, which was challenging to obey in countries where bribery was normal practice. Thou shalt not "book" (take) orders for business that were never going to materialize or take credit for existing orders not known to be solid.

Field organizations kept receiving training during the middle decades of the twentieth century. As a result, salesmen and customers kept current about trends in the computer industry, mainly because IBM had the largest sales force and the most customers. This circumstance helped make the "IBM Way" the de facto approach by which much of the industry worked. IBM's ethics, way of talking, and thinking became how things were done.

PERSONNEL PRACTICES IN THE AGE OF FULL EMPLOYMENT

As I was writing this chapter in 2018, IBM was shedding employees and moving work from one country to another, involving additional turnovers. Executives called it "workforce rebalancing" in response to changing "market dynamics." IBMers called it firings, and it had been going on for over a decade. IBM had also brought in tens of thousands of new people through over 100 acquisitions during the previous decade to rapidly deploy capabilities that in earlier decades would have been nurtured organically by retraining employees. In earlier times, management thought employees could learn quickly about some new technology, but it took time to understand how to do things at IBM, so understanding how the firm worked was believed to be more important than knowledge about some new technology. Most employees today would not recognize personnel practices from Watson Sr.'s day. None of those practices proved more central than IBM's full-employment policy. Today's employment practices represent some of the most dramatic divergences from nearly all of IBM's history.

Recall that central to the company's personnel policies was the implicit contract between the employee and IBM, which we can paraphrase as, "You give us the full measure of your talents, thinking, devotion, and time, and we will guarantee you lifetime employment with interesting assignments and a comfortable standard of living." Such a pact does not diminish the fact that it was always difficult to do. IBM management created and sustained personnel practices in support of full employment, net profits, revenues, and returns to shareholders. For the most part, they were successful until the late 1980s.

In the post–Watson Sr. period, Tom Jr. continued his father's paternalism, which he passed on to the next generation of executives. IBM's senior managers of the 1950s to 1970s lived by IBM's values and practices and remained more committed to his values than subsequent generations of management would be. Managers at all levels were keepers and promoters of the culture. They were also punished if they did not adhere to it. Managers hired employees, ensured they were trained, and had to generate enough revenue to support them. Benefits remained stable and funded through the middle decades of the century. These included bonuses, starting salaries roughly 7 percent above competitors' and with increases, medical insurance paid for by IBM, vacation-like events for high achievers, additional funding to take care of handicapped children and immediate family members in crisis, the Watson Scholarship for college-bound IBM children who exhibited outstanding academic performance, IBM stock purchases at a discount, and a pension, among others. Employees could apply to have the company fund local community projects in which they were involved. In exchange for benefits, IBMers were expected to support the company and to embrace IBM's culture and its rules.

An element of all of IBM's personnel practices concerned how it treated what today are called "protected groups," including ethnic and religious minorities, people with disabilities, and women. IBM had a long history of protecting, nurturing, and recruiting such people. Altruism served as a reason, but another was the hard fact that they represented pockets of potential employees. Beginning in 1943, when the pool of potential male employees in the United States dried up because of the military draft, IBM began hiring handicapped people, including blind and mentally challenged workers. They were offered ever more opportunities. In the early 1930s, service staff in factories included women. Women entered field engineering's ranks in growing numbers in the 1940s and became systems engineers and salespeople in the 1960s. Women worked their way up the management ladder. By the early 1970s, IBM had formalized hiring and promotion of women to tap into a talent pool already in the firm and in response to affirmative action laws in the United States.[29] In 2012, IBM appointed its first female CEO, Virginia "Ginni" Rometty, who started her IBM career as an SE. By the end of the 1980s, nearly a third of IBM's managers were women.

IBM's response to minorities and women was an example of how it often embraced practices widely adopted by other large U.S. and European corporations. The civil rights and women's rights movements in the United States in the 1960s, followed by U.S. federal civil rights laws and regulations mandating inclusion of protected groups in employment, reinforced the authority of personnel departments to implement the kinds of formal processes described here. Over 95 percent of corporations with 5,000 or more employees already had personnel departments by the early 1930s. By the time IBMers were developing affirmative action processes in the 1960s, other firms were doing the same to avoid legal battles with individuals and federal authorities, while personnel managers were touting the benefits of tapping into a larger, more diverse internal hiring pool.[30] By 1970, 20 percent of all large corporations had formal programs similar to IBM's, and not until 1991 did even half of all large U.S. companies have processes that included protections against discrimination, training on diversity, and measurement systems to track progress toward diversity.[31] While the U.S. government backed off forcing corporations to implement such programs during the Reagan administration, these had proven so effective that many companies continued with them, including IBM. IBM's affirmative action initiatives started at the same time as the 20 percent, but built on its earlier experiences more extensively than most and then shared its experiences with customers, burnishing its image as a progressively managed enterprise.

On the U.S. side of the company, prior to the 1950s, most IBMers were white men. The first observable change came with the influx of Jewish scientists and engineers in the 1950s, with the increase in women soon after. The inclusiveness of various groups occurred worldwide. IBMers worked in a meritocracy that valued results and adherence to IBM's values. A great sales manager who abused his employees would go nowhere in the company. At the other extreme, someone closely tied to a rising executive could ride up the corporate ladder but still had to be competent and exhibit strong interpersonal skills. IBM was not, however, egalitarian. A slight caste system existed. At the top of the social order were sales personnel from sales people to senior executives. IBM's CEOs were all in sales at one time. IBMers and customers thought the importance given to leadership from sales was one of IBM's success factors, because these people paid less attention to the features of a technology and more to solving a customer's problems. The majority of senior executives were U.S. citizens, to the consternation of ambitious IBMers in Europe during the Golden Age, an issue discussed further.

Managers comprised a powerful minority within IBM's population. Less than 5 percent of IBMers became executives, while approximately 12–15 percent were managers during the Golden Age, the percentage being lower in the 1950s, higher in the 1980s. A manager hired, fired, and controlled the work of employees. In the 1960s and 1970s, one had to have two or more employees to be a manager, but later some held the title but had no employees reporting to them. By the late 1990s, as budgets tightened and organizations flattened, some managers had as many as 50 employees reporting directly to them. Managers were not treated gently the way employees were. They were expected to perform, and when they didn't, they were brutally pulled out of their jobs, some literally overnight. If union activity took place within one's organization (*unit*), that manager could easily be taken out of his or her position. An executive whose organization failed to accomplish its objective could be pressed into early retirement, be denied further promotions, or be put into the "penalty box," especially executives. The penalty box remained widely used, including during the Golden Age, when, for example, the PC side of the business became a career killer for potential CEOs who had difficulty in making that business prosper. They could wait it out or, as many did, leave IBM. So managers remained an insecure lot, especially as the Watsonian paternalism began to wear off. As one IBMer observed, "The nearer you get to the center of IBM, the more you have to conform. More of your attitudes are determined for you up there."[32] Branch managers were saying the same thing by the early 1980s. Nevertheless, they were expected to be "tough," whereas being "soft" harmed one's career advancement. While being tough, they had to be gentle with their employees, persuading and motivating them. Early female executives had to be even better than men at these two roles.

One unattractive part of IBM's managerial practices was the paucity of non-U.S. senior management either at corporate headquarters in Armonk, New York (the new HQ since the early 1960s), or on the board of directors. The one exception repeatedly trotted out by IBM apologists was Jacques Maisonrouge (1924–2012), who joined IBM in 1948, worked his way up in sales in Europe to become chairman of the board of World Trade in 1976, and retired in 1984, but even he complained about the lack of international representation.[33] The wholly owned national subsidiaries, however, were often 95 to 99 percent populated with local nationals. American management worked in a national subsidiary at critical moments, as in Europe just after World War II, if it experienced a round of corruption or if it was not performing as required.

Nothing attracted more attention from management than a personnel problem. If an individual "open doored" his management, there was a process involving immediate appointment of an investigator, who reached out to the offended employee within 24 hours of the employee's lodging of a complaint. In the Golden Age, these complaints ranged from a perceived unfair appraisal to sexual harassment, and occasionally bias on the basis of age or race. To avoid the first problem, IBM developed a process that described each employee's job and objectives, ideally to gain the employee's commitment to the desired goals, and included mandatory appraisals at midyear and at the end of the year. The process was designed to avoid having anybody being surprised by an appraisal. Employees were given formal and informal opportunities to improve their performance. Managers learned to "keep book," documenting an employee's performance; otherwise, if they fired someone, invariably the lawyers and human resources staff would overturn their action.

All employees were anonymously surveyed for their opinions of their management, jobs, and about IBM.[34] Their local management met with groups of them to discuss how to address areas of concern, some of which they feared might lead to establishment of unions.[35] Meticulous records of these events were kept. If management became aware of union organizing, investigatory teams formed to find ways to discourage formation of a union, unless required by law. Unions did not exist in most of IBM's national companies. Management believed unions would interfere with the company's ability to change the roles of their employees or to move them about as needed. Salaries and benefits were hardly issues, since IBM paid competitive salaries and offered benefits similar to those of unionized companies.

Opinion surveys informed management about the mood of employees. In 1968, despite the stresses of S/360 on everyone at IBM, 40 percent of surveyed employees thought IBM was one of the best companies to work for, although their work life was filled with tensions and long hours. In 1972, at the time of a global computer industry downturn, that 40 percent had shrunk to 27 percent. As the firm grew in the 1960s, it also became bureaucratic and too process and rule driven. In 1968, already 49 percent of employees reported their managers were insisting that people adhere to company rules rather than to the intent of company practices. In 1972, that number climbed to 72 percent, and it remained there or at higher levels through the 1980s. Employee morale dipped in the late 1960s to early 1970s and rose in the second half of the 1970s and early 1980s. That earlier feedback concerned corporate officials. As the era of the S/360 receded, younger employees complained that their work was not as challenging as they wanted, again an aspect of working at IBM uncovered through opinion surveys. These employees reported that work pressures and objectives increased.

What happened when business conditions warranted reductions in headcount, given the full-employment operating principle? The recession that began in 1970 made it clear to Corporate that it had too many employees, so hiring slowed or stopped. But IBM could not dismiss thousands quickly, nor could it avoid the problem. DPD in the United States, for example, needed to shrink by 14,000 people. The bulk of the excess employees shrank through normal attrition, such as dismissals for poor performance, retirements, and people leaving IBM to work for other enterprises. "Excess resources" became a recurrent topic at staff meetings up and down the organization worldwide until the recession ended a year later. Task forces addressed the problem arising in the early 1970s and mid-1980s by offering early retirement programs in exchange for additional accruals to their pensions or outright one- to two-year salary bonuses. Programs were funded out of operating budgets and gross profits and worked to reduce the number of employees. A less successful second strategy, called "back to the field," by which overstaffed division, plant, and corporate staffs were transferred to branch offices to help sell as a way of keeping them employed, did not work well, as not all employees adjusted well to working in branch offices.

Changes in IBM's products and organizations encouraged employees to leave. Annual turnover ranged between 5 and 7 percent, higher if there was an emphasis on reducing "headcount." In the second half of the 1980s, the process sped up, although as late as 1983, *Think* magazine, now only for employees, carried an article assuring all of IBM's continuing commitment to full employment, while staffs in Poughkeepsie and other sites were being offered "early out" programs. Walter E. "Walt" Burdick, IBM's vice president of personnel, told employees that "the antithesis of respect for the individual would be to take somebody's job away because of factors he or she had no control over—say, a recession, the loss of a contract, a declining workload." That issue of *Think* led with the tag line, "When the economy runs into stormy weather, it's nice to know the commitment is there"—just several years before IBM entered a near-death crisis that ended "full employment."[36]

A dark underbelly of IBM's full-employment policy was its effect on ambition. For example, if someone had not made it to middle management in sales by age 40, they understood that they had plateaued and needed to decide whether they could accept another 15 to 20 years without further advances or should leave IBM to pursue other opportunities. Since career paths had become so rigid by the mid-1970s, one could reasonably project how far they were going to go and through what jobs. Many felt so comfortable in "Mother IBM" that they remained.

Bob McGrath (b. 1929), an American IBMer in the 1950s and 1960s, began publishing an alumni directory of ex-IBMers in 1972.[37] By 1973, his list had 1,500 names, a number that grew for decades. McGrath thought that in the early 1970s, on average, 2,000 people worldwide left IBM each year out of a population of 250,000 to 260,000 people.[38] His numbers seem too low, since many people did not appear in his database. By the 1970s, annual turnover hovered at between 5 and 8 percent, below the average for most large U.S. corporations but higher than in Western Europe.[39] Some went into wonderful jobs, such as vice presidents, presidents, and chairmen of companies; IBMers who knew they could not become CEOs at IBM, for example. Over a third of those McGrath tracked stayed in the data processing world, which helped to reinforce IBM's dominance. They took their IBM ethics and business practices with them, along with IBM's long-standing policy of not participating in corrupt practices.

We have looked inside IBM during its Golden Age and seen how a large, successful enterprise built on its corporate culture and earlier efforts, thereby facilitating a period of profound, if difficult-to-achieve, growth, but to complete a full picture of that era, we now explore external manifestations of IBM's activities. Through that exercise, we uncover seeds of its future problems, too.

10 "THE IBM WAY": WHAT THE WORLD SAW, 1964–1993

> In an interdependent organization, a community of effort is imperative.
> —THOMAS J. WATSON JR.[1]

IBM BECAME A large firm along with other American and international ones. Each employee learned how to do that as they went along, from senior executives to the newest IBM salesperson, sharing insights with each other, so much so that part of IBM's success can be attributed to its creation and dominance of an information technology ecosystem in the 1960s to the 1980s involving most large businesses and many democratic government agencies. Its influence and behavior expanded and changed, driven by such nontechnical issues as strategy development, accounting and financial strategies, and managerial worldviews, often in response to regulatory and legal regimes. The greatest number of large firms were headquartered in the United States, within easy reach of over half of IBM's employees. By 1973, IBM ranked among the ten largest corporations, along with General Electric, Chrysler, Mobil Oil, Texaco, ITT, Royal Dutch Shell, General Motors, Exxon, and Unilever.[2] Historians observed that part of the success of IBM and other firms was their ability to leverage emerging technologies, while the Chandlerian model of how large enterprises worked endured.[3]

To situate IBM in the institutional histories of corporations, this chapter addresses four topics in the following order. First, we review what it did to justify our calling the middle decades of the twentieth century IBM's Golden Age, when it went from being an up-and-coming computer company to being *the* dominant firm in that market. Next, I describe the emergence of the IBM ecocenter, suggesting that the company's success was partly the result of its influence on a wide range of views and activities that take academic debates about "path dependency" beyond traditional accounts of that notion. Discussion of its ecosystem contributes insights into how companies succeed and fail, particularly where new technological regimes emerge quickly. I then discuss IBM's financial results. This chapter ends with a description of the price IBM paid for its successes in the Golden Age, what I label undercurrents, which disrupted the trajectory of IBM's success, the subject of all subsequent chapters.

THE GOLDEN AGE OF MAINFRAMES

The late 1950s to the mid-1980s were IBM's Golden Age of mainframes, when it dominated the large worldwide computer market. In this period, IBM became known as *the* computer company. It was a glorious time of market dominance; rising stock prices, earnings per share, revenue, and profits; and sheer size. Many business professors and the business media saw IBM as the smartest-run enterprise in the world. Newly minted MBAs wanted to work for IBM; a job there was very "cool." Watson Sr. would have been proud to see that IBM had become one of the most respected firms on the planet, but, as Watson knew, too, there existed dangerous currents of legal, technical, and competitive turbulence to navigate. But in the 1960s, IBM was on a roll.

The heroes two chapters ago were the engineers who developed the S/360. Would the R&D momentum they had built propel IBM through the 1970s and 1980s? The relentless march of new technologies kept them on their toes. But now they had created the base technologies underpinning the S/360. In the next two decades, the sales staff at IBM took the lead, with senior management driving further expansion. The late 1960s, 1970s, and 1980s became almost as frenetic as the early 1960s, but in different ways.

In the 1960s, competitors entered the market with peripherals and, later, computers. Lawsuits over patents, but mainly about IBM's growing market dominance, proved so serious to IBM that we discuss them as a group later rather than as piecemeal parts of IBM's growing market presence. In the end, they did not stop IBM's momentum, nor did national governments bent on promoting their "national champions," but one legally affected issue needs immediate attention. IBM's bundled software was convenient for customers. IBM's bundling practice hindered, but did not stop, the emergence of software firms or software service providers. Recall that to stop an impending antitrust suit by the U.S. Department of Justice, in 1968 IBM unbundled software from hardware leases. Customers could pick and choose from 17 software products.[4] IBM presented an image that it was giving its competitors the opportunity to sell products and services.

Customers were surprised and confused. One branch manager remembered that "mass trauma swept through many of IBM's largest customers as they realized they had to pay forty dollars per hour for a systems engineer who most knew only earned from fifteen to twenty-five thousand dollars per year. IBM's major accounts stayed awake nights trying to figure out how many millions of extra dollars they might have to spend."[5] This branch manager, Max Beardslee, recalled that sales offices also went through similar angst as they sorted out implications of the announcement, "since most major customers wanted to digest this fundamental change in IBM's pricing before moving ahead with any new purchase commitments. Computer installation decisions were delayed at every level, wreaking havoc on the commission-dependent sales force and throwing plant shipment schedules into an unpredictable mess."[6] Customers for smaller systems were relatively immune from the crisis, because their costs were small.

In manufacturing, Bob Evans and his colleagues were still fixing S/360 problems and reacting to evolving technologies when Corporate was becoming concerned about new threats to IBM. Recall that in 1964 the core modules in the computer were based on SLTs, early computer chips, but the new technologies that were emerging were better in many ways, most notably monolithic chips, which used one silicon chip for an integrated circuit, unlike SLT, which required four chips to do the same work. Engineers inside and outside of IBM embraced the new technology. In June 1970, IBM introduced two computers that relied on the new technology, and it gave these machines a new name: System/370 (figure 10.1). The first two, Models 155 and 165, were aimed at the high end of the market. These proved popular

Figure 10.1
IBM System 370 Model 158, introduced in 1972, became a computer workhorse for large organizations. Photo courtesy of IBM Corporate Archives.

because they were reliable, cost-effective, fast, and the right size for many new uses of computing.

IBM improved price performance by using monolithic chips and new memories (called *cache*), and additional models of the S/370 relied completely on these chips. In September 1970, virtual memory became available with the Model 145, making it possible to run several copies of an operating system (or applications) within the same system as if the one computer were several. The Model 145 was also popular for the same reasons as the Model 158. This went on just as the computer industry experienced its first global recession. The introduction of so many new computers came more quickly than IBM's rivals could respond to, especially in Europe, and so IBM was able to expand at the expense of its rivals. But the cost of computing hardware also was dropping quickly, so management worried about how best to proceed.

Just as with the SPREAD task force, senior management launched another one, called FS—Future Systems. It began meeting in the summer of 1971. Its members were tasked with figuring out new ways of organizing computer memory, the feature most subject to technological change, and with addressing the cost of developing software, which remained labor intensive. Problems with software were actually more urgent, since about two-thirds of the cost of operating a computer system was driven by software and related services, in some data centers about 80 percent. Could FS come up with a replacement for S/370? As with earlier "new" technologies, sales and customers expressed concern about the cost of transition but were equally interested in new functions. By the end of the 1960s, IBM's S/360 operating system and architecture were de facto global standards. Even the Soviets, who decided not to create their own computer technology, standardized on IBM's S/360 by retroengineering IBM's machines and illegally copying its software. FS dragged on in the early 1970s, leading Corporate to shut it down and to continue introducing new S/370-based models.

Radically new mainframe computing was not to be. In 1975, IBM introduced the System 370 Models 158 and 168, which proved to be just as popular as the earlier Models 155 and 165. They cost less, had more capacity (memory, ability to process more data, speed), and provided a pathway for current users of smaller IBM computers needing to increase computing capacity. Beginning in 1977, IBM began introducing a family of computers to replace the S/370s at the high end, called "303X" processors and named the 3031, 3032, and 3033. Their operating systems were updated versions of those used by large S/370s and, earlier, in the S/360s. These machines were designed to compete against Amdahl Corporation, offering a wide breadth of processing capability. For example, the 3033 represented about a 100 percent increase in processing power over that of the 3032. Large corporations and government departments were the intended users.

In the late 1970s, IBM introduced new mainframes at the low end of its S/360-S/370 heritage markets, the 4331 and 4341. These were popular with sales reps and their customers. They used existing peripheral equipment and operating and application software, were relatively inexpensive, and took up little room—about the space of a home freezer. They were so inexpensive that the cost of computing from all vendors dropped over the next several years. Customers swapped out midsized and smaller mainframes for them or acquired several of the smaller models (4331s) as remote processors to "talk" with larger ones in the main data centers.

As in the 1960s, rivals responded in familiar ways. Some dropped out, notably RCA and GE, while others introduced machines to compete with S/370s and 4300s. But the majority wanted to protect their existing "install base" by bringing out machines that allowed their customers to continue using new, less expensive technologies without having to shift to IBM. Those retaining a strategy of using systems incompatible with IBM's included Burroughs, Honeywell, Sperry Rand, and NCR, the vendors that competed against IBM in the 1960s.

Amdahl followed a different path by providing "plug compatible" machines that could be swapped out from IBM S/370s. That strategy proved successful because the machines were priced low enough relative to IBM's to warrant a customer taking a hard look at them, and because they offered momentary technical advantages, tit-for-tat, all through the 1970s and 1980s. Amdahl's rivalry with IBM unfolded at the high end, particularly against the IBM S/370 168, although battles over Models 158s, 145s, 148s, and the remaining 165s were not uncommon. The "mainframe wars" were conducted with dueling financial arguments waged in the offices of financial executives more than with "feeds and speeds" in the data centers. Gene Amdahl did well in the 1970s, less so in the 1980s. The Data Processing Division (DPD), where IBM housed its largest accounts, conducted most of IBM's warfare, less so the General Systems Division (GSD), home to smaller customers.

Plug-compatible peripheral vendors also went after IBM, often using ex-IBMers who could make larger salaries and bonuses by bringing to these new rivals their IBM know-how or went on to establish their own firms.

Some events seemed to attract a great deal of attention. For example, twelve employees opened up Information Storage Systems in San Jose after collectively quitting IBM in December 1967. That was unheard of. Before that event, an IBM office or laboratory would lose an engineer here or there. There had always been a low but steady turnover in sales, all quite normal for that profession in any industry. Cases of desertion from the mother company always seemed shocking. People rarely quit IBM voluntarily. The fact that employees frequently left other vendors did not matter. It was simply not done at IBM, so when it happened, management saw it as a bigger problem than other firms would have, for departures struck at the heart of IBM's way of doing things.

Unplanned departures occurred in strategically sensitive parts of the company, too. For example, in July 1969, four employees at the Boulder, Colorado, plant established Storage Technology Corporation. That same year, Alan F. Shugart (1930–2006) joined Memorex Corporation as vice president for product development, which allowed him to transfer his IBM experience to new storage products. Shugart recruited over 100 IBM employees over the next several years and established two additional firms selling similar products, Shugart Associates (1973) and Seagate Technology (1978); both became successful rivals to IBM. Then there was also Gene Amdahl with his mainframes. Plug-compatible peripheral vendors owned about 10 percent of the market for tape drives and 3 percent for disk drives by the start of 1971.[7]

While IBM was focusing on mainframes, still a fast-growing market in the 1970s, a new market developed for minicomputers. In large companies, engineers and others in marketing and research sought their own systems if they wanted to break away from the financial community that controlled access to computing and were more interested in supporting accounting and inventory control than in, say, computerized modeling or manufacturing scheduling. Smaller computers were becoming more affordable because the cost of integrated circuits kept dropping at an almost predictable rate of nearly 20 percent every 12 to 18 months, a reflection of Moore's Law, named after Gordon Moore (b. 1929), who famously predicted that rate of decline. In 1968, he and Robert Noyce (1927–1990) cofounded Intel

Corporation, which became the world's largest producer of semiconductor chips. Declining costs meant physically smaller computers. DEC dominated the new "mini" market, but several dozen others soon battled it. Key players included Wang, founded in 1964, Data General in 1968, and Prime in 1971. One of the more popular new entrants was Hewlett-Packard (H-P), which had produced measurement tools since the 1930s and had many engineering customers. It deployed a sales force made up largely of engineers selling to fellow engineers.

As customers learned how best to use computers and cost justify them, and when to swap out one system for another, they automated functions that lowered labor costs, increased sales, managed inventory turnover, leveraged national capital gains taxes, and so forth. Their increased skill, when married to changes in the expense of technologies and maintenance, made the *relative* cost of computing attractive. Thus, while a mainframe might have cost more in raw dollars in the 1960s than in the 1950s, because the newer machines were significantly larger in capacity, the manager acquiring one had more work to pump through it, which reduced the cost of systems.[8]

Controversy persisted about whether IBM "missed" the minicomputer market because it did not respond aggressively to this emerging market until other vendors were succeeding in it. However, there is more to the story. IBMers read the same trade publications as others in the industry, and corporate and engineering communities in IBM hired industry watchers, such as IDG and Forrester, to tell them about new developments. IBM became more bureaucratic in the 1960s and 1970s, causing engineering and sales to present cases for new products to growing layers of management working in an increasingly cautious climate. Lawsuits and the U.S. antitrust suit stimulated this slowing decision-making behavior.

However, as one IBM DPD executive put it, "If we have $1 to invest and we get an 80 percent return on that by putting it into improving an existing product, why would we want to put that $1 into a new system that might only yield a 30 percent return on investment?" Every technology-based company faced that dilemma. In the late 1990s, the idea eventually acquired its own name, the "Innovator's Dilemma."[9] The answer, of course, is that some investments have to be allocated to emerging markets; otherwise a company ran the danger of missing these markets or not being armed with the capability to participate in them, a concept understood within IBM. DPD advocated for large systems, while GSD and its manufacturing allies advocated for smaller ones. Both, however, were keen on having products for distributed computing across a customer's enterprise, linked to each other under control of the account's IBM sales team.

Both obtained what they wanted, even DPD, which was allowed to sell minisystems as well. In 1970, IBM brought out the System/3. IBM Germany had crafted its architecture, and it was different from the S/370's. It used a 96-column card, had its own operating system, was aimed at small companies, went into engineering departments and manufacturing and process plants, and required less staff to take care of them than systems in large data centers required. In time, IBM replaced S/3s with newer, less expensive products, notably the S/32 (introduced in 1975) and the powerful S/38 (1979). The S/38 proved massively popular, wiping out the majority of its competitors during the 1980s and leaving others crippled survivors (such as DEC). Customers replaced their products with newer, powerful desktop processors, too, including the PC. The size of this market hovered at 275,000 minicomputers for all types in the United States by the end of 1978, with 38 percent from DEC, 15 percent from Data General, 8 percent from H-P, and a third from IBM.[10] IBM's AS/400 replaced the S/38 beginning in 1988. It went on to become the most popular minicomputer, selling over 400,000 units.

Senior management decided in the 1970s to concentrate its software initiatives on operating systems and reinforced that strategy in the 1980s. It would also leverage its successful telecommunications tools, notably CICS (Customer Information Control System), used to transfer data in online systems. It was—and is—hardly known outside of IBM's customer ecosystem, but as historian Martin Campbell-Kelly described it, CICS "is indispensable for thousands of online transactions, and—since its commercialization following unbundling in 1970—it earned IBM billions of dollars in profits."[11] Occasionally IBM dabbled in application software for accounting, manufacturing, and banking work, but this was an on and off activity over the decades, because hundreds of firms specialized in software tools that ran on IBM's systems. For IBM, these niche markets were too small, the old problem of where best to invest for the highest yield,[12] while software providers drove up demand for IBM's hardware.

IBM continued to engage in large, government-funded software systems, such as U.S. air traffic control systems in the 1960s and 1970s and later those for other countries. Many space flight systems were developed or managed by IBMers, notably computing on the spaceship that landed humans on the moon in July 1969. It built avionic and navigation systems for the U.S. Navy and U.S. Air Force in collaboration with defense contractors. Armonk used its Federal Systems Division (FSD), established in 1959 to replace the earlier Military Products Division, to handle these low-profit government projects.

While much of IBM's success played out in similar fashion around the world, which we will look at in subsequent chapters, the world market for computers grew sharply. Markets in which IBM operated consumed more computers from all vendors than those in which it did not. Rivals appeared, although IBM dominated, often controlling between 60 and 80 percent of a national market.[13] The S/360 essentially kicked off IBM's global expansion, far more than the 1401 had done. Between 1965 and 1980, IBM and its U.S. rivals enjoyed rapid worldwide growth outside the United States, with many customers embracing computing for the first time. That is one reason why IBM World Trade grew faster than Domestic. But the same was true for other firms. By 1975, approximately 46 percent of the value of the world's stock of computers lay outside the United States.[14] In 1960, there were 5,500 computers installed in the United States, but in 1983 there were some 400,000. This was a huge rate of growth. Looking at Western Europe for the same years, there were 1,500 in 1960 and 225,000 in 1983. Japan, which industrialized enormously in the same period, had a similar experience, having only 400 computers in 1960 but 70,000 in 1983.[15] These numbers signaled that IBM was changing as it became more globalized.

IBM, THE CENTER OF AN INFORMATION ECOSYSTEM

Aspects of IBM's way of thinking about information technology and how to operate a company became a major source of a larger computing ecosystem that included customers, computing professionals, industry watchers, and management in all facets of corporate life in large companies and government agencies. Diffusion of the "IBM Way" was a by-product of a conscious effort to influence IBM's customers, started by Watson Sr., but also a result of IBM's dominant presence in many industries and large organizations across the industrialized world. These realities present a powerful case for why we can argue that IBM was an iconic firm, although one could argue, too, that its sound business practices, successes over so many decades, and the quality of its people were driving forces. A combination of these factors led to the diffusion of IBM's corporate culture to other organizations, largely through the data centers that used its products and services. One way to see that process at work is by looking at the actions of individual employees, circulating back to an idea Watson Sr. had, that individuals made a difference, the notion that IBM was all about people, and why retirees at their farewell parties waxed emotionally about the privilege they had of working with such individuals. It was IBM culture at its best and most passionate.

James Martin (1933–2013) was an imposing English IBMer, standing 6 feet 5 inches tall. With his accent and commanding presence lecturing or delivering a speech, he caught an audience's attention. He became an expert in software development, programming languages, database management, telecommunications, and, later, what he called the "wired society," publishing dozens of books on these topics. Martin reflected the growing role of IBM's ideas and knowledge about computing that so influenced data processing professionals between the 1950s and the end of the 1980s. He joined IBM in England in 1959, soon shipped off to New York to work on the American Airlines SABRE system, the first large commercial real-time reservation system, still used to book flights online. In England, he worked on similar projects before returning to New York at IBM's Systems Research Institute (SRI). At SRI, IBMers and customers attended seminars on all manner of computing technology and its management.

In 1965, Martin published the first of ten books on technical issues that he wrote while at IBM. He published dozens more after he left the company. Martin's early books became standards in the field for programmers, software analysts, and other technical data processing professionals. In 1977, *The Wired Society* became an international best seller. Martin left IBM the following year to pursue a career in writing, lecturing, and consulting that led him to publish over 60 books in his lifetime. Almost all were published by Prentice-Hall, one of the top two or three publishers on computing. Many of their titles were written by IBMers and were thus a trusted source for data processing professionals. Most of what Martin wrote reflected the collective thinking of IBMers and their customers. As late as 1987, nearly a decade after leaving IBM, he coauthored a book about IBM software (VSAM) that connected computers to telecommunications systems, evidence of his persisting IBM worldview.[16]

Martin was emblematic of many IBMers as sources for much thinking about how to work with IBM's technologies and managerial practices. Some, like Martin, published, whereas others, such as Bob Evans, met with customers to explain IBM's thinking. These people worked at IBM's more than two dozen plants and laboratories in the 1950s through the 1980s, when they developed technologies and products and spoke with IBMers and customers. IBM researchers published in key academic and technical journals and were active in technical societies, such as IEEE's Computer Society. There was hardly a technical standards committee for computing that did not include an IBM member.

A second source of IBM influence that contributed to making IBM a "go-to" source for much thinking was sales and general management. The charismatic Buck Rodgers lectured and published on how IBM functioned, particularly in sales at the apex of IBM's influence with general management at large corporations,[17] but he was not the only one to do this. A bigger influence were the thousands of salesmen who brought into their accounts experts on a particular industry, personnel management, supply chain management, and so forth, to share what IBM was doing and to explain the rationale for its actions. Most customers required their IBM salespeople to keep them informed on business and technological trends.

All senior IBM executives were expected to call on customers, even if they were not in sales. Some had their secretaries monitor their calendars to determine what percentage of their time they devoted to this activity. IBM CEOs befriended CEOs of leading customers, IBM vice presidents in manufacturing did the same with their cohorts, and so it went. Performance appraisals included the extent to which one engaged with customers. IBM established a network of managers and experts to interact with public officials from city councils to country presidents and prime ministers; others worked with regulators and legislators to influence the shaping of laws and tax policies.

One could see IBM's growing influence on customers and others. Martin's thinking and writing were shaped by his experience at IBM. Another example was Watts S. Humphrey (b. 1927), a contemporary of Martin's. When he left IBM after a 27-year career, he continued to publish on data processing while working at Carnegie Mellon University. He was named a Fellow by industry organizations (IEEE, ACM) and served on the Malcolm Baldrige National Quality Award Board of Examiners. Humphrey's publications were an extension of his thinking and experiences at IBM.[18]

Emerson Pugh, an IBM engineering executive who worked on the S/360, became president of the IEEE in 1989 while still an employee of IBM. The IEEE, then as now, was one of the world's largest organizations of technical professionals and computer scientists. It had hundreds of thousands of members around the world. Pugh had worked in various leadership roles in the IEEE since 1964. He recalled that while president of the IEEE, he "put in 40 hours a week for IEEE and 40 hours a week for IBM."[19]

Figure 10.2 depicts the information ecosystem that included IBM, its customers, and other organizations. Several observations become evident. For one thing, it included a large variety of participants, not simply a great number of members, of which there were thousands. For another, IBM had a physical presence, with people interacting with each other every day, such as sales representatives and field engineers, and with its hundreds of lawyers, lobbyists, and media staff. Most of these constituents also employed ex-IBMers, such as data processing managers. Salesmen worked

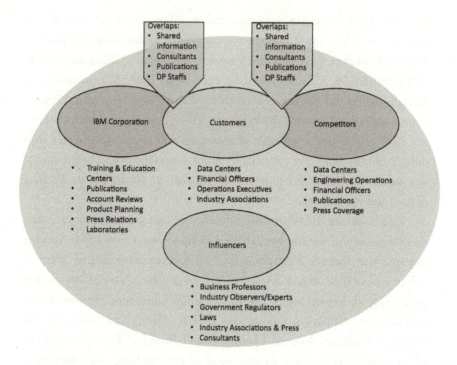

Figure 10.2
IBM's information ecosystem, 1960s to 1980s.

for IBM's competitors, most in leasing or in companies that sold IBM plug-compatible products, such as Telex, Memorex, Amdahl, and Fujitsu. Lawyers who worked at IBM appeared elsewhere, while thousands of IBMers from other lines of work became managers, senior executives, or CEOs elsewhere, maintaining contacts with IBM. If one wanted to work for a computer industry consulting firm or as an expert on IBM, that individual needed to have worked at the company, as Gideon Gartner, founder of Gartner Associates, did in the 1970s.

Whenever IBM did something, people paid attention. It was routine for leading business and technical publications to report on IBM's activities and what these meant for other organizations. Frequent topics of discussion included IBM's business strategies, reorganizations, and the economic and strategic significance of one product or action versus another. Gartner became wealthy doing that kind of analysis. *Fortune, Forbes,* the *Wall Street*

Journal, Computerworld, Datamation, Harvard Business Review, the *Economist,* and publications in other countries published stories on IBM. Sales staffs and senior management across IBM were routinely asked by customer executives or officials to explain why IBM was doing something, how it managed the acquisition of components, or was able to operate worldwide single-product strategies in the face of so many different national cultures, tax laws, and regulations. Other multinational corporations faced these issues as well, influenced by similar considerations, managerial fashions, and musings of Harvard Business School professors and other experts, but when IBM embraced an idea or a strategy, it was like putting a seal of approval on it.

Hundreds of authors of business books discussed what IBM was doing as justification for what the writer was proposing. *In Pursuit of Excellence* was typical. Even after IBM had entered a period of crisis that dulled its previous reputation, authors still relied on it. The most widely sold business book in the 1990s, *Reengineering the Corporation: A Manifesto for Business Revolution,* by James Champy and Michael Hammer, included a chapter on IBM's recent near-death experience, describing how its senior management was executing a turnaround when it was clear in that book how badly IBM had recently misstepped.[20]

IBM was not alone in nurturing an IBM-centric information ecosystem. Its competitors did the same, but theirs were smaller and less pervasive in their effects. For example, both Burroughs Corporation and RAND Corporation published books about data processing and programming. Customers of Sperry Univac in the 1950s, but also all of IBM's large and small computer rivals, established user groups with newsletters and annual conferences. Like IBM, a few vendors established briefing centers around the world. Customers visited IBM's competitors' manufacturing sites, too, to be briefed on the technologies underpinning their products.

All European, British, and Asian "national champions" maintained close ties to their political elites in order to burnish their images and gain support against IBM. This was a particularly important activity that should be considered part of IBM's information ecosystem because what occurred behind closed doors became data in IBM's market research. The surge of

IBM products into Europe in the 1960s led Arthur Watson to write to his brother that IBM now "owned" 64 percent of the mainframe market.[21] That share would increase before diminishing in the 1980s. IBM was able to introduce new generations of equipment in the 1950s, 1960s, and 1970s faster than local computer companies could, a topic we take up in a subsequent chapter. It could do this because of its effective sales force and attractive products but also because of its information exchange and infrastructure.

For example, in 1969, at the height of its shipment of S/360s, and just before the start of a worldwide computer recession, IBM had six laboratories in Europe, including in Great Britain, West Germany, and Sweden; there was one near any customer. IBM operated 13 manufacturing plants scattered over Europe. They had conference rooms and well-run cafeterias. That year, IBM operated 157 sales offices in Western Europe. Customer staffs trained at many of IBM's employee training centers at laboratory, educational, and manufacturing locations in Europe and in the United States. Others existed in Japan, Brazil, and Mexico. Each shared information and provided lectures, publications, and hands-on experience with IBM's products and computing.

Not everyone was happy with IBM's rapidly expanding presence, such as General Charles de Gaulle, who ordered the French government to consider local vendors before IBM. Meanwhile, the French army standardized on IBM because that technology was also NATO's. It knew NATO would collaborate with France to push back a Soviet invasion but that such an effort would require using compatible computing and telecommunications systems. Europeans saw IBM and other U.S. corporations as pushing their way through Europe with their (American) way of doing things. Nevertheless, Europeans and Asians learned about computing the same way Americans did, and in the center of much of that information exchange stood IBM. That circumstance extended the process Watson Sr. had started in the 1920s when he wanted to create a global brand. The critics' voices seemed hardly heard and unable to slow IBM.

BUSINESS RESULTS AND CONSEQUENCES

As IBM grew, so did its profits, the value of its stock, and its standing in the world. In 1961, IBM crossed the $2 billion mark in sales ($2.2B) at about the time that Tom Watson Jr. was pondering why people thought that maybe IBM was losing its momentum when the IBM 1401 was generating revenue, to be followed by the S/360 and then the S/370, and the company was massively expanding globally. In 1973, IBM passed the $10 billion revenue mark, and in 1981, the year in which it introduced its PC, it turned in revenue of $29 billion. Its last year of continuous growth occurred in 1990, with revenue of $68.9 billion. In 1961, IBM reported $254 million in net earnings, which continued to rise steadily. In 1970, IBM turned in its first year of billion dollar net profits ($1.2B), with profits peaking in 1984 at $6.6 billion. Then alarm bells went off at Corporate in 1985, when revenue continued to climb (to $50.7B) but net earnings dropped slightly, to $6.582 billion. While a profit decline of $27 million seemed minor since revenue increased, that decline demonstrated that something was wrong. A drop in profits had not occurred at IBM in living memory.[22]

We should care about the consequences of the Golden Age because out of it came the start of IBM's wild ride to near death in the early 1990s. Subsequent chapters explain what happened, because after development of the S/360 it was the biggest event in the history of IBM and shocked all participants in the company's ecosystem worldwide. Life at Armonk took an ugly turn. It was not long before the rest of the company felt the crisis. Table 10.1 shows net earnings for 1984 through 1990, before the company entered a new phase it had never experienced before: running the business at a loss. IBM's culture had never been so challenged.

Recall that generations of managers controlled financial performance by doling out budgets annually and managing headcount in bits and pieces, tinkering with them over the course of a year. Headcount is the easiest to track. IBM ended 1961 with nearly 76,000 employees in the United States and a worldwide total of just over 116,000, so Domestic was still the center of IBM's universe, despite its effort to be a global company. Fast-forward to 1970, when IBM and its customers had finally digested

Table 10.1

IBM net earnings, 1984–1990 (in billions of dollars)

1984	6.58
1985	6.56
1986	4.79
1987	5.26
1988	5.74
1989	3.72
1990	5.07

Source: Emerson W. Pugh, *Building IBM: Shaping an Industry and Its Technology* (Cambridge, MA: MIT Press, 1995), appendix A, 324.

the bulk of the S/360s. Worldwide, IBM had 269,291 employees, of which 156,859 worked in the United States. Outside the country, that population kept increasing, reaching 113,000 in 1970. The source of IBM's business had shifted substantially to outside the United States, while the U.S. market continued to grow. IBM's employee population declined a tad before growing again in the second half of the 1970s and first half of the 1980s. It peaked in 1985 at just over 242,000 in the United States and 405,000 worldwide. So again the non-U.S. part of the business continued to expand, adding 50,000 workers. Then the combined U.S. and non-U.S. employee populations began to decline from just over 403,000 in 1986 to 373,000 in 1990, largely through normal attrition. It seemed no extra effort was required, just managerial intent not to hire while nudging normal forces that led to turnover and retirements.[23] IBMers noticed the slowdown in business and that beginning in 1985 early retirement programs were being offered to select groups, while the corporation assured everyone that full employment was still IBM's operating principle.

Outside of IBM, stockholders, stockbrokers, and the industry press paid increasing attention to what was happening at IBM. Like utility stocks, IBM's stock was what brokers and relatives advised for "orphans and widows," as it was safe, just like AT&T (until 1984), General Motors, and some European manufacturers. As the number of investors in the United States and Western Europe increased, interest in IBM's stock increased beyond the closed circle of IBM's employees, institutional investors, and the wealthy.

All through the 1960s and 1970s, people held onto their shares, with an uptick in sales during the global computer recession in the early 1970s. In the 1980s, turnover of shares doubled because there had been a stock split in June 1979 in which the owner of one share now owned four, and even earlier, in April 1969, with a 2 for 1 split, so the number of shares available for purchase increased faster than the quantity sold in the 1970s and 1980s. The exception came in October and November 1987, when U.S. stock exchanges declined precipitously resulting in a tripling of disposals of shares. The announcements of the S/360, S/370, and, in August 1981, of the IBM Personal Computer (PC) had almost no effect on the value of the stock or its trading volume. During IBM's Golden Age, it paid out a small dividend. For most investors, IBM was a safe bet.

However, inside the computer industry—IBM's ecosystem—the ground was shifting beneath the company's feet. While the number of S/360s IBM sold was significant through the 1960s, recall that by the late 1960s its market share for computers was actually decreasing as rivals entered with their new systems. IBM's revenues increased less because of the number of machines placed and more because it sold greater quantities of its largest systems to existing customers, meaning that the percentage of new systems sold to new users was declining. No senior executive wants to see a decline in market share, even if being pursued by the U.S. government for creating a monopoly. In addition to rising competition, most fiercely in the United States, the declining cost of computing technologies meant more computing per dollar could be done in a system. Diffusion of easier-to-use programming languages helped dampen the costs of creating new software, too, although that improvement also encouraged development of software that was more complex. Such innovations encouraged the emergence of a commercial software market. All these trends combined partially masked fundamental changes in the economics of computing.

IBM's senior managers were aware of these changes. The combination of factors affecting the economics of the company's products goes far in explaining why they introduced new products more quickly than their competitors did in the late 1960s and 1970s. Their objectives remained fairly constant, however: to lead as a "total system provider," offering everything customers needed; to support strategies that allowed IBM to continue growing revenue, net profits, and market share; and to use excess resources wisely to invest in R&D, spend on dividends, and expand into new countries and markets. The effort required determining how to redeploy excess employees into these ventures or to eliminate them without violating IBM's full-employment strategy. Their objectives were not easy to accomplish, as one affected the other. For example, as chip technology improved, one consequence was further automation, requiring fewer employees to make integrated circuits. So, did one make so many additional improvements that the staff doing the work could remain the same size, or do improvements in manufacturing techniques increase faster than the increased volumes needed, meaning a reduction in the number of employees? These were tricky issues to deal with. As long as Watson Jr. remained in charge, IBM sought growth, a mantra his successors embraced but found difficult to achieve.

As IBM entered the 1970s, a sense of crisis began to pervade the ranks of senior management. Employees did not like it either. Apathy increased, as did turnover, with IBMers joining other firms. Management continued to seek growth, however. In the early to mid-1970s, IBM increased the number of salesmen. An overarching problem was that IBM generated significant amounts of profit in the late 1960s and 1970s that needed to be spent wisely so as not to increase its taxes or affect the ongoing U.S. antitrust suit. IBM routinely enjoyed a pretax return on its leasing business in the range of 25–30 percent until the late 1970s. Its rate of return on profits hovered closer to 6.5–6.7 percent, which while not spectacular was healthy. IBM explored investing in new ventures, such as TV maintenance, home typewriters, even wristwatches, until the early 1990s, when it ran out of profits and cash. Until then, IBM continued to collect vast amounts of money for which it had to find a purpose. As one well-informed observer put it in 1973, "If IBM were a bank, it would rank as one of the country's largest."[24]

IBM made a few acquisitions in the 1970s and 1980s. An important one was Science Research Associates (SRA), which published technical literature, where some IBM engineers and computer scientists published books and customers attended seminars. Finding strategic investments proved difficult for senior managers trying to stay focused on core businesses, particularly in the United States. In Europe and Asia, markets for existing products still grew in the 1970s and 1980s, so finding strategic investments was less of an issue. By the early 1970s, just over 40 percent of IBM's business came from the United States, 39 percent from all of Europe, 10 percent from Latin America, 5 percent from Japan, and the rest from other parts of the world. Not included in the U.S. 40 percent was an additional 3 percent generated by sales to the U.S. government, continuing a 75-year tradition of the U.S. government being IBM's largest customer.[25]

How did IBM spend its money in the 1970s and 1980s? Just over half went to sales and operations (SG&A).[26] These included the funding of capital investments in the equipment leased to customers. About 80 percent of IBM's hardware products fit into this category; the rest it sold. Leased equipment had to be depreciated over time. Increasingly during the 1970s, financial analysts within IBM began questioning the costs and benefits of IBM's long-standing practice of leasing rather than outright selling of equipment. Depreciation consumed 12–15 percent of IBM's expenses. Retained earnings—profits saved for a rainy day—hovered at 8–10 percent. IBM's tax rate hovered at 13–14 percent, and investments in R&D were 6–7 percent of revenues until the late 1980s, when they temporarily shrank. Dividends sustained IBM stock's value, and they cost about 6 percent of the company's budget. In the 1970s, IBM had the added expense of legal fees to fight a barrage of lawsuits. In some years, that expense consumed 2 percent of the budget.[27]

DISTRESSING UNDERCURRENTS

IBM's success and culture were not without their limitations. These were difficult to identify in its Golden Age, when so much work resulted in achievements that the long hours, problems, and existential threats failed to slow the company's momentum. There were distressing undercurrents that needed attention. Employees, observers, and historians could be caught up in the hubris of a successful strategy and a magnificent balance sheet.

Gus Kane, a salesman with over two decades of experience who was speaking to a class at IBM's Sales School in Poughkeepsie, New York, in 1983 borrowed a line from Charles Dickens: "It was the best of times and the worst of times." Kane argued that life in the "field" was pressure-filled, that "as you were celebrating a big sale at one end of your territory, a nuclear bomb was going off at the other end." His message was that IBM constantly managed its business in an environment of extremes. Salesmen increasingly faced off against IBM rules that made it difficult to consummate a sale, such as with pricing that frequently remained 20 percent higher than a competitor's, especially a leasing company that could depreciate the same IBM equipment over 10 years instead of 4. They faced myriad competitors for every little and big piece of business. There were dozens of competitors to fight off weekly in the United States and increasingly in Europe.

When Telex sued IBM, one of the by-products of that case involved the court order that vast amounts of IBM documents be made public. That is how historians learned that IBM's senior managers worried about a problem they and others were creating: computers dropping in cost, becoming commodities. Technical innovations resulted in cheaper, faster, and better computer chips, while IBM's computer architecture and software were the primary standard for many competitors' products. Vendors increasingly competed on price, less on differentiating functions. The problem of changing economic fundamentals spread from mainframes to minis in the 1970s and to PCs in the 1980s. IBM's profits from mainframes peaked at the same time it was selling every S/360 it could manufacture.

If a supplier depreciated a leased machine, would that lessor have enough time to recoup its initial investment as newer, less expensive replacements came to market? Of course not, if for no other reason than that in response to competitive pressures IBM replaced its products at a faster rate than it could recoup investments and desired rates of profits of earlier machines. If new computer chips appeared every 18 to 24 months at nearly half the cost of the prior generation of components, and if IBM was amortizing a computer or disk drive in four to five years, the financial circle did not close. Prices dropped faster than depreciation. That is one reason why IBM chose to urge customers to acquire all their computing equipment from IBM, not just bits and pieces of a system, because some units had a more stable price and profit, such as keypunch machines, printers, and tape drives, but these paled in cost when compared to a million dollar mainframe.

Competitors experienced similar problems, but IBM more so, as it came to dominate markets. When looking at a multiyear list of IBM's revenues and net earnings, it becomes evident that earnings were not rising as quickly as a percentage of revenues as revenues themselves were growing. Gideon Gartner's consultancy spent the last third of the twentieth century explaining this structural problem. Gartner also educated commercial consumers of computers about the implications of their strategies on how best to finance these rapidly evolving capital goods. Everyone understood that the economics underpinning IBM's products were shifting. All were trying to make sense of this, second-guessing each other.

Gideon Gartner, considered by the end of the 1970s to be the leading expert on IBM's finances and product strategies, observed that if rumors suggested IBM was about to introduce a new product in, say, six months, customers knew to wait for the new machine, while vendors stewed because their customers also wanted to wait. IBM would prefer that nobody know its plans for new products, while Gartner and his staff spent enormous effort working out the financial schedules and costs. He recalled that by the 1980s "turbulence roiled the computer industry. The traditional vertical model, epitomized by IBM, in which a single company designed, produced and put together all the components of a product, was shifting to a horizontal model in which different companies manufactured specific components at sharply reduced prices" and newer rivals "were emerging and grabbing market share at a frightening rate," which by the end of the decade had reduced IBM, "the world's most successful, most profitable, most powerful, most influential, and best-managed company," to "just another large corporation struggling to adjust to forces beyond its control."[28] In other words, the economic/technological puzzle brought forth by the S/360 was never solved.

IBM became increasingly arthritic as the result of a rising tide of bureaucracy. Behaviors were constraining performance beyond what the federal antitrust suit was causing. As IBM grew in the 1960s, it followed its long-standing tradition of, first, controlling (some called it microman-aging) and, second, measuring everything for sound reasons to ensure its long-standing ethical standards were not compromised in an era filled with lawsuits and because the field/staff structure led to the growth of both con-trolling and measuring. With ten layers of management, each with staffs, it was probably inevitable that bureaucracy would grow. Decisions slowed, the Wild Ducks had to fly more tightly in formation, authority to make deci-sions drifted upward again after Watson Jr. was no longer at IBM, and much was being centralized. By the mid-1970s, it seemed to employees that there was a policy or procedure for almost anything. One could conclude that IBM was well run. It had spent the 1960s so dominating its markets that it exuded the appearance of stability, a circumstance that encouraged expanded use of procedures and formalized policies. The problem of bureaucracy was well recognized. Every few years, a task force studied it, but little was done. It seemed intractable. In 1978, Domestic ran such a task force in DPD, which had a couple of hundred branch offices, and discovered that salesmen spent nearly 40 percent of their time in the office filling out forms such as multiple forecasts, processing orders, and attending team and branch meet-ings. They were required to spend at least two weeks in training each year and, depending on their seniority, had anywhere from one to six weeks of vacation coming to them, in addition to national holidays, leaving only half their time to work with customers. Attempts to fix the problem failed. Another study reported similar findings in 1985.

The Telex exposures documented growing centralization of decision making. As discussed further in a subsequent chapter, management worked diligently to coordinate product development and manufacture worldwide to optimize local resources and tax incentives. It could do that since IBM's national companies were wholly owned subsidiaries. Laboratories were given responsibility for developing new models, such as in Germany for S/370s, Hursley in Great Britain for software components, Zurich for databases, San Jose for disk drives, and so forth. European factories still bought components from and sold them to each other, leveraging import/export tax laws in Europe before the continent created the European Union. By the end of the 1960s, global product management was an integrated operation, reinforced by moving IBMers back and forth across organizations in one- and two-year assignments that improved personal and information networking and collaboration. IBM's culture made that possible, a capability that large companies increasingly cultivated.[29]

Some of the internal meetings and paperwork would benefit one side of IBM at the expense of another. For example, in the 1960s, IBM adopted a set of worldwide forms for reporting expenses. These were easy to use, and their data could be consolidated. Sales reporting and forecasting had been standardized for decades. Order processing and rules for what constituted "confirmed orders"—that is, a customer committed to a machine—were also standardized, along with terms and conditions and the wording of contracts for all manner of goods and services. All required enormous amounts of work to conceive, impose, and maintain them. Employee and customer opinion surveys of the 1950s and 1960s became invigorated with professional pollsters developing surveys, which became annual events, just like Fall Planning across the entire corporation. "Spot surveys" about specific issues were added, too. As new organizations were created, or reorganized into new regions, areas, and divisions, everyone in those new structures had to meet to "kick off" the new year or organization and to develop a collective understanding of the new mission. A product manager in Poughkeepsie would worry about getting a new product designed, approved, and funded to get it going, while a salesman in Paris or Tokyo worried that the local government and competitors were going after his customers.

In the mid-1970s, journalist Nancy Foy studied how IBM operated, interviewing scores of IBMers, at many levels of the enterprise, who worried about the way the organization was responding to a growing repertoire of threats and problems:

> The few men in Armonk's interlocking committees are getting older. These men—the nearest one can find to be a personification of "IBM"—set the strategies. In recent years these have been reactions to outside forces far more than they have been initiating action for internal reasons. The men who are taking over from Tom Junior are gifted managers, powerful men, responsible citizens—but as products of IBM they tend to be organization men rather than innovators.[30]

Could younger people be brought in along with their new ideas? Foy suggested that "IBM needs a new flock of wild ducks."[31] New people joined IBM, innovations were introduced, but the culture inherited from the Watsons proved both a blessing for momentum and a burden exposing another generation of IBMers to enormous challenges. Overcontrol from Armonk became a growing problem as IBM continued to expand.

OTHER CONSIDERATIONS ALSO IN PLAY

In sum, IBM engaged with smaller companies and more competition over mainframes in large ones. Commercial software and competitors selling services came into their own, challenging IBM's monopoly on mainframe computing.[32] During the 1960s to 1980s, IBM had unbundled its software, putting its programs into the market to compete against more specialized software houses. IBM had locked itself into its S/360 technical standards. To understand further the significance of those developments, we need to explore what happened to Arthur Watson's World Trade, expanding our understanding of IBM's status as a behemoth, or the global extent of the "IBM Way." World Trade was a large piece of IBM's business but a part that seemed to live in an alternative reality alongside Corporate and IBM Domestic.

11 IBM ON THE GLOBAL STAGE

> When we and other progressive firms do something new, its effect spreads
> and changes the character of an area of the economy. Little by little, our
> example spreads over a wide area.
> —FRENCH IBM MANAGER, 1960[1]

WHEN WORLD WAR II ended, IBM picked up the pieces of its worldwide operations. In a staff meeting, Thomas J. Watson Sr. declared the
company's performance outside the United States "nothing short of a dis-
grace."[2] Tom Watson Jr. thought demand was strong; it was just that IBM
could not deliver products because of shortages in supply. IBM took the
quick step of sending equipment no longer needed by the U.S. military in
Europe to its local factories for refurbishing. The stratagem worked and
also provided employment for European IBM veterans returning to the
company. Watson Jr. recalled that "with a few hours' work and a new coat
of paint, those machines were something they could sell."[3] But the "Old
Man" wanted more, so he poured resources into Europe, reestablishing
offices and contacts with customers.

Watson Sr. settled on two strategies for jump-starting business in
Europe. Picking up the story of World Trade from chapter 7, first he created his own internal common market a decade before the Europeans did.
He ordered his tiny European factories to make parts for both their own
country's market and for export to IBM factories and suppliers in other
nations. For example, 60 percent of the parts made in Germany would be
for the German market, leaving 40 percent of the output available for sale

by IBM in other European countries. An IBM country company earned foreign exchange credits, which it used to import parts, making it possible for IBM to avoid high national tariffs for finished products. It rarely had to ship a completed machine that had no local parts. Watson Jr. explained, "This trading around allowed us to operate on a much larger scale, and far more efficiently" than any company constrained within one country.[4] It is a crucial idea in understanding IBM's global strategies, because for the next half century IBM developed increasingly integrated global product plans, production, and marketing strategies.[5] This approach helps to explain how IBM could move quickly against slower-moving European "national champions" in the 1960s to 1980s. Second, Watson Sr. hired local nationals to run and staff national companies to optimize local cultural and legal traditions and to leverage the local language and "know-how." On the whole, he chose effective country leaders. They and their staffs grew the company at remarkable rates in the years that followed.[6]

Recall what some historians noted was an act of nepotism, that Watson Sr. divided IBM into two halves: the U.S. market for Tom Jr. to run, and everything else, to be run by Tom Jr.'s younger brother, Arthur. In October 1948, Watson Sr. told Tom Jr. of his plan, adding that Domestic would retain worldwide responsibility for finance, research, and product development. Tom Jr. disliked the idea, but several days later, his father told the brothers what he wanted to do. Tom Jr. admitted later to being jealous that his less experienced younger brother was about to be made his equal. Tom Jr. relayed to his father reasons for not forming World Trade (WT) Corporation: redundant staffs and overhead, that WT would likely reduce IBM's manufacturing productivity, and so on. Watson Sr. stood up and barked at Tom Jr., "What are you trying to do, prevent your brother from having an opportunity?" That is how IBM World Trade came into being.

The rest of this chapter would be anticlimactic if we just reported the new structure of 1949 with WT becoming a wholly owned subsidiary that owned country companies, and likewise if we just reported that Tom Jr. considered the move a success: "It capitalized on Europe's economic recovery, financed itself through its own profits and foreign borrowings, and grew as fast as the American company."[7] But it was a momentous event. The story is more interesting because of how IBM ran WT. When one fills an organization "with some of the most talented businessmen in Europe," things become complicated.[8] The same happened in Latin America and Asia. By 1953, these "most talented businessmen" employed 15,000 people, about half the size of Domestic. Arthur Watson could take credit for this rapid growth, too, blending the best of Domestic with local national opportunities, and with both sides of the business collaborating enough to leverage each other's assets and capabilities. Watson Sr. was pleased. Under Tom Jr.'s command, the decentralization of authority and responsibility articulated in Williamsburg, Virginia, extended into WT. In various iterations over the next half century, World Trade divided itself into additional geographic companies. Within them, they established regional offices and branch offices, with laboratories and factories reporting to global manufacturing or research divisions.

This chapter focuses on a broadly diverse group of issues. It is a history of IBM's non-U.S. operations. Historians and others writing about WT comment as if it were almost a separate company from IBM Domestic.[9] While this view is convenient when writing a chapter or an article, it is misleading, because Corporate operated a globally integrated firm, a point insufficiently recognized by students of the company's history.[10] Senior executives viewed WT as an extension of the network of factories, laboratories, and sales regions that existed in Domestic. For this reason, the story told here includes what otherwise would be left out of the story of IBM's foreign operations, notably the work of CEO Frank Cary, who I rescue from obscurity and argue was one of the most powerful and best CEOs in IBM's history. IBM evolved into a global behemoth more complex in structure than the company Watson Sr. ran before World War II. IBM's non-Domestic business grew to where half of the company's revenue came from outside the United States.

Historians have recently paid increased attention to emerging economies, looking at what happened in areas such as Asia and Latin America. Crucial to such investigations is how multinational corporations interacted with businesses and governments in these economies. This chapter is a detailed case study of how one firm did that. As Geoffrey Jones, Gareth Austin, and Carlos Dávila argued, foreign influence on local economies was extensive; it could even be called "foreign domination." As this chapter demonstrates, that domination included adoption of U.S. managerial practices, such as those proffered by IBM.[11]

We begin by describing the core of IBM's immediate postwar foreign operations—Europe and the formation of WT—followed by brief histories of IBM's operations in Asia and Latin America. Those discussions represent the first story.[12] We then turn to the rising tide of global competition and the role played by Cary in creating the IBM international behemoth, describe IBM's departure from India as part of the global evolution of the firm rather than as a result of IBM's Asia's experience, and analyze how globalizing changed IBM. We summarize the discussion by analyzing IBM's global financial results.

EUROPE: WORLD TRADE'S GLOBAL EPICENTER

Between the 1940s and the end of the 1980s, IBM's non-U.S. operations were centered in Western Europe and Japan. IBM's European core consisted of the United Kingdom (largely England), France, West Germany, and to a lesser extent Italy, Sweden, Austria, Switzerland, and Spain. IBM dominated computer sales in Europe to a greater extent than in the United States, with sales surging in the early 1960s, compelling European rivals to restructure and to ask their home governments for support and protection.[13] In the late 1960s and 1970s, IBM retained its dominance, with its market share rising to more than 80 percent, in contrast to the more competitive U.S. market, where its share vacillated between 40 and 60 percent.[14] The third phase of the Personal Computer as well as mainframes in the 1980s saw the rise of German, Japanese, and U.S. rivals.

IBM World Trade, presaged in earlier chapters, was about creating a business similar to the U.S. company. While Arthur Watson balanced conformity to company-wide practices with those of national companies, he took advantage of global product strategies and developed local capacity to invent and manufacture. WT was held accountable for generating *profitable* revenue and, just as important, for maintaining or expanding market share.[15] Local IBMers knew where every system was installed, including

Figure 11.1
Arthur K. Watson, the first leader of World Trade Corporation. Photo courtesy of
IBM Corporate Archives.

their rivals', and how many were on order from IBM and other vendors.
IBM's definition of market share remained nuanced, as it included share by
product, size of enterprise, and industry. IBM's accountants sliced revenue
and profit data in every conceivable way and then used this data to recommend financial actions to leverage profits *and* market share.

The U.S. government's antitrust case influenced IBM's actions around
the world. The logic of its suit influenced European regulators and companies competing against IBM. The criticism against IBM is straightforward
and is discussed in detail in chapter 12. If a company had a high market

share, it could make products in sufficient quantity to drive down production costs below those of rivals while maintaining higher prices, generating expanding profits from each sale and from more sales. Government economists argued that IBM did this to such an extent that its competitors could not compete against Big Blue. U.S. government lawyers argued that violated antitrust laws.[16]

WT reflected a parallel IBM universe that operated alongside Domestic, almost out of sight for most U.S. IBMers. In Europe, Domestic seemed always present, even though the majority of employees were local nationals. In the early 1950s, Watson Sr. spent up to four months at a time traveling through Europe to jump-start business and, of course, his son—an American—ran WT; his successor, Gil Jones, was also American. By the mid-1960s, when over 10,000 Europeans worked at IBM, fewer than 200 Americans worked in Europe. Nonetheless, European citizens, their governments, and local employees thought of IBM as an American company.

Ties bound both sides of the Atlantic, less so Japan, and nowhere more than in creating and manufacturing products. Product developers in U.S. and European laboratories and factories discussed products in face-to-face meetings. Beginning in the late 1950s, European laboratories assumed responsibility for worldwide development of IBM's offerings, such as Hursley, England, for CICS software. Since the 1960s, CICS had made it possible for mainframes to send data to each other over networks. Thousands of European customers visited factories and laboratories in the United States with their IBM salesmen. They attended seminars in Poughkeepsie and Endicott until the 1990s and subsequently at briefing centers in Palisades, Hawthorne, and Somers.[17]

IBM's customers were similar around the world. The largest organizations were overwhelmingly customers. IBM cultivated midsized organizations with the 650, 1401, and smaller S/360s. While not as profitable, since smaller systems were priced less expensively and required additional "hand-holding" to introduce first-time users to computing, they represented the future of IBM. Some became large enterprises, while the majority increased their computing. It was essential, however, to get all accounts to use IBM's technologies, because their dependence dampened growth in the future cost of selling to them and constrained competition. With remarkable speed, IBM dominated the Western European market. How did that happen? The answer turns on the mundane routine of well-executed business practices that valued speed of execution, effectiveness, good salesmanship, and creative and knowledgeable pricing, contractual terms and conditions, marketing, and advertising. A review of the experiences of several countries illustrates how.

Early on, in the United Kingdom, most notably in England, IBM had been selling time-recording equipment and leasing Hollerith hardware through local agencies. In the 1940s, Britain led the world in developing early computer technology and became the earliest extensive user of computing in Europe.[18] Two British electronics manufacturers sold computers: English Electric and Ferranti. A third company, J. Lyons, a food manufacturer that also ran a chain of teashops, did also.[19] Its machine, called LEO (Lyons Electronic Office), became available in 1951. British Tabulating Machine (BTM) and Powers-Samas sold punch card equipment—the first, Hollerith products, and the second, Powers's own—in the same markets chased by IBM and Remington Rand. Both U.S. firms terminated contracts with these British firms and set up their own operations, beginning to sell locally in 1951. The British firms that had these earlier American alliances remained in their traditional data processing markets in the 1950s, while IBM and the others moved into computers. Prodded by British officials, BTM slowly dabbled with computing, while IBM pushed aggressively ahead. In 1959, BTM and Powers-Samas combined to form International Computers and Tabulators (ICT).

IBM's 1401 killed off the punch card tabulator business, allowing it to grab the lead from British vendors for computers. British computing in the 1960s was about accommodation of this new reality, with the result that IBM permanently destroyed any possibility of local vendors in Britain or elsewhere seriously challenging it. The 1401 bought IBM 40 percent of all computers installed in Great Britain. Until the end of the 1960s, ICL retained 49 percent of the local market.[20] IBM's hold on the high end with S/360s continued, and likewise in the 1970s with S/370s and 4300s. The number of users increased, too.

France offered a potentially larger market. IBM's presence there became subject to greater national and public discussion than in Britain. The French saw IBM as a threat to its economic and cultural independence sooner than Britain had. SEA (Société d'Electronique et d'Automatisme), a French computer start-up, introduced its first computer in 1955. CBM (Compagnie des Machines Bull), like the British BTM, entered the computer business in the second half of the 1950s. CSF (Compagnie Générale de Télegraphie sans Fil) and CGE (Compagnie Générale de Electricité), two large enterprises, sold computers in the early 1960s. Alarm bells went off in Paris because before anybody could stop IBM, it was growing rapidly.[21] In 1949, IBM had 166,000 square feet of French manufacturing and laboratory space, not including sales offices or repair centers. It employed 2,186 people in France. In 1960, just before introducing the 1401, IBM's manufacturing and laboratory space had grown to 553,000 square feet and it employed 6,200 IBMers in France, making it one of the larger companies in France.[22] Its employees worked in one factory, two card-manufacturing facilities, two development laboratories, and 32 sales and service bureau centers scattered around the country, even in French Africa, Madagascar, and Vietnam. The French plant outside the little town of Corbell-Essonnes, 20 miles upstream from Paris on the Seine River, had just been built. It exported parts and equipment to 64 countries and became one of France's largest industrial facilities. IBM's firepower proved even greater, however, because of its 6,200 employees, of whom only 23 percent worked in manufacturing, the rest being engaged in R&D or sales. So even before the magic of the 1401 (later the S/360), IBM had a formidable presence in France.[23] A similar story could be told of IBM's even larger presence in West Germany and its expanding operations in Italy, Spain, Sweden, Finland, Ireland, and the Netherlands, among other nations, all made possible by reinvesting locally generated profits back into the country organizations, augmented by additional funds from company-wide R&D and manufacturing.[24]

But the great battle for the European market was fought in France. Step back a half dozen years before IBM introduced the 1401 and see how its rapidly expanding infrastructure made it possible for it to enter the French market in 1956 with the 650, where it found an active, competitive computer market. It proved to be what observers called an "epic struggle IBM is waging to hold its own in the crucial electronic data processing field."[25] When the 1401 came to France in 1961, it caught all vendors flat-footed. As in Britain, the French government encouraged local firms to step up their game, expand further into computing, and form alliances and mergers, but it was too late. IBM gained control of 50 percent of the market.[26] In the 1960s, other U.S. firms entered the market, notably GE and Control Data, while CMB licensed RCA equipment to sell.

The French government anointed a "national champion," Compagnie Internacionale pour l'Informatique (CII), in the second half of the 1960s. While officials encouraged local customers to consider buying French first, even government agencies bought from IBM, notably its largest departments and the military. The government initiated the first of several Plans Calculs, a national strategy for developing a local computer industry. It portrayed IBM as an American firm, even though it was one of the largest corporate employers in the country and always ranked in the top half dozen French exporters of machines and parts. Officials and the media fixated on threats to the nation's business and culture from American businesses, lumping IBM into that milieu. Meanwhile, GE took control of Machines Bull, a major local company, in 1964.

In 1966, the U.S. National Security Administration (NSA) determined that a CDC system should not be sold to the French military, so the U.S. Department of Defense, which handled the formal export permission process, prevented Control Data from doing so. NSA was concerned that technological information relevant to national security could leak out. That so infuriated President Charles de Gaulle that he launched his Calcul plans in 1967. These efforts failed to stop IBM. IBM's aggressive pricing, quick introduction of new products, and effective "account management" ensured that it dominated the French mainframe market. In the 1970s, French studies discussed the role of IBM and other multinationals in society. The public learned that IBM owned over 70 percent of the market and that no French company held even 10 percent. The government invested over one billion dollars in its local industry between 1967 and 1982, but to little avail.[27]

IBM steamrolled across Western Europe. The larger the enterprise, the quicker IBM penetrated it. Countries with smaller firms were slower in using computers. Not until PCs came into wide use in the 1980s and 1990s did the market for computing dramatically expand across Europe. By the early 1980s, WT had assumed the organizational structure it retained until the end of the century. WT consisted of two parts. First, there was EMEA (Europe, Middle East, and Africa), with Europe the largest portion. The second part, AFE (Americas, Far East), consisted largely of Japan and everyone else. As of the mid-1980s, EMEA was twice the size of AFE. Both were subject to Armonk's dictates on products, revenue targets, and pricing. Hundreds of employees at WT headquarters, in the country organizations, and at IBM's two offshore WT quasiheadquarters in Paris and Tokyo tracked expenses and prospects, and coordinated assignments for the development and manufacture of goods. Europe dominated EMEA, and Japan dominated AFE.

EXPANSION INTO ASIA

Japan came out of World War II devastated. Following the war, it was occupied by Allied military forces for a half decade. Its economy lay in a shambles. Use of data processing remained largely the purview of the occupation forces. Telecommunications and electronics companies came back in the early 1950s, including Nippon Electric (NEC), Fujitsu, Hitachi, and Oki. Unlike their European counterparts, these remained in the computer industry, challenging IBM. How did Japan's computer industry differ from Western Europe's? The industries in both regions initially did well because of national reconstruction, a process that unfolded more quickly in Japan than in many parts of Europe. By 1954, Japanese transistorized computers appeared. The government arranged for investments in its local industry beginning in 1957. Japan's Ministry of International Trade and Industry (MITI), its powerful economic development agency, invested in the economy and in individual companies, and coerced collaboration and increased competition within industries, exercising more authority than its European counterparts. MITI's staff did not hesitate to use their power.

IBM's records are filled with complaints about MITI's heavy-handed treatment of foreign companies, including IBM. MITI slapped tariffs on foreign computers of between 15 and 25 percent. To participate in the local market, IBM agreed to license patents of interest to Japanese companies. IBM was not allowed to bring in capital or technology to manufacture in Japan. In 1960, MITI licensed IBM computer patents for a 5 percent royalty fee.[28] MITI negotiated similar licensing agreements with other firms, such as TRW and Sperry Rand. It used subsidies, low-interest loans, grants, and other financial tools to nurture the local computer industry. It forced Japanese companies to compete against each other. MITI did not choose "national champions." Japanese authorities made it difficult for IBM to sell. Customers needed permission to bring in a "foreign" computer, and they first had to consider local suppliers. By the early 1960s, all foreign vendors combined owned about 60 percent of the Japanese market, but that had slipped to less than half by the late 1980s. Local companies learned how to compete at home and abroad. They were able to compete against IBM's 1401. After IBM introduced its S/360, Japanese vendors responded quickly with compatible systems. Hitachi, NEC, and Toshiba entered the market against IBM. By 1968, Fujitsu was the leading computer vendor in Japan.

MITI's initiative to develop advanced computer technologies, called the "Very High Speed Computer System Project," generated consternation among IBM's scientists, vendors on both sides of the Atlantic, and even in the U.S. Department of Defense. In the mid-1980s, European and U.S. manufacturers worried about Japan's ability to penetrate their markets with inexpensive high-quality television sets, stereo equipment, automobiles, personal computers, other electronic devices, and even wristwatches, creating the same angst in corporate America as the French and British experienced in the 1960s and 1970s regarding U.S. vendors.[29]

A feature of IBM's relations with Japan was the constant and complicated negotiations for permission to operate in the country. All agreements existed only for a few years, yet IBM was able to retain 100 percent ownership of IBM Japan and to manufacture in the country.[30] Despite constraints, IBM remained profitable over many years. IBM Japan employed local nationals from top to bottom. IBM concluded that its Japanese customers would support it against government insistence on partial local ownership and thus never had to surrender it.[31] After the government backed down on the issue in the 1970s, IBM increased its investment in local manufacturing and education.

IBM managers believed that many of the business practices in Japanese companies had been borrowed from them, largely in the 1950s. As one IBM manager mused, "IBM was probably also a key model ... for the Japanese corporations," thinking of IBM's and Japan's similar full-employment policies, job enrichment programs, continuing training, quality control, intense customer service, and ethics.[32] That did not make doing business in Japan any easier. American IBM executives resented Japanese policies and the brevity of its own Japanese employees when reporting results to IBM Corporate. Given the competitive environment and MITI's hostility, the company still held 30 percent or more of the mainframe market in the 1970s and 1980s.[33]

As other Asian economies industrialized in the 1960s and later, IBM expanded into them. These included Indonesia, Singapore, Taiwan, and South Korea.[34] Australia and New Zealand were already active markets in the 1950s, similar to those in the United Kingdom and Canada. IBM's relative success in Japan, however, allowed it to expand across Asia in the 1950s to 1980s, opening sales offices that for a time reported to IBM Japan until they had critical mass to establish themselves as country companies.

ELUSIVE LATIN AMERICA

It seems that every large North American corporation plans and hopes for massive success in South America, and IBM was no exception. The region had a population comparable in size to North America's. It had natural and mineral assets similar in volume and diversity. Nevertheless, the reality of 21 countries with French, Spanish, Portuguese, and English cultures, varying business traditions, and unstable economic and political circumstances made it impossible for U.S. corporations to achieve the massive growth they could in North America, but enough business existed that no major enterprise could ignore it. WT's experience proved complicated for reasons largely unique to the region, but, as with Europe and Asia, its activities in Latin America were both about its actions and the company operating as an internationally integrated enterprise.

On January 1, 1959, Fidel Castro completed his six-year revolution in Cuba against the government of Fulgencio Batista. Just 33 years old, bearded, and wearing combat fatigue–styled uniforms, Castro seemed wild looking to middle- and upper-class Cubans and to the people IBMers sold to in Havana and in Santiago de Cuba. Their personal and professional situations deteriorated because, within months of gaining control, Castro announced his intention to run a socialist, then a communist, state. Within barely a month of taking power, his government began confiscating properties of wealthy Cubans, including private companies. Then, on August 6, 1960, Castro nationalized all foreign-owned businesses.

That action put Marcial Digat, IBM's manager, out of business, because the company stopped operations, could no longer send products to Cuba, and now had Cuban employees who needed to leave the island for fear of being arrested as political enemies of the state. In the 1950s, he represented the company in Cuba, selling to government agencies, banks, insurance companies, and manufacturing firms. Prior to that, he had held important positions in the Cuban government. Like so many of his social class, Digat was suspected of being an enemy of the new state and so with just a few dollars to his name, he, his wife, Anita, and their children fled Cuba, leaving behind their home and possessions. Arthur Watson gave Digat a job in WT headquarters in New York. From that posting, Digat extracted other employees and placed them in various Latin American IBM offices. As one Latin American IBMer recalled, these Cubans "ended up having better jobs than what they had within IBM of Cuba."[35] Meanwhile, IBM was no longer selling data processing goods and services in Cuba.

Revolutions in Latin America disrupted routine business. Bigger challenges usually came in the form of runaway inflation that harmed IBM's ability to extract its earnings out of a country. Brazil, so important to IBM in Latin America, chronically suffered bouts of stagflation or inflation and economic turmoil. Superficial reforms, lack of political will, and corruption made business there challenging. In 1990–1993, for example,

Brazilian employees checked daily to see what the rate of inflation was and then determined whether to spend their money immediately to buy groceries, gas, or other items before they increased in cost over the next several days. How does a company pay its employees or charge customers under those conditions? Each financial crisis raised such issues across the continent and in the Caribbean.

Despite these problems, IBM's activities in Latin America mimicked routines evident in other parts of the world. Its customers were large organizations that took delivery of IBM's computers at roughly the same time as North American users, they just took fewer since there were fewer customers. Expansion in Latin America followed the familiar pattern of agents followed by local IBM companies. Branch offices opened in capital cities, then in other large urban centers. As WT expanded across Latin America, it opened regional offices to provide coordinated control and the kinds of resource sharing occurring in Europe and, through Japan, with other parts of Asia.

In the post–World War II period, both Watson Sr. and his son Arthur traveled throughout the region, meeting with employees, customers, and political leaders. They participated in IBM rituals such as 100 Percent Club meetings and Family Dinners. It was not always easy to carry out IBM's rituals. For example, in 1950, Watson Sr. visited Bogotá, Colombia. As was customary, local IBM leader Luis A. Lamassonne prepared for his arrival. He explained, "We had already inspected the only hotel where we could hold the reception, the Hotel Estacion! We found it in complete shambles, and had to arrange to renovate and paint the dining room, as well as change all of the curtains.... We even had to buy the china that would be used."[36]

In almost every country, national economies slowly evolved into forms that fit IBM's profile for customers. Large enterprises and government agencies were core to IBM's business in Brazil, Argentina, Mexico, Chile, and to a lesser extent also in Uruguay, Colombia, and Cuba. In each country, IBMers had cultivated business since the 1920s and, as that grew, they had established a local presence. By the early 1950s, IBM operated in Argentina, Brazil, Ecuador, Costa Rica, Chile, Colombia, Mexico, Peru,

Uruguay, Venezuela, Cuba, and all of Central America. Elsewhere, it had agents, such as in Trinidad, until it opened a sales office there in 1957. IBM set up a South American Area headquarters in Montevideo to play the same role as Paris and Tokyo. WT managed all of Central America as one region, and likewise with the Caribbean Area and the South American Area. At the height of 1401 sales, the South American Area established two regions, with the highly unimaginative names of Region One and Region Two. Region One consisted of Argentina, Brazil, and Uruguay, while Region Two controlled Bolivia, Chile, Colombia, Ecuador, Paraguay, and Peru. Local managers who had came up through IBM led offices in countries and regions.

Sales of 1401s led to major growth in the 1960s. Local manufacturing of parts, and later machines, followed the same pattern as in Europe for the same reasons. Additional activities included manufacturing punch cards and electric typewriters. Just as IBM was getting ready to deliver S/360s, IBM Brazil was exporting to other Latin American countries parts and products valued at $1.8 million. IBM's business grew along with its infrastructure. First came the 1401s, then S/360s (beginning in 1966), while the older product remained Latin America's computer workhorse. IBM dominated its southern markets to the same extent it did in Western Europe.

As the number of branch offices, manufacturing facilities, service bureaus, and customer briefing centers increased, so did WT's structure. On April 2, 1973, IBM launched a new organization: Americas/Far East Corporation (AFE), a wholly owned subsidiary of the company. In 1974, Ralph A. Pfeiffer Jr. (1926–1996) became its chairman. He worked at IBM for 37 years, starting as a salesman in Cleveland, Ohio, in 1949 and rapidly rising up the sales side of Domestic IBM. In 1970, he became president of the Data Processing Division, a highly prized job. He brought to AFE well-regarded managerial skills that helped him impose the same discipline and practices in the rapidly growing Latin American operations that had served IBM elsewhere. As Latin American business increased, so did the area's presence in Corporate. In 1983, Pfeiffer became a member of the corporate management board, and the following year he became chairman and chief executive officer of IBM World Trade Corporation.[37] Early in his management of AFE, Pfeiffer ran four regions in Latin America, Northern, Central, Eastern, and Western, mimicking names used for U.S. regions. He encouraged closer ties to North American operations, for example having customers visit U.S. operations. In 1977, AFE launched an educational tour for 30 Latin American and Asian educators from 24 countries to visit IBM's research center, the T. J. Watson Research Center, nestled in Westchester County, New York, and universities in New Hampshire, Tennessee, and Florida.

IBM's 4300 computers proved as popular in Latin America as in the United States and for the same reasons. PCs also did well, although they remained largely stand-alone systems without telecommunications until the 1990s. A litany of reorganizations throughout the 1980s and 1990s accommodated an ever-growing number of branch offices. Almost every year in the second half of the century, IBM opened up offices, manufacturing facilities, or education centers in Latin America. IBM had country general managers assigned to 20 nations by the early 1970s, all of them locals, managing thousands of employees, a population that expanded until the mid-1980s.

But not all went well. By then, local IBMers were complaining about "bureaucracy that continued to grow without limits."[38] Years after retiring, one Latin American IBM executive observed that in addition to the problem of bureaucracy, another had grown worldwide, not just in Latin America: "the arrogance of the Company amidst its grandeur". In time, IBM paid a price for its problems, and not just in South America.[39]

RISING TIDE OF GLOBAL COMPETITION

IBMers looked at competition through several lenses. Corporate, sales, and product division headquarters had since the 1920s maintained staffs whose sole purpose was to learn as much about competitors as possible: product features, prices, contracting terms and conditions, customer attitudes, sales volumes, and who their customers were worldwide. Computer scientists, engineers, and product developers did the same, but with a particular eye on developing responses to competitors with better, faster, or less expensive products. Sales staff, the "field," represented the third lens, the group that watched what was happening within their accounts. Normally, historians of IBM treat Corporate, Domestic, and WT solely in terms of the company's strategy, such as how it leveraged national tax laws, drove down costs of manufacturing and marketing, and organized resources to have sufficient firepower aimed at entire markets worldwide. IBM, however, was a complex organization with different communities and regions that independently viewed competitive forces through their parochial lenses. Over time, however, the roles of WT, Domestic, and Corporate became more integrated, more monolithic, with respect to how IBM *as a whole* responded to a rising tide of global competition. As rivals scaled up to challenge IBM around the world, it responded with more integrated approaches to product development, pricing, terms and conditions, marketing, advertising, and sales. By the 1970s, WT increasingly functioned within that context of the behemoth.

When an industry observer, U.S. antitrust lawyer, or economist looked at IBM's performance against the competition, they either viewed the number of times IBM faced competitors at the account level or at the top of the organization, where product pricing decisions were being made. They drew conclusions largely on those bits of information, but all segments and layers of IBM spent almost as much time worrying about actual or potential competitors as they did in understanding what customers wanted. It is a central observation about IBM's culture, and no more so than for the years after the commercialization of computers, when so many *types* of rivals took on IBM. For that reason, all three spoke a common language, that of specific products versus those of rivals. While the higher up the organization one went, the more strategy and markets (hence market share) caught interest, all levels focused on two priorities: preserving the base of machines (hence current revenues) in every account and increasing market share. The definition of market share varied as one moved up and down the organization. At Corporate, executives talked about what share of all installed machines of a particular class IBM "owned," such as mainframes (1950s–1990s), PCs (1980s–1990s), distributed processors (1970s–2000s), and so forth.

WT thought in terms of how much of Germany's IT "spend" went to IBM. At the branch level, it was all about how many competitors were kept out of its territory or how many competing machines were still installed that IBMers planned to displace. At that level and often at regional and division levels in sales, IBMers still knew by customer enterprise what competitors had installed, how long they had been there, often the enemy salesman's name (not just the vendor firm's), and exact terms of their offerings, and had plans for surmounting them.

As IBM increasingly used business partners for ever-larger products and accounts, it attempted to impose such competitive disciplines on them. This strategy yielded mixed results, as for example with minicomputers in the 1970s, PCs in the 1980s, and application software from the 1980s to the first decade of the new millennium. Mixed results arose out of the uneven performance of IBM's partners and frequent rivalries with local IBM salesmen if their compensation terms did not clearly delineate who was responsible for specific types of sales. Nevertheless, business partnerships remained a tool used by WT, harkening back to a strategy used by Watson Sr.

One mechanism facilitating further integration of all parts of the company involved standardization of company-wide policies and practices, which spurred bureaucracy in the 1960s and 1970s. That meant there were employees whose primary job did not involve engaging with competition or whose objectives were seemingly in conflict with other parts of IBM battling competitors. By the 1960s, "marketing practices" departments approved proposed terms and conditions, such as pricing, that a salesman wanted to use against competitors. Often these departments said "no" because of some general rule or out of fear that if they gave in to one individual then "everyone" would want the same terms. Such a turn of events was seen as threatening IBM's high profits across a product line.

Lawyers represented another class of employees often more concerned about aspects of IBM's well-being than about competition, although when engaged in a specific customer situation they could be counted on to be helpful, especially those in a sales region or division. Lawyers working outside a direct sales organization might hold other views. For example, during the U.S. antitrust suit in the 1970s, lawyers counseled senior executives not to "own" more than 50 percent of any national market for fear that regulators would want to interfere. No self-respecting sales executive would ever want to obey such guidance; nonetheless, they heard it anyway. A third group—finance and planning (F&P)—might advise against an expenditure or a perceived affordability in order to control expenses or to implement a strategy to sustain a certain level of profitability, regardless of market realities.[40] The influence of all three communities—marketing practices, "Legal," and F&P—ebbed and flowed, depending on immediate realities. When American, Western European, and Japanese officials were concerned with IBM's market dominance, lawyers held sway. When IBM dominated a market, marketing practices became more influential. When profits were under pressure, F&P played an increased role. It is remarkable, however, how so much of IBM's culture and behavior had remained consistent worldwide from one decade to another since the 1950s. Responses to competitive pressures globally, nationally, and locally could vary as circumstances changed and new rivals came and went.

In Western Europe in the 1950s and 1960s, three types of mainframe rivals went after IBM's tabulator customers: office appliance manufacturers, electrical device suppliers, and newly established computer firms. Many left the market when it became evident that the investment required to build computers, let alone go up against IBM, proved too rich for them or their home governments to fund. As business historians Martin Campbell-Kelly and Daniel D. Garcia-Swartz put it, "By the late 1940s, no other company in the world had developed a combination of capabilities that mattered for success in electronic computers as comprehensive as those of IBM."[41] The same abilities applied to events in the 1950s, 1960s, and 1970s.[42]

By 1980, American rivals were operating in IBM's non-U.S. markets, a new development. By then, the world was calling IBM "Big Blue," while in the United States its rivals were pejoratively still referred to as "the Seven Dwarfs." IBMers argued that they had scores of rivals worldwide in each market niche. By then, about 46 percent of all computers were installed outside the United States, evidence of a growing global market. As in the now large U.S. computer industry, valued at over $6 billion, additional billions were being spent worldwide. All this occurred prior to the arrival of the PC. Mainframe markets remained essentially the same worldwide in the 1980s as the PC platform rapidly infiltrated markets and customers.

Customers did not distinguish between World Trade, Domestic, or Corporate; IBM was simply a large U.S. firm. Global coordination of IBM's operations increasingly attracted other large international corporations that also were integrating operations and thus appreciated IBM's ability to provide coordinated account support worldwide through its Selected International Accounts (SIA) program. SIA managers in Switzerland told American salesmen what to do with respect to ABB, another in the Netherlands gave advice regarding IBM's operations in Indonesia with Shell, an American in Detroit advised with respect to General Motors in Latin America, and so forth. Customers learned from IBM how to integrate their own globalized operations, while IBMers also learned from them.

However, we still face the question, what were IBM's comprehensive responses to its growing list of rivals around the world? The answer to that question inserts us into the core of IBM's global business strategy in the period from the 1960s to 1990 and the role of a new CEO.

FRANK T. CARY AND THE GROWTH OF A BEHEMOTH

By the early 1970s, in addition to focusing on rivals selling mainframes, plug-compatible computers, and leasing companies, IBM was also entering a new era. Thomas J. Watson Sr. was dead. Arthur Watson had resigned in 1970 and was soon followed by Tom Watson Jr. in 1971, the latter for health reasons. All of a sudden, there were no Watsons at IBM! The Old Man's office at 590 Madison Avenue in New York existed almost as a shrine. In 1974, Arthur Watson fell down the stairs in his home and died of his injuries at the age of 55. His last few years had been sad, marred by alcohol abuse and a short-lived post-IBM tour as U.S. ambassador to France that ended after an incident on an airplane. No other members of the Watson family worked at IBM.

IBM's senior executives had all come up in Watsonian IBM, with a heritage they applied through the 1980s, but the reality of their changed circumstances became evident when new people sat atop IBM's throne: Vin "T. V." Learson as chairman and, more importantly for day-to-day operations, the mild-mannered, gentlemanly Frank T. Cary (1920–2006) as CEO. Looking at what Cary's generation accomplished contradicts myths that the U.S. government's litigation against IBM in the 1970s slowed (or stopped) the company in its pursuit of worldwide revenues. Caution seeped into the company's culture and behavior, but that was after a raft of lawsuits had been settled in the second half of the 1980s and early 1990s in the United States, not while lawyers were compelling IBM to spend tens of

Figure 11.2
More than any other IBM CEO, Frank T. Cary turned IBM into a global behemoth. Photo courtesy of IBM Corporate Archives.

millions of dollars annually fending off competitors and government prosecutors. WT was not immune to IBM's continued globalization, nor was its new CEO, who oversaw that transformation. Because IBM's worldwide business grew substantially during Cary's tenure as CEO, it is appropriate to discuss his role within the context of our review of World Trade and to emphasize that he was a global CEO, not focused only on U.S. operations. Observers of the IBM of the 1970s have ignored his broader role.

Cary lived through the era of the birth and diffusion of mainframes. He was in the thick of the rough-and-tumble battles that made the 1401 and then the S/360. Like so many of his generation, he came to understand the power of grand strategy as practiced by large multinational enterprises, especially regarding how IBM priced products, a secret he and a tiny coterie of executives learned from T. V. Learson and pricing experts in the central Hudson Valley of New York. It was perhaps more than ironic that the first long-serving CEO in the post-Watson era was not from the East Coast. Born in Gooding, Iowa, raised in Inglewood, California, and graduating from the University of California at Los Angeles, Cary went on to complete an MBA from Stanford University in 1948. That same year, he joined IBM as a salesman in Los Angeles. Cary rose quickly through the ranks from sales manager, to branch manager, and then, in 1964, to president of the Data Processing Division, which led the charge in selling S/360s in the United States. Two years later, he became general manager of the Data Processing Group, in effect running all U.S. sales. In 1967, he became a senior vice president. After two more promotions, in March 1971 he became a member of the company's senior roundtable, the Executive Committee, and three months later was named president of IBM.

With this background, Cary knew about IBM's competition and how to sell computers, deploy people, and allocate budgets. His most important midcareer duties involved selling S/360s. He learned about the product's pricing dynamics at a time when the cost of computing was dropping so quickly that the technology was evolving into a commodity, creating a major problem waiting to blow up in Armonk's conference rooms. Plug-compatibles and leasing companies were Cary's crosses to bear. A quiet, efficient financial executive, Hillary Faw, responded to Cary's request for insights in a note that in time U.S. antitrust lawyers flaunted as proof of IBM's strategy for dealing with rivals, a memorandum that helped Cary pull back the kimono hiding useful strategic ideas that informed future management teams. Faw wrote that leading with prices and controlling them was key to IBM's success:

> IBM has established the value of data processing usage. IBM then maintains or controls that value by various means: timing of new technological insertion; functional pricing ... refusal to market surplus used equipment; refusal to discount for age or for quantity; strategic location of function in boxes; "solution selling" rather than hardware selling.
>
> The key underpinnings to our control of price are interrelated and interdependent.... These interrelationships are not well understood by IBM Management. Our price control has been sufficiently absolute to render unnecessary direct management involvement in the means.[43]

Some of these precepts were modified in the 1980s but not during Cary's tenure.

Two years later, in 1969, the U.S. antitrust suit had begun, in time shaping what Cary did in the 1970s, but he already knew about the power of pricing, setting higher prices for computer memory upgrades when facing little competition while holding down the cost of mainframes, and of pricing disk drives using IBM's own manufactured components, adjusting prices and configurations with new computers, just as Faw had argued IBM had done in the 1950s and 1960s. In other words, while sellers were selling, Corporate focused on pricing and configurations of equipment. Cary aimed his weapons at leasing companies in Europe and North America by cutting prices, charging for software that used to be free to customers of both leasing companies and IBM, and forcing lessors to lower prices even though both they and leasing customers had signed long-term contracts based on prior higher IBM ones. Midsized customers found their costs for computing dropping thanks to IBM's pricing. When the price of S/360s dropped at the start of the 1970s, IBM killed off this product line, replacing it with S/370s that cost little enough to destroy demand for S/360s and charging for upgrades of memory and peripheral equipment larger computers called for. These actions came as demand for computing by new and existing customers was expanding worldwide.

Concerns regarding litigation in the United States and potentially in Europe also influenced how Cary and his executives reacted to competition. Worries about litigation hounded his generation, beginning before he was CEO, while IBM was in the thick of S/360 sales. How litigation influenced IBM's relationships with competitors is illustrated by the firm's unbundling decision in 1969. In 1968, IBM faced antimonopolistic lawsuits in the United States filed by competitors. The U.S. Department of Justice was pressured by them to sue IBM, most aggressively by CDC. As a preventive action against possibly losing cases, IBM explored unbundling software; that is, charging customers for some software and other services while offering lower leases for hardware to smooth out the total costs to users. That strategy would allow leasing companies to sell machines to customers and possibly take the air out of a potential federal case and possibly private lawsuits in Western Europe and Japan. It is an important point because historians of IBM's unbundling decision described it as an American event, but by the end of the 1960s, all pricing and product strategies in the company were weighed against broader considerations of a global market.

In mid-1969, IBM announced unbundling, to begin January 1, 1970, drawing the attention of customers and competitors worldwide as they pondered the implications of this change in software pricing. While designed mostly as a response to U.S. litigation circumstances, IBM's international ecosystem took note, especially large multinational customers with data centers outside of the United States that coordinated with IBM on a global basis. Meanwhile, U.S. customers thought IBM had not done enough to even out costs, that hardware prices had not dropped sufficiently to compensate for what they now would have to pay in total. Competitors, too, were not happy, arguing that IBM had not done enough to open up markets for them. Unbundling failed to dissuade the federal government from pursuing an antitrust case against IBM, discussed in detail in chapter 12. IBM made no immediate profit on the deal, as its costs for developing software were already sunk so they could not quickly be recovered, because software was to be leased, not sold. The industry entered its first global recession in 1970–1971. Burton Grad, a member of IBM's two task forces that prepared the details of this announcement, recalled that "IBM acted from fear that antitrust actions against it would succeed because of IBM's previous discriminatory bundling of services with computer products," with unbundling designed to mitigate this problem, IBM "acting in its own, primarily defensive self-interest when it unbundled."[44]

Pricing, litigation, competitive pressures, an international economic recession, and now customer expressions of opinions about how IBM should offer all manner of products and services complicated decision making for Cary and his senior leaders. Cary had learned that problems required varied and continuous fixes, that pricing strategies were never enough, no longer the silver bullets they seemed a half decade earlier. Too many circumstances had changed quickly, and Cary had to do more.

To set the scene, Cary became CEO in 1973 and ran IBM's operations until 1981, a fact that is a bit confusing, as he was also chairman of the board from 1973 to 1983. He held all the global reins of power and control, even though, as in any large corporation, he still needed to persuade other executives to go along with his ideas, and he still relied on task forces to work up the details on an issue and make recommendations. Nevertheless, he could look at the entire world and think about how to play IBM across the map. Even Tom Jr. had only some of that power after his father died, as he had to share it with his brother. Cary had a worldwide operation up and running. WT was real, with organizations, factories, branch offices, and experienced IBMers on the ground. Not since Watson Sr. had so much authority been invested in one person. Even then, the "Old Man" never ran a company as big as the one Cary was running. In 1973, Cary had over 150,000 employees in the United States and another 120,000 around the world. That year, IBM generated almost $11 billion in gross income and net earnings of nearly $1.6 billion. When Cary retired in 1983, the company had almost 370,000 IBMers, generating over $40 billion in revenue and $5.5 billion in net earnings.[45]

At the beginning of Cary's tenure, it was not clear that he would be the strong leader to follow Watson Jr. or could push forward a large, bureaucratic organization. One knowledgeable computer industry watcher, Ernest von Simson, sided with the doubters, but decades later, when reflecting on those times, concluded that, "All of us were wrong. Frank Cary was the first professional manager to head a traditionally entrepreneurial company that had outgrown its traces. His style may have been more modest than [that of] his predecessors." He was not flamboyant.[46] Watson Jr. agreed: "The fact was that for eight years he ran the company as well as it had ever been run."[47] Cary epitomized the "Organization Man" of his time.

His first challenge concerned the leasing companies gaining on IBM, since their ability to sell secondhand equipment at lower cost constrained IBM's ability to charge higher prices, threatening the controlled revenue and profit growth IBM so cherished. Cary had already experienced rounds of meetings over several years before the S/370s were introduced, internal battles and "non-concur" blocks to one form of technology or other, and considerations of various strategies. IBM documents made public in lawsuits from the period recorded his frustration. For example, Cary wrote Learson on November 5, 1971: "Organization indecision was intolerable." So it went, with other memos expressing annoyance in the months ahead.[48] Cary advocated introducing less expensive S/370s in response to competitors, even if it meant taking a short-term hit on revenues and irritating customers who had installed early S/370s. He got his way. Customers in the early 1970s swapped out their 370 Model 155s and 165s for replacements sooner than they had planned. Leasing companies were stuck holding warehouses of these now technologically obsolete systems, which dropped in value by 20–40 percent from their original purchase price. They did not learn their lesson and came back in the mid-1970s, leasing the new Models 158 and 168. Cary & Co. again introduced new computers and peripherals at lower cost and with new features, again chasing off leasing companies in Europe and North America.

But Cary knew IBM's process for introducing products was deteriorating. Every S/370 decision proved cumbersome, slow, and risked not being made in time to counter rivals. Senior sales executives feared salesmen were losing control over their accounts. In the 1970s, the game was turning on who had the least-expensive machines, a change from the 1960s, when it was all about price/performance. Cary pushed for resolution of a number of problems a task force had identified in 1971: a broken product-planning process, "complexity" emanating from IBM and its rivals, not to mention a growing variety of "vested interests," software development (now a profit center) at odds with the hardware divisions (also profit centers), quality of the staffs involved, and too much interference by senior executives. The task force even blamed Learson by name for too much meddling, a breach of company etiquette but obviously necessary to call out. Cary chose to decentralize operations to speed IBM's response to changing market conditions.

On January 13, 1972, Cary split the Data Processing Group in two, with sales, maintenance, and planning in one part and components and software product development in the other. He named the first cluster the Marketing and Services Group, the second the Data Processing Product Group. John Opel, Cary's future successor as CEO, took charge of the second group. A third organization, the General Business Group, focused on smaller customers, while the existing Office Products Division sold typewriters and other word processors. However, this reorganization created a problem that lasted through the 1970s. Customers were now being visited by Data Processing Division sales staff for large systems while salespeople from the General Business Division called on them for midsized ones, sometimes in competition for the same business as DPD's, and, of course, the typewriter salesmen from OPD called on them as well. Customers worldwide complained about this problem for a decade. Cary had created three vertically integrated groups essentially autonomous of each other. His decisions had little to do with lawsuits or the antitrust case. They were about responding to rivals around the world.

The organizations created by Watson Jr. were hardly recognizable. Big breakthroughs with systemwide products were no longer relevant. Now IBM faced worldwide markets where it had to compete for every piece of business while costs of computing (e.g., computer chips) continued to decline. Introductions of technology would be done in an evolutionary, incremental manner. In May 1975, Cary took the extra step of reorganizing the specialized business units into self-sufficient product divisions. For example, software came under control of the product divisions. Bob Evans, long IBM's advocate for technological compatibility across systems, left his job, replaced by Allen Krowe (b. 1932). Krowe was a high-energy financial executive who later served as IBM's chief financial officer in the early 1980s, when he was credited with inventing the euphemism "negative growth" to put a positive spin on poor financial performance. Subsequent reorganizations slowed advanced product planning activities, while mainframe development was split into two parts: one to produce products to compete against Amdahl and Japanese rivals, the other to compete against minicomputers. Jack Kuehler (1932–2008), another engineer who in the late 1980s served as president of IBM, led the latter. An IBM observer in 1978 summed up the situation: "IBM is now in the box business, not total systems," because "we can't afford the delays, confusion, lack of software accountability, and endless coordination it takes to deliver total systems."[49]

Setting aside potential antitrust consequences, the new decentralized organizations attacked their competitors with what can only be described as a blizzard of product announcements in the late 1970s and early 1980s that seemed to appear almost monthly or quarterly, including the iconic IBM PC, discussed later. To clarify who IBM's rivals were, there were four types: manufacturers of plug-compatible mainframes; a growing collection of vendors selling plug-compatible peripheral equipment; leasing companies, which ranged from one-man operations to nationally based financial companies; and scores of minicomputer suppliers. This competitive landscape remained unchanged in the 1980s. By mid-decade, IBM encountered a fifth rival: PC-compatibles, such as Compaq. Apple, already active, was a minor player at the time.

In January 1981, having reached the customary retirement age of 60, Cary stepped aside from day-to-day operations. The board of directors replaced him with John Opel as CEO, while Cary stayed on as chairman for two more years and as a member of IBM's board for ten more years. During his tenure as CEO and chairman, he had decentralized product development and midwifed IBM's PC, introduced in August 1981, and had grown the company (figure 11.3). Cary should be remembered for hammering plug-compatible rivals and leasing companies, too, although they never went away. Amdahl, for example, periodically infused with new

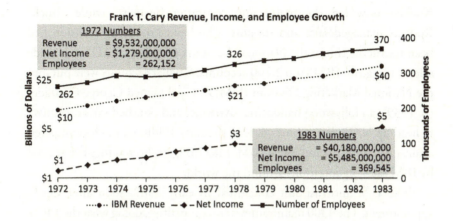

Figure 11.3

Revenue, income, and employee growth under Frank T. Cary, 1972–1983. Courtesy of Peter E. Greulich, copyright © 2017 MBI Concepts Corporation.

funding from Japanese investors, continued to needle IBM's mainframe business into the 1990s.

Opel quickly focused on competition. Articulate and methodical, he, too, had come up in U.S. sales in a career that paralleled Cary's. Thanks to IBM's strategies, thousands of rivals had either gone out of business or consolidated into fewer, more muscular ones requiring new responses. The new names that kept appearing on competitive analysis reports in the 1970s and early 1980s included DEC, H-P, Wang, and, by the mid-1980s, a raft of PC rivals, notably Compaq. Opel consolidated operations to drive down costs and increase focus. He established three major entities: large computers, midsized ones (he put PCs in with this group), and all field operations. He dissolved specialized units, such as those selling typewriters (Office Products Division) and General Systems, which had sold a new distributed minicomputer called the S/1 as a quick, if anemic, response to rising mini competition.

Senior leaders were of Opel's generation, notably John Akers (1934–2014), a future CEO of IBM who had come up in sales the same way as Cary and Opel. Akers took over the midsized computer and PC pieces of the business and brought Krowe over as his vice president of finance.

Kuehler now led the mainframe computer business, while "Buck" Rodgers managed sales and support. The Data Processing Division had been restructured into the National Accounts Division (NAD) to provide sales coverage for IBM's top 2,200 accounts. Smaller accounts were put into the National Marketing Division (NMD). Opel named George Conrades (b. 1939), a Hollywood handsome, dynamic, and polished sales executive, to head up NAD. For a short while in the early 1990s, Conrades competed against Akers for the top job at IBM. Like Rodgers, he was highly regarded by IBM sales organizations around the world.

The U.S. antitrust suit concluded in early 1982, soon after Opel's appointment. The 4300 mainframes were competitive, doing what the 1401s had earlier, expanding the base of new accounts and users within existing accounts. Sales of PCs were doing well, so Opel reverted back to IBM's old practice of setting controllable annual growth targets of 18 percent. Things looked fine, but quickly the product divisions again began creating incompatible products that often proved uncompetitive. These included minicomputers and, later, newer models of PCs. As Simson wrote, "It was creativity run amok that would bedevil John Akers a decade later."[50]

To expand business and continue hammering the intrusion of small and large competitors, IBMers, particularly those in NAD, focused on expanding their footprint within existing large accounts. While they tussled with plug-compatibles in the "glass house," normally controlled by an MIS director reporting to the CFO, IBM's sales force began calling on other departments. These included engineering, factories, and distribution centers, leveraging their growing industry knowledge to sell new applications. They taught "end users" how to apply computers to improve operations or to lower labor costs. IBMers had become captives of the management information systems (MIS) directors in glass houses who did not want them drumming up new business that would bring more work to them, while IBMers felt compelled to break away from these data processing directors who threatened to do business with plug-compatibles. Most customers continued to use IBM equipment. While only a third of all business opportunities in IBM "glass house" accounts were contested (this was more common with end users), that was still a large number for a company that wanted "account control." Opel, and later Akers, retrained field staff to sell applications; the approach worked. IBM's revenue kept growing. In 1984, IBM had 405,000 employees worldwide. Its high-water mark came in 1990, after a decade of continuous growth, culminating in nearly $69 billion in revenue and almost $6 billion in profits, but with a smaller population of employees, because it was already feeling the pinch of declining business and margins, so it ended the year with 373,000 workers.[51]

Executives worried about the surge of Japanese imports into the United States, but with no radical changes anticipated in technology, it seemed IBM's existing pricing strategies remained effective. Between the 4300 and IBM's PCs, revenue grew rapidly in the early 1980s, jumping from $29 billion in 1981, Opel's first year at the helm, to $46 billion just three years later. It seemed to employees, customers, competitors, and the business press that IBM could do little wrong. It was a darling of the stock market and often the number one company on anyone's list, but the future was being compromised. To increase revenues when computers were still dropping in cost, IBM decided to shift from leasing equipment to encouraging outright purchase of its products. IBM increasingly favored the earlier, larger cash infusion that resulted from outright sales, weaning itself off the leasing business model it had embraced for over 90 years. In exchange for that shift, IBM lost the predictability of cash flows that came from leases. The sales organization worldwide disapproved of this change in strategy. Conrades & Co. even had to entice the field with bonuses to sell rather than lease products. Leasing companies could buy a flood of secondhand equipment by the end of the decade, which they could lease to IBM's customers in competition with the company's new products. Another cost to IBM involved the decline of account control as long-term relations greased by the lock of a lease on both IBMers and customers declined, transforming relationships into transaction-based ones rather than the more collaborative services-centered relationships of old.

History likes to blame Akers for IBM's decline and near death, but IBM caught the deadly infection in Opel's day. Because the largest competitive battles still occurred inside the glass house over mainframes and peripheral equipment, salesmen, and their leaders in the corner office of the CEO, focused more attention on these aspects of the business than on PC sales or other opportunities. It seemed to many employees that IBM was running on autopilot. Akers succeeded Opel as CEO in February 1985, and his story will be told later, since he is credited with single-handedly nearly destroying IBM, resulting in his firing in January 1993. However, we are getting ahead of our story, because we must first understand how going global during the Watson Jr. and Cary years affected IBM, contributing to the malaise Akers confronted.

IBM had become so large by the end of the 1960s that it kept growing seemingly in a world of its own making. It had its own vernacular, processes, and rules for everything, and its customers were largely cocooned within IBM's technologies and technical standards. Competitors could not scale up. Governments the size of Great Britain's, France's, and Germany's could not assist their national champions, with Japan being the exception. While Latin Americans did not see IBM as a threat to their economic survival, with the muted exception of Brazil, in Europe more IBM equipment was already installed. A handful of IBM corporate managers could make decisions affecting whole nations. Perhaps the most interesting example is what happened in India.

IBM LEAVES INDIA, THEN RETURNS

In the 1950s and 1960s, India was one of the world's largest poor countries. Its industrial base looked more like Europe's of the pre-1860s, and its use of data processing equipment remained minimal. After gaining independence from the British in 1947, it followed the Soviet model of building up heavy industry, resulting in growth of the local economy of about 3.5 percent each year, while its population expanded faster. Famine always seemed a threat, and poverty the nation's hallmark. The national government had committed itself to socialism, implemented through autarkic practices. This was not good for U.S. companies like IBM, which functioned best in open market economies.

The Indian government wanted to leapfrog economic and managerial phases nations went through to apply the kinds of advanced technologies represented by computers and other industrial equipment. In the mid-1960s, the government accused IBM of dumping old 1401s into India instead of making available the new, more sophisticated S/360s. Local task forces called for India to become self-sufficient in supplying the nation's computer needs. One study, prepared by the Bhabha Committee, laughably suggested the nation's entire needs could be met with an investment of $4.2 million on the latest technologies, but, in 1967, its recommendations became public policy. The committee failed to account for the lack of local computing skills, experienced managers, and even business conditions that could benefit from computers.

One by-product of this naive approach to computing hit IBM hard. Indian regulators came to IBM in the late 1960s to discuss sharing part ownership of IBM India with local investors. It was not a new idea; European governments had broached that possibility, but IBM turned them away without hesitation. IBM's executives, both local and those from New York, turned down India's proposal, arguing what turned out to be the truth of the matter. They told the Indians that IBM managed a worldwide, integrated product development and manufacturing process. To make that process work, it had to manage in a centralized fashion, and IBM was organized around that construct. To divert some of IBM's control to a local IBM company's operations by selling off part ownership would compromise the efficiency of that process. IBM executives believed that argument so much that they were prepared to do the unthinkable: walk away from the second-largest country in the world. As talks continued in 1968, executives warned they were prepared to exit if necessary. The Indians backed down.

Indian officials had also been talking to other companies, and the British company ICL caved in. It agreed to allow an Indian-owned manufacturing plant, as it did not have a highly integrated worldwide manufacturing process comparable to IBM's. In those years (1968–1972), the Indian government failed to wrest control of its tiny computer industry from foreign companies; it had no indigenous industry yet. Perhaps two locally built systems had been sold in India, while another 185 came from other countries.[52] India wanted foreign companies to manufacture locally, which foreign manufacturers resisted. Instead, some decided to bring in older products, much as IBM did with 1401s. IBM's practices meant India would not get the latest technologies, such as IBM's S/360s and later S/370s, which IBM, and India's actions, blocked from coming into the country and would prove too expensive for local customers anyway.

IBM's position did not stop the Indians. They came back to IBM in 1973 and again in 1974, raising the same issues. Both sides talked into 1978, with neither budging. At most, IBM offered to manufacture small things locally, such as typewriters. Both local and WT IBMers still did not feel the Indian market could absorb modern equipment such as S/360s, more realistically now S/370s, because the logical candidates for such systems had little or no prior experience with computers. Most railroads, all government agencies, and banks, for example, still choked on paper, while labor was so cheap that few incentives existed to automate their work. The business case to motivate IBM to act differently was simply not there. IBM's corporate records demonstrated that the IBMers were adamant that the Indians would not know what to do with an S/360 or S/370. As yet, no case existed for perhaps building them there and exporting them to other parts of Asia, which, in the 1970s, were just as incapable of using this technology as the Indians were. It all came to a head in 1977, with officials pushing hard on the matter. Meanwhile, whatever business IBM had going on in India had come to a halt, as everyone waited to see the outcome of the talks. Permits to import IBM equipment stopped being issued. Other U.S. and English companies slowed their activities. Burroughs, to avoid that trap, negotiated an alliance with Tata for shared ownership. It made little difference.

Lost in all the discussions, except to the IBMers in WT, was the size of IBM's Indian market. It was tiny, so IBM had little incentive to break its worldwide policy of not selling equity in a local company. Furthermore, if it did it here, it would have to in France for sure and also in other countries. Its last order in India for equipment had come in December 1974—three years earlier. Rental and other revenues hovered at only $6 million annually from all of India. The staff used to refurbish machines totaled 219

IBMers. In all of India, IBM had 803 employees, less than the number they had in a midsized U.S. state or midsized European country. In fall of 1977, WT staff figured out how to pull out of India if the government persisted in its demands. Indian officials felt IBM's presence would impede development of a local industry, while IBM focused on the issue of ownership. They were talking past each other.

In New York, WT staff told senior management that IBM had in India 362 data entry customers, 479 unit record equipment users, and 139 computers (1401s). The grand total of all machines was 7,881, with a net book value of just $5.6 million that could be sold off. This information convinced WT management that they could dispose of the inventory, stop supporting it, and walk away with no measurable impact on the corporation's balance sheet.[53] When the staff calculated severance packages for local employees should they choose to stay, travel and moving costs for those wishing to remain with IBM in other countries, and other related expenses, these totaled $5.9 million. In other words, IBM could walk away from India at a cost of $300,000. When negotiations broke down in November 1977, IBM announced it was leaving, and the following June it did so. The Indian government felt it was best for that to happen so that the Burroughs-Tata and other potential start-ups could thrive, including a local national champion, Electronics Corporation of India Limited (ECIL). Quickly, other firms formed, including one made up of local ex-IBM employees, International Data Machines (IDM).

This is a remarkable story on many levels. India developed a local computer industry, although it remained small, largely for the same reasons as at IBM. IBM was able to demonstrate to any government that cared that it would not break up its organization, while its integrated product development approach remained intact. Employees who chose to leave India were assigned to similar jobs in Australia, Canada, Great Britain, and the United States, continuing the normal progression of their careers. The Indian episode gave us a view into how IBM analyzed situations and "staffed out" issues before making decisions. The story also pointed out that senior managers could tightly operate globally—an objective Cary wanted and that Opel supported—and also that they could not afford to act otherwise.

IBM had become a global behemoth, with the good and bad that came with such a distinction.

When the announcement went public, there was of course much buzz worldwide, but not at World Trade headquarters. IBM's media machine defended the decision, and other large corporations took note. The global power of IBM made it comfortable for U.S. executives to look at the world's map and pick and choose where to participate. In the 1990s, IBM returned to India after the government gave up its socialist economic practices and welcomed back foreign corporations. By the early years of the new millennium, IBM had a couple of thousand Indian employees, and by the early 2010s, over 100,000, or 25 percent of all people working for IBM worldwide.

Obvious losers in this story were potential customers who needed IBM's training and services style of selling used worldwide so effectively for decades in introducing thousands of organizations to every generation of new data processing. One global study of the diffusion of computing demonstrated that where IBM operated, local organizations acquired more computing earlier than in nations in which IBM did not have a presence. The pattern held regardless of the role IBM's competitors played.[54] India's expenditures on computers in the 1980s were just slightly more than those of the Philippines and Indonesia. Taiwan spent more than India as a percentage of its national economy as late as the early 1990s. India's computer takeoff waited until the last decade of the century.

HOW GLOBALIZATION CHANGED IBM

As WT expanded, what were the effects on IBM's culture? To help answer that question, we have the results of Geert Hofstede's opinion surveys conducted in 40 countries between the late 1960s and early 1970s. Because many of the issues he explored as an IBM personnel manager did not change over many years, we can accept that his findings reflected circumstances early in the 1960s and later in the 1970s.[55]

As WT grew, its managers learned that a U.S.-centric corporate culture and organization needed adjustment to meet local behaviors and beliefs.

Hofstede observed that having common technologies or sets of practices at IBM contributed "to the shaping of organizations" but were "insufficient for explaining how they work."[56] Technological and process introductions, while they facilitated changes in corporate culture with broad adoption of similar behaviors across countries in an international firm, did "not wipe out differences among societies and may even enlarge them" because of "preexisting value systems societies cope with."[57] Multinational corporations had a "home" national culture in which executives lived and made decisions. In IBM's case, it was the United States. Volvo had a Swedish "home culture," Mitsubishi a Japanese one; even churches had them, such as the Mormons (American) or Roman Catholics (Italian). A few corporations had transnational cultures, meaning they shared national cultures, such as Unilever (British and Dutch). Hofstede called out "the importance of shared value patterns for the functioning of organizations."[58] Companies with one dominant national culture proved easier to manage than those with competing ones. As employees accepted a dominant culture, its influence was, as one might say in the United States, "the way we do things around here." In Hofstede's words, "They are taken for granted."[59]

To succeed in WT, one needed to be bicultural: American and local. That was because local management needed to be able to work with decision makers at Corporate, as was the case with non-American employees interacting with Americans at WT in the United States. Hofstede observed that local IBM companies went about much of their work using host country cultures, however, since most employees did not interact directly with the Americans, only with their processes and technologies. He considered bicultural managers in national firms "linking" into Corporate and to other countries an essential reason why WT worked.[60] He was one of those links, Dutch, working all over the company, yet reporting to Americans in New York. IBM, like other U.S. firms, put the burden to be bicultural, and hence also English speaking, on WT employees, not requiring Americans to be bilingual or even nominally bicultural. The occasional tour of duty in a foreign country for one to five years barely exposed Americans to the more than 40 national cultures in which IBM operated between the 1950s and 1980s.[61]

On some matters, however, employees shared a great deal. Examples Hofstede reported make the point. In the 1960s, IBM opinion surveys reported that employees felt overworked; it was the boom period when IBM was installing and fixing S/360s in many countries. As the decade was ending, opportunities for promotions improved, adding to the stress of working long hours and wondering where the rewards were in exchange for that added effort.[62] Local situations also affected attitudes. In the 1960s, France entered a period of enormous political and social upheaval, culminating in the May Days of 1968. It was a period of expanding union activism, too, which IBM Corporate, WT, and country managers resisted. While not a problem in the United States, it was bubbling up in Europe, most of all in France. One IBM union activist noted that the "IBM Way" "was very centralized and had created an internal bureaucracy incapable of adapting to changing circumstances," causing "internal trauma" in those years.[63] WT was a difficult business to run. So, how did it do?

RESULTS OF IBM'S GLOBAL BUSINESS, 1949–1990

"IBM World Trade Corporation has been phenomenally successful," a researcher reported in 1961.[64] He could have written the same in 1971, or 1981, but not in 1991. By then, it would not have mattered, because worldwide IBM was in deep trouble. But before then, IBM's parallel universe of Domestic and World Trade had evolved from an extension, an appendage of IBM Domestic, into a wholly owned subsidiary that had it been an independent enterprise would have made the *Fortune 1000* list by the late 1960s. How big WT became was always a fact buried in IBM's reporting. IBM's annual reports contained one or two sentences about it in the Chairman's Letter, which ran two to four pages, while breakouts of its financials were hidden in data-packed pages near the end of these publications. American IBMers could not care less. European employees knew their neighbors and customers considered IBM an iconic American firm. Latin Americans felt like a backwater operation micromanaged by North Americans. The mystique of the "IBM Family" was global and survived until the 1980s. IBM Japan kept its own counsel, while African activities involved servicing data centers of former colonial powers' corporations. South Africa was a growing annoyance because of worldwide criticism of apartheid, so U.S. corporations started pulling out, as IBM did in 1984, only to return in the 1990s.

A tour through the numbers demonstrates how effective IBM's worldwide strategy was, which in its simplest terms involved projecting the company's way of doing business to the rest of the world, with minor modifications to accommodate local practices with essentially the same products at almost the same time worldwide. British, French, and German firms executed similar strategies in the nineteenth century, which large U.S. corporations emulated in the post–World War II period. At the risk of a little tedium, examine the financials in table 11.1. For a corporation, there are two fundamental metrics that must be positive: what is left over as income (profit) after accounting for revenue and costs, and current assets, resources that can be converted into cash or similar liquid assets within a year. Like all large enterprises, IBM tracked many other items, notably the

Table 11.1

World Trade net income, select years, 1949–1990 (in millions or billions of dollars)

Year	Net income	Comments
1949	6,257M	First year World Trade is in business
1953	9,423M	Largely European sales, a few in Latin America and Japan
1959	40,202M	Increases begin sharply because of outright sales, not leasing
1964	123,998M	Last full year before IBM began shipping S/360s
1966	174,606M	First year of full impact of S/360 sales begins
1968	270,546M	First year of WT gross sales exceeding $2 billion
1969	397,783M	S/360 outright sales in full swing, high volumes
1970	512,520M	U.S. and global computer industry slows
1974	919,836M	S/370 installations in full force, also national recessions
1980	1.737B	Last year before IBM introduced the PC
1981	1.541B	Decline caused by global inflation, lower demand, competition
1983	2.164B	Global recovery, growing PC sales (largely in United States)
1985	3.078B	World Trade has over 163,000 employees
1988	4.079B	On gross revenue that exceeded prior year's by $5 billion
1990	4.574B	On gross revenue of $41 billion, with 168,000 employees

Source: International Business Machines Corporation, *Annual Reports*.

total value of its assets, buildings, inventory, number of employees, and gross sales (cash taken in before deductions). Each measure told "the business" something about its affairs. To understand the extent of WT's performance, look at net income and a couple of other measures.

The year 1949 was the first year of reporting WT results. By building on prior momentum, it reported a solid performance of over $6.7 million in net income. Much of that stayed outside the United States, plowed back into WT. To put that number in context, in 1949 IBM as a whole generated $33.3 million in net income. In other words, over $26 million in profit came out of U.S. operations. The company outside the United States kept growing. In 1964, the year before IBM began installing S/360s but when the effects of 1401 sales had already positively affected results, WT generated almost $124 million in net income. In other words, in 15 years, it grew from $6.7 million to $124 million, a remarkable performance. In 1964, its current assets hovered at $197 million on gross sales of $933.4 million. IBM's total gross sales that year reached $3.2 billion, so already WT was on its way to contributing a third of total sales. IBM's net income in 1964 came in at $431 million versus WT's $124 million, so WT was contributing slightly less than a quarter of the total. It was already a big company in its own right, staffed with 50,000 employees. Then the S/360 generated revenue, with sales bumping up beginning in 1966.[65]

That year, WT's net income reached $174.6 million, and it kept increasing so quickly that the rate of growth of the 1950s seemed slow in comparison: $209.4 million in 1967, $512.5 million in 1970 (more than doubling in four years), $686.6 million in 1972, and reaching $919.8 million in 1974. In 1974, IBM's net earnings reached $1.84 billion. In other words, WT's contribution now amounted to 50 percent of the total. It also had 132,000 employees out of a total of more than 260,000. A decade later, with John Akers at the helm, WT generated $2.6 billion in net income and sat on $11.89 billion in net assets, while IBM as a whole generated $6.6 billion in net earnings. During the second half of the decade, WT's "headcount" leveled off, then shrank. Nonetheless, net income kept growing, reaching $4.57 billion in 1990, the year before IBM suffered its first loss in modern times. In 1990, WT drummed up $41.89 billion in gross revenue, a figure that then flattened before declining in the early 1990s.[66] So, IBM's strategy for expanding business outside the United States worked, surmounting competition, economic disruptions, revolutions, wars, and regulatory attempts to constrain the company in many countries.

Why did IBM's strategy work? Good execution, to be sure, played an important role. Most of its failed rivals could be chastised for not doing that, or for thinking too small, focusing too narrowly on small market niches or just national markets. While good execution was necessary, it was not sufficient. There is an old IBM salesman's saying that applies here: "90 percent of a sale is about showing up." Implied in that aphorism is the assumption that there first needed to be demand for one's products and, once identified by the *peddler*, whoever offers it likely wins. That happened to IBM. The company rode a worldwide wave of demand for computing in the second half of the century wherever it existed, with a few exceptions, discussed later. That demand was caused by industrialization in many countries, even during the Cold War, when many nations embraced Soviet-style managed economies, and even there, computing proved attractive for the same reasons as elsewhere. For all, these included improving labor productivity, driving down costs, and performing functions not possible without the capabilities of information technologies. IBM's problem, to quote an internal survey from 1984, was to keep up with its customers, whose "data processing workloads will continue to grow at the greatest rate we have seen for a long time. With this comes the demand for additional capacity to meet those workloads."[67]

In projecting to the world what it created in the United States, its style of selling proved ideal for what happened. In large enterprises and government agencies, where the greatest amount of knowledge about computing existed, IBMers knew how to collaborate with their customers' experts, learning from them and developing products relevant to them. It could build supercomputers for military organizations; manufacturing systems relevant to the automotive, industrial machine, and transportation industries; and still others for banks and large insurance companies. But it also could sell to smaller organizations just getting into computing, teaching them how to use this technology and motivating them to take the plunge into computing through salesmanship and cost justification. IBM was able to hold its customers' hands as they adapted their operations to computerization and to increase their reliance on this technology. In some countries, there were numerous large institutions, as in the United States, while many organizations in Latin America and in Mediterranean Europe were smaller. For each, IBM adapted, expanding its abilities to deal with large or smaller enterprises, specializing in local industries, and offering products relevant to its markets.

Countercurrents of competition and legal and regulatory problems proved strongest in the United States, less so everywhere else, with the possible exception of Japan. Competitors challenged about a third of IBM's sales efforts and, even then, it won well over half of them, which speaks to IBM's account control, solid sales and service execution, effective product introductions, and pricing. The combination proved essential.

As positive as the story about its performance was, a dark, dangerous cloud of litigation hung over IBM, threatening to shatter everything, including the very structure of the company. That cloud hovered over the company for half the careers of 300,000 IBMers, with potential consequences affecting the professional careers of others working in thousands of companies competing against IBM. The problems were so grave that few in IBM dared discuss them openly. Yet most in the computer industry and its customers were gripped by the events unfolding around IBM. It would be difficult to imagine any corporate lawyer in, say, any *Fortune 1000* company not paying attention to the unfolding drama, most of which took place in New York City and Washington, D.C.—the longest antitrust suit in U.S. history and other cases related to it. It is time to take the wrapper off that story because by its conclusion IBM, its competitors, and how customers interacted with computing had changed, with consequences still unfolding in the twenty-first century. That is why a chapter about corporate lawsuits is so necessary, though so filled with drama.

12 TWO DECADES OF ANTITRUST SUITS, 1960s–1980s

> In effect, the government complaint against IBM was that because it was so
> big it must be an antitrust violator even though no illegal behavior could be
> shown. In other words, the company was guilty of making a good product
> and pricing it right. Horrors.
>
> —THE MEMPHIS PRESS-SCIMITAR, 1982[1]

FRANK CARY SPENT much of the 1970s in court. There were many days
when his driver showed up at his house early in the morning to take
IBM's CEO either to an office filled with lawyers and IBMers working on
lawsuits at 1133 Westchester Avenue—DPD HQ—in White Plains, New
York, or to the federal courthouse at Foley Square in Manhattan, where he
was grilled by hostile Department of Justice (DoJ) attorneys or by IBM's
own. Some court sessions lasted many hours. Either way, Cary had to be
attentive, careful in how he spoke, and always stick to a rehearsed approach.
He then attended post-testifying debriefings back at Armonk before his
driver took him home, pouring out the exhausted Cary at his front door.
The CEO had attended thousands of meetings sprinkled around the world,
often dealing with contentious issues, so he understood how to behave in
front of the government's lawyers. In this instance, if he and his company
failed to defend their behavior, IBM could be split into multiple companies
or pay a frightfully large financial penalty. There were days and weeks when
he spent up to 80 percent of his time focused on *U.S. v. IBM* (1969–1982),
the longest antitrust case in U.S. history.

Besides the disruption to IBM's affairs, Cary must have been irritated by the fact that the lawsuit concerned the company's activities with the S/360. In the 1960s, both he and John Opel had expressed skepticism about the strategy of building systems in modular fashion that could be tailored to a customer's needs. Their experience with the S/360 led him to join a generation of senior executives who never again wanted to engage in such a massive project. IBM created new classes of competitors, notably plug-compatible mainframe and peripheral vendors, as well as 250 rival leasing companies, so despite the enormous increase in revenue and the placement of over 18,000 S/360s by the end of the 1960s in the United States alone, generating $16 billion in revenue and $6 billion in profits,[2] he occasionally wondered if it was worth it. Now he had to deal with a raft of lawsuits. For most of his tenure as the head of IBM, the DoJ was hot on IBM's heels.

IBM's experience was not unique in American industry. As new technology firms emerged in the late nineteenth century, early entrants such as AT&T, DuPont, and US Steel gained great market dominance, which was protested by regulators and then government lawyers, who wanted them to scale back to encourage competition and innovation. While Americans loved their litigation, other nations had other methods of dealing with such issues: the Japanese used MITI to govern industrial rivalries, innovation, and imports, while European regulators altered or prohibited specific practices. European and Asian governments invested in local vendors and created favorable regulations to support them. The U.S. government did, too, while simultaneously trying to contain the competitive surge that accrued to companies like IBM. That dual approach was unique to the United States, and such behavior continued right through the twentieth century. Economists have studied the implications of these kinds of litigation, and we encounter their work in this chapter. Business historians, however, have a great deal of catching up to do, so this chapter should provide insight about the effects of litigation on their favorite topics: strategy, organization, R&D, corporate cultures, and information ecosystems. The problem is part of the larger one labeled by Matthias Kipping and Behlül Üsdiken as being "stuck elsewhere: business history between history and economics."[3] While interest in business-government relations has enjoyed a recent boom, antitrust and other iterations of lawsuits remain outliers in that broader discussion. Litigation needs to be further integrated into the histories of companies because, as Matthias Kipping put it, "governments have played an important role in business matters."[4] My point is less of a criticism than a recognition that litigation is profoundly influential on a corporation, and IBM is a case in point.

On May 18, 1998, the DoJ filed an antitrust case against Microsoft Corporation, accusing it of behaving as a monopoly in violation of U.S. antitrust law. Twenty U.S. state attorneys general joined the suit. The particulars of the case were less important than that government lawyers focused on the issue that had concerned them about IBM: practices that reduced the ability of competitors to sell to Microsoft's customers and that blocked entry of new rivals. Microsoft and the government went to trial and on November 5, 1999, the company was found guilty of maintaining a monopoly over its operating system for PCs and of constraining rivals, such as Apple, Lotus (owned by IBM), Netscape, and others. The following June, the court ordered Microsoft to split into two firms. Microsoft's lawyers appealed, and the company and the Justice Department negotiated a settlement. The trial judge approved the deal in June 2004.

So IBM was not alone in experiencing the U.S. government's love/hate relationship with big business. It did not end with Microsoft. In April 2012, it became Apple's turn, when it was accused of raising the prices of e-books. Trade publishers and high-profile authors joined the case, filing their own suits. These mimicked earlier ones: appeals, negotiated settlements, and court approval of parts of agreements, although the U.S. Supreme Court let stand a fine of $450 million in a ruling handed down in March 2016.

After being relatively quiet on matters concerning information technology companies in the 1990s, in the 2010s European regulators probed Apple, Facebook, Google, and Amazon, as well as IBM, over a variety of issues related to their market dominance and behavior. So the issues involving IBM were part of a much larger topic involving how high-tech companies gained control and operated in information technology markets. These usually concerned data privacy and "foreign" dominance of national markets.

Could regulators and lawyers keep up with markets and technologies that continued to change faster than the wheels of justice turned? This chapter adds evidence that a disconnect existed between changing technologies and markets on the one hand and how quickly the legal system could respond, a phenomenon that IBM's experience demonstrated.

The more important story, however, is not a legal one but rather how litigation affected the daily operations of a firm. The task before us is to reconstruct IBM's perspective on litigation and how its employees were affected, because for decades afterward their behavior was conditioned by the legal events of the 1950s to 1980s. Our purpose is less to add new insights regarding antitrust law and more to appreciate what occurred inside one corporation. To do that, the story is organized into three discussions. First, I briefly describe the legal landscape in which IBM operated in midcentury; second, I discuss the private antitrust lawsuits and the federal case; and third, I examine the consequences of the federal case. For students of IBM's history, the events of the private and federal cases will be familiar, as they are routinely discussed in company histories, although here points of emphasis differ, as we take advantage of the passage of time, providing perspective and insights on internal operations. The consequences of the federal case described here represent new material, with the notable exception of historian Richard S. Tedlow's observations about how IBMers talked about their business, reported on in this chapter. Central in much of the discussion of the federal case has been the economic assumptions underpinning the government's argument against IBM, also reviewed in this chapter, challenging the effectiveness of government economic assumptions and emphasizing the cost to all parties involved in both private and public cases.[5]

With the federal case, the broader issue of how to apply century-old antitrust laws in an economy that appeared so different by the 1950s and 1960s, when technological and economic changes came more rapidly than the legal system could keep up with—a point discussed here but only recently taken up by legal scholars—is informed by the role of information as an economic influence on events.[6] Not discussed in this book are patents and copyrights, but they are discussed by others.[7] IBM's experience with antitrust litigation is not well understood, hence our focus on it here.[8] Historians have paid more attention to antitrust activities of the 1950s than to the more important ones of the 1970s. The earlier event takes on importance, historians say, because it resulted in Thomas Watson Sr. turning over control of IBM to his son, Tom Jr.[9] Historian Robert Sobel was one of the few to point out that antitrust activity at IBM should be seen as a whole, not as bits and pieces scattered in histories of IBM.[10] I agree with him.

Finally, we correct the chronology of this story. This case did not begin in 1969, as historians have asserted. It started years earlier, when the DoJ began exploring the possibility of a suit against IBM. In fact, it is not completely clear when that process began. Why is this distinction about dates important? When IBM lawyers and senior management learned that the DoJ was entertaining antitrust questions, they responded to this turn of events with concern. The DoJ's activities affected IBM's strategy, the terms and conditions of its offerings (such as unbundling), and the behavior it expected of its employees. More than any other company in the information technology world, then or now, it had experience in such matters. In less than a decade, IBM management knew it faced an existential threat to the firm's survival.[11]

THE LEGAL LANDSCAPE, 1950s–1970s

Large U.S. corporations had fretted over antitrust issues since 1890, when the Sherman Antitrust Act became law, followed by subsequent legislation in the Clayton Act of 1914 and other patent, trademark, and copyright laws. As time passed, firms in an increasing number of industries took into account essentially three antitrust issues when developing their products and marketing strategies. First, the law forbade companies from exercising monopolistic control over their markets, and they could be found guilty of violating the law even if they were perceived to have the power to do so. As the largest companies gained such power, it proved impossible for them not to exercise it. IBM was no exception. Second, government lawyers and judges sought to stop "tie-ins," practices that forced customers to buy one or more goods or services when acquiring a specific product, such as when

IBM required a tabulator customer to use IBM cards. Third, as companies developed patents they were allowed to convert into commercial products, officials wanted them to share (lease out) rights to competitors, such as when the DoJ forced AT&T to do so in the 1950s after it invented the transistor.

By the mid-1950s, enough cases had gone through the courts to make all three considerations relevant for senior executives to keep in mind when formulating product development strategies and in shaping the structure of their organizations. IBM shared these same concerns with other U.S. enterprises, notably Alcoa, AT&T, and United Shoe Machinery Company, firms that tangled with antitrust litigation. IBM's experiences in 1936 and 1956, in which its activities were restrained by consent decrees, became high-profile examples of the federal legal community working to nurture competition within the U.S. economy.

Section 2 of the Sherman Act was the main event. It forbade companies from stifling competition, which could be caused by becoming large or dominant in a market. That notion was at the center of the DoJ's case. The Clayton Act of 1914, in the words of a student of that law, "brought greater specificity to antitrust by enumerating the forms of corporate activity that were subject to prosecution," such as outlawing discriminatory pricing, "exclusive dealing," and "tying contracts," among other actions.[12] In 1914, the U.S. Congress established the Federal Trade Commission (FTC), giving it broad authority to advise and regulate on antitrust matters. The economic issues stimulated considerable discussion among economists in support of either IBM or the DoJ, providing a detailed plot to the case.[13]

Competitors who sued IBM focused additionally on Section 3 of the Sherman Antitrust Act, which extended the law to cover actions in the District of Columbia and in all U.S. territories. In 1977, Congress passed the Foreign Corrupt Practices Act, which essentially said that one could not do overseas what laws prohibited a company from doing in the United States. When an Argentine IBM executive was charged with bribing a local government official a few years later, it was as much a criminal offense for his U.S. manager as it was for him in Argentina. Regardless of whether another country chose to implement similar antitrust laws, management in New

York had to take U.S. practices into account when operating World Trade or in implementing anticorruption practices around the world. The "Business Conduct Guidelines" that governed the behavior of all IBM employees worldwide were a direct outgrowth of U.S. anticorruption laws. In practice, the two fused together within IBM.

It made sense that this would happen. Recall that Thomas Watson Sr. had been convicted of violating the Sherman Antitrust Act largely because of business practices at NCR that in future decades might have been viewed also as acts of corruption. The case against IBM in the 1930s did not have the tinge of bribery or corruption but certainly had the feel of constraining competition and the look of tie-ins to control markets. The case leading to IBM's consent decree in 1956 had a patina of illegality in addition to the more formal concerns about antitrust behavior. In the 1950s, one response by IBM was to make sure all employees understood the terms of its consent decree with the DoJ and to prescribe the kind of behavior employees could not engage in, integrating into its guidelines responses to concerns over antitrust, corruption, and business ethics, making them part of the "IBM Way." In time, these became the Marketing Practices Guidelines that every employee has been required to adhere to ever since.

American legal battles of the twentieth century were often dramatic and the source of much corporate rhetoric, posturing, and press coverage, but they were usually resolved within a few years. The cases IBM faced in the 1960s and 1970s were of long duration and of high cost to the federal government and IBM. In the federal antitrust case, taxpayers footed the bill. IBM spent in excess of a quarter of a billion dollars. We may never know for sure what this case cost the nation.

Government policies remained remarkably consistent throughout the twentieth century. The desire was to break up links in commercial behavior that at best were, to use Usselman's word, "tenuous," always to ensure competitors' survival.[14] Their survival rested on the belief that competitive behavior led to technological innovation, competitive prices, and quality products. Practices such as bundling goods and services were forbidden; unbundling became a solution. No company seemed to have done more to inject the word "unbundling" into the American business lexicon than IBM.

By 1970, most data processing managers around the world understood the concept. Not until IBM introduced the term "Personal Computer," in 1981, did so many people become exposed to an IT phrase emanating from one company.[15] To avoid confusion, however, there is a difference between policies and practices. The U.S. government went through periods when it enforced antitrust laws more firmly than at other times, such as during the Progressive Era and again right after World War II, but less so during the 1920s and 1980s. But when it did, what it enforced and how it interpreted legislation remained relatively consistent.[16]

The legal environment enveloping the cases discussed in this chapter can be summarized quickly. On the one hand, federal prosecutors, regulators, and courts spent enormous energy to ensure the economy was vigorous in its ability to sustain competitive activities. The United States did this more than any other nation. To put it in blunt terms, if a country wanted to know how best to manage national antitrust laws, regulate patents and trademarks, and control corporate corruption, they turned to the United States. On the other hand, no nation did as much to encourage development of new sciences, technologies, and products, funding them with hundreds of billions of dollars buttressed by laws to protect, yet regulate, these innovations. Such investments led to the creation of the computer industry in the United States, and its growth was faster, more vigorous, and occurred earlier than anywhere else. One could argue the same about telecommunications, medicine, air travel, and weapons systems in the post–World War II period. In summary, corporations like IBM were encouraged to do well, and when they did, they often had their market power challenged. Corporations and government officials learned how to navigate this seemingly contradictory behavior. IBM became a master player.

CDC, TELEX, AND ALL THOSE PRIVATE LAWSUITS

Recall Control Data Corporation (CDC), one of the post–World War II start-up computer companies that began by specializing in large scientific computing, successfully producing large-end computers that competed against IBM's largest computers. It ran head-on against a problem when

IBM discussed producing larger S/360s that CDC management concluded were designed to dislodge CDC's products. In 1968, CDC's management decided to open a legal front against Big Blue, accusing IBM of announcing higher-end models of the S/360 aimed at CDC's 6600.[17] CDC's management had cause to be suspicious about IBM because the CDC 6600 did fine until IBM told potential customers for CDC's system that it was about to bring out an S/360 Model 90 that would outperform CDC's machine.

In fairness to IBM, it did in fact work on such a machine and in fact built and delivered 13 of them, but it is also true that these machines did not perform as promised by IBM and experienced technical difficulties during development, all of which led IBM to lease them for less than originally planned. IBM lost about $100 million on that effort. IBM documents revealed during legal proceedings demonstrated that its executives were upset with the project and with the Product Test Department (responsible for quality control), which refused to sign off on a machine built largely in response to competitive pressures, notably the Models 90 and 91.[18] But IBM's announcement of the forthcoming Model 90 had its effect. Customers waited for IBM's computer, so CDC's sales of the 6600 slowed. In its annual report in 1965, CDC blasted IBM's "frequent announcement of changing characteristics and new models, at reduced prices, of large computers reported to be under development."[19]

CDC's president, William Norris (1911–2006), referred to IBM's S/360s as "phantom machines" because they did not exist at the time of their announcement. CDC's lawyers accumulated case studies of IBMers selling this product, documenting what IBM told customers about how effective it would be. This had three consequences. First, other firms embraced the idea of fighting IBM's market dominance in court, so over the next few years they launched their own suits, listed in table 12.1. Evidence and arguments from one case resurfaced in others. Second, the DoJ, barely ten years after settling with IBM in 1956 to stop market-dominating practices, again began exploring what IBM was doing with the S/360s. That investigation led to its antitrust suit, filed in 1969.

Third, IBM agreed to a rapid settlement of the CDC case. It sold its Service Bureau Corporation (SBC) to CDC for a fraction of its value, which

Table 12.1
Chronology of antitrust lawsuits filed against IBM, 1969–1975

Case filing date	Case name
1969	*U.S. v. IBM*
1969	*Greyhound v. IBM*
1972	*Telex v. IBM*
1973	*CalComp v. IBM*
1973	*Hudson v. IBM*
1973	*Marshall v. IBM*
1973	*Transamerica v. IBM*
1974	*Forro v. IBM*
1974	*Memory Tech v. IBM*
1975	*Sanders v. IBM*

Source: List modified from Franklin M. Fisher, James W. McKie, and Richard B. Mancke, *IBM and the U.S. Data Processing Industry: An Economic History* (New York: Praeger, 1983), 379–380.

added to CDC's own service bureau business, and paid CDC an additional $101 million in compensation in cash and contracts. In exchange, CDC turned over its case studies to IBM, evidence that other litigants would have loved to use.[20] In his memoirs, Tom Watson Jr. admitted being persuaded by his lawyers to destroy the file before it could become evidence. "I had no choice," he wrote, "'Burn it,' I said."[21] It was done that night. In hindsight, he noted, "Even though the best lawyers money could buy assured me I wasn't breaking any law, it made me feel uneasy."[22] He had denied the DoJ and IBM's rivals a major body of evidence.

The Telex case was another matter. Formed in 1936 to sell hearing aids, in the 1960s it entered the computer peripheral equipment business. In 1972, it filed an antitrust suit against IBM along the lines CDC had four years earlier, and three years later, the U.S. government filed its own suit. Unlike CDC's case, this one came down through history as a sleazy attempt at judicial redress by a vendor unable to sell competitive products.[23] It asked that IBM be broken up because Big Blue was selling and leasing machines at prices Telex could not match. Its complaints piggybacked off the federal case. Telex won its case in the initial trial, being awarded a sum five times its gross revenue, but which the court later lowered. Meanwhile, in a countersuit, Telex was found guilty of infringing IBM patents and stealing trade secrets. In 1975, a federal court overturned the conviction against IBM. IBM agreed not to collect the penalty levied against Telex, so the legal fight ended. The case took three years and seven months to settle.[24]

The industry trade press covered it blow by blow. *Computerworld*, the premier trade newspaper in the industry, covered every twist and turn.[25] The other leading publication, *Datamation*, did, too. Industry watchers provided running commentary. These included Gideon Gartner, who made a living interpreting IBM's actions for the brokerage industry. Everyone in the computer industry paid attention to these cases because, as Gartner put it, IBM was the largest vendor: "Big Blue ruled the info-tech industry and vendors and users alike danced around IBM like courtiers at Louis XIV's Versailles. When IBM made a product announcement, everyone listened."[26] Fanning interest during the Telex trial, a judge, over IBM's objections, ordered all documents in the case made public, resulting in 40,000 pages of memoranda, minutes of IBM meetings, product plans, notes, and other IBM ephemera becoming available to reporters, industry watchers, prosecutors at the DoJ, and the other firms suing IBM. The Computer and Communications Industry Association (CCIA) came into existence to supply the anti-IBM community with information. It sold many copies of these documents to IBM's rivals for $5,000 a set.[27] These documents damaged IBM's cause.

The Telex drama was not the only legal activity under way. In 1972, CEOs at CDC, Univac, NCR, and Honeywell called on the DoJ to get on with its case against IBM, offering to assist to move it forward; that is, paralyze IBM's ability to compete against them. Reporters favorable to IBM tended the minority view: "The most recent case [IBM vs. Telex] is a classic illustration of the slimy function and goal of antitrust: the sacrifice of ingenuity and ability and success to mediocrity and incompetence and failure. In ruling against IBM, Judge A. Sherman Christensen has sanctioned the sacrifice of IBM's ingenuity and ability and success to the mediocrity, incompetence and failure of a virtually bankrupt little fifth-rate company, Telex." This reporter's argument was that, rather than attacking the firm, IBM's rivals should thank it for inventing the computer industry and thus, "Consequently, it is IBM that made and makes it possible for them to succeed." The writer blamed Telex for "poor management and a colossal failure to produce a product that very many people care to buy."[28] Another observer commented that the "Telex case inspired several small companies to get in on the pickin's."[29] In other words, some saw litigation as an opportunity to reach a cash settlement with IBM based on the Telex documentation.

Table 12.1 shows IBM's competitors joining a growing list of vendors complaining about Big Blue's actions, relying on the expanding body of available trial evidence. While the majority of these cases had ended by 1980, during the 1970s they added to the cloud of IBM's legal problems. IBM survived them all. For example, a U.S. district court dismissed the *Greyhound v. IBM* case, one of the first filed against the company, in 1972. On appeal, a federal appeals court called for a new trial. To cut back on the anticipated expenses of such a trial, IBM's lawyers negotiated a settlement, paying out $17.7 million. Both parties agreed that IBM would admit no wrong.

Other cases were resolved similarly. The CalComp case went to trial in 1976, but the court dismissed it in 1977 because of a lack of evidence of wrongdoing, even before IBM's lawyers could mount a defense. Forro went to trial in 1977 and, a month later, the judge threw out that case. The following year, IBM's lawyers were back in court, this time with Memorex, with the judge handing down a verdict for IBM. In 1979, the same happened in the Transamerica trial. Smaller cases involving Marshall, Memory Tech, and Sanders were settled out of court. No private case had established that IBM monopolized any market for mainframes or peripherals or had illegally crushed leasing companies.

IBM's lawyers had private U.S. cases to deal with every year from the late 1960s until the early 1980s. Duane W. Krohnke, a young lawyer at IBM's antitrust legal firm (Cravath, Swaine & Moore, better known as CS&M inside IBM), recalled what it was like to work on these cases, citing the example of the Greyhound litigation. As a young father of two, he found IBM's cases grueling. He left home very early in the morning and did not return until after his children were asleep. Working weekends became routine. One lawyer supposedly reported 27 hours in one day as a result of working across three time zones!

Greyhound wanted to question IBM officials under oath. IBM spent large sums on lawyer fees to look at vast quantities of its own documents to prepare for that questioning. As Krohnke described,

> One of the IBM officials to be deposed in the Greyhound case was its President, Thomas J. Watson, Jr., and I was put in charge of assisting Tom Barr in preparing Mr. Watson for his deposition. This was a daunting challenge. It meant collecting and analyzing as many IBM and public documents as possible that were potentially relevant to the Greyhound and other cases, figuring out the possible questions that might be asked of Mr. Watson by opposing counsel and then meeting with him and IBM's General Counsel, Nicholas Katzenbach, to go over these documents and questions, all in a relatively short time period.[30]

To get Watson Jr. prepared, he and Tom Barr (the young lawyer's boss) had to meet with him on IBM's jet flying back from California to New York, after the two lawyers flew out to California so that they could fly back with Watson. Inside IBM, such cases always involved a similar tedious process of research, endless rounds of meetings, and years of depositions.

That IBM had been aggressive, clever, and determined in competing was never in question. The plaintiffs and IBM argued over the sizes of the markets, its rivals wanting a definition that made IBM look like it dominated, while IBM contended that, by its definition of market size, its share was smaller.[31] The lack of common definitions caused much confusion in each case and led to hung juries and to judges tossing out cases. The key point IBM made to its customers, the public, and its employees is that the firm was never found legally guilty after all the verdicts were handed down and appeals ended. As irritating and time consuming as they were to IBM, all those cases proved to be the legal sideshow of the 1970s. The main event was the federal case.

THE FEDERAL ANTITRUST CASE: *U.S. v. IBM,*
69 CIV. 200 (S.D.N.Y. 1969)

The federal case ran so long that when it ended in January 1982, half of IBM's employees had not been at the company when it began. They never knew a time when the case was not hanging over them. European and Asian IBMers were not immune either, because the effects seeped out worldwide. It was a case that had its fits and starts, stops and progress, quiet periods and frenetic moments, its ups and downs, but remarkably the key players in the case remained involved for over a decade. Admirers of federal judge David N. Edelstein (1910–2000) considered him a kind and fair man, but IBM's legal team saw him as being prejudiced against the company and big business in general. Many of his rulings gave them much to worry about. He adjudicated the government's case for ten years. IBM's lead lawyer was Thomas D. Barr (1931–2008) of Cravath, Swaine & Moore, who in time directed the work of some 200 people on the case. His counterpart at IBM, Nicholas Katzenbach (1922–2012), a senior vice president, became involved after joining the company in 1969.

Then there was the cast of over 1,000 other participants. The government brought 118 people to the witness stand. IBM brought a similar number, plus there were 97 IBM depositions of government officials. All these people needed to be prepared for their roles and played their parts, often more than once, as did Frank Cary. The list of IBMers deposed or brought into court read like a Who's Who of IBM: John F. Akers (vice president and group executive), George B. Beitzel (general manager of the DP Group), Frederick P. Brooks Jr. (formally of IBM and a software manager on the S/360), Frank Cary (then chairman of IBM), Bob O. Evans (vice president of engineering programming), Hillary Faw (who had advised senior management about pricing strategies), Ralph E. Gomory (director of research), Gilbert E. Jones (chairman of the board of World Trade), T. V. Learson (retired chairman of IBM), John R. Opel (senior vice president), Ralph A. Pfeiffer (corporate vice president and president of the DP Division), Paul Rizzo (vice president, Finance and Planning), "Buck" Rodgers (vice president, Marketing), Tom Watson Jr. (retired chairman), and so many lesser figures. In other words, an entire generation of IBM executives participated.

Figure 12.1
Thomas Barr led IBM's defense against the federal antitrust suit in the 1970s and
early 1980s. Photo courtesy of IBM Corporate Archives.

But it did not end there. Other luminaries from the world of computers were drawn in as well. These included J. Presper Eckert of Univac, developer of the ENIAC and UNIVAC I; Edward Feigenbaum, an academic and
rising star in the emerging world of artificial intelligence; one-time IBM
employee Gideon I. Gartner, then Wall Street's leading authority on IBM;
John W. Mauchly, cofounder with Eckert of their own computer company
(later called Sperry Rand); William C. Norris, chairman of the board and
CEO of CDC; Frederic G. Withington of Arthur D. Little and, like Gartner,
an industry expert; and an assortment of executives from IBM's rivals, plus

the 97 officials deposed for the case. All were cast for the longest antitrust case in U.S. history.

When it started with IBM's rivals urging the Justice Department to open an inquiry into the company's behavior, Attorney General Ramsey Clark (b. 1927), a progressive New Dealer in President Lyndon B. Johnson's cabinet, became interested. In 1967, his department began exploring the computer industry and soon realized IBM's central role. IBM's lawyers felt it would become obvious that the computer industry was competitive and therefore IBM had not violated any antitrust laws. Discussions with IBM began almost immediately, with the company's lawyers cooperating in 1967 and 1968. It was their belief that the industry was open to competition and could be accessed by many new rivals, contradicting the DoJ's concern that IBM was constraining trade. Management wanted to quickly close the case. IBM presented the DoJ with 15,000 pages of supporting evidence. Federal lawyers chose initially to define the market in narrow terms (mainframes and associated peripherals), while IBM advocated for a broader definition. By the DoJ's definition, IBM had few competitors. To use one expert's description of the DoJ's thinking, "Market concentration and the existence of substantial barriers to entry carried with them the presumption of illegality."[32]

By the end of 1968, it was clear that the DoJ would probably file an antitrust case against IBM. In early January 1969, the government's lawyers met in Clark's office to weigh the issues. The Johnson administration was to end in a couple of weeks, so if after two years of work they were going to file a case, they had to move quickly. They knew the next administration, a Republican one, would undoubtedly not press charges, so they acted. On their very last day in office, January 17, 1969, a Friday, Clark's DoJ filed suit against IBM and then everyone went home for the weekend, leaving it to the next administration to deal with it.

How did the DoJ inform IBM, and how did its employees learn about it? On that last day of the Johnson administration, Edwin M. Zimmerman, assistant attorney general in the Antitrust Division, called IBM's vice president and general counsel, Burke Marshall, just as the parking lot at Armonk was emptying, with everyone going home. Zimmerman informed him that the case was being filed in New York City. Marshall then called various senior executives to share the news. Almost instantly, the news media began broadcasting the announcement; IBMers driving home up and down the east coast of the United States began hearing the news on their car radios. IBM quickly sent a notice to every IBM facility in the United States through its internal network and then around the world. Within minutes, IBM's response was also being broadcast, over "the wires" of United Press International, Associated Press, and Dow Jones.

When the wider IBM community learned about the filing the following week, employees suspected something was not right; the announcement did not look good. Just the fact that the DoJ filed its case on the very last day of an administration did not pass the sniff test, tainting the suit right from the beginning and leaving a lingering odor of suspicion for the life of the case. By early February, IBM was explaining to employees the details of the case, the government's position, and IBM's, all in a matter-of-fact manner.[33] The actions by the presiding judge added to the widely held belief within IBM that the case was bogus, but IBM's lawyers quickly realized it would be the most important one of their careers, although none thought it could go on for more than three to four years. On the hopeful side, a Republican administration was about to take office the following week.

What was the complaint? The DoJ argued that IBM had violated Section 2 of the Sherman Act, which stated that no firm can "monopolize or attempt to monopolize ... trade or commerce." It summarized its case in 12 double-spaced typed pages. That was it. As the case lumbered along over the next decade, those 12 pages launched what U.S. solicitor general Robert Bork famously called "the Antitrust Division's Vietnam." The DoJ dived into the never-ending case, which consumed vast resources, filing the case in Manhattan in the U.S. District Court for the Southern District of New York, then let it sit there for nearly three years.

IBM's lawyers wanted to get going on tussling with the DoJ. Tom Barr, IBM's lead lawyer, already working on other antitrust cases for IBM and now responsible for this one as well, recalled that, "The antitrust division did nothing, and I mean absolutely nothing. They wouldn't do anything to prosecute the case, and they wouldn't talk to us about settlement."[34]

Actually, some activity occurred, because in 1970 IBM began providing the DoJ with pretrial information, as is customary before a lawsuit, where both sides collect—"discover"—evidence needed for a trial. Soon, however, the DoJ's lawyers stopped the process, deciding simply to use the information gathered for the CDC case against IBM, though it dated back to 1968 and that case had already been settled out of court. In January 1972, Judge Edelstein, chief justice of this court, assumed responsibility for presiding over the case.

Progress slowed again. IBM wanted a different census of the industry's activities used, one that had already been developed by the federal judge involved in the CDC case. The New York court upheld the DoJ's objection to IBM's request. A new census was created that involved interviewing—deposing—800 people to create a file describing the computer market. The one not used included a survey of 1,700 companies. The cost to all parties to create this new census ran into the millions of dollars. The DoJ now submitted a broad definition that, as the trial unfolded, became too unclear for the case to progress in its favor, but the judge allowed it, while denying IBM's request for a more precise definition of the market. Next, the DoJ asked the judge to order IBM to produce thousands of pages of material from the CDC case, even though the government's lawyers had agreed earlier not to do that. Judge Edelstein agreed to the DoJ's request. The U.S. Supreme Court sided with the judge, even though IBM claimed many of the papers involved privileged communications between clients and lawyers.

In October 1972, IBM asked that a trial be held quickly to define the market, and then hold the main trial for the antitrust charges on the basis of that first trial's result. The judge refused. In 1974, the DoJ broadened the charges to include evidence that came out of the Telex suit. The DoJ wanted to add these to its case, since IBM was initially found guilty. Edelstein approved the DoJ's request. Soon after, the 10th Circuit Court of Appeals in Denver threw out IBM's conviction in the Telex case, but it was too late; the DoJ could now use the massive file. That summer, the DoJ secured permission to depose more witnesses; IBM was prohibited from doing the same.

Accounts of the suit routinely ignore one important constituency: everyone's customers. What did they think? Their actions spoke loudly in the late 1960s and 1970s. They acquired computing products and services from every vendor in ever-larger quantities, but were they agnostic about the performance of one firm over another? In 1973, *Datamation* set out to provide insights by surveying 400 data processing managers concerning the eight largest computer manufacturers. The magazine focused largely on "after-sales service," "product reliability," "support," and whether the company could "live up to claims." IBM ranked number one and far ahead of all the others across the first three categories. In a separate question about cost versus performance, it came in lowest. In other words, customers thought IBM's products and services were the most expensive. It asked respondents to rank a company's ethics, and IBM came in a close second. Since the DoJ and other firms were hammering IBM on ethics, why were customers happier with IBM's performance?[35] The survey never resolved that mystery, but two conclusions were either they did not think the charges against IBM had merit or everyone else was worse than IBM.[36]

On the charge that IBM controlled the market, respondents disagreed. The survey asked them to vote to what degree they believed the statement "People are reluctant to buy something new until IBM gives its blessing." Eighty-three percent of the respondents disagreed with the statement, because they believed they were qualified to judge the value of a new technology for themselves. *Datamation's* writer expressed skepticism over their responses, but it was quite an emphatic result, and the respondents were knowledgeable about computing. They were the people most affected by market realities, by whether IBM had a stranglehold on the market's behavior.[37] Finally, since litigants accused IBM of driving rivals out of business, often citing the highly publicized case of RCA, an iconic U.S. corporation that had entered the computer business but without deep knowledge about how to compete in the world of computers, what did respondents say about RCA? They ranked RCA lowest in four out of six categories of performance. They hammered RCA over its ethics, inability to honor its claims, and the quality of its after-sales and support services.[38] Their responses begged the question: Did RCA just not compete as well as other firms, including IBM?

Finally, on May 19, 1975, the trial began in the Manhattan court-room. All parties assembled at 10:30 A.M., to begin what it would take the DoJ three years to do—present its case.[39] The DoJ brought in 52 witnesses, 32,000 exhibits, and 72,000 pages of transcripts. File cabinets lined the walls of the courtroom. IBM's motions for mistrial, submitted as the case shifted, were denied, so the trial continued. On April 26, 1978, the DoJ completed its presentations, and IBM began its defense that afternoon.

Meanwhile, the DoJ had swapped out its prosecutors, so it wanted to reinterview IBM's witnesses. Edelstein approved their request. IBM had by now delivered to the court 300,000 pages of materials, so many in fact that to manage this huge file it created an online database for use by its lawyers. Later, it sold this software as a product to law firms. What the DoJ had now asked for would have entailed creating five billion pages of text drawn from the files of some 2,000 locations worldwide, which IBM estimated would cost it $1 billion to gather. The judge agreed to a compromise: Cary would testify about pre-1974 activities at IBM and about evidence from his prior depositions. Nevertheless, his driver had to bring him down to the courthouse for 10 days just for this phase of the trial. By now, IBM's lawyers were fed up with the judge, and in July 1979 it asked him to recuse himself because of "bias and prejudice" against Big Blue. He declined to do so and was upheld on appeal. However, even the appellate court observed that perhaps a settlement would be in order. Nothing came of the recom-mendation, despite a few meetings.

Meanwhile, in January 1981, the Democratic administration of President Jimmy Carter ended, and a new one, led by President Ronald Reagan, a Republican, came into office. That meant new DoJ leadership and different priorities at the White House. Both sides completed present-ing their cases in June. All through the trial years, IBM maintained its inno-cence. Cary stated, "I want all IBMers to understand that our competitive practices are fair and ethical. That is the way we have always conducted our business and the way we always will."[40] He never missed an opportunity to repeat the message. Each year, IBM included a one or two sentence update in its annual report to stockholders. It was almost unnecessary, as the busi-ness trade press routinely covered every step.

Regardless of IBM's position, the bigger drama unfolded outside the courtroom. The case lasted so long that most of the circumstances on which it was based—actions of the 1960s—no longer existed. The industry had fundamentally changed. S/360s and S/370s were history. The industry now had a vibrant software market, another for midrange systems, yet another for desktop computing (largely PCs, worth billions of dollars), and a rapidly expanding IT services industry. Most of the competitors affected in the 1960s and early 1970s were gone. The major players in the early 1980s did not exist when the case began: Amdahl, Apple, and Data General, among others. Japanese competitors were vigorous and active in the U.S. market. The press was already describing the case using terms such as "anachronistic" and "irrelevant." It was costing the DoJ millions of dollars and becoming a source of embarrassment to the White House.

Then, just after 4 P.M. on January 8, 1982, on another Friday afternoon, a deputy assistant attorney general, Abbott Lipsky, raised his tall, thin frame before the now aging Judge Edelstein in that familiar courtroom number 1105. Lawyers from both sides of the case, newspaper reporters, and industry watchers packed the room. The buzz for months had been that maybe the case would end soon. Lipsky uttered the words IBM's defense team had wanted to hear for so many years, that "the case is without merit and should be dismissed." A week earlier, on Wednesday, IBM's legal team heard that the DoJ was about to bring the case to a close, so conversations began. On Thursday evening, Assistant Attorney General William F. Baxter, the chief of the Antitrust Division, signed off on shutting down the case. That fateful Friday morning, Tom Barr added his signature to the "stipulation of dismissal." Baxter and his staff had spent a couple of months reviewing the mountain of evidence from the case and could not see sufficient reason for continuing. Barr felt vindicated, exclaiming later that day that, "Sixteen Federal judges have decided in our favor." He added, "These claims are without merit. IBM has been completely vindicated."[41]

Four hours before Lipsky stood up in that courtroom in New York instead of Baxter, who normally would have uttered those fateful words, the latter was in Washington, D.C., where he announced the conclusion of an out-of-court settlement of the government's antitrust suit against

AT&T, the world's largest company. That suit had gone on for seven years, and its settlement resulted in the company's breakup into 32 operating companies, forever changing how telecommunications evolved. The Reagan administration had decided to clean house of old antitrust cases and open a new chapter in the federal government's relations with large corporations. Baxter found time to comment about the IBM case, saying simply that dropping it was "the only sensible thing to do," since it had been based on "flimsy" evidence.[42] He acknowledged that in addition to being a poor case, it had cost the U.S. government between $1 and $2 million per year for 13 years. His cost estimates seem low; nonetheless, it proved expensive.

IBM CEO John Opel was thrilled, calling the decision "wonderful news," a "burdensome" case for IBM now over. Everyone at IBM Corporate seemed relieved. IBM's media machine got out all the usual press announcements, arranged for interviews, and every IBM bulletin board around the world carried the news by Monday morning. Years earlier, Cary had called it the "Methuselah of antitrust cases," and Baxter, the new U.S. attorney general, agreed. The case unfolded across four presidential administrations, the tenures of nine attorneys general, and three IBM chairmen (Watson Jr., Cary, and Opel). The New York Times called the conclusion of the AT&T and IBM cases "the end of an era in antitrust law and very likely the beginning of an era in information and telecommunications technology." Business Week wrote that "Justice [Department] deserves the thanks of the country for blowing the whistle on a case that was weak to start with and became weaker with the passage of time."[43]

But not everyone was happy. Richard T. DeLamarter, an economist who worked for the Justice Department on the case, published a book-length retrial of it, savaging IBM's activities of the 1960s. DeLamarter wrote that "IBM is in fact a major problem for practically every country in which it does business, even the United States. By maintaining everywhere a self-perpetuating, lopsided market structure in which it towers over all competitors, IBM has amassed entirely too much power to be considered 'good' for any nation as a whole."[44] Five economists who worked on IBM's side of the case defining the size of the computer market took the opposite view in two fat books. Three of those economists were blunt about the matter: "The government's argument was based on erroneous conceptions of competition and a grossly inadequate understanding of the facts, particularly in respect to the nature and definition of the market in which IBM operated, the experience of other firms in that market, and the significance of IBM's introduction and pricing of new products in the context of market developments."[45] Among the beneficiaries were business historians, who ended up with access to hundreds of thousands of pages of information about the computer industry.[46]

No event of this magnitude just ends on a Friday afternoon. Consequences for IBM unfolded over the next quarter century, casting a shadow over the company. But first, what happened to the key players? Attorney General Ramsey Clark, under whose watch it all began, went on to support various liberal political causes and to provide legal defense services to Saddam Hussein, among others. Born in 1927, as of this writing (2018), he was in his nineties. Judge David N. Edelstein retired from the bench in 1994. When the IBM case ended, he was three weeks shy of his seventy-second birthday. He died on August 19, 2000. William F. Baxter (1929–1998), who had his moment of fame with this case in 1981–1982, was applauded by economists and criticized by some in political life and law for not taking on large, vertically organized corporations. He spent most of his life as a law professor and in legal practice and died at the age of 69. IBM's lead attorney, Thomas D. Barr, had joined Cravath, Swaine & Moore, IBM's law firm, in 1958 and remained with the practice for 40 years. He died in 2008, one day after turning 77. IBM's senior legal official, Nick Katzenbach, had been a prisoner of war during World War II, a Rhodes Scholar, a lawyer after the war, assistant attorney general in the Kennedy administration, deputy attorney general from 1962 to 1965, and then attorney general. IBM hired him as its general counsel in 1969, and he retired from IBM in 1986, after which he turned to private practice. Like so many of the players in the antitrust story, he, too, led a long life, passing away at age 90.

Cary and Opel rarely spoke in public about their time at IBM, and never about the antitrust suit. The only IBM CEO who did was Tom Jr.:

Looking back I see a lot of sad irony in the whole affair. I think a lot of people would agree that at the outset the Justice Department's complaint had merit. IBM was clearly in a commanding position in the market, and some of our tactics had been harsh. We eliminated many of these practices ourselves, and our overall record during the case was pretty clean. But I've always thought that if Judge Edelstein had carried the suit along rapidly, we'd likely have ended up with a consent decree in which we might have formally agreed to hold back from announcing our machines until we were a little further along with their development, to loosen our grip on the educational market, and so on. Instead, the case stretched on unresolved for so long that before it was over history showed my arguments to Ramsey Clark to have been right. IBM kept growing, but the computer industry grew even more, and the natural forces of technological change etched away whatever monopoly we may have had.[47]

WHAT THE ANTITRUST CASE DID TO IBM, THE COMPUTER MARKET, AND OTHER CORPORATIONS

Inside IBM, accountants and executives were tabulating the costs of all these federal and private lawsuits. The U.S. government was doing the same. At IBM, the cost of a constantly expanding legal staff in the 1960s and 1970s became a permanent feature of IBM, with a population of dozens of attorneys expanding to hundreds. Historian Richard S. Tedlow estimated IBM's costs just for the litigation of the 1960s–1970s in the tens of millions of dollars.[48] A more accurate cost would easily be ten times that amount.[49] Various observers spoke of the damage done to IBM's confidence, its way of acting, and weakened *élan vital*. While the antitrust case was still ongoing, Watson Jr. had this to say about the rise of the lawyers: "It depressed me to see IBM back in the lawyers' hands. The antitrust case began to color everything we did. For years every executive decision, even ones that were fairly routine, had to be made with one eye on how it might affect the lawsuit."[50]

Tedlow cleverly picked up on a subtle change in how IBMers spoke and wrote since the end of the case. Certain phrases could not be used, such as "market share" and "crush our competition," yielding to a new corporate language filled with code words. Slide decks carried less text, bulleted lists instead of sentences.[51] Tedlow stated that "the antitrust suit traumatized IBM for more than a decade. The special 'code' being developed to deal with normal business situations introduced an element of unreality into the company."[52] While all of this was true, as we will see later when discussing the history of the Personal Computer, executive management also proved eager to reenergize the company in the 1980s. With new leadership coming during the 1990s, the effects of the lawsuits began to wane.

Step out of corporate headquarters and one could see others fretting over the rising power of lawyers at IBM. After all, it was the job of lawyers to keep IBMers out of jail and the company out of court. Sales thought the legal community was overly cautious. Every executive had assigned to them a lawyer they could or should go to for every significant decision, even to review comments to be made outside the firm. David Mercer, a British IBM manager, wrote in 1987 about doing business in World Trade: "One department that is uniquely powerful in IBM, where it probably barely exists in most other companies, is Legal. IBM has a long history of almost continuous legal battles with the U.S. government, typified by the decades long anti-trust suits. As a result it is pathologically nervous of the legal implications of almost any decisions or activities; details that other companies would not even consider contentious. That is reflected in a unique, and important, offshoot: the Business Practices department." While the Business Practices Department was normally seen as a constraining force, Mercer admitted that the resulting "Business Conduct Guidelines" used worldwide made it easier for IBMers to know what they should and could not do.[53] He also reminded us that the rise of the lawyers and their influence dated to before the antitrust suit, to the time of the consent decree of 1956.

Lost to history was another antitrust case that should be acknowledged. For reasons similar to those the U.S. Department of Justice had used, the European Union also explored the possibility that IBM had violated its laws. The charges were similar. Its litigation process took a couple of years and, in August 1984, IBM and the European Commission settled the case, with IBM agreeing to end some of its practices. The European Union started a new investigation of IBM's mainframe maintenance practices in 2010. The regulatory probe ended in late 2011 when IBM agreed to modify how it provided information to its competitors regarding mainframes. The Europeans had learned from the U.S. cases. Joaquin Almunia, European commissioner for competition, explained: "Timely interventions are crucial in fast-moving technology markets."[54]

Historian Steven Usselman made the point that the combative relations between the DoJ and IBM "never devolved into a simple doctrinaire feud between habitual adversaries." Their disputes "involved complex questions regarding the ways in which market structure and firm organization shaped incentives and promoted or impeded technological change." These U.S. suits involving IBM "essentially provided a forum in which lawyers, economists, and other experts actively worked through the issues" concerning how a modern corporation could function and the parameters set by the law.[55] It is a discussion still under way, occurring with the EU in its dealings with Amazon and Facebook in the 2010s. Usselman was not alone in pondering the significance of the earlier cases. Lawyers and economists did, too, publishing scores of lengthy articles about the effects. A general cooling of antitrust prosecutions permeated the work of the Antitrust Division at the DoJ for the next quarter century.[56] Economists debated the effects of emerging technologies on national economics and corporate behavior.[57] Commentators combined the cases of IBM and AT&T, the first as a winner, the second often as a loser, in the high-stakes game of antitrust litigation.

But Watson Jr. may have come closer to the ultimate truth of the matter, that however more cautious IBMers became at all levels of the corporation, the markets kept growing. Opportunities kept expanding to such an extent that the company could increase revenues, expand profits, and grow its global footprint in the 1980s while still carrying the psychological burdens imposed by caution, slowed innovation, and increased bureaucracy. Tom Jr. hinted at the hit to IBM's confidence and bravado that occurred. IBMers living through the period felt chastened, and when the government's case ended, they were more relieved than excited. For most, it meant the company would not be broken into two or more pieces, as was happening to AT&T. Did the case affect other large corporations, particularly American ones? Any major U.S. corporation that was doing well in the United States was vulnerable to litigation either from its less successful adversaries or by the DoJ. Nobody could ignore the risks, especially when the DoJ experienced success over the course of the second half of the century.

Was the exercise of so many lawsuits worth it? The U.S. Department of Justice spent a fortune, yet the IBM case was essentially a loss. However, it got what it wanted out of the AT&T case. While the IBM case certainly diminished its appetite for antitrust suits, if it intended to foster more competition, it succeeded, as the 1980s and 1990s turned into a Golden Age of innovation in information technologies, although much of it would have come regardless of what happened to IBM. We know that because the company was not broken up or severely hampered, while new technologies came along, evolving rapidly into viable commercial forms. They surfaced from many sources, across numerous industries and countries. The most spectacular one, of course, was the explosive use of the Internet, which we now realize was one of the major events of human history.

Breaking up AT&T released pent-up demand for digital telecommunications waiting in the wings in Canada and Europe, which gushed forth in digital telephonic switches, cell phones, and mobile computing. Would IBM have unbundled its software if there were not concerns over potential antitrust moves by the DoJ? The evidence suggests potential government litigation pushed IBM to take that action. The antitrust cases facilitated the emergence of a large commercial software industry that might otherwise have remained far smaller for a very long time.

IBMers in the 1980s widely believed that the cost to IBM's spirit and energy unquestionably had been severe. The dollars involved proved ultimately less of a factor than how the company operated. IBM could afford to carve out blocks of Cary's time for the case because customers kept acquiring IBM products for all the reasons they had always done so. Stockholders remained supportive as well. Nevertheless, it would be difficult to find an IBMer who lived through the period who thought it was a positive experience. IBM's U.S. employees remained critical of the U.S. Department of Justice for the rest of their careers and normally did not discuss it, even among themselves.

The Antitrust Division and the Department of Justice both changed over the course of the lawsuit. The IBM case was widely described as the DoJ's "Vietnam," the idea being that it lost its war against IBM and that the case lasted as long as the U.S. war in Southeast Asia, at enormous cost to the nation. However, Marc Allen Eisner, in his study of the DoJ's antitrust activities, argued that it practiced poor economics in the 1960s but did far better by 1982. The Reagan administration limited the antitrust activism of the department that had so marked its activities from the 1950s through the 1970s,[58] although the DoJ never gave up its valuation of the importance of market power in determining whether to pursue antitrust litigation.[59]

Historical accounts of IBM move from the antitrust cases to narratives of IBM's experience with the Personal Computer. However, one large, unfilled part of the history of the company ignored or glossed over by journalists, economists, historians, and IBMers was IBM's interactions with Communist Europe. If someone thought IBM World Trade lay slightly outside Domestic—the core of IBM—then what would they think of the Cold War world that existed on the other side of the Berlin Wall? The company's experience there did not parallel what the rest of IBM underwent in Western Europe or the United States, and it is to that story we must turn next.

13 COMMUNIST COMPUTERS

The vast majority of Soviet managers and administrators had little or no perception of the practical and potential value of computers.
—SEYMOUR E. GOODMAN, 1979[1]

THE COLD WAR hung over billions of people like a dark cloud. It had started secretly during World War II when the Soviet Union and the Allies lined up on opposite sides to shape the postwar world with rival brands of a global order and did not end until the Soviet Empire imploded in 1989. In the intervening nearly half century, the world came close to nuclear holocaust several times, while both sides fought numerous surrogate ground wars in Africa, Latin America, and Asia. Both sides monitored and controlled what companies could buy and sell to each other, because they were always concerned about espionage and the exchange of technologies that might provide military advantages to the other side. For example, Polish computer users liked British technologies, and Soviet officials thought Poles and East Germans might share communist computer architectures with the West. The Russians sold a handful of machines to the West, largely through Finland, but the majority of sales went from West to East. Charles de Gaulle's clash with the government of the United States over a French effort to acquire a CDC computer was typical of much larger forces at work that shadowed the activities of IBM and other large corporations around the world.

During the first decade of the Cold War, Josef Stalin (1878–1953) micromanaged relations between the East and West. Between 1953 and late 1964, Nikita Khrushchev (1894–1971) ran the Soviet Empire. The 5 foot 3 inch, bald-headed leader gave the appearance of being jolly, a solid peasant, but he had grown up in the rough-and-tumble world of Stalinist politics and union labor movements. IBM was about to encounter this Soviet pounding his shoe at a United Nations podium and shouting to the West, "We will bury you." For months afterward, IBM employees were reminded of his warning, because public buses posted his picture and the quotation alongside other advertisements. However, in the late 1950s, Khrushchev was dismantling the harsher elements of Stalinist rule. He encouraged calmer relations with the West, despite his bellicose rhetoric.

In a milder moment, a "thaw," the premier visited the United States in September 1959. Upon hearing that he was coming to America, Tom Watson Jr. invited Khrushchev to visit an IBM plant, and Soviet officials showed up at IBM San Jose. Before arriving at IBM, things had gone poorly for Khrushchev. While at an exhibit of American products in Moscow, Vice President Richard Nixon had his famous "kitchen debate" with the premier over the benefits of capitalism as reflected in the appliances in modern American kitchens. The Soviets had difficulty believing Americans could afford them; certainly Russians could not. So there was much to see in the United States, but things did not always go according to plan. The mayor of Los Angeles denied the Soviet leader permission to visit Disneyland for security reasons, which really irritated the premier. Even the leader of the communist world wanted to meet Mickey Mouse. Hungarian IBMers brought to the United States after the Russians occupied their country in 1956 were not happy about Khrushchev's impending visit to their plant. On San Jose factory bulletin boards, IBM had posted a notice that the visit was in the spirit of building friendship between the two countries and that if anyone did not want to be part of that gesture they could take two days off from work with pay. Twenty did. IBM was currently exhibiting a RAMAC system in Moscow and was trying to establish sales with the Soviets. At the time, a ban on U.S.-Soviet sales blocked such activity. Watson wondered whether the visit would be a mistake. Would the premier use the visit to criticize IBM, the United States, or the American way of life?

On the big day, September 21, 1959, the premier and his entourage showed up at the new San Jose plant, built three years earlier as the manufacturing site for the state-of-the-art RAMAC, just in time for lunch. Watson shrewdly wanted to break the ice with lunch first, followed by a tour of the facility and a demonstration of the RAMAC. Watson would feed Khrushchev in the company cafeteria, where both managers and workers ate, not as in Soviet plants, where the two classes of employees ate in segregated dining areas. Watson had instructed the cafeteria to serve normal food, nothing fancy. The staff trotted out fancy vegetables and the best salads California had to offer. In his memoirs, Watson described how much Khrushchev enjoyed selecting what to eat and helped himself to generous portions, smiling as he did it. The guests could see several hundred IBMers having lunch there also. Watson later recalled that Khrushchev was constantly touching people, shaking hands like a U.S. politician. Walking through the plant, he managed to make a personal impression on employees. "My father was the only other man I ever knew who could affect a large crowd that way," Tom Watson Jr. recalled in his memoir.[2] Khrushchev talked with IBMers, asked them about their work, how much they were paid, and what they spent on groceries. In reaction to the computer demonstration, he commented on how the Soviets also had advanced computers. In 1959, nobody knew that in just over a decade, Soviet "advanced" computers would be IBM clones.

The lunch made an impression. The leader of the communist world had onion soup, fried chicken, a fruit salad, ice tea, and orange juice. Later, back in the Soviet Union, he encouraged factories to implement American-style cafeterias but did not speak publicly about IBM's computers. The idea of self-serving cafeterias was alien to the Soviets but clearly resonated with communist sentiments about "self-service." Khrushchev paid less attention to American computers than to such issues as standards of living, agricultural practices (he was raised on a farm, and agriculture was a major public policy concern), and, of course, IBM's cafeteria. He never mentioned IBM in his memoirs, but the company was on the minds of other Soviets and Eastern Europeans.[3]

Communist regimes comprising the Union of Soviet Socialist Republics (U.S.S.R.) ruled a vast landmass from the end of World War II in 1945 until the 1990s. China and India, and various other countries around the world, hovered around the Soviet orbit with communist or socialist states, embracing Russia's economic strategies as much as its data processing technical standards. In that environment, IBM operated almost as if in an entirely alternative reality, one characterized by limited sales and few competitors, as it understood competitors operated. It was an environment where the majority of computers were IBM clones, illegally copied using stolen machines, software, and user manuals, duplicated in scores of factories producing thousands of machines based on IBM's models or acquired through legal means. These modeled the S/360s, S/370s, and IBM PCs, as well as minicomputers from other U.S. vendors. Nothing in IBM's past prepared it for this bizarre situation.

Much about IBM-Communist relations remains shrouded in mystery, although new historical research is beginning to change that.[4] Historians focus on cybernetics in the Soviet Union, revealing a vibrant movement with discussions framing the thinking of senior Soviet officials regarding communist computing.[5] A second line of research involved the role of Soviet networks, in which proposals for such communications schemes were developed, but, as Benjamin Peters has demonstrated, "stumbled due to widespread unregulated competition among self-interested institutions, bureaucrats, and other key actors."[6] As mentioned briefly in this chapter, the poor diffusion of personal computers in communist countries was one of the few instances (as currently understood) where ideology played a profound role, because the Soviets did not want dissidents to be able to communicate or share information. A third line of historical investigation concerning Soviet computing has proven to be the most prolific, focusing on specific computer projects. Many Eastern European memoirs demonstrate that far more attention was paid to creating Soviet computers than Western scholars appreciated until recently.[7]

IBM is notably absent from this literature, and its own records provide few insights. The U.S. Central Intelligence Agency (CIA) and other expert reports offered more details about computing, while communist records remain largely closed. One important finding of these studies is the enormous exchange of information back and forth between the West and East. Elsewhere I have likened Winston Churchill's "Iron Curtain" more to a chain-link fence through which information about computers passed than a solid wall, while other researchers documented the rise of the scientific world of computing as a community from Japan to Russia.[8] Despite limited records about IBM, we can construct an account of communist computing in which IBM played an important if unusual role. After the lunch with Khrushchev, IBM was there but not central to what happened, distanced from crucial events of communist computing, indirectly influential but with almost no benefits to the company. Here there were limits to IBM's iconic status, and World Trade could barely generate business in communist-controlled Europe.

To address this chapter's topic, it is essential to understand major computing activities in Communist Europe to provide the context in which to situate the appropriation of IBM's technologies there, our second discussion. We then turn to what IBM did in the region, correcting notions that the firm only had its technologies "stolen" by the Russians. IBM's activities there after the end of the Cold War round out our survey.

INTRODUCING COMMUNIST COMPUTING

The evolution of computing in the Soviet Union can be summarized quickly. The Soviets used less computing than the West or Japan during the second half of the twentieth century. Technological evolution from one generation of computing to another lagged the West by between 6 and 15 years, yet Soviets used computers in areas of the economy similar to those of the United States: defense manufacturers, military and weapons research, space, development of nuclear weapons, later in civil manufacturing, and in limited form in office work, accounting, and centralized planning. The Soviets were particularly aggressive in using computers to do national economic development planning, which failed as much because the technology could not yet handle the necessary large, complex calculations and data management as because of insufficient appreciation of the economics required.[9] User organizations varied widely from those in the West, with priorities set differently. Military and atomic weapons research in the 1950s and 1960s claimed high priority, though commercial uses also blossomed. In the 1970s and 1980s, Soviet manufacturing used computers in personnel and payroll management, master production and plant scheduling, logistics, coordinating transportation, and air traffic control. Normally, decisions to use computers were made by centralized government authorities mandating uses for specific purposes. These authorities then shipped machines and software to specified users. Decision makers ignored issues concerning installation of these systems or allocation of time and funds to train users and maintain equipment and software. These practices existed in all nine states of the Soviet bloc: Russia, Poland, Hungary, Czechoslovakia, German Democratic Republic (East Germany), Romania, Bulgaria, Yugoslavia, and Albania. While the last two countries eventually broke with the Soviets, their technological profiles matched those of other communist states.

The Russian and Soviet capital, Moscow, was ground zero for critical decision making about the kinds of computers to use. Russian officials negotiated with the eight other countries about the roles they should play in the development, manufacture, and diffusion of computers. Poland, East Germany, and Russia remained the most advanced users of computers and the most influential in Soviet computing policies and practices. As in the West, homegrown projects to build a few computers popped up in the late 1940s at mathematical, scientific, and engineering institutes. Russian cybernetics took off in the 1950s, as both the subject of serious research and political discourse, despite periodic bans and objections by officials. Ultimately, interest in the subject prevailed within computing circles and among many scientists, resulting in what Slava Gerovitch, the leading student of the subject, called the "cybernetization of Soviet science."[10]

In Moscow, groups of engineers began acquiring knowledge about computing from the West. By the end of the 1960s, the Soviets routinely translated into Russian and other languages over 2,500 Western scientific and engineering publications, so people interested in computing had access to key Western publications, which included the majority of U.S. journals on technical and scientific issues as well as books. Beginning in the 1950s, computer scientists from the United States and Eastern Europe visited each other's countries, computer vendors, and universities, engaging in candid exchanges about technical challenges and issues. Both sides wrote trip reports and, in the case of Western visitors, often published them in technical journals such as those produced by the IEEE Computer Society and the Association for Computing Machinery (ACM).[11] Soviet electrical engineers and computer scientists had access to these articles. Great Britain's early computers became the most widely mimicked by Eastern Europeans. American influences increased in the 1960s, especially IBM's technologies. From the 1950s through the 1980s, each country expanded training and research, though to a lesser extent than in the West.

Why did Soviet computing lag the West's? The U.S. Congress asked William J. McHenry, an American expert on Soviet computing, this question in 1987. He responded with a half dozen reasons that differed from the experiences of IBM, its competitors, and their customers. Other observers confirmed McHenry's opinions. He observed that users had more difficulty using computers than in the West, because of "slow, unreliable hardware, small main memory sizes, and small disk sizes." Communist users complained about "hardware failures and difficulty of obtaining service." They had to repair their own machines and software. There were no IBMers or other service personnel to help out. Nor did government agencies provide sufficient assistance. Repair work meant increased costs, as offices and factories had to hire their own maintenance personnel. A major problem McHenry pointed out was "the difficulty of obtaining new machines and help in migrating from aging ones, leading to a tendency to hang onto old systems longer than necessary." Users complained of their "inability to procure packaged software," often leading to "unusable products" being delivered to them. McHenry's final observation was perhaps most lethal: "poor user training and difficult-to-use systems which alienated users." His answers in 1987 would have been the same for the prior two decades.[12]

McHenry described the absence of what computer users in the West took for granted. To use any complex product like a computer, IBM and others had to provide a set of machines and software in sufficient quantities and in a timely fashion. IBM and its rivals had to explain to customers why they should deploy these offerings, train them in their use, and then provide maintenance. Vendors could do this better and less expensively than users. The Soviets never fully understood the necessity of building this complex ecosystem around computing, and the results showed. The communist experience is a telling lesson of how right successful Western computer vendors were in focusing on their information technology ecosystems. In IBM's case, it had been a priority since Hollerith's day. Users east of the Iron Curtain did not have salesmen pushing them to use computing, enough technology to make data processing attractive, or crucial handholding. Western observers noted that much work was under way to develop computing but was fundamentally a flawed exercise. One of the leading experts in the West, Seymour E. Goodman, observed that "the Soviets opted for a distant relationship with the U.S.-dominated international computer community. As a result, they denied themselves many of the benefits of computing that were available elsewhere, and the indigenous industry of the U.S.S.R. rapidly fell behind that of the United States. Soviet policy reflected both a desire to develop an independent capability in an important strategic technology, and a rational but somewhat short-sighted perception of computing and its value to the U.S.S.R."[13]

While the history of Soviet computing was cluttered with machines and innovations, the structural problems McHenry and Goodman identified kept Communist Europe from being economically able to compete with the West. For example, centralized planning (done partially using software modeling) meant that some computer factories did not have the right parts or had production targets that did not match demand. Despite this, production managers built machines and shipped them whether needed or not, because it was their job to do so. It was like receiving a camera and being told to use it but not having film. Stories abounded of printers arriving with no paper, or either no disks for the disk drives accompanying a new computer or only one or two, not the three or four needed to boot up a system. There were also tape drives without tapes, and computers that had some or no software. In some instances, staffs did not know how to install a system so the machines were left outside in the snow, still in their crates. Universities and the military did better, as they had better-trained staffs and more funding, especially the military and scientists working on national security issues, as exemplified by their successful development of nuclear weapons and the Soviet space program.[14]

The results of all their problems could be seen in the number of installed systems. Remember, the Soviets' European geographic footprint was as large as Western Europe.[15] The year 1970, midway through the era of the computer, is a good time to assess how things were going. That year, the entire Soviet bloc had about 6,500 installed computers, the United States nearly 70,500, and France, West Germany, Japan, and Great Britain each between 5,000 and 7,000 systems. East Germany had 360, West Germany 6,700.[16] China had even fewer computers and less industrialization than the Soviets.

EMBRACING THE "IBM WAY"

By the late 1970s, almost all mainframes used by the Soviets were near copies of IBM's S/360s and soon after S/370s, right down to their physical construction, components, and software. Adoption of IBM's architectures extended to almost all essential peripheral equipment as well, such as printers, disk and tape drives, and control units. IBM's documentation on the architecture and use of its hardware and software had been translated into Eastern European languages without the company's permission but nevertheless became the basis of communist computing into the late 1990s. Had the Soviets acquired IBM's products legally, as done in the West, IBM might have been larger by 25 percent or more as measured by its number of employees, revenue, and profits. Central and Eastern Europe would have used far more computers of advanced design than they did. What was going on was widely known, and while co-opting IBM's designs (patent and copyright infringement) was illegal in the West, that situation posed no problem in Eastern Europe. The Russians, in particular, had a long history of retroengineering products, going back as early as the 1930s, famously with American aircraft and military vehicles. They also had computer scientists who added their own innovations, such as software functions, or modified machines at individual data centers out of necessity to fit software into computers with inadequate memory. So, to say the Soviets completely duplicated IBM's machines and software is not strictly correct but also not far from the truth. How did they do it?

This story had its roots in the 1960s, out of practical concerns about catching up with Western technology when computing was becoming crucial to national security and to the military on both sides of the Atlantic and across Central Europe. As many as 20 incompatible systems were under development in the Soviet bloc. They had the same problems as IBM's machines: they were not upgradable, were incompatible, and were often too small to handle the work required of them. The development costs for so many different systems proved too great, and the diverse skills needed were unavailable. Many Soviet computers were specialized for satellites, military applications, and the space program, so they were unavailable for other applications. From their earliest days, IBM and other vendors had developed "general-purpose" systems that could be used for a variety of purposes, not solely for a specialized purpose. Prior to the 1970s, the Soviets designed systems that were for single (or few) purposes. It was not until over a quarter century after the West started developing more flexible systems that the Soviets did the same.[17] In the Soviet Union, computer scientists and users discussed the benefits of having modular systems, too, just as IBM and American computer scientists, engineers, and customers were doing. These debates accelerated as demand for computing increased.

At the highest levels, officials were ordering all parts of the economy and government to use computers. Premier Khrushchev promoted this agenda in the early 1960s. By then, he also was keen on improving the quality of Soviet computing. They were moving into the second generation of computers, while the West was entering the third. Something had to be done quickly. The answer seems simple in hindsight: don't reinvent the wheel. The decision to copy IBM's S/360 was made in 1967 and, as a CIA report noted, the RYAD (better known in Soviet circles as ES) series was to be "a direct copy."[18] Designs for an upward-compatible family of computers designed roughly along the same lines as IBM's S/360 emerged, called the "Unified System," began in the late 1960s. The lion's share of that early work took place in

Russia, followed by agreements and establishment of enterprises to participate in its construction in Bulgaria, Hungary, East Germany, Poland, Romania, and Czechoslovakia. The scale of the resources was as substantial as that of a large U.S. corporation. Some 100 organizations, close to 300,000 workers, and over 46,000 engineers and scientists were assigned to the Unified System project.[19]

Debates about RYAD's architecture ensued in all these countries, ranging from advocating copying the IBM S/360 to others proposing a unique communist computer. The Soviets established the Council for Economic Mutual Assistance (CEMA) to manage this and other economic and technical initiatives. The initial plan to mimic IBM's architectures called for construction of three compatible systems of different sizes, called ES followed by a model number, such as the ES 1020, ES 1035, and so forth (much as IBM was using the common name S/360) to indicate increasing sizes of computers. These were to include compatible peripheral equipment for all RYAD computers. Table 13.1 provides technical comparisons of various Soviet machines to IBM's S/360.

The RYADs have come down in history as if they represented one design that totally co-opted IBM's architecture. These Soviet systems continued to evolve through four generations, much as in the West systems like the S/360 and S/370 changed over time, along with their software. Clearly, the first generation of Soviet systems closely matched IBM's, as demonstrated in table 13.1. When the decision to move ahead with the S/360 architecture came, another decision allowed the Soviet military to have supervisory control over its implementation, a responsibility yet to be studied by historians. Ultimately, the decision to embrace IBM technology turned on its more advanced software, especially its operating system, although the Soviets recognized IBM's hardware architecture as the de facto world standard for general-purpose computers. In the 1970s, new waves of computers emerged from that standard: the ES-1020 (1971), ES-1030 (1972), ES-1040 (1973), and ES-1050 (1973). IBM's operating system (OS/360) for large systems became ubiquitous, although modified extensively from one edition (release) to another (OC EC), followed by adoption of the company's operating system for smaller systems in the 1970s as well.

Table 13.1

Technical specifications of early RYAD and IBM 360 series computers

Model	Add time (microseconds)	Memory cycle time (microseconds)	Input/ output rate	Storage capacity (kbytes)
IBM 360-20	58	3.6	160	4–32
ES-1010	200	1	140	8–64
IBM 360-30	40	1.5	400	16–64
ES-1020	25	2	200	64–256
IBM 360-40	12	2.5	800	32–256
ES-1030	6.5	1.25	700	128–512
IBM 360-50	4	2	1,200	128–512
ES-1040	1.4	1.35	1,300	256–1,024
IBM 360-65	1.3	0.75	1,200	256–1,024
ES-1050	0.65	1.25	1,300	256–1,024
IBM 360-75	0.8	0.75	1,300	256–1,024
ES-1060	0.5	0.6	1,300	256–1,024
IBM 360-85	0.16	0.08	1,300	512–4,096

Notes: Add time = time required to execute one addition. Memory cycle time = time required to read and restore a specified number of bits. Input/output rate = maximum speed of input-output operations. Storage capacity = number of units of addressable internal storage available. kbytes = kilobytes; a byte is a basic unit of memory used to form words.

Source: Directorate of Intelligence, U.S. Central Intelligence Agency, "Soviet Bloc Computers: Direct Descendants of Western Technology," June 1989, 6, https://www.cia.gov/library/readingroom/docs /DOC_0000500644.pdf.

These systems had compilers for Western programming languages, initially for FORTRAN-4, COBOL, PL/1, RPG, Assembler, and Algol.[20] Systems developed in the late 1970s and 1980s took advantage of changes in IBM's architecture and operating systems but also increasingly used Soviet technical innovations. New computers appeared on a regular basis, such as the ES-1022 (1975), ES-1032 (1974), ES-1033 (1976), and ES-1052 (1978). The Soviets were following paths similar to those of Amdahl, Fujitsu, and Hitachi, all producing machines compatible with IBM's.[21]

In sum, the Soviets produced three generations of systems along the IBM style: the first, in the late 1960s to early 1970s, closely modeling IBM System 360; the second, in 1977–1978, reflecting changes IBM introduced with System 370; and a third, appearing in 1984, which still relied on

S/370 but with the largest number of Soviet enhancements and modifications. A fourth generation under development barely went through design and testing before the end of the Soviet era. Some 20 of these last machines were manufactured; the ES program ended in 1998.

When it was over, the RYAD consisted of 32 models and over 200 different peripheral machines. The Soviets used 12 versions of IBM's operating system over nearly three decades. Eastern Europeans borrowed Western Europe's Algol programming language more than American languages such as COBOL, later PL/1. The Soviets probably used every IBM software product that ran on its S/360s and S/370s, and included the majority of commercial software products sold in the West, most without licensing or purchasing them. RYAD systems proved popular, and an estimated 15,000 were installed in the Soviet sphere. By the early 1980s, users relied on IBM software tools, such as IMS, IDMS, CICS, and OS, forcing communist computer developers to remain strongly wedded to IBM's architecture. Obtaining IBM machines to test Soviet versions of the software proved difficult, so some of that work was done using more easily obtainable Japanese systems from Amdahl and Fujitsu, especially for third-generation systems in the mid-1980s (ES-1016, ES-1026, ES-1036, ES-1046, and ES-1066), the machines most in use until the end of the Soviet era.[22]

East Germans were particularly enthusiastic about building RYADs modeled on IBM's systems, while the Poles favored British ICL systems. Everyone else took up positions all over the architectural map, from American, to British, to Soviet-unique systems. Most of the early systems were more compatible with IBM's 1401s than with S/360s, because the skill levels of the available workers were more in line with the capabilities of the 1401s and less developed to handle S/360 hardware and programming. This was especially so in East Germany, because of the greater ease in replicating the older, simpler system. It quickly became evident that duplicating S/360s was going to be a difficult task, and it was never fully achieved. Furthermore, early RYADs did not include time sharing, whereas IBM's eventually did.[23] In the years in which IBM built S/360s (1964 through the early 1970s), the company manufactured 35,000 of them, the Soviets an estimated 5,000.

A crucial reason for mimicking IBM concerned software. Recall that communist computer engineers accessed Western technical literature and conversed with Western scientists and engineers, so they understood IBM's difficulties in stabilizing its operating systems in the 1960s. They reasoned that if IBM, with its skilled engineers, was having difficulty creating this new software, then imagine how difficult it would be for the Russians and East Germans. They also concluded that it would be less expensive. It turned out to be a good decision, as it helped to push along development of local systems, even if at a slower rate than at IBM. Without IBM's software, the Soviets feared their computing would remain stuck in the 1950s. IBM was a convenient shortcut, despite challenges in adopting its software.

The economics involved proved interesting as well. Soviet systems were capable of running only one application at a time. In the West, S/360 systems could run several concurrently. To do so required large amounts of computer memory, more sophisticated operating systems, and other complex software. So, in addition to avoiding having to create such software, CEMA and others avoided the massive investments made by the West in computing. IBM's S/360 project cost the company over $5 billion. That amount did not include additional billions of dollars spent by commercial software companies and customers on related products and their adoption or the tens of thousands of man-years involved.

While all of this seemed practical on the part of the Soviets, even wise of policy makers in centralized economic planning departments, implementation did not include creating the kind of information and support ecosystem in which IBM enveloped its customers. That broad level of support ultimately made it possible for customers to operate IBM's S/360s, even when challenged by the problem-plagued operating systems in early releases. That IBM ecosystem was missing in Communist Europe. Goodman noted that, in the late 1970s, "Repair or replacement of faulty parts that in the United States would take hours or at most days may still take a year in the Soviet Union."[24] It was a bigger problem than just response time. The Soviets failed to appreciate how much a user of any mainframe needed a breadth of services. Decision makers had little or no personal experience running data centers the way IBMers, their competitors, and customers did. Faulty configurations of input/output machines with mainframes and software, insufficient peripheral equipment and supplies, air conditioning, and adequate supplies of electricity in data centers compounded problems into the 1970s. It took almost a decade before such practical matters became evident at senior levels of centralized planning and manufacturing agencies. By then, government departments were making peripherals, such as disk drives, that duplicated functions, so they were becoming increasingly incompatible. Nonetheless, what they had proved to be better than what existed before they started borrowing from IBM.

Not to be overlooked is the fact that by standardizing on IBM the East could use thousands of commercial software products that they could copy and share. Over time, Soviet computer scientists were able to weave into them developments occurring in computer science and technology in the West, so they kept up, reducing the gap between what IBM and others were producing and what became available in Communist Europe. Lags with IBM often shrank to the point where they paralleled those between IBM and its competitors. CEMA and others grossly underestimated how difficult it would be to co-opt IBM hardware and software, which goes far in explaining why the Soviets never fully caught up with IBM. With the lack of dynamic and effective relations between developers and users in the West, the Soviets always had to wait to see what IBM and others developed before they could determine what they wanted to do next.

While all of this was going on, communist countries obtained copies of IBM's equipment, often in Western European countries or in Latin America. But, as one informed observer, Seymour E. Goodman, noted, "The Soviets have demonstrated that, if they are willing to try hard enough, they can illegally obtain entire I.B.M. computer systems."[25] A CIA report as early as 1973 made a similar observation: "The task of copying may have been aided by the clandestine acquisition of embargoed 360 series computers and associated documentation. This probably decreased the time and effort needed to achieve a Soviet prototype," but this same report also made the point that "the availability of the hardware for inspection does not reduce the effort needed to go from laboratory to mass production."[26] How many computers were smuggled into the Soviet bloc remains unknown.

Occasionally an IBMer would report a customer "losing" a system or piece of equipment, or needing a fresh set of manuals for an entire system for some inane reason.[27]

The same story could be told about IBM's PCs.[28] When they became available in the early 1980s, the Soviets embraced their architecture the same way but installed fewer of them for fear they would be used to share information within the U.S.S.R. that was hostile to the state. This paranoia was particularly intense in Russia, East Germany, and Hungary, but it existed in all communist republics. The Soviets also borrowed minicomputer technologies from the West, standardizing largely on DEC's VAX systems. An unintended consequence evident when IBMers came back into Eastern Europe in the 1990s was that they found many facilities somewhat familiar with IBM systems and therefore not disposed to try other brands.

IBM'S ROLE BEHIND THE IRON CURTAIN

IBM did not stand by as its S/360 was illegally replicated. It complained to U.S. and Western European authorities, but they could do little to block these practices, let alone the illegal shipment of products east. IBM's ties in Eastern Europe dated to Hollerith's days. One of Hollerith's earliest contracts provided the Russians with punch card equipment for their census in 1895. During the 1920s and 1930s, IBM established branch offices in Central Europe, including in Moscow. During World War II, Tom Watson Jr. flew in and out of Russia as a U.S. Army pilot. From 1979 to 1981, during the administration of President Jimmy Carter, he served as U.S. ambassador to Moscow.

During the Cold War, IBMers found it difficult to conduct business in Soviet Europe. Many of IBM's properties and equipment had been destroyed during World War II or confiscated by new regimes. U.S. and Western European governments swiftly limited exports of advanced technologies to the Soviet Union. Those regulations imposed constraints on IBM's ability to establish local sales offices, let alone sell equipment, but it was able to establish agency-like relations in each communist country. Soviet politics periodically also reared its ugly head, causing IBM to pull local employees out of the region. IBM's head in Poland in 1945, Janusz Zaporski, moved to IBM Brazil. IBM Czechoslovakia collapsed after it came into the Soviet sphere in 1948. Soviet regulations blocking importation of Western technology also inhibited IBM. Some projects were implemented, however. IBMers in Hungary assisted with a census in 1950, even though that same year Soviet officials arrested IBM's local manager, Julius Sandorfi. IBM typewriters, knockoffs also from government-run factories, were popular in Eastern Europe. In 1956, IBM World Trade headquarters stopped sales of computers to the Eastern bloc because the U.S. government considered many of its products too advanced to let the Soviets obtain them.[29]

IBM's competitors proved more aggressive in selling in the region. European manufacturers were more able than IBM or other U.S. firms to bring machines into this market. They seemed less constrained by the delicate problem of balancing standardization and copying of IBM technologies, illegal smuggling of IBM products, and sales deemed to be possible security risks by Washington officials. In 1965, IBM worked with U.S. regulators in the Department of Commerce and Department of Defense to establish protocols for how to request permission to sell to the Soviets. These built on practices used during World War II.

IBM established a small office in Moscow, periodically staffed with IBM employees, during a period of détente in the 1970s, managed out of WT's European headquarters in Paris. From there, IBMers forayed into the Soviet Union. Later, that mission was transferred to Vienna, where IBM established a regional headquarters responsible for Communist Europe. An early leader of the Austria Control Center was Ralph R. Stafford, an American. In the 1970s, one of the salesmen who went in and out of Moscow was Jim Donick, an American who spoke Russian and had honed his sales skills in a branch office in West Orange, New Jersey. As business increased, the IBM center was folded into IBM's Europe-wide operations, known as the Regional Office Europe Central and East (ROECE). It was structured the same way as other regional staffs, populated with Austrians, other Europeans, and Americans on temporary assignment from Domestic. What they sold came from IBM in Western Europe.

IBMers participated in the business fairs popular in Central Europe in the postwar decades. Recall the RAMAC on exhibit in Moscow in 1959. These events provided IBMers with opportunities to meet potential customers. In 1967, the Hungarian government acquired its first IBM computer, an S/360 Model 20. By 1973, IBMers were working in Yugoslavia, Bulgaria, Czechoslovakia, East Germany, Hungary, Poland, Romania, and Russia. IBM's two largest customers were Russia and Yugoslavia, with some 150 systems sold to these countries by 1976 and another 150 to the rest of the region. At the same time, communist copies of IBM-based machines, largely Unified System, occasionally competed against IBM's systems in the West, through a Finnish-Soviet venture called Elorg-Data Company.

These actions beg the question, however, of how IBMers sold computers to the Soviets when their customers were also making copies of IBM's machines. How did IBMers deal with U.S. regulators, who had to approve every sale behind the Iron Curtain? Sales began with a willing government periodically interested in détente with the Soviets. The Nixon and Ford administrations encouraged U.S. corporations to increase trade with the Soviets, facilitating approvals and the formation of joint ventures with Russian organizations. The U.S. government established the U.S./U.S.S.R. Trade Council, with American CEOs and Russian senior officials as members. At the dawn of the 1970s, IBM's CEO, Frank Cary, established a small team to work with the Soviets, named IBM Trade Development, based in Paris and run by Ray Fentriss, who had many years of experience selling computers outside the United States. In 1975, Brad Lesher (1935–2014), another American experienced in running IBM operations outside the United States, replaced him. He left a short record of how IBM sold in the Soviet Union:

> This unit worked on a project by project basis and each computer delivery was completed only after lengthy reviews by the U.S. government and its NATO partners. This review could result in project delays of 6–12 months or even more before an export license to ship the computer would be granted. This prompted we Russian hands at that time to draw the analogy of doing business in Russia with the mating and subsequent gestation period of elephants. You conduct business at a very high level and there is a lot of noise,

foot stomping, and kicking up dust at the onset. You then wait for up to 27 months for the result.[30]

While sales remained low, one in particular gained some visibility: IBM computing for the 1980 Olympics, hosted by the Soviets but boycotted by the United States. Lesher explained why: "They were installed a year earlier for the Eastern Bloc games" and "were fully paid for and licensed and installed" and after the games were redeployed in Moscow to handle various administrative applications.[31]

How systems were sold came right out of IBM's playbook. Lesher's staff of marketing representatives and SEs worked in classic project style but with a Russian twist:

> Our modus operandi was to have our technical teams from Paris and Munich fly in and work on projects for several weeks at a time and then on an average of once a month the executive team would fly into Moscow for project reviews on the spot and a series of high level government calls to solidify existing business and pursue new opportunities. This would normally involve intense negotiation sessions beginning with vodka early in the morning, continuing through lunch and vodka and sometimes followed by dinner with vodka. It was a monumental effort to argue each point incessantly to a final agreement and contract but once the contract was signed a supplier couldn't find a better business partner than the Russians to live up to the deal and make the appropriate payments on a timely basis.[32]

The permanent staff in the 1970s remained small: three IBMers and their families. Jim Donick was an example. Germans also periodically served in Moscow. Participants from IBM in the 1970s and early 1980s periodically included up to a dozen additional employees in Moscow. That mode of operating continued until the collapse of the U.S.S.R. and the opening of a local market in a much wider, more conventional way.

There remains one more open question to round out our discussion: Did Watson Jr. help IBM while serving as U.S. ambassador to Moscow? He was busy dealing with the Soviet invasion of Afghanistan. That war alone consumed him night and day. IBM's corporate records likewise did not contain any evidence of any IBMer attempting to reach out to him for assistance. Rather, employees worked with lower-level officials in the U.S. embassy on routine administrative matters required by U.S. and Soviet regulators dealing with import/export matters.

But the old salesman in Watson popped out at least once. When the Russians invaded Afghanistan, the Carter administration wanted to punish Moscow. While at a meeting at the White House in early 1980 with the president and his security advisers, Watson spoke up probably more like an IBMer than as a diplomat. The idea on the table was to block all sales of U.S. products to the Soviets. Watson objected that these companies, in his own words, "weren't even going to be allowed to send spare parts to fix equipment that was still under warranty." Watson recalled telling "the president that didn't make sense; if you want to declare war or have a boycott, fine, but breaking a commitment to a customer is always wrong."[33] Carter ordered sales stopped, as he wanted to punish the Russians. Carter's edict included IBM. Had Watson subconsciously thought about IBM's relations with the Soviets at that moment? It is hard to tell, but clearly his reaction reflected the long-held value of customer service so ingrained in IBM's sales culture. International tensions ultimately made U.S. corporations cautious about making too many investments behind the Iron Curtain. IBM was not alone in its limited initiatives; Dow Chemical, ITT, AEG Telefunken, and ICL, among others, kept investments within the Soviet Union low, choosing instead to work with local business partners on a limited basis.[34]

AFTER THE BERLIN WALL FELL

Berlin, occupied by Britain, France, and the United States as one sector and the rest occupied by the Soviets, was surrounded by East Germany. Since 1961, a wall had divided the city, built by the East German government to prevent young, educated workers and their families from migrating to West Germany. By August, when it began to build the wall, nearly 50,000 people had moved to the West. That was too much of a brain drain for the East German government to ignore. The wall quickly became a global symbol of communist oppression. Over the decades, East German guards killed 171 people attempting to escape to the West; an estimated 5,000 succeeded.

Six hundred escapees were wall guards. It seemed that every time someone was shot or made it out, Western media carried their story. In a visit to Berlin on June 26, 1963, President John F. Kennedy declared "Ich bin ein Berliner," "I am a Berliner." In June 1987, President Ronald Reagan stood before it and demanded of Soviet premier Mikhail Gorbachev, "Tear down this wall."

On November 9, 1989, evidently confused by instructions from on high, a spokesman for the East German Communist Party announced that citizens would be able to pass through the wall beginning at midnight. News spread quickly through the city; thousands of young East Germans gathered at gateways at the wall. Local guards were confused but began opening the gates. Thousands flooded through while thousands of others climbed the wall that evening and all night celebrated their newfound freedom. They also began tearing down the wall. That weekend, over two million people poured through checkpoints, some returning home the next day after sightseeing and shopping in West Germany. Communist regimes, already under siege, began to collapse.

The Cold War fell of its own weight, and new governments formed across the region. Holdouts like East Germany and Russia could not stand for long. The process was chaotic, complex, yet peaceful. The direction rapidly became clear: toward more open democratic and capitalist societies. It happened so quickly that everyone was caught by surprise. The Russians chose not to clamp down as they had when the Hungarians, East Germans, and Poles tried to break the Soviet hold over their countries in earlier times. Many U.S. and Western European officials learned about the fast-moving events by watching television, while Western TV cameramen scrambled to get footage. IBMers in Vienna and all over the company were just as mesmerized as everyone else. It took a few days for them to realize that perhaps a fabulously new market was about to open. It turned out not to be fabulous, took nearly a half decade to enter, and remained tenuous, but with toeholds already in place, IBM was prepared to enter this new world. Expanding telecommunications with the West, in part using PCs, may have helped growing numbers of dissidents hostile to communist rule, suggesting a new world opening up.[35]

IBM's history in Central Europe and Russia mirrored the company's experience when it had expanded into Western Europe in the 1910s and 1920s and reestablished its presence in post–World War II Western Europe. Business partners and employees searched for customers, initially government agencies but later newly privatized factories and companies. IBM established a PC manufacturing plant in Russia but competed with over a half dozen local rivals with unmatched inside connections. Nonetheless, during the early 1990s, it became a successful reentry into local markets, overcoming the lack of effective legal enforcement of contracts so crucial to the successful functioning of a capitalist economy, or clarity in existing business laws.

Business grew slowly, yet as it did IBM in Vienna committed resources to the region. The company had a banner year in 1994, when IBM World Trade Europe/Middle East/Africa Corporation established local IBM companies in Bulgaria, Poland, the Czech Republic, Slovenia, Slovakia, and Russia, with one in Croatia being added the following year. Other countries followed: Latvia and Estonia in 1997, Lithuania in 1998. Each became responsible for expanding IBM's customer base and branch offices beyond its capital city. Besides the Russian PC factory, IBM opened a few manufacturing facilities that also served as places to bring customers and IBMers for training. In Hungary, IBM began constructing a disk drive factory in 1995. By then, a new era had opened in Russian-IBM relations (see table 13.2).

But old behaviors died hard. The mysterious, often questionable events of Cold War days continued, especially in Russia. In the 1990s, Russia attempted to evolve from communist authoritarian government into democratic parliamentary administration. By the end of the decade, Russia was drifting back into authoritarian practices. Throughout the decade, business behavior remained corrupt. American and European companies, subject to U.S. and Western European anticorruption laws, sometimes got into trouble. IBM's Russian subsidiary broke no Russian law but led IBM Corporation and its subsidiary into a federal courtroom on July 31, 1998, to admit guilt in having exported 17 computers that ended up at a Russian nuclear weapons laboratory. A fine of $8.5 million came out of Domestic's budget. IBM

Table 13.2
Chronology of IBM-Soviet activities, 1949–1995

1949	IBM formed World Trade Corporation
1956	IBM introduced 305 RAMAC and 650 RAMAC
1959	IBM displayed RAMA at an industrial fair in Moscow, Russia
1959	Thomas Watson Jr. met with Nikita Khrushchev in San Jose IBM plant
1959	IBM introduced 1401 data processing system
1964	IBM displayed an IBM 1140 data processing system in Russia
1964	IBM introduced S/360 family of computers, peripheral equipment, and software
1967	U.S.S.R. decided to standardize Soviet computing on IBM S/360 design
1967	Hungary acquired its first IBM S/360
1972	IBM Europe organized within World Trade
1973	IBM opened a branch office in Moscow, Russia
1980	Russia used IBM computers in Olympics; United States did not participate in the games
1989	Berlin Wall comes down, communist regimes begin collapsing in Eastern Europe
1991	Formation of IBM CSFR, a wholly owned subsidiary in Czechoslovakia
1991	Formation of IBM Poland
1991	Formation of IBM USSR Ltd.
1993	IBM began manufacturing Personal Computers in Russia
1994	IBM opened branch office in Vladivostok, Russia
1994	Formation of IBM subsidiaries in Czech Republic, Poland, Slovenia, Slovakia, Bulgaria, and Russia
1995	Formation of IBM Croatia
1995	IBM opened PC manufacturing plant in Czech Republic
1995	IBM started manufacturing disk drives for Personal Computers near Budapest, Hungary

had never been convicted of violating federal import/export laws before. Russians had quietly acquired the systems in 1996 and early 1997. The *New York Times* reported the Russians thought the deal was legal since its government had signed a test ban treaty on nuclear arms in 1996.[36] However, the ban did not absolve the company from adhering to regulations.

The fine caught IBMers off guard. Federal investigators found no evidence that Americans knew of the deal, let alone participated in it, and declared that the IBM Government Relations office in Washington, D.C., had been completely cooperative. The assistant United States attorney for the case, Eric A. Debelier, reported that "IBM acted in a highly responsible manner."[37] World Trade executives cleaned house in its Moscow operations, while Russian officials "refused to assist us in any way."[38] Silicon

Graphics also landed in a similar bind. Congress reacted to these and other sales of advanced technologies in other industries by tightening laws regarding exports, despite IBM and other firms lobbying against such legislation.

LIMITS OF DIFFUSION

IBM's experience with Communist Europe teaches us much about this company and about computing. Writing in the late 1970s, Goodman placed a great deal of blame for Soviet failures in economics at the foot of its centralized mismanagement in the deployment of computers. Too few Soviet managers could properly appreciate the role of computers, at least as understood in the West. Goodman argued that, "Extensive use is being made of Western products, but the Soviet industry seems satisfied with the short-term goals of recreating selected Western systems at a rate that is slower than that at which the West built them in the first place."[39] He correctly blamed the Soviets for being "clearly dependent on a substantial and sustained transfer of technology from the West, and particularly from the United States," its supposed mortal enemy.[40]

Its approach to dealing with Western technology kept it isolated, since officials in each of the communist states showed little inclination to connect to the global computer industry the way the rest of the world had already done. While many countries wanted an indigenous computer industry, as did communist states, their political, technological, and economic ecosystem was perhaps too centralized, run by individuals not adequately in touch with users or technologies, so they failed to leverage IBM's technology effectively. If one were going to be dependent on Western computers, would it not make sense to establish close ties to those creating the technology, such as IBM? For most of a century, IBM's largest customers had found that useful to ensure vendors developed goods and services relevant to them. It is how IBM achieved iconic status. Missing inside the Soviet bloc in the halls of power was the "voice of the customer." IBM's experience with Communist Europe contrasted sharply with its role in the rest of the industrialized world, where the company influenced events. IBM thrived in capitalist economies, not in state-dominated ones.

The company's context was not always a positive force. Capitalist economies evolve constantly, and nowhere was that seen more frequently than with underlying technologies. If a company responded well to these winds of change, so much the better. If not, the seeds of their potential death were sown. IBM's destiny over the next several decades was planted in a few conference rooms in Armonk and White Plains and in a nearly secret operation in Boca Raton, Florida. By the time all that played out, IBM had introduced the most iconic product of the late twentieth century: the Personal Computer. Bill Gates became a household name and the richest human on the planet while IBM's nearly unbroken record of successes over an entire century shattered. It all began with Charlie Chaplin. It is to the "Little Tramp's" story that we turn next.

14 "A TOOL FOR MODERN TIMES": IBM AND THE PERSONAL COMPUTER

We screwed up. ... We did not see the PC as a platform.
—SAMUEL J. PALMISANO, 2015[1]

PHILIP DONALD "DON" Estridge (1937–1985) introduced IBM's PC to the world on August 12, 1981, at the Waldorf-Astoria hotel in Midtown Manhattan. With that announcement, IBM brought forth another computer revolution; however, few realized that at the time. As the press generally put it, "OK, so IBM now, too, has a microcomputer product. Big deal." Soon the world embraced little computers by the millions. IBM's share of those sales dominated for several years, but by 1986 the company was at risk of becoming a PC also-ran. In 2005, Chinese computer maker Lenovo purchased IBM's PC business.[2] What occurred in the intervening years between IBM's success entering the PC business and exit from it nearly a quarter of a century later? From IBM's perspective, in the first half of the 1980s, something terrible began happening, turning a new and vast market into an ugly battleground with many rivals. From the second half of the 1980s until its end 20 years later, the PC story degenerated into a disappointing chapter in IBM's history. IBM's customers became unnerved, the company stumbled badly, and the PC business became the graveyard for the careers of a slew of employees and potential future CEOs. Over time, it became clear that the disappointing story of IBM's PC mirrored the declining performance of the entire company.

The triumphant tone of IBM's history from the 1910s to the 1970s ended in the 1980s. In the 1980s, IBM operated in over 150 countries.

Customers and investors considered IBM an American treasure. However, IBM's prior success with the mainframe business did not avert the decay in most parts of its business, with shrinking mainframe sales, an inability to take on minicomputer vendors like DEC, and the frustrating story told here about PCs. IBM's early history with PCs unfolded at the company's high-water mark, when its revenues were still growing, the company's mainframes continued to dominate, and the firm captured a significant market share in the PC business.

Today we know that IBM's PC experience revealed an internal corporate sclerosis. Most of the decisions and actions taken in the 1980s occurred in the United States. IBM's decline is a story of a corporation that became too big, too bureaucratic, and too insular. As the 1980s unfolded, IBM's PC activities were influenced by events in its mainframe business, while the effects of its PC products came to play a central role affecting the general affairs of the company. That was not supposed to happen, because the PC business was intended to be a small sideline activity, not a threat to the company's mainframes or to its position as the industry's iconic vendor. In the process, the company's PC business suffered, contributing to the declining performance of the entire company. Histories of IBM and PCs have yet to link together the performance of the two businesses or fully appreciate events at IBM in the 1980s and early 1990s. This chapter begins to integrate events across the company and the PC.

A generation of senior executives stayed out of touch and psychologically unprepared to remake the company in the way that Tom Jr. had responded to the development of large computers. The momentum in emerging computer technologies shifted from IBM, settling on Microsoft, Intel, and Apple. New participants in the computing world, such as Compaq, Dell, and later H-P, caught everyone's attention. IBM lost its position as the center of the world's IT ecosystem.[3] A smaller, less prosperous company might have collapsed. IBM's slow response to changing technologies led to a decline that extended for over 30 years, the entire career of a lifelong IBM employee. For many of those years, the firm sustained itself with cash flow from mainframe sales that, although declining, remained large. In the early 1990s, IBM almost went out of business, rebounded quickly for over a decade, but then struggled to retain its stride. It would be difficult to overstate the magnitude of that experience on customers and the computer industry.

Historians have yet to document the general history of personal computers, with much of the work so far left to journalists and memoirists.[4] To describe more fully IBM's role, the effects of the PC on the company's overall performance, and, conversely, how the firm's culture and mode of operations affected the PC business, this chapter describes the birth of the PC, its glory years (1982–1985), and then how it contributed to IBM's decline (1985 to the early 1990s).

Lessons culled from IBM's experience link closely to observations made by Alfred D. Chandler Jr. regarding commercialization of complex technologies. He observed that "successful high-technology firms were those that were able to combine and coordinate technological knowledge with that of product development, manufacturing, marketing and distribution into an integrated learning base."[5] IBM did a great deal of what Chandler described, although with much difficulty and internal infighting. IBM's experience demonstrated that first-entrant advantages could only be maintained, in Chandler's words, "so long as they continued to commercialize new products based on their initial competitive advantage."[6] IBM was unable to do that for a sustained period of time. Chandler's admonition that a successful company adheres "to definite paths of learning" did not occur at IBM either.[7] Larger issues were related to IBM's internal operations, errors in judgment, and faster responses by competitors exploiting changing technologies. This chapter demonstrates that failure in a large multinational corporation is a far messier affair than Chandler suggested and much closer to what a new generation of scholars realize.[8] Woven into issues related to corporate culture were concerns regarding competition and innovation, both discussed here as a contribution to the interests of economists regarding "industrial leadership."[9]

The personal computer disrupted the computer industry in a good way by vastly expanding the number of individuals and organizations that used computers. While IBM faced many challenges in this new market, its involvement went far in explaining why the world embraced this new technology in the 1980s. Explaining IBM's role helps explain why its initial activities had a greater effect on the PC's acceptance by users than did the early actions of rivals such as Apple, Compaq, Dell, or even Microsoft, and many hundreds of rivals in hardware and software. IBM's essential contribution was to position the technology as suitable for wide use, compelling rivals to meet what became a demand grossly underestimated by all vendors. IBM contributed a technology standard—a format or model—that made sense to users and rivals. It also lent its eminence to this form of computing. If IBM had not participated in PC technology, these machines would eventually have spread, only more slowly and possibly in some other form, such as Apple's alternative design.

IBM did not invent the first desktop computer. Its origins dated to the period between 1969 and 1971 when Intel Corporation developed the microprocessor, a computer chip that could be programmed similarly to a big computer. Technologists were rarely known for giving their inventions exciting names, so this device was called the Intel 4004. It sold for $1,000, making it affordable for many people. Improvements in speed, capacity, and performance came rapidly. In 1974, Intel introduced the 8080, dubbed a "computer on a chip." Individuals, followed by start-up companies, began putting together desktop computers. Most users were hobbyist counterculture individuals and small groups, not the Caltech or MIT PhDs one saw at IBM. They developed a new class of computers. In January 1975, the Altair 8800 became what was probably the first computer kit in the world; it sold for less than $400.

Other vendors entered the market. Apple Computer succeeded better than all the others in the 1970s in developing commercially attractive machines. Its products caught the attention of IBM and some of its large customers. Its founders, two electronics geeks, Stephen Wozniak (b. 1960) and Steve Jobs (1955–2011), built their own personal machines and taught themselves how to write software. In 1976, Apple was part of a handful of tiny companies trying to enter a potential new market, with Jobs recognizing interest in such a machine could extend far beyond the hobbyist community. In order for it to succeed, it had to be easy to use, come out of a box, plug into the wall, and run when turned on. That idea was the origin of Apple Computer's ease of use. The company achieved this with the Apple II, which when it was introduced in 1977 became the first widely accepted personal computer. It faced two competitors, Commodore Business Machines and Tandy. Most historians agree that the personal computer revolution probably began in April 1977 at the West Coast Computer Fair, attended by early PC developers and hobbyists. Here, Jobs introduced the Apple II and Commodore unveiled its PET machine. Both were designed to meet the needs of consumers, not just hobbyists or technically skilled individuals. The Apple II cost $1,298, while IBM's large mainframes cost over a million dollars. In August, Tandy entered the consumer market with its TRS-80, sold with games. These new "appliances for the home" barely had a recognizable consumer/hobbyist market yet, with most software consisting of video games and a few programming tools.

To take off, this new market needed software. By 1980, the "killer apps" were becoming evident: spreadsheets, database management tools, and word processors. Early machines were not equipped to communicate with each other over networks. That function appeared over a half decade later. The first "best seller" software package came from Daniel Bricklin (b. 1951), a Harvard MBA student, who conceived the idea of using one of these machines to perform financial analysis. The result was VisiCalc, for *Visible Calculator*, introduced in December 1979. Running on an Apple II, Bricklin's app became the first practical tool a department or individual could use for an affordable $3,000 purchase price without having to depend on an IBM "glass house" for computing. In its first nine months, 25,000 Apple II computers used Bricklin's software out of a total of some 130,000 machines sold by Apple in the same period. The following year, packages for word processing appeared, once it became possible to display more than 40 uppercase characters on a screen. Soon hundreds of consumers every month in 1980 bought the Wordstar word processor for $450 a copy. It allowed users to type in both uppercase and lowercase.

So, a market emerged that did not exist before and did not grow out of the existing computer industry. The shift from hobbyists to people using spreadsheets and word processors led commercial users to acquire these machines also. Quickly, IBM's large U.S. commercial customers faced the implications of this emerging technology: Who would maintain the equipment and its software? How secure was data in these devices? How much control was the data processing department losing to engineers and others now going off on their own? What was IBM's position with respect to these machines: should they be taken seriously or not? By 1980, customers in many industries were telling their IBM contacts to enter the fray with a product that could be bought and controlled by their data processing managers. IBM employees agreed. Hobby clubs at IBM plant sites were forming in the United States, where on Sunday afternoons engineers gathered to build, use, and learn about these machines in places such as San Diego, Endicott, and Poughkeepsie. Even Frank Cary, IBM's CEO, was hearing about the need for an IBM "response."

How IBM responded has now gone down as one of those remarkable events in history, as it should be characterized, for it became on the one hand a shining moment at IBM but on the other hand came about because of the company's internal problems. IBM had dabbled with smaller machines in the 1970s, the Datamaster and 5100, both poorly conceived, but in 1980–1981, it was not clear what the arc of IBM's experience would be. Even as late as 1987, over a half decade after IBM had entered the PC market and was then experiencing considerable difficulties competing, economists were pondering the central managerial issue of "whether IBM can adapt to an era when the bases of competitive advantage in the computer industry are shifting."[10] IBM was not alone in being positive that it could meet that challenge. Boeing, a customer with close ties to IBM at the highest levels, was able to embrace new aircraft and market conditions and even meet the threat presented by the European Airbus consortium. The U.S. automotive industry, while late in responding to the challenge of less expensive, smaller Japanese vehicles, also had begun its transformation to maintain its market share, but like IBM, these firms faced stiff winds within their own organizations from those resisting fundamental changes in products and markets. Returning to the economists just quoted, the operational challenge IBM faced concerned how to enter the PC market in an effective way. As Stephen S. Cohen and John Zysman put it, "The American production tradition—with its rigidities, its inattention to quality, and its high overhead—is not well situated for competition," a circumstance that would "depend so critically on maneuverability and flexibility."[11] One could argue that IBM was part of that world, but it proved equal to the challenge for half a decade, again reminding other large multinationals that it had something to teach them about how to enter new markets.

The logical place to build a successful small computer was inside the General Products Division (GPD), but it had many other priorities and hence no budget or people to allocate to yet a third machine. It focused on minicomputers and its successful typewriter business. Cary decided simply to fund its development out of his own budget. He turned to William "Bill" Lowe (1941–2013), who was already inside GPD and had given some thought to the design of such a machine. Quiet, a bit stiff socially, but the personification of the white-shirted, blue-suited IBM executive, he could think "outside the box." When Cary asked him to come back in several months with a plan for developing a machine in a year, he did. Cary ordered him to find a facility to put it together that would be away from Big Blue and operate outside of IBM's product development process. Lowe reported directly to Cary, bypassing the complex product development bureaucracy, which had grown massively during the creation of the S/360 and S/370.

To go through the normal process to get the new product to market would have required four or five years, but the incipient PC market was moving too quickly for that. Lowe left Cary's office with instructions to find 40 people from across IBM and locate them in Boca Raton, Florida. Lowe's plan called for his team to buy existing components and software and bolt them together into a package aimed at the consumer market. The product also had to attract commercial users, although it was not clear how many corporate customers there would be. Mainframe system salesmen

Figure 14.1
Bill Lowe. A lifelong IBMer, Lowe was the "Father of the PC" at IBM. Photo courtesy of IBM Corporate Archives.

could be expected to ignore or fight these little intruders, so the project was kept reasonably secret. Possible competitive dangers with the consumer market added more reason to keep quiet. Over the next 15 years, IBM made Bill Gates one of the richest people in the United States. When Lowe, recognized as the "Father of the IBM PC," left the company, he had little wealth to show for his efforts.

After the birth of the IBM PC, the hunt was on for a design and components. A friend of Bill Lowe, Jack Sams, a software engineer who gets credit for some of the thinking about buying parts and software for the machine, vaguely knew Bill Gates. He reached out to the 24-year-old Gates, then living in Bellevue, Washington, to see if he had an operating system that might work for the IBM PC. At that point, Gates ran a 31-person company. He had dropped out of Harvard to get into the new microcomputer business as a hacker, programmer, and hands-on expert in the new technology, and while he thought of programming as an intellectual exercise, he also had a sharp eye for business. He met with the IBMers in July. They assessed each other, neither believing a partnership might lead to a huge new business opportunity. The IBMers were not greatly impressed with Gates, so they turned to Gary Kildall (1942–1994), president of Digital Research, Inc. (DRI), the most recognized microcomputer software company at the time. Kildall then made what historians may have to consider the business error of the century. He blew off the blue-suiters so that he could fly his airplane, leaving his wife—a lawyer—to deal with them. The meeting went nowhere, with too much haggling over nondisclosure agreements, so the IBMers left. The negotiations with DRI were over. Kildall had missed the opportunity to personally earn many tens of billions of dollars. Gates was now the only option, and he took the IBMers seriously.

The next month, Lowe presented his plan to the management committee in Armonk. In those days, it met a couple of times each week to set priorities and adjudicate issues among competing divisions regarding allocation of resources and to set strategic and operational priorities. Building on Cary's idea of putting together a PC outside of IBM's development process disturbed some members of the committee. Nobody at that meeting foresaw how big an opportunity the PC business could be, or how little IBM would be contributing to its software and hardware: there would be no homegrown operating system or IBM-made chips. Committee members were more interested in retail dealers, a distribution model with which IBM had no recent experience. Even IBM's typewriters went through dedicated sales channels in the Office Products Division (OPD). The committee also knew that IBM had failed to properly build its own tiny machines, specifically the Datamaster and the 5110, but Lowe was offering an alternative strategy and already had Cary's support.

With memories of S/360 software problems also part of their personal experience and acknowledging there might be programming issues for Lowe, they nevertheless approved his plan. Lowe negotiated terms, volumes, and delivery dates with suppliers, including Gates. To meet IBM's deadline, Gates concluded he could not write an operating system, so he acquired one called QDOS ("quick and dirty operating system"). IBM wanted Gates, not Boca Raton, to have complete responsibility for making the operating system work. That meant not buying his software but leaving him the rights for how best to use it. Microsoft acquired QDOS for $75,000. By the early 1990s, that investment had made the firm worth $27 billion. IBM made the strategic error of not insisting on retaining rights to or ownership of DOS, which proved far worse than giving up the $27 billion opportunity, because it meant that when Gates successfully converted QDOS to DOS, he set the technical standards in the market. In fairness to IBM, nobody at the time thought the PC business would turn out to be so big; nor did Gates and his tiny company. In future years, Gates said he had been "lucky."

Back at Boca Raton, the pieces started coming together. The team designed the new product, lined up suppliers, and in August 1981 introduced the IBM Personal Computer, one year after gaining the management committee's approval to move ahead. How was IBM able to do this? To a considerable extent, credit goes to one IBMer, Don Estridge. He was a rebellious engineering manager known for being disrespectful of the company's norms. He liked to wear cowboy boots instead of wingtip shoes. He would not show up at the endless rounds of review meetings so typical of product development at IBM, nor return phone calls. Estridge made decisions quickly and told Lowe and Cary about them later. Cary provided Lowe and Estridge with their internal political "air cover," frustrating engineering and product development departments elsewhere in IBM, but there was nothing those departments could do. Estridge turned out to be the perfect choice to ram this project through. He staffed up with like-minded rebels, later nicknamed the "Dirty Dozen." They put in long hours and built a beautiful machine. By the fall, Lowe had moved on to a new job, so it was Estridge working with Cary. Estridge obtained chips from Intel, made sure

Figure 14.2
Don Estridge, the popular PC executive who ran the IBM PC business during its successful period. Photo courtesy of IBM Corporate Archives.

Microsoft kept the development of DOS from QDOS secret, and quashed rumors that IBM was building a system.

When Estridge introduced the PC to the world, IBM's competitors would have to respond quickly, so they, too, increasingly would have to use DOS and Intel chips. It seemed IBM had climbed into the driver's seat. The bigger challenge for the IBM team was acquiring application software, because without it their product would not appeal to users. They lined up Lotus Development to provide their 1-2-3 spreadsheet package; other software products followed from multiple suppliers. Estridge had to find a manufacturer for his machines; neither he nor other IBMers consistently did a good job of forecasting capacity needs, as demand always exceeded supply. Their original forecast called for 1 million machines over three years, 200,000 the first year. In its second year, customers were buying 200,000 per month. Meanwhile, the IBMers kept acquiring, or encouraging others to provide, games and business software. IBM's advertising used the friendly figure of Charlie Chaplin's "Little Tramp" as the face of this system (figure 14.3). The character gave the ad a human, whimsical quality, with its simple white table, red rose, and punch line, "A Tool for Modern Times."[12] IBM's application software business was soon generating revenue of $100 million annually. Software vendors began writing software for the IBM PC, embracing DOS as the primary industry standard. As one reporter put it, poor "Kildall and DRI became answers to trivia questions."[13]

The big day came on August 12, 1981. Press releases were distributed to the media. Similar announcements were made in countries where the PC was to be sold. Salesmen in U.S. branch offices had received packets of materials on the afternoon of the previous day. Branch managers had already scheduled employee meetings for 10 A.M. eastern time and later that day would meet with customers to introduce everyone to the PC. Estridge wondered if the media would show up. After all, the PC was a small product, not in IBM's traditional space, and certainly not yet a big deal in the world of computers. Some 100 people crowded into the Waldorf-Astoria hotel. Estridge described the product, had one there to demonstrate what it could do, and answered a few questions. That was it.

Figure 14.3
Charlie Chaplin. The PC/1, introduced in 1981, had one of the most iconic advertising campaigns in IBM's history. Photo courtesy of IBM Corporate Archives and Charlie Chaplin Estate. Charlie Chaplin™ © Bubbles Inc. S.A.

In the branch offices, salesmen had slides but no sample machines. Along with their customers, they collectively scratched their heads, wondering how they could use it. It was one thing for data processing managers to worry about engineers and others in their companies buying such devices, quite another when they now had to participate in their use and management. For most customers and IBMers, it was a new world. The trade press treated it with nonchalance because IBM had been expected to introduce a PC. Customers got what looked to them and their salesmen at first blush like something pretty clever. It had the right amount of memory, so they thought, to run various software application packages, combined with a nice collection of commercial and consumer tools, including the accessible BASIC programming language. That consumers could acquire these at

ComputerLand, a popular computer equipment retail chain in the United States, added another level of simplicity.[14] For some corporations, the fact that IBM now had a product was recognition that these little machines were not some crazy geek-hippy fad but were in fact a new class of serious computing.

THE GLORY YEARS OF THE IBM PC, 1982–1985

Nobody at IBM, ComputerLand, or in the computer industry predicted what would happen next. In its first year (1981–1982), with initial shipments made in October, the IBM PC generated $1 billion in revenue. That money was over and above what IBM had planned on before the PC came online. For the moment, Estridge and Lowe could do no wrong. Cary's decision to avoid the long and bureaucratic product development process had paid off handsomely. Encouraged by their success, the IBMers in Boca Raton released a sequel in early 1983, called the XT. They considered other ideas for home computers and games, too. While Estridge managed to get out the AT, the XT's successor, in 1984 without being ensnared by IBM's processes, it was the last PC designed and produced outside IBM's product development process. His PC business was folded into IBM's bureaucracy, as rivals within the firm wanted to constrain his successes or co-opt his business with a new chairman's approval. In 1980, John Opel had inherited control of IBM from Cary and endorsed reining in the PC business.

Opel remained out of touch with the PC. One executive reporting to him bought a PC and opted for the maximum amount of memory he could put on it. When the executive told Opel of his experience with the machine, Opel asked, "Why do you need so much memory, when lesser is more than enough?" His employee walked away from the conversation convinced that Opel did not fully understand the significance of this technology.[15] Opel never did e-mail, use a terminal, or have a PC. Gates and other PC executives in the industry not only had machines but had personally built them, written software for them, and used them at work.

We could conclude that in those early years Opel and senior management did not need to know much because business overall was outstanding. IBM's revenue reached $29 billion in 1981 and climbed to $46 billion in 1984.[16] No other company in the world had done so well in such a short period of time. It seemed to Opel & Co. that they could do no wrong. The company was routinely ranked one of the best run, while critics accused it of corporate arrogance. IBM's stock more than doubled, making IBM the most valuable company in the world, at a whopping $72 billion, but some executives still did not understand why the company had to come out with such a machine. One executive quietly let a reporter know that he had asked the question, "Why on earth would you care about the personal computer? It has nothing at all to do with office automation," adding that these were not "real computers" and that in his opinion IBM did not "belong in the personal computer business to begin with."[17]

It did not help that the media only wanted to talk about IBM's PC or that customers, too, were falling in love with the new machines, ignoring the rest of IBM's senior executives and their lines of business. The sales force and product divisions stayed focused on selling mainframes, minicomputers, and typewriters. Historians and journalists wrote extensively about the internal battles over career issues among senior executives and jealousies with Estridge, but in hindsight those rivalries only involved a few dozen individuals. Estridge faced incessant calls to report on his activities in Armonk, diverting his attention away from the PC business, slowing development of new products at the same time that other firms began to speed up introduction of their own offerings. This slow, almost imperceptible shift in cadence proved in the long run to be unhealthy for IBM.

The first visible sign of the change came on August 1, 1983, when Estridge's skunk works was designated the Entry Systems Division (ESD). That shift subjected it to IBM's rules covering behavior and product development. In other words, Estridge's operations became ensnared in the bureaucracy that Cary had temporarily bypassed. Unfortunately for Estridge, his 4,000 employees exploded in size to 10,000, seemingly overnight. He managed to get out a new product, the XT ("extended technology"), which had been designed before this organizational change. With it, IBM reached its high-water mark in PC market share, at 75 percent. The PC software industry grew as thousands of programs aimed at commercial and consumer markets appeared over the next few years. In January 1983, *Time* magazine named personal computers, not a person, "Man of the Year." Once again, and despite itself, IBM was changing the world, and other vendors.

Why was the product so successful? As demand increased among corporate users who did not want to rely on their centralized data centers, they turned to these machines. They had been purchasing them before, almost secretly, out of their own budgets, often without notifying their data processing organization, which normally had ultimate responsibility for them and were in a position to negotiate quantity discounts for their purchase. Every variety of little computer came into these companies and, in some firms, at such a rate that they equaled in quantity the amount of computing power already in data centers in 1984 and 1985.[18] When IBM brought out its PCs, data center managers saw that they could have a standard device, hold IBM's feet to the fire for configuring them the way users wanted, and negotiate bulk prices. In the decades that followed, however, historians were able to report that the market for such technologies had already existed before the IBM PC. The company was playing a fast game of catch-up with its own device so as not to lose any opportunity in that market or, worse, "account control."[19]

What about the rapidly emerging consumer market, with which IBM had no experience? Management thought the company should go after it, but mistakes occurred. One afternoon before the PC Jr. was introduced to the world in March 1984, IBM salesmen in branch offices in the United States were going about their normal routine of opening up a box of announcement materials for use the next day: slides, literature, photographs, and handouts. Inside, at the top of the box, however, was the keyboard for the PC Jr. Something had gone terribly wrong. As these salesmen went through the technical descriptions of the new machine, it got worse. On that day, IBM lost its PC charm and never gained it back. The design and approvals for this machine went through IBM's multilayered product development and review process, with the eventual design shrinking— literally—and not just in function.

The PC Jr. had a tiny keyboard, so small that it was for children. The IT and business media, dealers, IBMers, and customers scornfully nicknamed it the "Chiclet keyboard." Much of its software was incompatible with that of other IBM PCs. The same situation held for its peripheral equipment, memory boards, and other extensions, so users could not exchange information and switch devices with others at home or at work. During the review process, the price of the machine rose, killing prospects of working with retail dealers. It seemed everyone mocked the machine. The company's salesmen ignored it, not wanting to make a "bad" or "irresponsible" recommendation to customers. They believed their personal credibility was on the line, a situation they had rarely faced before. IBM lowered its price, added functions, and persuaded dealers to promote it, but to no avail. Estridge took the blame. Rumors inside IBM suggested it had spent $250 million to develop it! ESD sought to sell unwanted leftovers to employees as potential Christmas presents for a few hundred dollars. That ploy failed.

In addition to IBM's onerous product development process, other changes in the economics of the technologies embedded in PCs were under way that were not fully understood outside of Estridge's organization. The cost of microcomputers kept falling faster than anyone predicted while simultaneously they were becoming more powerful—Moore's Law, which held that the processing speed of chips doubled and chip prices halved roughly every 18 months, was at work. Compaq and others introduced ever lighter and more powerful machines without anything like IBM's review process. In the early 1980s, IBMers consistently underestimated the size of the PC market, how fast it would grow, and how its base technologies were evolving. Although it sold many PCs in the early 1980s, IBM failed to expand quickly enough to stay in step with the expanding demand. By the mid-1980s, IBM was facing numerous rivals and was falling into the practice of responding to their introductions, not setting the pace, as it had done with mainframes. IBM was also experiencing a combination of internal rivalries for resources and attention among the product divisions and imposition of high internal overhead charges to cover the costs of its corporate headquarters and to provide a financial buffer for the year's balance sheet, which led to adding budgetary burdens on each division. The budgetary surcharge added costs charged to the PCs that competitors did not have. IBM's slow appreciation of what customers wanted did not help either, nor did its lagging insight into how the technology was advancing, except for a small community of IBM's computer engineers.

IBM's relations with its two most important vendors, Intel and Microsoft, remained contentious through the 1980s, as much because of differing worldviews as because of clashing personalities, such as between the older Bill Lowe and the young Bill Gates and later the abrasive James A. "Jim" Cannavino (b. 1945) with the Microsoft community. Gates sold competitors the same operating system that IBM used, and Intel provided them with identical chips. Both companies made a fortune. Rivals figured out that IBM had set the de facto technical standards for PCs, so they developed compatible versions they brought to market more quickly and sold for less. Vendors that had not latched onto that insight about standards or proved unwilling to embrace them suffered, such as Wang, Digital Equipment, and AT&T. Meanwhile, Estridge was not getting along with senior executives at IBM, particularly those on the mainframe side of the house. In early 1985, Opel replaced him as head of the PC business with Bill Lowe, who was seen as being more able to work with the rest of the firm.

Even the weather did not cooperate. On August 2, 1985, Estridge, his wife, Mary, and a handful of IBM salesmen from Los Angeles boarded Delta flight 991 headed to Dallas. Over the Dallas airport, 700 feet off the ground, a strong downdraft slammed the plane to the ground. One hundred thirty-seven people died. IBMers were in shock. The sales region in Los Angeles went into mourning, as did Estridge's division. Despite his troubles with senior management, he had been popular and highly respected. Not since the death of Thomas J. Watson Sr. nearly 30 years earlier had employees been so stunned by a death within IBM. Hundreds of employees attended the Estridges' funeral. Boca Raton and Austin, Texas (Entry Systems Division HQ), were quiet that day. The magic of the PC had died before the airplane crash, but if there had been any doubt before, the tragedy at Dallas confirmed it.

IBM's experience mirrored patterns of technological innovation observed by historians of technology. Robert Friedel, for example, pointed out that innovations, offered up in the form of incremental changes, came from many anonymous individuals.[20] In IBM's case, thousands of employees worked on the PC. Between 1981 and 1986, they introduced 11 models, ranging from the original PC (5150) in 1981, to the XT (1983), PC Jr (1983), AT (1984), and others (1986). These included software, media, computer chips, channels, and ports.

THE PC'S CONTRIBUTION TO IBM'S DECLINE, 1985 TO THE EARLY 1990s

Lacking the outgoing personality and "out-of-the-box" behavior of Don Estridge did not help the more formal, "old school" IBMer Bill Lowe. Despite his early experience with the PC in Boca Raton, many around him did not think he understood the PC market, arguing that he had grown up with mainframes in Cary's generation. The closest he came to small computing was in bringing out the successful mini system S/34. He had just spent several years in Armonk immersed in its internal workings and in establishing ties with the Old Guard, who, like him, did not fully understand the PC world. Gates had a far deeper appreciation, as both companies tried to collaborate on a new operating system for IBM, called the OS/2. Gates was also developing what became his highly successful replacement for DOS, called Windows. The two companies haggled over royalty payments and how to work on OS/2, debating in an atmosphere of mistrust, especially by IBM regarding Gates's intentions for Windows. Gates was selling software to Compaq and Tandy. While IBM continued to sell millions of machines, over time their unit profit declined, and just as bad, IBM's market share shrank from roughly 80 percent in 1982–1983 to 20 percent a decade later. Lowe could not break out of his mold of introducing new products more slowly and less competitively, leaving on the table billions of dollars in lost revenue. By the early 1990s, that lost business hovered at $15 billion per year.

How computers were used changed in ways IBM proved unable to respond to effectively enough, most notably in controlling the shift from stand-alone machines to networked PCs in the 1980s. Just as mainframe computing exploded in growth once database packages and telecommunications came into use in the 1960s, in the 1980s a similar phenomenon

occurred when users pressured their data processing departments to provide links to databases housed in mainframes. They also wanted access to
files outside the company, for which technology was coming online during
the second half of the 1980s. During the same period, Microsoft and IBM
began to respond to an emerging new way of interacting with computers
that moved from programming languages to icons and natural language
commands, which came to be known as graphical user interface (GUI,
pronounced("gooey") interactions.

Such developments portended a break from the technical standards
of the mainframe, with the high priest of the "big iron" approach, Earl
Wheeler, who controlled all of IBM's software in the second half of the
1980s, ruling with an iron fist. He had joined IBM in the 1950s as an engineer. He wanted IBM's software and networking to make it possible for all
IBM machines to "talk" to each other. Unfortunately for him and IBM,
customers were telling him they wanted telecommunications that "talked"
with all computers in their organization, which meant also with machines
from IBM's competitors, from PCs on up, including those from Digital
and Compaq, hated by IBM. Wheeler responded in 1987 with a blueprint,
not a product, called Systems Application Architecture (SAA). As part of
SAA, mainframe software developers at the Hursley laboratory would
develop the GUI for all machines. This facility specialized in mainframes
and large-system telecommunications, not PCs. What could go wrong?

Meanwhile, Microsoft and IBM could not fully connect on the development of OS/2, although they kept working at it on and off into the early
1990s. Software developers outside of IBM were frustrated with IBM's
software standards and direction. OS/2 came out in late 1988, priced at
$340. It also required $2,000 of additional memory. Application software
took an additional year to make it to market. OS/2 began to acquire "the
smell of failure."[21] Dealers and customers headed for the exits. By 1987,
IBM had over a thousand programmers assigned to that project and to
developing telecommunications, costing an estimated $125 million a year.

Known to few outside of IBM and Microsoft, in mid-1986 Gates had
offered to sell IBM a portion of his company. He needed cash to fund
development of new operating systems. Such a sale might have bonded the

two companies into a more collaborative relationship. Bill Lowe declined the offer, making what was perhaps the second-biggest mistake in IBM's history up to that time, following his first one, not insisting on proprietary rights to Microsoft's DOS operating system or similarly for the Intel chip used in the PC. It was already becoming clear that Microsoft was going to become one of the most successful firms in the industry. In fairness to Lowe, he remained nervous that such an acquisition might reactivate the U.S. Department of Justice's antitrust concerns. Would its lawyers view an IBM-Microsoft partnership monopolistic, since each firm still had over 50 percent of their respective markets? Possibly, but probably not. The Reagan administration was not inclined to tamper with the affairs of large multinational corporations. More to the point, Lowe, Opel, Wheeler, and other senior executives did not adequately understand the PC market. The purchase price probably would have been around $100 million in 1986, an amount that by about 1993 would have yielded a return of $3 billion and in subsequent decades orders of magnitude more. The gain to $3 billion alone would have exceeded the profit IBM made on PCs from August 1981 to the mid-1990s.[22] Lowe's fateful decision came as IBM's market share was declining, already down to 40 percent by that summer of 1986.

Lowe had the mindset that PCs, and especially their software, should undergo the rigorous testing the rest of the company's products underwent. That meant no software should be introduced until it was as close to being bugproof as possible. All other PC software developers valued speed to market over quality. They contended that it was better to get something out sooner that worked pretty well, let users identify problems, and then fix them quickly. Lowe was aghast at that strategy, yet it was how the software business grew outside of IBM.

Meanwhile, both in his division and across the top of the firm, executives wanted to extract as much revenue and profits from existing products as possible before being forced to bring out new ones. Rivals did not have an installed base of products to worry about, so in mid-decade they introduced plug-compatible machines and software as fast as the market could absorb them. IBM's old, measured way of growing its business by a controlled 15 percent annually was collapsing. Salesmen were coming forward with proposals to sell PCs in bulk, in some cases literally by the truckload, at discounted prices, but were being pushed back by executives and their marketing practices and legal staffs. For example, the sales team assigned to American Standard, a firm that made bathroom fixtures, wanted to sell 6,000 PCs to their dealers. Executives at American Standard agreed to that within a dozen meetings. IBMers had requested permission to do the sale for over a year, in scores of meetings, before IBM's contract and legal teams authorized them to offer these new terms.[23]

Lowe's team was also slow to embrace faster chips Intel was producing, most notably the 80386. These made PCs run "wickedly fast" by the standards of the 1980s, making it possible to run more complex software. IBM's own faster chips never met with Lowe & Co.'s support either. The new Intel chip turned out to have just the right speed and functionality for the next generation of computers. Without IBM as a partner, Intel owned the next-generation platform for chips, and Microsoft owned the operating system standard in the late 1980s. The product divisions debated all manner of ideas in IBM's management committee and within various divisions. Nevertheless, to its credit, IBM managed to bring out the PS/2, using OS/2, in April 1987, with the hope that it would be the magic to restore IBM's glory in the PC market. IBM's new CEO, John Akers, required that this PC be called a *system* to give it the patina of more heft, like a mainframe. Its graphics were excellent and sharp but otherwise it was of no particular significance, as the market was already flooded with attractive clones. Lowe thought he had a clone killer on his hands and that his patent lawyers could serve as his shock troops to fight clone manufacturers. Instead, he had an expensive machine that ran slowly.

Compaq outmarketed Big Blue in 1987–1988. Customers pushed back on IBM's insistence that they start using the machine's new three-and-a-half-inch disks. They wanted machines with Intel's 386 chips, and that did not come from IBM until later that year. IBM's market share continued to slide over the next several years. Compaq brought out new models of IBM PC–compatible machines, priced cheaper, and marketed them well throughout the 1980s and 1990s. Compaq was unencumbered by the bureaucracy and overhead costs at IBM and focused on one hardware market. Compaq's senior management deeply understood the technology; IBM's still did not. IBM irritated customers by attempting to force them to embrace the technology embedded in the PS/2, such as its microchannel bus (how it moved data in and around the machine). By 1990, IBM's behavior had cost it another 20 percent of market share.

All of this happened as IBM's mainframe profits declined. Many of its large customers had recently replaced their systems in the mid-1980s as prices kept dropping. At the same time, the cost of performing a calculation on a PC dropped so much that it was often 100 times cheaper to do work using a little machine than on a mainframe. Customers were beginning to understand that economic reality, particularly large enterprises that had a choice of using one or the other. Often they had no option but to support both, as so many of their end users had already acquired PCs (many of them clones). This was a worldwide phenomenon, not limited to the U.S. market. Meanwhile, IBM's cost of producing PCs remained too high. Results began to creep onto the balance sheet. In 1986, earnings declined by 27 percent over the previous year's, while revenue went up only 3 percent. Opel escaped just in time, since custom called for him to retire when he turned 60, in 1986. John Akers inherited the company's declining fortunes. The year 1987 was shaping up to be another so-so or bad year. Akers recognized that the mainframe business had entered a long, slow decline, the PC business had gone into a more rapid fall, and the move to billable services was just beginning. The U.S. market was saturated with all manner of products, while Europe, Asia, and Latin America represented growth areas.

As a result of its various issues, IBM had about 10,000 too many employees in the United States. Akers approved a voluntary early retirement program to lower U.S. operating costs while maintaining IBM's overseas population, now about 60 percent of the company's workforce. Employees oversubscribed to this severance package, an unwelcome, unintended consequence, since the majority were among the best employees in the firm. Subsequent voluntary severance programs in the late 1980s and 1990s triggered similar results: too many people accepted them, and too many of them were among IBM's best and brightest, who were confident they could find employment elsewhere.[24] In that first wave of departures, 80 percent had the highest appraisal ratings one could get at IBM. Simultaneously, to increase sales, many staff members were pushed back into sales offices, with mixed results. Branch managers started firing underperformers; training them had not always worked. Their career progression slowed, or they retired.

To help replace shrinking revenues from the PC business and to fight rivals in the midrange market, in 1988 IBM brought out the midrange AS/400 in various-sized models. It took a long time to design and build them, but customers liked them. Over the next decade, they acquired over 400,000 of them. The AS/400 was one of the few shining lights in the hardware product line during that critical period of the late 1980s and early 1990s. By the end of the 1980s, the AS/400s generated $14 billion in revenue annually, slightly more than IBM's archrival Digital Equipment.

Nevertheless, business remained soft. None of this helped Bill Lowe, of course, and he was passed over for promotion. One rival promoted over him was Richard "Dick" Gerstner (1939–2012), who became a senior vice president. He was the brother of IBM's next CEO, Lou Gerstner, who had yet to join IBM. The year before Lou's arrival, Dick Gerstner had contracted Lyme disease, and he retired from IBM in 1993. Lowe resigned from IBM in December 1988 and took a job at Xerox. Jim Cannavino replaced him as head of the PC business. He spent the next couple of years wrestling with it and Bill Gates. He had what one journalist correctly described as "a prickly management style," which did not help matters, especially in management committee meetings or with Microsoft.[25] OS/2 did not catch on in the market, despite Cannavino's efforts; Gates launched Windows.

One episode exposed the structural problems management and product developers faced. IBM always had technologies in various stages of development, and never more so since even the early 1950s. What eventually became the RS/6000 was one by-product of IBM's capabilities. John E. "Jack" Bertram (1928–1986), better known behind his back as "Blackjack," provided leadership. A cigar-smoking, irascible, foul-mouthed terror, he was probably the engineer most admired by other IBM engineers in the 1970s and 1980s. He hated salesmen and marketers, thought they did not understand customers' problems, and wanted engineers to "get off their butts" and out of their labs to solve them. He also had a new computer chip he wanted the lab in Austin, Texas, to develop. To do that, he brought in another like-minded renegade, R. Andrew "Andy" Heller, a classically trained pop singer and engineer at IBM from 1966 to 1989, who rose rapidly through management. He developed IBM's UNIX operating system and the RS/6000. He had a beard, wore cowboy boots, hated ties, was loud, did not care for the niceties of IBM's political behavior, and counted Steve Jobs among his friends.

Heller wanted to build a powerful workstation and to that end brought in another imaginative engineer, John Cocke (1925–2002), who in time became known as the "father of RISC architecture." Cocke worked at IBM from 1956 to 1992. For his work, he received all the major engineering awards, including the Eckert-Mauchly Award (1985), ACM Turing Award (1987), the National Medal of Technology (1991), and the National Medal of Science (1994), among others. He felt that working within the confines of IBM's product development culture limited his ability to implement new ideas. That was a nearly insurmountable challenge. He was too much of a wild duck for IBM.

RISC stands for reduced instruction set computing, essentially a way of reducing the number of built-in instructions on a computer chip. The RISC approach reduced the processing a computer chip had to do by shifting more of the work to software, which meant one could optimize a system by packing more processing into a smaller space and perform work more quickly and less expensively. Engineers thought this architecture could be put into all of IBM's systems from mainframes to laptops, lowering development costs, building faster computers, and offering less expensive products; in short, a unified product line, echoes of the S/360. What could go wrong?

For one thing, John Opel resisted imposing one standard chip across the entire hardware product line. IBM's many divisions would have fought such a mandate. The midrange people, however, found the idea appealing in the 1970s to early 1980s because they had so many product lines; the Office Products Division also liked the idea for its typewriters and word processors. The politically powerful mainframe community would fight it, largely because many of its engineers questioned Cocke's calculations about dramatically increased performance. Also, in the early to mid-1980s, the mainframe business was in great shape. Because of these differences, product development remained fragmented. Akers lived with that situation, believing the divisions should be creative and that the diversity of thinking would help keep them that way.

Cocke and RISC limped along. IBM missed the huge market that soon developed for powerful desktop computers. Management worried more about competition from Fujitsu, Hitachi, and NEC, not emerging desktop processing rivals, such as Apollo and Sun, and several thousand start-ups. Sun in particular became a problem. Founded in 1983, it fundamentally shifted the nature of computing during the 1990s with powerful desktop workstations, making PCs of the 1980s look like limp performers. With its new products, engineers could finally get off midrange systems to design products (CAD) and run manufacturing (CAM) systems. IBM did not respond to the new market until 1986, several years after Sun was already there. IBM's RISC was underpowered. IBMers did not sufficiently believe in Cocke's design. IBM's RT machines in the late 1980s could not compete effectively with Sun's, even though IBM used a watered-down version of the RISC technology Cocke had invented in the 1970s. Again things went too slowly. Meanwhile, Heller quit IBM out of frustration. His skunk works to develop a workstation was pushed into the PC Division, under Cannavino's control. The *New York Times* reported that Heller's departure symbolized "the wrenching changes now taking place at IBM as it attempts to respond to new developments that are sweeping the computer industry."[26] Note the term "respond," meaning following.

Design and production delays, reviews, and in-house contention contributed to the late announcement of a solid RISC workstation, the RS/6000, to replace the RT product line, which did not happen until February 1990. Customers and the media gave it a thumbs-up because pilot projects with customers had gone well and software developers had created products to run on it. Demand proved excellent, with the RS/6000 generating $1 billion in revenue during 1990, $1.8 billion in 1991, and $2.5

billion in 1992, its performance a success story. But because of the slowness of IBM's product development process, its technology came too late to save the PC, minicomputer, or mainframe businesses. H-P and others responded to the RS/6000 with less expensive, powerful machines. The RS/6000 remained in IBM's product line and was renamed and updated as the e-Server p Series in October 2000. In the process, the PowerPC microprocessor had fulfilled the original dream of having a basic processor far more powerful than when conceived a quarter of a century earlier.

Meanwhile, the PC market matured. The gold rush of the late 1970s and early 1980s gave way to a more stable market, with shakeouts reducing the number of players. By the mid-1980s, IBM's technical standards had become the norm for the majority of PC vendors, with the notable exception of Apple, which retained its small market share for years. A large software industry grew up with practices different from those of the more traditional mainframe-centric suppliers. The new programmers had to have the same kind of machine-software knowledge that programmers in the 1950s did with mainframes, as both had to figure out how to cram small memories with sufficient software to do useful work. By the 1970s, mainframe programmers could not think small enough, while a new generation of developers came along, such as Bill Gates.

Gates's introduction of Windows 95 on August 24, 1995, was a major media event. The launch cost a whopping $200 million. By the mid-1980s, technological barriers to new entrants had appeared that called for hardware and software that were more sophisticated, so know-how for creating new software for PCs now settled into a few firms, locked up with patents and good salaries, and giving competitors limited access to distribution channels. In 1983, how did 35,000 software products compete for the 200 shelf slots at a PC retail outlet?

To answer, let's sum up events. Frank Cary recognized the onerous system his company had created for product development and the fiefdoms around it. Flexibility in these early years proved crucial to winning Round One of the PC battle. IBM learned, however, that it did not know how to develop and price PCs for the retail market—those 200 shelf slots. Round Two of the PC battle started on October 25, 1984, when IBM announced that it would provide an integrated set of midrange products. This technology would be compatible from the PC up through the mainframe. That act drew the PC back into the main product development tent and its bureaucracy. IBM's attempt to integrate networking capabilities across all products failed to win customers who wanted computing products to network, and for that they had to look outside of IBM. Other stumbling steps did not help either, most notably the PC Jr. Estridge's death symbolized the end of Round Two.

Round Three featured a rising tide of customers and software vendors irritated at IBM's efforts to develop the proprietary OS/2 operating system. In both Rounds One and Two, IBM let Microsoft, which sold to IBM's clone competitors, keep the rights to its operating system. Customers found clones to be just as good as IBM's products and with plenty of software and networking tools. It did not matter that Microsoft's software was notorious for having bugs or that IBM's was far cleaner. Speed to market was the most critical success factor. Risks of "buggy" software surfaced, which customers and developers proved willing to take. Technical standards pursued by IBM in the mid-1980s created new problems. It took IBM too long to settle on the Intel 386, as it remained wedded to the slower 286 chip, giving Compaq a year's lead. IBM was still trying to sell to both consumers and businesses, which added more confusion. Lowe was focusing on software for commercial customers but also some OS/2 graphical functions for consumers, which delayed introduction of new products. In the late 1980s, IBM and Microsoft could not collaborate. There were too many clashes of personalities and corporate cultures, their widening differences too obvious. Mistrust ruled the day. OS/2 failed to bring back the primacy in the market that IBM's Cannavino so wanted.

By 1992, the writing had been on the wall for some time. Microsoft had shipped 105 million copies of DOS, 15 million that year alone. By that time, 20 million copies of Windows sat inside new PCs, 10 million in 1992 alone. Apple's Macintosh claimed 10 million sales, 3 million that year. In 1992, IBM reported only 2 million copies of OS/2 shipped, many free.[27] In other words, about 85 percent of all PCs going into the market used a Microsoft operating system. In 1993, Microsoft enjoyed revenue of

$3.7 billion. The prior year, IBM had experienced a $5 billion loss on total revenue of $64.5 billion. Louis Gerstner, IBM's CEO in the 1990s, later wrote that, "Consumers didn't care much about advanced, but arcane technical capability. They wanted a PC that was easy to use, with a lot of handy applications." Marketing and merchandising skills were crucial, and IBM had neither. Gerstner argued that "Microsoft had all the software developers locked up, so all the best applications ran on Windows."[28] His successor, Sam Palmisano, commenting on the performance of IBM's rivals, admitted, "They really outexecuted us."[29]

The end of the saga came in October 1995, when large corporate customers told senior IBM executives they were deserting OS/2. State Farm Insurance, Caterpillar, and UPS, among others, were turning to other suppliers. One long-time industry watcher concluded that, "In the end, the contest was one that IBM was totally unsuited to enter—never mind, win. Decades of IBM culture, good and bad, had thrown up too many roadblocks along the way."[30] Consumer and commercial markets required different rates of speed and quality of hardware. Gerstner stated, "What my colleagues seemed unwilling or unable to accept was that the war was already over and was a resounding defeat—90 percent market share for Windows to OS/2's 5 percent or 6 percent."[31] Thousands of IBMers had worked on the OS/2 and were emotionally invested in what they believed would be a new era of IBM success. Gerstner had to end "the religious wars against Microsoft. We lost."[32] One could criticize Opel and Akers for not managing the PC episode. Two Harvard business professors did.[33]

The company soldiered on until Sam Palmisano, who once worked in the PC organization, took charge. In 2005 he sold the PC business to Lenovo, the rapidly growing Chinese manufacturer of IBM laptops. The terms of the sale represented a clever, indeed creative, resolution of the long-standing problem of the PC for IBM. Before describing that deal, understanding the circumstances faced by IBM helps clarify the relevance of its terms.

Over the first quarter century of the PC business, as personal computers continued to drop in price, becoming commodities, they continued to evolve into more powerful devices. IBM's competitive advantage for a century was its ability to help its customers use complex systems. PCs had become a commodity business by the end of the 1980s. IBM struggled to squeeze a profit out of that business, for good reason. As late as 2005, IBM was still the third-largest producer of such devices, including laptops, so demand lingered; it was just that IBM struggled to make profits from these products. Palmisano and his senior executives had the courage to set aside emotional attachments to their "Tool for Modern Times" and end it.

Into the early years of the new millennium, IBM had done all the normal things to drive down the cost of making and selling PCs: outsourcing parts and manufacturing, collaborating with Lenovo. IBM was eyeing the growing market for more advanced forms of information technology in China. IBMers had already learned that to work effectively in the Chinese market on anything they needed local alliances, such as with Lenovo. The media gave Palmisano considerable credit for selling off the business, even though many employees lamented the end of the PC at IBM. The deal with Lenovo was far more than the unloading of what Palmisano publicly admitted was an unprofitable commodity business. It was a strategic strike, increasing IBM's access to Asia's largest economy, which was growing. Critics within the firm worried that loss of this PC product would weaken account control, the perennial concern of IBM's sales force. Employees in the PC Division fretted about being transferred to another firm.

But Palmisano & Co. had already committed to getting out of low-profit markets. They understood the need to constantly move to higher-margin ones. It was the central overarching strategic initiative of Palmisano's term as CEO and the initial one of his successor, Ginni Rometty. The PC did not fit into that schema. As Palmisano explained, "If you decide you're going to move to a different space, where there's innovation and, therefore, you can do unique things and get some premium for that, the PC business wasn't going to be it."[34] The obvious option would have been to sell the business to a better-fitted manufacturer of commodity products, such as H-P or Dell. Dell and other suppliers had offered to discuss such a purchase with IBM. IBM was already working closely with Lenovo and eager to improve its hand in China in the now more attractive IT services business, so Palmisano and his management team chose a different path.

As the *New York Times* explained, this sale "signals a recognition by IBM, the prototypical American multinational, that its own future lies even further up the economic ladder, in technology services and consulting, in software and in the larger computers that power corporate networks and the Internet. All are businesses far more profitable for IBM than its personal computer unit."[35]

If it was a strategic decision, and not simply an attempt to dispose of a losing product line, what deal did IBM negotiate? In December 2004, IBM announced it was selling its business to Lenovo for $1.75 billion, to take effect in 2005. IBM would continue to maintain its existing share of ownership in Lenovo for three years, with an option to acquire more equity in the firm, which was partially owned by the Chinese government. The head of Lenovo's PC business would be IBM's senior vice president, Stephen M. Ward Jr., while his new boss would be Lenovo's chairman, Yang Yuanqing. Lenovo acquired a five-year license to use the IBM brand (its tricolor IBM logo) on such products as the popular laptops (Thinkpad) and PCs, and to hire IBM employees to support the Chinese company's sales and services to existing customers in the West, where Lenovo was virtually unknown. IBM would continue to design new laptops for Lenovo in Raleigh, North Carolina. Some 4,000 IBMers in the division already worked in China and would switch to Lenovo, along with the 6,000 in the United States.

The deal ensured that IBM's global customers had familiar support while providing a stable flow of maintenance revenue to IBM for five years. For Lenovo, the deal provided a high-profile partner. Over the years, it had sold 18.9 percent of its equity to IBM, a low price for IBM to get a partner respected in the Chinese market. Palmisano wanted to expand his IT services business to large Chinese corporations and government agencies. Now IBM was partnered with China's largest computer manufacturer, which controlled 27 percent of the Chinese PC market, and Asia's largest vendor. IBM's PC revenue was nearly $13 billion and barely profitable. The deal was one of the most imaginative crafted in IBM's history, yet it remained for many IBMers a sad close to a quarter-century chapter in IBM's history. The PC business had destroyed careers and exposed the underbelly of a large company to a world that had not existed the last time it enjoyed enormous success. By then, technology was already transforming as the world quickly woke up to the arrival of a new one: the Internet.

THE LONG DECLINE OF IBM AND ITS PC BUSINESS

It can be difficult to imagine the enormous changes the world underwent in that quarter century. Just in the realm of PCs, the unimaginable happened. No company dominated and almost anyone could participate in the early years. Few barriers stood in the way of an energetic person eager to enter the market. College students like Bill Gates could get a box of parts and with some programming savvy get into the business. IBM assigned hundreds and then thousands of employees to similar projects. Estridge protested, arguing angrily that, because of IBM's "full-employment" policy, Corporate had transferred thousands of programmers to him who knew nothing about PCs. Chips could now be purchased for pennies, while for less than $10 memory could be had that would have cost over $1 million for a mainframe in the mid-1980s. In Africa in 2005, one could acquire a fully built PC made in China for as little as $200, and even then it was considered expensive. Computer scientists at MIT were distributing a simple hand-cranked laptop for children.[36] While IBM's annual count of the number of mainframes placed during that quarter century was in the low thousands and that for midrange systems in the tens of thousands, everyone was counting PCs sold in the tens of millions. Hundreds of millions connected to the Internet and private networks by the early years of the new millennium. The dominance of the United States as the largest market for PCs in the 1980s soon diminished as Western Europeans acquired these machines in the 1990s, joined by users all over Asia, Latin America, Eastern Europe, and parts of Africa by the time Palmisano decided to sell off the PC Division.

IBM employees looking back remarked on how few people were involved in the decisions that led to the initial successes and subsequent failures by IBM. It was overwhelmingly an American IBM drama, situated in Armonk, White Plains, and Poughkeepsie, New York, Boca Raton,

Florida, and Austin, Texas, too, and to a lesser extent Rochester, Minnesota, home of most of IBM's midrange systems, and Raleigh, North Carolina, which made terminals, laptops, and other screens. Engineers, salesmen, dealers, and customers played minor roles in this saga. Essentially three to four dozen senior IBM executives were involved, plus their entourage of staffs. Cary, Opel, Akers, Estridge, Lowe, Cannavino, Palmisano later, and a few others dominated the story. At Microsoft, a similar tiny group also played crucial roles, but then the company was small, with only 31 employees when the blue-suited IBMers showed up. Compaq and Apple were also diminutive firms, so only a few leaders in each made the critical design and business decisions. If one added up all their names, including the IBMers, the list only comes to about 150 players.[37]

What about all the bureaucracy that got in the way? There were hundreds more people involved who worked in the product divisions. Each had its own constituencies and fiefdoms to protect, regardless of whatever customers were saying in public or in the privacy of their meetings with IBM executives and their salesmen. IBM's internal constituencies shifted to the sidelines fairly quickly, because each fiefdom took a stand on an issue and then punted to the next level of management. Staffs working for higher-level executives prepared their bosses to present to the management committee to settle. Since these senior leaders had come up in the mainframe era of the 1950s and 1960s, they lacked the personal touch, the feeling one had if they had tinkered with PCs as high school or college students. Many managers and executives at IBM in the early 1980s did not even use e-mail, because that was a task for their secretaries and assistants.

E-mail spread widely from top to bottom at IBM in the second half of the 1980s, so decision makers at the highest levels began acquiring at least a crude sense of the technology's implications by the time they made it to the management committee in the late 1990s. It took a veteran of that transition, Palmisano, to ultimately give up on the PC. Even his predecessor, Lou Gerstner, who understood the problem in the 1990s, found it impossible to shut down that business. Internal rivalries ensured narrowly focused decision making that harmed IBM's ability to stay in the market for PCs. Journalists reviewing the PC experience routinely brought up this factor. The historical evidence is understandably sparse, but IBM's CEOs, in particular, gave considerable thought to the overall problems and success factors for the firm. While they largely misunderstood the PC market, even once it unfolded before their eyes, as happened to Opel and Akers, they did not ignore it. They worried about it. Cary had the advantage of being CEO at the beginning of it, so he only needed to know that a new market was emerging and that he had to get people in there right away. No other CEO could deal with this market as easily, because it quickly became too complicated.

Other executives were going to push their technical standards—IBMers and customers alike—whether they wanted them or not, such as Earl Wheeler. Executives such as Jim Cannavino, who thought they understood the market and also had a history of success, pushed forward thanks to their forceful personalities. Then there were those who came up in the existing manner of doing business and honestly thought it was the best way, such as Bill Lowe, who believed IBM's product development process was good, even if slow.

OBITUARY OF IBM'S PC BUSINESS AND WHAT CORPORATIONS COULD LEARN FROM THE EXPERIENCE

Employees, customers, and business school professors have not considered IBM's experiences with the PC as history but have drawn lessons from them as events unfolded. These continue to be referenced each time IBM sells off an old piece of its business, such as the sale of another part of its computing organization to Lenovo in 2014.[38] So what were some of the lessons that began to emerge? In a thoughtful, well-informed, if scathing, attack on IBM's business practices in the 1990s, buttressed by interviews with key protagonists at Big Blue, D. Quinn Mills and G. Bruce Friesen dissected the company's experience with the PC. According to Mills and Friesen, the PC was part of senior management's failures: "Its relinquishment of control of the new personal computer technology to competitors [was] clearly top management's responsibility."[39] They noted that Apple, Intel, and Microsoft "benefitted from errors made by IBM's executives," who proved incapable of capitalizing on shifting technologies. They pointed out, with some basis in fact, that "IBM's fear of antitrust prosecution caused it to cede the microprocessor in the general marketplace to Intel."[40] However, evidence that the fear of antitrust problems had shrunk by the mid-1990s suggests other reasons for IBM's problems, to be considered in chapter 15.

The central failure did not come from fear of government prosecutors. Rather, according to Mills and Friesen, "IBM's failure to see that market standards for personal computers would be set by software and not hardware led IBM to cede control over the personal computer operating system to Microsoft."[41] The Harvard researchers blamed these errors on executive management, not rank-and-file employees:

> Had IBM's executives aggressively backed the personal computer, had they marketed an IBM version of the Intel processor, and had they quickly displaced Microsoft's personal computer operating system, IBM's share price would never have taken the dive it did. And the company's traditional culture, with its emphasis on employment security, would have continued in place, to be admired throughout the business world.[42]

The company's severe problems in the 1990s were caused by many circumstances, but clearly a central failure still plaguing the company was how it dealt with its employees. But the essential problem was clear: IBM's decline and subsequent crisis originated in the way it handled the PC opportunity.

Other lessons from the PC experience kept surfacing. By the time IBM sold the PC business, one could be more specific about the "Little Tramp's" "Tool for Modern Times." When we talk about the role of senior management, we enter the realm of strategy. In the case of the PC, the first question to ask about any new technology was whether it was fundamentally transformative. It took a while to appreciate that the PC was as transformative as magnetic tape had been when it replaced punch cards in the 1950s. IBM's early desktop computing focused on consolidating typing pools, just as data entry on cards had done 30 years earlier. Each had the wrong focus. The PC distributed typing out of typing pools or clusters of secretaries. In fairness to all involved, the minicomputer was less a technological end game and more of a step along the way to the PC. We know that more clearly today than in the 1980s. Distributed processing with minicomputers masked the fact that computing was being dispersed. Emerging economics and the functionality of the new Intel chips and the PCs that could be built with them made possible the dispersal of computing across an entire industry and into the private lives of hundreds of millions of people.

We read a great deal about "first-mover advantages" in technology, a concept that gained wide popularity in corporate circles in the 1990s.[43] A great deal of the dot-com phenomenon of the 1990s centered on the belief that the first company to reach a new market would dominate it, so get there as fast as you can, even if you cannot make a profit on the first day. This mantra stated that if a company won market share, profits would follow. But the reverse could also be true: arrive too early and you become trapped in products that prove uncompetitive. That is what happened to many pre-IBM PC vendors in the 1970s. Tandy and Commodore failed for reasons tethered to coming in too early. By the time IBM arrived, the focus on standards was beginning, and Estridge's contribution was to establish them. After that happened, it became a footrace to see who could consolidate the largest market share. Strategy rapidly shifted to focus on speed of execution and dealing effectively with business partners and suppliers. IBM got the timing right, established the standards, but lost the footrace. Latecomers, such as Dell, saw more clearly what needed to be done. Over time, IBM learned similar lessons.

All of IBM's competitors carried less corporate baggage than IBM did. Their operating costs were lower, and they had fewer views and behaviors formed in earlier times to influence new circumstances. IBM then, as is largely the case now, had an accounting practice whereby the costs of operating the corporation were shared in varying degrees across the entire enterprise, regardless of what types of businesses they were in. A piece of the business with a high profit margin would contribute a proportion nearly equal to that of a lower-margin or low-volume division. While proportions varied over time, every division paid a tax to Corporate. In the case of the PC business, it began a year either with more staff than it might otherwise need or with a cost burden exceeding that of its rivals outside IBM. In 1987, Microsoft had 1,816 employees, of which an estimated several hundred were developing its operating system, while IBM had several thousand assigned to its own PC software. That skewered the business model, imposing a cost burden on it as well as a need for management reviews and hence additional staff work, and slowed decision making. All of these factors combined to hobble the business. That reality also existed long before one could criticize senior management for being "out of touch" with this new business.

The second form of baggage consisted of a worldview nurtured by the "big iron" business of mainframes. All senior leaders had honed their managerial skills and perspectives largely in the S/360 days and 1970s. DEC, Wang, and others had the same problem and struggled to reduce the number of employees when their businesses had to respond to the changing economics of small and midsized computers. IBM executives tangled with the idea of using a non-IBM operating system (Microsoft DOS and later Windows). In the end, they invested hundreds of millions of dollars in OS/2, which they never got right. Their heritage called for a 100 percent IBM operating system as a way to remain the dominant "go-to" source for computing. Even though Microsoft worked for a while on OS/2, it largely became an IBM-made package.

Recall that IBM never behaved like a monolithic company the way the public thought it did. It operated more like a city made up of communities (divisions) of alternating and conflicting interests. CEOs in many companies usually focused more attention on the future direction of the company than line management did, and IBM's chairmen were no exception. Divisions promoted their worldviews and advocated intensely for their current and proposed next products. They believed in them, and the careers of their senior and middle managers depended on the corporation allowing them to finish and launch their products. So just as tabulating people resisted the arrival of digital computers, mainframe factions competed for attention and resources with the midrange, and later the PC, constituencies. Because of these large, diverse communities, CEOs at IBM engaged in far more operational matters than in many other companies. The existence of a senior management council such as the management committee, chaired by the CEO, ensured they would be engaged far more than Watson Jr. would have thought wise, yet probably more in line with how his father retained a hands-on approach until the end of his life. Contradictions, rivalries, and competing perspectives could be managed.

Now there seemed to be a contradiction here. On the one hand, divisions, each with different scales of costs, profits, and revenues, competed for attention and resources. Sometimes they competed in the same markets, as when two parts of the company would show up at a customer's office with mini and mainframe proposals to bid for the same project. On the other hand, the management committee and IBM's CEOs exercised considerable if not absolute authority over the business, being able to crush guerrilla operations against their decisions. What are we to make of this paradox? IBM tried to manage the PC business in a Chandlerian way, in which managerial hierarchies controlled events. The PC business evolved more quickly and responsively toward fluid, market-oriented, networked models of behavior. In that world, managerial hierarchies proved insufficiently dynamic. Their objective was to respond to changing circumstances, not to shape them. Market conditions and networks of users and technologies became inputs for products that commoditized rapidly. This phenomenon was not unique to IBM or to the world of computers; it existed in other industries also. The evolution of the automotive industry as Japanese rivals entered it in the 1970s and 1980s is a familiar example. Ultimately, mainframes, such as those of the 1970s and by Earl Wheeler in the 1980s, ran against the new notion of PC markets.

These dynamics were barely visible at the time because everyone focused on the immediacy of whatever they were dealing with. One might have thought that IBM's CEOs would have seen the future, but they did not understand well enough the technological realities IBM faced or how to translate what they knew into what needed changing at IBM. The exception was Frank Cary buttonholing Lowe to create the PC in Boca Raton. Even then, it was a one-off fix to a problem, not a systemic transformation.

IBM's fabled sales forces, always led by conservative management with a penchant for striving for stability in their markets—account control— and predictability in the product line, often resisted new technologies and machines. Confused for a while by a new type of technology (as occurred with the PC), its members could normally be counted on to urge caution, even resistance to the new, especially if they thought these could become an alternative standard (platform) to what they already knew and controlled. Enhancements to existing technologies, on the other hand, were enthusiastically welcomed, such as a new generation of mainframes, operating systems, and software utilities. Middle managers in sales were close to their customers and deeply understood the role of competitors. Their customers were largely glass house data processing managers who initially saw the PC, too, as a threat to their authority. They and their IBM sales representatives embraced the PC slowly, but PC users held both accountable when the new technology did not function as they expected. IBM sales too often demonstrated an inability to grab the lead in pushing use of PCs with the certainty they did with mainframes. In the mid-1980s, IBM had to pay them extra bonuses in addition to normal commissions to get them to focus on this product.

That both customers and salesmen shared the same issues, values, and lack of understanding can be explained. They grew up together. As Watson Sr. wanted, sales got "close to the customer," living in the same neighborhoods, sending their children to the same schools, socializing on off hours, playing golf, and attending conferences to learn together about a new technology. Recall that since the 1920s IBM's mantra had been service, service, service to customers. IBM's value to customers came when IBMers showed them how to use a data processing technology and then helped them implement its use. A lesson one could draw from that experience is that new technologies and business-to-business (B2B) sales organizations do not mix well. The PC experience became a cautionary example. Management failed to provide proper training about the implications and use of the PC, too, while they and their employees responded according to how they were being measured and paid. Harvard professor Clayton Christensen, a leading authority on the disruptive effects of new technologies, demonstrated that "good managers consistently made wrong decisions when faced with disruptive technological changes," because they "played the game the way it was supposed to be played," by the rules of the prior paradigm.[44] His insight applied to IBM and its large corporate customers, who made up the majority of its business.

Less appreciated by outside observers and IBMers then and now was the effect on IBM's position at the center of the global IT information ecosystem. Recall that when it came to tabulating data processing and mainframe computers, IBM served as the primary source for insights about technology—how to use it, pay for it, and gain a solid return on its use. IBM dominated many of the industry's attitudes and practices. It appeared in 1981–1985 that IBM might continue this historic role, now to include PCs, but it lost that opportunity as competitors led in introducing new models and uses, software development, and development of critical tele-communications infrastructures. *PC Magazine,* a voice of the new world, decreased its coverage of IBM over time when conversing about this new technology. Beginning in the mid-1990s, the PC as a focal point for discussion about uses of information technology also declined. Customers had migrated to new platforms, such as tablets, mobile computing, and smart-phones, and to Internet-based ones, too. All were further afield than IBM's core areas of influence.

Tensions between an older and an emerging corporate culture played out in the 1990s and the following decade, a period as rocky as any in IBM's history, a story we take up next. The company's experiences and responses unfold in chapters 15–17. That story begins by discussing how IBM almost could have gone out of business. For that, we go to chapter 15.

Part III

A TIME OF CRISIS, 1985–1994

15 STORMS, CRISIS, AND NEAR DEATH, 1985–1993

The expansion of IBM's worldwide business took many forms in 1980. Among the most visible were the 8 million square feet of plant and laboratory space under construction in eight countries at the end of the year.
—*IBM ANNUAL REPORT, 1980*[1]

BEHIND IBM'S DOMINANCE of the mainframe business, its annual rankings by business magazines as the most admired corporation, and the whimsical ads of the "Little Tramp" and IBM's PCs hid a story of corporate failure of gigantic proportions. Beginning in the late 1980s and extending over two decades, IBM dismissed or retired some 200,000 employees, more than half of whom were located in the United States. A generation of executives and middle managers left, too, including John Akers, the first chairman to be terminated in IBM's history. The tsunami of layoffs and retirements proved so massive that an employee walking through almost any IBM office in North America saw entire floors of empty cubicles and offices, an old IBM telephone directory tossed on the floor, an IBM coffee mug perched on a window sill, or perhaps a half dozen IBMers working in a space that used to hold over 100 colleagues. At least there was more than enough parking. It did not matter whether the location was a sales office, factory, divisional headquarters, or laboratory. IBMers gauged the extent of the layoffs by the number of cars parked out front. Ironically, most of these empty buildings were relatively new. A construction boom at IBM during the 1970s and 1980s added skyscrapers in such cities as Paris, Chicago, New York, Minneapolis, and Detroit, and new factories on both sides of the Atlantic and in Asia. It seemed executives needed their own tower, especially sales executives.

Inside IBM, rumors and grumbling increased sharply in the early 1990s, while it was not uncommon for employees to devote an hour or more each day to spreading those rumors, gossiping and grousing about potential lay-offs. They asked when the board of directors was going to act, what group would be laid off next, whose "dumb" idea it was to break up the company, and whatever happened to the Basic Beliefs. Wall Street analysts were fuming: "What was happening to IBM's profits and revenues?" "Why aren't more employees being laid off?" "Why is the stock dropping in value?"[2] Customers were complaining of too many IBM proposals conflicting with each other, deteriorating service, inability to get things done with IBM, and prices that were too high. Nobody was happy; something had to be done.

Increasingly, everyone wanted to blame one person: John Akers. In the New York area, rumors had it that Frank Cary and John R. Opel, both still on IBM's board, were not pleased with his performance; Tom Watson Jr. reportedly wished he were still running the company. Even Akers barked at staff. Exactly one year before his departure, he yelled frustratingly at a room full of managers in a training class, asking them, "What [have you] done for the company recently?" One of those managers took notes and spread the news of Akers's outburst around the company through e-mail. Never had an e-mail traveled so far so fast or been read by so many so quickly.

Yet the board kept issuing public assurances that things were under control and that it had full confidence in Akers's leadership, until IBM announced on January 26, 1993, that he would "retire" on April 1, a full year early. Akers appeared on the internal IBM TV station and in press photos standing next to board member James E. Burke (1925–2012), who led the cabal pushing him out, as he announced the change of command. Burke said the board would now start a 90-day hunt for a new CEO, including looking outside of IBM. Watching the proceedings of Akers's retirement and later the introduction of his replacement, Louis V. Gerstner Jr., on IBM's internal TV network was surreal. Most of the North American IBM population clustered around these TVs. The majority believed Akers had been fired for good cause.

Figure 15.1
John F. Akers was the first CEO at IBM to be dismissed by the company for poor performance. He was IBM's chairman of the board from 1986 to 1993 and CEO from 1985 to 1993. Photo courtesy of IBM Corporate Archives.

Akers, too, was upset long before he was forced out. In that April 1992 managers' class, he burst out that he was "goddam mad" with how IBM was losing market share for various products. He criticized the assembled managers for not trying harder, saying, "The tension level is not high enough" and that IBMers "can't change fast enough."[3] Periodically, internal e-mails with similar messages attributed to him leaked out, irritating and frustrating employees, but by then it seemed "everyone" knew the company was failing. Akers complained about the decline in IBM stock's value.

Observant employees, customers, and industry watchers were in denial or remained confident that Akers would fix the problems. He said he would do so in every annual report during his last five years at IBM.

When IBM's profits started falling by billions of dollars beginning in 1990 and then it started posting losses in 1991, everyone seemed shocked, stunned that the great IBM was really in trouble. This company was the great American multinational. Writers at *The Economist* reported that "IBM was always more the model of an all-conquering American multinational than such other heavyweights as General Motors or Proctor & Gamble. It pervaded every market it was allowed to enter; it was more widely visible, more scrutinized, more admired. ... IBM was the best."[4] Another observer pointed out that "IBM unquestionably created a strikingly vigorous and usually profitable industry."[5]

What happened at IBM cannot be fully understood as being just about declining costs of mainframe technologies, new entrants into the PC market, or the tiring effects of a decade of litigation, although all were factors. We have to understand the problems in a broader context, addressed in this chapter. Then, chapter 16 looks at how IBM responded and the results, even at the risk of repeating points made earlier. There is much to learn, beginning with a review of the financial performance of the company to demonstrate the magnitude of the crisis it faced. Then, we move to an explanation of how IBM's growth strategy failed, which will be useful to those who consider corporate strategy crucial in understanding business history. It is the cautionary tale that strategy created by smart, well-intentioned, successful executives is no guarantee of success. IBM's experience reinforces the importance of strategy linked to execution, the limits of strategy, and the uncertainties of directing even a well-run company in uncertain times. IBM's story reminds us that strategy is about making choices, mitigating risks, and giving employees a direction, a purpose. Realities and choices shaped subsequent events here. Historians observe that incremental decisions often are the determinants of a company's strategy and performance. Control—a central intent of strategy—is an aspiration, not a guarantee of success. As William Lazonick argues, understanding decision making in creating strategy is essential. It is the lens through which this chapter examines IBM, because its experience reinforces his argument.[6]

WHAT THE FINANCIAL RECORD SHOWS

By beginning with the financial record, we can see the stark shift from the well-run company to one in deep trouble, and the swiftness of that transition. The combination of extent and speed of change that so shocked people highlighted the feeling of betrayal on the part of customers, stockholders, and especially employees. The numbers illustrate that a large corporation can change quickly, so much so that normal causes of largeness and old attitudes can only partially explain what happened at IBM. American automotive companies were also under enormous pressure beginning in the late 1960s; high-profile tire manufacturers failed. Many firms in various industries were also in trouble in the 1970s and 1980s, so while IBM managed to delay its difficult time, it ultimately was not alone.

Just as Louis V. Gerstner Jr. and a small group of executives were able to formulate a rescue of IBM in the 1990s, a handful of earlier senior managers, perhaps as few as two dozen, had led IBM into the abyss in the 1980s. The only way IBM could move swiftly enough in one direction or another was through the personal actions of these executives, and none more than those of its CEOs. They were never pleased with the speed at which their vast organizations transformed, but IBM evolved. With the benefit of hindsight and the historical record, it is clear that both Opel and Akers can be held responsible for much of what happened, not the employees who Akers blamed but who were powerless individually to turn the ship around. They could only do their jobs and watch the disaster unfold.

Nevertheless, there was plenty of blame to go around. Wall Street gave terrible advice to IBM and its board, then pressured the board to fire Akers.[7] Board members ignored their responsibilities and listened too much to Akers and to stock analysts. None of these groups—IBM executives, board members, or Wall Street analysts and large institutional stockholders—paid enough attention to the company's customers or to its competitors. Their behavior ran contrary to the Watsonian practices of being attentive to their customers and ruthless in neutralizing competitors, behaviors that won IBM customer loyalty, if also continuing to attract the attention of antitrust lawyers.

Regarding Akers's complaint that IBM was losing market share all over the world, what did the facts show? Recall that, on the surface, the first half of the 1980s was great, even though the economics of mainframes, minicomputers, and PCs were changing and IBM was struggling to keep up. Table 15.1 shows the revenues and profits (earnings) IBM reported for 1980 through 1985. IBM still dominated the mainframe and PC markets. Table 15.2 paints a different picture. While revenue continued to pour into the company, total earnings became uneven for the first time since the 1930s. To an informed observer, this data indicated growing volatility in the company's operations and its deteriorating performance in the marketplace but not necessarily in the quality of the company's strategy. The decline in the number of employees, however, sent up red flags among employees, while Wall Street and the IBM board saw this as evidence of management taking steps to control expenses. Meanwhile, IBM's management kept sending the world soothing messages of confidence. Even the terrible performance of 1989, which could not be hidden from the public, did not stop Akers from declaring that "demand for IBM's products and services remains good … we look forward to a more competitive IBM" and that "IBM is planning for growth in all major geographies in 1990," built on the opportunity to acquire "new" (additional) customers and take advantage of new uses of computers.[8]

Table 15.1
IBM's good years: Financials and number of employees, 1980–1985, select years (revenues and earnings in billions of dollars)

Year	Gross income	Net earnings	Year-end global workforce
1980	26.2	3.4	341,279
1982	34.4	4.41	364,796
1984	46.3	6.58	394,930
1985	50.7	6.55	404,535

Source: Emerson W. Pugh, *Building IBM: Shaping an Industry and Its Technology* (Cambridge, MA: MIT Press, 1995), 324.

Table 15.2

IBM's transition years: Financials and number of employees, 1986–1990
(revenue and earnings in billions of dollars)

Year	Revenue	Net earnings	Year-end global workforce
1986	52.16	4.79	403,508
1987	55.26	5.26	389,348
1988	59.6	5.74	387,112
1989	62.65	3.72	383,220
1990	68.93	5.97	373,289

Source: Emerson W. Pugh, *Building IBM: Shaping an Industry and Its Technology* (Cambridge, MA: MIT Press, 1995), 324.

Table 15.3

IBM's disaster years: Financials and number of employees, 1991–1993
(revenue and earnings in billions of dollars)

Year	Revenue	Net earnings	Year-end global workforce
1991	64.77	−2.86	344,396
1992	64.52	−4.97	301,542
1993	62.72	−8.1	256,207

Source: Emerson W. Pugh, *Building IBM: Shaping an Industry and Its Technology* (Cambridge, MA: MIT Press, 1995), 324.

Now look at table 15.3, where in a three-year period revenue, earnings, and number of employees all shrank. Note the extent of the change from 1990 through 1991: a $4 billion drop in revenue, $8 billion freefall in earnings, and a substantial decline in the number of employees, although Wall Street observers thought that the employee population should have shrunk further. Performance in 1992 and 1993 reflected that continuing trend in deteriorating effectiveness that had started when the number of employees began to shrink in 1987.

However, the deterioration proved more subtle than the public evidence suggested. A closer look at IBM's annual reports in 1991 through 1993 reveals that it actually had operating earnings of $3 billion in 1991 and 1992, although they dropped sharply to $300 million in 1993. The reports of IBM losing money resulted from the huge write-offs it took to cover the cost of severance for the tens of thousands of employees pushed out of the company. If it had not let so many employees go, earnings in 1991 and 1992 would have been lower than in the past, but not so bad. The problem in 1993 was the precipitous decline in earnings and what it foretold about 1994, which is what set off alarms. From 1991 through 1993, IBM claimed $24 billion in restructuring costs. Those were massive write-offs by any measure, made more frightening because they came quickly, in the short span of three years.

Instead of capitalizing such expenses over several years, as is normal for U.S. corporations, IBM claimed ("recognized") them in the years in which they occurred. The company wanted to lower its overhead costs quickly and put these expenses behind it as part of the process of "turning the ship" in a new direction. Akers and his colleagues did not believe there would be further write-downs year after year. Their accounting tactic created more chaos sooner and of a greater intensity than might otherwise have been the case, fueling concerns that IBM was headed for disaster. That fear surfaced even with the first charge to earnings but grew as others followed. In defense of Akers, who made this decision one year at a time, he did not think this would happen more than once. As business management experts D. Quinn Mills and G. Bruce Friesen summarized it, "What began as a prudent fiscal practice became a burden under which IBM's finances and Akers's own career collapsed."[9] Another expert on the company, *Wall Street Journal* reporter Paul Carroll, summed up IBM's situation: "By fall 1992, things were out of control." In the third quarter, "business died in the last couple of weeks of the quarter," despite Akers's prediction that it would be a good quarter. The last quarter of the year "turned into IBM's biggest disaster ever."[10] That was the bad news. The good news was that Akers's successor thus came into IBM with a great deal of the restructuring costs behind him that otherwise he would have taken. Recall that all this activity occurred while the company had experienced a decline in operating margins dating to the 1970s. In the 1950s, a dollar's worth of revenue spun off 55 cents in earnings. That rate of return kept dropping steadily to below 40 cents by 1993, with mainframes by then a diminishing contributor to IBM's finances. IBM prudently sought to reduce operating expenses and moved heaven and earth to do so, cautiously in the beginning but with a brisk sweep through the business by the time Gerstner joined IBM.

How did it go? By 1990, IBM's selling, general, and administrative (SG&A) expenses consumed 30 percent of the company's revenue. That was a bit high, but very high if you take into account the long-term decline in the profits of the mainframe business when customers were also acquiring other forms of computing. By 1993, IBM had only reduced its operating expenses by 1 percent. Restructuring had amounted to shrinking an existing organization, not a fundamental redesign of the company. Akers had thought of a fundamental reboot of the company. In the early 1990s, margins still remained high and expenses lower. Margins remained in the 16 percent range, not bad, though dropping, while expenses were not falling fast enough. When IBM hit its financial wall in 1993, its margins came in at 39 percent and its operating expenses at 29 percent, leaving 1 percent profit after accounting for all other costs. If we layer on the charges for shutting factories and discarding employees, we arrive at the numbers in table 15.3. The company was unable to cut expenses as quickly as it needed to, because it had too many factories and employees and too much bureaucracy. The top 200 executives had not been sufficiently aggressive in redesigning their operations and slashing expenses.

IBM's stock value reflected the company's changing circumstances, shocking investors who saw it as the safe stock for "orphans and widows." From 1943 to 1974, its value had risen continuously and the company had paid out a dividend. The years 1975 through 1981 were turbulent as IBM's stock price declined, as did the value of the entire market. From 1982 through 1987, IBM's stock value rose, at which point it began to decline into the 1990s, dropping to levels not seen in a decade. A deeper dive into the numbers shows that, adjusted for inflation, the stock had stagnated in the 1970s and 1980s, and of course in the early 1990s. The market had kept the stock's value artificially high because its quarter-to-quarter forecasting made it look like the company's business was improving. It was the point Akers made each quarter and in each annual letter to stockholders.[11]

A more fundamental influence on the value of IBM and hence on its performance was the changes in information technology, with cycles different from the financial flows that were of greater interest to Wall Street. This forced companies like IBM to better manage balances between mature technologies and their revenue and profit streams as the former technologies became obsolete and new ones surfaced with different costs and profits. That balancing act was at best difficult to achieve for any firm. IBM struggled with that balance all through the 1970s and 1980s. Mills and Friesen explained the connection with stock values: "In periods when IBM is pioneering new technology projected earnings will be good and real growth positive; the markets therefore overvalue potential and elevate the stock above long-run equilibrium."[12] The bottom line was that the stock was overvalued for too long. When problems with IBM's performance became obvious, its value quickly declined by double digits.

What about Akers's complaint regarding market share—what happened? Between the mid-1980s and the end of 1991, IBM lost market share in slow-growing markets, specifically in mainframes and minicomputers. The more serious problem concerned mainframes. In 1986, IBM generated $17 billion in sales from mainframes, but by 1991 that business had declined to $15 billion. IBM's market share shrank by nearly a third. IBM's revenue *shrank* by 2.4 percent, while all its rivals' revenues *grew* on average by 3.3 percent. That was alarming, but in an industry where changing technologies required vendors to ride new waves of technology, the bigger problem for IBM occurred with those new forms of computing, the most rapidly expanding markets at the time. Numbers proved deceiving. In 1986, for example, IBM sold $6 billion in PCs and workstations, and in 1991 sales of these products were $10 billion. While impressive, in those intervening years IBM grew sales by 11 percent while all other vendors combined expanded theirs by 21 percent.[13]

IBM's relatively weaker growth was not for lack of trying. The $6 billion per year IBM spent on R&D was more than almost all its rivals combined, but its shrinking percentage of market share continued across the product line. All of this was made worse by new customer managers coming to power who were increasingly comfortable buying from multiple vendors, suppliers who offered newer technologies at lower cost that performed well and conformed to industry standards.

Akers was right to be frustrated. IBM faced declining demand for what it was selling. Its executives were staring at a death spiral that if not corrected meant the end of IBM. Similar problems had destroyed many of IBM's rivals. Was IBM next? More to the point, how did IBM get into this mess in the first place? It is the central question to ask because its senior executives understood the economic dynamics underpinning IBM's mainframe and PC businesses. Despite this, the majority demonstrated a reluctance to reduce the power and cultural influence of their portions of the firm as technological changes suggested new directions, new opportunities not seized on as quickly as they might have been, the story introduced in chapter 14.

A GROWTH STRATEGY GONE WRONG

IBM had a business strategy that failed because of suppositions underpinning it. A junior executive in the strategy department at Corporate walked into a Sales School classroom in Poughkeepsie, New York, in 1982 to introduce sales trainees to IBM's business plan. He had his collection of slides ("foils" in IBM's language), which he assured his audiences were the same ones he used with the CEO and his most senior managers. They were so secret, he said, that the students would not be given a copy of them. After discussing market trends, IBM's plans for new products, and so forth, he put up a slide showing what all this meant for IBM's financial future. It showed that IBM's revenue would grow from $29 billion in 1981 to $100 billion in 1990. Figure 15.2 is a representation of that chart. Half a dozen Sales School instructors were sitting in the back of the class. All had been successful salesmen. One dropped his coffee, while several others looked surprised. Following normal practice with guest speakers, none asked questions; none of the students who should have did. After the strategist left, the instructors asked each other if they had ever seen such a chart that unwaveringly pointed straight up. The slide did not show wavering lines to account for years of more or less revenue growth. It was a mathematically compounded, even growth line to $100 billion.

In other words, it was IBM's old view of controlled growth, much as it enjoyed in the 1950s through the 1970s, imposed on the 1980s, when the

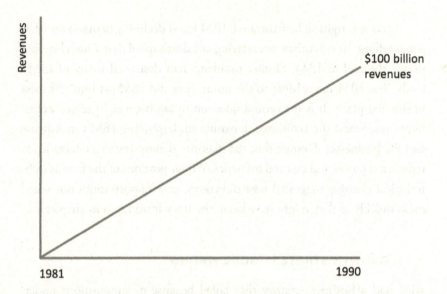

Figure 15.2
A representation of the chart used in the 1982 sales meeting that forecast revenue growth to $100 billion by 1990.

instructors sitting in the back row knew that emerging technologies guaranteed a different growth pattern. What that would be remained foggy. That same chart appeared all over the company and soon was even used by industry pundits. By late 1983, anyone who cared to know had probably seen or heard about it. In annual reports, John Opel and John Akers spoke about an industry whose growth would reach over a trillion dollars worldwide, so on the surface IBM's projection seemed reasonable and conservative. Opel was excited and had explained to his board how the oil and global economic crises of the 1970s were behind them and that IBM would increase revenue each year by an amount equal to DEC's revenues. Only Japanese mainframe vendors, whom he worried most about, stood in his way, constantly drawing him back to the locus of his career, mainframes.

Akers's strategy for riding the anticipated wave of new demand and for addressing the Japanese threat revolved around becoming the low-cost provider of machines and key components. That meant building factories that could produce in quantity. That additional construction called for more factory employees, salesmen, and other support personnel. Because of the large barriers to entry for manufacturing semiconductors, Akers saw that building such capacity in support of mainframes would play to IBM's technological strengths and economies of scale. IBM's financial power would allow it to capitalize its investments over the long haul. Akers's strategy meant all these new employees represented an unavoidable expense, and their subsequent dismissal created enormous churn in the company for the next quarter century.

The thinking that went into his call for massive growth had been worked out in the late 1970s. In 1980, for the first time, IBM published a public corporate strategy. Opel told stockholders that, "We see many indications that the growth of IBM's business will remain strong" and that "the majority of IBM's growth will continue to come in data processing and office products." He added that, first, to execute the strategy, IBM was "investing heavily in the several dozen key technologies that drive the information processing industry ahead," including "placing a high priority on designing and building quality into every product." He intended to be the "low-cost" provider, to invest in "sales and service innovation," and to add facilities.[14] The following year, using almost the same language, he repeated the mantra for IBM "to be the product leader," relying on such descriptors as "foremost in quality," products that were "defect-free," and of best "value." Second, he stated that it is IBM's "goal to be the most efficient company in our industry," and third, "to compete in, and grow with, the information industry in all its aspects."[15] He then devoted the next two pages of his letter to stockholders to a description of plans for new products, higher-volume marketing, expansion of the company's global footprint, and optimizing the number of employees.

Akers kept tuning the message. In 1983, he described four objectives. IBM was now going to grow with the industry, meaning at the same speed. IBM would demonstrate leadership across the entire product line, with technology, quality, and value. IBM would be the most efficient by being the low-cost producer and low-cost seller, and have the lowest cost of administration. IBM would maintain high levels of profit. How did Akers do with his four-part plan? During his watch, IBM lost market share in all its markets. Better, more innovative, less-expensive technologies appeared first outside of IBM. Akers's cost of doing business remained one of the highest in the industry. Profitability evaporated, but it could almost be excused in the euphoria that enveloped the company. IBM had been accused of hubris and "arrogance" throughout the 1970s and 1980s. Both Watsons would have found this most curious, but in part the conceit had been fueled by more than IBM's success with the S/360 and S/370, or even later in the early years of the PC. As Robert Heller explained,

> The IBM of the early Eighties was a place of inexhaustible pride. Like the Roman Empire at its zenith, IBM was rich with the fruit of past conquests and supremely confident of new victories. To admirers, inside and outside the empire, its actions and ideas seemed to fit together with an innate perfection, like some vast Swiss watch.[16]

In their best-selling business book of the decade, *In Search of Excellence*, McKinsey and Co. consultants Thomas J. Peters and Robert Waterman Jr. cited IBM as one of the greatest companies on earth.[17] They celebrated IBM's bias toward action, continuous ties to customers, productivity, innovative actions, and emphasis on business values, ethics, and a combination of loose and tight controls. That in hindsight they were more wrong than right did not become obvious for half a decade, but for the moment, IBM was fabulous, ranked the best-run company by *Fortune* magazine year after year. It seemed IBM could do no wrong.

Buck Rodgers's mantra, "The IBM Way," seemed absolute in its confidence and relevance, and it was widely emulated even late in the 1980s. Liberated from the constraints of the antitrust suit of the 1970s, IBM was now free to expand, to manifest its excellence in all that it touched. IBM's public relations machine seemed to work overtime to promote this image of excellence. Read *Think* magazine, annual reports, and transcripts of interviews with executives, and the same messages continued. Every success called for its own press release, every failure well couched in language dismissing its relevance. College graduates wanted to work for IBM, just as in the 2010s they saw Google, Amazon, and Apple as the "go-to" destinations for the smart and ambitious. That was the environment in which John Opel stepped in as IBM's leader.

FLAWED EXECUTION

Curiously, in none of Opel's public statements about IBM's new strategy did he mention what customers wanted, only what IBM desired. It is against this background of growth that we can come back to the fateful decision to shift IBM's long-standing practice of renting equipment to outright sale of its products.[18] Recall that Opel wanted the faster influx of revenue from outright sales to fund his expansion. IBM began reporting leases as

Figure 15.3
John Opel was the CEO who expanded IBM's factories and number of employees in the belief that the company would grow massively in the 1980s. Photo courtesy of IBM Corporate Archives.

increased sales, an accounting gimmick, which nonetheless made it possible for the company to generate additional funding for the growth strategy. All over IBM, management obtained permission to hire thousands of employees, while billions of dollars went into new factories, sales headquarters, and training facilities. Employees and construction companies described IBM's expenditures in the 1980s as "lavish." Mills and Friesen correctly called it "wildly optimistic; even negligently so."[19] While overconfidence and arrogance prevailed, customers began complaining about the changing terms of acquiring equipment, concerned that the ties with IBM that so bound them together through leasing would deteriorate. They were right.

To pull off the financial strategy, revenue from renting and leasing had to drop from 85 percent of IBM's sales to 12 percent. The surge in income that would come from selling equipment outright instead of accumulating revenue over the life of a lease was a bubble. By the early 1990s, only 4 percent of IBM's revenue came from the steady flow of rentals. The rest had to be earned every year against rivals and in the face of fluctuating economic conditions. It had to take into account the seemingly ever-changing technologies underpinning everyone's products. IBM became increasingly marginalized as customer loyalty declined as a result of Opel's fateful decision to transform IBM's offerings from a relationship-based business grounded in leasing to a transaction-based one relying on purchases. IBM no longer served as the center of the data processing ecosystem. Industry observers opined that the shift away from leasing did not need to occur, because the 4300 computers were generating a good deal of new revenue.[20] IBM sped up the move to the purchase strategy for new and already installed equipment. If properly managed, PC sales would have provided additional manna from Heaven.[21] Instead, purchase revenue cannibalized the installed leased equipment, sacrificing predictable cash flows for uncertainty and short-term gains.

It did not help that the fundamental problem with IBM's strategy was its overdependence on one assumption: that mainframes would dominate computing in the 1980s. Instead, a world of telecommunicating computers emerged using PCs, desktop processors, and minicomputers. In the 1980s, customers worldwide spent more on PCs (including software and maintenance) and telecommunications than on mainframes. So, instead of the $100 billion forecast for 1990, IBM brought in $69 billion, still a good performance but far from what Opel had planned on in 1980 and 1981. IBM acquired a great deal of modern manufacturing and sales capacity—for the wrong products. Its resource imbalances were real, and widening by huge amounts. As early as 1983, some of IBM's senior executives saw that they had already missed the opportunity to control the software business for PCs. When Sales School instructors saw that fateful slide, one could understand their shock. As one industry observer insightfully noted, the shift "represented a mortgage on the future," while revenue expanded fabulously and account control began a deep, rapid decline.[22]

In February 1985, Opel turned over control of IBM to John Akers, while remaining chairman. Other senior leaders included Paul Rizzo (b. 1936), now vice chairman, and Jack Kuehler (1932–2008), corporate vice president for products. All grew up in the mainframe era. Akers inherited a company that could not sustain Opel's growth strategy. Several immediate events forced the switch away from his plan. IBM introduced the 3090 mainframe in February 1985, which contained few innovations but doubled performance versus price, the expected norm for new computers. The 3090s were uncompetitive when pitted against Amdahl's and those of IBM's other Japanese rivals. Revenue from mainframes remained soft. The 3090's attractions were insufficient to convince customers to replace recently acquired equipment with this one. Second, IBM still did not have its act together with respect to minicomputers, so it was losing share to other vendors. Third, IBM went through the embarrassing PC Jr. episode. Akers's first year resulted in weak profits. Famous for not liking bad news, he seemed in denial about softening mainframe sales in 1985 while declining PC profits put pressure on his margins. The square-jawed former Navy pilot seemed to lack the certitude called for under the circumstances, a bias for confident action.[23]

The year 1986 unfolded as another lackluster year. In January, an IBM executive told *Fortune* that IBM had "a revenue problem."[24] Costs, too, were disconcerting. Akers and his cohorts initially resisted laying off employees, respecting IBM's historic full-employment practice. Akers and his generation of executives kept riding technologies and practices that needed changing. The same *Fortune* article observed that IBM "persisted in trying to sell them [customers] products when what they wanted was solutions, help in getting their thousands of computers to talk to each other, help in wringing both productivity gains and competitive advantage out of their investment in data-processing equipment."[25] That same month, *Fortune* announced its annual ranking of the most admired firms, and IBM was now number seven. While that was still a good ranking, as the magazine explained, "The world does not expect mere competence from IBM; it expects heroics. The company has been a near-icon. Millions of Americans rate it a national asset and prize it as a symbol of managerial and technological excellence."[26]

In fairness to Akers, IBM responded to its failed strategy, the subject of chapter 16. Akers and his circle had responded to the error of their strategy in two phases, the first involving the management team that had implemented the failed strategy and then a second designed to correct this first attempt, the latter led by Louis V. Gerstner Jr. Accounts of IBM's crises of the 1980s and 1990s describe IBM's history as one combined phase of decline and Akers's faulty response, Gerstner's rescue of IBM as a separate event, and his postrecovery activities as an extension of his rescue. The evidence suggests a different chronology, as we will see in subsequent chapters. This chapter discussed the problems and crisis facing IBM. Chapter 16 recounts what Akers did in more detail than in this chapter, providing a different narrative than what has been available previously. Subsequent chapters will deal with the turnaround in IBM's fortunes Gerstner initiated (the second response). I then demonstrate that the second half of Gerstner's tenure was not about rescuing IBM but rather about developing and implementing a new strategy, so it deserves to be treated separately from the initial rescue. I present that in chapter 18, continuing the arc of his new IBM through the chairmanship of Sam Palmisano to 2012.

16 IBM'S INITIAL RESPONSE, 1985–1993

> As you know, the Board has also accepted my recommendation that the selection process begin for a new chief executive officer of IBM.
> —JOHN AKERS, JANUARY 26, 1993[1]

THE DAY AFTER Akers's bombshell announcement, the *New York Times* reported that IBM "also cut its dividend payments to shareholders for the first time in IBM's 79-year history, reducing the quarterly payout to 54 cents from $1.21."[2] Much happened along the way to that announcement. For decades, revenue came into IBM's coffers, thanks to leases and the size of the firm. If one region of the world was in recession, then another enjoying good times picked up the slack. IBM management practiced a form of quasisocialism: if one part of IBM was prospering, then that prosperity was shared. If the company as a whole suffered financially, or some division's results became a drag on IBM's performance, then all divisions, or the most prosperous ones, received a tax either in the form of budget cuts or increased quotas. Financial adjustments were usually made on an annual basis, but during the 1980s they were made quarterly and in the early 1990s were made monthly. That way of managing financials was part of the combination of loose and tight management styles that had worked for decades.

When the financial strains proved too great in the early 1990s, managerial controls broke down. Too many parts of IBM no longer delivered sufficient revenue to support the structure of the firm. The dividend paid to "widows and orphans," to large institutional investors, pension funds, employees, retirees, and individual investors, could no longer be sustained.

The finance and planning (F&P) managers in Armonk brought their shocking analysis to John Akers with the recommendation that the board cut the size of the dividend. It was the hardest of blows, because there would be no hiding the extent of IBM's problems. Now the board would be held accountable for IBM's problems. If there had been any doubts before, Akers and his lieutenants now confronted a large fire burning down the company.

How IBM reacted to its failed strategy is about facing the reality that they had taken steps to rectify the situation too slowly and too late. Those steps were necessary, though painful. If the megastrategy launched by John Opel had been more humble, if there had not been so many new technological innovations in the 1980s, if competitors had not been so good, if customers had simply obeyed their IBMers, and if European governments had not picked on IBM so much with their "national champions" programs, maybe none of this would have happened. But none of those "ifs" happened. IBM operated in a world of multiple existential threats compounded by its own mistakes, and it believed its own hubris too much. To its credit, senior management accepted the need to respond to these threats, and how they did took over a decade to play out. The first half of that tale is the subject of this chapter, continuing the review of events from the previous one.

IBM could not hide its problems, as the extensive press coverage of the company's difficulties demonstrated, but we can put some hard data to the matter. In the early 1990s, IBM ranked eighth in the world as measured by revenue, being beaten out in size only by such peers as General Motors, Shell, Exxon, and Ford, plus a few others. Using our measure of number of employees, IBM ranked fourth, exceeded in size only by General Motors, Siemens, and Daimler-Benz. Its footprint could be found in over 100 countries.[3]

To understand how Akers and his senior executives addressed IBM's problems, we need to explore four issues: the steps they took; why they failed to provide effective leadership; the crucial role of the board of directors; and then the lessons to be drawn from their actions. The last point is important not only for informing business historians but because these lessons were being cataloged and presented to IBM's executives in the years immediately following Akers's departure. The subjects of this chapter are also of continuing interest to historians and experts in business management. These include the role of individual leaders, a topic discussed in greater detail in chapter 17; the role of corporate governance, specifically of the board of directors of this large multinational corporation; and how change unfolds in moments of crisis.

Culture and personal leadership continue to serve as contending themes in this chapter, perhaps not fully satisfying business historians focused on the social history of corporations or their continuing concerns about the role of individual leaders, but this chapter demonstrates that both are interrelated. When Roland Trempé studied nineteenth-century French coal mining, he made clear that contention and industry/work cultures were central issues to explore; his thinking still informs historians and my approach here.[4] Alfred D. Chandler Jr. observed that organizations respond to market conditions and that large institutions could be discussed as nearly monolithic entities even though, in practice, they were collections of constituencies operating under a corporate banner, an approach continued in this chapter.[5] While not purposefully replicating William G. Roy's approach to examining the behavior of American corporations, the story unfolding here mirrored his concerns about the role of economic power, again institutional behavior, his sociological approach, prior history, and contingency. It is useful to keep in mind his observation that a corporation's activities are "the work of specific individuals and groups acting within the context of constraints and facilitators, setting goals, mobilizing resources, and influencing others to act in concert" and "shape meanings," because "the form of the modern industrial corporation abounds in contingency."[6] He could have been describing IBM in any decade. We also explore the role of IBM's board, relying on the research of business management scholars and sociologists.[7] Many of IBM's board issues turn on roles and the scope of responsibilities, themes discussed in earlier chapters and increasingly in the remaining ones.

THE RESPONSE

When circumstances compelled Akers to dismantle Opel's growth strategy, he began slowly and then took increasingly more drastic measures. Recall that IBM gave up its historic full-employment practice, decimated employee loyalty and morale, caused some 200,000 employees to leave, emptied out buildings all over the world, plunged Poughkeepsie and Endicott into recessions, irritated customers, made it possible for new rivals to thrive, and replaced a generation of management. IBM's culture was riddled with holes. All three "Basic Beliefs" of respect for the individual, customer service, and excellence became barely recognizable. Akers's successor crafted a replacement for these beliefs that was more suited to the realities of the 1990s.

Until late in 1986, Akers assured everyone that things were going well. Then came his new message: "1986 was a difficult year for IBM." He acknowledged that "the information industry has achieved a remarkable record of growth. That record is not a line moving straight up, and it reflects several previous downturns." The $100 billion chart vanished. "The past two years" in Akers's words, "have been as difficult as any in our experience—a period of significant restructuring and retrenchment." His response was to speed up new product introductions and move employees from staff jobs to sales and service positions while "streamlining our operations." He spoke about a "stronger product line," finally serving up a statement about "commitment to customer partnerships," with a "leaner, more vigorous company." He admitted getting rid of "unneeded capacity" but said, "We continued to maintain our tradition of full employment."[8] While his public messages represented a departure from his usually highly optimistic communications and demonstrate that the heavy lifting of unwinding had yet to start, nonetheless everything seemed large now at IBM. For example, redeployment of people "back to the field" involved 12,000 employees in 1987. Many of IBM's competitors did not have anywhere near that number of workers.

IBM executives realized quickly that all divisions needed to shrink. In the process, the corporation spent billions of dollars. Just as it expended cash and took on debt to expand capacity, doing so incrementally as it sought to get to some equilibrium that would make possible $100 billion in revenue, it now incrementally shrank to "right size," to be a company of the size needed to earn a profit on the volume of revenue it was making. Eliminating employees was the most important lever management could pull to lower costs. To even touch that lever required them to abandon IBM's nearly hundred-year implied contract with its employees, releasing frightfully ugly and dangerous problems that the corporation still lives with. Right into the late 1980s, IBM had practiced the most thorough paternalism one could find in a large corporation. If a worker's job went away, IBM found them another in the company rather than lay them off. That last commitment became the rubbing point in the 1980s, because it was the element of the implied bargain management had to break if IBM was to unwind its excess capacity in a timely fashion.

Incrementally, Armonk approved dozens of actions that reduced the number of employees during the second half of the 1980s. With every new round of layoffs and voluntary separation programs, terms became less generous. Ever-larger groups in the United States and Europe were made eligible to participate; many did voluntarily. It would be difficult to underestimate the disruption to employee loyalty and focus on work that resulted from the possibility of being pushed out at any moment, the inability to plan based on some fixed separation package since these kept changing, and not knowing whether one was working in a part of the business safe from dismissal either because of their role, personal performance, or local labor laws protecting their jobs. In a company where such circumstances had not existed since the early 1920s—65 years earlier—the new work realities were unprecedented. Employees felt violated, cheated. Their new work atmosphere poisoned a great deal of Akers's efforts to fix IBM's problems. His second step involved reducing salary increases and then restructuring job classifications in order to lower salaries for specific categories of positions to drive down the cost per unit of work, regardless of merit. By the mid-1990s, IBM was differentiating salaries by location, allowing countries to set compensation based on what other firms paid locally. For example, someone working in Idaho would be paid less than a resident in New York City with the same job and rank. These otherwise normal steps had the effect of reinforcing employees' inability to focus on their work.

"Pay for performance," long an IBM mantra, evolved. Until the mid-1980s, the goodwill of loyal IBMers motivated them to do well what the company needed done. That involved personal commitment, acceptance of individual responsibility for excellence, solving problems, addressing wants of customers, and protecting IBM's interests. Those who embraced such behavior were rewarded with job advancement and increased income, using annual performance reviews as the tool to assess behavior and performance. Supposedly, performance reviews allowed managers to weed out poor performers. In reality, it did not, because assessments were of the employee against his or her objectives for the year, not in comparison to other employees. So, it became nearly impossible to dismiss poor performers. By the 1980s, bloated staffs were the norm. The concept of "starve the turkeys to feed the eagles," an aspiration, never came to fruition. Salaries flattened, even becoming uncompetitive. As severances began, self-motivation to do well deteriorated, with consequent erosion of labor productivity and quality of performance.

In the early 1990s, IBM introduced employee rankings, a practice already used by many corporations. Each manager ranked the effectiveness and value of every employee from best to worst. No level or rank was immune from the process. This ranking influenced appraisal ratings, the amount of bonuses, and salaries, and in its wake spun off extensive guidelines about how to tie together all three. Rankings made it easier to select who should be laid off. If a department had an outstanding staff, that is to say all its members were better performers than, say, others in similar levels in other parts of the company, someone still had to be ranked the lowest and hence subject to lower appraisals, income, and bonuses, and be exposed to being laid off. IBM's adoption of employee rankings corroded teaming behavior, as employees now saw each other as potential rivals. It was a slow, subtle transformation. Morale dropped. It did not matter what one's performance was, because it was what position they held that determined whether they were dismissed. For example, early targets for downsizing were headquarters and administrative staffs. If a specialist who was an expert in competing against mainframe rivals happened to be located in Atlanta in the National Marketing Division (NMD) while a similar expert was in the National Accounts Division (NAD) in White Plains, New York, the one in Atlanta lost his job in 1987, regardless of whether he was a better performer than his counterpart in White Plains. Both were in this role because they had been identified as better sales performers than their peers in branch offices.

So managers had fewer workers but were still required to do the same work as before. IBM slashed its billion dollar training budget, too. By the mid-1990s, one simply hired someone who already had a desired skill and dismissed IBMers who did not have it. That practice has continued to the present. It made sense if the company was no longer hiring for lifetime employment. The change quickly became obvious to Americans when IBM closed a facility in Greencastle, Indiana, forcing local IBMers to take what was then a generous severance package. It did not take employees long to realize that the IBM world beneath their feet was changing. Even European employees protected from such actions by national laws became concerned.

Akers sought to transform the culture of the company. Changes in salary and appraisal administration represented part of this effort, but Armonk also began tinkering with the centralized management structure it had found effective over many decades. The absolute authority over work activities managers had was now challenged by a new managerial transformation entering American, Asian, and European firms, called total quality management (TQM), which IBM referred to as market-driven quality (MDQ). These practices required that a company be willing to change its practices, that employees continuously be trained and learn about the effectiveness of the work they did, and that workers have the authority to change how they worked, hence transforming the notion of teaming from rhetoric to practice. That new philosophy struck a blow at the heart of management's authority, indeed at the need for managers. Instead of executives running the business from the top down, they would be required to shift responsibility down the organization and facilitate practices up from the bottom. That last change alone was nothing less than a revolution at IBM. Some welcomed it, mostly nonmanagerial employees and highly self-motivated managers. Many shied away from the increased responsibility or, more often the case, resisted losing their authority. Beginning in the mid-1980s, MDQ became a company-wide campaign.[9]

Employees were encouraged to submit more suggestions for improvements than ever before. Teams across the company looked at how to streamline work processes, making both minor and significant progress, such as the first attempts at creating a global procurement process.[10] However, some topics remained taboo. For example, if in the early 1990s an IBM sales organization experimented with a new peer appraisal process, its manager could be guaranteed a visit from divisional or corporate personnel management shutting down that innovation. Products still came to market late, despite the implementation of process redesign practices. Employees focused their attention on avoiding layoffs, participating and keeping up with the changes in processes and practices, and figuring out how they fit into the frequent organizational changes under way in all corners of the company. Customers saw their IBMers spending more time focusing on internal issues than on their needs.

Internally, consensus management bumped up against teaming that worked faster. So, senior management pushed implementation of MDQ in how work was done. They used every means to force the transformation, but they continued to operate a centralized management process while attempting to decentralize decision making. MDQ did not work well, despite a heroic effort across the firm from top to bottom. The most serious problem concerned the confusion over authority and continuous incremental cuts in budgets and staffing that played havoc with the initiative. Akers extolled individual leadership, while an employee read company publications cautioning them not to go too far, meaning not to spend too much money, because their organization had to live within its budget. The reason for concern about distributed authority is because quality management at its core called for companies to rely on teams of employees closest to a situation or with the greatest knowledge of a circumstance or process to manage their own work. That meant authorizing them to establish metrics of performance, judge their own work against those metrics, and modify processes as quantitative data led them to conclude that changes were needed. Those behaviors ran contrary to IBM's way of doing things.[11] However, that was the situation during Akers's time. By the end of the 1990s, many MDQ practices were working in other multinational corporations, where they were no longer called MDQ but rather TQM.[12]

Meanwhile, IBM's financial performance deteriorated. Akers pressed for further reductions in bureaucracy, a subject of interest to every CEO at IBM. The press began noting the changes he was pushing, some positively, such as when the *Wall Street Journal* reported in November 1988 that IBM was reducing its operating costs and increasing earnings.[13] A year later, the same publication criticized IBM's financial performance, reporting that Akers was going to lay off another 10,000 employees and cut more expenses. IBM's efforts had addressed symptoms, not the root causes of the company's problems.

Akers was not alone in his frustration. Better performers left with every new severance package, managers resisted changes, and most employees did not feel empowered to fix problems. New deals with customers could not be put together in a timely or flexible fashion. For example, if a customer wanted a specialized PC, say 200 or 300 of them, the PC Division would refuse to build them, saying it could not afford to do that for quantities less than 1,000. But Compaq did.

To a great extent, what survived the 1980s and early 1990s was a set of attitudes and behaviors that Akers just could not break. These included notions of excellence not aligned with those held by customers. The endless stream of managerial meetings, which consumed as much as a third of someone's time, distracted them from their intended work. Members of the corporate management committee were not the only ones trapped in conference rooms several times a week. There was insufficient urgency to get things done, with employees still seeking permission and instructions, all contrary to the operating principles of MDQ/TQM. Too many were being pushed out because they held jobs no longer considered relevant and were given no opportunity to transfer to more urgently needed positions. Staffs often were still too big. Akers knew about each of these failures, but he focused more on obtaining immediate results than on changing the culture of the firm. He was part of the problem, not fully understanding the change needed. He stated, "We are clearly putting competition into the IBM system," meaning employees competing against each other, when what MDQ advocated and many other corporations were finding was not the way to operate. Rather, practitioners of TQM and their managements advocated increased collaboration and teaming.[14]

Akers decided to reorganize the firm to shake things up. He sold off units of IBM. One of his earliest and most visible was the printer and printer supply business, which IBM sold in 1991 to the investment firm of Clayton, Dubilier & Rice, Inc., in a leveraged buyout, creating Lexmark. IBM retained 10 percent ownership in the new company and allowed it to use the IBM logo. IBM occupied one seat on its board. To run Lexmark, IBM and the new owners turned to a 32-year veteran of IBM, Marvin L. Mann (b. 1932). Mann, now liberated from IBM's management ways, turned Lexmark into a successful operation, going after H-P's laser printers, building a state-of-the-art manufacturing business supporting a $2 billion line of revenue with 5,000 employees, a workforce Mann later trimmed to 3,000. This IBM veteran turned out to be highly entrepreneurial, perfect for this spin-off, which he ran for nine years.[15] In time, industry observers questioned whether Lexmark had become the best at making and selling printing technologies that were rapidly becoming outdated. One reporter called its key PC printer a "Ferrari engine in a pickup truck body," a bit clunky.[16]

Key to our story is the typewriter piece of Lexmark, considered the best in the world. These typewriters were also the most expensive, but secretaries and typing pools did not care, for the machines were "the Mercedes-Benz of the executive suite," and without them, top secretaries could not be recruited.[17] During the 1970s and 1980s, this business suffered from benign neglect because it was "only" a $2 billion business for IBM. The rest of the company thought it was a sideshow.[18] Salesmen in DPD paid little attention to it, as their quotas were too large for them to waste time on typewriters. Neglect by management destroyed this wonderful business. When Akers began spinning off less profitable pieces of the company, typewriters were thrown on the pile of discards. The Lexmark transaction made it possible to package together printers, keyboards, printer supplies, and the old typewriter business. That worked for Lexmark but was, of course, more evidence that IBM was having difficulty managing what had been an important piece of its business.

Employees and customers were frustrated with Akers's earlier moves: 15,000 semiforced departures in 1987 and then 21,000 staff sent back into sales branch offices. This cadence of reducing the number of employees continued in 1988 and 1989. At the dawn of the new decade, another 8,200 staff and 16,000 factory workers lost their jobs, and an additional 11,000 were transferred to branch offices; 7,700 programmers were redeployed. The sales organization had been reorganized three times in four years, and another "reorg" was pending. It seemed nobody in sales knew anyone anymore anywhere in the company. Telephone directories were out of date; Rolodex files were more useful if they listed *home* telephone numbers of colleagues.

IBM had rarely made broad reorganizations until Tom Watson Jr. began doing so in the late 1950s, again when the company grew in size and complexity, thanks to the S/360. Because of the increased number of reorganizations, it makes sense to explain their forms. Reorganizations of divisions involved creating new ones dedicated to specific markets or products, whereas smaller reorganizations involved departments within a division. To draw an academic analogy, think of a division like a college within an American university. IBM divisions could either be just within the United States or global. As the company grew, clusters of divisions were organized into "groups," such as a combination of sales and product manufacturing divisions aligned to address a specific market, such as for large or small systems and customers. Senior vice presidents (later called general managers) managed groups, while presidents, ranked one level below them, ran divisions. This combination of divisions and groups came into use more frequently to align resources with IBM's strategies.[19] In Akers's early years at the helm in the mid- to late 1980s, IBM's slowness in bringing out new products and lowering costs proved nearly insurmountable. He had to try something else. For many executives in other companies, major reorganizations represented an almost nuclear option, and so it was at IBM. In IBM's centralized managerial culture, such reorganizations were intended to diffuse responsibility and authority. While used frequently, they had less effect over time, because as they became too frequent, they disrupted networks of collaboration and focus.

In early 1988, IBM began implementing a new approach. To move decision making closer to customers and products, IBM created five independent business units (IBUs), each with its own general manager and range of authority. All reported to one general manager, Terry R. Lautenbach (1938–2004). He had the impossible task of running these IBUs plus all of the sales and service organizations located in the United States. One would have thought that at least he was now the number two executive at IBM. This was not so, because in addition to Akers (chairman), two vice chairmen and one executive vice president joined with the chairman to form a committee to which Lautenbach reported. The same group also oversaw all World Trade marketing and manufacturing.

"Cumbersome" was the polite word used by some employees close to Akers to describe this arrangement. Recall that the current iteration of the corporate management board dated to 1985, with 18 members who also oversaw operations, or at least broke up disputes and allocated resources. The smaller group quickly dominated decision making, marginalizing the larger committee. Earlier groups were now dissolved, including the Information Systems Group (ISG), which had concentrated authority over all of the company's hardware and software decisions from typewriters to mainframes. The new, smaller committee met two or three times a week for meetings lasting all day. Akers had hoped to better integrate decision making using his reorganization with ISG, but that organization did not work, so he reversed course by decentralizing further. His new structure also failed, so in December 1991 he announced yet another new structure similar in form but now increased to nine organizations. At the same time, he created four non-U.S. (World Trade territory) marketing and services companies.

If the reader is becoming confused, so were thousands of employees, customers, and industry watchers. In mid-1992, *Fortune* acknowledged Akers's promising intention but asked, "But is he pressing the message hard enough? Probably not."[20] In fairness to him, the same article acknowledged, "Think your company has troubles? IBM faces practically every challenge known to management."[21] By now, much of the business press had turned against Akers. In a thorough analysis, *Fortune* concluded that the reorganization would not foster more autonomy across IBM, nor would it replace the culture of complacency, but the magazine liked that he was keeping a unified sales force, which would have no effect on the working style of manufacturing divisions. *Fortune*'s reporters admired the company's increasing shift from products to services, embedded in the reorganization, and IBM's renewed focus on customer issues. They most appreciated that the reorganization promised to reduce staff by possibly100,000.

Each of the nine organizations was large. Enterprise Systems generated $22 billion in mainframe and related product sales, essentially twice the size of any other "Baby Blue." Akers created Adstar for storage and tape drives and some software largely for sale to mainframe users. Personal Systems became responsible for PC sales and $11.5 billion in revenues. To manage the minicomputer business, largely the AS/400, Akers created Applications Business Systems (ABS).[22] He formed four smaller organizations, each with its own branding and name: Pennant Systems to sell printers and related software, Applications Solutions for services and software, Technology Products to make microelectronics, and Networking Systems, which derived most of its business from mainframe customers. Each was treated as if it were an independent company. Did that mean the "PC Company," as it was called (in practice, still a division), could compete against ABS with its RS/6000, asked one observer?[23] The answer was not clear. However, Akers shared his thinking about the broader reorganization: "The role of corporate management will be to oversee our portfolio of businesses" and "disengage from declining or less profitable businesses to maximize IBM's financial returns."[24]

Customers were already being visited by representatives of most of these divisions and now had to deal with the little IBM companies, too. Large-account salesmen were now serving as gatekeepers, while everyone wanted the right to come in and see their customers. From 1991 to 1993, increasing numbers of new sales personnel, all on incentive compensation plans designed to have them sell only their organization's products, were banging on doors at IBM's large customers while scrambling to find a second tier of smaller customer enterprises. Morale kept dropping, as did customers' confidence in their ability to do business with IBM. IBM's costs remained too high, while sales and profits kept dropping. By now, it was widely believed inside the company and elsewhere that Akers had latched onto a strategy for breaking up IBM in the belief that the various components would collectively operate less expensively and generate more revenue, and that IBM Corporate was evolving into a holding company. It seemed the only people pleased were the heads of these new lines of business (LOBs). They were the tiniest minority at IBM. Akers's organizational changes between 1988 and 1992 were the most unpopular with employees in IBM's history.

Corporate turmoil also plagued these organizations. For example, out of the five organizations created in 1988, by 1992 four of their leaders had left those organizations: one retired, two became senior VPs, and Conrades had been pushed out of the company; the fifth (Ellen Hancock, IBM's highest-ranking female executive at the time) would soon leave as well. Terry Lautenbach departed in 1992. Other departures included Kaspar V. Cassani, who retired, and Allen J. Krowe, who went over to Texaco. Only Akers and a handful of the old guard remained. Employees scratched their collective heads wondering at all the turnover in the groups and at Corporate. Every week or two, a major leadership change was posted on bulletin boards and communicated via e-mail.

It was difficult to find sufficient constancy of leadership to make possible any meaningful reforms. By then, the industry press was in the groove of criticizing Akers and IBM's actions. These included *Computer Industry Report, Datamation,* and *Computerworld,* and such business journals as *Fortune, Business Week, The Economist,* and the *Wall Street Journal.* The press and customers complained that almost all the reorganizations seemed to be on the sales side, while product divisions still were not delivering new cost-effective offerings quickly enough to satisfy users' needs. IBM's status kept dropping from frequently being ranked first, to seventh, and then tenth by 1992. Industry reporters still acknowledged IBM's technical prowess but harshly criticized its inability to convert lab wizardry into products. IBM's growing list of patents did not seem to matter anymore. It appeared that "everyone" was waiting for these problems to be solved. Who could do it? Not Akers. Where was the board of directors? Why was IBM not fixing its problems?

At the October 1992 board meeting in Tokyo, Akers got the word that it was time for him to leave. The facts are shrouded in mystery, but his close colleague Sam Palmisano intimated that such a conversation occurred.[25] The scenario made sense, as the board had chief executive officers who would have understood when a corporate crisis had broken out that required their attention. IBM's mainframe revenues had dropped almost in half since 1990, putting IBM on a path to destruction. In his memoirs, Lou Gerstner confirmed the fear inside the board.[26] Members of any board can be counted on to become agitated when stock values drop precipitously. IBM's stock had lost $77 billion in value since 1987. Shares dropped in value from $43 in the spring of 1987 to $12 in early 1993, with their value dropping by half just in the previous year. After a long board meeting on January 25, 1993, Akers resigned. Frank A. Metz Jr. (b. 1934), IBM's "nice guy" CFO, left, having "retired." The board believed he was in over his head with IBM's financial issues. Jack Kuehler, at the time president under Akers, became vice chairman, with essentially no responsibilities, while Paul J. Rizzo (b. 1928) came out of retirement to keep things running until a replacement for Akers could be appointed.

After the arrival of a new chairman, Louis V. Gerstner Jr., from outside IBM on April 1, other senior executives left, most in the same year or in early 1994. Akers completely disappeared from the business world. He died of a stroke on August 22, 2014, four months before his eightieth birthday. Gerstner and Burke did not invite him to join the board, as was customary with former heads of IBM, although Opel still served, along with Paul Rizzo. It had been a bad first quarter for IBM's senior U.S. executives. The week Akers announced his resignation, a bloodbath of a reorganization occurred at the large U.S. retailer Sears, Roebuck and Co. Problems had recently plagued General Motors as well.

In 1994, Opel retired from the board, leaving Gerstner (chairman) and the new CFO, Jerome B. York (1938–2010), as members. Akers's resignation was by any measure a sad day for the company, but for employees and IBM watchers his departure held out the hope that the end of the worst chapter in IBM's history was near. It seemed that all employees blamed this one man for everything that had gone wrong. The media did, too. A quarter century later, what do we know?

THE FAILURE OF LEADERSHIP

Much debate has taken place over who, or what, to blame for IBM's troubles in the 1980s and early 1990s. Many events stand out:

- IBM's increasingly slow ability to respond to market needs with newer, better-priced products, such as the late arrival of the PS/2 and the reluctance to embrace the Linux operating system.
- Elimination of IBM's social contract of lifetime employment, which destroyed loyalty and productivity.
- The continuous dribbling flow of layoffs in what Gerstner later characterized as "Chinese water torture," brought about by incremental responses to IBM's ongoing declining fortunes.
- A performance appraisal process that had eroded so far that dismissing incompetent people proved nearly impossible, dismissals amounting to about 1 percent of all employees per year.
- Increasing internal emphasis by IBMers at all levels, but particularly by middle management on up, on their careers and the interests of their corner of IBM rather than what was happening outside of IBM with customers and rivals.
- Expanding bureaucratic sclerosis that made it difficult for well-meaning IBMers or concerned customers to get things done within IBM relevant to those concerns.
- Rising independence of customers increasingly willing to make hardware and software acquisitions from IBM's competitors and also to align with technical standards out of sync with IBM's Systems Application Architecture (SAA).
- Continuing high cost of IBM's goods and services relative to that of its more agile rivals.

The list is long. Eventually historians may boil the list down to a shorter one, but at the time, these eight themes captured the attention of those concerned about IBM. Most commentators spoke of IBM's corporate culture as a major source of the company's problems because it proved insufficiently flexible in accommodating technological and market changes. Employees paid more attention to the lingering effects of the antitrust suit, yet historical evidence demonstrates that the company exploded forward with new initiatives after the litigation ended: global expansion, the PC product line, and initiatives to add new customers in ever-smaller companies.

But at its core, we come back to IBM's central problem of a flawed strategy that called for the company to expand massively in the 1980s within the context of a mainframe world. The notion that the market would remain centered on the mainframe was simply wrong. That is why it was possible to accuse senior managers at IBM of being "out of touch."

What about the stock market or the media? What credit, or blame, can be laid at their feet? As IBM's financial performance declined after Akers took the top job in 1985, their recommendations were superficial: cut costs, lay off employees. These prescriptions stood in contrast to those from customers: better products, more networking to all vendors' machines and software, improved price/performance. Neither the stock market nor the media focused on structural problems with IBM's processes—its way of working—or on challenging its strategy of expanding the company to become the low-cost provider to fight Japanese rivals. In fairness to them, it seemed many industries in the West were obsessed with Japanese competition in the 1980s and had yet to realize that the post–World War II economic Golden Age had essentially ended. By the early 1990s, it did not help that all of IBM's global and product markets had simultaneously entered a period of economic stagnation, or recession. As a national economy's fortunes rose or fell, so did IBM's. In the past, one or more markets might have done that, but not this time. Too many industries and national economies were linked together—globalization's fundamental feature.

For a better answer, we need to search inside IBM. Its key strategic decision makers came up in a homogeneous sales culture. They took for granted IBM's strong technological prowess but viewed the world as a place to inject their products, particularly as the company shifted to a strategy of being a low-cost producer and away from leasing and toward purchase. That mentality broke Watson's cardinal rule: they dismantled IBM's close ties to its customers. Periodically, management realized it, as when Akers declared 1988 as the "Year of the Customer."

But it was too late. As explained in the previous chapter, the relationship with customers had evolved into a more transaction-centered one, away from the service- and solution-oriented one of the past, reinforced by computers now becoming commodities to be purchased at the lowest cost, which were interchangeable across brands and no longer customized. In a survey of 1,000 customers conducted in 1994, 37 percent reported that IBM had "lost touch with the marketplace." This finding represented a massive departure from the past. One customer reported that IBM "got too far removed from the day-to-day issues facing customers." Another customer argued that "IBM got into trouble because of greed and stupidity. They thought about themselves and not the customer."[27] IBM entered the 1990s with distraught customers and a demoralized workforce. However, there was plenty of business to be had; it was just that IBM was no longer winning it. Interestingly, in the same survey, only 6 percent stopped buying from IBM because of its high prices; instead, nearly twice as many complained about Big Blue's arrogance.[28] A few IBM executives in the early 1990s reacted privately, with such comments as, "Employee morale will increase when the revenues rise" and "Customers need to get back in line with IBM." IBM's system of doing business had unraveled.[29]

Customers had more specific issues. Large-company chief information officers (CIOs) complained that IBM did not defend the relevance of mainframes, letting PC apologists dominate the narrative. It did not help that IBM's mainframes sometimes were as much as 40 percent more expensive than Japanese ones. Within his first 90 days on the job, Louis Gerstner lowered the cost of many products, including mainframes (largely the S/390 at the time), and launched a public relations campaign to defend the importance of the mainframe. Along with significant changes in the base technology, those actions dramatically improved price/performance, and mainframe sales turned around in 1994.

We are left with the conclusion that in IBM's highly centralized, top-down way of doing business—its culture—as reflected in the behavior of its most senior managers, lay the source of the company's central problems. They developed the failed strategy of the 1980s. They were unable to sustain, or enhance, a more customer-focused or agile approach, although they tried. They failed to protect employees from layoffs. It is difficult to change a large company's course. At about the same time, Charlie Brown, chairman of AT&T, famously said that transforming his company was like turning the course of an oil tanker. Lee Iacocca at Chrysler and later Jack Welch at GE made similar comments.

IBM's homogenous senior managers were both prisoners of their experiences of an earlier but now different market and of decisions made by earlier CEOs. Decisions made by Cary affected Opel's realities; Opel's realities affected Akers's circumstances. Akers's decisions shaped what IBM looked like on the day he retired. Their sales-centric heritage embedded in a sales culture either made it impossible for them to understand the culture they needed to change or, more to the point, that IBM's problems were more than issues with competitors and markets. Looking back, Walter E. Burdick, a group executive at IBM in the early 1990s, may have captured the essence of how the company's executives looked at the situation:

> I felt that the previous CEOs [Cary, Opel] had made three major mistakes in the technical and financial areas. They had let Microsoft dominate the software field, while IBM still focused on the shrinking hardware business. They had helped the Intel Corporation survive against the Japanese competition in the 1980s and had actually owned nineteen percent of that firm, only to sell their interest in what would become worth tens of billions of dollars. Finally, they allowed Apple Computer and Compaq Computer to dominate the personal computer business before IBM seriously entered the field.[30]

On Akers, Burdick admitted to his family, "It was a very difficult time for the chairman, and I was his personal confidant during that troublesome time."[31]

All lived in a world of management by committee, the results of the Watsonian contention/consensus system that allowed various divisions to escalate issues. Akers followed the examples of Cary and Opel in promoting consensus, because as the center of a complex company each had to avoid the serious problem of unintentionally making a decision that could harm the company or its customers, that for some reason could not be implemented, or that employees would not carry out.[32] They wanted to avoid someone becoming an autocrat, running an imperial chairmanship. Tom Watson Jr. had taught them to be collegial, and his lesson worked during the 1960s and early 1970s. Consequently, successes and failures could be laid at the feet of a small team of senior executives.

When that managerial inner circle became overconfident as a result of their personal and corporate successes of the 1960s and 1970s, they stretched too far to sustain their paradigm of mainframe products and customers. As late as 2000, one member of the corporate management board, elected to that committee in 1990 when the company was in serious trouble, still waxed almost nostalgically about the role: "It was a significant honor to be added to the top management board in the company."[33] Complex issues became increasingly intractable, leading to "kicking the can down the road" behavior on some issues and avoidance of possibly different strategy options. By the mid-1980s, these behaviors had fostered complacency in dealing with the erosion in IBM's ability to respond to new customer needs and changing markets. Executives became too cautious when entertaining innovations. Recall how they backed off supporting Future Systems's plan to replace the S/370 with a new platform. They still felt the pain of their experiences in bringing out the S/360. The same happened with RISC, which was developed in the 1970s but did not make it out of the lab until the late 1980s to early 1990s. There would be no more "bet your company" decisions coming out of this generation of executives.

The company remained unable to transform its way of operating, despite its efforts to do so. It remained a command-and-control world of centralized authority from on high. Paris and Tokyo were interesting places to work, with large staffs responsible for directing the work of IBM in large geographic spaces, but as Jacques Maisonrouge reminded us, the key decisions were made in Armonk by a small cadre of executives who lived in Connecticut and spent time at IBM HQ down the road in Westchester

County, New York. This occurred as the computer industry was segmenting into smaller, more specialized forms. Its physical footprint had moved to new localities: Silicon Valley in California, increasingly Texas, London, Taiwan, parts of Japan, and the outskirts of large European cities. By the early 1990s, Akers had concluded that in response to these new circumstances the company had to be broken up. His vision called for fracturing the singleness of IBM's one common face to the customer, pointing IBM toward a future as a holding company. He began implementing his new approach in the face of almost universal hostility below the senior ranks of the corporation, division and group management, and IBM's customers.

Meanwhile, several hundred thousand employees worried about losing their jobs or working with a vast collection of operating processes, some the by-product of MDQ but most the result of a much longer process of product development. Everyone's attention to longer-term strategies diminished. One set of informed observers noted that "no one on IBM's top management team was watching the strategic development of technology; they were too busy managing a process."[34] Those IBMers who noticed were either not heard or ignored, as happened to those involved with Future Systems and RISC technologies. When Akers and his colleagues did pay attention to strategy, they focused too much on mainframe threats when industry observers and IBMers should have focused on Apple, Intel, and Microsoft and, if necessary, less on Amdahl, Fujitsu, and Hitachi. Gerstner's take on this behavior was that IBMers had developed a "foxhole mentality" and that senior management did not have a company-wide strategy.

As these senior executives witnessed IBM's deteriorating stock price and financial performance, it appeared they paid more attention to the advice of Wall Street and less to that of their customers. They were unable to ignore the likes of *Fortune, Business Week,* or the *Wall Street Journal,* which called for layoffs and lower operating costs, even at the risk of altering the positive aspects of the company's culture. One Harvard Business School professor close to many of IBM's issues at the time declared that its "executives lost confidence in their long-term strategy and bowed to Wall Street's wishes, accepting record restructuring charges to make rapid short term changes," with the media able to break "the concentration of IBM's management on the technology cycle—something it [media] had been unable to do in 1950, when the tabulator technology was dying."[35] The Watsons may have read these publications, but they did not take advice from journalists on how to run IBM.

The massive write-offs in the early 1990s shocked customers into asking whether it still made sense to use IBM products if the company was running the real danger of going out of business, which would mean no new releases of software and no maintenance for hardware or its operating system. The write-offs caused both IBM's employees and its senior executives to lose confidence and to get out of sync with the natural ebb and flow of technological innovations. For the first time in IBM's history, senior executives paid attention to the wants of capital markets. Until the early 1990s, IBM had steadfastly done the opposite—ignored them—and instead paid attention to the cadence of technological transformations and economic opportunities these presented to customers and the company. For that reason, we can conclude that many if not all of IBM's most senior executives in the early 1990s were just as complicit as John Akers in making strategic errors of judgment. They, too, proved too slow to respond to market conditions and, given the speed with which they evolved, too late.

THE ROLE OF IBM'S BOARD OF DIRECTORS

Like all publicly traded companies, IBM belonged to its board of directors, which had legal responsibility for managing the investment made by stockholders in the firm. It hired the CEO to run the company on its behalf. Directors had the obligation to inspect operations of the firm and to approve major strategic initiatives. Their loyalty lay with the stockholders, not with employees of the firm, unless, of course, the workers also owned stock, which many did. During periods of crisis, when employees asked why the board did not act, they often did not understand the directors' loyalties and priorities. It did not help that a board's priorities were not clearly communicated or simple to describe. Taking care of employees and thinking of the long-term interests of a corporation and its customers often represented solid and appropriate concerns for board members, in alignment with their legal responsibilities. It was normal practice to have as members current or previous senior officers of the company, such as retired CEOs. In IBM's case, these included Cary and Opel, and Akers before his retirement.

What role did the board have in IBM's troubles? IBM's board has a history of operating in the background, drawing almost no attention. IBM's acted like almost every other board of a large multinational corporation, but that began to change in the late 1980s, as both employees and Wall Street asked what the board was doing to fix IBM's problems and to replace its leadership, most notably Akers. In the early 1990s, blogs were still a thing of the future, so there is no massive trail of employee missives complaining about their CEO, unlike in the 2010s concerning the performance of another IBM CEO under siege, Ginni Rometty. But the hue and cry for the board to act existed.[36]

In 1988, IBM's board consisted of 18 members, 6 of whom were active or retired IBMers (CEOs, senior vice presidents, vice chairmen), 6 CEOs from other companies (two were in the health industry and two from media), 2 outside lawyers, and 4 from higher education. None came out of the computer industry external to IBM, and all were on the older side (50s–60s). All had been handpicked by IBM CEOs who followed the tradition set by Thomas Watson Sr., where the head of the company populated the board with like-minded people who could be counted on not to interfere too much. With so many decades of continuous profitable financial results by IBM, there seemed to be no urgent need for its members to act independently. IBM's CEOs held meetings in interesting places and nurtured collegiality with its board members. The board's lack of expertise in an industry undergoing enormous changes contributed to its hands-off style.

By late 1991, the media was pressing IBM's board to do something. Its membership remained remarkably the same as in 1988, consisting of 18 members, of whom 5 were IBMers, 1 was a lawyer, 2 were from higher education, 2 were European CEOs, and the others were U.S. CEOs, even some of the same people as in 1988. The Executive Compensation Committee, made up of CEOs, had the same members as before. Importantly,

Figure 16.1
James E. Burke, member of the IBM board of directors, who negotiated the resignation of John Akers and recruited IBM's next CEO, Louis V. Gerstner Jr. Photo courtesy of IBM Corporate Archives.

James E. Burke (now retired CEO of Johnson & Johnson) chaired that committee. He would come to play a crucial role in replacing Akers. So again IBM's board was a stable, cozy group.

In 1992, the board finally had to begin wrestling with leadership and strategic issues facing IBM. As one observer put it, "The board was far too large for an effective committee; it was headed by a chairman who was also chief executive; it was stuffed with retirees; and it was short on relevant business experience."[37] Ten members each owned fewer than 10,000 shares of IBM stock. One could reasonably have expected them to have had larger investments in IBM. Their economic ties to IBM were the $55,000 retainer paid to each of them for serving on the board. In short, few had economic incentives to rock the boat.

Then came the fateful year of 1993, when, in the first quarter, the board dismissed Akers and searched for a new leader from outside of IBM. That board ended the year smaller, with 14 members, one of whom was the new chairman, Louis V. Gerstner Jr. Opel and Rizzo were the only IBMers remaining. One lawyer and three members from higher education were still on the board. But the action required from the board came from the seven CEOs. All already had served more than one year, most for many years. The long-term members included James E. Burke of Johnson & Johnson, Thomas F. Frist Jr., then chairman of the Columbia/HCA Healthcare Corporation, and others with two or more years of service. Again, with the possible exception of Gerstner, who had managed IT projects and had run American Express, and therefore knew something about IT credit card operations, the others still had no experience with computing. Their knowledge of IBM's operations still came largely from IBM's CEOs and staff.

Boards do not like to fire CEOs. When they do, they come to the decision after a protracted period of observing the stock price dropping, as complaints from Wall Street or the media become increasingly critical, or if a scandal envelops a senior official. In the case of IBM, Akers had compounded the problem because he pushed out potential rivals, so no heir was obviously waiting in the wings. This was a rare situation at IBM, which always prided itself on having succession plans at all levels of the firm. Akers was 59 years old when the board acted, just one year away from IBM's customary retirement age, which further aggravated the succession problem. So what finally pushed the board to act? Akers's failures were simply too obvious and too public. It did not help that the stock's value continued to drop by nearly 10 percent between 1987 and 1991, and even further in 1992 and 1993. Publicly and behind the scenes, the board collectively and its members individually continued to voice support for Akers. So month after month he endured public criticisms and declining support from IBM's employees and customers, but his board stuck with him. It acted, just later than it should have. That it failed to fix IBM's problems or help Akers suggests that collectively the board proved unwilling, complicit, or simply incompetent to carry out its fiduciary and ethical responsibilities until forced to by circumstances. When a company operates well, a benign board is a useful one, as during the Watson Sr. years, but when IBM entered a turbulent era, it needed to be more activist and be populated with individuals familiar with the technologies and operational considerations relevant to the company.

Did the board understand how dysfunctional IBM had become by, say, 1991? Obvious signals that should have been familiar to the CEOs on the board were ignored, such as the exits of 30 corporate officers between 1986 and 1992. That does not even include the well-known technical stars, notably Gene Amdahl, who built a successful company to sell a rival to the S/370. The list of senior leaders leaving was publicly known and routinely reported by the press. It included Allen Krowe (executive vice president), Ed Lucente[38] (president of World Trade, Asia), Mike Armstrong (chairman of IBM World Trade), and George Conrades (who at the time of his departure led corporate marketing). Other large corporations benefited by acquiring these and other IBMers: Krowe by Texaco, Armstrong by Hughes Aircraft (where he had an excellent career), and others by Northern Telecom and even Microsoft.

Large reorganizations at any major corporation are normally subject to review by a board. It is unclear how IBM's board reacted to the many reorganizations Akers introduced, which the other sitting CEOs would have understood levy a short-term cost in employee productivity and so are done cautiously and as infrequently as possible. The "musical chairs" nature of his reorganizations was, as one observer put it, "clumsy" at best. When Akers migrated toward making IBM a holding company of a portfolio of firms, not divisions, it took his board over a year to grasp the strategic implications of that transformation. If accepted by the board, that strategy should have led it to insist Akers staff his senior positions with people more skilled in running such an organization. It did not. More of the same kinds of executives as had always worked at the highest levels kept occupying top positions, while potential heirs to Akers kept leaving. One can blame the board for allowing that to happen. Over the eight years of Akers's rule, it seemed complacent.[39]

In the year before the board deposed Akers, past and present members kept putting out statements supporting him. Irving Shapiro said, "I applaud what IBM is doing." Richard Lyman declared Akers had "the full confidence of the board." Yet by then the stock had dropped in value by 25 percent. In December 1992, Jim Burke, considered the most influential board member, praised Akers also.[40] In the days and weeks before Akers's ouster in late January 1993, board members kept making supportive statements despite the fact that, as reported by the *New York Times*, "the pressure on Mr. Akers had been mounting for months, with large institutional shareholders" becoming "increasingly outspoken as they watched I.B.M.'s share price drop ... in the summer."[41]

When the board finally acted, to its credit, it did so quickly. It kept the planning surrounding Akers's departure secret, a remarkable feat given the number of people who watched every move made by anyone associated with IBM Corporate. Burke, known best for how his company deftly handled the tainted Tylenol crisis in 1982, led the effort to end Akers's chairmanship. Less than a board coup, the effort appeared more a collaborative process with the CEO, according to Burke. It is possible that many of the supportive comments made about Akers by board members in the 60 days before his ouster might have been made to provide cover for what Burke and others were doing behind the scenes. We may never know, as most of the board members either are now deceased or did not leave a public record of their roles. Ultimately, everyone on the board wanted Akers to resign, and in the end that result was achieved. The way it was done mirrored the manner in which U.S. multinational boards normally dealt with such issues. With a set of experienced CEOs on the board, they were capable of shepherding the process to a logical, clean conclusion.

In sum, however, many employees felt the board had behaved badly, from being too complacent since the late 1980s to making complimentary comments about Akers's rule in the weeks leading up to his announced "retirement." It did not help that employees were also grousing about all the changes under way at IBM. They felt disenfranchised, left out of decisions, suffering the consequences of actions taken by others. The press and students of IBM's behavior agreed.[42] IBM's centralized operation made it clear that Akers and a small cadre of executives were to blame for IBM's failures.[43] Akers, the board, and his senior executives proved unable to change IBM's way of doing business or update its corporate culture. The next CEO went directly after those two problems in a forceful manner that left no doubt about what he was going to do, discussed in detail in chapter 17.

SOME FINAL LESSONS

An analysis of IBM's experience conducted at the Harvard Business School soon after Akers's departure is a useful guide on how to think about events at the company.[44] IBM was accused of ignoring its customers, focusing too much on internal debates and issues. Competitors paid a great deal of attention to their customers; IBM did not. To prioritize customers before all others was Watson Sr.'s mantra and that of CEOs right through Cary, but decreasingly thereafter. All decisions should take into account customers' wishes, not be purely financial, as occurred when IBM switched from lease to purchase of its products. That action diminished the relationship between IBM and its customers, as it evolved from service and partnership to transaction based. A quarter century later, it has not recovered from that transition. Understanding one's customers required a deep knowledge of how their business worked. Not appreciating that customers really wanted a partnership with IBM damaged the company Watson Sr. and his sons built and caused Gerstner endless angst as he worked to rebuild it.

Then as now, a fundamental structural problem existed with senior leadership. Akers had been the CEO and the chairman of the board but also an operational manager within IBM's management structure. A CEO should push a company in a direction but retain sufficient distance from its daily operations to be able to judge how well the firm is accomplishing his or her wishes. At IBM, all these positions were consolidated into one, a situation that was essential when an imperial leader needed to move quickly, as in the cases of Thomas Watson Sr. and Tom Jr., and later with Gerstner, but not in most periods. All modern CEOs at IBM were, to quote Ginni Rometty's title(s), "Chairwoman, President and CEO of IBM." A decade earlier, the Harvard team concluded that "delegating many decisions to divisional or subsidiary executives can help to achieve the proper balance."[45] Gerstner's successor, Sam Palmisano, took steps to foster delegation, in much the same manner as Watson Jr. Overreaching with strategy seemed a temptation hard to resist. In IBM's case, the S/360 stretch worked, but not expansion in the 1980s. Overreaching remained an internally created habit—threat—in large corporations that are financially strong and whose leaders have a history of success, others would say arrogance, but may not be fully in touch with current realities.

Another lesson from IBM's experience is that reorganizations do not fix bad strategies. IBM has had a penchant for reorganizing to fix problems, especially since the 1980s. Some of that activity, of course, was required as circumstances changed, but did IBM need to reorganize sales operations four times in the 1980s and again repeatedly in the early 1990s? Reorganizations should be conducted to implement strategy. They are no substitute for a good strategy. IBM forgot, or never knew, that lesson; nor did its board of directors, which should have paid more attention to Akers's growing use of this managerial tool. When it did, as he was marching forward with the breakup of the company, it did the right thing, but barely in time. To the credit of every CEO in IBM's history, they all fought growing tides of bureaucracy, some more successfully than others. Opel could have done more but did not. By the time Akers took charge of the company, it was vast, powerful, and unstoppable. He may have just dealt with it halfheartedly;

it is difficult to tell because the historical record is inconclusive and he had so many fires to extinguish from the first day of his tenure.

Opportunities were wasted or cast aside. Future Systems and RISC are the two examples IBMers of the period always cite, as do business professors and members of the computer industry. But we can add IBM's struggle with OS/2, chipping away at its functions to drive down its selling price, and overstaffing programming projects.

Circumstances compelled Akers, more than any previous CEO, to discard employees. To his credit, he did so reluctantly, as he knew the value of having dedicated lifetime employees, but incrementally disposing of them killed morale. One could trace this process by noting the declining support for IBM in opinion surveys conducted every year all over the world. Management had a long-standing practice of sharing results with employees, but now sharing information about declining morale and operational challenges reinforced negative employee views of the company. Dealing with a financial issue by laying off employees, while problematic, does not leave behind long-lasting negative consequences if it is a one-time event and effectively executed. In IBM's case, Akers's ever-expanding layoffs broke IBM's implied contract with its employees. Executives kept telling employees at all levels that this is "the last one," only to be ordered to implement another two months later, so management lost credibility. The next three CEOs increasingly continued layoffs.[46]

Finally, we come back to Akers himself. Ernest von Simson, a seasoned strategist knowledgeable about the computer industry, argued that the biggest mistake that can be laid at the feet of John Akers was his failure to force the changes in mainframe pricing and technology that his successor embraced. Simson also asked, "Why hadn't Akers replaced his subpar executives, especially when the company was clearly in trouble?"[47] Ultimately, Akers, a prisoner of IBM's culture, could not sufficiently distance himself from the problems to take appropriate actions. Walter E. Burdick, one of his eight senior vice presidents, may have inadvertently reinforced this conclusion in his memoirs, intended only for family reading: "While it was apparent the problem we encountered in the 1980s had been created by Akers' predecessors, he inherited the total burden of transformation. He and I were both proud of the way we handled the transformation because it preserved the values and principles of the corporation."[48] Akers fought a losing battle with his employees, and more so with the market. Simson's list of problems Akers could not overcome included lack of a creative ideology for the business; what he called "the burden of assets," meaning decisions and actions he inherited from Opel; resistance to change from within the company all through the many layers of IBM; distractions caused by competition, especially Akers's fixation with Japanese mainframe vendors who ultimately were deposed, while other rivals in the PC world should have attracted more attention; and failure to create an effective succession plan for the top positions, especially his own.

Historians will debate whether Akers exhibited a steadiness of leadership, what others called a "constancy of purpose," undistracted by Wall Street pundits giving bad advice. Watson Jr. displayed that concentrated focus when he fixated on getting S/360 done. Gerstner had it when he was determined to keep IBM intact and to rebuild relations with customers, regardless of advice that might have distracted him. But toward the end of his tenure, Akers did not exercise constancy of purpose. He inherited Opel's faulty strategy, even if he, too, had been one of its architects. Hardly anyone at IBM understood the degree of change required to reverse the strategy during Akers's first two years at the helm, only that change was needed quickly. Likewise, industry watchers, customers, the media, and stock analysts failed to appreciate the extent of the changes required or the consequences that resulted. All the criticisms heaped on Akers came after he had been in charge for well over a year, and they increased over time, rightfully so since with the passage of time, the ineffectiveness of the response could be laid at his feet.

Finally, as we will see in chapter 17, some of the remedial steps taken by Gerstner to turn the company around had been launched during Akers's time, such as the move into services and outsourcing. Personally, I liken it to what happened with President Franklin D. Roosevelt and the New Deal of the 1930s, when FDR implemented reforms to mitigate the Great Depression by taking some steps worked out by the previous administration of President Herbert Hoover. Roosevelt moved more quickly than

Hoover and received credit for the results. Gerstner moved more quickly than Akers and likewise won credit for his efforts. In both cases, the successful leader made decisions that led to positive results, while the failed leader made strategic mistakes: Hoover in thinking that the U.S. economy would rebound with only a modicum of federal assistance, Akers in thinking IBM would rebound with only a few actions required by Corporate. The key difference in these cases is that Akers had more time to deal with his problems than Hoover did. Nevertheless, both were complicit in not being able to contain the causes of their crises: Hoover the onset of the Great Depression, Akers the rapid decline of IBM.[49]

So IBM tumbled onto hard times. After Gerstner came to IBM on April 1, 1993, the company remained in its dismal state because, as Charlie Brown said, a large corporation can only turn as fast as a large oil tanker. It would take Gerstner time, too, to turn Big Blue around. How he did that has become a mythical tale of success. With the passage of time, we can more dispassionately explore his achievements, the topic of chapter 17.

17 HOW IBM WAS RESCUED, 1993–1994

Fixing IBM was all about execution.
—LOU GERSTNER[1]

IBM WAS A lucky firm. When John Akers fell from grace, the board of directors announced that it would start a worldwide search for a new chairman/CEO and that it would get the job done in 90 days. That triggered a frenzy of press coverage, with Wall Street analysts pontificating about what had to be done and others opining on who that individual should be, all leaving customers and IBM's employees hopeful, curious, confused, anxious, but engaged. In the spring of 1993, one would have been hard pressed to find any company that received as much attention from the business press as IBM. Conversations between IT vendors and their customers invariably included speculation about IBM's hunt for a knight in shining armor. Investors were the most hopeful, concluding that "finally" IBM's board was doing its job. Customers had become less dependent on IBM over the previous decade, so they frequently took a more distant interest in the IBM drama. Competitors knew IBM was wounded but not down for the count. Perhaps the interest was also a result of its being such a rare event. In any given year, only 3.8 percent of all CEOs were fired, fewer if the board was large, heavily staffed with the firm's employees, and if the CEOs had close social contacts with board members, three features of IBM's boards.[2]

IBMers had the most at stake. They eagerly anticipated a change in leadership. Some hoped for a "fresh face" from outside who could "shake things up, kick out the old guard," and give the company direction, because the majority felt IBM was adrift or, worse, about to go out of business. Few knew how true that last observation had become within the inner circle of IBM's most senior executives. Executives were at personal risk of losing their jobs. Many were leaving IBM on their own, as were employees at lower levels, some forced out, others having given up on the firm. But most IBMers were simply anxious, knowing their futures were insecure.

Many parts of the company had almost come to a halt, as people traded rumors and gossip for untold hours each day, while others took matters into their own hands. Open management positions took longer to fill, while some employees took the initiative to address their local situation without seeking the usual permissions of old. For example, in the sales organization in Wisconsin, over 500 employees lacked a clear purpose. A handful created a consulting practice within the firm to sell strategy consulting. Their practice proved successful; the IBM payroll system kept paying them, and it took 18 months before anyone figured out that this "rogue" practice existed. Others had done the same elsewhere until Corporate finally began to corral all of these entities into what became known as the IBM Consulting Group. Product groups kept manufacturing goods and pushing them out to market while not introducing new ones from late 1992 until the first half of 1993. People went through the paces. The IBM community lacked a shared sense of what the company needed to do. American employees, raised in a culture that included decisive leaders and a tradition of personally taking charge of their destinies, hoped for a new leader, not just a new CEO. European and Japanese employees, while more secure in their jobs because of local labor laws, were also anxious, although their management tamped down their fears. American managers seemed frozen in the glare of a fast-moving train wreck headed in their direction.

IBM got its new leader, Louis V. Gerstner Jr., on time. He was a good fit for this moment in IBM's history. He rapidly formulated a plan for revitalizing IBM, executing a turnaround with a combination of long-serving IBM managers and new ones he brought into the company. He persuaded IBMers to go along with his moves and introduced a new, if blunt, style of management (some called him "rude" and "brutal"), needed to "urgently" (his word) fix IBM. There was no time for the polite, calm manner of a Frank Cary, John Opel, or John Akers. Gerstner managed like Watson Sr., acting with confidence, with a will intolerant of dissent, and intensely impatient for action. Probably unknown to him, he resurrected the autocratic, centralized leadership culture of pre-1956 IBM. He overcame obstacles and pushed IBMers to success before their rivals could rally. How did all of that happen so quickly, essentially in two years? Most turnarounds in larger enterprises took closer to a decade or more. One could argue that IBM's current turnaround—called a "transformation" in polite business language—had been under way either since 2014 (the CEO's perspective) or for closer to a decade (the view more widely held by employees), so answering that question is immediately important.

Because he was new to IBM, we introduce Gerstner and why he appealed to the board, and then examine his biography. The hunt for Gerstner was a highly visible event in the business world, so the search for a new CEO is discussed next, shedding light on how corporations recruit leaders. The chapter then shifts to a detailed discussion of the company's plans for recovery under Gerstner and how these were implemented, and concludes with an assessment of results, which ranged from financial success to significant changes in IBM's culture. This chapter presents a blow-by-blow account of a successful turnaround.

For this narrative, we have the benefit of the leading protagonist—Gerstner—having written his memoirs, providing insights into his thinking.[3] Although his book must be used with the usual caution historians apply to such publications, the historical record aligns closely with his version. In part, I think that is because when he wrote his book, other publications had already appeared based on wider sets of interviews and press coverage that he could draw on, including investigatory journalism. Such evidence makes it possible to provide more balance, for example, by demonstrating that he faced opponents to his proposed changes, a criticism he barely mentioned in his account. His is the only quasiofficial primary source we have for the period, as archival records remain closed, and no senior or middle managers of the 1990s have yet commented publicly on the period.

A PERSPECTIVE ON GERSTNER

Gerstner had acquired useful experience that taught him how to resuscitate faltering companies and then put them on a trajectory for financial growth and expansion. He acquired this know-how in various situations as a consultant, then as a senior manager at McKinsey, but more importantly through his subsequent work at American Express with credit cards and retail financial systems, and finally at RJR Nabisco with manufacturing and more branding. These were the decisive events preceding his arrival at IBM. He succeeded at each of these assignments, and when added to what he did at IBM, he became a darling of Wall Street and the subject of numerous profiles and two books.

He became as good a CEO as either Watson Sr. or Tom Jr. The trajectory on which he set IBM continued essentially unchanged for nearly a quarter century, marked by expanding revenues from services and software and a long, gradual retreat from the sale of hardware. He introduced more changes to IBM's corporate culture than any previous CEO had since Watson Jr. Part of his legacy involved criticism by long-term IBMers who thought changing IBM's values, as embodied in its Basic Beliefs, was a colossal mistake,[4] but Gerstner argued that he intentionally changed many of IBM's old ways of doing things, returning IBM to the core values embraced by the Watsons, such as a fierce commitment to customer service, excellence in sales, and purposeful actions as opposed to blind adherence to processes and rules.

SO WHO WAS LOU GERSTNER?

Gerstner's friends and colleagues said he was intelligent, energetic, and ambitious at every turn in his life, from competing in sports in high school to chalking up excellent grades in high school, college, and at the Harvard Business School. When he came to IBM, he did not look the part of an executive, as he was short and stocky, built like an aging football player. Smiling did not come naturally to him; neither did small talk. He seemed impatient and became legendary at IBM for resisting long-winded slide presentations or "corporate-speak." IBMers close to him thought that he

Figure 17.1
Louis V. Gerstner Jr., while CEO and chairman of the board of IBM in the 1990s.
Photo courtesy of IBM Corporate Archives.

behaved rudely; others found him a bit frightening but refreshing. Friends saw that much of that behavior was already evident by the time Gerstner was a teenager, while his success as an adult reinforced his confidence and forceful style. Raised in a close-knit Catholic family, he exhibited a work ethic and a "no nonsense" approach to school. He enjoyed sports as a student and before college adhered to strict household rules. Gerstner held to his Catholic beliefs throughout his working career.

Louis V. Gerstner Jr. was born on March 1, 1942, the second of four sons. His parents, Louis V. and Marjorie Gerstner, raised him in Mineola,

New York, where his father worked as the night traffic manager at the Schaefer brewery. His mother worked at the registrar's office at a nearby community college and as a real estate agent. She lived a long life, passing away at the age of 96 in 2013, so she witnessed her son succeed at IBM. In the 1950s, Mineola was a small, working-class community in Nassau County on Long Island, on the fringe of New York City. Gerstner attended a local Catholic high school, for which he retained affection as an adult, donating money to it over the years. His teachers, many of whom were priests, maintained strict rules of behavior. The school environment taught him to excel. The oldest of the four boys, Dick Gerstner (1939–2012), also had the same education and went on to a full career at IBM, which brought him close to being a contender for the top job in the late 1980s before illness cut short his work. Years later, he learned that he had suffered a severe case of Lyme disease, a poorly understood illness afflicting many IBMers in the Connecticut-New York area in the 1980s.

Lou Gerstner chose not to attend a Catholic university, accepting a scholarship to Dartmouth in Hanover, New Hampshire. He majored in engineering and earned a reputation for being diligent. Gerstner chose a career in business, so upon graduating magna cum laude, he enrolled in the MBA program at the Harvard Business School. Graduating in 1965, he joined the prestigious management consulting firm of McKinsey and Company in New York. In management consulting, then as now, one had to learn a disciplined way to become a quick study of a client's business and its issues and problems, and be able to develop and recommend specific actions to address them.[5] Gerstner was a natural for that kind of activity and over the next decade did good work, established a network of contacts, and rose rapidly within the highly competitive world of McKinsey. He was admired for his work and talent, but colleagues also thought him brash. One McKinsey partner recalled that Gerstner "did have this tendency to boast and to brag ... he can't help it," perhaps a response to those blue bloods in the firm by a young man in a hurry who came from a more modest social background.[6]

At the tender age of 28, Gerstner made principal (1970), and more quickly than his peers he became a director at the firm. It was in those two roles that his later famous confrontational, blunt, impatient style became most evident. This, combined with his penchant for working diligently, served him well at IBM. Part of how he succeeded at IBM involved behaving like a McKinsey consultant, asking questions, listening, understanding issues, and recommending solutions—and, because he was in charge at IBM, implementing his own solutions. Gerstner married a southerner from Danville, Virginia, while working at McKinsey. They had a boy and a girl, and Gerstner retained a firm commitment to his family even when challenged by the long hours of work at IBM.

Gerstner's career took off in 1978, when he accepted an executive position at American Express to run its credit card business. There he gained senior management experience, learned who he could trust and work with, and learned how to apply his analytical approach to issues. He gained a reputation for being a "control freak." Despite competition from Visa and MasterCard, he introduced new credit cards and services and, important for the IBM story, modernized computing infrastructures. His relations with IBM's account team became strained as the complex transformation of his company's major IT applications unfolded, and in the process Gerstner had his first taste of how IBM operated. Frustrated at his inability to move up quickly enough at American Express, largely because there were others already ahead of him, he became restless.

On March 13, 1989, RJR Nabisco announced that Lou Gerstner had been hired as chairman and CEO, a position he held for four years. His move shocked friends, colleagues, and Wall Street, as his departure was considered a significant loss for American Express. In his new job, he dealt with the four Cs of the business: cookies, crackers, candies, and cigarettes. He honed his branding skills, learned how to reduce by half a monstrous corporate debt of $29 billion, and learned how to repopulate top echelons of the company with fresh leaders. His predecessors left him a company in disarray, but he was able to improve the business. He learned how to reshape corporate bureaucracy, launching a fundamental corporate restructuring. He reportedly commented that the exercise had been "traumatic" for him, "like crossing the Sahara. It just goes on and on."[7] The cookie business was fine; the cigarette part stabilized, and in the process Gerstner improved the quality of the iconic Winston, Camel, and emerging Salem products. If Gerstner thought selling "cigs" and cookies required creative management, a bigger challenge would be a firm in worse shape, larger, and known to everyone: IBM.

FINDING LOU GERSTNER

If Gerstner seemed well prepared to take on the IBM challenge, someone first had to recruit him. When we last left IBM's board, its members had woken up to the fact that they had not properly supervised senior management, removed John Akers and his CFO, Frank A. Metz Jr. (b. 1934), and announced the search for a new CEO. For that, it needed a plan and a team. The board set up a search committee and then hired two executive search firms. James E. Burke led the process for the board, while every major business publication and all of Wall Street focused unbridled attention on the search. How do you find someone to take over an iconic firm on the brink of going out of business? How do you find someone with enough prestige and experience willing to take on such a risky mess, one that could probably lead to the dismantling of a great corporation with all the public embarrassment that would accompany that calamity? Who would hundreds of thousands of employees follow, given their frustrated, mad mood about everything? Internal candidates were nonstarters because so many were seen as part of the problem at IBM. Robert J. "Bob" Labant, 47 years old and in charge of sales, was not well regarded by his sales organization, particularly by his branch managers; the more respected James A. Cannavino, a year older, ran the troubled PC Division; and none of the other product executives had the right credentials.

From the outset, the board favored an outsider, even though Burke had openly informed IBM employees he would consider an internal candidate. Rumormongers and the press had a field day suggesting who was being considered, or should be. Their lists included all the industry stars of the day: Robert M. Kavner (Compaq), Ben Rosen (GE), Jack Welch (GE, the dean of American CEOs at the time), Bill Gates (Microsoft), George Fisher (Motorola), John A. Young (H-P), Ross Perot (EDS), John Sculley (Apple), and Morton Meyerson (Perot Systems), to mention the most obvious. The search committee had a list of over 100 potential candidates, reached out to many, but found no takers, even among second-rank candidates. All were Americans. Among the luminaries, there were few turnaround artists, and that was what IBM really needed, not a technology wizard from Silicon Valley as so frequently recommended by industry watchers.

Back in January, Burke had contacted Gerstner but to no avail. As time passed, Burke circled back to Gerstner. One of the search firms, Heidrich & Struggles, now found Gerstner more willing to consider the position. Gerstner began to think he could manage one more enterprise, and IBM would be an enormous step up from RJR Nabisco. Timing was excellent, as he could exercise his RJR stock options, worth $22.5 million. His 54-year-old brother, Richard (Dick), had been at IBM for his entire career, having recently run IBM's operations in Asia and the Personal Computer Division, so he had a source for trusted insight.

The search intensified, with Lou Gerstner meeting in secret for an hour and a half with Paul Rizzo of IBM, who Gerstner knew and admired, and Jim Burke on February 24 at the Park Hyatt hotel in Washington, D.C.. Gerstner asked many questions. In his memoirs, he reported that the conversation "was very sobering. IBM's sales and profits were declining at an alarming rate. More important, its cash position was getting scary. We went over each product line." Gerstner concluded that "the odds were no better than one in five that IBM could be saved."[8] At the time, he was Burke's only lead for the job, and the 90 days were clicking by, with the press speculating every day about finding Akers's replacement. IBM's employees wanted to discuss nothing else but the hunt. The firm seemed to have come to a halt, floating in some suspended animation.

Burke even used the most ego-flattering argument to Gerstner that "You owe it to America to take the job."[9] He agreed a few days later. Now Burke had to convince board members that Gerstner would be their savior. Some questioned whether he was the best that could be had, and a few were concerned, perhaps, that they would likely become casualties. Burke remarked later that, "Lou was tougher than nails. Hard things needed to be done, and I knew he could do them. We needed somebody who was by instinct, training, and interest very strategic in his thinking. Everybody knew that was one of Lou's hallmarks. He thinks strategically about everything."[10] Word got out about his style. People seemed intimidated when he swept into meetings with an entourage. As one analyst put it, people were not afraid of Akers but they were afraid of Gerstner.[11]

By the third week of March, the press had sniffed out that Gerstner was the target; an intensely private man, he kept mum. When the *Wall Street Journal* reported on March 24 that he was going to be IBM's next leader, it was a done deal. The usual haggling over his contract received considerable public attention in late March, to the annoyance of some IBM employees. He was taking care of the details of his compensation, as he should. After he retired from IBM in 2002, the issue came up again when reports surfaced that his compensation totaled $500 million to $600 million. By then, most employees thought Gerstner was worth the price because he had saved the company. With his acceptance of the job, the "media circus" ended.

What the press and employees did not know at the time (1993) was that the "haggling" included far more important issues, notably Gerstner's range of authority. He wanted to be named both CEO and chairman. He questioned Akers's strategy of breaking up the company and wanted support for an alternative course of action. He wanted to change the membership of the board, obviously a very sensitive subject. Board members knew they were ending their sinecures. With those issues resolved, IBM had its new leader.[12] When on March 26, 1993, John F. Akers and Jim Burke introduced IBM's new CEO to the world, the company had not given up all its old ways or sense of dignity. The dismissed Akers had to stand up before the world and say, "I'm pleased to turn over leadership of IBM to Lou Gerstner, a proven, effective leader who will accelerate IBM's drive to improve competitiveness and profitability."[13] Gerstner and his new crew had yet to dampen IBM's corporate-speak.[14]

DEVELOPING AN EMERGENCY CORPORATE RESCUE PLAN

By 1998, when IBM's recovery had long been completed, a bit of the old hubris returned in lengthy slide presentations explaining how IBM turned around. Looking at the slides today, one would think that on April 1,

1993, his first day on the job, Gerstner arrived at Corporate headquarters in the old building in Armonk with a comprehensive plan that he merely had to execute flawlessly. Decks entitled "Reinventing IBM" had the classic classroom case study style: The Case for Change, The Strategy, The Results, and The New Paradigm. Few IBMers took them seriously. Only at conferences did someone trot out such presentations, because customers expressed interest in how IBM's survival had unfolded. The implication was that IBM could help others do the same. On day one, it was not clear how to resuscitate IBM. We have Gerstner's own memoirs as Exhibit A as evidence of the lack of clarity, of the need to continually invent. Recovery was as much an act of discovery and invention as of the sense of the new CEO and others around him that the company needed to stop hemorrhaging cash and profits and to identify and execute actions that played to its strengths.

One day during Gerstner's first month on the job, when he got into the back seat of his chauffeur-driven IBM company car to go to work, there sat 79-year-old Thomas J. Watson Jr. He lived across the street from Gerstner. As Gerstner told the story, "He was animated and, perhaps better stated, agitated. He said he was angry about what had happened to 'my company.' He said I needed to shake it up 'from top to bottom' and to take whatever steps were necessary to get it back on track." He urged Gerstner to move quickly, to be bold.[15] During his first 90 days at IBM, Gerstner met with his key executives, learned about each part of the business, spoke at town hall meetings, issued messages of calm, delivered measured calls to take action, and met with customers. He was introducing himself to Big Blue. He quickly came to several conclusions: that IBM had to stop spending so much, ensure 1994 was a profitable year, and convince customers that the company was "back serving their interests, not just pushing 'iron' [mainframes] down their throats to ease our short-term financial pressures," complete the "right-sizing" started by Akers, and develop a business strategy.[16]

Gerstner began to build his own team of executives, recruited from American Express, Nabisco, and elsewhere. The most crucial for the turnaround was Jerome B. "Jerry" York (1938–2010), just shy of 55 years of age, who was then chief financial officer at Chrysler Corporation. York joined IBM in late April, not even a month after Gerstner.

York came in to analyze the byzantine and confusing financials of IBM, find near-term opportunities to lower costs, and help "right size" the company. He had worked at GM and Ford as both a line executive and in manufacturing, and had experience cutting costs. An intense, short, small man, often profane (unique among senior IBM executives before he came), he was a high-energy manager. York willingly used fear as a tool, did not hesitate to fire people, and was a severe disciplinarian. If Gerstner was impatient, York was flagrantly so. Over the next year, he turned over every carpet at IBM looking for inefficiencies in order to understand in detail the company's finances and to find opportunities to implement changes. He was more of a chief operating officer than a CFO, and he took the brunt of the "tough guy" heat from employees and others off Gerstner. It was York who determined which groups of employees needed to be laid off and under what terms, and what lines of business needed to be starved or fed, working closely with Gerstner. He did as much as anyone at IBM to turn around the company.

Gerstner needed to fix IBM's terrible image, so his first hire was David B. Kalis (b. 1947). Kalis had a mustache (unusual among IBM executives) and was a strapping, imposing individual, tall next to Gerstner. He had grown up in Ohio, considered becoming a Catholic priest, served in the Peace Corps, and had a reputation for hard, thorough staff work. One colleague commented that, "David's very good at sensing where the land mines are."[17] Gerstner pulled Kalis's predecessor at IBM, Mary Lee Turner (b. 1945), out of her job as the corporate communications executive after a negative article on IBM appeared in the *Wall Street Journal.* She literally was shipped off to faraway China. Kalis was "incredibly rude and unforgiving," noted a journalist.[18] His job was to protect Gerstner from the press and to restore the company's image, tasks he executed with speed and professionalism. He was IBM's first professional marketing executive.

Gerstner also brought in Abby F. Kohnstamm (b. 1954), his executive assistant at American Express in 1986 and 1987, as his chief marketing officer, where she would serve for 12 years. At American Express, Kohnstamm developed a reputation for being smart and aggressive, and got along with Gerstner. When she joined IBM, she was 39 years old, unassuming and genial, in sharp contrast to the louder, more intimidating other new hires. Her father, Charles Francis (1924–2009), had worked at IBM from 1957 to 1987, becoming the company's senior advertising executive, essentially the role she now had, though her title was different. One of Francis's claims to fame was the development of the Charlie Chaplin PC ad campaign. Kohnstamm's claim would be the consolidation of all of IBM's myriad advertising efforts, run individually out of each product division, into one global cohesive and integrated initiative using the Ogilvy and Mather agency. She joined IBM on May 1, as part of David Kalis's team; later she reported directly to Gerstner.

The final early major hire was someone to work on IBM's personnel issues: to manage layoffs, create incentives that motivated employees to become more results oriented and competitive, and align compensation with business objectives, all while helping to create a new corporate culture absent lifetime employment. For that task, Gerstner turned to Gerald "Gerry" Czarnecki (pronounced *char*-nuh-kee) (b. 1940). He had a background in general business management in the banking industry. Most important, he had experience restructuring a large organization, Honolulu Federal. There, he cut the bank's staff by a third while improving its revenues and customer services. He also had been an IBM customer. He had to do at IBM what he had done at Honolulu Federal: downsize while protecting what worked well. His casual, more unstructured style of managing led to clashes with York, who cared not a whit about IBM's corporate culture. As one reporter put it, "Czarnecki was all psychologist but no drill sergeant. And IBM needed tough love." That was an interesting assessment, since Czarnecki had been a U.S. Army officer in the early 1960s.[19]

With his team settling in, Gerstner turned to assuring Wall Street, IBMers, and stockholders that the first steps were to control costs and restart normal product and selling activities. At his first annual IBM shareholders meeting, held at the end of his first month in office, he heard complaints about his board and company. Gerstner realized that he would have to start replacing board members. The press clamored for a vision. They and Wall Street wanted a roadmap. The media made much about a comment he made that the last thing IBM needed was a vision. He was all about execution, but he began making decisions. One of his first was to reduce the price of mainframes, even though it meant losing revenue precisely when he needed more cash, because he concluded that IBM relied too much on mainframes for revenue and not enough on other end products. Quickly, however, sales of mainframes improved sufficiently to hurt IBM's rivals. Tied to that decision, Gerstner was persuaded by senior IBM technology executives that moving from bipolar to CMOS technology for the S/390 mainframe would reduce the cost of the computer while not sacrificing profits. Either the technology would deliver as promised or the mainframe business was over. It worked. Each subsequent year, IBM enjoyed double-digit increases in the amount of computing customers acquired, thanks to the twin decisions involving pricing and technology.

That same spring, Gerstner paid attention to the role of the management committee, the council of senior executives at the pinnacle of IBM's contention system. It still met once or twice weekly and had six members. Gerstner decided to kill it in April, a casualty of his penchant to make decisions personally. Gerstner's take was that "the rise and fall of the Management Committee symbolized the whole process of rigor mortis that had set in at IBM," but "the problem was that over time, IBM people learned how to exploit the system to promote their own agendas," leading to a culture of "prearranged consensus" worked out by the division staffs. So the management committee only saw one proposal, and thus its role had evolved into "a formality—a rubberstamp approval."[20] In time, Gerstner learned that the company was too big and complicated for him to run, so he created a new management committee, one that continues to the present.

IBM's revenue kept declining. Gerstner was instilling a sense of urgency to "right size" the firm and was encouraging executives and managers to make decisions, take actions, and hold each other accountable. By the fall of 1993, his sense of urgency and energy had spread through most parts of IBM, even though the company's financial performance had yet to reflect the change. By July, Gerstner had already stepped up his efforts, because the bleeding continued, employees were still impatient for him to set a direction, and the media was getting ready to assess his first 100 days. Each circumstance called for substance. In his words, he made decisions to "keep the company together, change our fundamental economic model, reengineer how we did business," and "sell underproductive assets in order to raise cash."[21] He was moving to the specific.

While several of his decisions reflected normal practice in such situations, such as selling assets to raise cash, one stood above all others: his decision to reverse Akers's strategy of breaking up the company. Gerstner later wrote that it was, "I believe, the most important decision I ever made—not just at IBM, but in my entire business career. I didn't know then exactly how we were going to deliver on the potential of the unified enterprise, but I knew that if IBM could serve as the foremost integrator of technologies, we'd be delivering extraordinary value."[22]

A quarter of a century later, it remains his defining, crucial contribution to IBM. If one were to make up a list of five or less "bet-your-company" decisions made by an IBM CEO, this would be one of them. It would sit next to Watson Sr.'s decisions to focus on tabulators and punch cards and to keep expanding products and sales during the Great Depression, and Watson Jr.'s decision to build the S/360. Perhaps one might also add Frank Cary's decision to develop the IBM PC as a skunk works. No decision made by an IBM CEO since Gerstner rises to that level of strategic importance.[23]

What was the actual decision? Beginning in July, more informally than in some grand pronouncement, Gerstner, in his own words, "began telling customers and employees that IBM would remain one unified enterprise." In his memoirs, he wrote that, "The response from our executive team was mixed—great joy from those who saw the company as being saved, and bitter disappointment from those who saw a breaking apart as their personal lifeboat to get off the *Titanic*."[24] It took the better part of several months before the wider IBM community realized what he had done.[25] IBMers thought keeping the company together was manifestly the right thing to do. They criticized Akers for doing the opposite, more than for any other action that he took. One would have been hard put to find a customer who thought breaking up IBM was a good strategy for the firm, let alone in their own best interests. If it seemed to be the intuitive grasp of the obvious by Gerstner, remember that he did not come up in IBM, so he had to learn who was for or against Akers's strategy.[26] Gerstner and his new executives would have been partially insulated from the passion over the issue in the industry, other than for the snippets of insight gained from other company executives, e-mails employees sent to Gerstner that he may or may not have read, or the few hundred customers he talked with.

The transition back to IBM's historic enterprise-wide services and coordination within IBM took time to implement, but because there was so much support for that approach, particularly at the divisional and field levels, it went more quickly than it might have otherwise. But why was the change needed? As computing came in the 1950s, users needed a vendor to offer a complete package of mainframes, peripheral equipment, software, installation, maintenance, training, and planning for future uses. Their primary need centered on IT integration. By the late 1980s, thousands of companies were offering specialized equipment and software. That reality forced users to integrate all these new IT machines and software with their existing computing systems, often using new products not available from IBM.

As we saw in earlier chapters, the retreat from vertical integration by IT vendors became a primary source of IBM's long-term decline, because the company, not just Akers, began thinking more about offering products without their full integration, leading to fragmentation of its product lines. IBM thus contributed to the fragmentation occurring in the computer industry in the late 1980s and early 1990s and, by extension, to Akers's idea that IBM should likewise be fractured into independent businesses by type of product.

Customers also contributed to the shift. Many wanted to reduce IBM's stranglehold on the market, which they knew propped up higher prices and profits for the company at their expense.

IBM's competitors encouraged this line of thinking and the "groupthink" about the wisdom of having more choices. Customer managers scattered about an enterprise sought distributed processing because they wanted to break up the centralized computing power of the CFO and their "glass houses." That meant shifting attention to telecommunications—not core to IBM's product offerings in the 1980s and early 1990s—and supporting products from various providers. To quote Gerstner, "IBM was slow, very slow, in delivering distributed computing," a gap filled quickly by start-up firms. Intel and Microsoft did the same with IBM. Customers wanted more competition in order to get better pricing and innovative products. Tens of thousands of vendors flooded the market. IBM's market shares declined, while the amount of computing installed rose. But now customers had to do what IBM had done for them for so many decades: serve as their own integrators. The cost of managing a company's computing ecosystem began rising as they hired necessary staff. The cost of hardware shrank as a percentage of a company's IT budget. Personnel expenses expanded sharply.

An IT industry secret at the time was the lack of technical standards to make machines and software from multiple vendors work together.[27] Everyone, including IBM, worked to create their own technical standards to block rivals. Think of today's power cords for an Apple device that cannot be used on a rival's and you begin to understand their problem.

Gerstner and a large swath of IBM understood that customers still needed an integrator. Gerstner wanted IBM to provide that integration, because it translated everyone's hardware and software into something of value, a service customers were willing to pay for. His thinking is worth recalling: "Given IBM's scale and broad-based capabilities, and the trajectories of the information technology industry, it would have been insane to destroy its unique competitive advantage and turn IBM into a group of individual component suppliers—more minnows in an ocean."[28] That is why his decision to keep IBM together was crucial. On that decision he could now build a recovery and convince IBMers to execute it. They would have their vision, their call to arms, and would be able to do what they did best, carry out specific tasks. That combination of factors and institutional skills helps explain why Gerstner could now fix IBM, using his surly new executive hires, increasingly confident that the majority of his employees supported the strategy, and that leveraged the core skills of the firm.

EXECUTING THE RECOVERY

In that same summer of 1993, Gerstner concluded that he had to change the business, which he told employees was good in bringing in $66 billion of revenue in a year—but it had cost $69 billion to do so. IBM's rivals were spending 31 cents to make one dollar of revenue, IBM 42 cents. That translated into a $7 billion expense problem. Gerstner was also reducing the price of mainframes. York advised the company to reduce expenses by $8.9 billion. Part of his plan called for the rapid, one-time dismissal of 35,000 employees over and above the 45,000 Akers had already eliminated. Gerstner defended the layoffs as "a matter of survival, not choice."[29] He told employees that this action would end the "Chinese water torture" of incremental layoffs that had so characterized the last several years. The company laid off the 35,000 in 1993. For a while, Gerstner's intention remained true, but by the second half of the 1990s, incremental layoffs came back as new skills were brought into the company, reigniting a personnel practice of continuous layoffs and hiring of new employees that intensified in the following decade, resulting in tens of thousands of additional dismissals and new hires.

New ways of reorganizing IBM's work emerged rapidly as a by-product of his thinking. Cost cutting just kept the lights on, the firm alive, but would not be sufficient for the longer term. At the time, most large enterprises had already concluded that their largest transnational processes, spanning across divisions, were too labor intensive, slow, bureaucratic, and expensive, such as for personnel, manufacturing, and purchasing. IBM was no exception. The fashion at the moment was "process reengineering," in which one completely reimagined how a specific process should operate to speed up work, improve quality, and reduce labor content. In the end, most successful reengineering projects resulted in substantial layoffs and more automation, yielding productivity increases in the range of 15 to 40 percent.[30]

IBM initiated similar efforts during Gerstner's tenure, although prior to his arrival, some work had started under the MDQ banner. York got the assignment to lower operating costs beyond his initial recommendations. Gerstner reported correctly that, "We were running inventory systems, accounting systems, fulfillment systems, and distribution systems that were all, to a greater extent or lesser degree, the mutant offspring of systems built in the early mainframe days and then adapted and patched together to fit the needs of one of twenty-four independent business units."[31] Examples

Figure 17.2
Jerome York, a leading architect of IBM's recovery in the 1990s. Photo courtesy of IBM Corporate Archives.

of redundancies and wasted efforts abounded. For example, instead of one chief information officer (CIO) for the firm, IBM had 128. CFOs proliferated all over the company, too. Each had their own unique systems, although they shared a modicum of practices. IBM did not have an integrated financial system (software) that rolled up all the charts of accounts into one set of books. To move from one division to another, an employee had to be dismissed by their current division, and hence moved off its books, before another one could acquire that individual, especially if he or she was moving from one country to another. So, a South African IBMer who had worked for the firm for 15 years, upon moving to London, for example, became a new employee of IBM U.K. and started the pension clock again. He was paid whatever the going rates were in Britain and received British IBM medical benefits.[32] Such circumstances were by-products of IBM's bureaucracy and earlier growth.

York moved quickly. At one point, he had 60 reengineering projects under way worldwide. These included core initiatives in hardware development, software, fulfillment, development of one global integrated supply chain, customer relationship management (CRM, where information on sales and forecasts resided), and an additional process to manage consulting services, largely in support of hardware and software. Many of York's reengineered processes, such as CRM, remained in use 20 years later. Others under development or redesign were considered enabling processes, such as for personnel, procurement, finance, management of real estate, and even one for information technology. It turned out that York was the impatient, detail-oriented executive to launch these initiatives.

IBM spent $4 billion annually just on IT, causing Gerstner to complain "yet we didn't have the basic information we needed to run our business," such as the ability for him to send out an e-mail to all employees at the same time.[33] IT staffs scrambled. By the end of 1995, IBM had saved $2 billion from upgrading its own IT operations and shutting down dozens of little-used data centers. Not since the early to mid-1960s had IBMers experienced a similar level of energy and urgency. To many it felt that IBM was finally fixing its problems. The plethora of IT had developed in all the divisions created over the years, which were encouraged to be independent, vertical operations. Of course, an IT company would be expected to serve itself with such tools, but as a consequence it reinforced barriers between divisions, such as between mainframes and PCs, and later, in the post-Akers era, between services and consulting. These barriers were as much operational as technical, since computing and processes were intertwined.

York pushed on other fronts, too, with Gerstner's blessing. IBM continued to reduce the amount of real estate it owned at an accelerated pace after 1993, such as by selling off those urban towers that every senior sales executive seemed to have. Even IBM's facility at 590 Madison Avenue in New York went on the block; IBM became a tenant for the few floors it needed. It reduced the number of training centers near New York from four to one. York even slashed the staff that managed real estate. Unproductive assets had to go, and that included much of the art collection started by Mr. and Mrs. Watson Sr. in the 1910s. The art collection, auctioned in 1995, generated $31 million in cash, but a few pieces were saved, such as portraits of IBM's previous CEOs, which soon graced the stairwell at a new, smaller corporate headquarters Gerstner built to replace the drab, large one, located on the same IBM campus in Armonk. He made it known that IBM was sending a message to its workforce that headquarters functions had to be smaller and leaner. An impressionist painting of a snowy Times Square with a Ford Model T car coming at you that used to hang in the living room at the IBM Homestead in Endicott now hung just outside the door of Gerstner's new office.[34] At the end of the 1990s, IBM reported that its reengineering activities saved it $10 billion.

Gerstner's most controversial sale involved the Federal Systems Division (FSD), which was sold to Loral Corporation in January 1994. It was also his biggest, generating $1.5 billion. Recall that this division did IT work for the U.S. government. Its employees were the ones who managed the development and use of software to put the first men on the moon in July 1969. They wrote the software for the FAA's air traffic control systems and did secret projects for the U.S. military and spy agencies, but it was always a low-margin business. At the time, many in IBM bemoaned the sale because there were so many individuals in the FSD that other consulting practices in IBM would have wanted when large swaths of the company were already moving toward more technical services. On the other hand, Gerstner's number one priority remained stopping the cash hemorrhaging, and this sale helped. In the second half of the 1990s, IBM began a long process of recreating many of the skills lost in the FSD sale, including establishing practices that today only service the U.S. government. Into the new millennium, that sale remained one of the most controversial actions taken by the Gerstner team.

Gerstner knew he had to explain to employees, and to a lesser extent to customers, what was being done and why, and to fend off continuous skepticism from Wall Street and the media. He had four messages to deliver. He created a certain amount of buzz that first summer with his initial message, in which he told reporters that, "What IBM needs right now is a series of very tough-minded, market-driven, highly effective strategies for each of its businesses—strategies that deliver performance in the marketplace and shareholder value. ... Now, the number-one priority is to restore the company to profitability." Second, IBM had to improve service to customers. Third, IBM would lead in the client server market and, fourth, be the full service provider, which came out of his thinking of keeping the company together.[35] The press and some Wall Street pundits did not see those comments as a vision, but IBMers, customers, and competitors did.

Observers of the company approved of Gerstner's immediate cost-cutting measures, almost all of which he explained to IBMers before they read about them in the press. He was less interested in playing the blame game and more in getting employees urgently fixing problems. However, he did not want to speak too openly about what was going on, he explained, "because I did not want our competition to see where we were going." IBM's key strategic decisions, all made in 1993 and 1994, included keeping IBM together, revitalizing the mainframe through new technologies and capabilities, remaining in the semiconductor business, preserving and leveraging R&D to get products out of the labs, and making sure that all that the company did reflected what customers believed was of value to them. Gerstner reminded employees that IBM's problems were theirs, not just Armonk's, to fix.

For the rest of his time as CEO, Gerstner regularly wrote short notes to employees in which he explained what IBM was doing. These were not stiff missives filled with platitudes and corporate-speak. One example from his first week on the job, discussing the issue of layoffs, set the tone: "I am acutely aware that I arrived at a painful time when there is a lot of downsizing. I know it is painful for everyone, but we all know, too, that it is necessary. I can only assure you that I will do everything I can to get this painful period behind us as quickly as possible, so that we can begin looking to our future and to building our business."[36] That candor, known in the company as "straight talk," never appeared in a note from Akers to employees.

By the end of the year, Gerstner was also rebuilding his management committee and restocking the board. Like Watson Sr. before him, he understood the need to have a capable board but one that would not slow him down. By the end of 1994, only 8 of 18 members of the board remained from the prior year. In 1993 and 1994, and all through the 1990s, IBM did what one would expect under the circumstances: it initiated reorganizations, launched a new advertising campaign that spoke to the future of IBM and its technological prowess, eliminated many of the senior executives who had grown up with Akers, hired thousands of new employees with fresh skills, extended stock options down the organization to focus people's attention on generating revenue and profits, and personalized commitments and plans with personnel appraisals based on a combination of their own, their business unit's, and IBM's financial performance to promote individual responsibility and collaboration. Those changes triggered many changes to IBM's culture, discussed in chapter 18.

When did the hemorrhaging end? When did revenues start growing again? For shareholders, when did the world declare that IBM had recovered?

COUNTING IMMEDIATE RESULTS

The year 1993 remained miserable at IBM. No CEO could turn around such a severe situation in months, but the actions taken after Gerstner came in, along with the intense work by York and others, led to a rapid turnaround by the end of 1994. As 1995 began, it was not yet clear that the immediate crisis had been resolved; only the passage of time would lead people to conclude the corner had been turned. By the end of the year, the company's performance signaled that the recovery was yielding positive results, and by the end of 1996, IBM's improving performance had "legs." Table 17.1 can be viewed as a report card of Gerstner's first five years at IBM, with 1992's data included to demonstrate that things were so bad that the board finally had to push Akers out of the company. Most observers dwelled on the speed of the recovery—remarkable in itself—but the bigger story is the *depth* of the turnaround.

Gerstner stanched the bleeding of cash by laying off employees, selling assets, and spending less. Even ordering office supplies became a challenge in the second half of 1993. The earnings picture, value of the stock, and so forth were financial by-products of steps taken in 1993 and 1994. Controlling the cost of employees was then, as now, the biggest and quickest lever Corporate could pull. The data shows Gerstner and his team reduced the number of employees far more than the 35,000 he promised. Buried in the year-end number of employees in each year during his entire tenure through 2002 was the fact that IBM hired many new workers with such skills as business consulting and IT services. By the end of 1994, half of all IBMers on the payroll in 1987 were gone. Some were never replaced, while others were hired to do new things. The greatest number of dismissals and

Table 17.1
IBM's business performance, 1992–1997
(revenue, net income, and cash flow in billions of dollars)

Metric	1992	1993	1994	1995	1996	1997
Revenue	64.5	62.7	64.1	71.9	75.9	78.5
Net income (loss)	(5.0)	(8.1)	3.0	4.2	5.4	6.1
Earnings per share (dollars)	(2.2)	(3.6)	1.2	1.8	2.5	3.0
Cash flow from operations	6.3	8.3	11.8	10.7	10.3	8.9
Return on stockholders' equity (%)	(15.4)	(35.2)	14.3	18.5	24.8	29.7
Number of employees (thousands)	301.5	256.2	219.8	225.3	240.6	269.5
Stock price (year-end)	12.59	14.12	18.37	22.84	37.87	52.31

Source: IBM annual reports, also conveniently summarized in a series of charts in Louis V. Gerstner Jr., *Who Says Elephants Can't Dance? Inside IBM's Historic Turnaround* (New York: HarperBusiness, 2002), 356–362.

new hiring occurred in the United States and Great Britain, where labor laws were the most flexible in allowing firms to swap out employees. This transformation of the workforce made it possible for Gerstner and his team to change the company's culture, particularly from 1998 through 2002. Older employees retired, quit, or were laid off, so they were not there to resist the changes, midcareer IBMers were still able to adapt to new conditions and survive, while tens of thousands of newly hired workers had no experience with IBM's Watsonian culture.

IBM's changing corporate culture received considerable attention from the media in the 1990s and became the focus of a considerable portion of Gerstner's own memoirs. Gerstner realized that many of IBM's critics did not properly understand the company. He quickly realized that IBMers were not soft, lazy, or uncompetitive. He had a different take on the source of IBM's problems. He blamed "the run-away success of the System/360" because "when there's little competitive threat, when high profit margins and a commanding market position are assumed, then the economic and market forces that other companies have to live or die by simply don't apply." Then, "the company and its people lose touch with external realities, because what's happening in the marketplace is essentially irrelevant to the success of the company."[37] Another result, according to Gerstner, was that "IBM forgot that all the trappings of its culture … were a function of the franchise created by the System/360. It wasn't really the product of enlightened management or world-class processes."[38] IBM was its own ecosystem and while not impervious to competition, it acted almost as if it was. That was the trap Opel had fallen into.

Gerstner also had a second take on the culture: the effects of the antitrust suit of the 1970s, which affected everyone's behavior over that 13-year period of litigation. To make his point, he cited the example of how people spoke and wrote: "While IBM was subject to the suit, terms like 'market,' 'marketplace,' 'market share,' 'competitor,' 'competition,' 'dominance,' 'lead,' 'win,' and 'beat' were systematically excised from the written materials and banned at internal meetings." The same points were made by Usselman and Tedlow in chapters 14–16.[39] IBMers had used all of these phrases before the antitrust suit; all were normal terms found in business and had come back into use at IBM by the end of the 1990s. As Gerstner pointed out, if you could not even use that kind of language, what was "the dampening effect" on IBMers? It made them more cautious, less innovative and aggressive. Employees and Gerstner agreed on this point. By the time Gerstner came in, lawyers, paid to mitigate risks to employers, were having far too much say over decisions, from corporate strategic initiatives down to the negotiation of a routine sales contract between a sales employee and a customer. IBM's fighting spirit was drained out of its "gene pool" just as technology's constantly evolving form reared its head again with the arrival of open source operating systems such as Unix, which challenged IBM's proprietary approach to technologies.[40] As early as 1994, Gerstner and his senior executives had to respond to such changes in the marketplace, which made it possible for IBM to grow its profitability from 1995 onward.

A book could be written about how Gerstner responded to the company's culture, with which he saw many flaws. He admired its integrity "in a way I've never seen in any other company,"[41] but he concluded that the Basic Beliefs no longer worked. Just as they were central to what had come before him, they were central to what he did differently. He thought "superior customer service" evolved from focusing on the needs of customers to making sure IBM's machines worked well. Many IBMers in sales and field engineering disagreed with his assessment, but it was his view that stimulated his actions. "Excellence in everything we do" had become "an obsession with perfection," evolving into "a stultifying culture and a spider's web of checks, approvals, and validation that slowed decision making to a crawl."[42]

The third Basic Belief, "respect for the individual," was the most sacred of all of IBM's beliefs. To the present, it still resonates, and it was the belief Gerstner had to transform the most. His take on the notion was that "it helped spawn a culture of entitlement where the individual didn't have to do anything to earn respect—he or she expected rich benefits and lifetime employment simply by virtue of having been hired."[43] Most long-term IBMers disagreed with his assessment, as many had invested decades in their careers, often working 50 to 100 hour weeks, especially in the 1960s and 1970s. He never won that argument; however, he did have a point that was often overlooked. As he explained, "The real problem was not that employees felt they were entitled. They had just become accustomed to immunity from things like recessions, price wars, and technology changes." So, it worked against them, for example, with some employees not being paid as well as their counterparts in other industries or as much as the best-rated workers.

Gerstner concluded that employees were often doing whatever they wanted. He certainly saw that with division heads not concurring on one issue or another. As he was quoted as saying earlier, there were too many regulations and checks to allow people to do as they willed, but he fired senior executives who got in his way. Such "hangings" were made known through word of mouth. So, Gerstner got the assessment only partially correct, and as a result it remained a source of low-intensity criticism of his actions in the late 1990s, particularly when he attempted to change the pension program so much that U.S. employees sued IBM, winning their case that the changes were a form of age discrimination just to save the corporation $250 million in costs. At the end of his tenure, he had concluded that corporate culture was the central source of strengths and weaknesses in any company, and managing it was the most difficult, yet essential, component of any corporate recovery.

Outsiders at the time held different opinions about IBM's culture. Most analysts thought IBM was bloated, that it needed to lay off more employees and become more competitive. While Gerstner, too, thought the culture needed changing, he was driven by different insights. He added a sense of urgency, mimicking IBM's style of operating in the 1960s more than that in the early 1990s in order to complete the transformation before the company went out of business. An expanded interest in shareholder value existed outside the firm. Reporters and industry analysts dutifully reported on every benefit taken away from employees, and the rise of resistance against those actions in the 1990s, especially in IBM's U.S. factories. Activities at the Endicott plant drew particular attention, where union organizing began and failed but triggered much debate in IBM company towns, even spawning an underground newspaper, the *Resistor*.[44]

The level of press coverage remained frequent and detailed. For example, a *Business Week* article published on October 4, 1993, just five months after Gerstner arrived at IBM, accurately described the problem of continually rising costs at IBM despite employee layoffs. "One day, York walked into Gerstner's office with some surprising numbers," the article noted, showing that while employee costs were dropping quickly, other expenses were rising by up to $7 billion. It added, "Too much inventory was being written off. Benefits, warranty, and purchasing expenses were rising" beyond what York thought normal: at IBM, 7 percent of revenue, versus an average of about 2 percent at other U.S. companies. IBM's CEO jumped "off his chair."[45] Gerstner often commented that press coverage was so intense that changing the wallpaper in an IBM ladies' bathroom became headline news. *Business Week* detailed steps taken by York and others to identify problems with inventory control, providing a level of detail not ordinarily made public. How did the story end? Long after the publication of the article, inventory management practices had improved across the firm, and with the implementation of a nearly 10-year project to manage IBM's worldwide procurement, too. The company never again wanted to be caught with a warehouse of unsellable PC Jr.s or old parts.

The highly regarded publication *The Economist* credited Gerstner with compelling employees to focus more on customer solutions than he thought they had prior to his arrival, stating, "Now after five years of purgatory under Lou Gerstner," that focus laid out the promise of permanent recovery.[46] The *Washington Post* paid less attention to IBM's culture and more to Gerstner's strategy and, most pointedly, to his decision to keep the company whole and to the massive cost cutting and write-offs executed by York.[47] In an article published by the *Harvard Business Review* in 1995, highly respected professor John P. Kotter published a list of steps a CEO needed to take, without skipping any, in order to engineer a turnaround. IBM was not mentioned by name, since Kotter was trying to generalize about his observations of some 100 companies. However, Gerstner's turnaround was the biggest, noisiest, and most studied one at that time, along with the less successful one at General Motors. Unless Kotter was living in a monastery in the middle of the Sahara Desert, he would have had on his mind IBM, and its CEO, an alumnus of his business school at Harvard.

Kotter's list serves as a near mirror summary of Gerstner's actions: establish a sense of urgency; form a powerful coalition of senior executives to lead the execution of change; create a vision (Gerstner said he had none, but it was obvious he did); communicate it (he thought in terms of telling people what needed to be done and why); empower others to execute the plan; implement short-term wins, such as what Gerstner did in selling off FSD and lowering the price of mainframes; consolidate improvements and continue making changes; and institutionalize new approaches.[48]

The turnaround, as remarkable as it appeared, reflected a broad recovery that had *started before* Gerstner came to IBM but that he and his executives accelerated. He added new elements to it, such as changes in how IBM treated its employees and what new businesses it entered, all leading to growth.[49] Those steps called for reconnecting IBM back into the center of competition in an IT industry profoundly changing, as networking and soon the Internet became pervasive. To miss any of these changes would have returned IBM to its dark days of decline. How IBM avoided that fate is the subject of chapter 18, about the most recent phase in IBM's history, which began with Gerstner's second five-year term as chairman and remained IBM's trajectory for over two decades.

Before moving to that story, we can ask to what extent his immediate actions in 1993 and 1994 were unusual. Some were normal, such as bringing in his own team from outside of IBM and then combining them with other workers promoted from within—actions well documented for other companies.[50] Gerstner's blunt manner also was not unusual, except at IBM.[51] As CEOs in other successful turnaround cases found essential to understand, Gerstner realized that IBM's culture had become toxic, what Eric G. Flamholtz and Yvonne Randle, two students of corporate behavior, described as a "culture of arrogance" that dated to the 1980s but that we have shown in earlier chapters dated to the start of the 1970s.[52] It was crucial to address the problem of a culture gone wrong or, as they described it, when the mainframe constituency in IBM "had won the battle but lost the war" to control the company after Gerstner arrived.[53] Gerstner's reorganizations, necessary in his early months at IBM as tens of thousands of employees exited the company and later as he solidified how his management team wanted to serve their chosen markets, paralleled what IBM executives had done before. The two great differences emphasized in this chapter were the speed and urgency with which he addressed IBM's problems.

John F. Padgett and Walter W. Powell, two sociologists expert in the emergence of organizations and markets, when explaining how corporations reorganized, could have been describing what Gerstner and other executives did at IBM, including Akers, when they wrote, "All new organization forms, no matter how radically new, are combinations and permutations of what was there before," arguing that their evolution "is not a teleological progress toward some ahistorical (and often egocentric) ideal." Almost echoing Alfred D. Chandler Jr.'s thinking, Padgett and Powell state that the act of transforming an organization, and hence restructuring it, "is a thick and tangled bush of branchings, recombinations, transformations, and sequential path-dependent trajectories."[54] But what historians and other scholars need to consider also when studying how organizations change are the passion, urgency, and speed that a CEO manifests in what are otherwise well-documented actions. These three behaviors were essential elements in this story. Had they not been there, would Gerstner's behavior have been similar to that of Akers and thus ineffective? Akers did not have the passion or the speed, only the sense of urgency, and one without the other two was insufficient, as IBM's experience demonstrates.

The point of this last discussion is not to minimize what Gerstner did, because he did bring back IBM from the brink of disaster and, as we will see in chapter 18, made it thrive. At their core, these are monumental achievements for any CEO by any standard, which his peers, the media, and employees recognized at that time. Rather, the point here is to suggest that Gerstner's actions, and those of several hundred executives at IBM, fit patterns that historians, economists, management consultants, and sociologists have identified as reflecting familiar patterns of corporate behavior. Keep that in mind as we turn to what he did in the second half of his tenure, actions that mimicked many of Thomas Watson Sr.'s during the latter's first decade at C-T-R.[55]

Part IV

IBM IN THE
NEW CENTURY

18 A NEW IBM, 1995–2012

> Our greatest ally in shaking loose the past, as it turned out, was IBM's own precipitous collapse. I decided to keep the crisis front and center. ... I didn't want to lose a sense of urgency prematurely.
> —LOUIS V. GERSTNER JR., 2002[1]

> It is also consistent with our DNA that we have paid equal attention to the continual reinvention of IBM itself—most importantly, reexamining and applying our core values to how we run the company.
> SAMUEL J. PALMISANO, 2011[2]

IN THE WINTER of 1994–1995, December and January could never have been more different at IBM in any decade. In December, sales pushes hard to get equipment, software, and services projects purchased, installed, or completed to make their revenue targets. The fourth quarter generated more revenue than any other, because of the twin pressures of making "one's numbers" and tax laws in many countries concerning purchases of capital goods, such as computers. IBM's factory employees worked to get all machines that had been tested shipped to customers. Field engineering worked night and day, as well as weekends, to get everything possible installed to make their targets and to reinforce the accounting practice for recognizing revenue. Some salesmen stood vigilant in their offices until after 10 P.M. on December 31 to make sure a customer did not cancel an order at the eleventh hour. Weeks earlier, IBM's CFO called on Chairman Louis V. "Lou" Gerstner Jr. to review how the year's numbers should be reported, as the accountants already knew how much money IBM made and had several ways to report it. They were pleased with what they could report to Gerstner in December 1994. Then there was January. It was normal for employees to go on vacation. IBM announces its prior year's financial results and opines about the year ahead in the third or fourth week of January. December 1994 and January 1995, however, were different from prior years because Gerstner was in a hurry to transform IBM but was not sure if the efforts to "stop the bleeding" had taken hold. He set the tone that 1995 would not be a year to coast when, on January 9, he announced a reorganization of the company.

As we approach the present in IBM's history, we confront the lack of conventional sources, such as archives, and the fact that corporations work to block information about current operations from seeping out.[3] Such are the challenges we face in this chapter and chapters 19 and 20.[4] Here we describe the transition from crisis management in 1993–1994 to a period of expanding business. We then explore how IBM transformed into a services business. Because sales of hardware as the dominant source of revenue declined in this period, we look at how IBM responded to that circumstance. The 9/11 tragedy was an existential event that could not be ignored. The transition from the end of Gerstner's tenure to that of a new CEO was far different from what occurred in 1993. How that happened was as much a process of effective management as it was a reflection of old and new corporate norms. We offer an answer to the central question of how IBM transformed so much in such a short period of time. For most scholars and employees, almost all this story is new, as it extends beyond the chronological boundaries of earlier histories of IBM.[5]

TRANSITIONING FROM RECOVERY TO GROWTH

January was a good month for IBM. Only the PC business disappointed. Bill Gates had won the war for the desktop. OS/2 was a lost cause, although many in IBM still did not recognize that fact. Everything else was humming, and the company had billions of dollars. In the fall of 1994, Gerstner was figuring out the next phase in the company's activities, and that meant hunting for growth. One key decision involved emphasizing *services,* since someone had to pull together various technologies and integrate them. Customers looked to large IT firms to do that work, and IBM was well positioned to perform the task. Gerstner's decision increased services revenue during his tenure.

Gerstner arrived at a second conclusion, too: that computing was rapidly becoming more networked and distributed and, when the Internet became an obvious new tool for business to use in 1996–1998, he knew IBM had to be in the middle of that transition. That event called for open standards—contrary to company-proprietary standards—and few existed. Customers wanted to plug anything into anything, hence the need for "open" standards. In a networked world, the PC would decline in importance, because computing could be done on mainframes within a network, not just on a machine sitting on a desk. IBM had to plan for that eventuality. Its marketing campaign, "solutions for a small planet," built on the notion of IBM providing integrated services. As historian Steven W. Usselman observed, "The new emphasis restored sales and customer service to a preeminence they had not enjoyed since the days of the elder Watson."[6] How did IBM do that?

On January 24, 1995, the same day that IBM announced the previous year's revenues and earnings, Gerstner told employees and the public that, "We are beginning to win in the marketplace." He also announced changes at IBM. Over the previous year, he had worked out who among the long-term IBM executives were keepers and who needed to go. Worldwide sales and services, already reporting to veteran IBMer Ned C. Lautenbach (b. 1944), now would consist of three parts. Gerstner appointed a general manager for all of North America (United States and Canada), the highly experienced, tough-minded Robert "Bob" Stephenson (1938–2011), who most recently had run IBM's operations in Asia, and moved David M. Thomas (b. 1950) into Stephenson's old job, which suited his skills better than running the AS/400 business. In perhaps the most important change, Gerstner appointed Dennie M. Welsh (1943–2004) to run Global Services, which in those days handled the outsourcing business.

Robert "Bob" Dies (b. 1945?), also a highly respected executive within IBM, took over sales operations. Gerstner retained Nick Donofrio (b. 1947), a long-serving, respected engineering executive, and John Thompson (b. 1949) on his senior management team to run other hardware parts of the business. He kept two holdovers from the Akers period: Irving Wladawsky-Berger (b. 1945), an imaginative and articulate technology executive, to run the technical side of the mainframe product line, and a sales executive, Sam Palmisano (b. 1951), to head the PC business. Palmisano would eventually replace Gerstner as chairman. In late 1995, Gerstner brought in Bruce Harreld (b. 1951) as his senior vice president of strategy. This last appointment brought to IBM a high level of professionalism in the development of business strategy. In September, York left IBM, having concluded that his work in cost cutting was over. G. Richard "Rick" Thoman (b. 1945) took his place, becoming the first CFO in IBM's history with international experience. All these executives had to increase sales of hardware, software, and services. In the mid-1990s, IBMers viewed software largely as a PC opportunity, a footrace with Microsoft. Hardware seemed the least mysterious, while services remained an opportunity to be developed.

The year 1995 thus brought a shift in activities and attitudes from defense to offense, from cost cutting to increasing business. That year, IBM generated $70 billion in revenue, growing the fastest and the most in a decade, while earnings per share doubled. The number of employees increased slightly, while the value of the stock rose by 24 percent. Of IBM's revenues, 57 percent came from a combination of PCs, software, and services. These were IBM's potential growth areas for the second half of the 1990s and the early years of the new millennium. The arc of IBM's expansion during the second five-year term of Gerstner's leadership had been set.

IBM's mood turned more positive, which one could see in the tone of Gerstner's messages to employees. All IBM CEOs routinely sent a note to employees when they announced quarterly earnings to congratulate them on a job well done or to urge them to do better. So what did Gerstner's messages in the late 1990s look like? An example was his second-quarter earnings announcement, made on July 18, 1995, which documented more growth in revenue and profits:

> Clearly, we're moving in the right direction and accelerating our pace in getting technology solutions from lab to market, in helping customers integrate

their information systems, in developing network products and services, in understanding and serving critical markets, and in our willingness to become a multi-dimensional company that delivers value to customers.[7]

But he did not let them off:

That said, let me add a cautionary word or two. We're seeing signs that demand may be slowing somewhat in the U.S. Several key European markets remain sluggish, and the gains we realized in the second half of 1994 will make our 1995 year-to-year comparisons more difficult. ... This is hardly the time to ease up. We must hone our strategies, implement them even faster, and continue our focus on both growth and productivity.[8]

In January 1997, in another announcement to employees, Gerstner heralded "record revenues along with very strong profits. ... We're growing, our turnaround continues, and we're rolling into 1997 with new momentum." Mainframes, services, even PC and storage products did well around the world with the exception of Europe. Again, Gerstner had a charge to the troops: "We have a strategy and the resources to lead. What we must demonstrate now is the will, the commitment and the personal dedication to take the strategy to the streets of the marketplace and win. If any team can do it—this one can."[9] Not since Watson Jr. had a CEO communicated so much with employees.

In early 1999, Gerstner broadcast a message over IBM's internal communications network to 305 locations around the world. After recapping a successful year of growth in 1998 across all lines of business, he opined that the value of the company had increased by $68 billion, but he shared worries for 1999: "distress in Asia and Latin America; the first full year of commerce with the Euro," and major transitions in important product lines such as servers, software, and disk drives. The company, indeed the world, was knee-deep in preparing for "the biggest 'X factor' of them all," the year 2000, or Y2K. Gerstner and other IT CEOs were commenting about Y2K; IBM was busy selling billions of dollars of services to prepare customers for that transition.

Y2K was an odd problem few outside of computer circles had heard about. When people wrote software in the 1950s to 1980s, whenever they had to have a place in the program for a date, say 1988, and have the software conduct calculations based on that or future dates in the twentieth century, programmers provided that capability. What they did not do was accommodate a date change to the 2000s, believing that whatever software they wrote would be replaced long before that. This proved incorrect, as old programs were still working in the mid-1990s. Technologists began worrying, then panicking, that such software might not work on January 1, 2000. Dates might revert back to 1900 or worse. Government regulators around the globe ordered banks, stock markets, and other critical institutions to update their software to work in a post-1999 world. All got the job done; only a few minor problems surfaced. The hysteria built up in 1998 and 1999 did not result in the end of the world as predicted, but in the mid-1990s nobody knew that. Fixing the problem would be easy but time consuming. IBM prepared a combination of over 800,000 reports, proposals, and projects to address Y2K. It seemed every bank and financial institution was fixing Y2K. Competition to help increased, too. Gerstner urged personal leadership, "charting the direction for our customers and our industry," based "on the reality of our performance."[10]

IBM'S TRANSFORMATION INTO A SERVICES AND CONSULTING FIRM

How do you change a company's business? A vast body of literature addresses this question, but how did IBM do it? It is easy to view IBM's history of the 1990s and beyond as a series of product introductions, stories of eccentric, even badly behaving, executives, and dramatic accounts of customer service. Several factors continued to make IBM iconic. It was a big company, employing hundreds of thousands of people, who called on businesses in over 150 countries to sell general-purpose technologies that changed how societies and economies worked.

There were also deeper trends affecting IBM's destiny that transcended any one CEO, division president, or employee. The most important of them ultimately surfaced where IBM earned its revenue and profits. Figure 18.1 displays the core of IBM's reality from 1980 to the present, a

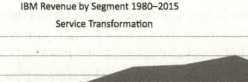

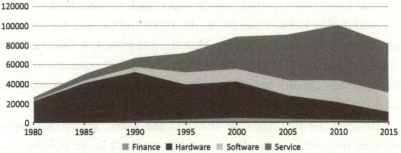

Figure 18.1
IBM's revenue by segment, 1980–2015. Courtesy of James Spohr.

period of over 35 years. The data transcended the careers of most IBMers, the terms of all CEOs and senior executives, boards of directors, most customer managers who worked with IBM, the entire careers of most IBMers, reporters' time on the IBM beat, and even the careers of individuals whose purpose in life was to "watch" IBM and report their findings to Wall Street, IBM's customers, and the press. The chart reflects what happened at IBM over the better part of four decades.

As trends rumble slowly over the decades, they increase momentum or slow, a process called *cycles* or long-term *trajectories*. They leave us with a sense that they are the result of forces beyond human control, as happens with the ebb and flow of earth's ice ages. As this book has demonstrated so far, however, these trends are more the result of actions taken by IBMers, their customers, competitors, and officials. The result of everything anyone did, or that commentators focused on, boils down to the three trends reflected in figure 18.1. It is a snapshot of what they chose to do. When IBM's CEOs took steps to set IBM on a path for future growth, they kept such trends in mind. The chart shows that the lion's share of IBM's revenue in 1980 came from the lease and sale of hardware (no surprise) but that over many decades both the dollar amount of revenue from these businesses and their contribution as a percentage of IBM's sales declined steadily. Blips up and down were considered serious and interesting when they occurred but did not alter the long-term trend. The shaded area above the hardware data accounts for software revenue from products such as those used in mainframes and PCs, and additionally, in the 1990s and beyond, for networking and Internet-related products. That revenue grew as a dollar amount and as a percentage of IBM's total revenue. The volume expanded so much that in the new century both IBM and its rivals thought of the company as either the largest or second-largest software firm.

However, services made up IBM's largest sector. By 2005, it overwhelmed revenues from hardware, yet the company's image still was that of a computer company. Services revenue grew right through 2011. In chapter 19, I discuss why IBM's total revenue declined beginning in 2012, but even then, the trend of greater contribution from services held. Income from product purchase financing was trivial; it was a service customers could use to finance purchases of equipment, much like a bank, or an airline when it sold airplanes to IBM and then leased them back to improve their own balance sheets. Observers point out that IBM entered the IT services and consulting business in a substantial way in the 1990s, but that would not have been possible had IBM not started down that path earlier, because it takes years to develop offerings, discover what customers would pay for and need, develop contractual terms, accumulate necessary skills, and determine how to make a profit from that business.[11]

Across 35 years, IBM transformed as profoundly in what it sold as it did when it moved from selling tabulating equipment to selling computers. Why the slow rate of transition? IBM was a much larger firm in the 1980s and beyond than in the 1950s and 1960s. The transition imposed itself on the company, customers, and competitors through newly emerging, complex technologies, from the PC to the Internet. However, the transition also occurred as conscious decisions made year after year by IBM's leadership, who moved in that direction as new opportunities presented themselves. At a tactical level, decisions mattered. For example, when Gerstner revived the mainframe in the mid-1990s, hardware revenues rose until the end of the century, after which they declined following Y2K investments in new hardware and economic recessions in various parts of the world.

IBM's start into services was not smooth. Its computer outsourcing deals of the mid-1980s were not always profitable, leading IBM to alter terms and conditions as it learned the business, especially about outsourcing. Observers commented that IBM still had deep pockets and vast resources that Gerstner could tap into, but it appeared that much of these resources were lodged in the services side of the business, its R&D capabilities, and in an experienced sales force working with customers. Gerstner's software business remained a fledgling operation, although it received much attention during his tenure, while hardware received too much. So the headline for the 1990s and early the following decade should be that IBM had become a services powerhouse. For employees living through this transition, it must have felt as if an automotive manufacturer had converted from a company that built cars to one that only repaired them. In such an analogy, only the customers would possibly be the same, and they, too, would have scratched their heads figuring out how to leverage new technologies and service requirements.

How did IBM move from being the computer industry's leading supplier of hardware to being one of the largest services firms? While IBM had a heritage of providing free services and software prior to 1969, its expanded role reflected an overall increase in demand by customers for such services, such as the "integration" Gerstner spoke about so frequently in the 1990s. By the early 1980s, major services involved IT support activities, such as installing or repairing malfunctioning software or machines, connecting and integrating systems, application software and data files, and consulting, such as writing software and implementing it or designing processes that operated with products from multiple vendors but that also resulted in new procedures and practices. IBMers built on prior experiences and knowledge. Worldwide revenue from these software and services activities grew to $31 billion. IBM was not alone in these emerging markets. In 1982, providers of services included Computer Sciences Corporation (CSC), with $420 million in revenues, Electronic Data Systems (EDS), with $250 million, Burroughs Corporation, at $232 million, and Arthur Andersen and Company, generating $187 million, as well as IBM with $195 million.[12]

After termination of the U.S. antitrust suit in 1982, IBM began expanding its services business to include outsourcing, time sharing, and its more traditional IT services. In the late 1990s, the Internet created additional opportunities for services, and time sharing appeared in new form by 2005, called the "cloud." Since then, outsourcing to the cloud has remained a growing opportunity for Microsoft, Google, IBM, and others. Demand for global IT services continued to grow. In 2003, it generated $570 billion for all vendors, growing even faster than IBM's own services business. In 2011, worldwide revenue reached $848 billion.[13]

In the Akers period, IBM ran data centers for a few firms, such as Kodak and Hibernia National Bank (both beginning in 1989). Such events gave the firm confidence to start thinking more broadly about developing a worldwide services strategy in 1991. Step one involved converting the Systems Services Division into the Integrated Systems Solution Corporation (ISSC), part of Akers's "Baby Blues" strategy of splitting the company into pieces. ISSC took responsibility for systems integration, writing software for customers, and running data centers. IBM created the Consulting Group, nestled within the sales organization, with 1,500 consultants to provide traditional management consulting, such as strategy (especially with high IT content) and process reengineering in 29 countries. IBM recruited many hundreds of new employees into this business from Ernst & Young, Booz Allen Hamilton, Nolan Norton, and McKinsey, among others. While a hodgepodge of consulting methodologies and corporate cultures came with them, IBM's customers welcomed the company's new offerings.

The Consulting Group corralled into its fold all the ad hoc consulting practices scattered about the company. Many long-term IBMers were purged from the group, literally out of the company.[14] For a couple of years, a guerrilla war took place at the lowest rungs of the new organization among IBMers who felt they could work in a services culture and those who came in convinced they could not. There were exceptions, of course, among the new arrivals. For example, North American Consulting Group general manager Michael Albrecht (b. 1940) blended new hires and long-time IBMers into a large and effective business. He had been a salesman and manager at IBM between 1965 and 1974, left to run the IT department at Michigan Gas, became a management consultant at Nolan Norton, and then returned to IBM in 1990. His experiences taught him the wisdom of blending sales and consulting together, since he knew IBM was large, his realm of authority relatively small, and that he would have to integrate with the sales organization if his employees were to succeed. Other consulting GMs did the same.

ISSC kept adding IT customers, including large U.S. retailer Sears, Roebuck and Company, United Technologies, and State of California, for instance, and began long-lasting relationships with health providers and users of medical computing. Contracts frequently ran into the tens of millions of dollars for many years, often a decade, while an increasing number also were so small that IBM's cost of obtaining new consulting projects began increasing. IBM's services business expanded into Central Europe, the United Kingdom, Japan, and Canada.[15] Through the 1990s, IBM's services business grew rapidly. Hardware maintenance, long a core service business, reliably brought in between $6 billion and $7 billion each year. That level of revenue remained impressive because during the 1990s IBM's hardware continued to improve, resulting in less maintenance needed per machine.[16] Maintenance revenue did not decline, because so many new machines were installed.

All services combined totaled roughly 20 percent of IBM's revenue in 1991. To build on its early momentum, in 1995 Gerstner created the IBM Global Services Division (GSD). In 1998, its consultants generated a third of IBM's revenue, but IBM needed a stronger industry-centric focus for consulting, and to jump-start that, in 2002 it acquired the consulting arm of its auditing firm, PriceWaterhouseCoopers Global Management Consulting and Technology Services (PwC). At the time, all major auditing firms were splitting apart their auditing and consulting practices largely because of regulatory requirements on both sides of the Atlantic, so PwC put its consulting arm up for sale. IBM bought it for $3.5 billion in stock and cash, a bargain given that in 2000 H-P had tried to acquire it for $17 billion. IBM's acquisition doubled its consulting staff, bringing 30,000 consultants into IBM overnight. Virginia M. "Ginni" Rometty (b. 1957), a future IBM CEO, then in charge of IBM's consulting services, led the acquisition effort and essentially turned over to the new hires operation of IBM's management consulting business. She assigned Frank Roney (also a recent hire into the company a few years earlier) operational responsibility for integrating PwC into IBM. Services revenue expanded rapidly, from $36.4 billion in 2002 to $55 billion in 2014. Consulting's contribution to IBM's revenue increased from nearly 45 percent in 2002 to over half in 2006 and then to almost 60 percent in 2014.[17]

IBM's transformation into a services business was a remarkable achievement, one hardly discussed by observers of IBM's history of the 1990s and the early part of the following decade. Gerstner acknowledged in his memoirs the disaggregation of the IT industry into thousands of vendors working in niche markets, concluding that customers were calling for someone to integrate these offerings. However, his vision and that of others in the early 1990s focused largely on IT integration. By the end of the century, it was evident that integrating IT into industry-centric and business processes would be at least as attractive an opportunity for IBM, hence the acquisition of PwC's industry practices. As opportunities changed, so did IBM's services. Outsourcing was the fastest and largest piece of the business; it played to IBM's IT strengths. The second largest was its business consulting services, the capability reinforced by PwC. As a percentage of the total services business, technical services and networking support shrank but then remained stable, as did the roughly equal in size maintenance business. The beauty of the shift from hardware to software and services was that the latter two segments always enjoyed higher profit margins than machines did. The impact is worth understanding. In 2000, services turned in pretax income of $4.5 billion. Just eight years later, that segment generated $7.3 billion. Software performed well, too, going from $2.8 billion in pretax income to $7.1 billion. Hardware shrank from $2.7 billion to $1.6 billion.[18]

In IBM's parlance, the firm had shifted from "components to infrastructure to business value," a strategy launched in the 1980s and continued into the new century. The mix changed largely because of acquisitions of software and consulting firms and by disposing of less-profitable hardware segments, such as printers, PCs, and disk drives. The high drama of good storytelling about the role of individuals is important, but, stripped bare,

IBM's success depended at least as much on its cold analysis of market conditions and purposeful implementation of strategies based on understanding markets. Gerstner augmented the disciplined approach already started earlier, and his successors continued to do the same. A point to reinforce is that IBM entered the management consulting business several years before Gerstner came to IBM. J. Bruce Harreld's (b.1950) arrival in 1995 reinforced a direction already under way, adding discipline to it.

Much of the credit for the early start also has to go to Robert M. "Bob" Howe, who IBM recruited from Booz Allen Hamilton in 1991 to run the IBM Consulting Group. A character by IBM standards, he frequently wore red suspenders and—shocking to some—took off his suit jacket in the middle of a public presentation. He knew his audience of IBMers was conservative and therefore enjoyed using blunt, sometimes crude, language to differentiate the culture he was attempting build within his own organization. He created a business that went from almost zero to $250 million in annual revenue by the time he changed roles in 1994. From almost no employees, he ended 1994 with 3,500. His organization nestled in Dennie Welsh's larger services empire. Before IBM's acquisition of PwC, both men were also responsible for aligning management consulting and some IT services offerings by industry. In July 1994, they reorganized these businesses into 12 industry specialties, such as for finance, manufacturing, health, and telecommunications; Howe took over the financial arm. It was that early experience of going to market by industry that helped convince senior executives eight years later that they needed to expand that approach, which is how they arrived at the conclusion that buying a large, industry-centric consultancy like PwC made sense.

Other individuals made a difference, too. Dennie M. Welsh (1943–2004), Howe's manager, worked at IBM for 33 years, following service as a U.S. Army pilot (1964–1966). An engineer by training, he spent his early years at IBM working on such projects as the NASA Apollo and Shuttle space programs, later managing the U.S. government's GPS development, the technology that made it possible for people today to get driving directions from their smartphones. During the Cold War, it was an extraordinarily important tool used by the U.S. military and intelligence agencies. Highly regarded, smart, and effective as a technology manager, Welsh rose quickly through the ranks in the 1970s and 1980s. In 1983, he took over many of IBM's commercial systems integration projects, and two years later he became vice president and general manager of IBM's important semiconductor laboratory in Manassas, Virginia. Welsh continued to manage many of IBM's contracts with the U.S. military. He became IBM's president of ISSC in 1991. When Gerstner created IBM Global Services Division (GSD) in the mid-1990s, he tapped Welsh to run it. Its initial business centered on outsourcing, a business Welsh understood. Just as important, he increased IBM's consulting and services capabilities. Consultants in Global Services remember him as an effective, enthusiastic leader of 90,000 IBMers, or about 40 percent of IBM's workforce. Disarming with his southern Tennessee drawl, no executive at IBM had as much knowledge about integrating hardware and software as Welsh, and IBM's largest customers welcomed his consultants.

Besides being IBM's first high-profile services executive, Welsh was one of the earliest in the modern period to suggest that IBM do in the private sector what he and FSD had done in the public sector. He had risen high enough in the company by the time Gerstner came to IBM to have access to the new chairman. He persuaded him to expand the services business. Gerstner took credit for coming up with the idea, but he also implied in his memoirs that when there was a strategic initiative under consideration, someone did the homework to figure out its elements. Harreld, for example, had that as his job, but before he arrived individual executives had to lobby for their ideas. Welsh's contribution was to make IBM move aggressively into IT services. Timing and good staff work were always crucial. In IBM's case, on July 2, 1996, the company announced that the U.S. Department of Justice had agreed to rescind a number of terms of the 1956 consent decree, the most important of which was the prohibition against offering computer services. Welsh could now leverage the company's knowledge of so many products and types of computing. IBM quickly became the world's biggest provider of computer services, but in 1998 Welsh had to take medical leave, and he retired in 1999. On January 1, 2004, he passed away at the age of 61, a sad ending to what had been a long career during which he had pushed IBM onto a services course. Samuel J. "Sam" Palmisano, a rising star at IBM who came up in sales, took charge of the services business, successfully expanded it, added process reengineering to its capabilities, and enhanced its networking services through partnerships with telecommunications firms. The services business expanded globally. By the end of the century, Global Services employed 140,000 people.

However, a problem began to develop in the late 1990s and early the following decade: customers increasingly wanted *industry-specific* consulting and IT services, while much of what IBM was offering was still IT-centric. The company began nurturing industry-specific services within the Consulting Group, but the effort proved insufficient, a problem the PwC consultants were supposed to fix. Over the next few years, some PwC people decided that life in a publicly traded company was not for them, others migrated to other jobs at IBM, and new hires came into the firm. In the decade following its purchase, the PwC contingent proved just big enough (30,000 people in a 300,000+ employee company) to nudge IBM into acting in more industry-specific ways. Goods and services offerings, advertisements, marketing materials, and technical and managerial R&D became more industry-specific. IBM remained at its core an IT firm, but it slowly gained expertise in services aimed at specific industries. These included manufacturing, large retail, banking (finance), insurance, telecommunications, government (mostly the U.S. government and European national governments), and medical industries. These industries had long been extensive users of computing, and of Dennie Welsh's IT services. These customers (by then, fashionably called "clients" by IBMers) provided connections and insights when, after 2010, IBM offered products and services in artificial intelligence (such as Watson Computer) and "Big-Data" analytics.

RISE OF SOFTWARE, DECLINE OF HARDWARE

Software and hardware remained the second and third legs of IBM's business. While operated through individual divisions devoted to each type of offering, and with services prepared to merge the two as integration projects, these two legs remained crucial and visible to customers and IBMers alike. The software business consisted of more than simply operating systems for mainframes and the continuing war with Microsoft over OS/2, which Gerstner finally quit fighting. While software contributed greater portions of IBM's revenue, few in IBM or the computer industry gave it as much thought as they believed the company did for hardware. The majority of employees, observers, rivals, and customers kept thinking of IBM as a hardware vendor, relegating software to a peripheral part of the computer business. Software sales were an afterthought until after 1993, when IBM responded to the "open source" debate, the continuing problems with Microsoft, the continued rapid expansion of networking by its customers, the rise of competitors serving that market, and the wider use of the Internet—all developments that took place during the 1990s. When IBMers focused on software, many did so too narrowly. The view from Corporate was that "IBM's executives were almost obsessed with the effort to unwind the decisions of the 1980s and take back control of the operating system from Microsoft."[19]

So, after the OS/2 war, Gerstner turned his attention to IBM's otherwise fragmented and disorganized approach to software. The changes that soon came remained in effect for over a decade. First, IBM gathered into one organization all of its software activities. What John M. Thompson (b. 1942), the new GM for this collection of goods, found in 1995 when he took control of it was horrible. As his manager explained, "IBM had 4,000 software products, all of which were branded with separate names ... made in more than thirty different laboratories around the world. There was no management system, no model for how a software company should run, and no skills in selling software as a separate product."[20] Thompson proved a good choice. A Canadian, he had joined IBM in 1966 as a systems engineer, the same role in which future CEO Rometty began 16 years later. In 1986, he took over IBM Canada as its president and chief executive officer, and in 1991 he became the corporate vice president responsible for helping to put together IBM's services strategy. Two years later, he took over the mainframe and midrange computer business. Then, in 1995, Gerstner put him in charge of the IBM Software Group, a position he held until 2002, when he was elected vice chairman of the IBM board, the company's second in command under Palmisano. Creative and decisive, he succeeded in all of his assignments.

Thompson's software group quickly hired and trained over 5,000 people to sell software. By 2000, Thompson had 10,000 people selling and supporting software. He reduced the number of software development labs from 30 to 8 and the number of brands from 60 to 6. Yet the range of competitors remained broad, from Microsoft to others aiming products at mainframes, notably SAP, PeopleSoft, and JD Edwards. Many others sold software to manage databases, transactions, utilities, and so forth, called "middleware." These sat between the extremes of small PC software packages and high-level applications sold by the likes of SAP. Much of IBM's software needed to be rewritten so as not to be proprietary in order to work on non-IBM platforms, such as those sold by H-P, Sun, and Microsoft, as part of IBM's newly embraced open systems approach.

In 1995, the software group proposed acquiring Lotus Development Corporation to fill a gap in IBM's middleware offerings. IBM needed a network offering, and Lotus Notes was an ideal product to meet that need. Thompson and his management team realized that this popular product, used for e-mail and online file management in a networked environment, would require a hostile takeover. IBM had never done that before. Gerstner earlier had personally tried and failed to buy Apple, so one could forgive him for being cautious about buying another high-profile company. Thompson, however, pushed for it. Gerstner had to learn about the company from scratch because, as one executive witnessing the takeover put it, "Lotus was just a flower to Lou."[21] In May, the board of directors approved the hostile takeover, with a maximum bid of $65 a share.

Gerstner and his team began developing their game plan, messages to the world, and how to execute the takeover. When IBM bid $60 per share, senior executives at Lotus pushed back. Gerstner told the press he was making the bid because Lotus would not consider a friendly takeover, which was never quite true. IBM won. Lotus's senior executives lost control of their company, although many were kept on as part of the takeover to get new releases of their products out the door—which was crucial for

IBM and its customers, too. Key to the deal was keeping the legendary Lotus product developer Ray Ozzie (b. 1955) in the belief that otherwise there would not be a new release of Lotus Notes. Without that new release, and retaining other crucial people, IBM would have acquired a hollow firm of little value. An intense week of negotiations and of lawyers writing agreements culminated in a deal that included keeping key personnel and defining the role Lotus would play in IBM. IBM acquired Lotus for $3.5 billion, or $64 a share. Jim Manzi (b. 1951), head of Lotus, became a senior vice president reporting to Gerstner to run his old company. On June 11, 1995, everyone signed the necessary paperwork.

The takeover was a big event. IBM acquired an essential product for its emerging software strategy. More important, IBMers learned lessons about how to take over a software firm that would inform the over 100 software acquisitions it would make in the next two decades. Lotus and IBM software people initially viewed each other with suspicion. It did not help that the Lotus people were housed in their own building in Cambridge, Massachusetts, while IBM's were scattered around the world. Nevertheless, for a few years, IBM honored its agreement to allow Lotus management to run its own operation. By the end of the century, however, Lotus had been integrated into the wider IBM software world; its name was retired in 2013. Ozzie remained at IBM for two years, completing the highly successful Lotus Notes 4.0. Notes did well from its earliest days with IBM because of its access to the larger firm's customers. In 1995, Lotus had 4.5 million users. By early 1998, that number had grown to 20 million, including all of IBM's employees.[22]

Nine months after acquiring Lotus Development, Thompson suggested a second acquisition, Tivoli Systems. Senior IBMers were more willing now to take that on. It proved a success, giving IBM new products in the distributed systems arena. Tivoli generated about $50 million in sales annually when it was acquired by IBM, but this had risen to over $1 billion per year by the start of the new century. IBM's total annual software revenue climbed to $13 billion by the end of 2001, spinning off an attractive $3 billion in pretax profits. It did not hurt that the Internet's wide adoption in the late 1990s energized corporate sales and that IBM was able to reorganize to sell software. By the end of the century, IBM had moved into the networked world, branding its offerings as "e-business." All parts of IBM participated: software, hardware, and consulting.

By 2001, IBM had its software organization well structured, with revenue and profit targets, and a broad set of products and strategies. IBM employees sold directly to the company's largest customers, as they had for decades, but they concurrently cultivated a worldwide network of 24,000 business partners, who sold to all other enterprises and public agencies. The Software Group organized into five lines of business: application and integration middleware (such as WebSphere); data management (such as DB2 and IMS), largely for mainframes; pervasive computing, which sold middleware enabling software; Lotus, which provided peer-to-peer communications (such as e-mail) and other collaborative tools for sharing data and files; and Tivoli, to provide systems management software. To put the Software Group into context, the other major pieces of IBM included Global Services (outsourcing and technical services), sales, marketing, hardware manufacturing, component technology manufacturing (but separate from computers), financing, research, and an assortment of internal support organizations. That structure remained essentially intact past 2010, although IBM constantly tinkered with divisions within each group in response to changing markets and products.

What happened to outsourcing, which had motivated many of the early movers to consulting, technical services, and new software tools and products? That business had grown steadily during and after Dennie Welsh's tenure. While in the early 1990s companies outsourced IT as a way of lowering or controlling the growth in costs for computing, by 2001 they had changed the kind of outsourcing they wanted. By then, a third of companies were outsourcing some IT functions because they did not have enough staff to operate or develop uses (applications) their users wanted, such as to mitigate Y2K issues or to add new software applications. A quarter of IBM's customers did not have the right skills or time to hire or train those who did. Nearly a quarter believed someone else could develop these skills more quickly. By 2001, only 4 percent of companies outsourced to save money. The world of IT was changing so quickly and expanding so rapidly that outsourcing seemed a reasonable response. In surveys conducted by IBM, usually the top five functions outsourced ranked from most to least were application development, website development, website hosting, network design/infrastructure build-out, and application integration—all classic activities of highly networked organizations in the thick of embracing the Internet.

Software loomed ever larger in importance at IBM. In the 1990s, open systems were rapidly becoming the new norm. Networking was expanding to everyone and to every computing device, and that was before the Internet and smartphones really made their presence felt as one of the key technological developments of the early years of the new millennium. Gerstner may have seemed harsh to his managers in 1993 and 1994 when he accused them of not having a "software mentality." It was true. IBMers still

Figure 18.2
Dennie Welsh, IBM's services leader during IBM's transformation into a services firm. Photo courtesy of IBM Corporate Archives.

fixated on "boxes," hardware, mainframes, and, to a certain extent, PCs. Once Gerstner ended the OS/2 war with Microsoft, he still faced down a fragmented software business. With the company set on a new course on the twin trajectories of networking and open systems, IBM entered the post-Gerstner era able and willing to acquire specialized software firms by industry and technology that could be blended together with consulting.

Under Sam Palmisano between 2002 and 2007, many dozens of small firms came into the IBM fold, although none as spectacular as Lotus and Tivoli. Both those acquisitions became important components of IBM's software tool kit in that decade because they had already created demand for their products before IBM acquired them. Each enhanced IBM's products for both large and midrange computer systems. IBMers found it easier to acquire a company than to integrate it into the firm's operations, because of differing cultures and insufficient appreciation of one another's capabilities and roles. IBM's senior leaders stayed the course, expanding software capabilities.

A key decision senior software executives made, which was implemented by Gerstner's successors, involved exiting the application software business. These programs did something specific, such as factory production planning or accounting. IBM shifted instead to software that provided companies and governments with their general digital plumbing. Database software and e-mail are examples. These kinds of software could reside on all manner of hardware and networks, including within the Internet. Markets for these products were larger than for packages that were more specialized. During the first decade of the twenty-first century, IBM's strategists, technologists, consultants, sales personnel, and customers began thinking of new uses for computing.

Next, in 2012–2014, IBM developed capabilities and offerings involving mobile computing, increased deployment of analytical tools, management of large bodies of data (Big Data), and software security. Since 2014, cognitive computing (use of artificial intelligence and the ability of a machine to learn from its own experiences) has also been part of the mix; it is discussed in chapter 19. Those initiatives were rooted in software but could not have surfaced on their own without the shift made in the 1990s to more universal uses of software (open source) and the increased generation of revenue that resulted. Sales provided the economic and managerial rationale for moving further down the software path. IBM's announcements of new products and reorganizations related to them characterized much of its activities since the mid-1990s, but the bigger transformations involved the incremental shifts in emphasis culminating in the long-term shift out of the hardware business while IBM kept introducing new mainframes and its highly successful midrange AS/400, PCs, and laptops into the new century.[23] A remaining unanswered question at the dawn of the new century was the same one Akers and Gerstner had asked: What should IBM do about its hardware business?

In the midst of that mystery, it was time for Gerstner to retire, as he had reached the age of 60, when IBM's senior executives customarily retired. IBMers, customers, industry observers, Wall Street, and the media asked: Who will be next? Would IBM's board look outside the firm for a new leader? After all, it had done well in finding Gerstner, lionized as one of the great turnaround executives. His picture appeared on the cover of major business publications with a smile or mischievous look of delight. Or, would the board promote someone from within? To hire another outsider might be seen as refreshing but could also indicate that maybe IBM's senior leadership problems had yet to be solved and that the company's recovery had not been completed. To appoint someone already at IBM had its benefits also, as a signal to the world that IBM had fixed its problems, that it again had a strong bench of qualified leaders, that IBM's business direction was solid and confident, and that someone from inside could manage from the first day, thanks to their knowledge of the firm. Gerstner and the board felt good about promoting from within.

They chose Sam Palmisano, who had a good run managing the PC company in 1997–1998, Global Business Service in 1998–1999, as head of the computer hardware business in 1999, and earlier in having gained a reputation as an amenable, effective sales manager and more recently in IBM's outsourcing business, which became part of GBS. Palmisano had joined IBM in sales right out of college in 1973, came up in the business through its various transitions from the large-account culture of the 1970s, and sat on top of enough parts of IBM in the 1990s and early the following decade to understand the company's various parts and where it was going. He was well liked and had avoided making enemies. The product of an Italian-American family raised in Baltimore, his father owned an automotive body shop. His son did well, graduating from Johns Hopkins University, where he played football and majored in history. He was also a bit of a musician, playing saxophone. He was smart, had a reputation for doing his homework, and could "sell upward," impressing management above him.

IBM's board approved Palmisano's appointment as chief operating officer (COO) in October 2000. He moved closer to total control of IBM

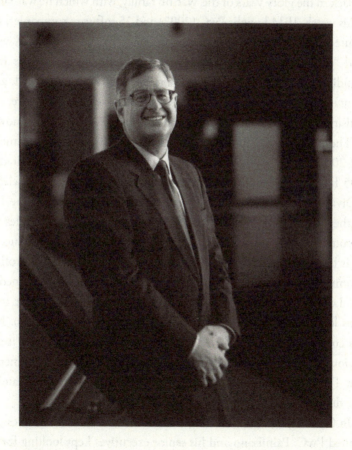

Figure 18.3
"Sam" Palmisano, IBM's CEO after "Lou" Gerstner, led IBM deeply into the IT services industry. Photo courtesy of IBM Corporate Archives.

in March 2002, when the board promoted him to chief executive officer (CEO), and finally as chairman on January 1, 2003. The board expanded his authority as Gerstner relinquished his, all to signal to the world a rational, calm transition, what investors, customers, the media, and employees wanted. At the other end of Palmisano's tenure as CEO, he did the same for the incoming Ginni Rometty. Palmisano faced the task of resolving IBM's hardware conundrum. He needed to maintain the arc of IBM's now successful business, which Gerstner had developed. He faced the challenge of figuring out how to expand IBM's iconic role in modern economies, harking back to the glory years of the Watson family, with which he was familiar. On his watch, IBM bought PwC (2002) and 25 software companies, slowly nurtured cloud computing, updated outsourcing, and expanded what it called "e-business" initiatives already launched in the face of the rapidly expanding use of the Internet.[24] It seemed things were going well, and he maintained a low profile during the first couple of years of his tenure, yet the acquisition of PwC reminded people that he and IBM were still innovating.

The first shoe Palmisano dropped was IBM's announcement in June 2002 that it had sold its anemic hard drive business to Hitachi for $2.05 billion and would lay off 1,500 workers from the Microelectronics Division. What a shock. IBM had invented hard drives in the 1950s, and they had been a great source of technological pride for decades across the company, not just within R&D, but the business was so successful that it became commoditized. IBM did not do well squeezing profits out of commodity businesses. Other firms did that better, as happened with PCs. Long-term employees who felt an emotional attachment to disk drives leveled a surprising amount of criticism against Palmisano. Newer hires could not understand the fuss. Business media considered it a wise decision. The layoffs, however, reminded people that full employment was gone. They signaled the start of an increasing number of layoffs, and even more during Rometty's time at the helm.

In October, four months after the sale of the disk drive business, IBM acquired PwC. Palmisano and his senior executives kept looking for other low-margin businesses to get out of and higher-margin ones to enter. In

2004, IBM sold the PC business to Lenovo, bringing to an end a quarter-century struggle to make it profitable. The sale created consternation inside IBM, as did the earlier disposal of disk drives. It also seemed that many in the computer industry symbolically had to take off their hats, for the end of an era had come.[25] Industry observers again applauded the disposal of yet another low-margin business. Customers paid little attention, as they had moved on to other vendors and platforms.

Employees in the PC group acquired new ID badges from Lenovo. Ironically, at the time IBM sold the PC business, the PC group was enjoying a period of some profits, generating $20 billion in annual revenue. But Palmisano knew it had no future. Few fully understood at the time that smaller mobile devices would soon compete against all PCs, not just IBM's. But IBMers at the highest levels clearly appreciated that smartphones, ever-lighter laptops, and tablets would quickly make their way into the market. Scientists and engineers in both research laboratories and the product divisions were making presentations on the future of these technologies, often proposing that IBM enter those markets.[26] More immediately, the sales of disk drives and PCs contributed to the overall decline in IBM's hardware revenues during the second half of Palmisano's tenure.

Human drama and tragedy played roles. The death of Tom Watson Jr. on December 31, 1993, the sad news that the popular Dennie Welsh was leaving IBM because of deteriorating health, and the anguish over IBMers being laid off reminded employees that they lived in changing times. Gerstner taught everyone that change was essential, that it needed to be relentless so that the company could thrive and not fall back into its old ways. Most managers who lived through the late 1980s and early 1990s were prepared to hold employees and management above them accountable to never repeat mistakes of the past, even to the point of risking their own careers, since they knew the alternative meant loss of their jobs anyway. IBM was becoming a tougher environment, with gentility a thing of the past. Fragility seemed to be everywhere, and never more so than on September 11, 2001.

Every IBMer knows where they were that morning. I was at my desk at home in Madison, Wisconsin, hosting a conference call with colleagues in France, Great Britain, Japan, and the United States that began at 8:00 A.M. New York time. My wife, who never interrupted my IBM conference calls, rushed into the room and blurted out, "You have to see this," and turned on a little TV set I had on a nearby shelf. There was the iconic image of the two World Trade Center towers in Lower Manhattan, with one on fire and soon after an airplane crashing into the second one. I had the volume muted on my phone because I was confused about why she would interrupt me, and then I instantly realized, "Oh My God!" I turned up the volume and over the speakerphone stopped whoever was talking to announce that it looked like the United States was being subjected to an attack in New York. There was silence, and then everyone started asking the same questions at the same time. I started to relay what was on the screen for a minute or so and then simply said, "All of you get to a TV or radio. This is serious. This meeting is over."

Four hours later, drained by the experience, I drove over to the local IBM office. There everyone was pale, sullen, shocked, scared, confused, and depressed. Nothing got done. The phones did not ring, the volume of e-mails dropped to almost none. Over the next several days, IBM worldwide remained shocked; few really worked unless they were in the Washington, D.C., and New York regions. An IBMer was killed on the flight that crashed into the Pentagon, while members of employees' families were killed on the other airplanes. Hundreds of customers died in the World Trade Center towers; data centers evaporated. The U.S. government announced that it wanted the stock market restored by Monday morning and called on the financial industry to move Heaven and Earth to show the world how resilient Americans could be.

That meant whole data centers had to be put together in days, with software, computers, peripheral equipment, cables, telecommunications hookups, and new staffs. Normally that took months. IBM had 1,200 customers in the World Trade Center towers and within two blocks of the site. Backup facilities had to be activated, all in days. IBMers scrambled all over the United States, in particular in New Jersey, snapping up empty warehouse space and office facilities that could be commandeered, rented, or borrowed. They went through their warehouses pulling in equipment, borrowing other machines from customers, and giving up sleep. But, on Monday, new data centers operated all over the country to support the finance industry. IBM built 20 new data centers in less than a week and found thousands of ThinkPads and workstations for its New York customers. Thousands of employees worked on the data centers and in providing support for relief organizations and government agencies. IBM immediately pledged $5 million in cash, technology, and technical assistance to a hastily established September 11 Fund in New York. Gerstner sent notes to the entire company, updating employees on IBM's role and complimenting them on what they were doing to help customers and communities.

Gerstner wrote a lengthy "Dear Colleague" note to all of IBM's management on September 18: "Your responsiveness helped us account for our people—over 2,000—in a fast but thorough way. I've heard stories of managers that arranged for medical attention, food and clothing for their people, and of others who personally provided transportation for employees who were stranded when mass transit systems shut down.... Many of you took the time to talk to each individual on your team and listened to our people express their feelings and fears. It was a superb job under conditions that none of us could have imagined, let alone practiced or prepared for."[27] Managers took decisions into their own hands. One first-line field engineering manager at 12:36 P.M. (central time) on the 11th sent out an e-mail to all his colleagues, "We are not officially closing the IBM location, however, as always, we encourage you to use your own discretion in terms of your personal safety," adding that wherever IBM operates, "the regional crisis management team is assembled right now."[28] In days, thousands of e-mails inquiring about people flowed through the company network, such as, "Nabil, thank you for your concern and good wishes. All the Global Sales Ops team members are safe. Marie-Claire lives in New York City but is safe. Catherine lives near the Pentagon, but is also safe. It is comforting to hear from our friends outside the U.S. Merci beaucoup." Another wrote, "To my US colleagues: I hope yourselves, your families, relatives and friends are in good shape. All over the world, we all consider ourselves as Americans in such a horror situation."[29]

On the afternoon of 9/11, Gerstner and his senior team scrambled to get messages of assurance out to IBMers, to call on them to use good judgment, assist customers, and donate blood. He first communicated world-wide with IBMers at 3 P.M. eastern time, barely six hours after the tragedy, next just after 5 P.M., and again the next day, and so it went all week. It seemed every executive and manager within hundreds of miles of New York was now figuring out what to do in the city; the same was true in the Washington, D.C., area, where IBM had 10,000 employees. A major effort that afternoon involved identifying the location of all employees in and around the disasters, following an extensive telephone tree process long in place at IBM. The employees were right to worry. As one colleague at 590 Madison Avenue wrote the next day: "I am … was in my office at 590 when it all happened … drove out around midday … no one on the roads except people covered in soot walking north on the FDR from Wall Str … friends of mine were there and are hysterical … many IBMers still unaccounted for … a tragedy of unbelievable proportions!"[30]

Air traffic came to an immediate halt for two days across North America, so IBMers moved machines by truck to affected areas, but the shock and pause in many activities extended into the following week. Some U.S. IBM sales executives began to worry that business forecasted for September—the last month of the third quarter, historically IBM's weakest because of summer vacationing—was in jeopardy. In the United States, one executive sent an e-mail in the third week reminding sales management of their commitment to their pre-9/11 sales forecast and to "close that business" with customers. It may have been one of the most quickly deleted e-mails in IBM's history.

The 9/11 tragedy was the most dramatic event of the early years of the new millennium, but it was not the only one, because life at IBM continued into turbulent times. Quickly, U.S. IBMers in the military reserves began to be called to active duty, upsetting consulting projects and normal workflows within IBM, but, with its prestige back and its influence in the corridors of corporations rising, management faced the delicate challenge of continuing the arc of its successful transition of the 1990s. One of the most important influences on it was the dot-com economic crisis that erupted near the end of Gerstner's tenure, but first a personnel change was in order.

A SMOOTH TRANSITION

The last thing anyone in Armonk wanted was more high drama in the changing of the guard when it came time for Gerstner to move on. The world needed to see that everything was working fine at IBM, and there was no better way to signal that than to appoint a "lifer" as the next CEO. On January 29, 2002, Gerstner wrote to all employees announcing that the board had selected Palmisano as the next CEO, effective March 1; that the current vice chairman, John Thompson, would retire on September 1; and that he (Gerstner) would stay on as chairman of the board until the end of the year. A transition could not be made any smoother than that. Gerstner put a fine point on the nature of the transition: "Over the past two years, Sam and I have forged a strong partnership to prepare the company for a transition in leadership. Supported by a fine Board of Directors, we have undertaken a process that has been disciplined, transparent, and thorough." He endorsed his replacement as competent and experienced, and declared that "Sam bleeds Blue. And because he does, he understands the character of our company at its soul."[31] The media, customers, and Wall Street approved, for it meant IBM's current strategy would remain intact.

IBMers and observers looking back on the 10 years Palmisano served as CEO and chairman used the word *incremental* a great deal, but it was a relative term—incremental to what? For example, as India began producing competent programmers and technologists who cost only 20 percent of what they did in the United States, many U.S. IT companies began hiring them in large numbers. In 2002, IBM employed about 2,500 Indians, in 2004 that number grew to 9,000, and in 2006 it expanded to 41,000.[32] By the end of Palmisano's term, although kept confidential by IBM, many in the computer industry believed IBM employed nearly 150,000 Indians. Just as important for the effect on IBM, as the Indian population increased, the number of American employees, who were more expensive, declined. They either incrementally retired, their divisions were sold off, or they were laid off. Continuous layoffs occurred in small numbers to keep IBM out of the media with ugly headlines about thousands of departures. During Palmisano's decade, the U.S. employee population shrank by an estimated 60,000 to 70,000, setting a pattern of ongoing "resource balancing" (IBM's PR term for layoffs) that extended almost on a quarterly basis to the present.[33] It became routine for IBM's CFOs to announce that IBM would be setting aside funds for "resource rebalancing" activities, although they never actually said how many people would be let go. Industry watchers translated dollar amounts into generally accurate numbers, however. Without accurate numbers coming from IBM, speculation ran rampant for years.

It seemed the new CEO took a couple of years to get his own voice, but by 2006 he was speaking in his words about IBM and its largest customers becoming "the emerging globally integrated enterprise," an institution "that fashions its strategy, its management, and its operations in pursuit of a new goal: the integration of production and value delivery worldwide. State borders define less and less the boundaries of corporate thinking or practice."[34] More than explaining a trend, he was describing IBM's operations. He clarified how it was possible to employ tens of thousands of Indians to displace U.S. IBMers to work less expensively for clients in the United States and in Western Europe. Swapping employees created enormous discontent in the U.S. and later in Western European workforces, but it went on anyway. To operate globally, IBM created transnational processes, metrics of performance, and improved profits. IBM moved from low-profit to higher-value market opportunities in the new millennium.

Palmisano launched a corporate "make-over," as IBM publicists called it in mid-2005, named Roadmap 2010, which initially was not controversial. An IBM publication explained that it was

> aiming to build on the company's previous success in wringing $5 billion per year in inefficiencies from its global supply chain. The goal was to use a combination of business process redesign, technology upgrades and redeployment of global labor to improve quality and responsiveness and drive annual productivity gains of 10 percent to 15 percent across the company's entire service portfolio.[35]

Work shifted to less expensive employees in Eastern Europe, Latin America, and Asia. Service centers provided programming and other consulting support on a global basis; manufacturing took place in China and later elsewhere in Asia. IBM was following the practice of other global companies in integrating around the world, told others about it, and became a model of how to accomplish that transition. What made it a remarkable move, however, is that outside of IBM the roadmap was a public statement of what financial targets IBM would aim for by 2010 and, if achieved, how it would continue to increase the value of IBM stock. With Wall Street's confidence, and customers acquiring its goods and services, it proved an effective tactic. The value of IBM's stock rose, helped by the simultaneous buyback of shares by the company.

However, it may have been too much of a good thing, because at its successful completion, Palmisano, with the help of his successor, Ginni Rometty, crafted a sequel, called Roadmap 2015, to extract further efficiencies. While the first Roadmap strategy met with some pushback from U.S. IBMers who saw their jobs disappear, that resistance escalated, went global, and involved executives high in the corporation who thought it had become a perverted strategy. Why that happened, and its consequences, is one of the central stories of the next chapter, but in the process of making additional changes during the period of Roadmap 2010, Palmisano had continued to move IBM toward becoming a services and software firm, while increasing revenue, profits, and the value of its stock. He spent $25 billion on software companies while selling the least profitable pieces of IBM. He was able to control the cost of the 426,000 IBMers under his command.

The smooth transitions could be seen elsewhere in the firm; for example, inside IBM's board of directors. Members came and went quietly and smoothly: two left in 2003, next two others in 2005, another two the next year, one each in 2007 and 2008, two in 2009, none the next year, and a final two in Palmisano's last year, in 2011.[36] Their replacements slipped in quietly, too, a mixture of CEOs of major customers and a few leaders from nonprofits. Members included CEOs of global enterprises, such as American Express, CEMEX, Eli Lilly, Emerson Electric, and Caterpillar. The board grew in size, too.

A reading of Palmisano's cover letters to investors in each of his annual reports demonstrated that IBM's strategy remained essentially unchanged. The language he used from one year to the next seemed almost repetitive. IBM's financial performance in the first decade of the twenty-first century remained consistently solid. That occurred during the dot-com crisis of 1999–2002, which drove thousands of IT companies out of business, and again in 2008–2011, when a severe global recession had the same effect on other companies. IBM's market share increased in all its core businesses, with the company spinning off billions of dollars to be reinvested in R&D, to cover the expense of swapping out existing IBM workers for others, to be returned as cash to investors through dividends, and to be used for buybacks of billions of dollars of IBM stock.

The tone of Palmisano's letters centered on financial strategies. He spoke of moving IBM into high-value markets, which meant moving into thriving economies in Central Europe and in Asia. He wrote of customers wanting to engage in another round of IT integration, with which IBM was assisting. He kept referring to trends and constancy. For example, in 2004, he wrote: "Over the past several years we've taken aggressive steps to remix our business" and "since 1997, exited or reduced our presence in such areas as application software, hard-disk drives, networking hardware, low-end printers and retail PCs" and moved into other lines of business, such as more services, moving into China, India, Russia, and Brazil, and adding 730,000 new accounts, largely smaller firms.[37]

The following year, Palmisano began a highly detailed description of IBM's strategies, which remained the same for the rest of his tenure. He spoke of IBM's move into "a high-value model" with three pillars—systems and financing, software, and services—the same trilogy that would characterize IBM from the late 1990s up to the present. Again, IBM declared that "the company has steadily shifted its business mix toward more profitable, innovation-based segments," with emphasis on the remix of where revenues came from (as figure 18.1 shows) and sources of profits, with software the most profitable and hardware the least. Palmisano's closing argument was that IBM was "capturing growth opportunities and increasing efficiency," such as by pursuing the emerging markets of China and Brazil, increasing its involvement in health care, travel, transportation, and consumer products industries, and focusing on small and medium-sized businesses to find new customers. He kept pushing global integration to lower costs for delivering services, manufacturing, and corporate functions. By 2005, it had become common for a manager to have staff scattered all over the world.[38] IBM reduced its layers of management, yet the number of managers kept rising, while divisions returned to old habits of competing for resources.

In the annual report for 2006, Palmisano delivered the same message. On generating higher value, he wrote, "Several years ago, we saw change coming, we remixed our businesses to move to the emerging higher-value spaces," which were services, systems and finance, and software, "and we decided to become a globally integrated enterprise in order to improve IBM's overall productivity and to participate in the world's growth market. As a result, IBM is a higher-performing enterprise today than it was a decade ago."[39] Palmisano's constancy is reflected in the following statement: "To many of us, IBM's transformation of the past few years, while dramatic, has not yet felt unfamiliar. For me and others in my generation, the experience has not been one of entering uncharted waters, but of returning to a pace of change, a level of impact and a type of thinking that drew us to this company in the first place."[40] For several years, the messages just quoted were repeated with updated statistics. After 2008 and the global downturn, Palmisano remained committed to IBM's strategy, still promoting it as change, the same as in previous years.[41] There seemed to be no reason to change the fundamental strategy, because it worked.

Beneath the consistent messaging, however, changes of a more tactical nature were under way. In 2010, IBM announced a set of priorities that grew in importance in subsequent years. IBM expanded its presence in growth markets, operating in over 170 countries, with revenues from outside the United States increasing their contribution to the total by 1 percent per year, with over half from outside North America. IBM began investing in software and services that specialized in analytics in business, health, and government. IBM paid attention to cloud computing, although its move into that market was slower than Amazon's and Google's, with Microsoft just behind them. IBM heavily promoted its campaign to wire up a "smarter planet" as a way of thinking of the world as having more intelligence (computing) injected into its activities. In January 2011, as IBM began a centennial celebration of its founding in 1911, Palmisano remained focused on revenues, income, margins, earnings per share, cash flows, and returns to shareholders, with his three-legged strategy of services, software, and systems.[42]

IBM's greatest source of revenue, as in earlier decades, came from the largest, most iconic firms around the world in over a dozen industries. They read like a list of the most well known: ABB, Aetna Life and Casualty, Air France, Banco Bilbao, Bank of Japan, BASF, Bell Canada, Bristol Myers Squibb, Caterpillar, CIGNA, City of New York, Coca-Cola, U.S. Department of Defense, Delta, Deutsche Bank, Disney, Exxon, Ford Motor, General Motors, Goldman Sachs, Japan Post, Kaiser Permanente, Lenovo, Matsushita Electric, Mazda, Nestle, Nissan, Nokia, Novartis, Pepsi-Cola, Pfizer, Reuters, Rockwell International, SABRE, Shell, Sony, Tata, Time Warner, Toyota, Visa, and Volvo, among others. IBM could claim all *Fortune 1000* enterprises as customers, and every democratic national government. A similar list could have been created for 1990 or 2000. Its breadth of accounts meant IBM had maintained and expanded its presence in organizations, and its geographic footprint, around the world.

IBM's senior vice president for communications, Jon Iwata (b. 1963), kept reminding IBMers that IBM was one of the world's most valuable brands, worth over $57 billion in 2007–2008. That value placed it with the likes of Coca-Cola, Microsoft, GE, and Nokia as the most valuable on the planet, buttressed by customers saying they trusted their personal relations with IBMers, that IBM produced "innovations that matter," and that its employees were dedicated "to every client's success." During Palmisano's tenure as CEO, those quotations became new elements of IBM's Basic Beliefs. The third echoed Watson Sr.'s: "trust and personal responsibility in all relationships."

IBM's research on the attitudes of customers revealed that the single largest influence on them was their personal experience with a company's employees, followed in descending order of importance by views of analysts or professional organizations and opinions of colleagues, peers, or friends. Watson Sr. would have smiled, because these were the same influences on IBM's customers in the 1920s to 1950s. IBM could influence customers on all manner of issues through its 200 worldwide briefing centers, which hosted 10,000 meetings per year by 2008, most running anywhere from a half day to two days each. Much depended on personal and institutional relations. IBM's iconic status, restored by Gerstner and his team, remained intact through the Palmisano years. IBM had made strides to quietly restore its traditional role of being an information ecosystem for the IT world and for senior executives in many other industries, but IBM paid a price for its successes—one considered worth spending at the time—that shaped how it behaved toward employees and how other firms could and did. Its corporate culture changed significantly in the process.

HOW IBM'S CULTURE CHANGED

Edgar H. Schein, a scholar of corporate culture, argued that transforming institutional cultures represents some of the most challenging work of senior leaders, efforts that vary by the stage of the company, from birth to "maturity and decline." His typology informed earlier chapters, and his model of how turnarounds occur—the story told in chapter 17—links to corporate cultural change. What IBM's leaders did reflects behavior he identified in other companies and that we will follow here.[43]

Everything at IBM always seems to come back to its Basic Beliefs, regardless of whether it is Watson's version, Gerstner's eight principles, or Palmisano's updated three points. They all dealt with quality of work, maintaining a focus on customers and listening to their needs, and relations between the corporation and its employees. IBM's culture—how employees behaved and what they believed—remained the source of all company policies, beliefs, and practices, so when Gerstner made substantial changes to the company's strategies in the 1990s, which Palmisano and his team continued in the next decade, it was inevitable that these changes would affect the three areas of beliefs. IBM was still evolving as this book was being written, with employees still experiencing churn in its culture.

Gerstner and his management team successfully increased IBM's focus on customer needs, arguably returning to one of the company's longest-cherished practices. In the 1990s, employees reported in opinion surveys that they understood the overall strategy, thought they were increasingly getting tools and products in support of the company's objectives, and saw their performance evaluations, rewards, and job opportunities align more closely with corporate strategy. They understood that the workforce would have to change as IBM shifted away from hardware sales to services and software. Although concerned about their pension rights (even successfully suing IBM to restore some) and job security, they were more willing to accept personnel turnover than they would be in the decade that followed. That pushback happened after 15 years of layoffs, begun under Akers, which resulted in turning over half the workforce and replacing survivors with new people.

The central cultural change, the one that cannot be ignored in any history of IBM, was the issue of layoffs, the turnover of personnel, as IBM became a more globally integrated enterprise. The incremental reduction of employee benefits was a second concern, particularly regarding pension, health, and severance packages. As IBM moved through the 1990s and the first decade of the new millennium, with layoffs and diminished benefits, employees intensified their complaints, while the corporation increasingly pursued these changes. The polite language used by employees to express "concerns" about these changes turned to harsher language, while product and service organizations increased their internal rivalry for resources.

It did not help that Asian economies in the late 1990s entered an economic downturn and crisis, that Western economies went through their own economic recession in 2001–2002, or that the world went through the Great Recession of 2008–2011. In each instance, demand for IT products and services suffered. Large companies in most industries responded by rapidly laying off people. In the United States alone in 2001, employers laid off some 100,000 workers each month. Layoffs and cost cutting did not end when economists declared a recession over, because the end of an economic crisis arrived at different times in different countries. For IBM, it seemed some national market was always in recession.

Globalizing work to lower operating costs characterized much of the activity inside IBM and other firms. Economists argued that the recent U.S. recession ended in 2011, while many large companies continued to shed employees in many countries. That explains why IBM kept transferring work from countries with expensive employees to others with lower salaries, such as its outsourcing to China in the 1990s, India early the following decade, and later Vietnam and elsewhere. Recessions reinforced the case for further automation and process reengineering to increase a corporation's ability to quickly move work around the world. IBM's competitors did the same. In the first half of 2001, for example, Dell abruptly let go some 2,000 workers, Winstar Communications shed over 40 percent of its staff, and AOL Time Warner eliminated 2,400 workers. As in prior decades, IBM behaved like its peers. When it did, IBM's behavior reinforced similar practices in other enterprises.

That behavior toward employees reflected the post-Opel world. At IBM, reducing the number of workers and their benefits had taken severe but lesser twists and turns under Akers. American workers who had grown up in the full-employment world of the Watsons became concerned, and talk of union organizing started during Akers's tenure in the mid-1980s.[44] Once full employment was gone and benefit reductions had begun, there was no return to the paternalism of the past. The twin practices sped up under Gerstner. They were implemented more abruptly under Palmisano, and a near firestorm marked the time of his successor, Rometty, whose chairmanship was viewed as one of laying off workers to achieve her operational targets by cutting expenses. That had been her reputation within the services and consulting side of IBM since the 1990s. Her reputation, however, did not diminish Armonk's admiration for her intelligence and her ability to communicate with customers and the all-important financial markets.

Nevertheless, as late as the fall of 2001, employee surveys from across the company showed general satisfaction with IBM. There remained high levels of understanding of IBM's strategy, communications by senior executives were rated as clear, and employees gave a strong personal compliment to Gerstner. Employees were reporting, however, that working conditions were deteriorating: more working hours, increasing pressure to achieve results, and compensation not matching these two realities. Roughly half of IBM's services personnel felt sufficient teaming and collaboration existed across internal organizations to accomplish their goals—an operational/cultural change Gerstner sought. In the late 1990s, roughly 60 percent of employees reported no problem with their work/life balance. It became an issue in the next decade, however; particularly worrisome to employees was when Corporate stopped reporting results of such surveys to workers late in Palmisano's tenure.

While senior management focused on an evolving organization and work processes to meet the growing attraction to customers of IBM's three-prong offerings in hardware, software, and IT support services, employees became more concerned about their jobs. That issue became so contentious in the United States in the first decade of the new millennium, and after 2010 in Europe and Asia, that it drew increased press coverage. Customers noticed that support from IBM could suddenly shrink, disappear, or simply deteriorate in quality. A U.S. worker would suddenly be replaced with an Indian, local support would be transferred to a help desk in Asia or Russia via telephone, or the number of employees assigned to the customer would be reduced. Complaints of language barriers cropped up for the first time in IBM's history. In the first decade of the new millennium, IBM stopped announcing how many employees it had in any country and, more irritating to employees and reporters, how many were being laid off. Corporate remained mum on the issue, although it continued to issue press releases that it was hiring. IBM did so as it brought in new people able to implement analytics or run a cloud operation in a less expensive country. Existing employees only saw layoffs.

Starting in the United States in the 1990s, employees did the unthinkable: they attempted to organize a union in communities where IBM had factory operations, such as Burlington, Vermont; Endicott and nearby towns; Austin, Texas; Raleigh, North Carolina; and on the West Coast. Groups formed, such as the IBM Global Union Alliance, which entered the fray along with the earlier Alliance@IBM. This latter organization was sponsored by the Communications Workers of America, which had been trying to unionize IBM's U.S. factory workers since the 1970s. Employees failed to organize a union at any facility, although in the process they created websites that collected information about layoffs, answered questions about terms of severance packages, and discussed rumors. Thousands of IBMers and ex-employees visited these websites and added comments. While participation originated in the United States, by 2010 such efforts had gone global. During some periods of frequent employee layoffs, more IBMers were visiting these sites than others sponsored by IBM about its products and news.

With the turnover of so many employees, why did IBMers fail to unionize to slow layoffs or cuts to benefits, or even to fight charges IBM and other chip manufacturers faced of polluting water in Fishkill and Endicott, New York? Lee Conrad (b. 1949), the most visible organizing leader among IBM employees, concluded that several reasons accounted for their failure. First, IBM initiated too many reorganizations, including the sale of whole businesses and divisions. Second, IBM's strategy of incremental rather than massive layoffs kept the issue of dismissals constantly on people's minds as the new normal rather than as an immediate crisis. Third, Conrad observed that IBM workers were too conservative and fearful of losing their jobs to risk organizing, and this was coupled with a decades-long suspicion of unions. Fourth, many IBMers remained in denial that they would be next to go (the old Basic Belief lingering). Management, largely human resources departments, carefully worked to limit the influence of union organizing, and they proved more successful than the organizers. In Conrad's words, the fundamental reason why IBMers were unable to organize unions in the United States was the structural changes that kept things "topsy-turvy" for three decades.[45] In many European countries, employees had been members of unions and worker councils for decades, as required by national laws.

Employee complaints remained remarkably consistent during the new century. Workers criticized IBM's CEOs for being paid vast sums while laying off workers. Palmisano was to be paid $5 million, but a union organizing website stated on March 6, 2006 that, "We are told at the IBM Fishkill Plant that there is no additional overtime allowed and no pay raise in sight." The same complaint surfaced in 2014, when Rometty was paid a multimillion dollar bonus, although IBM's revenue and the stock's value had declined in the previous year. Complaints by employees about working conditions went out over the Internet. A posting from January 28, 2006 stated: "I sat in on a number of calls which were formerly staffed in the US or by people who spoke and could understand fluent English. Now a lot of those calls are staffed from Brazil or Argentina. No one knows what the heck the other person is saying half the time."[46] Pointing out that all CEOs were living in a period when CEOs in general were being well paid, and even making the case that IBM's were not as generously compensated as others (with the exception of Gerstner, who was very well compensated), did not affect employee attitudes toward executive compensation. Many thought executives were overcompensated for poor performance, while nonexecutive employees were denied salary increases and were laid off to reduce IBM's SG&A.

While those complaints continued into the 2010s, increasingly the conversation turned to layoffs. The majority occurred in the United States, which had the largest population of employees in the 1990s and early the next decade, and the least restrictive labor laws. The Alliance tracked these layoffs through feedback from employees laid off and press reports. IBM employee organizer Conrad reported that in the mid-1980s IBM had 230,000 employees in the United States but by 2016 only about 78,000, many replaced by "lots of contractors, H1b visa and offshore workers with us.ibm.com addresses."[47] Some went away with the sale of divisions, such as several thousand transferred to Lenovo in 2014 when IBM sold additional pieces of its business to the Chinese firm, joining thousands who had departed earlier with the disposal of the disk drive and PC businesses.

Employees used harsher language: "If anyone at the highest level of IBM has half a brain (which I've come to doubt)" (November 30, 2014). The reason for layoffs (called resource actions or RAs) was widely believed to be "so CEOs and Executives can get their bonuses at the end of the year. IBM US employees need a union to stop this corrupt practice" (October 13, 2014). Between 2006 and 2016, older workers seemed targeted for layoffs, so employee websites began reporting this problem: "It is a way to remove older employees from the payrolls" (May 1, 2012). They accused Corporate of trying to cut expenses to support the stock's value and did not hesitate to get personal about it: "Ginni will be the only employee left" (April 2, 2016).[48] The overall complaint from thousands of commentators was neatly summarized by one British employee in early 2016: "Losing shareholders money, firing thousands of employees, clients abandoning the company like rats from the Titanic, and giving top management bonuses. IBM management is giving the middle finger to everyone. I can't think of a more disgusting and insulting organization. Corruption reigns at Big Blue" (January 31, 2015). Such rhetoric would rarely have appeared in writing even in the mid-1990s. Conrad found many personal criticisms of CEOs and managers too vulgar or mean-spirited to post. Watson Sr.'s notion of the "IBM Family" was gone.

But it was not for lack of trying by Palmisano. Recall that during his first two decades at IBM the Basic Beliefs were still alive. When it was his turn to run the company, he still believed that shared values could play a powerful role, so he updated the Basic Beliefs in 2003. He explained in late 2004, "I feel that a strong value system is crucial to bringing together and motivating a workforce as large and diverse as ours has become. We have nearly one-third of a million employees serving clients in 170 countries. Forty percent of those people don't report daily to an IBM site; they work on the client's premises, from home, or they're mobile." Important to him was that "half of today's employees have been with the company for fewer than five years because of recent acquisitions and our relatively new practice of hiring seasoned professionals." He could not order them around. Top-down management had failed in the 1980s, while a set of values embraced by employees would make it possible for people to go about their work when management was not there to tell them what to do. "People—rather than products—become your brand," taking us back to Iwata's point.[49] When Palmisano published his three new values, over 200,000 employees quickly downloaded them, and responses back included severe criticisms about how IBM was not living up to them but very few that were critical of what these three ideas stood for. IBM had preserved some of the Watsonian

DNA of the Basic Beliefs. It was the gap between values and execution that had created so much tension during Palmisano's tenure and that of his successor.

KEEPING SCORE

The media paid less attention to IBM's churn in personnel and layoffs than current and former IBMers wanted. The company deflected interest by not releasing data on the number laid off and usually dismissed employees in low enough numbers on a continuous basis to avoid regulatory reporting. Gerstner and Palmisano displayed greater interest in discussing "shareholder value" and dividends. Rometty continued that focus on financials. The bigger story outside the firm was its business success. Customers acquired IBM's products and services, stockholders enjoyed rising stock values and growing dividends, and IBM was back in the business of being iconic. Table 18.1 reports the company's financials, reflecting results for both Gerstner's and Palmisano's efforts.

Revenue grew, with dips caused largely by the sale of low-profit businesses. Net income increased, especially during Gerstner's tenure. Management intensified its focus on what is delicately called "financial reengineering," an emphasis on increasing earnings per share, dividends, and

Table 18.1

IBM's business performance, select years, 1998–2011

(revenue, net income, and cash flow in billions of dollars)

Metric	1998	2000	2002	2004	2006	2008	2011
Revenue	81.7	85.1	81.2	96.3	91.4	103.6	106.9
Net income (loss)	6.3	8	5.3	7.5	9.5	12.3	15.9
Earnings per share (dollars)	3.3	4.4	2.4	4.4	6.1	8.9	13.4
Cash flow from operations	9.3	9.3	10.5	12.9	15.3	12.9	19.9
Return on stockholders' equity (%)	32.6	40	22.8	29.8	34	13.6	20.2
Number of employees (thousands)	291	316	316	329	356	399	434
Stock price (year-end)	92.2	85	77.5	98.5	97.15	84.16	183.8

Source: IBM annual reports, numbers rounded. Some dramatic changes were the result of changes in accounting's reporting practices, such as return on stockholders' equity between 2006 and 2008.

stock value, even buying back IBM shares. Cash flows improved, largely from a growing portfolio of long-term outsourcing contracts and services, ensuring a steady stream of money. After Gerstner's tenure, the number of employees kept increasing, although who they were changed as thousands left and other thousands were hired. Annual reports always spoke to investors, less often to customers, and hardly at all to employees. Each year, Gerstner, then Palmisano, emphasized returns to stockholders, hence the efforts to reduce expenses to increase profits, move into new markets, and report on new products and services.

With Palmisano's time as CEO ending in 2012, Corporate worked to end his term on a high note. IBM celebrated its centennial in 2011, using the occasion to claim the right to speak from a position of financial strength by which the world could learn from its experiences. Palmisano argued that, "We believe the lessons of our history apply more broadly. Whether you seek to understand the trajectory of technology or to build and sustain a successful enterprise or to make the world work better, there is much to learn from IBM's experiences."[50] One can forgive the hubris and celebrating the centennial, because it is rare for a company to last as long as IBM.

The media, customers, and industry observers acknowledged the company's milestone, regardless of criticisms they had about its financial practices, layoffs, and difficulty of doing business with it. *Bloomberg* captured much of Wall Street's assessment when it summarized changes the chairman had made, all of which "helped Palmisano realign what was once the largest computer company into a service and software powerhouse. The maneuvers made the company predictably profitable, boosting per-share profit for more than 30 quarters. Since 2001, Palmisano has boosted sales by 20 percent, while keeping costs of the 426,000 employee behemoth little changed."[51] Regarding Roadmap 2010 results, Palmisano proclaimed, "Over the past five years, we have increased our market capitalization by $70 billion, and returned $50 billion to shareholders in net share repurchases and $14 billion in dividends—creating approximately $135 billion in value for our owners."[52] Five years earlier (2006), 65 percent of IBM's profit came from services and software, now 84 percent, while he had invested $70 billion in

R&D since 2000. In the same period, IBM acquired 130 firms. It seemed the company was in good shape, but the celebration would not last long.

The end of Palmisano's period at the helm coincided with the dawn of a rapid reversal of the momentum and successes achieved in the post-1994 era. The next one, under Rometty, was fraught with financial shortfalls and concerns, more churn in IBM's employee population, a faltering strategy that ushered in a more widely supported one, what Rometty called a "reboot," and the birth of a new approach for sustaining IBM's business. Those who thought IBM could continue to ride a wave of success based on the actions taken by Gerstner and Palmisano were mistaken. What happened? How bad was it? Because IBM was a company that so many customers depended on, answering these questions became crucial to them, to hundreds of thousands of IBMers, and to the future of how humans could possibly understand the weather, solve fundamental health problems, and rely on artificial intelligence, better known as cognitive computing. Those are subjects of chapter 19.

19 HARD TIMES, AGAIN, AND ANOTHER TRANSFORMATION

We no longer expect to deliver $20 operating earnings per share in 2015.
—IBM CFO MARTIN SCHROETER, OCTOBER 2014

ON JANUARY 19, 2017, IBM's CFO explained that for the nineteenth consecutive quarter of Ginni Rometty's stewardship, IBM's revenue shrank, and the company's hardware business had declined even faster. Yet many analysts and stockholders applauded because the source of its revenue showed IBM was transforming away from low-profit businesses to others with larger profit potential (software, analytics, and artificial intelligence), notably cloud computing, which was even better when combined with artificial intelligence. It was essential for a major IT provider to be participating in this area. Since 2012, IBM's revenue has continued to shrink, and the company has laid off thousands of employees while thousands of others have entered the firm. Employee morale declined, too. Only half the company's employees would recommend to their friends that they work at IBM.[1] In earlier decades, thousands worked to get their children into Big Blue. The media and customers complained loudly in 2013 that things were not going well at IBM. Employees had been making the same point for over a decade. In their defense, senior executives argued that the company was shifting away from hardware to services and software, such as cloud computing and analytics, later into security and mobility, counseling patience and understanding. Analysts applauded these moves but complained about execution: hardware sales were dropping faster than revenues were increasing from the new "imperatives." They wanted results in the current quarter, while executives understood that big changes took years to accomplish. The question was could they shift—in their words "transform"—quickly enough to keep up, then set the pace in changing the buying practices of their customers and changing information technology?

Industry observers complained that IBM was late to the party, particularly to cloud computing. Roadmaps and their targets predominated for too long as the company's operational mantra. Finally, in the fall of 2014, the company dropped its roadmap strategies, a half decade after complaints from thousands of employees that they perverted IBM's ability to succeed, diverted attention from focusing on customers and product innovations, and encouraged excessive cost cutting and large layoffs. IBM was under siege, playing catch-up with changing competitors, emerging technologies, and hence what customers were buying, while mad ex-employees were becoming customers, possibly future poison pills for the company. The timing of changes to new technological regimes is also of great interest to business historians, and not just to economic historians interested in technological innovations and their impact. While much work has been done in studying, say, R&D practices, such as by Margaret B. W. Graham, David C. Mowery, and Richard Nelson, to mention some of the most obvious, fewer studies have addressed how individual senior management teams respond, so this chapter expands the aperture on the issue of change management.[2]

By 2014, even the culture and practices of the Gerstner period were barely recognizable at IBM, with its sales culture seriously undermined and senior leaders relying too much on financial and accounting strategies as they plodded toward new sources of revenue. They bailed water out of the blue boat to maintain high cash flows from service contracts and to sustain profits and the value of the company's stock. Senior leaders focused on quarter-to-quarter management of the business out of the Corporate, services, and software parts of the business. This chapter will have much to say on each of these points, drawing on statements by executives and employees. It seemed like the financial and human resources staffs were dictating what everyone had to do. Layoffs were mandated, even for fully engaged service personnel billing their time, all to drive down expenses. In

Canada and the United States in 2016, employees were reporting layoffs of salespeople responsible for promoting Watson computing, one of IBM's focus areas. Growing numbers of employees seemed to express a collective quizzical look. IBM's history reminds us that Big Blue had overcome adversities before, that it was frequently late to a new technological revelry, something Watson Jr. reminded in his memoirs, but once in a market, it was often a dominant player. Each time, it was not clear whether the company would survive. Too many observers prematurely wrote off the firm. Yet, here we are with a company that generated $80 billion in annual revenue, so while IBM was again in trouble, it was also doing well. IBM's old culture was gone; a new one that employees, customers, the media, and analysts could see would sustain the company had yet to solidify. The CEO since 2012, Virginia M. "Ginni" Rometty (b.1957), clearly had as rough a time on her watch as John Akers had on his or Thomas Watson Jr. had. In Rometty's case, she enjoyed less employee support than Watson Jr., or even Akers.[3]

Understanding recent events at IBM is as important as ever, because IBM continues to play an extraordinary role and draws the attention of scholars, employees, and other business observers. It is involved in shaping national economies and the future of robotics, medicine, artificial intelligence in augmenting human behavior, and computing itself. We face the problem of the company's future remaining unclear. There is a history lesson to help in our assessment: IBM is so big, powerful, and able to accumulate billions of dollars that it cannot be written off as some technological has-been. To kill the old computer dinosaur would still require an army of dragon slayers. The old dinosaur had evolved into a more advanced form that required different hunters, while naysayers were also transforming into new competitors, such as Google and Amazon.com; new partners, such as Apple; and new investors, such as the Sage of Omaha, Warren Buffett (b. 1930), and his company, Berkshire Hathaway, until he chose to reduce his investment in 2017.[4]

This chapter focuses on recent events at IBM, even though the story told lacks the clarity made possible by the hindsight of history. IBM remains a company filled with bright, highly educated, experienced employees, even if too many of them are disgruntled, yet cheered on by the market, stock analysts, investors, and customers. What are we to make of this situation? It begins with a failed strategy that took too long to rectify but— and this is an essential quality of IBM—in time management changed and faced the necessity to acknowledge, retire, and replace old practices. I describe the company's strategy to the point where it needed replacement, assess an enormous problem within the firm of laying off employees and hiring new ones, and assess these actions within the context of IBM's old Basic Beliefs and the exigencies of current realities. Then I describe IBM's current business strategy. It is essential to wrap up with a discussion of artificial intelligence—IBM's Watson system—as that is the central technological and marketing focus of the firm today. While the events described are still unfolding as this book goes to press, the description is done in the language of the historian. Those familiar with the work of Alfred D. Chandler Jr., Louis Galambos, and Geoffrey Jones, among historians, and such industry watchers as Gideon Gartner in the 1970s and 1980s and Kevin Kelly in the 1990s and the next decade, will see that they shaped my discussion of post-9/11 IBM. We see a demonstration of what Martin Campbell-Kelly and Daniel D. Garcia-Swartz demonstrated in their history of the computer industry, that "the persistence of companies is, in an overworked but fundamentally true phrase of our era, constant reinvention," and only those that "responded to rapidly evolving technologies and markets have been able to survive and thrive."[5] IBM was transforming in a century that continued to see improvements in the lives of people that were made possible by the continued development of information, knowledge, and wealth, which historian of optimism and progress Steven Pinker based on the call "dare to understand!" IBM's offerings continued to be at the center of that 250-year pursuit of the Enlightenment by humankind.[6] That is the central theme of IBM's history during the twenty-first century. The reader will notice that the tone and depth of detail change in this chapter, as we shift to what management intends, with less emphasis on what IBM did. That is because of the immediacy of unfolding events.

FROM ROADMAP 2015 TO ROADKILL 2015

In the first decade of the new millennium, the company's most senior executives deemphasized Gerstner's focus on the needs of customers, concentrating greater attention on delivering "shareholder value" as their prime mission, trumpeting less the needs of other stakeholders, notably employees. While many other large, publicly traded U.S. corporations embraced similar priorities, IBM seemed to be an extreme case, the poster child for financial engineering. That is not to say IBM turned its back on its customers—far from it. It seemed to employees that the firm lowered its appreciation for their contributions as well. Nothing so dramatically demonstrated the shift from earlier priorities than Roadmap 2010, and more so Roadmap 2015. The first one worked, the second one caused declines in revenue. IBM's productivity shrank and its market shares shrank for nearly half a decade in such key segments as cloud and mobile computing. The magnitude of the effects of the two Roadmap strategies on IBM's performance is comparable to the effects of those initiated by John Opel in the early 1980s. In the case of the roadmaps, the remnants of Watson-era culture deteriorated sufficiently to again raise questions about the long-term viability of the company. So, how did the roadmap strategy come to IBM?

Recall that in 2006 Sam Palmisano announced Roadmap 2010, which set as a financial target increasing earnings per share (EPS) by 2010, which IBM achieved largely through a combination of layoffs, the sale of poorly performing parts of the company, buybacks of its stock, and routine culling of wasteful and redundant expenses. In the process, the company became addicted to layoffs and increased use of financial strategies, which IBMers and stock analysts increasingly called gimmicks. Efforts to grow IBM with sales and new offerings slowed. Palmisano explained his rationale for that first roadmap in mid-2015, when employees were attacking the second one, joined by a growing number of market analysts, industry watchers, and investors worried whether IBM had driven toward its goal with such force that it reduced its ability to compete. He argued that while investors demanded quarter-to-quarter improvements of all companies, this attitude made no sense when managing a firm. He admitted, "However, that investors want some direction as to where you'll be so they can measure you and decide whether to invest in you or not. That's a very fair request." He continued, "So, we came up with something we felt we could live with and that made sense, which was a 2010 road map to go from $6 to at least $10 a share." He denied it was a financial target, arguing it was "a long-term perspective of where the IBM Company could be in four to five years. It was a way to be shareholder friendly, but not quarterly driven." But, put a number in front of an IBMer and they will chase it like a dog after a rabbit.[7] The roadmap became *the* target driving many decisions and actions from 2006 through 2010.

The value of IBM's stock remained elevated, as did profitable cash flows. IBM continued to pay generous dividends, and its senior executives enjoyed growth in their stock options, but IBM paid a hefty price for these results: a slowing response to new market conditions, such as its delayed entry into cloud computing.[8] In the past, IBM's ability to respond to changing market circumstances was normally at the rate it needed to optimize sales and profits or to be slightly ahead of its competitors, as in the 1960s and 1970s. In fairness to Palmisano, the company acquired PwC's consulting arm, which was a true investment in the future of the firm, and worldwide manufacturing and service delivery systems were implemented. These actions worked.

Wall Street loved the boldness and confidence with which Roadmap 2010 was announced and carried out, because it promised predictable returns on IBM stock, but employees became hostile toward it, as they came to link it with layoffs of expensive U.S. employees to support the strategy almost from the time it was announced. Customers at first did not see any impact on their service from IBM, but by 2010 that was no longer true. Meanwhile, the press marveled at how well IBM seemed to be run, a pleasant circumstance as much attributable to their naive understanding of what was happening inside IBM as it was to excellent marketing and media management. As one Wall Street insider put it, "No public company we can think of does a better job of schmoozing Wall Street's Finest and convincing them that there's a there, when in fact the there is not quite as there as it might seem."[9] Armed with a detailed plan for how they were going to make "the numbers," the strategists and financial community in Armonk recommended to Palmisano a new roadmap: $20 EPS by 2015. He and his board embraced it for the same reasons they had the first one, with the added incentive that Roadmap 2010 worked, overachieving its targets (reaching $11.52) and making its original goal a year early.[10] The decision to announce this second roadmap involved many senior executives, but Palmisano took credit for it.

In 2009, when work on the next roadmap was under way, the executive in charge of IBM's strategy was Ginni Rometty, then senior vice president and group executive for sales, marketing and strategy. In other words, she and her organization were primary authors, along with Mark Loughridge (b. 1953), who had worked in IBM's financial communities since joining the company in 1977. Outside of IBM, he was credited as the creator of both roadmaps, with Palmisano's full support. Loughridge prepared various detailed presentations on how IBM would implement its roadmap. To make the target, IBM had to expand business into new parts of the world and with new products and services, which is where Rometty and her team came in. In the end, buybacks and layoffs contributed successfully to the first couple of years of the second plan, while her team turned in a less stellar performance. It is important to call out her role because when named president and CEO of IBM in October 2011, she had fully embraced Roadmap 2015. One might argue that Palmisano was still around as chairman so she had no real choice but to continue supporting it until he turned over the chairmanship to her in late 2012, but she continued to support Roadmap 2015 for another two years. She really owned it.

By then, financial objectives dominated Armonk's activities. The first line in Rometty's first chairman's letter, in the annual report for 2012, makes it obvious: "I am pleased to report that in 2012, IBM achieved record operating earnings per share, record free cash flow and record profit margins, with revenues that were flat at constant currency." She continued, "Operating earnings per share were up 13 percent, putting us well on track to our 2015 Road Map objective of at least $20 of operating earnings per share. Importantly, we continued to deliver value to you, our owners."[11] That year, IBM generated $104.5 billion in revenue. It was perfect; just keep doing what Palmisano had done. Investors loved it.

One analyst summed up investor views: "I've never heard anyone within IBM articulate the value of the company the way she does."[12] But the roadmap represented more than a "goal" (her term). Rometty explained:

> As before, the road map is not simply a list of targets, but a management model built on exploiting multiple ways to create value. Operating leverage will come from our continuing shift to higher-margin businesses and improving enterprise productivity—expected to be $8 billion over this five-year period. We will create value for shareholders through an anticipated $50 billion in share repurchases and $20 billion in dividends.[13]

Cutting the number of available shares would increase earnings per share (EPS). Rometty anticipated generating $20 billion from "growth areas" by 2015. This growth would come from new markets where local economies were expanding, business analytics, "cloud computing," and an array of uses of computing to improve human activities such as managing supply chains, farming, water, sewer systems, and urban operations, all under the clever marketing title of "smarter planet." Charts detailed how EPS would be achieved year by year, with plans being developed, implemented, and updated quarterly until IBM abandoned Roadmap 2015 in October 2014. EPS of $20 had become *the* target before all others.

Every annual report from this period, and many speeches by Palmisano and Rometty to employees and the public, made it clear that Roadmap 2015 was the focus. One participant in quarterly IBM analyst conference calls recalled that these were "run by the CFO and focused strictly on the numbers: on the revenue number, on the cash flow number, on the share buyback number, and on the earnings number. In particular, the per share earnings number." He added, "The CEO never graces the call, and no actual business operators discuss their business. No success stories are told, no customers highlighted. It is all about margins and currencies and so-called one-time charges and so-called one-time gains, and tax rates, and how all those things added up to the earnings per share that quarter. And, most especially, what that earnings per share means for *The EPS Roadmap*" (analyst's emphasis).[14]

Rometty was the longest-serving champion of Roadmap 2015. A graduate of Northwestern University with a science degree, she joined

IBM in 1981 as a systems engineer in a Detroit, Michigan, branch office. Articulate, bright, and filled with a confident energy, she quickly moved up the organization in the 1980s and 1990s, largely in services. In 2002, she became the executive most responsible for the acquisition of PwC's consulting arm, continuing to ride IBM's march into services and consulting. Colleagues noticed in the 1980s and early 1990s that she sported a large ego and drive. Once she entered management, she tended to use the word "I" instead of "we" to claim credit for accomplishments by her organization and developed a reputation for not being loyal to her employees. At IBM, it was more customary to be inclusive and in public to be humble about one's achievements. In one internal presentation, Rometty chastised her services executives and managers for being more interested in their families than in IBM's business. The next day, she sent the attendees an e-mail that may have been the closest to an apology she ever made in public. Her language and behavior dogged her throughout her career, and she increasingly drew criticism because she "never covers your back." One manager to whom she reported found her "not warm," lacking a strong "people leadership style."[15] People commented that she did not inspire employees, treating them, to use her word, as "resources," a term that irritated many IBMers. As she approached Palmisano's position as head of the company, she had rivals to contend with. One, Steven A. Mills, senior vice president of the profitable software business, was reaching the age of retirement. Another, Robert Moffat (b. 1956), Mills's peer responsible for the systems and technology (hardware) group, got caught up in a sex for insider trading scandal in 2009, was fired, convicted, and served six months in federal prison.[16] A close confidant of Palmisano, he was also responsible for many thousands of layoffs and was therefore unpopular among wide swaths of IBM's U.S. manufacturing workforce.

Rometty was qualified and faced no rivals, so it made sense to give her the CEO job. It helped that she had a charisma that worked well outside of IBM, so essential in dealing with customers, investors, and the media. Within the services business, she had a reputation for cutting expenses and laying off people to make her targets and for being weaker when it came to implementing revenue growth strategies. She focused more on financial strategies than Palmisano had, far less on expanding the business or nurturing the sales culture that had long worked for IBM. She embraced the move to software and services. She had tied her destiny to Palmisano's. On the occasion of her appointment as CEO in 2011, she announced that, "What you'll see is an unfolding of the strategy we have in place," and according to the *New York Times* took credit for having "a hand in creating it."[17] She proved more of a technocrat than an inspirational leader, more in the mold of Palmisano and Akers but more blunt.

Figure 19.1
Virginia Marie "Ginni" Rometty served as IBM's chairman, president, and CEO beginning in 2012, during a difficult period in IBM's history. Photo courtesy of IBM Archives.

The centerpiece of Rometty's leadership rested in managing financial results and shareholder value. In April 2012, she hosted her first shareholder meeting, in Charleston, South Carolina. She reported "weak" earnings for the first quarter—unfortunately for IBM a harbinger of things to come—but doubled down on the financial strategy already in play for a decade by reminding her audience of the value of the stock and the $15 billion spent on stock buybacks and $3.5 billion in dividends, up 15 percent over the previous year. She proudly announced that IBM had spent $6.3 billion on R&D, which seemed stingy in comparison to the other numbers she bandied about. She argued that, "Since the beginning of 2000, we have returned $133 billion to you in the form of dividends and share repurchases, while investing $81 billion in capital expenditures and acquisitions, and spending nearly $70 billion on R&D."[18] The global economy was in various states of recession or weakness. At this annual stockholders meeting, she reiterated her commitment to her "Roadmap to the Future."

By July, IBM's revenue fell only 3 percent, despite the continuing deterioration in the global economy, while net income rose by 6 percent, the latter made possible by stringent controls on expenses. Employees complained that Rometty made this possible by laying off colleagues. By October, it seemed that IBM was settling into a pattern of disappointments. Phil Guido, in charge of North American sales, admitted to his employees that "we had a disappointing quarter," because they had not grown revenue. He blamed customers for putting off decisions to buy while they waited for anticipated new products. He also blamed poor performance by sales teams, using phrases like "we had execution issues." The bad news kept coming in. First quarter 2013 saw no revenue growth, despite continued acquisitions of software firms by IBM. Already shrinking service revenue declined by another 4 percent.

Then a psychological bomb hit IBM HQ. The blast was eerily similar to the one that hit IBM in the early 1950s when its first customer, the U.S. Bureau of the Census, from which Hollerith had come with his tabulating equipment, which became the core of early IBM, chose to obtain its first computer from Univac, not IBM. If one had to pick one event more than any other that caused Watson Jr. to move quickly into computers, that was it. Now it seemed it was happening again, involving "cloud computing"—a form of mainframe outsourced processing. The U.S. Central Intelligence Agency (CIA), a massive user of computing, was moving to the cloud and put out a request for bids for that business. IBM made the short list of two potential suppliers. On February 14, 2013, the agency awarded the business to Amazon.com, the large online retailer, for which cloud services was not even core to its business. Amazon.com had made the case that because e-commerce was very much like cloud computing, involving millions of individuals accessing server farms to process data (orders), it could support the CIA's large number of employees. What made the award more shocking was that Amazon's bid cost a third *more* than IBM's. IBM protested, since it was the low-cost bidder, but government auditors responded that CIA officials had "grave" doubts that IBM could provide reliable technology and cloud computing, rating its capability "marginal." IBM was now, incredibly, too "risky" to choose. As one reporter put it, "The CIA butt kicking is a microcosm of larger problems IBM is having as it struggles to adapt to the cloud era," instead focusing too much on what the writer referred to, using an internal IBM employee term, as "Roadkill."[19]

Complaints leaked to the public. On the Internet, bloggers accused Rometty of not having a vision, of she and IBM executives being "out of touch" in going after the cloud opportunity, and of maintaining too many layers of management. One industry commentator, Steven Zolman, argued that "IBM's sales culture is poison" because so many in sales did not understand the products and services they sold, obsessing instead on closing higher-margin sales. Moreover, executive compensation was tied directly to whether the company made the earnings per share targets of Roadmap 2015.[20] Others worried that exporting services to other countries—offshoring—reduced the quality of IBM's performance in North America and Western Europe. Success at IBM had to start "with a strategy that's designed to impress more than just Wall Street investors"; instead Rometty was providing "more of the same" rather than a response to changing conditions in the market.[21] Customers were buying fewer machines and software housed on their own premises and more computing services through subscriptions to cloud-based offerings.

Headlines became uglier, such as "IBM's Sales Slump Turns Stock into Dow's Lone Loser of 2013," despite increases in dividends. Total sales declined in 2013 because of sluggish sales of hardware that could not be made up by growing revenues for software and services. Rometty was blamed for trying to cover these gaps by relying on job cuts, tax gains, and sales of assets in order to increase EPS. One portfolio manager, Todd Lowenstein, complained in late December 2013 that, "We don't think investors are going to be paying up for financially engineered EPS." They "want to see top-line growth, and IBM is just not part of that trend."[22] IBM's supporters among reporters, bloggers, and industry watchers were now making suggestions on how IBM could fix its problems.[23]

IBM's customers found a growing number of cloud service providers. IBM did not see growth in overall sales as measured by revenue for the next several years. On January 21, 2014, after releasing the previous year's disappointing numbers, Rometty announced that the executive team would "forgo our personal annual incentive payments for 2013."[24] But she was sticking with Roadmap 2015. It began to appear that customers were voting with their budgets for something IBM was having difficulty offering.

IBM's circumstances deteriorated more rapidly in 2014. Stockbrokers were tiring of IBM's focus on earnings and began paying more attention to its shrinking revenue:

> Even though IBM delivered 11% EPS growth in FY13, revenues declined, and the company saw a sharp decline in hardware profitability.... While IBM was able to offset much of the decline through cost savings and margin expansion in software and services, IBM also excluded a $1B restructuring charge from non GAAP EPS, a stark change from previous years when restructuring expenses ... were included in the P&L. Moreover, a lower tax rate ... generated over 85% of the company's EPS growth.[25]

Translated into nontechnical language, IBM used an alternative set of measures along with the required GAAP (generally accepted accounting principles) to emphasize its cash flow.[26] Another criticism of Roadmap 2015 was that, "It's a bit of a mystery why IBM is sticking to the EPS roadmap when it appears less and less relevant."[27] One stockbroker forecast that IBM would "repurchase $15B or more of its shares this year [2014], and rebalance its workforce by at least 13,000 heads. Many investors believe IBM should be investing in its future by buying new technologies and investing in building capability, rather than rightsizing the organization." The same commentator offered up the theory "that IBM's financial incentives (senior executives; incentive programs are based 60% on operating net income near-term and 80% of operating EPS long term) make the choice simple."[28] More sinister reports began circulating that IBM had stashed assets and employees in subsidiaries in low-tax countries, such as Ireland and the Netherlands: "The Dutch group [IBM] had three employees in 2008, a number that has since swelled to about 205,000 as of the end of 2012—only 2 percent of whom actually work in the Netherlands."[29] The press began reporting that IBM had accumulated $44 billion in profits outside the United States for which it paid no U.S. taxes. More analysts and industry watchers criticized IBM's fixation on earnings that spring and summer.

In first quarter 2014, revenue shrank again by 4 percent year over year. Rometty shifted her message to growth: "In the first quarter, we continued to take actions to transform part of the business and to shift aggressively to our strategic growth areas including cloud, Big Data analytics, social, mobile and security." She added, "As we move through 2014, we will begin to see the benefits from these actions."[30] Meanwhile, IBM's stock declined in value by roughly 20 percent. According to one critic, the market's support for IBM so far came "with [a] 25% reduction in IBM's workforce, most of which will be shed from the company's hardware business. When has that ever been good news? The company called it 'rebalancing its workforce' so that it can better focus on its new priorities including analytics, cloud and cognitive computing." The same critic, however, said the "company has finally come to terms with its history of underinvestment."[31] CNNMoney put the problem more succinctly: "Two years into Ginni Rometty's tenure as CEO, the company faces a double dilemma: Revenue is shrinking while the company is having trouble hitting its ambitious EPS targets."[32] Wall Street was becoming nervous about her priorities and ability to execute. Forbes got personal, saying, "IBM leadership appears to have lost its way," adding that "managing earnings is not managing for long-term success" and concluding that "the real problems—R&D cuts, higher debt, massive stock buybacks" were dampening optimism for the company. That other firms were doing massive buybacks did not matter; IBM was now seen as being in real trouble.[33]

Reports of "fed up" IBMers seeped into the press: protests by IBMers in France over working conditions in June, earlier complaints at various IBM plants in the United States and Latin America, downsizing reports out of India. In September, employees in various parts of the company were informed that their skills were not up to snuff and therefore they would have to take training to stay in the company and, while doing so, would be docked 10 percent of their salary. People were shocked because normally an employer paid for training, not employees. This action was seen as yet another act of penny-pinching financial engineering to drive down costs in the face of inadequate growth in revenue. People began asking, what is going on? Where is the board of directors when you need it? What does such an action say about IBM's values? Was IBM misleading customers when it said it had the skills needed to serve them, justifying IBM's pricing, yet accusing employees of not having those skills? One reporter wondered about Rometty's role. Was this a random act by an executive making "a boneheaded move without informing anyone?" The editorial conclusion to that question advised IBM's management: "Don't be jerks."[34] Headlines became hostile, even from sources historically friendly to IBM, such as *The Motley Fool,* which ran one that read, "Should the Dow Jones Get Rid of International Business Machines Corp?"[35] It all came to a head on October 20, 2014.

It was not going to be the usual quarterly conference call hosted by IBM's CFO to answer analysts' questions about earnings past and anticipated. For one thing, Rometty turned up on the call along with her CFO, Martin Schroeter. On the call were analysts from Goldman Sachs, Morgan Stanley, Sanford Bernstein, Barclays, UBS, Citi, and other institutions, including Cantor Fitzgerald, now back in business after losing almost its entire staff in the destruction of the World Trade Center towers on 9/11. Schroeter first went through the normal recitation of the numbers: a 4 percent decline in revenue this quarter compared to 2014's third quarter, and net income of $3.7 billion, also down from expectations. Services revenue was flat, margins declined, the company faced a "tax headwind," and it generated about the same cash as before ($2.2 billion). Hardware sales dropped precipitously. Schroeter blamed weaker software revenue, again on "some sales execution issues," and volatility in world currencies. He reported "strong growth" in revenue from IBM's focus areas, its "imperatives." A piece of news he wanted to emphasize but that the press paid hardly any attention to was IBM's sale of its microelectronics business to GlobalFoundries, the firm that would provide IBM with its future semiconductor technology. Schroeter said that IBM would move more quickly into higher-growth businesses. Schroeter said IBM would use more overseas "global delivery skills," code language for cheaper workers. Because of divestitures of slower businesses, he cautioned to expect revenue to be down $7 billion, with pretax losses of a half billion dollars. So far, this was a routine call about declining IBM performance and a strong defense of what it would do next.

As Schroeter was ending his prepared remarks, it became clear to everyone on the call why Rometty was on it as well. The CFO dropped a bombshell so quietly, so briefly that it took even IBMers several days to realize what had just happened. Schroeter announced, "Given our third quarter performance, the actions we're taking and with only 15 months till the end of 2015, we no longer expect to deliver $20 operating earnings per share in 2015." IBM had just announced that it was *abandoning* Roadmap 2015.

Events in 2015 and beyond would determine whether that was what Rometty and her team were doing. They already had a new strategy, one that many IBMers, investors, and customers liked—the "imperatives."[36] In response to a question, Rometty doubled down on the importance of IBM's cloud strategy, which included data and analytics, saying that IBM was going to move more quickly in transforming the company to pursue new growth areas. Asked about declines in the number of employees, the CFO acknowledged some occurred as a result of selling businesses but also because of relying on "global delivery centers," in which IBM did work remotely for clients. Rometty reinforced the need for speed, use of mobile and other technologies, and reducing layers of management. Toward the end of the call, Rometty repeated that, "We no longer expect to deliver the

2015 EPS objective." She admitted that Q3 of 2014 was bad, yet the company was "fundamentally better positioned than it was a few years ago."[37]

Once IBM released its numbers, the stock market responded quickly. IBM's stock dropped to a three-year low. The press picked up on the message about canceling the roadmap. Rometty sent a note to all employees announcing the weak performance, then pivoted to a reminder that the company would implement a three-part plan: establish a dedicated cloud business, introduce more flexible software offerings for customers and transform how services were delivered, and continue to streamline the company's operations to improve its speed and agility. Mark Cuban, an outspoken billionaire, blurted out his disgust: "IBM is no longer a tech company. They have no vision. What they've evolved into is a company that does [arbitrage] on acquisitions. It's stock buybacks. Who is IBM anymore?" He would "absolutely not invest in IBM," saying it was no longer a computer company but instead "they specialize in financial engineering." Just as bad in Cuban's opinion, "They are an amalgamation of different companies that they are trying to ar[bitrage] on Wall Street, and I'm not a fan of that at all."[38] He was expressing how many people reacted after the announcement. One reporter put it simply: "And now Rometty is left with no clear, articulated turnaround strategy."[39]

Andrew Ross Sorkin at the *New York Times* came partially to Rometty's defense by claiming that she was stuck with the prior strategy launched by Palmisano, but he was also tough on her: "All these 'shareholder friendly' maneuvers have been masking an ugly truth: IBM's success in recent years has been tied more to financial engineering than actual performance." Probably emboldened by the 7 percent drop in the price of the stock to $169.10, he criticized IBM's practice of buying back so many of its shares, citing $138 billion spent on share buybacks and dividends, while spending only $59 billion on its own operations (capital expenditures and $32 billion in acquisitions). These actions led him to conclude that "IBM has arguably been spending its money on the wrong things: shareholders, rather than building its own business."[40] He was not alone in this view. David A. Stockman, in an earlier life President Ronald Reagan's director of the Office of Management and Budget and a banker, posted on his website earlier in 2014 that "IBM is a buyback machine on steroids that has been a huge stock-market winner by virtue of massaging, medicating and manipulating" its earnings.[41] Sorkin argued that Rometty was "late" in reinventing the company, and shareholders should have pressured the company to implement needed changes instead of basking in the mirage of rising stock values and strong dividends.[42] Could Rometty turn the company around in time?

IBMers and ex-employees went to the Internet to opine: "Anybody who watched quarter after quarter of revenue declines while expecting the $20 target to happen must believe in magic"; "Give the company back to technology, taking it away from financial engineers … and treat their star employees well"; "Build organic products that companies and people want"; "Under the deal with GlobalFoundries, IBM will pay the semiconductor company $1.5 billion to take over chip manufacturing operations [true] so the business was managed to the point it had a negative value?"; "Buybacks are, in my view, a negative leading indicator that signals no other productive uses of capital are available." Some thought Rometty inherited a bad situation from Palmisano, that he had cleaned out much of the fat, leaving her to cut muscle to make the target. But a more widely held opinion was that, "She has had almost 3 years to make things better at IBM and has failed convincingly. When is the Board of Directors going to take some action? Is anybody at the helm or is the ship going down with the crew?"[43] Concerns about layoffs dominated employee comments: "Sure lay off all employees here in the US and offshore every job. See how fast this ship sinks then"; "If layoffs are necessary, so be it. But Rometty should be the first to go"; "Same old story at IBM, layoffs, layoffs.… They have no other tricks." The bottom line was that, "IBM has simply lost its edge." Harking back to her reputation for lacking empathy, one employee wrote, "She speaks to staff and customers as if they were toddlers in kindergarten.… It breaks my heart after 40 years to see the changes in IBM. They forgot their strength was their people."[44]

When Rometty reported to investors in the annual report for 2014, published in early 2015, she no longer led off with Roadmap 2015 but rather with the argument that IBM was continuing to move to higher-value businesses, with a growing consensus of approval among IBM's investors and business media. It was also her strongest set of statements about what would soon be called IBM's "imperatives," such as the move to cloud, analytics, and Big Data. Revenue had shrunk again, this time by 5.7 percent, to $92.8 billion. Now consolidated gross profits had shrunk as well, by 4.7 percent. Global Services, supposedly the growth part of the business, shrank by 3.5 percent.[45] The first quarter was marginally better, with EPS up over first quarter 2014 by 9 percent and net income up 4 percent on flat revenue. Of that revenue, the contribution from strategic imperatives rose by 30 percent. Rometty reported things were unfolding as planned. Meanwhile, she hired consultants to help develop a strategy to fight off activist investors bent on ousting her. The activists failed, but they caught the attention of Wall Street.[46] The year 2015 was turning out to be another bad year.

It proved far worse for employees who were laid off. "Resource actions," "RAs" as they were known at IBM, attracted increased attention from the media.[47] By late spring 2015, such stories were linked to IBM's overall performance. Instead of having 134,000 employees in the United States, as it did in 2005, it now employed roughly 78,000—Corporate no longer reported how many it had anywhere in the world, just the grand total. Analysts speculated on how many more would go based on charges to restructuring reported by IBM, leading to estimates that IBM had disposed of 15,000 U.S. employees in 2014 and might "only" eliminate 12,000 in 2015. As one analyst put it, "That's what it's come to at IBM. Cutting the jobs of 12,000 people gets shrugged off as business as usual."[48]

It was becoming difficult to find optimists. In October 2014, the board authorized another round of stock buybacks, while Rometty declared that, "We will continue to make the investments and changes necessary to manage our business for the long term and to shift to higher-value offerings." But, she also doubled down on the financial intent of remaining "fully committed to returning significant value to shareholders," hence the buybacks, dividend payments, and continued reduction in the cost of employees. Pondering all of this, one American analyst wondered "whether IBM will have enough cash flow to fund these buybacks organically, or if it will need to issue even more debt," which could cause rating agencies at some point to "downgrade IBM to junk."[49]

Revenue dropped by over $11 billion to $81.7 billion. Net income increased by a billion dollars, although income from continuing operations shrank by $2 billion. Net cash remained strong, at $17 billion; cash on hand was closer to $8 billion. Buybacks continued at nearly half the rate of earlier years. The board approved a slight uptick in dividends, but the value of the stock had dropped from $160.44 at the end of 2014 to $137.62 on December 31, 2015. IBM was positioned to lose many supporters. The story was becoming monotonous: investments in growth areas, continued layoffs, excuses about currency issues, and IBM's calls for patience from investors who had been extraordinarily patient during Rometty's tenure, probably because of consistent dividends and buybacks.

In 2016, IBM's revenue declined from $81.7 billion in 2015 to $79.9 billion, gross profit from $40.7 billion to $38.3 billion, and the all-important net income from $13.2 billion to nearly $11.9 billion. A combination of stock buybacks and increased dividends caused the stock's value to rise by over 20 percent, but the legacy business was still shrinking faster than the strategic imperatives were growing. However, imperatives now accounted for just over 40 percent of the company's revenue, which many felt meant IBM was finally getting traction in its latest transformation.[50] While the CFO explained last year's financial performance, Rometty was in Davos, Switzerland, at the World Economic Forum.

THE PROBLEM OF LAYOFFS

Dogging Armonk was the company's continual turnover of personnel. As the company shifted out of low-profit businesses and into others requiring new types of skills, IBMers left as part of what was sold off or transformed. Prior to such events, and over a period of years, layoffs occurred on a continuous basis in those parts of the business. No part of the business felt secure from layoffs, and not just the lower ranks. Increasingly, those in higher echelons, at divisional director and vice presidential levels, were laid off also. Manufacturing, software, and services divisions more aggressively shifted work to places where workers were less expensive. The poster child for that strategy was the move of thousands of jobs out of the United States to India.[51]

Layoffs could not be hidden in IBM's factory towns of Endicott, Poughkeepsie, and Fishkill, where IBM populations decreased by the thousands. In Endicott, IBM's presence went from over 10,000 to under 1,000 in less than fifteen years. Weeds grew in the empty parking lot at the closed IBM Country Club; paint peeled off the walls in the clubhouse itself. The Homestead became a privately owned hotel. Poughkeepsie's IBM population shrank just as dramatically. Similar stories of job losses could be cited in Germany, France, Canada, Great Britain, and Australia, among other countries. The thinning and replacement of IBM's population occurred in a recurring pattern. Those parts of the business that represented the past, the least profitable, contracted continuously, quarter after quarter, year after year. An employee's performance rating or skill played a decreasing role compared to what organization they resided in when it came to influencing their fate. By 2010, it seemed employees waited for the ax to fall, to be, in their words, "RA'ed" (meaning a "resource action" occurred). It began largely in those countries where labor laws provided the least resistance to such layoffs, notably nations of the British Commonwealth and the United States. As IBM worked to achieve its Roadmap 2015 goals, layoffs spread across France, the Netherlands, and Germany, despite local regulations making them difficult and expensive.

Four other trends accompanied layoffs. First, between the 1990s and 2017, severance payments shrank. For example, in the United States in the 1990s, someone leaving IBM would receive two weeks' salary for every year worked at the company up to six months of their current pay, in a one-time payment, plus medical benefits. By 2015, severance was one month's pay.

Second, benefits declined for those remaining. There was the case in the late 1990s when IBM attempted to replace its traditional pension plan with a new system that put money in an employee's 401(k) fund that discriminated against workers over the age of 40. A court ruled that illegal. In 2006, the company tried again. Fearful of rising and unpredictable costs for pensions and medical insurance in the United States, IBM announced that it would stop payments to its defined-benefit pension plan and instead make those payments into an employee's savings plan. In 2012, Corporate announced it would only make a one-time annual payment to the 401(k) accounts of individuals on the payroll as of December 15, so anyone laid off earlier in any year would not receive matching funds for pension purposes. Table 19.1 lists some of the obvious changes. Each step met with anger on the part of workers, who lit up websites with complaints. The layoffs continued.

A third, perverse practice seeped into IBM's behavior, noticeable by 2008 but blatant by 2010, involving the appraisal system. Every individual received a year-end performance appraisal that after text describing results included a rating—a grade—from "1" (outstanding) to "2+," "2" (average), "3" (underperforming), and "4" (not doing the job). There had always existed loosely defined guidelines as to what percentage of the workforce in a department, region, plant, or division should receive "1" appraisals, for example, much like an academic grade curve. As the years passed, guidelines and rules of thumb became hard targets imposed to keep labor costs down (a 1 was paid the most, a 2 received no bonuses or salary increases, and so forth). By 2010, even if a manager had an outstanding set of employees, the human resource community mandated that a certain percentage had to be rated a "3." The percentage to be rated a "3" evolved into specific targets;

Table 19.1
Changes in IBM's U.S. employee benefits, 1999–2014

1999	IBM pension plan replaced with a cash balanced account—later dismissed by court order as being illegal
2005	IBM announces it no longer will have a defined-benefit pension for employees; replaced with a payment to their 401(k) accounts instead
2007	IBM stops contributions to its pension fund, freezes all pension benefits, with no accruals for long-term employees;
	IBM announces enhancement of Tax Deferred Savings 401(k) Plan (TDSP)
2013	IBM announces that to receive TDSP matching grants an employee must be on the payroll on December 15, with funds to be deposited on December 31
2014	U.S. retirees on Medicare moved to extended health plan

Source: Peter E. Greulich, *A View from Beneath the Dancing Elephant: Rediscovering IBM's Corporate Constitution* (Austin, TX: MBI Concepts, 2014), 161–162.

for example, "You will appraise 5 of your staff a 3." When the next layoff was announced, those rated a "3" were the first to go. The appraisal system lost credibility. Employees and their managers did not take the exercise seriously as a means to motivate better performance and reward results. It got so bad that by 2015 the company had implemented a new appraisal system, promoted as providing continuous feedback to employees on their behavior and performance. Nothing changed; layoffs continued.

IBM was saddled with an appraisal system that many employees believed only worked to identify who to lay off next and was far from the Basic Beliefs one chose (Watson Sr.'s, Gerstner's, or Palmisano's). One employee's comments were typical, this one from October 2016: "Longtime IBMer. Always Top Performer 1+, 2—never a 3 in my career. Was put on a PIP [performance improvement plan, improve or you are fired] along with untold others. All high level and older. Instead of RA they were told their performance was not up to standard for the half and given incomprehensible targets for the PIP. 30 days severance."[52] By 2011, dismissed IBMers were complaining of age discrimination, largely in the United States. It did not help that Rometty and executives used the term *resources* to describe employees. The dehumanizing aspect of the word became an expanding affront, particularly to older employees. Thousands of employee Internet postings from 2007 to 2018 complained that morale was "terrible." From a human resources perspective, IBM was in as serious a period of personnel churn and crisis as it had been in since the late 1980s.

Fourth, layoffs were done gruffly, with an increasingly less sensitive approach to the feelings of individual IBMers. Their website postings were filled with accounts of the bluntness of layoffs, and these were now also beginning to filter into the economic and business literature. One early example from 1993 set the tone. An employee in good standing in Poughkeepsie, with 16 years of service, was told he was being laid off and was dismissed out of his building. His formal dismissal letter was both demeaning and reflected a betrayal of trust in his company: "You have been designated a 'surplus employee' effective immediately." This individual was one of 8,000 dismissed by IBM from the Central Hudson Valley area of New York.[53] That other large U.S. corporations were doing the same, including cutting back health benefits and retirement pensions, only bolstered senior management's belief that layoffs were a necessary and effective strategy by which to run the company worldwide. The old social contract had been broken. The chief economist at the U.S. Department of Labor in 2010–2011, Betsey Stevenson, observed that the days of taking care of one's employees were over, that "profits and efficiency have trumped generosity."[54]

With all the churn, it became increasingly difficult to know how many people worked at IBM. It is normal in a large enterprise for people to come and go, for the employee population to ebb and flow, and IBM is no exception. IBM, however, only publishes total population numbers and in 2018 it stated that the firm employed 367,000 worldwide.[55] In March 2018, a nonpartisan news outlet, Propublica, published a detailed report documenting age discrimination in how IBM chose who to lay off in the United States and in Western Europe, adding further controversy to its personnel practices.[56]

FIVE INITIATIVES AND THE EMERGENCE OF A NEW STRATEGY

With the obsessive roadmap focus diminished, the elements of IBM's strategy underpinning it became more obvious, easier to talk about, and increasingly made more sense to IBMers, analysts, and customers. Time would tell if Corporate had really retired Roadmap 2015 or simply continued it without explicitly discussing it. Rometty restated her financial objectives in ways that aligned more clearly with IBM's business strategy. For example, in early 2015, she set her sights on having IBM generate over 40 percent of its revenue in 2018 from five markets: analytics, cloud computing, cybersecurity, social networking, and mobile technologies. Older businesses, such as mainframes, would diminish, but IBM's challenge would be to grow revenues from new markets quickly enough to cover the retreat from the old while sustaining, and at some point growing, total revenue and profits. Units that IBM sold off, such as chip manufacturing, represented the elimination, in Rometty's words, of "empty calories," businesses that generated revenue but low or no profits. Hardware was not going away; rather, it was needed in new forms. Rometty said, "We can't hold on to our past." Some employees thought she was shedding IBM's core culture as much as old businesses when making such comments.

IBM got ahead of competitors with analytics software and with processes to manage and analyze massive bodies of data. While IBM arrived late to cloud computing, it slowly extended its presence among large enterprises in 2015 and 2016 with combinations of cloud services. Services involving cybersecurity represented a new market for IBM and most competitors in 2016, while a partnership with Apple Computer offered the promise of portable computing and app development platforms lodged in cloud servers. Social networking involved management consulting as much as software services. IBM's acquisitions were closely tied to supporting these areas of focus, particularly to catch up in cloud computing. IBM purchased a cloud computing firm called SoftLayer for $2 billion and opened a number of data centers to house cloud services. IBM amassed skills it did not have in cybersecurity, a new field for all IT vendors and customers, purchasing firms with those capabilities. Now Rometty had a strategy that resonated and played to her strengths in communicating their importance.[57]

Perhaps more interesting, yet still difficult to see, was a different transformation occurring with IBM's offerings, involving Watson, an artificial intelligence offering combining computing hardware and software. If it worked as engineers at IBM and its senior executives anticipated, it could be as important as System 360. More than a bundle of technologies, it consisted of a series of new services and capacities as well. These included analytics for Big Data, massive computing, and the ability of computers to learn, to teach themselves new facts, and to acquire new insights. It also combined technologies still troubled with start-up issues and much hype. Watson is a computer that answers questions presented to it in a human language. IBMers poured trillions of facts, entire libraries, and every medical article they could get their hands on into this machine's memory and armed it with tools to rapidly scan this data for an answer. As it responds to questions, it learns from the experience what better answers to offer. This is a simple description for an early, practical form of artificial intelligence converted into a commercial product, a service, and most readers have already heard about it.

In February 2011, on the popular American television quiz show *Jeopardy!*, two of the show's previous champions competed against an IBM computer named Watson.[58] Contestants were given broad clues to an answer and then had to phrase their response as a question. The humans had rapid command of large amounts of facts and excellent judgment, even instinct, about the right answers. Along with Watson, the contestant who responded the quickest won dollars. Over the course of two nights— February 14 and 15—Watson competed against these two champions. On the first night, it tied with one and got ahead of the second. On the second evening, Watson crushed the humans, winning $77,147 to their $24,000 and $21,600, respectively. The grand prize of $1 million went to Watson; IBM donated the money to charity. In the studio audience were IBM employees, from Palmisano to IBM scientists and engineers who had been working on artificial intelligence and computing for decades. It was not clear if Watson could win, although the engineers had played many games with it, even with the TV producers, who also wanted to know if it had a chance before putting it to the test on national television. It probably did not calm nerves that IBM's executive royalty showed up for the live contest. When Watson won, chests puffed at IBM for a moment, especially in the Research Division, for it had not enjoyed such a spectacular success in a long time.[59] IBM garnered much positive PR and goodwill. Winning was what so many people expected: "It was IBM, what do you expect?"

Why all the fuss at IBM, in the world of computing, and even by the press and the public? While critics would then, as now, point out the limits of Watson's capabilities, nonetheless something had changed. Almost everyone had known for decades that if you provided a computer with very specific instructions—software—it could carry out tasks, like moving data through the Internet, moving boxes on a conveyor belt, or rapidly calculating accounting numbers. That had been going on since the 1940s, but, as two IBMers commenting on that kind of computing put it, "Computers today are brilliant idiots," because all they could do was store large quantities of data and perform calculations on it. They could not understand, learn, or adapt the way a human could, and those were the capabilities computer scientists were beginning to bake into this new class of computers. That is why the *Jeopardy!* victory was so important for them, for IBM, and probably for the world.[60] The victory felt like IBM was back where it historically had always found itself—in the middle of the grand challenges of its time, and this one included big computers! As its developers improved Watson's capabilities, IBM's executives and computer scientists increasingly warmed to the realization that this technology had the potential of burnishing IBM's offerings, of answering a question Rometty asked often of her employees: How do we make IBM "essential"?

Beating two quiz champions was an important marker of progress, but the breakthroughs had been inching forward over several decades as engineers and computer scientists found ways to make computers accumulate vast amounts of information—essentially everything, for example, ever published in medicine or weather data going back decades, even centuries—explore possible answers to a question, determine the odds of one being more right than another based on prior encounters with similar questions, and then select the optimal one, all rapidly. Now imagine a doctor or a medical researcher collaborating on, say, diagnosing a cancer and then have the computer suggest to that doctor treatment options that had a high probability of being successful based on prior cases, while feeding researchers case information in support of their own research. That was a new form of collaboration between humans and machines. Tracking its prior transactions—experiencing—with a topic, a question, or an answer, that system would apply learning to its activities, simply repeat steps, and keep track of how often it did them, or how quickly, as in more traditional computing.

The technology in Watson had evolved to a level where its users had a machine that exercised learning, or cognition, to be more technical. Once IBM's marketing staff understood what the company's engineers had started to create, they came up with a way to promote this evolution with what appeared initially as a clumsy phrase that captured the essence of what was happening: *cognitive computing*. People would simply have to become comfortable with the term because for years to come this form of computing would characterize how information processing would be done and for what uses. All of a sudden, new possibilities opened up for IBM, its competitors, corporate customers, and everyone else. Now imagine, for example, one's smartphone connected to such a system answering questions individuals had that go beyond such mundane ones as getting driving directions or answering trivia questions to settle a bar bet. Imagine a doctor in a remote African village asking his smartphone to assess a lump in a woman's breast to determine if she has cancer, and do it quickly, cheaply, and so accurately that this doctor would want to use his phone regularly in his practice. An IBM-Apple alliance on mobility now made sense. IBM's early foray into massive computing to analyze and graphically present output of Big Data did, too, and so did cryptanalytics, for similar reasons. Today, with data being collected by sensors in quantities orders of magnitude greater than before, it could run through such systems to make it understandable to humans. As students of this computing put it, "A cognitive computing environment requires sufficient amount of data to discover patterns or anomalies within that data," enough "that the results of analytics are trustworthy and consistent." It was about acquiring insights, the thing that highly knowledgeable people did well.[61]

Kevin Kelly, a founder and editor of *Wired* magazine, is an unapologetic technoenthusiast. He visited the Watson system around 2015, four years after the *Jeopardy!* event. Watson's technology had moved from a purely experimental system to one that was beginning to seep into IBM's cloud offerings. It was setting up IBM's cloud offering to be more than a less expensive place where customers could process data without having to buy all of those old "idiot" technologies and pay for staffs to babysit them. Kelly found Watson was being used by customers with whatever tools they had: smartphones, tablets, and so forth. His reaction is worth reading:

> This kind of AI can be scaled up or down on demand. Because AI improves as people use it, Watson is always getting smarter; anything it learns in one instance can be quickly transferred to the others. And instead of one single program, it's an aggregation of diverse software engines—its logic-deduction engine and its language-parsing engine might operate on different code, on

different chips, in different locations—all cleverly integrated into a unified stream of intelligence.[62]

A great deal of progress had been made in a few years. It was also an example of an unintended consequence, because it was difficult to imagine it being so open to different platforms and input equipment if IBM had not made the decision in the late 1990s to embrace open source technology. Making IBM more agnostic about software and hardware used with its products facilitated development of Watson's technical architecture.

Other IT companies understood there was the same potential in medicine (IBM's initial focus area for Watson) and in other areas. Staff involved with Watson even published a cookbook based on the system's analysis of what ingredients are most enjoyed by people, including one for Indian paella.[63] Major cloud companies wanted this kind of technology; Amazon used cognitive computing in retail. By 2014, 322 companies were spending in excess of $2 billion to develop similar systems. All the key IT players were in the game: Google, Facebook, LinkedIn, Pinterest, Intel, Twitter, and Chinese firms such as TenCent and Baidu. All hired AI experts, even luring away some of IBM's Watson people. IBM's five imperatives were beginning to gain an identity different from the one they began with earlier. They started to dribble out—"escaped," as Gerstner said of IBM's laboratories—into concrete forms as machines, software, and specific services. If you have any lingering doubts, recall the history of RISC, which took years to evolve into products. As early as 2010, IBM strategists and technologists understood the potential: "The goal is to have computers start to interact in natural human terms across a range of applications and processes, understanding the questions that humans ask and providing answers that humans can understand and justify."[64]

IBM began to invest in commercializing this technology. IBMers reported on its use by big customers after 2012. Of particular interest to Watson's engineers and management, and to Rometty, was getting Watson working quickly in medicine. Here much patient data already existed in digitized form, where IBM had under way experiments and long-term projects and where the need for diagnostic tools and research was urgent, compelling, and could be financed by governments, universities, foundations, and pharmaceutical firms. IBMers formed collaborative projects with partners ranging from Nuance Communications on clinical decision support functions to doctors at Columbia University in New York to figure out where best to use such technology. A partnership created in September 2011 with WellPoint, an American health care provider, led to the development of early tools to suggest treatment options for doctors. Their initial product focused on lung cancer.

In January 2014, Rometty established the IBM Cognitive Business Group, committing the company to selling Watson-based services, with a staff of 2,000 and revenue targets. While its growth depended on continued evolution of Watson technology, offerings, and market receptivity in the face of growing competition, the group made progress, if more slowly than senior executives wanted. Nonetheless, Rometty bragged that it would generate $10 billion in annual revenue within a decade.[65] She possibly had her own technology "big bet."[66] At IBM, a big bet required massive attention and the muscle of the entire firm, such as when Thomas Watson Sr. bet on tabulating equipment, Watson Jr. on System 360, and now Rometty with AI. In each instance, it was not fully obvious at the time when bets were placed that they were, in fact, big bets. The one possible exception was Lou Gerstner's decision to keep IBM together, which he and everyone around him knew was major, but even this big bet did not have the risks of the others. System 360 did not start out as one but rapidly evolved into IBM's biggest.

As with all big bets, execution was always the main concern. Critics could always be counted on to question the wisdom of making them. IBM was no exception. For example, in 2016, Tom Austin at Gartner thought Rometty's "moonshot" would take years to unfold and said that, "It seems like they're swimming upstream with that."[67] He did not say anything IBMers all over the company did not already understand. IBM could afford to step up and maintain its "constancy of purpose," a phrase coined by quality guru W. Edwards Deming (1900–1993), whose ideas often reflected IBM's approach to a business or technology strategy. The market for such AI technologies drew IBM's attention as much as anyone else's. In 2016, IDC, a highly respected IT industry watch group, valued the AI market at $8 billion. Its analysts thought the number would rise to $47 billion by 2020. No wonder Rometty was in a hurry. Again, IBM was in a footrace, one that favored her company.[68] IDC opined that in 2020 the big winners would be Amazon, Google, Microsoft, and IBM. Although IBM was not sharing information about how much revenue it generated from each imperative, estimates by industry watchers speculated that revenue attributed to Watson technology hovered at $500 million in 2016. It did not matter whether this was a guess, hubris, or how IBMers coded their transactions in their CRM system. It remained their future.

IBM's strategy involved providing AI platform tools and hardware, but unlike the other major players, it leveraged large bodies of data (such as weather data) and experts (such as weather forecasters and doctors). Medical uses accounted for two-thirds of IBM's Watson revenue in 2016, and they seemed to be working. Steve Lohr of the *New York Times* reported:

> At the University of North Carolina School of Medicine, Watson was tested on 1,000 cancer diagnoses made by human experts. In 99 percent of them, Watson recommended the same treatment as the oncologists.

> In 30 percent of the cases, Watson also found a treatment option the human doctors missed. Some treatments were based on research papers that the doctors had not read—more than 160,000 cancer research papers are published a year. Other treatment options might have surfaced in a new clinical trial the oncologists had not yet seen announced on the web. But Watson read it all.[69]

Even though IBM's financial performance remained anemic in 2016 and 2017, Rometty had to be feeling better about her overall strategy, thanks to Watson, as she said, "Digital business is converging with a new kind of digital intelligence—what you will recognize as Watson. We call this Cognitive Business." You can forgive her hubris when she said, "We can literally build cognition into everything digital."[70] Rometty's dominant messages were increasingly about cognitive business, a mantra she continued throughout 2018. For better or worse, she may have found her voice. Now she had to execute with a company still troubled.[71]

20 THINK: IBM TODAY AND ITS LEGACY

> It is better to aim at perfection and miss it than to aim at imperfection and hit it.
> Our work is one of service.
> —THOMAS J. WATSON SR.[1]

> This is a company of human beings, not machines, personalities not products, people not real estate.
> —THOMAS J. WATSON JR.[2]

> I feel our purpose is to be essential to our clients.
> —GINNI ROMETTY

IT SEEMED THAT IBM's long history circled back on itself from time to time, from good times to bad times, facing challenges and opportunities, but always to a company adaptable to changing circumstances, if often too slowly. Herman Hollerith understood this essential notion; Thomas Watson Sr. was relentless about it, as was Tom Watson Jr. It is a behavior still being repeated today at IBM. As in previous decades, the larger ecosystem of multinational corporations still wants to learn from IBM's experiences. With so many new multinational companies entering the global economy, the number of interested parties is expanding, especially in Asia, learning from Western companies. When we step outside the consumer electronics and digital retail firms of Apple, Google, Dell, and Amazon, behind them all is the longest-surviving company: IBM. Over the course of its history, it has generated over $1 trillion in revenue.

When Tom Watson Sr. was a teenager in Painted Post, New York, it would have been impossible to predict the arc of his life. In his time, a farmer/lumber yard owner in rural New York would not have thought his son would be the best-paid executive in the United States. The only people who get things right are biographers of dead people, because they know how the story ends. Historians of defunct companies do, too, although they keep arguing about what it all means as more evidence turns up or new circumstances stimulate new thinking. Then there are companies like IBM that are still alive. This one has over 380,000 employees and literally millions of people they call customers. We do not know how IBM's story will end. Corporate biographers guess, while journalists and industry watchers too often predict its demise.

Business historians know that the longer a company survives, the greater the odds of it living for decades more. If placing a bet on IBM, one would prudently stake it on IBM being around, but we do not know what it will look like in 2040 or 2080. This exercise is precarious because of the exceptions. NCR, Burroughs, AT&T, and Kodak are four iconic U.S. corporations that had been around for a century, dominated their industries, were big, and went out of business. NCR and AT&T are names used by other firms, riding on the brand value of the old enterprises no longer around. IBM could always go out of business or be bought out and have its name picked up by another firm.

Did anybody contemplate acquiring IBM? The one publicly known occasion, which at best could only be called a rumor, came in 1975, when the *Wall Street Journal* reported that the Saudi Arabians were contemplating such a move. Recall that, at the time, oil-producing nations were cash-rich and were looking to diversify their investments. IBM denied anything was going on. A week after the rumor, CEO Frank Cary fulfilled a commitment he had made earlier to speak at an IBM DPD branch office in Cranford, New Jersey, and at the request of the meeting's organizers, who had a reputation for putting on skits (a tradition at IBM), came on stage wearing an Arab headdress. Having spent years in IBM sales offices, he knew of the custom, agreed to put on the costume, and after everyone stopped laughing and applauding said, "There is no basis for the rumors you heard about the

Arabs buying IBM," and after much laughter, added, "and I'll fire anyone who takes a picture of me today!"

Why do we care about IBM's fate? There are many companies that can fill in pieces of its market. Ginni Rometty had it right when she asked how IBM was relevant. We care for all the reasons this book was written. We learned that IBM usually had products crucial to the well-being of thousands of companies, even whole industries, that improved the quality of life in advanced economies, and that augmented the productivity and efficiency of humans. It was big and rich enough, filled with enough smart people, and positioned in just the right spots in the twentieth century to play a major role. IBM had to earn its iconic status and the more than one trillion dollars it generated. During its existence, humankind rapidly became wealthy, life spans tripled, death rates declined to a fraction of what they had been, and life became safer, more comfortable, and healthier.[3] Those were not easy tasks to accomplish, but IBM was in the thick of them. The story told here is not of a slick, always well-run, efficient company. Like biographies of great figures in history, this corporate biography has argued that IBM's feet were made of clay, yet it was smart and successful. All that history brings us to the present. What are we to make of this company?

We begin by diagnosing negative conditions that cannot be politely swept under the rug, then turn optimistic to understand what IBM has going for it. The weaknesses and strengths are so pervasive that they transcend any individual IBMer, CEO, or board of directors, so key to understanding IBM. After that analysis, we summarize IBM's legacy, which affected the work of one million employees over the past 13 decades across 178 nations. It is time to judge IBM's history in ways familiar to historians, economists, and business leaders. We first look at problems IBM is experiencing and then at realities making its future optimistic. We put a century's worth of experience together into a unified discussion set within the context of IBM's overall business performance. Because IBM's history is still unfolding, it is useful to look at the company's global role today. I end the chapter with a brief summary of IBM's legacy and key themes of the book.

IBM has two problems: financial performance and errors in strategy. First, its revenue dropped by over 20 percent from $105.5 billion in 2012 to $79.1 billion in 2017, and many wanted to blame the company's CEO, Ginni Rometty. It was not an unreasonable charge, since CEOs take credit for the good things their people do and therefore should be blamed for what they do not do well. As IBMers are wont to say, "It comes with the territory"; you take credit for the bluebirds and eat the bad business your predecessor graciously left for you. In a time when business cultures value growth, IBM's top-line revenue performance disappointed, even though the firm managed to generate good profits through careful management of costs and moves toward more profitable growth segments of the IT industry. In the face of diminishing revenue performance and market share, it shrank its workforce and turned it over, a painful exercise. That effort had the effect of weakening employees' morale and motivation to "give it their all" while creating a small army of bitter ex-employees, many of whom went to work for IBM's customers and competitors. Whatever defense one puts up for what IBM did to crawl through its current problems, Rometty & Co. will be scarred in the history books, whether historians ultimately decide they deserved it or not.[4] It was John Akers's fate, which is sad since we now know that he inherited the consequences of decisions his predecessor took credit for, even if he helped to implement them in his prechairman jobs and made the near fatal one of wanting to break up the company.

The obvious source of IBM's problems is also the most contentious issue—the increased emphasis on financial and accounting issues at the expense of investing in the technologies and skills needed to respond to changing customer preferences when technologies were continuing to evolve at a "wicked speed," a term used by Sam Palmisano. That fixation with financial strategies to bolster the company was the root cause of IBM's shrinking revenues and displacement of so many people who, in an earlier time, were called members of the "IBM Family." The "roadmaps" were not the start of that pivot toward shareholder value. That began during the 1990s, less with Akers, who had to cut expenses and lay off employees but did so less aggressively than his successors. A critic of IBM charged that

"IBM's leaders today [2014] are fully isolated and immune from the long-term consequences of their decisions. People who own companies manage them to be viable for the long term. IBM's leaders do not."[5] Palmisano convinced stockbrokers to support and increase the value of IBM's stock by predicting future earnings in both roadmaps. By 2014, investors and brokers complained that IBM was cutting expenses too greatly to fund development of new products and services or even to provide quality services for its current activities.

The second problem involved IBM's strategy between 2000 and 2015. Its core businesses were starved of resources to shift money and people to a few "big bets." Observers commented that IBM needed such bold actions to generate large near-term profits at the expense of the firm's long-term more secure businesses. There has long been a debate about that issue, but its customers settled it by how they spent on IT. They were shifting to cloud computing and, while senior executives at IBM were aware of this trend as early as 2007, they correctly understood that the majority of their customers still used computers in data centers. The situation did not begin to change until about 2010, when major cloud providers ratcheted up their offerings. IBM was slower to respond to this shift than Amazon was, for instance. IBM's executives admitted as much. Critics argued that IBM should have expanded its hardware business rather than selling off its computer assets for quick infusions of cash in the 1980s, 1990s, and early the following decade.

Similar charges have been levied against its software business, with critics arguing that IBM did not know how to provide agile new services quickly enough. They questioned its solution to buy 120+ companies that had skills and assets needed immediately, such as patents and products. As those purchases happened between 2006 and 2014, it seemed IBM was awash in all manner of firms, but Armonk wanted to acquire software houses that supported its imperatives. The challenge before IBM was to integrate these acquisitions to drive down costs while going to market coherently, an effort well under way by 2012. By 2016, the company's software business was largely about cloud and cognitive computing.

However, the biggest churn and source of criticism involved services, supposedly IBM's largest moneymaker. It was highly profitable in comparison to hardware. To drive down expenses, IBM shifted customer work to less expensive countries, such as India, where it cost 80 percent less than in the United States. So, paradoxically, many cuts in expenses and layoffs came from the services side of the business. IBM and other IT companies could afford to fly Indian workers to the United States. U.S. employees and customers began to complain about poor-quality service. Even how IBM ran its services business came under attack. For over a decade, it was accused of keeping its accounting and operational books on spreadsheets. While there was some truth to that, over time IBM invested in tools to track billable hours, for example, but the charges of insufficient investment in managerial tools never went away. To squeeze more productivity out of employees, targets for how many hours they should bill a customer increased. In the early years of the new millennium, billing 65–75 percent of one's time was considered about right in the IT services world. That practice left time for training, vacations, holidays, internal meetings, and illnesses. By 2012, billable targets in many cases had crept up to 95 percent and in some instances to over 100 percent. Employees complained but to no avail.[6] Those who were not billing at required rates were targeted for layoffs.

As IBM increased its focus on its imperatives, how it executed them became the subject of criticism, which executives took on in media interviews and in presentations at conferences. Critics saw IBM shifting too slowly to cloud computing and pricing its analytics services too high, while Microsoft pushed ahead technologically on mobile services, although IBM and Apple partnered to pursue that opportunity. The fact that IBM chairmen focused on the interests of investors in their annual reports was seen as another example of IBM moving away from its historic focus on customers first. The heart of what critics saw wrong at IBM in the post-2010 era was the quality of its transformation. It was responding too slowly to changing market conditions, investing too little, and remaining addicted to financial engineering. The weaknesses seen at IBM turned, however, on its obsession with shareholder value. Peter E. Greulich, a retired IBM employee, prepared a comprehensive analysis testing these financial issues. He concluded that by emphasizing shareholder value IBM's historic emphasis on its other stakeholders fell by the wayside. Thomas Watson Sr. defined stakeholder value as including employees and customers, not just investors or analysts. Watson's mantra survived until the early 1990s, although it declined in importance, suggesting a root of IBM's current difficulties in responding to market conditions. After studying IBM's financial performance, Greulich concluded that, "Since 1999, IBM has failed to optimize revenue, optimize profits, or provide attractive return to its shareholders." IBM instead "invested in paper, increased shareholder risk, destroyed employee morale, played financial games, and failed all its stakeholders."[7]

Greulich's assessment is difficult to ignore. In constant 1999 dollars, the productivity of IBM's sales force declined by over 40 percent, and in actual dollars by nearly 20 percent. Take the revenue of the company and divide it by the number of employees, and that is how you get such figures. Employees complained that declines in productivity could be attributed to insufficient internal processes and procedures helpful in their daily tasks. Like many other large enterprises, IBM was more interested in profits than in revenue, and hence in discarding less profitable businesses and acquiring those with greater potential.[8] Employees in 2017 were producing as much profit per capita as at the start of the century, meaning that IBM remained profitable but could not optimize profits. Rivals were optimizing profits to a greater extent than IBM was.

During Palmisano's tenure, IBM repurchased about $10 billion of its own stock each year, and only in his last year as CEO did IBM beat what one could have obtained by just investing those same dollars in an index fund. That same level of performance continued during Rometty's tenure. Complicating IBM's investment in its own stock was its 30 percent decline in value over the first 16 years of the new century. In the process, IBM removed from the market over 800,000 shares. Ironically, Gerstner issued splits in 1997 and 1999, and it was those extra shares that the company essentially bought back for $162 billion.[9]

In recent years, observers began worrying that the aggressive use of "goodwill" accounting practices also put the value of the stock at risk. Goodwill is an intangible asset, usually measured as the difference between what one paid for an acquisition (such as a software firm) and what it owned (such as buildings and furniture). In the case of the PwC acquisition in 2002 for $3.9 billion, only $0.32 billion was tangible assets, such as furniture. IBM claimed $3.2 billion for "goodwill." Thus 81 percent of the purchase price, Greulich pointed out, was for PwC's employees, "synergies from combining PwC and IBM," what he called the "premium paid to gain control." His analysis of 162 acquisitions showed that nearly 74 percent of their costs were attributable to "goodwill," so if any of them went out of business, they would have no residual value.[10] Even the best venture capitalists are thrilled if 10 percent turn out well. The value of IBM's total assets grew only because of increasing use of goodwill.[11] If one deducted goodwill from the value of IBM's stock, then the worth of these assets went negative starting in 2007. Most of its rivals did not face that situation, with the exception of H-P with its disappointing acquisitions of EDS and Compaq.

Goodwill is fine if where its value lies—in people's heads in the form of knowledge, experience, and skills—is retained and applied, but with all the layoffs at IBM, one should ask how much of that goodwill remained. There are no available statistics to support or deny the charge that many skilled people left the firm after their company was acquired by IBM, but there is a great deal of anecdotal evidence, largely from those who left and went public with their departures. Laid-off employees continuously complained that this was the case. Some of that is normal, as happened between 2003 and 2006, when many senior PwC consultants and executives left. So many departed that the audit arm of the business reestablished a new consulting practice staffed with many ex-PwC/IBMers.[12]

Greulich, like so many other critics, including thousands of employees, argued that IBM's behavior destroyed morale. While IBM's internal employee opinion surveys are not made public, it does publish an annual *Corporate Responsibility Summary Report,* which he mined for evidence directly from IBM, finding that it published an employee satisfaction metric for the last time in 2010's report. In it, IBM acknowledged that morale had declined when compared to its peers.[13]

Additional charges by employees, retirees, the press, and academics included IBM's historic propensity for bureaucratic behavior, with considerable micromanagement by Corporate, division headquarters, and management levels immediately below it. For example, it was not uncommon for edicts to come down banning all travel toward the end of a quarter or that small expenditures for travel or office supplies required signoff by a divisional vice president or general manager. In most divisions in most years since 2004, expenditures for training dropped, in some cases to negligible amounts. The decline of IBM's historic sales culture and respect for individuals—IBM's Basic Beliefs—remained a criticism that did not go away for over 30 years. No matter what Corporate did to deny or mitigate this criticism, it remained. Ultimately, it was the most contentious topic and the one raised most vociferously by long-term employees, along with their criticism of IBM's obsessive concern with financial strategies. However, for many critics, it was the combination of weakening financial performance, decline in sales from its legacy businesses, and slow revenue growth from its cognitive and other "imperatives" that ailed IBM.[14]

THE CASE FOR WHAT'S RIGHT AT IBM

If these charges represented the entire truth, one would expect the company to die soon. IBM's history and current circumstances demonstrate there are things right with IBM to place on the plus side of history's ledger. The case for what's right at IBM begins with size. At the start of 2018, IBM employed an estimated 378,000 people in over 170 countries. Critics pointed out that the number was down by 56,000 since 2012, when the company had 434,000 employees, with estimates that in the intervening period IBM ousted 78,000, some of whom were replaced by employees with different skills, many arriving as a result of acquisitions. Any way one looks at it, the number of employees remains high. Of those current employees, some 120,000 work in Global Business Services (GBS), the services side of IBM, most as IT experts.

IBM's Research Division, with a staff of several thousand, remains one of the largest collections of PhDs in computer science and technology in the world. This group represents a global treasure deployed in a dozen laboratories around the world. They have primary responsibility for developing

Watson's AI technology. The division's staff has received every distinguished award available to technologists and computer scientists. Staff members have a history of receiving Nobel Prizes, including Leo Esaki (1973), Gerd Bining and Heinrich Rohrer (1986), Georg Bednorz and Alex Müller (1987), and former IBMer William E. Moerner (2014). When IBM brags about its technology prowess, it is usually because of what its researchers do, but its small army of "IT Architects" are also highly regarded as they work directly with customers.[15]

Despite IBM's troubles in growing its business, its results remain impressive. It generates some $80 billion in revenue annually. Its profits are consistently large, and it came into 2017 with over $8 billion in cash. A reading of its annual reports for the past several years provides a counterargument to a pessimistic analysis. Its dividend payout, at about 3.4 percent, is as good as or better than those of other large enterprises, and it has been paid for decades. In 2016 and 2017, stock market analysts were warming up to IBM's stock again, suggesting it had a future.

More significant, IBM remains at the center of much of the global information technology ecosystem, a seat it has occupied for decades. While not the throne it was in the 1960s and 1970s, it remains a sofa shared with Microsoft, Google, Amazon, and Apple. IBM retains a reputation for contributing more to a business/technology ecosystem than just technology. That is why, for example, when IBM implements a new personnel policy, other firms pay attention. It is why, when it emphasized shareholder value, either others did or IBM followed what was considered wise practice. In short, it remains one of the iconic multinational enterprises, with an image broader than any one technology. Thomas Watson Sr. gets credit for starting to put IBM in the center of a business ecosystem in the 1920s. Every generation of IBM's leaders since then has sought to retain or enhance that position. Sometimes that exposure proved embarrassing, as when IBM had its near-death experience in the early 1990s and even recently.

IBM is one of the best-known brands. Since the 1930s, business media have routinely ranked it as one of the most admired corporations, later as the largest in computing. Rankings placed IBM in the top five largest companies globally, regardless of industry, a position it has rarely surrendered.

Interbrand, a leading brand consultancy, placed a value of $75.5 billion on IBM's brand in 2012. IBMers with many years of employment marveled at how those three little letters—I-B-M—gained them access to management at all levels in all industries around the world, something few other firms could do. Most IBMers working with customers have stories of how they were told that IBM was a "national treasure," even during the dark days of the early 1990s and again in the post-2012 period. Even some of its competitors did not welcome the thought of IBM not being around. Its image, cultivated over the course of nearly a century, reflected goodwill resulting from its accomplishments.

For a century, a greater asset was IBM's corporate culture. Much has been made about it in this book, for good reason: every generation of IBMers has considered it the single most important asset of the corporation, after its people. IBM's culture was one of optimism, of meritocracy, the core beliefs of any sales-dominated business. By culture is meant its values and its points of view, not just its behavior. Despite efforts of recent CEOs to modify and, during their term, "update" the company's three Basic Beliefs, in one form or another they survived. Watson Sr.'s sound bite "THINK" did, too, coming out of desk drawers after Gerstner's term ended and being celebrated by Corporate during IBM's centennial in 2011. Notions of customer service, excellence in all that one did, and respect for the individual (meaning employees) ebbed and flowed. In Gerstner's time, he reemphasized the importance of customer focus—IBMers saw it as meaning service to them as well. While Palmisano validated the importance of the Basic Beliefs to IBMers, they began to see him as violating the most important one for them—respect for the individual—because of the layoffs. Rometty is given little credit for valuing that basic belief, and only grudgingly for finally remembering who paid the bills: customers. Too many IBMers had been laid off during her tenure as CEO/chairman and earlier as head of IBM's consulting business.

IBM's culture evolved over time. From the 1920s through the 1970s, the center of gravity for much of the thinking, beliefs, and actions was the customer. Beginning in the 1970s and extending through the 1980s, products dominated. Gerstner shifted emphasis back to the customer, but those after him emphasized shareholder value. Movement in emphasis back and forth between customer and product occurred within the tenets of IBM's culture and Basic Beliefs, while the degree to which Corporate embraced shareholder value, always present, existed outside the boundaries of prior practices. The consequences of placing so great an emphasis on financial tactics help explain why so much of what happened at IBM in the first decade of the new millennium seemed to represent a departure from successful prior managerial priorities. For example, in that decade, IBM's senior management imposed a ranking system on all employees, leading to such practices as assigning quotas for low-ranking "3" appraisals. IBM added another ranking system, by which managers ranked from 1 to "n" all employees in a department. Rankings made it easier to identify who to quickly dismiss. Ranking did not result in employees engaging in competition among each other; rather, they resisted that behavior, because the complexity of their work necessitated their collaboration with colleagues.[16] After so many years, a new appraisal system in 2016 discarded the hated ranking process, bringing IBM closer to the core practices of old.

A bone of contention in the first decade of the new millennium among long-serving IBMers and those laid off or retired involved the sales practices of the firm, "The IBM Way" Buck Rodgers spoke about in the 1980s and that Thomas Watson Sr. before him had articulated for nearly a half century. From that focus on the role of sales and services came products customers wanted, assistance they believed they needed, and IBMers prepared to go to great lengths to help, protect, and support them. IBM factory workers sometimes resented the prestige that sales personnel enjoyed, but both sets of employees understood that they owned a collective responsibility toward customers. Customers, competitors, and industry observers credited that culture and the quality of IBM's salesmen as one of the most important reasons IBM thrived for decades. Today that sales culture has been under siege for over a decade, more often unintentionally but nonetheless so.

Rometty was never a quota-carrying salesperson, and by the time she had responsibility for running a sales organization, she was a senior executive who also operated a services and consulting business. She could argue that although she never came up in the sales culture the way someone like Cary, Opel, Akers, or Palmisano did, she understood it. That is not the same as living it, of course. It did not help to have IBM CFOs who worked for her complain to analysts that part of the reason for IBM missing a financial target was "sales execution issues," which the sales force saw as insulting. Nonetheless, such slights did not prevent them from attempting to live by the standards of that culture because their job, career advancement, and income depended on performing well. Their sales culture was not dead; those "resources" lay in waiting to bounce back from their diminished status. In tallying IBM's good side, its resilient sales culture makes the list along with its R&D prowess and technical capabilities.

Between the 1980s and the early years of the new millennium, senior management typically hosted one or two global meetings, plus internal conferences, attended by the company's most respected technical people. They included Nobel Prize winners, hundreds of PhD computer scientists trained at the finest universities in the world, and IBM's elite engineers, designated as Distinguished Engineers (DEs). The latter were granted executive status and the freedom to do whatever research and work they wanted, usually for up to five years. "IT Architects" attended the global meetings by the thousands. They helped customers put together entire systems of machines, computers, software, networks, and applications. Pound for pound, they were worth more than any other class of IBMers to customers and salesmen. To attend one of these meetings is to learn about the depth of IBM's technical prowess, because IBM had to use the largest convention centers in the world. Walk in and you would see between 3,000 and 6,000 people, and that only accounted for roughly half the population of IBM's top experts! Row after row of men and women in their 30s to late 60s, from around the world, greeted you. As late as the 1990s, you could meet engineers who helped develop the S/360, others who had figured out how to make computer chips out of one atom, and still others who were working on what eventually became the Watson supercomputer.

Thousands of similar people continued to come into IBM through acquisitions of specialized companies, sustaining the tradition of deep bench strength, even though many older IBMers argued that the company's technological muscle was weaker. The newer people brought in different skills in AI, cybersecurity, and analytics. Many still reported to technology managers who bridged the technological culture of an earlier IBM, even if "earlier" now meant the 1990s. So, along with a brand, R&D, and a sales force, one must add an effective community of technologists to IBM's list of positives.

An often underappreciated advantage for IBM, understood by senior management but less by employees at large, was the company's stockholders. They have been a patient lot in the post-2012 period, as the company turned in declining revenue. It became easier for them to support, or at least not fret too loudly about, IBM's extensive use of financial engineering. Institutional investors and mutual fund owners, a community of only 1,816 organizations, held 60 percent of IBM shares.[17] A few large holders became the subject of considerable press coverage, notably Warren Buffett, who defended the stock (his company owned 8.5 percent of outstanding shares until early 2017) and IBM's senior management, giving pause to some who might otherwise have been louder critics. Like IBM's customers, the majority demonstrated familiarity with the company and were professional investors.

But everything comes down to having a business strategy and implementing it. As this chapter was being completed in 2018, IBM had its five imperatives infused by increasingly powerful Watson technologies that IBM's IT ecosystem was feeling good about. As late as 2017, the same CFO who complained about sales execution, Martin Schroeter, was also quick to point out that IBM's customers had vast quantities of digital data that required blending cognitive computing with cloud platforms to effectively control the use of information.[18] IBMers understood that as well as any technologist. That combination represented IBM's future, and the company had the skills and capacity to seize that opportunity. A year earlier, he was arguing that the imperatives were generating over $30 billion in revenue and that would be just north of $40 billion in 2018.[19] Most analysts were skeptical, although they acknowledged that the company possibly had this capability. As one observer put it, "IBM is still a company in transition. Its strategic imperatives are growing as a percentage of its top line, but their margins are questionable, and they continue to be weighed down by the company's legacy businesses."[20]

Problems executing its five imperative strategies remained. Even Schroeter could not hide that fact. Take the case of IBM's services business, housed in GBS, and let him illustrate, perhaps by accident, an example of an execution problem, even though he may not have seen it as such:

> The revenue in GBS in any given period is going to be driven primarily, not solely but primarily, by the backlog. The backlog is built by signings. So we've gone through a process where we've taken again pools of people who are focused on signing clients to big contracts and shifted them into other areas. So we did see continuous signings declines in GBS, which meant the backlog was declining. Now we have gotten the signings piece back to growth again first time and so as signings grow, that will build that backlog and when that backlog grows then the revenues will start to grow.[21]

Any consulting executive will ask, why would you ever pull back sales of big deals, unless you cannot staff such projects? Salespeople were undoubtedly dismissed from IBM, if we are to believe posts by ex-employees in external websites, and not just transferred to imperatives, as Schroeter suggested. As the percentage of revenue from imperatives increased, a good portion of those sales would be translated into long-term projects or cloud "pay-for-what-one-uses" services that needed to be run by GBS.

A strong point in IBM's favor was Corporate's recognition that it could use new blood at the top of the house. In 2016, Rometty brought in executives from outside the firm to run marketing, another to expand IBM's ties to software developers, an Intel executive to lead a chip architecture initiative, new communications staff, even Microsoft's chief of sales and marketing operations, Karan Bajwa, putting him in charge of IBM's Indian operations soon after. Others in 2015 and early 2016 came in to run lines of business, such as GBS, still one of the company's largest customer-facing organizations. But they did not know their way around the very large Big Blue, so could they be effective? Rometty and her senior IBM-heritage executives said yes. Would she have their backs? Observers of the IBM scene asked the following questions:

Will they have the authority to stop the IBM zombies at the door and keep them from further damaging their organizations? Will the RAs stop? Will the divisions be allowed to run with less profit so that they will have the resources to fix things? Will people actually get raises? Will there be good business strategies and plans, and will they be communicated to the whole organization? Will information on business progress (sales, profit, budgets, etc.) be shared with the whole organization? Will everyone understand how their work will affect the bottom line? Will decision making and control of budgets be delegated?[22]

Some thought no; large investors like Buffett thought otherwise. They were pleased that Corporate was investing in technologies supporting AI, Big Data, and cloud computing as pillars of IBM's transformation. Critics focused on the daily operational issues that if not fixed would make investments in technologies, acquisitions, and new executives worthless. Write-offs would signal Corporate's ineffectiveness. Customers continued to spend nearly $80 billion with IBM, some happy with what they received in exchange, others disappointed and noisily expressing their concerns, as happened with large projects in Australia, Indiana, and the U.S. government. IBM remained in the center of much of what was going on, still a hub, and increasingly, if too slowly for many, playing a growing role in those areas of computing of concern to large organizations.

FROM BUTCHER SCALES TO COGNITIVE COMPUTING

IBM evolved into a behemoth multinational corporation by intent and as a result of unintended consequences that unfolded over 13 decades. It helped that three little companies operated in a crucial sweet spot of the Second Industrial Revolution—data processing. Large organizations were swept up in the larger forces of the "Control Revolution" that proved so essential in making large enterprises and government agencies possible.[23] As IBM emerged out of three fragmented businesses, it facilitated creation of larger enterprises, and these made IBM possible as well. If IBM needed customers, customers needed IBM, too. Technological imperatives in all periods became the basis of IBM's "value proposition."

Technological evolutions were not always controlled by IBM, however, as Herman Hollerith learned when rival James Powers kept evolving punch card technology in the early 1900s, when Univac gave IBM a run for its money in the early 1950s, when Compaq did the same with PCs in the 1980s, or when three generations of computer scientists and engineers developed computer chips that relentlessly followed Moore's Law, forcing basic technologies and uses to change. The alternative was corporate death. When the dot-com bubble burst at the dawn of the new millennium, over 6,000 IT firms went out of business. So did scores of office appliance manufacturers in the 1930s to 1950s, minicomputer vendors in the 1960s and 1970s, and several thousand PC hardware and software vendors in the 1980s and 1990s. So, getting the technology right was important for success, and that meant dealing with what was often a nemesis, since life would have been easier if technologies did not change so quickly. But they did, and that is why Thomas Watson Sr. gave up on scales and went all out on tabulating equipment.

Changing technologies upended well-laid product strategies and "go-to-market" plans for all vendors, not just IBM, but both they and their customers faced the trauma of technological changes not seen since the arrival of steam engines in factories and in transportation in the nineteenth century and later transformations brought about by the internal combustion engine and electricity. Information technology met everyone's definition for the word *revolution.* It was radical, turning a lot of things on their heads and changing how the world worked in one lifetime. A few numbers hint at the impact. Between 1986 and 2007, the amount of information—data—one could store in a computer increased by 23 percent *each year.* The amount of information transmitted through telecommunications grew by 28 percent *each year.* The raw computing power of computers grew by 58 percent *each year.* All the data transmitted through telecommunications in the entire year of 1986 could be pushed through a network in two thousandths of a second in 1996. Put another way, the increase in the volume of data in one year (2006 to 2007) was greater than all the data sent over telecommunication lines in the entire previous decade.[24] While there already existed reliable "rules of the road" to predict such changes by the mid-1960s, translating those into products and uses proved difficult, and getting the timing right was always a challenge. In a study I conducted of how 18 American industries used computers, it was difficult to find any company or industry that correctly understood the transformations they would experience and planned for them. It seemed everyone was stumbling forward cautiously, excited but always uncertain.[25] It is surprising that any computer vendor survived the second half of the century; most did not.

That observation leads us to an equally important issue: the practical matter of running an IT business. The three little firms that made up C-T-R functioned at various degrees of efficiency but well enough to warrant creating a holding company. Bringing in an experienced big-company executive with talent in the form of Watson Sr. provided this holding company with a view of what it would be like if it became another NCR. Confidence, optimism, the growth of big businesses and large government agencies that were all voracious in their consumption of data, and an expanding global economy made it possible for IBM to grow. It was blessed with good leaders in that crucial period of 1914–1941 that set the firm to move out of its embryonic stage, making it possible for it to come out of World War II big, virile, and respected. The move from tabulating to computing set the corporation on its destiny. Today we know that in many countries upward of 70–80 percent of all installed computers came from IBM between the early 1960s and the 1980s. That is when IBM became the hub of the information technology ecosystem that so transformed work done before the spread of the Internet.

Historians rightly focused on the effects of technological changes on IBM and its rivals. Useful approaches in understanding IBM's experience came from historians and economists such as Alfred D. Chandler Jr., Richard R. Nelson, and Giovanni Dosi, who discussed the notion of "path dependency" in large enterprises. The essential idea is that once a firm is on a technological trajectory, it becomes wedded to it, enhancing it and living by its consequences. That dependency made it difficult to jump onto a different trajectory. For example, if you use Microsoft Word, you are reluctant to use a different word processing tool, if for no other reason than that you do not want to learn how to use a new software product.

Would you change your keyboard if the letters and numbers were arranged differently than they are today? If you were an IBM customer relying on System 360 or 370 mainframes, the cost to switch to a different platform was unaffordable. So path dependency is real and evident in all periods of IBM's history. For most users, it was a known technological path to follow so long as their suppliers provided continuous innovations and more cost-effective products, the reality IBM's customers experienced. On the other hand, it constrains, but not necessarily blocks, the move to a new platform, a possibility IBM faced in every decade of its life.

IBM lived through three technological platforms, protocols, or environments. Each consisted of groups of compatible products, and practices for their use and for how they were sold and serviced by IBM and competitors that determined how IBM was organized. Each required different skills, knowledge, and activities, so, as the company moved from one product to another, the entire organization and what its employees did changed, and the same happened with its customers. Examine figures 20.1, 20.2, and 20.3. They show that IBM traveled through three technological eras, with some overlap as it moved out of one and into another. The dates shown for each evolution are rough, since one can quibble about end dates. The essential observation is that IBM's three technological regimes went through the same phases economists, business managers, business professors, and historians rely on as a framework for describing technological evolutions: launch, growth, maturity, and decline. IBM's three regimes are obvious: tabulating, mainframe computers, and, for convenience, distributed computing, which sweeps up minicomputers, PCs, and other desktop machines and software. With any product, there were overlaps, but stepping back, we see three.

We can mine several observations from these graphical representations. First, the introductory period—the launch phase—lasted longer than one might have thought otherwise. With tabulating equipment, it took several years. But a decade to kick off a new technology seemed normal, such as the period Watson Sr. needed to turn C-T-R into the proto-IBM company. Second, the growth period slowed as one moved from an earlier regime to its next technological regime, which suggests path dependency

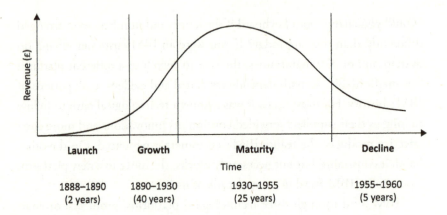

Launch	Growth	Maturity	Decline
1888–1890 (2 years)	1890–1930 (40 years)	1930–1955 (25 years)	1955–1960 (5 years)

Figure 20.1

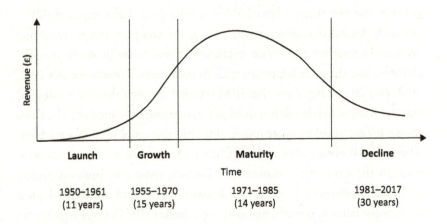

Launch	Growth	Maturity	Decline
1950–1961 (11 years)	1955–1970 (15 years)	1971–1985 (14 years)	1981–2017 (30 years)

Figure 20.2

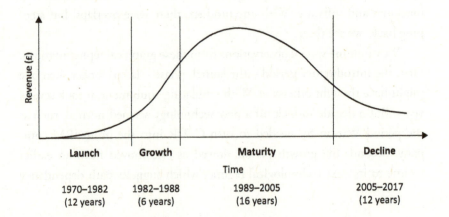

Launch	Growth	Maturity	Decline
1970–1982 (12 years)	1982–1988 (6 years)	1989–2005 (16 years)	2005–2017 (12 years)

Figure 20.3

dragging on the adoption of new equipment. This is exactly what salesmen and their customers experienced as they moved from one to another. Third, there is a period of maturity that occurred, path dependency's best feature—characterized by incremental, less disruptive changes. It is when vendors and customers understood the technology best and applied it most effectively and most extensively. Everyone's greatest dependence on it was maximized. Fourth, decline came as new technologies emerged that were compelling enough that both suppliers and users *had* to embrace them, and that resulted in enormous churn in the products, knowledge everyone had, business models, sources and volumes of revenue and profits, and individual careers disrupted or destroyed. This is the period of displacement and augmentation of one technology over another. It is the phase in a technology's life that has consumed the most attention of historians, economists, and business management experts.

IBM scientists, engineers, and management were familiar with many of the dynamics of technological regimes and transformations. Soon after its publication in 1997, Clayton M. Christensen's book *The Innovator's Dilemma* was being widely read and discussed inside IBM.[26] Quotations from it routinely appeared in slide presentations, including those prepared by strategists at Corporate and in product divisions, continuing a long-standing practice of understanding what academics and others had to say about technologies.[27]

Table 20.1 summarizes the number of years IBM spent in each technology's life cycle by phase. Notice also the total number of years IBM relied essentially on one platform. The durations of the first two phases are not so different. The third phase—distributed computing—one could argue is not yet over, so the learning point might be that the first two lasted 71 and 67 years, respectively. Life cycles were remarkably similar, longer than the table or figures would indicate, since mainframes are still being used that come from IBM, or earlier, tabulating equipment serviced by IBM was in use well into the 1960s, while IBM's laptops, although no longer being sold, were still being used a decade later. What this remarkable longevity demonstrates is that in sustaining it, IBMers organized, learned, and knew about one technological regime for such a long time that it was

Table 20.1

Timeline of IBM's technology life cycles, 1888–2017 (phases in years)

Phase	Tabulators	Mainframes	Distributed computing*
Launch	2	11	12
Growth	40	15	6
Maturity	25	14	16
Decline	5	30	12 (PCs only)
Total Life	72	67	47

*Phase still unfolding. Does not include mobile computing, such as smartphones.

able to optimize the business in support of it and forget or discard prior know-how and experiences.

There are other reasons for finding these behaviors of interest. For one, since IBM's dominance of so many of these markets influenced both the speed and shape of the use of a technology and the transition to its sequel, its cadence shaped the information technology (or earlier, computer) industry's behavior. It also influenced behavior in other industries that had existed for over a century, including roles of widely accepted protocols and standards, slow group movements to new ones, and the emergence of oligopolistic firms dominating technological regimes and businesses. In other words, the longer the IT industry exists, the more it behaves like other long-lived industries. There are few long-lived companies in this industry besides IBM, most notably H-P, which dates from the 1930s, but many IT companies are 30, 40, or 50 years of age. Microsoft and Apple come to mind, as do Cisco and Oracle. Scholars and journalists studying the industry tend to focus on the newest arrivals, such as Amazon, Google, and Facebook, but as the industry ages, the number of long-lived companies will increase. IBM is the oldest and so provides more perspective about what happens, or could happen, to a firm if it survives long enough. Most providers of IT have not lived long enough to transition from one techno-logical regime to another, although Microsoft's partial shift from being PC based to Internet orientation is one that is under way. Today, IBM's transi-tion to "cloud computing" is another.[28]

Understanding transitions from one regime to another is compelling not only for historians but also for journalists, economists, and managers, because technological changes still go on, most of which are viewed as being profoundly disruptive to prior regimes. These changes include the combination of artificial intelligence (AI) and cloud computing (what IBM is doing with Watson combined with cloud); Big Data with analytics, which in turn mixes with AI; and blockchain technologies. Any combination of these could result in the next technological life cycle model, a future figure 20.4. IBM's difficult transitions from one regime to another have much to teach historians, economists, and managers about current and future ones already emerging but not fully understood. This insight is made more compelling because of the increasing number of IT firms and customers reaching ages of sufficient duration to experience multiple transitions in their IT path dependencies. Their transitions involve the technologies, products that grow out of them, what people know about computing and how to use it, the economics involved for both vendor and user, and the consequences on business performance and society at large.

THE CENTRALITY OF IBM'S EXPERIENCE

The history of IBM from the 1880s to the end of the 1980s was triumphant because it nestled into the center of much of the growing, crucial, and dominant roles of larger organizations. That was because of the quality of its leadership and the fact that it was always recognized as one of the best-staffed corporations in the world. It also managed to attain iconic status by being like its customers. More than just encouraging salesmen and executives to dress like their customers, live in the same neighborhoods, intermingle socially, and cultivate a nation's elite, IBMers adapted ideas and practices from these groups. "Groupthink" regarding management practices became a two-way street: customers borrowed ideas from IBM, and IBMers borrowed from their customers. When Japanese companies embraced W. Edwards Deming's total quality management in the 1950s and 1960s, IBM did likewise, leading fans and critics to accuse IBM of being obsessed with processes, or what its critics called "bureaucracy."

But IBM and its customers learned from each other. Part of that exchange of ideas crucial to IBM's success was the notion implanted by

Thomas Watson Sr. that IBM's value was in helping customers use data processing effectively. Its strategy was to teach, show, and demonstrate. It did this well by training employees, developing products in collaboration with customers, and timing their offerings to coincide with when customers would be receptive to new ways of doing data processing. As companies learned, especially those involved in complex technologies, they traveled through what is known as the "experience curve," even documenting improvements as they came to appreciate the results of changes, such as the manufacture of a delicate product or service. In manufacturing, for instance, experts knew that productivity could improve 20 to 30 percent each time a firm doubled the volume of units sold. One quickly concludes that a firm's success is based on its experiences, on the information and knowledge employees have. Since the 1970s, the ability of a company to

Figure 20.4
IBM service personnel rode these vehicles in large urban centers, quickly delivering parts. This British example from the 1920s symbolized IBM's commitment to customer service. Photo courtesy of IBM Corporate Archives.

compete has rested on experiences. Today it is nearly impossible to accumulate and apply such knowledge without using all manner of computing, and increasingly application of artificial intelligence and massive data collection procedures and tools.[29] Customers came to think of IBM as well run.

Inside its walls, and sometimes outside them, IBM went through its first century facing many challenges. Building a successful business is complicated, and IBM's experience was no exception. Harnessing and then innovating technologies was always a dicey affair characterized by short-term confidence in how they would evolve. Unintended consequences interfered with grand strategies and activities. Existential problems and opportunities affected IBM, such as two world wars, the Cold War, recessions, depressions, and globalization, none of which IBM could control. Recall IBM's attempts to manage its subsidiary in Nazi Germany, in Europe during the six years of World War II, or when it left India. The company had its scandals, too. Robert Moffat's arrest was only one of the latest, another occurring in India a few years later, just as at other companies, but as Louis V. Gerstner Jr. pointed out, he encountered genuine widespread adherence to business ethics at IBM.

That leads us to IBM's secret sauce for success. Was it a corporate culture from the 1920s through the 1980s or 1990s, or was it the quality of its workforce, one consistently praised decade after decade, even in the troubled years since the late 1980s? Previous students of IBM's history took sides on the question. IBM's executives, when confronted with the issue, universally embraced *both*. The sales culture with its focus on customer service was a key ingredient in IBM's success, because it made it possible for individual IBMers to make decisions on how best to apply data processing technologies around the world. *Every* memoir written by an IBMer speaks of this culture's power, and when they perceived someone deviating from it, they criticized them. Gerstner saw the transformation of this culture as his greatest challenge and in the end called it "*the* game" in IBM. It dominated because it had worked for so long. Because the culture demanded excellence and service, people were brought into the company who could fulfill those twin missions. As IBM grew and hence had more influence on companies, industries, and national economies, it became more essential

Figure 20.5

IBM's culture was also flexible. At a time when drinking alcohol was forbidden by IBM, here we see a group of Brazilian IBMers cheering on their 100 Percent Club achievement with mugs of beer. Photo courtesy of IBM Corporate Archives.

and easier for it to hire well. One could argue that everyone wants to hire the best, but IBM's ability to do that for so long has to be seen as one of the reasons why it did so well.

That was the first century for IBM. What happened later, beginning in the mid-1980s and extending to the present, initiated a different era in IBM's history. While IBM turned in strong financial results between 1995 and 2012, it ate its cultural and employee seed corn as it responded to growing problems of an existential nature, such as customers' shift from mainframes to PCs and then to cloud computing, and to two strategic errors. The first was Opel's thinking that IBM would keep growing based on mainframe computing. He expanded IBM, confident in his decision. To be fair, it was a group decision made collectively with his senior managers and the board of directors. It proved nearly fatal, and Akers took the blame.

The second error was possibly IBM's decade-long obsession with stockholder value in combination with a growing quarter-to-quarter mindset that made it possible to rationalize continuous dismissals of employees. Palmisano, Rometty, and others justified this last action as a result of rapid technological changes, but IBM had encountered rapid technological changes before, such as the move from office appliances and tabulating equipment to digital computers, yet it managed to navigate through those times, albeit painfully. IBM was also the victim of "groupthink" in that many of its customers also had embraced a focus on shareholder value, financial engineering, stock buybacks, and so forth, along with rapid turnover in personnel and shrinking employee benefits. It is difficult to imagine IBM having taken an alternative path. Regardless of the cause, IBM transformed greatly in the first decade of the new millennium, in every measurable way. Beginning in 2012, its problems and ongoing transformation burst the walls of successful financial performance, spilling out years of shrinking revenue. Its profits were built through every means except growth in the business, as it sacrificed the profits that could have accompanied that expansion.

IBM's financial performance raises a question: Is growth always a good thing? The mantra of American business, reinforced by decades of business professors teaching millions of students and managers, is that growth is desirable. I cannot answer the question here; however, we can say that IBM embraced that belief and the quarter-to-quarter insistence of brokerage houses and investors that IBM continue to grow revenue, profits, dividends, and stock value. That view proved detrimental to every implementation of a growth strategy since the mid-1980s. CEOs from Opel to Rometty complained about it because they knew one could not run a large enterprise on a quarterly basis; they had tried. That effort caused them to consume the company's seed corn, from continuously laying off employees to incrementally reducing benefits, bonuses, and salaries. They knew that growth for the sake of growth, revenue for the sake of revenue, was never good enough. Like Thomas Watson Sr., they knew that net earnings—profits—were more precious than more sales.

Laced throughout the history of IBM, even in its pre–C-T-R days, was an aspiration to help create a better world. The aspiration was more than noble; it was big, even when IBM was small. Watson Sr. spoke about

"World Peace through World Trade," while nearly a century later, Rometty asked how IBM could be "essential" to the world. These notions could be taken as arrogance or hubris run amok, but actually it was not, because for so many decades IBMers felt they had enough capacity and capability to change how the world functioned. To them, it was a moral responsibility, not just good business. We now know, for example, that the use of computing by countries in which IBM operated proved more extensive than in those in which it was absent, even if other suppliers were present. Today, IBMers think the potential to cure cancer using artificial intelligence—Watson—is possible. These people are not innocent of the ways of the world; they are educated, successful, bright, and armed with an organization capable of doing a great deal.

The core feature of companies like IBM—multinationals—to quote Robert Fitzgerald, a longtime student of their activities, is that, "They have the ability to transfer transnationally from their home economies or to develop transnationally in an overseas location. In many cases, it was the possession of these capabilities that bestowed on multinationals their bargaining power over host governments and overseas territories, which needed access to the know-how or resources controlled by foreign businesses. In some cases, the importance of a multinational gave it leverage over its own home government."[30] IBM increased its influence the same way as other multinationals did, by using information technologies and an increasingly educated workforce. Fitzgerald could have been describing IBM:

> Multinationals increased their control over cross-border value chains of supply, distribution, finance and production, and, through these, proved adept at utilizing national locations with differing competitive advantages and levels of economic development. Across these complex networks, they employed a mix of equity control, alliances, partnerships and contracts, different in character to the organizational trends of the immediate post-war decades when multinationals had preferred more direct supervision within a managerial hierarchy. The approach of the 1990s was resonant of the international networks so familiar to the trading, finance and utility multinationals of the nineteenth century. As a consequence, while enhancing their ability to manage greater degrees of uncertainty, modern multinationals could control or

influence ever greater concentrations of capabilities in management, technology and capital, with which to maintain their competitive lead, and to negotiate with host governments that sought to attract the assets they owned.[31]

Much of what he describes applied to IBM even in the 1920s, certainly by the 1950s, and clearly had been a way of life for longer than the living memories of current IBM employees. One other observation that is worth remembering is that "the multinational has undertaken the route of continuous change" as a source of its success, a lesson IBM learned, occasionally ignoring it at its peril.[32] In achieving its status as a multinational, IBM brought hundreds of other firms down the same path with its products, attitudes, and practices.

These played out in individual events. Take, for example, those beliefs that periodically went public, such as IBM's "smarter planet" marketing campaign early in the new millennium. One IBM manager writing about the role of leadership in 2012 pulled out an example of the role of aspiration from his own company: "IBMers are committed to building the future—a better world, and a better IBM."[33] He linked that notion to operations in ways that would have been familiar to generations of employees: "IBMers are systems thinkers. We help our clients, our colleagues and the world understand and design the essential dimensions of any system—how it senses, maps and analyzes information, detects underlying patterns, and translates that knowledge into belief and action," into sound framing of problems.[34] IBM's history demonstrates that these statements represented long-held beliefs and patterns of behavior with, of course, exceptions in every decade.

Like other multinationals, IBM helped shape globalization. Computing made it possible for manufacturing firms to desegregate the production process, shipping work to the most cost-effective corners of the planet, thanks to the cheapness of transferring know-how and communications. Expensive Northern Hemisphere workers lost out to less costly ones in the Southern Hemisphere, while both continued to acquire know-how and information, using IT to coordinate activities. What IBM sold to so many nations was the ability of a small number of developing economies to industrialize rapidly, joining the more industrialized nations of old that, to quote economist Richard Baldwin, "reshaped the world economy." To be specific, Baldwin pointed out that the G7 nations (IBM's customers since the dawn of the twentieth century) "deindustrialized" while others industrialized (Taiwan, China, Indonesia, and Brazil, for example), with the new nations experiencing "spectacular growth takeoffs," largely starting around 1990. This caused "a boom in commodity exports and prices," resulting in industrializing nations' share of world GDP returning by the early years of the new millennium to what it had been at the start of World War I. "Almost all developing nations massively liberalized their policies on trade, investment, capital, services, and intellectual property," Baldwin noted. That is why IBM could hire tens of thousands of Indians and uncover demand for its products in every transforming economy on the planet. I agree with Baldwin that "at the base of all these gigantic changes was the evening out of the very uneven distribution of production know-how that had emerged" between 1820 and 1990.[35]

IBM's history offers insights on the matter of leadership, too, which played such a major role in facilitating the kinds of changes described by Baldwin and others. While much has been written about IBM's managerial practices, a company that long lived offers more. When a company has been around long enough, it is ruled by many CEOs. IBM's CEOs ran the company for between 4 and 10 years each, with the exception of T. V. Learson, who was a placeholder for Frank Cary when Tom Watson Jr. had to relinquish authority after a heart attack. Three of IBM's CEOs were confident visionaries who ruled with the certainty of an emperor: Thomas Watson Sr., to a lesser degree his son Tom Jr. (and to an even slightly lesser extent his other son, Arthur, in World Trade), and Lou Gerstner. They knew what they wanted to do and imposed a strong hands-on corporate authority over the company. While they said much about delegating *authority*, they were more inclined to delegate *accountability* for actions taken and for failures. Frank Cary played the company's culture and organization like a master violinist. He knew how to "work the system" to get what he wanted. Sam Palmisano exhibited some of those traits but did not hesitate to ride Gerstner's wave and compromise the Basic Beliefs when he thought another transformation was needed.

If we appraise the other CEOs the way employees were doing, then the lesson is that just because someone held a powerful position of centralized authority did not mean they were omnipotent. John Opel, a technocrat, made the mistake of expanding the company without understanding what was happening to the technological underpinnings affecting IBM's destiny. His successor, John Akers, less capable of working the IBM organization and frustrated by that fact, had to clean up Opel's mistake, and if he had done only that, we could have appraised him as average. But he was the CEO who agreed with those in the company who wanted to break up IBM, so the board of directors became willing to push him out of his job. They were fair to appraise his results as failing. Palmisano provided a modicum of stability.

Then there was Ginni Rometty. The first several years of her rule would have earned her the boot out the door, because IBM shrank and she remained fiercely in denial about the ineffectiveness of her actions. But then she faced her failures and embraced a strategy that increasingly made a great deal of sense to employees, customers, investors, and the business media, because it represented a good marriage of emerging technologies and IBM's capabilities. Redemption was in the air by 2016, but Rometty's performance in 2017 represented the continuation of the problems of 2015 and 2016, quite understandable since you do not turn a large company around so quickly. On a positive note, she ended 2017 with the fourth quarter turning in revenue growth when compared to the same quarter in 2016. However, Rometty cannot solely be blamed or complimented for whatever happened at IBM. She worked for the board of directors, so its members must share the blame and credit. They believed she performed better than employees, Wall Street, or the media thought. A careful reading of IBM's annual SEC filings for these years reveals what behavior and performance by senior executives the board rewarded. That filing essentially is the compensation plan for top executives, much like sales staff had their "Sales Plan." For 2016, "the Board approved an annual incentive payment of $4.95 million for Mrs. Rometty, which represented 99% of target. The payout level considered significant progress in the implementation of IBM's strategy, with continued growth in Strategic Imperatives, momentum in cognitive, and the creation of new businesses in health care, Internet of Things, and financial regulatory compliance." The Compensation Committee of the board noted "major steps taken to realign workforce skills and strengthen senior management."[36] She did as instructed by her board.[37]

It is a curious feature of IBM's appraisal system that the higher one sat in the organization, the less attention was paid to how they dealt with their employees, as it was all about the numbers, the results. So Rometty's behavior toward employees, as reflected in her language (referring to employees as "resources") and layoffs, was overlooked, as was Gerstner's blunt manner. Akers received no points for his politeness toward employees and sensitivity to the Basic Beliefs. T. V. Learson may have been the rudest IBM executive, at a time when personal style was important, and yet he got a pass because he got the S/360 to market. A lesson from IBM is that good manners are only essential with customers, Wall Street, and politicians. Having a view about where the company needs to go and accepting that it must continue to change at the speed with which technologies and customers do is central to the success of a firm and its senior leaders.

Throughout IBM's history, one important group remained in the shadows, thought about only when the company was in trouble: IBM's board of directors. Employees rarely spoke about it, and never in public. For members of IBM's ecosystem, the board was simply out of mind, invisible. Over the past century, it has numbered no more than a couple of hundred people. It was not uncommon for a board member to serve for nearly a decade. Retired IBM chairmen routinely were elected to it, except Akers. Minutes of their meetings never became public, although once in a while a board member spoke about IBM events, such as James "Jim" Burke did when Akers stepped down in 1993. Membership consisted of CEOs of companies comparable to IBM in status and size; all were IBM customers. Few members knew much about the technology IBM was selling, but they knew how to run large enterprises. In the second half of the twentieth century, the IBM board had a sprinkling of U.S. government officials, a few academics, and leaders of nonprofit organizations. These three sets of members were often seen as window dressing to make IBM appear socially conscious, yet they provided practical insights on how to deal with the U.S.

government, especially when it came to antitrust matters in the 1970s. In the last third of the century, European and, later, Asian members joined the board. In all periods, the head of IBM and other senior executives also sat on the board. Members were older than senior executives in the firm, usually in their 60s.

IBM's chairmen recruited members who supported their initiatives and made sure they stayed committed. Rarely did chairmen and boards argue in public. In his first half dozen years at C-T-R, Thomas Watson Sr. contended with an activist board, and in the 1930s members questioned the wisdom of his decision to expand IBM's business while its competitors were pulling back. But, even then, they let him have his way. Tom Watson Jr. managed to control his board through the long years of System 360's development. Akers enjoyed the support of his board even when the media and investors were questioning IBM's direction in 1990–1993. Only when faced with the prospect of IBM falling apart and with investors howling did the board act. Even then, it took an activist minority to prod other members. In his memoirs, Gerstner explained how he remade IBM's board, shrinking its size, eliminating members, and restocking it with people more compatible with his views. Palmisano and Rometty carefully tended their boards, with the result that their boards remained supportive. With many analysts and employees noisily complaining about Roadmap 2015 in 2012–2014, the board stood by Rometty, backing the transition she was espousing.

We know too little about the board's history. It put CEOs under contract to run IBM, often in five-year increments. It valued increases in shareholder value—meaning stock price—and delegated to CEOs how to accomplish that. It dismissed only one CEO in the history of the company. The occasional leaked discussion or slide deck suggested that IBM executives reviewed major strategic decisions with board members, although key decisions were made about IBM's future before board meetings, in those management committee sessions comprised of the senior executives and the chairmen. In recent decades, IBM's board consolidated under one hat an awkward set of titles: president, CEO, and chairman. It had become fashionable in many large enterprises to combine all three positions, consolidating much authority in the hands of one individual. At IBM, it reinforced the centrality of Armonk's control over the entire IBM empire.[38] IBM's most effective CEOs dominated their boards and company, strengthened by a confident view of what needed to be done and by the authority to implement their vision.

Board members rarely interacted with IBMers at large, except with those who made presentations to them or those being groomed for higher positions by a CEO. By the time a new CEO was appointed, board members were familiar with several potential candidates, so they could select the one they and the retiring chairman wanted, comfortable in the knowledge that they understood who they were appointing. They took succession planning seriously, and when IBM's bench strength weakened, they did not hesitate to grouse about it, even outside the boardroom in whispered comments to other CEOs and a few large investors, as occurred while Akers was consolidating his authority against rivals.

IBM's secretary managed a staff providing board members with information about the firm and arranging for their meetings. Since the 1980s, many of these gatherings have been held on the second floor of the IBM training center at Palisades, New York, just up the road from Armonk. Walking up the staircase to the room in the back where they sometimes met, they saw a portrait of a stern looking Thomas Watson Sr. looking down at them. At the top of the stairs, to their left, was a restored IBM parts truck from the 1920s, a reminder of IBM's early central mantra—customer service.

In the mid-1980s, IBMers began to publicly accuse their CEOs of being out of touch, most notably Opel and Akers. Did their complaint apply to the board? One retired senior vice president who wished to remain anonymous about the matter groused to me in 2015 that the current board was made up of "old" people who instead should be in their 50s and more attuned to what was going on with technology.[39] Historians who have studied the role of boards since the 1990s frame their research around the issue of "corporate governance" and suggest similar practices and issues at other companies. Board members invited IBM's most senior executives and chairmen to serve on their boards as well, which added to an older membership but also provided institutional knowledge about the company. Board behavior reflected the activities of a small community of closely knit members, whose roles remained tightly guarded, an information ecosystem of their own. The locus of IBM's actions remained centered in the chairman's office or across the hall in his or her conference room, less so in a boardroom. One senior vice president may have accidentally pulled back the curtain exposing discontent or differences of opinion within the board when, while helping to find Akers's replacement, he commented that Jim Burke "was very difficult to work with" and that members were troubled that he had invited "the media into the boardroom," a most "unusual" action. This executive's comments may have reflected the attitudes of other board members when he opined that "it was he, Burke, who probably said too much to the media."[40] Yet the board retained a positive reputation among executives in other multinationals and among industry experts.[41]

A tight link remained between employees and their board, who were glued together by shared beliefs, worldviews, and experiences, an invisible ecosystem. Jacques Rojot, a retired professor of business practices with considerable hands-on experience himself as a member of various boards, used an example from IBM to explain that corporate culture could have potential negative effects on decision making, putting "limitations on rationality":

> In the early 1970s IBM specialized in research and design of big powerful computers that it rented to clients. These orientations influenced the people IBM hired, the training it gave to employees, and the values that top managers espoused. IBM's resulting cognitive limitations in its research, engineering, and marketing conspired to make its forecasting ignore elements present in the technological and market environment that were allowing the design of a personal computer. It thus lost ground that was almost impossible to make up.[42]

The board was complicit because it had IBMers among its members and it had approved the CEO's recommendations. When trying to understand its patience with IBM's transitions in the post-Palmisano era, it remains useful to keep Rojot's observations in mind.

IBM'S LEGACY

Step into an elementary school classroom filled with children in Endicott, New York, or in any other IBM company town that has suffered devastating declines in the number of IBMers on the company's payroll, and you will see the children busily at work. Go to the local high school and you will see the same thing, with the vast majority graduating and moving on to college. In both schools, teachers will tell you that these children are bright, do their work, express curiosity about the world around them, and come from families that believe in work and accomplishments. You could argue, "Well, that reflects the heritage of the Polish, German, and Italian immigrants who migrated to that part of New York State in the nineteenth century," and you would be right, but only to a certain extent. Look deeper, ask which students had parents or grandparents who worked at IBM, and you will hear success stories about their children of IBMers becoming astronauts, politicians, academics, senior officials, military officers, actors, comedians, and business people who shared one common feature: they succeeded in their chosen professions. The same holds, for example, in Rochester, New York, with children and young adults raised in Kodak families, and in Japan with Toyota families.

So what is the point? What people learned at work, what they came to believe from their careers, they passed on to their families. Over a million people worked for IBM, involving a large number of families over the course of five generations. Some worked at IBM for more than three generations, often with multiple members being employed there at the same time. Pity the poor IBM salesman who did not make his numbers only to find when attending his family's Christmas celebrations that several brothers had. The Watson, Lautenbach, and McKittrick families staffed executive ranks for nearly a half century. Whatever goodness someone learned at work, they handed down to their children. Tom Watson Jr. remembers sitting in his father's office as a child, watching how the Old Man ran the company. Photographs show him and his brother touring IBM factories or on ships headed to Europe to inspect local operations.

It is not uncommon when meeting someone for the first time for an IBMer to hear from their new acquaintance that one of their parents or relatives had worked for the company, a statement always expressed in a tone of pride. It happens all over the world. Over many decades, customers took pride in telling an IBMer that he or she had been an IBM customer, announcing that they, too, had been part of this greater ecosystem in which IBM seemed normally at the center. The nobility of doing good things for the world, of knowing how to function efficiently, may ultimately explain why IBM was iconic, why its presence became important to understand. It may also explain how the company accumulated so many assets, grew to such size, and so controlled its markets. There are no guarantees that this will continue; big companies can go out of business in less than a year—think of Enron and Lehman Brothers—but children guarantee a legacy for this company, no matter what.

I have argued in this book that IBM became a corporate force of nature, retaining that status for over a century. It became so big that it could influence whole industries and economies. It became so admired that even in its hard times, people expected the best of business results. IBM has long been held to higher standards, which was irritating to some of its CEOs when the company did not live up to them. There were days when one could expect the likes of Akers or Rometty to go home frustrated by the criticisms they got, when what they were really interested in was leaving behind a healthy company in a better world, not simply accumulating cash and IBM stock.

It mattered what IBM's CEOs thought and did, because it was a company that they dominated. Historian Steven W. Usselman correctly cautioned that their dominance evolved over time, too. Watson Sr. "imprinted his personality upon a modest-sized firm looking to bring a fairly stable product to a wider market," but over time "the links between personality and enterprise grow much more muddled and complicated, however, as the size of the firm increases and its range of activities expands." At IBM, the closer one came to the present, the more important it became "to consider matters of structure and function."[43] Thus, the combination of CEO power, beliefs, and personalities on the one hand and the ecosystem comprising IBM, or to use Usselman's phrase, "structure and function," on the other, are essential ways to understand the history of this firm.

Ask employees what the company gave to the world, and they will say IBMers. It is impossible to attend a promotion party, retirement event, or funeral of an IBMer without all the other members of the company emphasizing people, IBM's people and their customers. This is more than pro forma ritual; IBMers can be seen shedding tears when publicly acknowledging colleagues.

A sales manager who ran the manufacturing branch office in West Orange, New Jersey, in 1981, who we will leave unnamed, was considered a hard-bitten, tough, demanding manager, often rude, and never satisfied with whatever you were doing. Most of his staff thought little of him. Veterans of both the Korean and Vietnam Wars thought him heartless. But the office performed well, made its numbers, and so in the fullness of time he was promoted to marketing director in Hong Kong, clearly an important promotion. Following long-standing tradition at the branch office meeting to announce his promotion, in the presence of his old boss, Tom Peronne, also a no-nonsense New York Italian-American executive, he stood up to thank the branch for its support, for making his promotion possible. So far, this was all routine behavior. Then, all of a sudden, in his ritual acceptance of the promotion, he broke out crying like a child as he reflected on his time in this branch, as he was speaking about the staff, the people. Up to that point, nearly 100 employees were sitting, arms folded, glad to hear he was leaving, eager to get back to whatever they were doing before this meeting was called. Shocked, one person in a louder voice than he probably intended said something to the effect of, "Oh My God, he cared about us!" There was a pause, a momentary silence in the room. The standing ovation he then received was loud and lengthy. His secretary was in tears. For days, the branch discussed this turn of events. In the end, the employee was just another IBMer, demanding and judgmental, but profoundly respectful of the company's people.[44]

Visit any external employee blog today where ex-IBMers vent about IBM, and you will find people saying that they were able to quickly find employment in other companies, many in the customer organizations in which they last worked. Their customers knew the same secret as IBMers: that this company nurtured people who were valued by companies, government agencies, and even national leaders. Watson Sr. used to say that his hobby was collecting good salesmen; he was not alone in that practice.

The story told in this book of the president of an office furniture manufacturing company in 1993 telling several IBMers "not to screw up, IBM is a national treasure," could have occurred in any decade or country. In the end, we must conclude that this company, with all its faults and blessings, was a remarkable institution. It took an industrial revolution to make it possible for it to exist. It will probably take a step change in the use of technology (artificial intelligence) to sustain it through a large part of this century.

Was the world better off because IBM existed? If the Second Industrial Revolution was worth it, by extending the life spans of humans by over 25 percent and by raising over three billion people out of poverty into more comfortable circumstances, then major institutional participants in that very global human story made our planet a better place. IBM helped, because it facilitated the dramatic diffusion of the kind of information economies required, which lowered the cost of transportation and manufactured goods, improved health and sometimes safety, and catered to the aspirations for human fulfillment, as when it managed computing that safely landed humans on the moon and then brought them back to earth. In the end, we must conclude that this iconic company helped to shape the modern world. It was no accident that Thomas Watson Sr. began the peculiar practice of referring to his firm as "The IBM Company," a tradition IBMers subconsciously still follow.

AUTHOR'S NOTE: IN THE SPIRIT OF TRANSPARENCY

AS AUTHOR OF this book, I have some confessions to make and want to share some information, because this is not an ordinary corporate biography. Historians write most corporate histories, and usually they are trained at the PhD level in business history. Many other histories are written by long-serving employees of a company who are not formally trained as historians but are clearly interested in and knowledgeable about the events of their company. The historians tend to write in the third person, never using the word "I," and are distant in their presentation of the history of the firm. The employees tell more stories, are more interested in the culture of the company, and could not care less about what theoretical constructs the academics are introducing or illustrating. The first group wants to demonstrate Chandlerian historiography or some other paradigm; the second group has only read other histories of the firm they are writing about.

Then there is me. I earned a PhD in modern European and American history and spent over 38 years at IBM in sales and consulting and in various managerial roles. Along the way, I simultaneously developed my career at IBM, working for the company in New Jersey, Poughkeepsie, New York, Nashville, Atlanta, and Madison, Wisconsin. I worked in international organizations and had staffs that straddled continents, but I also kept writing histories of the information technology world, including about IBM. By the time I came to write the book you are reading, I had spent 45 years studying the firm but wanted to present its history more as a professional historian than as a reminiscing employee. For decades, for my earlier history books, almost every time I had to come near corporate headquarters for some IBM meeting, I made it a point to carve out a couple of hours to work at the IBM Archives. In time, I came to understand that magnificent collection better than its wonderful staff did. I had stuck my nose into hundreds of cartons of old documents, probably touched every bound volume of company newsletters and magazines, and glanced at many hundreds of photographs. That was all made possible because of the convenience of going to White Plains, Somers, and Armonk as an employee. As an IBMer, I met many of the personalities that have walked through the pages of this book since the 1980s.

I talked with Frank Cary about his role a number of times, made two presentations to John Akers, did an analysis of process outsourcing opportunities for Sam Palmisano while he ran GBS, and Ginni Rometty was my second-line manager for two years. I had the thrill of spending an hour with Tom Watson Jr. in 1982 discussing IBM's history and his role in it. I made the point to him that if he ever wrote his memoirs, he had to discuss how he and IBM made the transition from tabulating to computing equipment. I was so pleased when years later he wrote his book and included a detailed and honest discussion of that very issue; the archival record confirmed that he did it accurately.

I personally embraced IBM's optimistic corporate culture, privileged to be one of those iconic DPD salesmen, and had nine 100 Percent Clubs and three Golden Circles to show for my efforts. I served as a manager for over 30 years of my time at IBM, so I experienced the lack of civil liberties we managers faced but had to ensure our employees enjoyed. I sat on enough perches in the company to have witnessed much of what unfolded in the last third of this book, but, like most IBMers, while I found much to admire in the company, I understood its warts and weaknesses and did not hesitate to deal with or complain about them while at IBM or hide them from this book, because it is the act of honestly attempting to understand both that makes it possible for historians, business professors, employees, and others working in large firms to appreciate the role of this company and possibly of their own.

Now, as to the company itself and this book, that, too, is a story. While much has been written about IBM, often encouraged by the company's media community, IBM is at its core secretive. IBM wants to control what is said about it and for decades did an excellent job of doing so. Its problems beginning in the 1980s, followed by the development of the Internet with all its many blogs and now the need to manage a workforce half of whom its own executives admit have been at IBM less than five years, mean that the company can no longer control what is said about it to the extent it did years ago. Good news is great, but bad news is plentiful. From the 1950s to the present, the company has had the policy of not supporting or assisting authors of books about IBM who are not currently employees. That rule applied to me as well. I began work on this book after retiring from IBM, and with just occasional exceptions for obtaining photographs and getting minor questions answered, much has been closed to me. Occasionally a historian gets in to see a few files, such as about IBM's operations in a particular company decades ago. Had I written this book while still at IBM, I would have probably been given much more access to the archives and other sources, as I had for decades, but I probably would also have had to submit it to someone at IBM to review the text before publication. That is why I waited until I left IBM, realizing I would not be allowed to see newer files, the records of the board of directors, and so forth. No matter; as the endnotes demonstrate, there was much material available about the company in external publications, databases, and blogs. I do not believe that I was denied any important fact about IBM's history by waiting. I also support the policy that IBM should husband its files so as not to inadvertently cause embarrassment to any IBMer, active or retired, assist a competitor, or compromise the privacy and confidentiality of a customer's operations. My contacts in IBM are wide and generous and always willing to answer my questions, especially with respect to events occurring inside IBM since my retirement at the end of 2012. My objective was to use only what I needed without compromising the company, especially if I heard about business forecasts and future product announcements. That is why you see no discussion about the future of IBM in this book, although I continued to learn much about that, even as these pages were being written in 2018. Should you have comments, critiques, or additional information about IBM that I should have, reach out to me. My e-mail address is jcortada@umn.edu.

Notes

PREFACE

1. Alex Planes, "Should the Dow Jones Get Rid of International Business Machines Corp?," *The Motley Fool*, July 16, 2014, http://www.fool.com/investing/general/2014/07/16/should-the -dow-jones-get-rid-of-international-busi.aspx.
2. Harold Evans, *Do I Make Myself Clear?* (New York: Little, Brown, 2017), 212.

CHAPTER 1: ORIGINS, 1880s–1914

1. Robert J. Gordon, *The Rise and Fall of American Growth: The U.S. Standard of Living since the Civil War* (Princeton, NJ: Princeton University Press, 2016), 570–571.
2. Mairi Maclean, Charles Harvey, and Stewart R. Clegg, "Organization Theory in Business and Management History: Present Status and Future Prospects," *Business History Review* 91, no. 3 (Autumn 2017): 457–481.
3. Geoffrey D. Austrian, *Herman Hollerith: Forgotten Giant of Information Processing* (New York: Columbia University Press, 1982); Lars Heide, *Punched-Card Systems and the Early Information Explosion, 1880–1945* (Baltimore: Johns Hopkins University Press, 2009). Heide neatly summarized much of this position in Lars Heide, "Shaping a Technology: American Punched Card Systems 1880–1914," *IEEE Annals of the History of Computing* 19, no. 4 (October–December 1997): 28–41. See also Friedrich W. Kistermann, "Hollerith Punched Card System Development (1905–1913)," *IEEE Annals of the History of Computing* 27, no. 1 (January–March 2005): 56–66. Hollerith continued inventing and interacting with the firm until his death in 1929.
4. Austrian, *Herman Hollerith,* 337–339; Robert Sobel, *IBM: Colossus in Transition* (New York: Times Books, 1982); Emerson W. Pugh, *Building IBM: Shaping an Industry and Its Technology* (Cambridge, MA: MIT Press, 1995); Rowena Olegario, "IBM and the Two Thomas J. Watsons," in *Creating Modern Capitalism: How Entrepreneurs, Companies, and Countries Triumphed in Three Industrial Revolutions,* ed. Thomas K. McCraw (Cambridge, MA: Harvard University Press, 1995), 349–395; Kevin Maney, *The Maverick and His Machine: Thomas Watson, Sr. and the Making of IBM* (Hoboken, NJ: John Wiley and Sons, 2003).

5. Hints of greater interaction can be found in the memoirs of early employees, notably Charles R. Flint, *Memories of an Active Life: Men, and Ships, and Sealing Wax* (New York: G. P. Putnam's Sons, 1923); Frederick Lincoln Fuller, *My Half Century as an Inventor* (privately printed, 1938); Walter D. Jones, "Watson and Me: Life at IBM," *IEEE Annals of the History of Computing* 24, no. 1 (January–March 2002): 4–18.

6. Most firmly described in Alfred D. Chandler Jr., *The Visible Hand: The Managerial Revolution in American Business* (Cambridge, MA: Harvard University Press, 1977), 377–417.

7. Gordon, *The Rise and Fall of American Growth*, 1–18.

8. U.S. Bureau of the Census, *Historical Statistics of the United States: Colonial Times to 1970* (Washington, DC: U.S. Government Printing Office, 1975), part 2, 598.

9. Gordon's central thesis. See Gordon, *The Rise and Fall of American Growth*.

10. James R. Beniger, *The Control Revolution: Technological and Economic Origins of the Information Society* (Cambridge, MA: Harvard University Press, 1986), 7.

11. Olivier Zunz, *Making America Corporate, 1870–1920* (Chicago: University of Chicago Press, 1990), 12.

12. For discussion of the problems with trusts and divergent opinions of historians on the subject, see William G. Roy, *Socializing Capital: The Rise of the Large Industrial Corporation in America* (Princeton, NJ: Princeton University Press, 1997), 18, 26.

13. He details many of these in his memoirs. See Flint, *Memories of an Active Life*.

14. No biography has been written about Flint, only the memoir he wrote, cited earlier.

15. Walter A. Friedman, *Birth of a Salesman: The Transformation of Selling in America* (Cambridge, MA: Harvard University Press, 2004), 107, 147–150.

16. Christophe Lécuyer, *Making Silicon Valley: Innovation and the Growth of High Tech, 1930–1970* (Cambridge, MA: MIT Press, 2007).

17. As if to reaffirm its New York roots, IBM built a new corporate headquarters on its Armonk, New York, campus in the 1990s, a decision lubricated by a new tax arrangement with the state and the involvement of the state government to retain IBM's headquarters. See Mary McAleer Vizard, "I.B.M. Planning a Scaled-Down New Headquarters," *New York Times*, August 20, 1995, http://www.nytimes.com/1995/08/20/realestate/ibm-planning-a-scaled-down-new-headquarters.html?pagewanted=all.

18. I found one still in use in Beloit, Wisconsin, in the 1980s!

19. For the most detailed analysis of patent issues, see Heide, *Punched-Card Systems and the Early Information Explosion*. For the father-son disputes, the best account is by Thomas Watson Jr. himself in his memoirs. See Thomas J. Watson Jr. and Peter Petre, *Father, Son & Co.: My Life at IBM and Beyond* (New York: Bantam, 1990). On the rivalries between both brothers and with their father, see Richard S. Tedlow, *The Watson Dynasty: The Fiery Reign and Troubled Legacy of IBM's Founding Father and Son* (New York: HarperBusiness, 2003).

20. Edward Aswad and Suzanne M. Meredith, *IBM in Endicott* (Charleston, SC: Arcadia, 2005), 12.

21. "Savage & Polite's Antique Clocks Identification and Price Guide," www.antiqueclockspriceguide.com. This lists the quantity made and their serial numbers by year from 1916 through 1949.

22. Sobel, *IBM;* Austrian, *Herman Hollerith;* Martin Campbell-Kelly, William Aspray, Nathan Ensmenger, and Jeffrey R. Yost, *A History of the Information Machine*, 3rd ed. (Boulder, CO: Westview, 2014), 3–40.

23. Desktop calculators and adding machines were used by the 1880s but did little to speed up the handling of massive amounts of numbers such as the U.S. Census Bureau processed. I explored this issue in James W. Cortada, *Before the Computer: IBM, NCR, Burroughs, and Remington Rand and the Industry They Created, 1865–1956* (Princeton, NJ: Princeton University Press, 1993), 25–78.

24. Daniel Boorstin, *The Americans: The Democratic Experience* (New York: Random House, Vintage, 1973), 172.

25. Beniger, *The Control Revolution,* 416.

26. It continued to grow, reaching 76.2 million, or another 21 percent increase over 1890's, according to the U.S. Census Bureau. For more details on the technical and managerial challenges that Billings faced, see Cortada, *Before the Computer,* 44–48.

27. Austrian, *Herman Hollerith,* 5–7.

28. James W. Cortada, *All the Facts: A History of Information in the United States since 1870* (New York: Oxford University Press, 2016), 148–152.

29. These included Remington Rand all the way through Sperry Univac.

30. The head of IBM in the late 1950s to early 1970s, Tom Watson Jr., recalled in his memoirs that his father often came home in a foul mood and yelled at everyone, creating tensions that extended nearly to the death of Watson Sr. in 1956, discussed in considerable detail in Watson and Petre, *Father, Son & Co.*

31. Austrian, *Herman Hollerith.*

32. Sobel, *IBM,* 12–13.

33. Austrian, *Herman Hollerith,* 325.

34. His extant business records make it evident that he spent considerable effort recruiting investors for the company's stock and that he kept detailed records of these transactions and produced monthly reports on C-T-R's performance. See Boxes 2–7, Flint Papers, New York Public Library.

35. $313,719 in total. See "Bulletin No. 61," October 22, 1913, in "Personal Miscellany Clippings," Box 7, Flint Papers, New York Public Library.

36. Charles R. Flint Papers, New York Public Library. A search aid and description are available at http://archives.nypl.org/mss/1032.

CHAPTER 2: THOMAS J. WATSON SR. AND THE CREATION OF IBM, 1914–1924

1. James C. Collins and Jerry I. Porras, *Built to Last: Successful Habits of Visionary Companies* (New York: HarperBusiness, 1994).

2. Kenneth Lipartito, "Business Culture," in *The Oxford Handbook of Business History,* ed. Geoffrey Jones and Jonathan Zeitlin (Oxford: Oxford University Press, 2007), 603–628.

3. Robert Sobel, *IBM: Colossus in Transition* (New York: Times Books, 1982), 49.

4. There were other times in IBM's history when a new CEO would take office and appear to employees, customers, and the media to coast along with sufficient revenue coming in for a year or two until market realities compelled them to do something or risk the health of the firm. In each case, if things seemed to be going well, they saw no reason to rock the boat,

rather than build on their perceived existing momentum. Later in this book, I describe a similar circumstance with CEOs John Akers in the 1980s, Sam Palmisano in the first decade of the new millennium, and Ginni Rometty in the early 2010s. In each case, the business was doing well with regard to revenue and profits when they took on their CEO duties, only to quickly find circumstances crashing, forcing them to go beyond managing day-to-day operations and start implementing fundamental changes.

5. James W. Cortada, *Before the Computer: IBM, NCR, Burroughs, and Remington Rand and the Industry They Created, 1865–1956* (Princeton, NJ: Princeton University Press, 1993), 64–78.

6. Sobel, *IBM,* 45.

7. That practice did not change until after his son Tom Jr. took over the firm in the mid-1950s.

8. In contrast, his son Tom introduced soft shirt collars into IBM, creating a sensation at headquarters the first day he showed up wearing one. It seemed that everyone ran out to buy new shirts. Tom Jr. was more adventuresome, enjoyed a lifetime of flying his own planes before and after doing so as a U.S. Army pilot during World War II, and participated in sports. For many decades, he also sailed. Thomas Watson Sr. never drank alcoholic beverages, but his sons did; his second son, Arthur, developed a drinking problem.

9. Bryson Ainsley interview by the author, August 10, 1982. Ainsley epitomized the classic IBM sales manager: tall, thin, wearing highly starched white shirts and dark suits, well spoken, smart, and conservative. At the time of the interview, he was the director of executive compensation at corporate headquarters. He had come up in sales and earlier in his long career had held the coveted position of branch manager.

10. Recounted in Kevin Maney, *The Maverick and His Machine: Thomas Watson, Sr. and the Making of IBM* (Hoboken, NJ: John Wiley and Sons, 2003), 12–13.

11. Remington Rand later became part of Sperry Rand when it bought the computer business and went on to manufacture Univac computers in the early 1950s, which momentarily challenged Watson Sr. and worried his son Tom. Watson's attitude toward problems was one he embedded into IBM's DNA and that is still widely observable in the firm. It was a classic sales management situation faced by generations of IBMers assessing how to deal with the complex operational problems of their customers and of their own company. That attitude was a primary reason why the majority of IBM's senior executives came up in sales. Most probably did not know that their way of thinking about problems was classic Watsonian IBM. It was just the way one thought about circumstances, and that mindset originated with Watson.

12. To hear Watson lecture on thinking in 1915, see http://www-03.ibm.com/ibm/history/multimedia/wav/thinkwav.wav.

13. IBM was the first company to mass-produce computers. In the early 1950s, Univac had orders for nearly 70 systems, building a few dozen, while IBM was just entering a period when it could manufacture hundreds of computers at a time. This innovation drove down production costs and even led to a new word, *manufacturability*, the art of designing a component or machine to make it easier to manufacture. See Emerson W. Pugh, Lyle R. Johnson, and John H. Palmer, *IBM's 360 and Early 370 Systems* (Cambridge, MA: MIT Press, 1991); John Harwood, *The Interface: IBM and the Transformation of Corporate Design, 1945–1976* (Cambridge, MA: MIT Press, 2011), 59–100.

14. By the 1950s, that function was a well-oiled machine within IBM's selling process.
15. Incidentally, share values and practices made it possible for the Chinese and Roman empires to function for centuries and for the Catholic Church to last for two thousand years.
16. Informed much along the lines argued in Trever Boyns, "Accounting, Information, and Communication Systems," in Jones and Zeitlin, *The Oxford Handbook of Business History*, 447–469. See also James W. Cortada, *All the Facts: A History of Information in the United States since 1870* (New York: Oxford University Press, 2016), where I argue that not just values but shared information facilitated development of personal and institutional cultures and common behaviors and values.
17. Thomas J. Watson, *Men—Minutes—Money: A Collection of Excerpts from Talks and Messages Delivered and Written at Various Times* (New York: International Business Machines Corporation, 1934), 71.
18. Maney, *The Maverick and His Machine*, 57.
19. Quoted in ibid., 63.
20. Ibid., 66.
21. Jones became IBM's treasurer in 1927, general manager of European operations (1930–1934), and then came back to his wife's home country of Canada as vice president of Canadian operations and director. He retired in 1944. See Walter D. Jones, edited by Don Black, "Watson and Me: A Life at IBM," *IEEE Annals of the History of Computing* 25, no. 3 (July–September 2003): 4–18.
22. All the quotations are drawn from Jones, "Watson and Me."
23. Sobel, *IBM*, 64.
24. Not until 1990 did they experience what Watson went through in 1921. Tom Jr. might have argued that he went through a similar experience in the 1960s when he scrambled for every possible dollar and penny to fund development of the world's most important computer—the System 360.
25. Sobel, *IBM*.
26. Watson, *Men—Minutes—Money*, 68. These kinds of messages were repeated down through the decades. Compare Watson's messages to IBM's value proposition published in its 10-K report filed in February 2016: "The company creates value for clients through integrated solutions and products that leverage: data, information technology, deep expertise in industries and business processes, and a broad ecosystem of partners and alliances. IBM solutions typically create value by enabling new capabilities for clients that transform their businesses and help them engage with their customers and employees in new ways. These solutions draw from an industry-leading portfolio of consulting and IT implementation services, cloud and cognitive offerings, and enterprise systems and software; all bolstered by one of the world's leading research organizations." See International Business Machines Corporation, "10-K Report," in *2015 Annual Report*, 22.
27. Watson, *Men—Minutes—Money*, 48.
28. While Watson Sr. and a handful of his closest advisers created the culture, his son Tom reinvigorated it for the computer age. Subsequent senior leadership teams relied on it for guidance and inspiration, at least until the end of the 1980s, but despite a century having passed, what Watson brought over from NCR and added has remained surprisingly intact.

29. Watson, *Men—Minutes—Money*, 15, 17, 19, 23.

30. Decades later, his son Tom would speak about the company's welcome of wild ducks as being good for the company, and he even published a poster showing wild ducks flying. Long-time IBMers said IBM loves wild ducks so long as "they fly in formation," capturing the essence of Watson Sr.'s attitude toward salesmen. He wanted them to think and act as he did, but creatively.

31. He published anthologies of these messages. See Watson, *Men—Minutes—Money*, *"As a Man Thinks ... ": Thomas J. Watson and His Philosophy of Life as Expressed in His Editorials* (New York: IBM, 1954).

32. Bryson Ainsley, born in 1928, joined IBM in sales in 1949 and retired from the company in 1987.

33. Over the next century, on occasion such problems occurred with devastating effects on customers, not to mention on the careers of the IBMers involved in the misapplication of IBM's products.

34. Paul Christ and Rolph Anderson, "The Impact of Technology on Evolving Roles of Salespeople," *Journal of Historical Research in Marketing* 3, no. 2 (2011): 173–193.

35. James W. Cortada, "IBM Branch Offices: What They Were, How They Worked, 1920s–1980s," *IEEE Annals of the History of Computing* 39, no. 3 (July–September 2017): 9–23.

36. Ibid.

37. As late as the 1980s, an employee could still join an IBM country club for that same $1 a year! Eighteen percent annual inflation rates in the 1970s did not change the amount.

38. Andrea Tone, *The Business of Benevolence: Industrial Paternalism in Progressive America* (Ithaca, NY: Cornell University Press, 1997).

39. John J. Schleppi, "It Pays: John H. Patterson and Industrial Recreation at the National Cash Register Company," *Journal of Sport History* 6, no. 3 (1979): 20–28; Elspeth H. Brown, "Welfare Capitalism and Documentary Photography: NCR and the Visual Production of a Global Model Factory," *History of Photography* 32, no. 2 (2008): 137–151; Helena Chance, "Mobilising the Modern Industrial Landscape for Sports and Leisure in the early 20th Century," *International Journal of the History of Sport* 29, no. 11 (2012): 1600–1625. Historians are increasingly studying these kinds of corporate rituals. See Philip Scranton and Patrick Fridenson, *Reimaging Business History* (Baltimore: Johns Hopkins University Press, 2013), 102–106.

40. The IBM Corporate Archives takes the position that it happened in 1933; however, a check of local city records by the author showed that IBM's presence began in 1935.

41. Even in the years immediately following the end of World War II, Watson would ride in a car with a regional manager, often with his wife coming along, seeking ideal places in the United States to rent office space for branches.

42. IBM's emphasis on innovation from almost the first day Watson entered the firm in 1914 offers more evidence to those business historians who argue that changing products and services contributed more to the expansion of the world's economy than the accumulation of capital did, the case summarized in William Laznick, "Innovative Enterprise and Historical Transformation," *Enterprise and Society* 3, no. 1 (2002): 35–54.

43. Alfred D. Chandler Jr., *Strategy and Structure* (Cambridge, MA: MIT Press, 1962); Pankaj Chemawat, "Competition and Business Strategy in Historical Perspective," *Business History Review* 76, no. 1 (Spring 2002): 37–74.

44. Specifically, see Chandler, *Strategy and Structure*.

45. Adam Smith, *Correspondence of Adam Smith*, Glasgow edition, ed. E. C. Mossner and I. S. Ross (Oxford: Oxford University Press, 1977), 55.

46. On the effects of purposeful strategies in the evolution of corporations, see Jonathan Zeitlin, "The Historical Alternatives Approach," in Jones and Zeitlin, *The Oxford Handbook of Business History*, 12–129; Scranton and Fridenson, *Reimagining Business History*, 102–107.

47. Chandler, *Strategy and Structure*, 14–15.

48. For example, see Naomi R. Lamoreaux, Daniel M. G. Raff, and Peter Temin, "Beyond Markets and Hierarchies: Toward a New Synthesis of American Business History," *American Historical Review* 108, no. 2 (April 2003): 404–433.

49. For discussion of them, see Matthias Kipping and Behlül Üsdiken, "Business History and Management Studies," in Jones and Zeitlin, *The Oxford Handbook of Business History*, 99–104.

50. I developed the ideas of information ecosystems as part of the social milieu of a company in Cortada, *All the Facts*. For the de facto sociological view of the firm, I was influenced by Scranton and Friedenson, *Reimagining Business History*, and by Kenneth Lipartito and David B. Sicilia, eds., *Constructing Corporate America: History, Politics, Culture* (New York: Oxford University Press, 2004).

51. Naomi R. Lamoreaux, *The Great Merger Movement in American Business, 1850–1904* (Cambridge: Cambridge University Press, 1985); William G. Roy, *Socializing Capital: The Rise of the Large Industrial Corporation in America* (Princeton, NJ: Princeton University Press, 1997).

52. I am thinking of Joseph A. Schumpeter, *The Theory of Economic Development*, English trans. from 1926 German edition (Cambridge, MA: Harvard University Press, 1934); Joel Mokyr, *The Gifts of Athena* (Princeton, NJ: Princeton University Press, 2002); Joel Mokyr, *A Culture of Growth: Origins of the Modern Economy* (Princeton, NJ: Princeton University Press, 2016); William Bauman, Robert E. Litan, and Carl J. Schramm, *Good Capitalism, Bad Capitalism, and the Economics of Growth and Prosperity* (New Haven, CT: Yale University Press, 2007); Deirdre Nansen McCloskey, *Bourgeois Equality: How Ideas, Not Capital or Institutions, Enriched the World* (Chicago: University of Chicago Press, 2016).

CHAPTER 3: THE EMERGENCE OF IBM AND THE CULTURE OF THINK

1. Thomas J. Watson, *Men—Minutes—Money: A Collection of Excerpts from Talks and Messages Delivered and Written at Various Times* (New York: International Business Machines Corporation, 1934), 82.

2. "Computing-Tabulating Changing Its Name," *Wall Street Journal*, February 15, 1924, 3.

3. For the text and an image of the letter, see George A. Fierheller, *Do Not Fold, Spindle or Mutilate: The 'Hole' Story of Punched Cards* (Markham: Stewart, 2006), 21.

4. "The Wall Street Journal Straws," *Wall Street Journal*, May 14, 1924.

5. Robert Fitzgerald, "Marketing and Distribution," in *The Oxford Handbook of Business History*, ed. Geoffrey Jones and Jonathan Zeitlin (New York: Oxford University Press, 2007), 397, 400–404, 408–410.

6. Mira Wilkins, *The Maturing of Multinational Enterprise: American Business Abroad from 1914 to 1970* (Cambridge, MA: Harvard University Press, 1974), 60–91.

7. Kevin Maney, *The Maverick and His Machine: Thomas Watson, Sr. and the Making of IBM* (New York: John Wiley and Sons, 2003), 89.

8. The conventional story is that Watson initiated business in Latin America. New evidence suggests that Latin Americans persuaded him to do so, particularly in Brazil, which became a large national market for IBM. For details on the Brazilian experience, see the video by Mauro Segura, *IBM No Brasil* (Sao Paulo: International Business Machines Corporation, 2017), available at IBM Corporate Archives, https://mediacenter.ibm.com/media/IBM+no+Brasil+-+how +everything+started-final-fixed2/1_bsq49uuo/51569082.

9. For a convenient source for these statistics, see Emerson W. Pugh, *Building IBM: Shaping an Industry and Its Technology* (Cambridge, MA: MIT Press, 1995), 323.

10. Nevertheless, there is a useful body of material on the technology and its industry. See M. H. Adler, *The Writing Machine—A History of the Typewriter* (London: George Allen and Unwin, 1973); W. A. Beeching, *Century of the Typewriter* (New York: St. Martin's, 1974); and the still useful Bruce Bliven Jr., *The Wonderful Writing Machine* (New York: Random House, 1954). But on the industry itself, the most useful work remains George N. Engler, "The Typewriter Industry: The Impact of a Significant Technological Innovation" (PhD diss., University of California at Los Angeles, 1969).

11. Jeffrey R. Yost, *Making IT Work: A History of the Computer Services Industry* (Cambridge, MA: MIT Press, 2017), 178–181.

12. Ibid.

13. Deirdre Nansen McCloskey, *Bourgeois Equality: How Ideas, Not Capital or Institutions, Enriched the World* (Chicago: University of Chicago Press, 2016), 105–106.

14. Quoted in Maney, *The Maverick and His Machine*, 99.

15. Quoted in ibid., 110.

16. Ibid., 112. Beginning in the 1980s and continuing into the 2010s, IBM kept drifting into complex matrixed organizations.

17. Not until his son Tom, who was not a founder of C-T-R, took over the business in the 1950s was it possible to create a normal divisional chain of command organization.

18. It remained in use right into the next century.

19. Andrea Tone, *The Business of Benevolence: Industrial Paternalism in Progressive America* (Ithaca, NY: Cornell University Press, 1997), on labor reforms, 16–65, on the response to unions, 182–198.

20. I have discussed the concept of information ecosystems in business extensively in James W. Cortada, *All the Facts: A History of Information in the United States since 1870* (New York: Oxford University Press, 2016).

21. Ibid., 97.

22. To hear IBMers sing this song, recorded in 1931, visit https://www-03.ibm.com/ibm/history /multimedia/wav/everonward.wav.

23. For a video of a performance dated 1983, see https://www.youtube.com/watch?v=tAKOjBhl1II.

24. Lars Heide, *Punched-Card Systems and the Early Information Explosion, 1880–1945* (Baltimore: Johns Hopkins University Press, 2009); Geoffrey Austrian, *Herman Hollerith: Forgotten Giant of Information Processing* (New York: Columbia University Press, 1982).

25. Watson, *Men—Minutes—Money*, 149.

26. Ibid., 177.

27. He received more than 50 patents while at IBM for 43 years (1917–1960) and was a major developer of the IBM 407 accounting machine, the first product at IBM to generate a billion dollars in revenue. See "Ralph Page, 95, Dies; Inventor with I.B.M.," *New York Times*, February 8, 1991.

28. Charles J. Bashe, Lyle R. Johnson, John H. Palmer, and Emerson W. Pugh, *IBM's Early Computers* (Cambridge, MA: MIT Press, 1986), 18.

29. Pierce was no longer contributing, as he had died suddenly in 1933, but kept being issued patents that he had applied for while still alive.

30. Pugh, *Building IBM*, 325.

31. Heide, *Punched-Card Systems and the Early Information Explosion;* James W. Cortada, *Before the Computer: IBM, NCR, Burroughs, and Remington Rand and the Industry They Created, 1865–1956* (Princeton, NJ: Princeton University Press, 1993), 128–136.

32. The number of customers IBM had is determined by looking at the country files for each of IBM's subsidiary firms housed at the IBM Corporate Archives, Somers, New York, all of which were required for decades to inventory the names of their customers and those of their rivals.

33. Watson, *Men—Minutes—Money*, 416.

34. William Henry Leffingwell, *Office Appliance Manual* (New York: National Association of Office Appliance Manufacturers, 1926), 179.

35. "Electrical Bookkeeping and Accounting," *American City* 30 (November 1935): 55.

36. Leffingwell, *Office Appliance Manual*, 179.

37. A practice continued to the present. See Wallace J. Eckert, *Punched Card Methods in Scientific Computing* (New York: Columbia University Press, 1940).

38. Cortada, *Before the Computer*, 128–136.

39. Ibid., 136.

40. For example, secretaries considered the Selectric typewriter, introduced in 1961, the best machine on the market. It remained popular for decades, largely because of the feel of the keyboard.

41. For a compelling argument about the economic importance and size of sweet talking (persuasion) activities, see McCloskey, *Bourgeois Equality*, 490–498.

42. On the centrality of this kind of activity, see Daniel Pink, *To Sell Is Human: The Surprising Truth about Moving Others* (New York: Riverhead/Penguin, 2012).

CHAPTER 4: IBM AND THE GREAT DEPRESSION

1. Thomas J. Watson, *Men—Minutes—Money: A Collection of Excerpts from Talks and Messages Delivered and Written at Various Times* (New York: International Business Machines Corporation, 1934), 473.

2. Quoted in Lorena Hickok, Richard Lowitt, and Maurine H. Beasley (eds.), *One Third of a Nation: Lorena Hickok Reports on the Great Depression* (Chicago: University of Illinois Press, 1981), 223.

3. In a speech delivered on September 27, 1933. See Watson, *Men—Minutes—Money*, 866.

4. To hear Watson deliver his message to IBMers, in this instance in 1937 to salesmen, visit http://www-03.ibm.com/ibm/history/multimedia/wav/opportunitywav.wav.

5. Watson, *Men—Minutes—Money,* 306.

6. Ibid., 308.

7. Mira Wilkins, *The Maturing of Multinational Enterprise* (Cambridge, MA: Harvard University Press, 1974).

8. International Business Machines Corporation, *Annual Reports,* 1935–1939.

9. Martin Campbell-Kelly, William Aspray, Nathan Ensmenger, and Jeffrey R. Yost, *Computer: A History of the Information Machine,* 3rd ed. (Boulder, CO: Westview, 2014), 39; Arthur L. Norberg, "High-Technology Calculation in the Early 20th Century: Punched Card Machinery in Business and Government," *Technology and Culture* 31, no. 4 (October 1990): 753–779; Lars Heide, *Punched-Card Systems and the Early Information Explosion, 1880–1945* (Baltimore: Johns Hopkins University Press, 2009), 211–219, 221–222.

10. We can go further and say that a similar dominance occurred in the European market after World War II. No other company in either the office appliance industry or hardly any other major industry in the United States so dominated its market for as long as IBM.

11. Robert Sobel, *IBM: Colossus in Transition* (New York: Times Books, 1981), 87.

12. For a film showing the equipment in use, see U.S. Social Security Administration, "The Systems Story—Social Security," https://archive.org/details/0888_IBM_Day_New_York_Worlds_Fair_May_4_1939_18_01_01_00.

13. Kevin Maney, *The Maverick and His Machine: Thomas Watson Sr. and the Making of IBM* (Hoboken, NJ: John Wiley and Sons, 2003), 156.

14. Watson, *Men—Minutes—Money,* 844.

15. Ibid., 845.

16. Sobel, *IBM,* 89.

17. Ibid., 91.

18. *International Business Machines Corp. v. United States* 298 U.S. 131 (1936).

19. IBM produced a movie of its role at the fair. To see this, visit https://archive.org/details/0888_IBM_Day_New_York_Worlds_Fair_May_4_1939_18_01_01_00.

20. Quoted in Maney, *The Maverick and His Machine,* 234.

21. Ibid., 237.

22. Watson, *Men—Minutes—Money,* 114.

23. Ibid.

24. Both quoted in Maney, *The Maverick and His Machine,* 879.

25. Deutsche Hollerith Maschinen Gesellschaft, *Festschrift zur 25-Jahrfeier* (Berlin: Dehomag, 1935), 31–50.

26. Quoted in Edwin Black, *IBM and the Holocaust: The Strategic Alliance between Nazi Germany and America's Most Powerful Corporation* (New York: Crown, 2001), 76.

27. Quoted in James Connolly, *History of Computing in Europe* (New York: IBM World Trade Corporation, 1967), 28.

28. Sobel, *IBM,* 135.

29. Connolly, *History of Computing in Europe,* 133.

30. Maney, *The Maverick and His Machine,* 204.

31. Sobel, *IBM,* 83–84.

32. While he sought publicity, he wanted to control what kind. Articles discussing his wealth were not among them.

33. Ironically, in 2016, IBM launched a worldwide marketing campaign touting the abilities of its Watson computer, which it branded as "Cognitive Business."

34. William Lazonick, "Understanding Innovative Enterprise: Toward the Integration of Economic Theory and Business History," in *Business History around the World,* ed. Franco Amatori and Geoffrey Jones (Cambridge: Cambridge University Press, 2003), 42–43.

CHAPTER 5: IBM IN WORLD WAR II, 1939–1945

1. Quoted in *Business Machines,* January 27, 1944.

2. Emerson W. Pugh, *Building IBM: Shaping an Industry and Its Technology* (Cambridge, MA: MIT Press, 1995), 323.

3. Kevin Maney, *The Maverick and His Machine: Thomas Watson, Sr. and the Making of IBM* (Hoboken, NJ: John Wiley and Sons, 2003), 291–326; Pugh, *Building IBM,* 89–107.

4. Most notably, B. Cohen, G. F. W. Welch, and R. V. D. Campbell, eds., *Makin' Numbers: Howard Aiken and the Computer* (Cambridge, MA: MIT Press, 1999).

5. Edwin Black, *IBM and the Holocaust* (New York: Crown, 2001).

6. Louis Galambos, *The Creative Society and the Price Americans Paid for It* (Cambridge: Cambridge University Press, 2012), 118.

7. I focused on IBM's U.S. operations and how the U.S. government managed the allocation of resources for the diffusion of office equipment. See James W. Cortada, *Before the Computer: IBM, NCR, Burroughs, and Remington Rand and the Industry They Created, 1865–1956* (Princeton, NJ: Princeton University Press, 1993), 189–205.

8. Recall that this is the industry that sold office machines, such as desktop calculators and adding machines, typewriters, and tabulating equipment. The term "office appliance industry" continued past World War II.

9. Thomas J. Watson, *"As A Man Thinks ... ": Thomas J. Watson, the Man and His Philosophy of Life as Expressed in His Editorials* (New York: International Business Machines Corporation, 1954), 95.

10. For an analysis of these various financial results, see Cortada, *Before the Computer,* 214–216.

11. Arthur Sanders, "Office Machine and Typewriter Industries in 1944" (Report of the Service Equipment Division, WPB, May 1945), in Burroughs Papers, Charles Babbage Institute, University of Minnesota.

12. David Kahn, *The Codebreakers: The Story of Secret Writing* (London: Weidenfeld and Nicolson, 1967), 300ff, 332–333.

13. Quoted in Peter E. Greulich, "The Story of Machine Records Units (MRUs) in World War II," MBI Concepts Corporation, http://www.mbiconcepts.com.

14. Ibid.

15. Pugh, *Building IBM,* 74.

16. Maney, *The Maverick and His Machine,* 338–339.

17. Thomas J. Watson Jr. and Peter Petre, *Father, Son & Co.: My Life at IBM and Beyond* (New York: Bantam, 1990), 136.

18. Ibid.

19. Richard S. Tedlow, *The Watson Dynasty: The Fiery Reign and Troubled Legacy of IBM's Founding Father and Son* (New York: HarperBusiness, 2003), 135.

20. Watson and Petre, *Father, Son & Co.*, 85.

21. Ibid.

22. Tedlow, *The Watson Dynasty,* 141.

23. Watson and Petre, *Father, Son & Co.,* 127.

24. Donald W. McCormick and James C. Spee, "IBM and Germany, 1922–1941," *Organization Management Journal* 5, no. 4 (2008): 214–223.

25. Robert Fitzgerald, *The Rise of the Global Company: Multinationals and the Making of the Modern World* (Cambridge: Cambridge University Press, 2015), 234–240.

26. Geoffrey Jones, "Globalization," in *The Oxford Handbook of Business History,* ed. Geoffrey Jones and Jonathan Zeitlin (New York: Oxford University Press, 2007), 155.

27. H. A. Turner, *General Motors and the Nazis* (New Haven, CT: Yale University Press, 2005); C. Kobrak and P. H. Hansen, eds., *European Business, Dictatorship and Political Risk, 1920–1945* (New York: Berghahn, 2004); F. R. Nicosia and J. Huener, eds., *Business and Industry in Nazi Germany* (New York: Berghahn, 2004); G. Aalders and C. Wiebes, *The Art of Cloaking Ownership* (Amsterdam: Amsterdam University Press, 1996).

28. C. Cheape, "Not Politicians but Sound Businessmen: Norton Company and the Third Reich," *Business History Review* 62, no. 3 (1988): 344–366.

29. Martin Horn and Talbot Imlay, *The Politics of Industrial Collaboration during World War II: Ford France, Vichy and Nazi Germany* (Cambridge: Cambridge University Press, 2014), 269.

30. David Martin Luebke and Sybil Milton, "Locating the Victim: An Overview of Census-Taking, Tabulation Technology, and Persecution in Nazi Germany," *IEEE Annals of the History of Computing* 16, no. 3 (1994): 34–35.

31. Heidinger was careful to cultivate the Nazis. For example, in 1934, when he opened a new manufacturing facility, he hosted a celebratory event for employees, customers, and local public officials, which included members of the military and of the Nazi Party. He subsequently published an elegant commemorative book distributed to attendees. See Dehomag, *Dentschrift* (Berlin: Dehomag, 1934), of which a copy is in the author's possession.

32. Maney, *The Maverick and His Machine,* 223.

33. Black, *IBM and the Holocaust.*

34. Michael Allen, "Stranger than Science Fiction: Edwin Black, IBM, and the Holocaust," *Technology and Culture* 43, no. 1 (January 2002): 152–153. Not until the 1990s did Germany begin automating its national card file.

35. Götz Ally and Karl-Heinz Roth, *Die restlose Erfassung* (Frankfurt am Main: Fischer Taschenbuch 2000), 120. But see also Luebke and Milton, "Locating the Victim," 25–39.

36. Ally and Roth, *Die restlose Erfassung,* 120.

37. Peter Hayes, "Did IBM Really Cozy Up to Hitler?," *BusinessWeek online,* March 19, 2001.

38. Allen, "Stranger than Science Fiction," 153.

39. On Nazi control over IBM France, see Geneviève Ollivier and Oscar Ortsman, *IBM ou la Tentation Totalitaire: Archives de Jean Ollivier* (Paris: L'Harmattan, 2006), 41–44, 71–73. IBM in France came under the control of Dehomag.

40. Horn and Imlay, *The Politics of Industrial Collaboration during World War II.*

41. Brad Lesher, *"Don't Forget the Peanut Butter, George!"* (No city: Xlibris, 2010), 62.

42. On events in postwar France, see Ollivier and Ortsman, *IBM ou la Tentation Totalitaire,* 72–73.

43. Ko Mizushina to James Connolly, June 7, 1966, "Biographical Files," Folder 28, Box 47, IBM Corporate Archives, Poughkeepsie, NY; J. T. Wilson memorandum to Thomas J. Watson, January 13, 1942, "1942 Watson Senior–Wilson Correspondence," Box 823, IBM Corporate Archives, Poughkeepsie, NY. On the occasion of IBM's fiftieth anniversary of its presence in Japan, it published a celebratory history, Nihon IBM, *Nihon IBM gofunen shi (A Fifty-Year History of IBM Japan)* (Tokyo: IBM Japan, 1988).

44. Ollivier and Ortsman, *IBM ou la Tentation Totalitaire,* 72–73.

45. James W. Birkenstock, "Pioneering: On the Frontier of Electronic Data Processing, a Personal Memoir," reprinted in Jeffrey R. Yost, ed., *The IBM Century: Creating the IT Revolution* (Piscataway, NJ: IEEE Computer Society, 2011), 101.

46. Ibid., 102.

CHAPTER 6: IBM GETS INTO THE COMPUTER BUSINESS, 1945–1964

1. International Business Machines Corporation, *1952 Annual Report,* 8.

2. Emerson W. Pugh, *Building IBM: Shaping an Industry and Its Technology* (Cambridge, MA: MIT Press, 1995), 323–324.

3. IBMers filled in details on the complexity of both the decision to get into computers and the launch of this new line of business. See, for example, C. J. Bashe, "The SSEC in Historical Perspective," *Annals of the History of Computing* 4, no. 4 (1982): 296–312; C. C. Hurd, "Early Computers at IBM," *Annals of the History of Computing* 3, no. 2 (1981): 163–182; J. C. McPherson, F. E. Hamilton, and R. R. Seeber Jr., "A Large-Scale General Purpose Electronic Digital Calculator—the SSEC," *Annals of the History of Computing* 4, no. 4 (1982): 313–326; B. E. Phelps, "Early Electronic Computer Development at IBM," *Annals of the History of Computing* 2, no. 3 (1980): 253–267; G. R. Trimble Jr., "A Brief History of Computing: Memoirs of Living on the Edge," *IEEE Annals of the History of Computing* 23, no. 3 (2001): 44–59; G. R. Trimble Jr., "The IBM 650 Magnetic Drum Calculator," *Annals of the History of Computing* 8, no. 1 (1986): 20–29. Kenneth Flamm makes clear how important the federal government's support was in funding early computer developments at IBM. See Kenneth Flamm, *Creating the Computer: Government, Industry, and High Technology* (Washington, DC: Brookings Institution Press, 1988); Kenneth Flamm, *Targeting the Computer: Government Support and International Competition* (Washington, DC: Brookings Institution Press, 1987). For the argument that computing and the military comprised an intimate, closed world and were dependent on each other, see Paul N. Edwards, *The Closed World: Computers and the Politics of Discourse in Cold War America* (Cambridge, MA: MIT Press, 1996).

4. The nearly definitive description of how that happened, based on extensive primary sources at IBM, is the very large book by Charles J. Bashe, Lyle R. Johnson, John H. Palmer, and Emerson W. Pugh, *IBM's Early Computers* (Cambridge, MA: MIT Press, 1985). See also Martin Campbell-Kelly, William Aspray, Nathan Ensmenger, and Jeffrey R. Yost, *Computer: A History of the Information Machine*, 3rd ed. (Boulder, CO: Westview, 2014), 124–127; David B. Yoffie, *Strategic Management in Information Technology* (Englewood Cliffs, NJ: Prentice-Hall, 1994), 272; Emerson W. Pugh, Lyle R. Johnson, and John H. Palmer, *IBM's 360 and Early 370 Systems* (Cambridge, MA: MIT Press, 1991), 443–444.

5. Paul A. David, "CLIO and the Economics of QWERTY," *American Economic Review* 75, no. 2 (1985): 332–337.

6. Jörg Sydow, Georg Schreyögg, and Jochan Koch, "Organizational Path Dependency: Opening the Black Box," *Academy of Management Review* 34, no. 4 (2009): 689–709.

7. Birger Wernerfelt, "A Resource-Based View of the Firm," *Strategic Management Journal* 5, no. 4 (1984): 171–180.

8. Mairi Maclean, Charles Harvey, and Stewart R. Clegg, "Organization Theory in Business and Management History: Present Status and Future Prospects," *Business History Review* 91, no. 3 (Autumn 2017): 462–467.

9. Pierre Bourdieu and Roger Chartier, *The Sociologist and the Historian* (Cambridge: Cambridge University Press, 2015).

10. Paul J. DiMaggio, "Interest and Agency in Institutional History," in *Institutional Patterns and Organizations: Culture and Environment*, ed. Lynne G. Zucker (Cambridge, MA: Harvard University Press, 1988), 3–22.

11. The argument that a commercial market existed and how it was pursued are themes described in Arthur L. Norberg, *Computers and Commerce: A Study of Technology and Management at Eckert-Mauchly Computer Company, Engineering Research Association, and Remington Rand, 1946–1957* (Cambridge, MA: MIT Press, 2005); Pugh, *Building IBM*, 131–182.

12. Steven W. Usselman, "Learning the Hard Way: IBM and the Sources of Innovation in Early Computing," in *Financing Innovation in the United States: 1870 to the Present*, ed. Naomi R. Lamoreaux and Kenneth L. Sokoloff (Cambridge, MA: MIT Press, 2007), 319.

13. Watson in a staff meeting held on July 6, 1943, quoted in Pugh, *Building IBM*, 118.

14. The most informed, reasoned account of IBM's aspirations at this time and how best to finance this shift is still Usselman, "Learning the Hard Way," 317–363.

15. The great successes of the 1960s, which were also profoundly transformative, were painful, personally challenging to tens of thousands of employees and nerve wracking for senior management. Men in their 40s with brown and black hair turned grey, careers were made and crushed in an instant, one Watson was broken, and another quit IBM after a heart attack. Smooth transitions never occurred at IBM.

16. Although he thought this technology would create new jobs.

17. Herb Grosch, June 1, 2004 commentary, http://www.columbia.edu/cu/computinghistory/mcpherson.html.

18. Quoted in Pugh, *Building IBM*, 133.

19. The subject in Richard S. Tedlow, *The Watson Dynasty: The Fiery Reign and Troubled Legacy of IBM's Founding Father and Son* (New York: HarperBusiness, 2003), given considerable attention in Kevin Maney, *The Maverick and His Machine: Thomas Watson, Sr. and the Making of IBM* (Hoboken, NJ: John Wiley and Sons, 2003), and also a subject of considerable discussion in Thomas J. Watson Jr. and Peter Petre, *Father, Son & Co.: My Life at IBM and Beyond* (New York: Bantam, 1990).

20. For a video of the machine and how it worked, see Krijn Soeteman, "Running IBM 604, 1948 Computer," March 11, 2012, https://www.youtube.com/watch?v=n58bu4CMSb8.

21. For a list of customers of the CPC version of this machine as of the end of 1949, see Pugh, *Building IBM,* en26, 358–359, and on the events of the period, 155.

22. Ibid.

23. Ibid., 155.

24. Usselman, "Learning the Hard Way," 334–336.

25. Hurd retired from IBM in 1962.

26. James Birkenstock, "Pioneering: On the Frontier of Electronic Data Processing, a Personal Memoir," reprinted in *The IBM Century: Creating the IT Revolution,* ed. Jeffrey R. Yost (Piscataway, NJ: IEEE Computer Society Press, 2011), 110.

27. For the quotation and a series of audio and video recordings about the 701, see https://www-03.ibm.com/ibm/history/exhibits/701/701_bites.html.

28. The availability of elevators often became a serious issue complicating installations of computers. If a customer only had a normal elevator, such as those found in the lobby of an old business building, a salesman had to order a crane and ask local police to block off the street on the day of delivery. This issue of a service elevator versus smaller-sized elevators remained until the introduction of physically smaller mainframes and peripheral equipment in the late 1970s.

29. Cuthbert C. Hurd, "Early IBM Computers: Edited Testimony," in Yost, *The IBM Century,* 77.

30. He went from director to vice president of sales in eight months.

31. Birkenstock, "Pioneering," 114.

32. Ibid.

33. IBM Archives, https://www-03.ibm.com/ibm/history/exhibits/650/650_pr1.html.

34. For a video of this machine, see IBM Education Department, "IBM 650 RAMAC, number 3," undated circa 1950s, https://archive.org/details/camvchm_000012.

35. Donald E. Knuth, "George Forsythe and the Development of Computer Science," *Communications of the ACM* 15, no. 8 (August 1972): 722.

36. Both quoted in Pugh, *Building IBM,* 208.

37. Its objective was to demonstrate the feasibility of having such an air defense system, in this instance to cover southern New England. Radar connected to this system was installed at Cape Cod, Massachusetts, with initial testing beginning in 1953.

38. Pugh, *Building IBM,* 215.

39. Ibid., 218.

40. Edwards, *The Closed World,* 102, and for his excellent account of the system, 75–112.

41. Referenced in ibid.

42. Steven W. Usselman, "IBM and Its Imitators: Organizational Capabilities and the Emergence of the International Computer Industry," *Business and Economic History* 22, no. 2 (Winter 1993): 1–35.

43. Quoted in Pugh, *Building IBM*, 223.

44. For a company promotional film describing the IBM 305, see IBM, "305 RAMAC," 1956, https://www.youtube.com/watch?v=zOD1umMX2s8. For an excellent film explaining the development and use of IBM 305s and 350s, see IBM, "RAMAC, the Search," 1956, https://www.youtube.com/watch?v=6coKh7vtpsY.

45. For example, see Usselman, "IBM and Its Imitators," 1–35.

46. Martin Campbell-Kelly and Daniel D. Garcia-Swartz, *From Mainframes to Smartphones: A History of the International Computer Industry* (Cambridge, MA: Harvard University Press, 2015), 39.

47. Paul Ceruzzi, *A History of Modern Computing*, 2nd ed. (Cambridge, MA: MIT Press, 2003), 70.

48. For a video history, see "IBM STRETCH: A Technological Link between Yesterday and Tomorrow" (Mountain View, CA: Computer Museum, 2008), https://www.youtube.com/watch?v=AvVrdQWZZLU.

49. Frederick P. Brooks Jr., "Stretch-ing Is Great Exercise—It Gets You in Shape to Win," *IEEE Annals of the History of Computing* 32, no. 1 (2010): 4–9.

50. Erich Bloch, "The Engineering Design of the Stretch Computer," *Proceedings of the Eastern Joint Computer Conference, Boston, December 1959* (Boston: IRE-AIEE-ACM, 1959), 45–58.

51. Other innovations included multiprogramming, memory protection, generalized interrupts, interleaving of memories, memory buses, I/O standard interfaces, and the 8-bit byte.

52. Quoted in Pugh, *Building IBM*, 237. Fred Brooks, a participant in the Stretch project and later the System 360's development, summarized Dunwell's fate: "Dunwell, in the corporate doghouse immediately after Stretch, was rehabilitated, apologized to, and made an IBM Fellow by Thomas J. Watson, Jr., when the true effects of his imagination and drive later became evident." See Brooks, "Stretch-ing Is Great Exercise," 9.

53. Pugh, *Building IBM*, 237–244.

54. For a video history of the 1401 system, see IBM, "A Century of Smart: The IBM 1401" (Armonk, NY: International Business Machines Corporation, 2011), https://www.youtube.com/watch?v=hQcaYvbwLPo.

55. Usselman, "IBM and Its Imitators," 2.

56. Ibid., 8.

57. The reason to pay attention to Freeland is that his study of General Motors covered many of the same decades as I do. See Robert Freeland, *The Struggle for the Control of the Modern Corporation: Organizational Change at General Motors, 1924–1970* (Cambridge: Cambridge University Press, 2001).

CHAPTER 7: HOW CUSTOMERS, IBM, AND A NEW INDUSTRY EVOLVED, 1945–1964

1. William W. Simmons with Richard B. Elsberry, *Inside IBM: The Watson Years* (Bryn Mawr, PA: Dorrance, 1988), 112.

2. Ibid.

3. Thomas J. Watson Jr. and Peter Petre, *Father, Son & Co.: My Life at IBM and Beyond* (New York: Bantam, 1990), 242.

4. Rowena Olegario, "IBM and the Two Thomas J. Watsons," in *Creating Modern Capitalism*, ed. Thomas K. McCraw (Cambridge, MA: Harvard University Press, 1997), 351–393.

5. Ibid., 340.

6. Ibid., 243.

7. Franklin M. Fisher, James W. McKie, and Richard B. Mancke, *IBM and the U.S. Data Processing Industry: An Economic History* (New York: Praeger, 1983), 22.

8. Discussed in more detail in James W. Cortada, *The Computer in the United States: From Laboratory to Market, 1930 to 1960* (Armonk, NY: M. E. Sharpe, 1993), 64–124.

9. David R. Clarke, "Production Planning at the Crossroads," *APICS Annual Conference: Proceedings of the 1964 National Technical Conference* (Chicago: American Production and Inventory Control Society, 1965), 1–7.

10. B. M. Gordon, "Adapting Digital Techniques for Automatic Controls," *Electrical Manufacturing* 44 (November 1954): 136ff, 322, and *Electrical Manufacturing* 44 (December 1954): 120ff, 298ff.

11. Charles J. Bashe, Lyle R. Johnson, John H. Palmer, and Emerson W. Pugh, *IBM's Early Computers* (Cambridge, MA: MIT Press, 1986), 190.

12. Both quotations are in Watson and Petre, *Father, Son & Co.*, 195.

13. Ibid., 196.

14. "Thomas J. Watson Sr. Is Dead; I.B.M. Board Chairman Was 82," *New York Times*, June 20, 1956.

15. All the surveys are summarized in Blaine McCormick and Burton W. Folsom Jr., "A Survey of Business Historians on America's Greatest Entrepreneurs," *Business History Review* 77, no. 4 (Winter 2003): 703–716.

16. Kevin Maney, *The Maverick and His Machine: Thomas Watson, Sr. and the Making of IBM* (Hoboken, NJ: John Wiley and Sons, 2003).

17. Richard S. Tedlow, *The Watson Dynasty: The Fiery Reign and Troubled Legacy of IBM's Founding Father and Son* (New York: HarperBusiness, 2003).

18. Steven W. Usselman, "The Watson Dynasty: The Fiery Reign and Troubled Legacy of IBM's Founding Father and Son and The Maverick and His Machine: Thomas Watson, Sr. and the Making of IBM (review)," *Enterprise and Society* 6, no. 1 (March 2005): 184–189 at 189.

19. Emerson W. Pugh, *Building IBM: Shaping an Industry and Its Technology* (Cambridge, MA: MIT Press, 1995), 324.

20. The one notable exception was Tedlow, *The Watson Dynasty*.

21. Like most large U.S. corporations, IBM encouraged employees to make suggestions for improving operations and products, even rewarding them with a percentage of the cost savings or profits gained.

22. Original in possession of the author.

23. Tom Watson Jr. to All IBM Managers and District Managers, two letters, January 21, 1952, original copies in possession of the author.

24. Ibid.

25. Maney, *The Maverick and His Machine,* 385–387.

26. I followed the account now considered the most authoritative on the case, Maney, *The Maverick and His Machine,* 385–387, 422–423. The Endicott welcome packet and story was derived from my own files.

27. Watson and Petre, *Father, Son & Co.,* 285.

28. Ibid., 286.

29. Ibid.

30. Ibid.

31. Ibid.

32. As an example, I started out as a salesman in 1974 (field), then taught new sales hires (staff), then became a sales manager (field), followed by a national marketing manager role (staff), followed by a stint as branch manager (field), then as a sales support manager (staff), back out into the field in consulting, followed by serving as administrative aid to a senior consulting executive (staff), then as an executive in another staff position before returning to the field as an operations manager for a new IBM start-up and finally ending in a staff position.

33. Bashe et al., *IBM's Early Computers,* 577.

34. Martin Campbell-Kelly and Daniel D. Garcia-Swartz, *From Mainframes to Smartphones: A History of the International Computer Industry* (Cambridge, MA: Harvard University Press, 2015), 37–39.

35. Ibid.

36. James W. Cortada, *The Digital Flood: The Diffusion of Information Technology across the U.S., Europe, and Asia* (New York: Oxford University Press, 2012).

37. Robert Sobel, *IBM: Colossus in Transition* (New York: Times Books, 1982). In fairness to him, however, he did write a volume about the Japanese computer industry and IBM's role, *IBM vs. Japan: The Struggle for the Future* (New York: Stein and Day, 1986), although he focused on the 1970s and 1980s, not the 1950s or early 1960s.

38. Campbell-Kelly and Garcia-Swartz, *From Mainframes to Smartphones,* 52.

39. Ibid.

40. Ibid., 53.

41. Jeffrey R. Yost, *Making IT Work: A History of the Computer Services Industry* (Cambridge, MA: MIT Press, 2017), 177–198.

42. Jeffrey R. Yost, ed., *The IBM Century: Creating the IT Revolution* (Piscataway, NJ: IEEE Computer Society Press, 2011), 6–7; Steven W. Usselman, "IBM and Its Imitators: Organizational Capabilities and the Emergence of the International Computer Industry," *Business and Economic History* 22, no. 2 (Winter 1993): 1–35; Watson and Petre, *Father, Son & Co.,* 242; Fisher, McKie, and Mancke, *IBM and the U.S. Data Processing Industry,* 3–167; Cortada, *The Computer in the United States,* 12–101; Paul Ceruzzi, *A History of Modern Computing,* 2nd ed. (Cambridge, MA: MIT Press, 2003), 13–78; Pugh, *Building IBM;* Bashe et al., *IBM's Early Computers;* Emerson W. Pugh, Lyle R. Johnson, and John H. Palmer, *IBM's 360 and Early 370 Systems* (Cambridge, MA: MIT Press, 1991); and the often least cited but perhaps most insightful of Pugh's studies on what may turn out to be the most technologically innovative period in

IBM's history, Emerson W. Pugh, *Memories That Shaped an Industry* (Cambridge, MA: MIT Press, 1984).

43. Yost, *The IBM Century*, 6–7; Usselman, "IBM and Its Imitators"; Watson and Petre, *Father, Son & Co.*, 242; Fisher, McKie, and Mancke, *IBM and the U.S. Data Processing Industry*, 3–167; Cortada, *The Computer in the United States*, 12–101; Ceruzzi, *A History of Modern Computing*, 13–78; Pugh, *Building IBM;* Bashe et al., *IBM's Early Computers;* Pugh, Johnson, and Palmer, *IBM's 360 and Early 370 Computers;* Pugh, *Memories That Shaped an Industry;* Alfred D. Chandler Jr., *Inventing The Electronic Century: The Epic Story of the Consumer Electronics and Computer Industries* (Cambridge, MA: Harvard University Press, 2005), 82–176. For citations of articles by engineers, see Yost, *The IBM Century*, 231–254. In the early 1970s, I was regaled with hundreds of stories about engineering, sales, and support during the 1950s and 1960s, and others by customers and users, the two latter communities normally overlooked in the accounting of IBM's technological history of the period.

44. Campbell-Kelly and Garcia-Swartz, *From Mainframes to Smartphones,* first quotation at 40, second at 41.

45. Usselman, "IBM and Its Imitators."

46. Watson to All IBM Managers and District Managers, January 21, 1952.

47. "The Brain Builders," *Time*, March 28, 1955 reprint, T. J. Watson Jr. to Fellow IBMer, April 5, 1955, copy in possession of the author.

48. For statistics and quotations, see IBM Data Processing Division, *Field Opinion Survey Results* (White Plains, NY: International Business Machines Corporation, undated [1960]), copy in author's possession.

49. International Business Machines Corporation, *Annual Reports*, 1946–1964.

50. Pugh, *Building IBM*, 326.

51. Ibid.

52. Pugh's numbers. See ibid., 323–324.

CHAPTER 8: SYSTEM 360: ONE OF THE GREATEST PRODUCTS IN HISTORY?

1. T. J. Watson Jr. "A Letter from the Chairman," *IBM News*, April 7, 1964.

2. "Consensus" was the word used by a student of the decision to go ahead with the S/360. See Peter Botticelli, "The System/360 Decision," in *Creating Modern Capitalism,* ed. Thomas K. McCraw (Cambridge, MA: Harvard University Press, 1997), 387.

3. On rare occasions, one would make a bad bet, as happened when CEO John F. Akers in the 1980s wanted to break up IBM into smaller, independent units. Increasingly from the mid-1980s on, however, CEOs proved more timid in making such decisions, delaying their timing, with the one exception being Louis V. Gertsner Jr., who in the 1990s had to quickly turn around a failing IBM before it went out of business.

4. Among the IBM commentators, see Emerson W. Pugh, *Memories That Shaped an Industry: Decisions Leading to IBM System/360* (Cambridge, MA: MIT Press, 1984); Emerson W. Pugh, *Building IBM: Shaping an Industry and Its Technology* (Cambridge, MA: MIT Press,

1995); Emerson W. Pugh, Lyle R. Johnson, and John H. Palmer, *IBM's 360 and Early 370 Systems* (Cambridge, MA: MIT Press, 1991). In addition to the Pugh volumes, which constitute the primary source on the technical history of the S/360, see C. Y. Baldwin and K. B. Clark, *Design Rules* (Cambridge, MA: MIT Press, 2000), which explores features of the S/360's architecture. For sources by participants, see B. O. Evans, "System /360: A Retrospective View," *IEEE Annals of the History of Computing* 8, no. 4 (1986): 155–179; J. E. O'Neill, "'Prestige Luster' and 'Snow-Balling Effects': IBM's Development of Computer-Time Sharing," *IEEE Annals of the History of Computing* 17, no. 2 (1995): 50–54; Martin Campbell-Kelly, William Aspray, Nathan Ensmenger, and Jeffrey R. Yost, *Computer: A History of the Information Machine* (Boulder, CO: Westview, 2014), 124 (see 124–133 for their account of the S/360, which is one of the most useful today).

5. William Lazonick, "The Innovative Firm," in *The Oxford Handbook of Innovation,* ed. Jan Faberberg, David C. Mowery, and Richard R. Nelson (New York: Oxford University Press, 2005), 29.

6. Keith Pavitt, "Innovation Processes," in Faberberg, Mowery, and Nelson, *The Oxford Handbook of Innovation,* 107–108; D. Leonard-Barton, *Wellsprings of Knowledge* (Boston: Harvard Business School Press, 1995); Alfred D. Chandler Jr., *Inventing the Electronic Century: The Epic Story of Consumer Electronics and Computer Industries* (New York: Free Press, 2001).

7. Paul J. Miranti, "Chandler's Paths of Learning," *Business History Review* 82, no. 2 (Summer 2008): 293–300.

8. Mira Wilkins, "The History of Multinationals: A 2015 View," *Business History Review* 89, no. 3 (Autumn 2015): 405–414.

9. Alan M. Rugman, *Inside the Multinationals: The Economics of Internal Markets* (New York: Columbia University Press, 1981); Alain Verbeke and Liena Kano, "The New Internalization Theory and Multinational Enterprises from Emerging Economies: A Business Perspective," *Business History Review* 89, no. 3 (Autumn 2015): 415–445. I take the position that Verbeke and Kano's perspective applies as well to corporations such as IBM that were not based in emerging economies.

10. Botticelli, "The System/360 Decision," 384–393.

11. Geoffrey Jones, *Entrepreneurship and Multinationals: Global Business and the Making of the Modern World* (Cheltenham: Edward Elgar, 2013), 200.

12. Pugh, *Building IBM,* 267.

13. Thomas J. Watson Jr. and Peter Petre, *Father, Son & Co.: My Life at IBM and Beyond* (New York: Bantam, 1990), 347.

14. Steven W. Usselman, "Learning the Hard Way: IBM and the Sources of Innovation in Early Computing," in *Financing Innovation in the United States 1870 to the Present,* ed. Naomi R. Lamoreaux and Kenneth L. Sokoloff (Cambridge, MA: MIT Press, 2007), 343, and for his account of the financial underpinning of that effort, 343–347.

15. Based on IBM documents exposed in U.S. court cases. See Richard Thomas DeLamarter, *Big Blue: IBM's Use and Abuse of Power* (New York: Dodd, Mead, 1986), 42.

16. Watson and Petre, *Father, Son & Co.,* 348.

17. Quoted in Pugh, *Building IBM,* 268.

18. Quoted in ibid., 269.

19. For a copy of the report, see http://archive.computerhistory.org/resources/access/text/2011/10/102713231-05-01-acc.pdf.

20. Pugh, *Building IBM,* 273.

21. Ibid., 274.

22. Ibid., 275.

23. The ability to emulate 1401 programs remained embedded in the operating systems of the S/360s, in the subsequent S/370s of the 1970s, and in subsequent processors, such as the 4331 and 4341 of the 1980s, although by the end of the 1970s there was little reason to call this fact to the attention of customers, except in less developed economies that still had a few 1401s local IBM salesmen had not yet dislodged.

24. Watson and Petre, *Father, Son & Co.,* 349.

25. Ibid., 350.

26. Frank Cary in response to a question from a DPD sales trainee, October 1975, Armonk, NY. I was present at that meeting.

27. Quotations in Usselman, "Learning the Hard Way," 362n102.

28. R. C. Warren, "IBM System/360," product announcement, Data Processing Division, April 7, 1964, IBM Corporate Archives, Somers, NY. Warren was the divisional vice president of marketing in the Data Processing Division, the part of IBM most responsible for the sale of S/360s.

29. Joseph H. Spigelman, "Implications of Recent Advances in Electronic Data Processing," *Financial Analysts Journal* 20, no. 5 (September–October 1964): 137.

30. Ibid.,138.

31. A concept used widely by IBM beginning in the 1950s and increasingly soon after by its customers, the idea was to look at all the costs of operating a computer: lease and rental of equipment, how much staff (and their cost) was needed to operate it, and the expense of space, air conditioning, and electricity, all weighted against the economic benefits delivered by the use of the computer, such as the ability to automate ever larger amounts of administrative work or lower the cost of inventory. For details, see G. Anthony Gorry and Michael S. Scott Morton, "A Framework for Management Information Systems," *Sloan Management Review* 13, no. 1 (Fall 1971): 55–70; Leonard Krauss, *Administering and Controlling the Company Data Processing Function* (Englewood Cliffs, NJ: Prentice-Hall, 1969); Ray Seth et al., "Information Resource Management Cost Justification Methods," in Guide International, *Proceedings* 45, pt. 1 (Atlanta, October 30–November 4, 1977), 183–196; and more specifically regarding hardware justification, Rodney L. Roenfeldt and Robert A. Fleck Jr., "How Much Does a Computer Really Cost?," *Computer Decisions* (November 1976): 77–78.

32. All quotations are from Robert B. Forest, "System/360's Initial Impact," *Datamation* 10, no. 5 (May 1964): 68–69, 71.

33. For an excellent lecture by Harvard historian Richard S. Tedlow about the System 360, see https://www.youtube.com/watch?v=DcqganpWfd8.

34. T. Wise, "IBM's $5,000,000,000 Gamble," *Fortune* (September 1966): 118; T. Wise, "The Rocky Road to the Marketplace," *Fortune* (October 1966): 138–143, 199.

35. For an excellent marketing film from IBM on the April 1964 announcement, released by the Computer History Archives, see https://www.youtube.com/watch?v=V4kyTg9Cw8g.

For an hour-long IBM movie about its operating system, *IBM Control Program of Operating System/360*, released in 1964, see https://www.youtube.com/watch?v=378S5Owi-BI.

36. For a well-thought-out discussion about how the financial underpinnings of the development effort were not as dire as the press and employees thought, see Usselman, "Learning the Hard Way," 346–348.

37. This practice later created problems for IBM in its antitrust suit with the U.S. Justice Department.

38. Pugh, *Building IBM,* 277.

39. Franklin M. Fisher, James W. McKie, and Richard B. Mancke, *IBM and the U.S. Data Processing Industry: An Economic History* (New York: Praeger, 1983), 140.

40. Watson and Petre, *Father, Son & Co.,* 351.

41. Ibid., 353.

42. Frederick P. Brooks Jr., *The Mythical Man-Month: Essays on Software Engineering* (Reading, MA: Addison-Wesley, 1975). It remained in print over a quarter century later.

43. Quoted in Pugh, *Building IBM,* 292.

44. Watson and Petre, *Father, Son & Co.,* 355.

45. Ibid., 358.

46. Ibid., 359.

47. Ibid., 360.

48. Pugh, *Building IBM,* 292–293.

49. Ibid., 294.

50. Wise, "IBM's $5,000,000,000 Gamble," 118.

51. Watson, *Father, Son & Co.,* 348.

52. Ernest von Simson, *The Limits of Strategy: Lessons in Leadership from the Computer Industry* (Bloomington, IN: iUniverse, 2009), 26.

53. Quoted in William Rodgers, *THINK: A Biography of the Watsons and IBM* (New York: Stein and Day, 1969), 285.

54. Ibid.

55. Watson and Petre, *Father, Son & Co.,* 355.

56. Martin Campbell-Kelly and Daniel D. Garcia-Swartz, *From Mainframes to Smartphones: A History of the International Computer Industry* (Cambridge, MA: Harvard University Press, 2015), 60–61.

57. Monty Phister Jr., *Data Processing Technology and Economics*, 2nd ed. (Bedford, MA: Digital Press, 1979), 36–45.

58. Usselman, "Learning the Hard Way," 348. He developed this notion in more detail in Steven W. Usselman, "Fostering a Capacity for Compromise: Government, Business, and the Paths of Innovation in American Computing," *Annals of the History of Computing* 18, no. 2 (Summer 1996): 30–39; Steven W. Usselman, "Computer and Communications Technology," in *Encyclopedia of the United States in the Twentieth Century,* ed. Stanley Kutler (New York: Scribner's, 1996), 799–829.

59. Campbell-Kelly and Garcia-Swartz, *From Mainframes to Smartphones,* 57–58, 66.

60. Ibid., 63.

61. Ibid., 64.

62. Ibid., 65.

63. Pugh, *Building IBM*, 324.

64. Simson, *The Limits of Strategy*, 34.

CHAPTER 9: "THE IBM WAY": HOW IT WORKED, 1964–1993

1. Thomas J. Watson Jr., *A Business and Its Beliefs: The Ideas That Helped Build IBM* (New York: McGraw-Hill, 1963), 7.

2. Buck Rodgers with Robert L. Shook, *The IBM Way: Insights into the World's Most Successful Marketing Organization* (New York: Harper and Row, 1986), 3.

3. Watson, *A Business and Its Beliefs*, 4.

4. Kenneth Lipartito, "Culture and the Practice of Business History," *Business and Economic History* 24, no. 2 (1995): 1–42.

5. Kenneth Lipartito, "Business Culture," in *The Oxford Handbook of Business History*, ed. Geoffrey Jones and Jonathan Zeitlin (New York: Oxford University Press, 2007), 604.

6. Victoria Bonnell, Lynn Hunt, and Richard Biernacki, eds., *Beyond the Cultural Turn: New Directions in the Study of Society and Culture* (Berkeley: University of California Press, 1999). See also Edgar H. Schein, *Organizational Culture and Leadership* (San Francisco: Jossey-Bass, 2010), considered the classic work on the subject and written by a business management professor.

7. Alfred D. Chandler Jr., *The Visible Hand: The Managerial Revolution in American Business* (Cambridge, MA: Harvard University Press, 1977), 6–12, 484–490. See also his sequel, too often overlooked, on the issue of how companies grow, Alfred D. Chandler Jr., *Scale and Scope: The Dynamics of Industrial Capitalism* (Cambridge, MA: Harvard University Press, 1990), 31–45, 90–145, 221–224.

8. Barry A. Turner and Nick F. Pidgeon, *Man-Made Disasters*, 2nd ed. (Oxford: Butterworth-Heinemann, 1997), 47.

9. Karl E. Weick and Kathleen M. Sutcliffe, *Managing the Unexpected: Resilient Performance in an Age of Uncertainty*, 2nd ed. (San Francisco: Jossey-Bass/John Wiley and Sons, 2007), 109–138; Edgar H. Schein, "Culture: The Missing Concept in Organization Studies," *Administrative Science Quarterly* 41 (1996): 229–240; Schein, *Organizational Culture and Leadership*; Jennifer A. Chapman and Sandra Eunyoung Cha, "Leading by Leveraging Culture," *California Management Review* 45 (Summer 2003): 20–34; and the study that includes IBM as a case study, Thomas J. Peters and Robert H. Waterman Jr., *In Search of Excellence: Lessons from America's Best-Run Companies* (New York: HarperCollins, 1982). But see also Charles O'Reilly, "Corporations, Culture, and Commitment: Motivation and Social Control in Organizations," *California Management Review* 31 (1989): 9–25.

10. Eric G. Flamboltz and Yvonne Randle, *Corporate Culture: The Ultimate Strategic Asset* (Stanford, CA: Stanford Business Books, 2011), vi.

11. Ibid., 102–104.

12. Watson, *A Business and Its Beliefs*, 31.

13. Ibid., 35.

14. Ibid., 39–40.

15. In the case of a salesman losing a sale to a rival, there was the "loss review," in which the selling effort was analyzed by the hapless rep, his management, and often others from regional or divisional headquarters to learn what could be done to prevent future losses of this kind.

16. An IBM human resources manager conducted over 40 surveys in the late 1960s and early 1970s across all of IBM, later reporting the results outside of IBM. See Geert Hofstede, *Culture's Consequences: International Differences in Work-Related Values* (Beverly Hills, CA: Sage Publications, 1980).

17. Nancy Foy, *The Sun Never Sets on IBM* (New York: William Morrow, 1975), 8.

18. Ibid., 9.

19. The feeling became more intense after 2000, when tough times were accompanied by large numbers of layoffs of employees around the world, as the company painfully shifted work to lower-cost countries or shed employees in favor of hiring ones already trained by other firms in the skills now needed.

20. Foy, *The Sun Never Sets on IBM*, 51.

21. Jay R. Galbraith, *Designing Matrix Organizations That Actually Work: How IBM, Procter & Gamble, and Others Design for Success* (San Francisco: Jossey-Bass, 2009), 129.

22. Ibid., 137.

23. Rodgers, *The IBM Way*.

24. For three examples out of many, see Rex Malik, *La IBM por dentro y mañana …?* (Barcelona: Ediciones Grijalbo, 1978); Buck Rodgers with Robert L. Shook, *El estilo IBM: Una autoizada y penetrante vision sobre la major organización de ventas del mundo* (Barcelona: Planeta, 1987); Luis A. Lamassonne, *Mi Vida con La IBM* (self-published, 1998); Jacques Maisonrouge, *Manager international 36 ans au coeur d'une multinationale de l'informatique* (Paris: Robert Laffont, 1985).

25. Jeffrey R. Yost, *Making IT Work: A History of the Computer Services Industry* (Cambridge, MA: MIT Press, 2017), 185–189, 193, 238, 280.

26. James W. Cortada, "IBM Branch Offices: What They Were, How They Worked, 1920s–1980s," *IEEE Annals of the History of Computing* 39, no. 3 (July–September 2017): 9–23.

27. That number managed to drift between five and seven layers during the 1990s and then early in the following decade crept up again.

28. Foy, *The Sun Never Sets on IBM*, 63.

29. For a description of this affirmative action process, written by an IBM HR manager of the 1960s to early 1970s, see M. Barbara Boyle, "Equal Opportunity for Women Is Smart Business," *Harvard Business Review* 51, no. 3 (May–June 1973): 85–95. The practices she described remained essentially in place for decades.

30. Frank Dobbin, *Inventing Equal Opportunity* (Princeton, NJ: Princeton University Press, 2009), 15–16, 66–67, 85, 101, 104, 136; Alexandra Kalev, Frank Dobbin, and Erin Kelly, "Best Practices or Best Guesses? Assessing the Efficacy of Corporate Affirmative Action and Diversity Policies," *American Sociological Review* 71, no. 4 (2006): 589–617.

31. Erin Kelly and Frank Dobbin, "How Affirmative Action Became Diversity Management: Employer Response to Antidiscrimination Law, 1961–1996," *American Behavioral Scientist* 41, no. 7 (1998): 960–984.

32. Foy, *The Sun Never Sets on IBM*, 118–119.

33. While his memoirs were published in English translation, the original French edition was more blunt about the problem of not enough senior European executives in corporate positions. See Maisonrouge, *Manager international*.

34. On the questions asked in the 1950s to 1970s, see Hofstede, *Culture's Consequences*.

35. It was not enough to meet just to understand issues; managers had to develop plans for addressing concerns and submit them to their human resources manager, who tracked progress toward resolving them.

36. Quoted in "The Payoff: No Layoffs," *Think* 49, no. 3 (May–June 1983): 3.

37. http://www.ibmalumni.com/.

38. Interview with Robert McGrath, May 24, 2016.

39. For numerous comments on how IBM employees felt about job security and employees' reasons for staying or leaving the firm, see Hofstede, *Culture's Consequences*. Hofstede, an IBM employee from the 1960s to early 1970s, hid the name of IBM by calling his case study HERMES.

CHAPTER 10: "THE IBM WAY": WHAT THE WORLD SAW, 1964–1993

1. Thomas J. Watson Jr., *A Business and Its Beliefs: The Ideas That Helped Build IBM* (New York: McGraw-Hill, 1963), 72.

2. *Fortune*, September 1973.

3. Youssef Cassis, "Big Business," in *The Oxford Handbook of Business History*, ed. Geoffrey Jones and Jonathan Zeitlin (New York: Oxford University Press, 2007), 189.

4. Jeffrey R. Yost, *Making IT Work: A History of the Computer Services Industry* (Cambridge, MA: MIT Press, 2017).

5. Max Beardslee, *International Business Marionettes: An IBM Executive Struggles to Regain His Sanity after a Brutal Firing* (Lancaster, OH: Lucky Press, 2001), 178–179.

6. Ibid., 178.

7. Emerson W. Pugh, *Building IBM: Shaping an Industry and Its Technology* (Cambridge, MA: MIT Press, 1995), 299–300.

8. An important finding in James W. Cortada, *The Digital Hand*, 3 vols. (New York: Oxford University Press, 2004–2008).

9. The idea was later formalized in a book by Harvard Business School professor Clayton M. Christensen, *The Innovator's Dilemma* (Cambridge, MA: Harvard Business Review Press, 1997).

10. Martin Campbell-Kelly and Daniel D. Garcia-Swartz, *From Mainframes to Smartphones: A History of the International Computer Industry* (Cambridge, MA: Harvard University Press, 2015), 80.

11. Ibid., 83.

12. The dilemma of whether to invest $1 in an existing product line that generates immediate profits or put that dollar into an emerging technology that will ultimately inevitably replace the older, still profitable technology but that in the short term will not generate the profits enjoyed with an existing product.

13. Contemporary commentators in Europe, for instance, tracked this pattern, well understood by IBM's historians. See, for example, Henry Bakis, *I.B.M.: une multinationale régionale* (Grenoble:

Presses Universitaires de Grenoble, 1977); Hermonn Relboldt and Raimund Vollmer, *Der Markt sind wir: Die IBM und ihre Mitbewerber* (Stuttgart: Buchmagazin Verlag Computer-Buch-und Hobby GmbH, 1978).

14. Campbell-Kelly and Garcia-Swartz, *From Mainframes to Smartphones,* 101.
15. Ibid.
16. James Martin with Joe Leben and Jim Arnold, *VSAM Access Method Services and Programming Techniques* (Englewood Cliffs, NJ: Prentice-Hall, 1987).
17. Buck Rodgers with Robert L. Shook, *The IBM Way: Insights into the World's Most Successful Marketing Organization* (New York: Harper and Row, 1986).
18. See, for example, Watts S. Humphrey, *A Discipline for Software Engineering* (Reading, MA: Addison-Wesley, 1995), and while he was still at IBM, Watts S. Humphrey, *Managing for Innovation: Leading Technical People* (Englewood Cliffs, NJ: Prentice-Hall, 1987).
19. Oral history conducted by Sheldon Hochheiser in 2009 for the IEEE History Center, accessible at http://ethw.org/Oral-History:Emerson_W._Pugh. This is the same Pugh who wrote *Building IBM.*
20. James Champy and Michael Hammer, *Reengineering the Corporation: A Manifesto for Business Revolution* (New York: HarperCollins, 1993), 185–201.
21. A. K. Watson to T. J. Watson Jr., December 13, 1967, Folder 1, RG 11: Employees, The T. J. Watson Jr. Papers/Administrative Records/personnel/Watson, A. K., Box 229, IBM Corporate Archives, Somers, NY.
22. Pugh, *Building IBM,* 324.
23. Ibid.
24. George Warren, "What Is IBM Going to Do with Its 'Trapped Riches'," *Computerworld,* August 3, 1973.
25. Nancy Foy, *The Sun Never Sets on IBM* (New York: William Morrow, 1975), figure 6, n.p.
26. SG&A refers to "selling, general, and administrative" expenses.
27. Foy, *The Sun Never Sets on IBM,* figure 6.
28. Catherine Fredman with Gideon Gartner, *About Gartner: The Making of a Billion-Dollar IT Advisory Firm* (New York: Lemonade Press, 2014), 128.
29. A major finding of a leading expert on corporate organizations of the period who was an ex-IBMer and had conducted similar studies while at IBM. See Geert Hofstede, *Culture's Consequences: International Differences in Work-Related Values* (Beverly Hills, CA: Sage Publications, 1980), 106–109.
30. Foy, *The Sun Never Sets on IBM,* 190.
31. Ibid.
32. Yost, *Making IT Work,* 231–272.

CHAPTER 11: IBM ON THE GLOBAL STAGE

1. Quoted in Boyd France, *IBM in France* (New York: National Planning Association, 1961), 61. The author's last name was indeed France.
2. Thomas J. Watson Jr. and Peter Petre, *Father, Son & Co.: My Life at IBM and Beyond* (New York: Bantam, 1990), 174.

3. Ibid.

4. Ibid., 176. The company still does that today.

5. This strategy had a history predating the 1950s, recently described with respect to the company's typewriter business. See Petri Paju and Thomas Haigh, "IBM Rebuilds Europe: The Curious Case of the International Typewriter," *Enterprise and Society* 17, no. 2 (June 2016): 265–300.

6. Many of my generalizations about IBM practices in this chapter are based on my examination of the IBM country files of 18 firms from 1945 to the 1980s, located at the IBM Corporate Archives, Poughkeepsie, NY, and used more fully in James W. Cortada, *The Digital Flood: The Diffusion of Information Technology across the U.S., Europe, and Asia* (New York: Oxford University Press, 2012).

7. Watson and Petre, *Father, Son & Co.,* 179.

8. Kevin Maney, *The Maverick and His Machine: Thomas Watson, Sr. and the Making of IBM* (Hoboken, NJ: John Wiley and Sons, 2003), 379.

9. For example, Steven W. Usselman, "Selecting Flexible Champions: Markets, Firms, and Public Policies in the Evolution of Computing in the U.S., U.K., and Japan," *Journal of Business Studies (Ryukoku University)* 35, no. 1 (June 1995): 27–43; Corinna Schlombs, "Engineering International Expansion: IBM and Remington Rand in European Computer Markets," *IEEE Annals of the History of Computing* 30, no. 4 (October–December 2008): 42–58; Petri Paju, "National Projects and International Users: Finland and Early European Computerization," *IEEE Annals of the History of Computing* 30, no. 4 (October–December 2008): 77–91; Nancy Foy, *The Sun Never Sets on IBM* (New York: William Morrow, 1975); Robert Sobel, *IBM, Colossus in Transition* (New York: Times Books, 1981).

10. Robert Fitzgerald, *The Rise of the Global Economy: Multinationals and the Making of the Modern World* (Cambridge: Cambridge University Press, 2015), 289.

11. Gareth Austin, Carlos Dávila, and Geoffrey Jones, "The Alternative Business History: Business in Emerging Markets," *Business History Review* 91, no. 3 (Autumn 2017): 537.

12. Based on examining individual country files of the period for IBMworldwide in the IBM Corporate Archives. Results are reported in Cortada, *The Digital Flood*.

13. The "national champion" programs in Europe have been the subject of much debate, most of it to explain why Europe could not succeed against the aggressive Americans, most frequently IBM. For a few samples of the discussion, see Margaret Sharp, ed., *Europe and the New Technologies: Six Case Studies in Innovation and Adjustment* (Ithaca, NY: Cornell University Press, 1986); Richard O. Hundley (ed.), *The Future of the Information Revolution in Europe: Proceedings of an International Conference* (Santa Monica, CA: RAND Corporation, 2001); Richard Coopey, "Empire and Technology: Information and Technology Policy in Postwar Britain and France," in *Information Technology Policy: An International Perspective,* ed. Richard Coopey (Oxford: Oxford University Press, 2004), 144–168; Eda Kranakis, "Politics, Business, and European Information Technology Policy: From the Treaty of Rome to Unidata, 1958–1975," in Coopey, *Information Technology Policy,* 209–246; Dimitris Assimakopoulos, Rebecca Marschan-Piekkari, and Stuart MacDonald, "ESPRIT: Europe's Response to US and Japanese Domination of Information Technology," in Coopey, *Information Technology Policy,* 247–263; James W. Cortada, "Public Policies and the Development of National Computer Industries in Britain, France,

and the Soviet Union, 1940–80," *Journal of Contemporary History* 44, no. 3 (2009): 493–512; Pascal Griset, "Du 'temps réel' aux premiers réseaux: une entreprise rêvée, une informatique à l'épreuve du quotidian (des années 1970)," *Enterprises et Histoire* 60 (September 2010): 98–121; Gerard Alberts, "Appropriating America: Americanization in the History of European Computing," *IEEE Annals of the History of Computing* 32, no. 2 (April–June 2010): 4–5; Arthe Van Laer, "Developing an EC Computer Policy, 1965–1974," *IEEE Annals of the History of Computing* 32, no. 1 (January–March 2010): 44–59; David Mercer, *IBM: How the World's Most Successful Corporation Is Managed* (London: Kogan Page, 1987).

14. Routinely cataloged by each country organization and reported to Corporate all through the period and preserved in the country records, IBM Corporate Archives, Poughkeepsie, NY.

15. Preserving market share protected existing cash flows and net profits; expanding market share offered the promise of higher net profits per dollar extracted from the increased revenue. It was not always axiomatic that one would strive for blind growth, always for controlled cash flows and profits, which in some instances required maintaining an existing market share, in others expanding it.

16. Henry Bakis, *I.B.M.: Une multinationale régionale* (Grenoble: Presses Universitaires de Grenoble, 1977), 25–52. For a similar discussion from a German perspective, see Hermonn Reiboldt and Raimund Vollmer, *Der Markt sind wir: Die IBM und ihre Mitbewerber* (Stuttgart: Buchmagazin Verlag Computer-Buch-und Hobby GmbH, 1978).

17. The chocolate chip cookies available at coffee breaks in Palisades became legendary on both sides of the Atlantic.

18. Described in John Hendry, *Innovating for Failure: Government Policy and the Early British Computer Industry* (Cambridge, MA: MIT Press, 1989). See also Mar Hicks, *Programmed Inequality: How Britain Discarded Women Technologists and Lost Its Edge in Computing* (Cambridge, MA: MIT Press, 2017).

19. John Hendry, "The Teashop Computer Manufacturer: J. Lyons, LEO and the Potential and Limits of High-Tech Diversification," *Business History* 29 (1987): 73–102.

20. Martin Campbell-Kelly and Daniel D. Garcia-Swartz, *From Mainframes to Smartphones: A History of the International Computer Industry* (Cambridge, MA: Harvard University Press, 2015), 44, 89.

21. Pierre E. Mounier-Kuhn, "French Computer Manufacturers and the Component Industry, 1952–1972," *History and Technology* 11, no. 2 (1994): 195–216; Pierre E. Mounier-Kuhn, "Genese de l'informatique en France (1945–1965): Diffusion de l'Innovation et transfert de technologie," *Culture Technique* (1990): 35–46; François-Henri Raymond, "An Adventure with a Sad Ending: The SEA," *Annals of the History of Computing* 11, no. 4 (1989): 263–277.

22. France, *IBM in France*, 25.

23. Jacques Vernay, *Chroniques des la Compagnie IBM France* (Paris: IBM France, 1988). See also Jacques Vernay, "IBM France," *Annals of the History of Computing* 11, no. 4 (1989): 299–311.

24. Described in considerable detail in Cortada, *The Digital Flood*, 91–237. See also Jacques Vernay, *Chroniques de la Compaignie IBM France, 1914–1987* (Paris: IBM France, 1988).

25. Ibid., 28.

26. Ibid., 47.

27. Richard Thomas DeLamarter, *Big Blue: IBM's Use and Abuse of Power* (New York: Dodd, Mead, 1986), 297.

28. Campbell-Kelly and Garcia-Swartz, *From Mainframes to Smartphones,* 50.

29. Tom Forester, *Silicon Samurai: How Japan Conquered the World's I.T. Industry* (Cambridge, MA: Blackwell, 1993); John Nathan, *Japan Unbounded: A Volatile Nation's Quest for Pride and Purpose* (Boston: Houghton Mifflin, 2004); Rodney Clark, *The Japanese Company* (New Haven, CT: Yale University Press, 1979).

30. Japanese IBMers told the author on various occasions that it was lobbying by their customers that made it possible for IBM to retain full ownership of the firm.

31. Other nations had sought similar terms, and in the case of India, IBM quit the country in the late 1970s rather than bow to such demands.

32. Mercer, *IBM,* 258.

33. The Japanese IBM story is far more complicated than explained here, so for a fuller account, see Cortada, *The Digital Flood,* 307–374.

34. IBM and other U.S. firms began doing business in Vietnam toward the end of the century.

35. Luis A. Lamassonne, *My Life with IBM* (Atlanta: PROTEA, 2001), 44.

36. Ibid., 79. It was the city's fanciest hotel, an elegant, turn-of-the-century structure, still in operation today as a high-end business hotel.

37. Pfeifer retired from IBM in 1986 but died from lung cancer a decade later at the age of 69.

38. Lamassonne, *My Life with IBM,* 198.

39. Ibid.

40. This became a major concern in the twenty-first century and was delicately referred to by the media and business observers as "financial engineering."

41. Campbell-Kelly and Garcia-Swartz, *From Mainframes to Smartphones,* 53.

42. As 1401s came off leases in the most industrialized countries, to be replaced with S/360s, the older computer systems were refurbished and then sold in developing markets not yet ready for larger, more sophisticated systems, such as the S/360.

43. Quoted from Faw's note as part of the legal file of the U.S. v. IBM antitrust case. See DeLamarter, *Big Blue,* 141.

44. Burton Grad, "A Personal Recollection: IBM's Unbundling of Software and Services," *IEEE Annals of the History of Computing* 24, no. 1 (January–March 2002): 71.

45. Emerson W. Pugh, *Building IBM: Shaping an Industry and Its Technology* (Cambridge, MA: MIT Press, 1995), 224.

46. Ernest von Simson, *The Limits of Strategy: Lessons in Leadership from the Computer Industry* (Bloomington, IN: iUniverse, 2009), 36.

47. Watson and Petre, *Father, Son & Co.,* 401.

48. Simson, *The Limits of Strategy,* 39.

49. Ibid., 47.

50. Ibid., 51.

51. Pugh, *Building IBM,* 324.

52. Joseph M. Grieco, *Between Dependency and Autonomy: India's Experience with the International Computer Industry* (Berkeley: University of California Press, 1984), 24–26; Om Vikas and

L. Ravichandran, "Computerization in India," *Electronics: Information and Planning* 6 (December 1978): 318–351.

53. In fact, the departure from India was not mentioned in the following year's annual report in either the Chairman's Letter or the financial overview.

54. A key finding I explain more fully in Cortada, *The Digital Flood*, especially at 509–510.

55. I was an employee at IBM from the 1970s to the 2010s and worked with scores of opinion surveys done inside the firm. Opinions in employee responses shifted very slowly, taking years for appreciable changes to be reflected in the surveys.

56. Geert Hofstede, *Culture's Consequences: International Differences in Work-Related Values* (Beverly Hills, CA: Sage Publications, 1980), 217.

57. Ibid., 234.

58. Ibid., 271.

59. Ibid.

60. Ibid., 271–272.

61. Ibid., 272.

62. Ibid., 232–233.

63. Geneviève Ollivier and Oscar Ortsman, eds., *IBM our la Tentation Totalitaire: Archives de Jean Ollivier, Traces d'une histoire* (Paris: L'Harmattan, 2006), 75.

64. France, *IBM in France*, 20.

65. International Business Machines Corporation, *1966 Annual Report*; Pugh, *Building IBM*, 224.

66. International Business machines Corporation, *Annual Reports*.

67. E. Roger Warmbir, "1984 NAD Large Systems Survey Findings," author's copy.

CHAPTER 12: TWO DECADES OF ANTITRUST SUITS, 1960s–1980s

1. Quoted in Geoffrey D. Austrian, "It's Over," *Think* 48, no. 1 (January–February 1982): 7.

2. Statistics based on evidence submitted by IBM in U.S. court cases. See Richard Thomas DeLamarter, *Big Blue: IBM's Use and Abuse of Power* (New York: Dodd, Mead, 1986), 59.

3. Matthias Kipping and Behlül Üsdiken, "Business History and Management Studies," in *The Oxford Handbook of Business History*, ed. Geoffrey Jones and Jonathan Zeitlin (New York: Oxford University Press, 2007), 102.

4. Yet even he pays scant attention to it. See Matthias Kipping, "Business-Government Relations," in *Business History around the World*, ed. Franco Amatori and Geoffrey Jones (Cambridge: Cambridge University Press, 2003), 372.

5. Well discussed in Marc Allen Eisner, *Antitrust and the Triumph of Economics: Institutions, Expertise, and Policy Change* (Chapel Hill: University of North Carolina Press, 1991).

6. For example, Mark R. Patterson, *Antitrust Law in the New Economy* (Cambridge, MA: Harvard University Press, 2017).

7. For examples of useful studies, see Lawrence D. Graham, *Legal Battles That Shaped the Computer Industry* (Westport, CT: Quorum, 1999); Gerardo Con Diaz, "Contested Ontologies of Software: The Story of Gottschalk v. Benson, 1963–1972," *IEEE Annals of the History of Computing* 38, no. 1 (2016): 23–33; Gerardo Con Diaz, "The Text of the Machine: American

Copyright Law and the Many Natures of Software, 1974–1978," *Technology and Culture* 57, no. 4 (2016): 753–779. The latter two are rich in bibliographic citations.

8. For example, Rex Malik, *And Tomorrow ... the World?* (London: Millington, 1975); William Rodgers, *THINK: A Biography of the Watsons and IBM* (New York: Stein and Day, 1972); Peter Halbherr, *IBM: Mythe et Realite: La Vie Quotidienne Chez IBM France* (Paris: FAVRE, 1987); Nancy Foy, *The Sun Never Sets on IBM: The Culture and Folklore of IBM World Trade* (New York: William Morrow, 1975).

9. For the most complete account, see Robert Sobel, *IBM: Colossus in Transition* (New York: Times Books, 1981), 90–92. See also Richard S. Tedlow, *The Watson Dynasty: The Fiery Reign and Troubled Legacy of IBM's Founding Father and Son* (New York: HarperCollins, 2003), 124–125; Emerson W. Pugh, *Building IBM: Shaping an Industry and Its Technology* (Cambridge, MA: MIT Press, 1995). Historians routinely dismissed this antitrust case with barely a comment when in fact it bothered Watson Sr. and at first made him unwilling to resolve the more serious case facing IBM in the early 1950s. In his memoir, Watson Jr. mentioned a number of times how irritating these suits were to his father, affecting his judgment regarding whether to settle them out of court. See Thomas J. Watson Jr. and Peter Petre, *Father, Son & Co.: My Life at IBM and Beyond* (New York: Bantam, 1999).

10. Sobel, *IBM,* 254–276. Sobel argues that all the lawsuits involving IBM and monopolistic behavior need to be understood together, not just the federal case. But historians did not totally ignore the issue. See, for example, Jeffrey R. Yost, *The IBM Century: Creating the IT Revolution* (Los Alamitos, CA: IEEE Computer Society Press, 2011), 21–23. Pugh, *Building IBM,* avoided discussing the case, but Watson Jr. did not and provides useful observations on its very earliest phases. See Watson and Petre, *Father, Son & Co.,* 376–389. For an excellent analysis of IBM's antitrust problems, see also Steven W. Usselman, "Unbundling IBM: Antitrust and the Incentives to Innovation in American Computing," in *The Challenge of Remaining Innovative: Insights from Twentieth-Century American Business,* ed. S. N. Clarke, N. Lamoreaux, and S. Usselman (Stanford, CA: Stanford Business School Books, 2009), 249–279. The leading authority on the history of the software industry documented the direct consequence of unbundling on the growth of business software products and services. See Martin Campbell-Kelly, *From Airline Reservations to Sonic the Hedgehog: A History of the Software Industry* (Cambridge, MA: MIT Press, 2003). For European coverage based largely on IBM archival sources and contemporary French publications, see James W. Cortada, *The Digital Flood: The Diffusion of Information Technology across the U.S., Europe, and Asia* (New York: Oxford University Press, 2012), 112–122. However, this topic and the large antitrust suit have not been adequately studied, despite the fact that during the proceedings IBM delivered to the court over a billion documents about the case and, more important, about the entire computer industry of the 1950s and 1960s, which are today available for study. A set may be found at the Hagley Museum and Library using the finding aid at http://findingaids.hagley.org/xtf/search?keyword=IBM.

11. Because I am speaking as an IBM employee who lived through the bulk of that chronology, this chapter may fail to convey to historians and others not there at the time the gravity of this case's influence on the operations of IBM. Ghosts of the earlier cases against IBM or its executives from the 1910s, 1930s, and 1950s loomed large, relevant, and recent.

12. Eisner, *Antitrust and the Triumph of Economics*, 22.

13. Franklin M. Fisher, James W. McKie, and Richard B. Mancke, *IBM and the U.S. Data Processing Industry: An Economic History* (New York: Praeger, 1983); Franklin M. Fisher and John J. McGowan, *Folded, Spindled and Mutilated: Economic Analysis and U.S. vs. IBM* (Cambridge, MA: MIT Press, 1983). For an account critical of IBM, see DeLamarter, *Big Blue*. For a broader discussion of IBM's role as part of the U.S. government's promotion of the computer industry in the 1950s to 1970s, see Kenneth Flamm, *Creating the Computer: Government, Industry, and High Technology* (Washington, DC: Brookings Institution, 1988); Kenneth Flamm, *Targeting the Computer: Government Support and International Competition* (Washington, DC: Brookings Institution, 1987); and an often overlooked economic analysis of IBM's performance in the 1950s and 1960s, Alvin J. Harman, *The International Computer Industry: Innovation and Comparative Advantage* (Cambridge, MA: Harvard University Press, 1971).

14. Usselman, "Unbundling IBM," 272.

15. A possible exception is xeroxing from Xerox.

16. Documented in clear detail in Eisner, *Antitrust and the Triumph of Economics*.

17. The same product the U.S. Department of Defense and NSA did not want CDC to sell to the French.

18. Plaintiff's Exhibits 1144B and 4079A in *U.S. v. IBM*, quoted in DeLamarter, *Big Blue*, 95.

19. Control Data Corporation, *1965 Annual Report*, 5, Defendant's Exhibit 14214, quoted in DeLamarter, *Big Blue*, 96.

20. CDC may have saved a detailed account of the file because in the CDC papers housed at the University of Minnesota in the Charles Babbage Institute archives there is a collection of these depositions. See CDC Papers, Record Group 80, Series 11, Box 1, "Legal Records," Folders 13–17.

21. Watson and Petre, *Father, Son & Co.*, 388.

22. Ibid.

23. Martin Campbell-Kelly and Daniel D. Garcia-Swartz, *From Mainframes to Smartphones: A History of the International Computer Industry* (Cambridge, MA: Harvard University Press, 2015), 74; Sara Baase, "IBM: Producer or Predator?," *Reason*, April 1974, 4–10.

24. "Telex v. IBM: Implications for the Businessman and the Computer Manufacturer," *Virginia Law Review* 60, no. 5 (May 1974): 884–909.

25. A useful summary of the case was provided in *Computerworld*. See Edith Holmes, "Three Years of Court Action Preceded Telex Reversal," *Computerworld*, February 5, 1975, 1, 4.

26. Catherine Fredman with Gideon I. Gartner, *About Gartner: The Making of a Billion-Dollar IT Advisory Firm* (New York: Lemonade Press, 2014), 125.

27. "Inside IBM's Management," *Business Week*, June 14, 1973, 46. For copies of CCIA's files on the Telex suits, see "Computer and Communications Industry Association Collection of Antitrust Records," Record Group CBI 13, Charles Babbage Institute, University of Minnesota.

28. Joe Wright, "How History Repeats Itself: The IBM Antitrust Case of 1972," *Capitalism Magazine*, July 20, 2002 (reprint of an article he wrote in 1972).

29. Baase, "IBM: Producer or Predator,"8.

30. Duane W. Krohnke, "The IBM Antitrust Case," *dwkcommentaries*, July 2011, https://dwkcommentaries.com/2011/07/30/the-ibm-antitrust-litigation/.

31. A line of reasoning developed in an earlier high-profile case involving Alcoa. See Donald F. Turner, "The Scope of Antitrust and Other Economic Regulatory Policies," *Harvard Law Review* 82, no. 6 (April 1969): 1207–1244.

32. Eisner, *Antitrust and the Triumph of Economics,* 115.

33. In the United States in *The IBM Newsmagazine,* February 10, 1969, 4–7.

34. Quoted in Austrian, "It's Over," 5.

35. Richard A. McLaughlin, "Monopoly Is Not a Game," *Datamation* (September 1973): 73–77.

36. I was an IBM salesman in the 1970s in the United States and, based on that experience, I believe the mystery is solved by the fact that IBM's relations with its customers were intimate, intense, friendly, and mutually reinforcing. In other words, Watson Sr.'s strategy of insisting on close ties may account for how customers felt about IBM.

37. The issue came up again with IBM's introduction of PCs in the 1980s, but then the IBM "blessing" may have influenced many more who were not data processing users.

38. McLaughlin, "Monopoly Is Not a Game," 76–77.

39. The DoJ set expectations for the court and IBM saying it could do it in a few months.

40. Ibid., 7.

41. Ibid., 4–5.

42. Ibid., 5.

43. Quoted in Ibid., 7.

44. DeLamarter, *Big Blue,* 326.

45. Franklin M. Fisher, John J. McGowan, and Joen E. Greenwood, *Folded, Spindled, and Mutilated: Economic Analysis and U.S. v. IBM* (Cambridge, MA: MIT Press, 1983), x. The second book is Fisher, McKie, and Mancke, *IBM and the U.S. Data Processing Industry.*

46. The Hagley Museum and Library and the Charles Babbage Institute at the University of Minnesota have large collections of papers from the period.

47. Watson and Petre, *Father, Son & Co.,* 389.

48. Tedlow, *The Watson Dynasty,* 261.

49. At best, that number might account for the billable hours from outside legal counsel, although probably not completely. The annual cost of running an office with, say, 150 to 200 hundred IBMers in Westchester County, New York, in the 1960s and 1970s would have been closer to $5 million, so across 13 years, that would mean another $65 million. Then what about the salaries of all those executives, middle managers, and scientists and engineers who were deposed, interrogated in court, or otherwise involved on and off over the period from 1966–1967 through 1981? Add in the cost of training every employee, manager, and executive on IBM's legal and marketing responsibilities since the mid-1960s. The training for all employees was the same—marketing guidelines—but in addition there was more for managers and then still additional discussions for executives worldwide. Periodically, IBM lawyers provided additional training and discussed changing circumstances and practices.

50. Quoted in Tedlow, *The Watson Dynasty,* 262.

51. A new generation of recent hires into the company in the 1990s brought back the cluttered charts and texts so evident today in PowerPoint presentations.

52. Tedlow, *The Watson Dynasty,* 262.

53. David Mercer, *The Global IBM: Leadership in Multinational Management* (New York: Dodd, Mead, 1988), 177.

54. Quoted in Stephen Castle, "I.B.M. Settles Antitrust Case with E.U.," *International Herald Tribune*, December 15, 2011.

55. Usselman, "Unbundling IBM," 250.

56. Eisner, *Antitrust and the Triumph of Economics,* 2–4, 184–185, 231–233.

57. Described in considerable detail in ibid.

58. Eisner, *Antitrust and the Triumph of Economics,* 135–149.

59. Patterson, *Antitrust Law in the New Economy,* 61.

CHAPTER 13: COMMUNIST COMPUTERS

1. Seymour E. Goodman, "Soviet Computing and Technology Transfer: An Overview," *World Politics* 60, no. 1 (1979): 551.

2. Thomas J. Watson Jr. and Peter Petre, *Father, Son & Co.: My Life at IBM and Beyond* (New York: Bantam, 1990), 330.

3. For a video of the premier's visit to IBM with commentary by his son, Sergei, see http://lakeshorepublicmedia.org/stories/american-experience-khrushchev-visits-ibm/.

4. For a discussion of the literature up to 2011, see James W. Cortada, *The Digital Flood: The Diffusion of Information Technology across the U.S., Europe, and Asia* (New York: Oxford University Press, 2012), 749–753.

5. The key pioneering work is by Slava Gerovitch, *From Newspeak to Cyberspeak: A History of Soviet Cybernetics* (Cambridge, MA: MIT Press, 2002).

6. He went on to argue further that the reason the West was able to create the Internet was because "capitalists behaved like socialists, while the socialists behaved like capitalists." See Benjamin Peters, *How Not to Network a Nation: The Uneasy History of the Soviet Internet* (Cambridge, MA: MIT Press, 2016), both quotations at 2.

7. For examples, see the collection of papers in John Impagliazzo and Eduard Proyadakov, eds., *Perspectives on Soviet and Russian Computing* (Berlin: Springer-Verlag, 2011); Stanislav V. Klimenko, "Computer Science in Russia: A Personal View," *IEEE Annals of the History of Computing* 21, no. 3 (1999): 16–30; Sergei P. Prokhorov, "Computers in Russia: Science, Education, and Industry," *IEEE Annals of the History of Computing* 21, no. 3 (1999): 4–15; Peter Wolcott and Mikhail N. Dorojevets, "The Institute of Precision Mechanics and Computer Technology and the El'brus Family of High-Speed Computers," *IEEE Annals of the History of Computing* 20, no. 1 (1998): 4–14; Anne Fitzpatrick, Tatiana Kazakova, and Simon Berkovich, "MESM and the Beginning of the Computer Era in the Soviet Union," *IEEE Annals of the History of Computing* 28, no. 3 (2006): 4–16; Hiroshi Ichikawa, "Strela-1, the First Soviet Computer: Political Success and Technological Failure," *IEEE Annals of the History of Computing* 28, no. 3 (2006): 18–31; Helena Durnová, "Sovietization of Czechoslovakian Computing: The Rise and Fall of the SAPO Project," *IEEE Annals of the History of Computing* 32, no. 2 (2010): 21–31; Helena Durnová, "Embracing the Algol Effort in Czechoslovakia," *IEEE Annals of the History of Computing* 36, no. 4 (2014): 26–37; Ksenia Tatarchenko, "Cold War Origins of the International Federation for Information Processing," *IEEE Annals of the History of*

Computing 32, no. 2 (2010): 46–57; Yuri Rogachyov, "The Origin of Informatics and Creation of the First Electronic Computing Machines in the USSR," *Proceedings, Third International Conference on Computer Technology in Russia and in the Former Soviet Union*, ed. A. N. Tomilin et al. (Piscataway, NJ: IEEE, 2014), 28–35.

8. Nicholas Lewis, "Peering Through the Curtain: Soviet Computing Through the Eyes of Western Experts," *IEEE Annals of the History of Computing* 38, no. 1 (2016): 34–47. See also Cortada, *The Digital Flood*, 238–306; Ksenia Tatarchenko, "The Anatomy of an Encounter: Transnational Mediation and Discipline Building in Cold War Computer Science," in *Communities of Computing: Computer Science and Society in the ACM*, ed. Thomas J. Misa (New York: ACM Books, 2016), 199–227.

9. R. W. Davis, *Soviet Economic Development from Lenin to Khrushchev* (Cambridge: Cambridge University Press, 1998), 79–82; Maurice Dobb, *Soviet Economic Development since 1917* (London: Routledge, 2012), 313–445.See also an older study, Antony C. Sutton, *Western Technology and Soviet Economic Development, 1945 to 1965* (Stanford, CA: Hoover Institution Press, 1973).

10. Gerovitch, *From Newspeak to Cyberspeak*, 83–141, 199–292, quotation at 199.

11. Tatarchenko, "The Anatomy of an Encounter," 199–227.

12. William K. McHenry, "The Integration of Management Information Systems in Soviet Enterprises," in U.S. Congress, *Gorbachev's Economic Plans*, vol. 2, *Study Papers Submitted to the Joint Economic Committee, Congress of the United States* (Washington, DC: U.S. Government Printing Office, 1987), 187.

13. Goodman, "Soviet Computing and Technology Transfer," 539.

14. David Holloway, *Stalin and the Bomb: The Soviet Union and Atomic Energy, 1939–1956* (New Haven, CT: Yale University Press, 1994), 204–234; David Hoffman, *The Dead Hand: The Untold Story of the Cold War Arms Race and Its Dangerous Legacy* (New York: Anchor, 2010).

15. Norman Davis, *Europe: A History* (New York: Oxford University Press, 1996), 1056–1136.

16. Cortada, *The Digital Flood*, table 6.4, 285.

17. The West built special-purpose systems, too, such as computers that fit into spaceships and aircraft and others embedded in large manufacturing process industry machines, but these represented a small portion of the population of computers used in the West. I discuss these machines and their uses in James W. Cortada, *The Digital Hand: How Computers Changed the Work of American Manufacturing, Transportation, and Retail Industries* (New York: Oxford University Press, 2004).

18. U.S. Central Intelligence Agency, "Soviet RYAD Computer Program," August 1973, 5, https://www.cia.gov/library/readingroom/docs/DOC_0000309585.pdf.

19. Ibid.

20. Victor V. Przhijalkovskiy, "Historic Review on the ES Computer Family," Russian Virtual Computer Museum, www.computer-museum.ru/english/es_comp_family.php.

21. Ibid.

22. Ibid.

23. Early System 360s did not either, but midway through its product life it did.

24. Goodman, "Soviet Computing and Technology Transfer," 565.

25. Ibid., 556.

26. U.S. Central Intelligence Agency, "Soviet RYAD Computer Program," 5.

27. It happened to me while I was an IBM salesman in the 1970s, when an entire S/370 Model 145 was "misplaced." I replaced it with an S/148, complete with fresh peripheral equipment and manuals. I spent six months trying to figure out what happened and to explain to company lawyers and auditors that I had nothing to do with what everyone knew had happened.

28. PCs in Communist Europe await their historian, although a few pieces of information can be gleaned in Gerard Alberts and Ruth Oldenziel, eds., *Hacking Europe: From Computer Culture to Demoscenes* (Berlin: Springer-Verlag, 2014).

29. Various U.S. government departments communicated back and forth with IBM regarding sales behind the Iron Curtain, this prohibition being only one of them. See World Trade Legal Records, Regional Files, European Headquarters, Box 108, RG6, IBM Corporate Archives, Somers, NY.

30. Brad Lesher, *"Don't Forget the Peanut Butter, George!": Fun and Funny Times Abroad* (No city: Xlibris, 2010), 86.

31. Ibid., 95.

32. Ibid., 96.

33. Watson and Petre, *Father, Son & Co.*, 433.

34. Robert Fitzgerald, *The Rise of the Global Company: Multinationals and the Making of the Modern World* (Cambridge: Cambridge University Press, 2015), 376.

35. Peters, *How Not to Network a Nation*, 159–186.

36. Jeff Gerth, "I.B.M. Guilty of Illegal Sales to Russian Lab," *New York Times*, August 1, 1998.

37. Ibid.

38. Ibid.

39. Goodman, "Soviet Computing and Technology Transfer," 569.

40. Ibid., 568.

CHAPTER 14: "A TOOL FOR MODERN TIMES": IBM AND THE PERSONAL COMPUTER

1. Quotation from an interview with Samuel Palmisano on the *Charlie Rose* program, December 17, 2015.

2. The sale was negotiated n 2004, but did not go into effect until early 2005.

3. IBM regained some of that position in the late 1990s, but it remains an open question as to what its stature is today, even though it continues to be one of the largest IT firms.

4. The links are at least acknowledged in Paul B. Carroll and Chunka Mui, *Billion Dollar Lessons: What You Can Learn from the Most Inexcusable Business Failures of the Last 25 Years* (New York: Portfolio, 2008), 160–161, 222.

5. Alfred D. Chandler Jr., "Commercializing High-Technology Industries," *Business History Review* 79, no. 3 (Autumn 2005): 603.

6. Ibid.

7. Ibid., 604.

8. Katia Girschik, "Machine-Readable Codes," *Entreprise et Histoire* (Autumn 2006): 1–14; Margaret B. W. Graham, "Technology and Innovation," in *The Oxford Handbook of Business History*, ed. Geoffrey Jones and Jonathan Zeitlin (New York: Oxford University Press, 2007),

365; Kenneth Lipartito, "Culture and the Practice of Business History," *Business and Economic History* 24, no. 2 (1995): 1–42; Kenneth Lipartito, "The Social Construction of Failure: Picture-phone and the Information Age," *Technology and Culture* 44, no. 1 (2003): 50–81.

9. David C. Mowery and Richard R. Nelson, *Sources of Industrial Leadership: Studies of Seven Industries* (Cambridge: Cambridge University Press, 1999).

10. Stephen S. Cohen and John Zysman, *Manufacturing Matters: The Myth of the Post-industrial Economy* (New York: Basic Books, 1987), 92.

11. Ibid., 149.

12. *Modern Times* (1936). To watch the movie, see https://www.youtube.com/watch?v=rvvJGCe 5NbM. It is worth taking the time to see this classic movie. Although it has nothing to do with IBM or computers, it does show a row of keypunch machines for "punching in" to work equipment and shows the negative consequences of automation on work.

13. Paul Carroll, *Big Blues: The Unmaking of IBM* (New York: Crown 1993), 41.

14. For a training video from 1982, see https://www.youtube.com/watch?v=9cXU94XNOJI.

15. This story was related to me by the executive in a private conversation.

16. Emerson W. Pugh, *Building IBM: Shaping an Industry and Its Technology* (Cambridge, MA: MIT Press, 1995), 324.

17. James Chposky and Ted Leonsis, *Blue Magic: The People, Power and Politics Behind the IBM Personal Computer* (New York: Facts on File, 1988), 107.

18. At the time, data center managers, IBMers, and the industry at large measured the amount of computing power in MIPS—millions of instructions per second—a computer's processing performance. Think number of answers per unit of time that came out of the machine.

19. "Account control" was IBM's language for salesmen controlling what kinds of equipment and software a customer acquired.

20. Robert Friedel, *A Culture of Improvement: Technology and the Western Millennium* (Cambridge, MA: MIT Press, 2007), 2–3.

21. Carroll, *Big Blues,* 117.

22. I developed a friendship with Lowe after he left the company. Even in the early years of the new millennium, he was still not able to recognize the colossal nature of his bad decision. He explained to me that the decision was not his alone to make, however, as it was shared with the management committee and the CEO. Fair enough; that was correct.

23. I was the manager of the sales unit that engaged in this transaction with American Standard.

24. In the United States, when a company offered a voluntary retirement package to employees, it had to make it available to all employees in the same business unit, such as a factory site or division. IBM could not offer it, say, to poor performers or select groups (such as older employees), or cap it at a specific number of employees. The company designed such offerings, however, to encourage specific groups but at that time (1980s–1990s) had little experience in gauging the extent of their popularity, especially with older employees who had strong performance ratings.

25. Carroll, *Big Blues,* 179.

26. John Markoff, "The Niche That I.B.M. Can't Ignore," *New York Times,* April 23, 1989, 12.

27. Ernest von Simson, *The Limits of Strategy: Lessons in Leadership from the Computer Industry* (Bloomington, IN: iUniverse, 2009), 226.

28. Louis V. Gerstner Jr., *Who Says Elephants Can't Dance?* (New York: Harper Business, 2002), 162.

29. Quotations from interview of Samuel Palmisano on the *Charlie Rose* program, December 17, 2015.

30. Simson, *The Limits of Strategy,* 229.

31. Gerstner, *Who Says Elephants Can't Dance?,* 139.

32. Ibid.

33. D. Quinn Mills and G. Bruce Friesen, *Broken Promises: An Unconventional View of What Went Wrong at IBM* (Boston: Harvard Business School Press, 1996).

34. Darryl K. Taft, "IBM's Palmisano: Sale of PC Biz to Lenovo Helped with China Expansion," *New York Times,* January 3, 2012.

35. Steve Lohr, "Sale of I.B.M. PC Unit Is a Bridge between Cultures," *New York Times,* December 8, 2004.

36. Nicholas Negroponte, "One Laptop per Child," *TED2006,* filmed February 2006, https://www.ted.com/talks/nicholas_negroponte_on_one_laptop_per_child.

37. One journalist wrote an almost day-by-day history of the PC through the early 1990s and included discussions about activities at IBM's rivals. His detailed index listed in total just over 160 people, many of whom remained central to the story right into the next century, such as Sam Palmisano, Steve Jobs, and Bill Gates. See Carroll, *Big Blues,* 371–375.

38. In 2014, IBM sold its x86 server business to Lenovo. For details of the sale, see the joint IBM-Lenovo press release, "Lenovo Set to Close Acquisition of IBM's X86 Server Business," September 29, 2014, Lenovo Newsroom, http://news.lenovo.com/news-releases/lenovo-set-to-close-acquisition-ibms-x86-server-business.htm.

39. Mills and Friesen, *Broken Promises,* 81.

40. Ibid., 133.

41. Ibid., 134.

42. Ibid.

43. Marvin B. Lieberman and David B. Montgomery, "First-Mover Advantages," *Strategic Management Journal* 9 (Summer 1988): 41–58.

44. Clayton M. Christensen, *The Innovator's Dilemma: When New Technologies Cause Great Firms to Fail* (Boston: Harvard Business School Press, 1997), 97–98. While it is not always an easy read, with not too much effort a manager can glean practical lessons from this book. In the late 1990s, the book enjoyed considerable popularity within managerial circles at IBM, but by early the following decade it was less consulted.

CHAPTER 15: STORMS, CRISIS, AND NEAR DEATH, 1985–1993

1. International Business Machines Corporation, *1980 Annual Report,* 7.

2. Such reporting repeatedly came from publications such as the *Wall Street Journal* and other institutional media, largely in New York, over the course of a half dozen years.

3. Charles H. Ferguson and Charles R. Morris, *Computer Wars: How the West Can Win in a Post-IBM World* (New York: Times Books, 1993), xi. There are still copies of this e-mail floating around, as many IBMers kept a copy because it was so sensational.

4. "Nerd Instinct," *The Economist,* June 10, 1995, 15.

5. Robert Heller, *The Fate of IBM* (London: Little, Brown, 1994), 202.

6. William Lazonick, "Strategy, Structure, and Management Development in the United States and Britain," in *Development of Managerial Enterprise,* ed. K. Kobayashi and H. Morikawa (Tokyo: University of Tokyo Press, 1986), 101–146.

7. The same occurred at General Motors and American Express in 1992–1993. See Stanley Buder, *Capitalizing on Change: A Social History of American Business* (Chapel Hill: University of North Carolina Press, 2009), 459.

8. International Business Machines Corporation, "Letter to Stockholders," *1989 Annual Report,* 4.

9. D. Quinn Mills and G. Bruce Friesen, *Broken Promises: An Unconventional View of What Went Wrong at IBM* (Boston: Harvard Business School Press, 1996), 87.

10. Paul Carroll, *Big Blues: The Unmaking of IBM* (New York: Crown, 1993), 229.

11. Mills and Friesen, *Broken Promises,* 141.

12. Ibid., 143.

13. Ferguson and Morris, *Computer Wars,* 84–86.

14. International Business Machines Corporation, "Letter to Stockholders," *1980 Annual Report,* 3–4.

15. International Business Machines Corporation, "Letter to Stockholders," *1981 Annual Report.*

16. Heller, *The Fate of IBM,* 62.

17. Thomas J. Peters and Robert Waterman Jr., *In Search of Excellence* (New York: Harper and Row, 1982).

18. When IBM switched from leasing equipment to selling it outright, including already installed products to increase immediate cash flow into the company.

19. Mills and Friesen, *Broken Promises,* 90.

20. At the same time, in the United States, tax credits and shorter depreciation schedules were available to motivate corporations to purchase new equipment.

21. Ernest von Simson, *The Limits of Strategy: Lessons in Leadership from the Computer Industry* (Bloomington, IN: iUniverse, 2009), 307.

22. Ibid.

23. It only returned with the arrival of Louis Gerstner nearly a decade later, described in chapter 16.

24. Carol J. Loomis and Susan Lindauer, "IBM's Big Blues: A Legend Tries to Remake Itself," *Fortune* 115, no. 2 (January 1, 1987), 34.

25. Ibid., 41.

26. Ibid., 34. For the ranking report, see Edward C. Baig and Barbara Hetzer, "America's Most Admired Corporation: The King Is Dethroned," *Fortune* 115, no. 2 (January 1, 1987), 18.

CHAPTER 16: IBM'S INITIAL RESPONSE, 1985–1993

1. International Business Machines Corporation, "Letter to Stockholders," *1992 Annual Report,* 5.

2. Steve Lohr, "Company News; I.B.M. to Replace Its Top Executive," *New York Times,* January 27, 1983.

3. Philip Mattera, *World Class Business: A Guide to the 100 Most Powerful Global Corporations* (New York: Henry Holt, 1992), 704, 706.

4. Roland Trempé, *Les mineurs de Carmeaux, 1848–1914* (Paris: Editions Ouvrières, 1971).

5. See, for example, Alfred D. Chandler Jr., *The Visible Hand: The Managerial Revolution in American Business* (Cambridge, MA: Harvard University Press, 1977), 203–205.

6. William G. Roy, *Socializing Capital: The Rise of the Large Industrial Corporation in America* (Princeton, NJ: Princeton University Press, 1997), 280.

7. I was particularly influenced by Jay W. Lorsch and Elizabeth MacIver, *Pawns or Potentates: The Reality of America's Corporate Boards* (Boston: Harvard Business School Press, 1989); Jonathan L. Johnson, Catherine M. Daily, and Alan E. Ellstrand, "Boards of Directors: A Review and Research Agenda," *Journal of Management* 22, no. 3 (1996): 409–438.

8. International Business Machines Corporation, *1986 Annual Report*, 2–4.

9. Corporate MDQ staff documented the concept and its practices in numerous documents, publications, and slides. For one of the most complete, see International Business Machines Corporation, *The Transformation of IBM: A Market-Driven Quality Reference Guide*, Version 1.0 (Stamford, CT: International Business Machines Corporation, June 1992).

10. A decade later, it had matured to the point where it became highly admired by other multinational corporations integrating globally fundamental processes. See Dean Palmer, "Lessons from an Early Adopter," *Works Management*, August 5, 2002, http://www.worksmanagement.co.uk /Continuous-Improvement/features/lessons-from-an-early-adopter-1/1714/.

11. For a history of the quality movement, see Robert E. Cole, *Managing Quality Fads: How American Business Learned to Play the Quality Game* (New York: Oxford University Press, 1999), which includes commentary on IBM's experience.

12. I have commented elsewhere on TQM as practiced at IBM and other multinational corporations. See James W. Cortada, *TQM for Information Systems Management: Quality Practices for Continuous Improvement* (New York: McGraw-Hill, 1995); James W. Cortada, *Best Practices in Information Technology: How Corporations Get the Most Value from Exploiting Their Digital Investments* (Upper Saddle River, NJ: Prentice-Hall PTR, 1998). TQM was also applied in such traditional areas as sales at IBM and elsewhere. See James W. Cortada, *TQM for Sales and Marketing Management* (New York: McGraw-Hill, 1993).

13. Summarized in Robert Heller, *The Fate of IBM* (London: Little, Brown, 1994), 30.

14. Quoted in ibid., 35.

15. For an autobiography by Mann, see Kevin Mann, "Biography of Kevin Mann," April 30, 2012, https://www.youtube.com/watch?v=C6D9WLH5vmo.

16. Peter H. Lewis, "The Executive Computer; Can I.B.M. Learn from a Unit It Freed?" *New York Times*, December 22, 1991.

17. Heller, *The Fate of IBM*, 281.

18. This business had slid greatly in importance. In Watson Sr.'s time, it had been a strategic revenue generator.

19. It might help to explain the ranks of IBM executives in this period. There were four levels. A Band D was a division-level executive, such as the individual to whom a dozen sales branch offices might report or was responsible for a major mission within a product division. A Band C was the next level up, normally a divisional vice president, who would have a number of Band Ds reporting to him or her. A Band B was normally a divisional president, later also a general

manager or managing director (by 2005), while a Band A was normally a senior vice president. CEOs, presidents of IBM, and chairmen were technically employees of the board of directors, not of IBM, while all the banded executives were direct employees of the firm. All banded employees were given stock options and salaries, and were eligible for bonuses and often also commissions. Below executives, there were also bands, expressed as numbers, which changed in numeration over time. But, like the executive bands, they were used to designate salary ranges, and terms and conditions for bonuses and stock options.

20. David Kirkpatrick and Jennifer Reese, "Breaking Up IBM," *Fortune* 126, no. 2 (July 27, 1992): 44–58, quotation at 58.

21. Ibid., 44.

22. International Business Machines Corporation, "Chairman's letter to stockholders," *1991 Annual Report,* 2–4.

23. Heller, *The Fate of IBM,* 297.

24. International Business Machines Corporation, *1991 Annual Report,* 4.

25. "IBM's Gerstner Spills the Beans … Unwittingly," *Truthinmedia,* December 16, 2002, http://www.truthinmedia.org/Bulletins2002/12-3.html.

26. Louis V. Gerstner Jr., *Who Says Elephants Can't Dance? Inside IBM's Historic Turnaround* (New York: HarperBusiness, 2002), 14–15.

27. D. Quinn Mills and G. Bruce Friesen, *Broken Promises: An Unconventional View of What Went Wrong at IBM* (Boston: Harvard Business School Press, 1996), 111.

28. Ibid., 113.

29. Stephen Schwartz (b. 1935), senior VP at IBM (1990–1992), in public comments to a group of sales managers, October 1991.

30. Walter E. Burdick, *Family Values—Walter E. Burdick—An Autobiography* (privately published, circa 2000), 310.

31. Ibid.

32. The notion of gaining "buy-in" from employees was an old one, dating back to the 1920s. Those executives who came up through sales knew from personal experience, for example, that if the sales force did not believe in a product, it would fail, as happened, for example, with the PC Jr.

33. Burdick, *Family Values,* 331.

34. Ibid., 132.

35. Ibid., 149.

36. No historian, employee writing about the company, or reporter has been allowed to view IBM board records. What few documents exist were exposed as part of the request for subpoenas by the U.S. Department of Justice in the 1970s as part of its antitrust suit against the firm. In the fall of 2015, I requested permission to examine those for the period 1987–1993 and was quickly denied access, even though the company had given me virtually free rein to use the company's corporate archives while I was still an employee.

37. Heller, *The Fate of IBM,* 303.

38. Pejoratively nicknamed "Neutron Eddie" by IBMers for having laid off so many employees.

39. My repeated requests to view board minutes were summarily denied over the course of a decade.

40. "IBM's Gerstner Spills the Beans … Unwittingly."

41. Lohr, "Company News; I.B.M. to Replace Its Top Executive."

42. Rosabeth Moss Kanter, Barry A. Stein, and Todd D. Jick, *The Challenge of Organizational Change: How Companies Experience It and Leaders Guide It* (New York: Free Press, 1992), 461.

43. Gerstner argued that just reversing this one decision—to break up the company—may have been the most important business decision of his entire professional life, discussed in more detail in chapter 17.

44. Mills and Friesen, *Broken Promises*, 183–184.

45. Ibid., 185.

46. Gerstner had to get the firm back to prosperity, so he told employees he would do one major layoff and then back off. He essentially did that, reducing the frequency of layoffs in the later years of his rule. Palmisano sold off chunks of the business along with its employees, such as the disk and PC parts businesses, but also engaged in incremental layoffs. Rometty became the most extensive user of incremental layoffs in the company's history. Compounding her use of layoffs was their size—many thousands of people every year—surrounded by secrecy as to the actual numbers. The worldwide furor that practice created was enormous. Employees established websites that documented her extensive use of this managerial tool. See, for example, https://www.endicottalliance.org/jobcutsreports.php and https://www.facebook.com/alliancemember. She argued that these employees were being swapped out for others who already had skills the company needed right now. The good people at the Harvard Business School would have disapproved, based on what they learned from Akers, but all those layoffs began in the 1980s, becoming a managerial practice for the next three decades.

47. Ernest von Simson, *The Limits of Strategy: Lessons in Leadership from the Computer Industry* (Bloomington, IN: iUniverse, 2009), 323.

48. Burdick, *Family Values*, 310, 313.

49. I thought of the Akers-Hoover/Roosevelt-Gerstner comparison in the 1990s. A recently published biography of Hoover reinforced the usefulness of that analogy. See Glen Jeansonne, *Herbert Hoover: A Life* (New York: Berkley, 2016), 251–269.

CHAPTER 17: HOW IBM WAS RESCUED, 1993–1994

1. Louis V. Gerstner Jr., *Who Says Elephants Can't Dance? Inside IBM's Historic Turnaround* (New York: HarperBusiness, 2002), 71.

2. L. A. Taylor, "Why Are CEOs Rarely Fired? Evidence from Structural Estimation," *Journal of Finance* 65, no. 6 (2010): 2051–2087; Graeme Guthrie, *The Firm Divided: Manager-Shareholder Conflict and the Fight for Control of the Modern Corporation* (New York: Oxford University Press, 2017), 23.

3. Ibid.

4. One still riling older employees in the second decade of the new century, retirees, and many laid-off workers, even 15 years after he retired in 2002.

5. Christopher D. McKenna, *The World's Newest Profession: Management Consulting in the Twentieth Century* (Cambridge: Cambridge University Press, 2006), 23, 192–215.

6. Quoted in Doug Garr, *IBM Redux: Lou Gerstner and the Business Turnaround of the Decade* (New York: HarperBusiness, 1999), 90–91.

7. Ibid., 114.

8. Gerstner, *Who Says Elephants Can't Dance?*, 15.

9. Ibid., 16.

10. Robert Slater, *Saving Big Blue: Leadership Lessons and Turnaround Tactics of IBM's Lou Gerstner* (New York: McGraw-Hill, 1999), 40.

11. Ibid., 158.

12. For details on his compensation, see Garr, *IBM Redux*, 27–28.

13. "Louis V. Gerstner Jr. to Become Chairman and CEO of IBM," *CHQNEWS Corporate Headquarters Bulletins,* March 26, 1993.

14. IBMers knew that defrocked managers were often compelled to make the same speech.

15. Gerstner, *Who Says Elephants Can't Dance?*, 37.

16. Ibid., 24–25.

17. Quoted in Garr, *IBM Redux*, 38.

18. Ibid., 38–39.

19. Ibid., 51.

20. Gerstner, *Who Says Elephants Can't Dance?*, 51.

21. Ibid., 57.

22. Ibid., 61.

23. The move to artificial intelligence and Watson computing may qualify as a comparable decision, but it is too early to tell as of this writing (2018).

24. Gerstner, *Who Says Elephants Can't Dance?*, 62.

25. That fall, he began to tell IBMers elements of the decision in town hall meetings, later through internal e-mail, and finally in January in the annual report. I observed a number of these communications.

26. Keep in mind that reversing a large firm's strategy is not to be taken casually, since so many smart people could have been presumed to have developed it and had embraced it. In IBM's corporate culture, such considerations were of paramount importance.

27. Although computer scientists, including IBM's, worked diligently to establish them, making some progress. See Andrew L. Russell, *Open Standards and the Digital Age: History, Ideology, and Networks* (Cambridge: Cambridge University Press, 2014), 197–261.

28. Ibid., 61.

29. Ibid., 63.

30. Thomas H. Davenport, *Process Innovation: Reengineering Work through Information Technology* (Boston: Harvard Business School Press, 1993).

31. Ibid., 64.

32. The experience of employee Gavin Roach, as he explained to the author.

33. Ibid., 65.

34. The very large Oriental carpet that had been in the same living room at Endicott for decades was rescued by local employees when the Homestead was sold off and can be seen in a tiny museum they set up to tell IBM's Endicott story, located in one of the company's buildings on North Street.

35. Gerstner, *Who Says Elephants Can't Dance?*, 69.

36. This and many others are reprinted in an appendix. See ibid., 79.

37. Ibid., 117.

38. Ibid., 117–118.

39. Ibid., 118.

40. Ibid.

41. Ibid., 183.

42. Ibid., 185–186.

43. Ibid., 186.

44. Copies of this rare publication are at https://web.archive.org/web/20160504150653/http://www.endicottalliance.org/. On the labor movement, see Steve Early and Rand Wilson, "Organizing High Tech: Unions & Their Future," *Labor's Crucible in the 1980's ... Organize!* 1, no. 8 (1986): 1–22. For details on the newsletter and the labor movement at IBM, see Lee Conrad to James W. Cortada, December 23, 2016, author's files. See also Chris Carlsson and Mark Leger, *Bad Attitudes: The Processed World Anthology* (London: Verso, 1990), 114.

45. Judith H. Robrjynski, "Rethinking IBM," *Business Week*, October 4, 1993, 86ff.

46. "The Rebirth of IBM," *The Economist*, June 6, 1998, 97–100.

47. Tim Smart, "IBM: How Another Titan Bounced Back," *Washington Post*, July 12, 1998, H15.

48. John P. Kotter, "Leading Change: Why Transformation Efforts Fail," *Harvard Business Review* 73 (March–April 1995): 61.

49. For video of Gerstner discussing his role at IBM in the early 1990s, see https://www.youtube.com/watch?v=YsNs3LA3QXE.

50. C. E. Fee, C. J. Hadlock, and J. R. Pierce, "Management Turnover across the Corporate Hierarchy," *Journal of Accounting and Economics* 37, no. 1 (2004): 3–38.

51. C. E. Fee, C. J. Hadlock, and J. R. Pierce, "Managers with and without Style: Evidence Using Exogenous Variation," *Review of Financial Studies* 16, no. 3 (2015): 567–601.

52. Eric G. Flamholtz and Yvonne Randle, *Corporate Culture: The Ultimate Strategic Asset* (Stanford, CA: Stanford Business Books, 2011), 184.

53. Ibid., 185.

54. John F. Padgett and Walter W. Powell, "The Problem of Emergence," in *The Emergence of Organizations and Markets*, ed. John F. Padgett and Walter W. Powell (Princeton, NJ: Princeton University Press, 2012), all quotations at 2.

55. Did he know what Watson Sr. did? Gerstner always expressed an interest in IBM's history, but was that simply a marketing interest to reinforce IBM's expertise? Several months after he joined IBM, as a courtesy, I sent him a history book I had just published on the early years of IBM and other firms in the office appliance industry. Two months later, I received the usual courtesy thank you letter, but with a couple of questions, which I responded to via e-mail. Had he read the section on IBM and Watson Sr.'s early actions? See James W. Cortada, *Before the Computer: IBM, NCR, Burroughs, and Remington Rand, and the Industry They Created, 1865–1956* (Princeton, NJ: Princeton University Press, 1993).

CHAPTER 18: A NEW IBM, 1995–2012

1. Louis V. Gerstner Jr., *Who Says Elephants Can't Dance?* (New York: HarperBusiness, 2002), 213.

2. International Business Machines Corporation, *2010 Annual Report*, 8.

3. For a recent example of how historians worked in this kind of environment, see William Aspray and James W. Cortada, "Before It Was a Giant: The Early History of Symantec, 1982–1999," *IEEE Annals of the History of Computing* 38, no. 4 (October–December 2016): 26–41.

4. Historians studying the history of computers, for example, have created a new intellectual and institutional infrastructure to support their work in contemporary history. For details, see James W. Cortada, "Studying History As It Unfolds, Part 1: Creating the History of Information Technologies," *IEEE Annals of the History of Computing* 37, no. 3 (July–September 2015): 20–31; James W. Cortada, "Studying History As It Unfolds, Part 2: Tooling Up the Historian," *IEEE Annals of the History of Computing* 38, no. 1 (January–March 2016): 48–59.

5. Although useful snippets and insights appeared in the business literature. See, for example, Geoffrey A. Moore, *Escape Velocity: Free Your Company's Future from the Pull of the Past* (New York: HarperCollins, 2011), 191–193.

6. Steven W. Usselman, "Unbundling IBM: Antitrust and the Incentives to Innovation in American Computing," in *The Challenge of Remaining Innovative: Insights from Twentieth Century American Business,* ed. S. N. Clarke, N. Lamoreaux, and S. Usselman (Stanford, CA: Stanford Business School Books, 2009), 270.

7. Lou Gerstner to "Dear Colleague," July 18, 1995, copy in author's possession.

8. Ibid.

9. Lou Gerstner to "Dear Colleague," January 21, 1997, copy in author's possession.

10. "Lou Gerstner's Worldwide Employee Broadcast," January 1999. This was his initial 1999 "kickoff" message to all employees.

11. Jeffrey R. Yost, *Making IT Work: A History of the Computer Services Industry* (Cambridge, MA: MIT Press, 2017), 232–242.

12. Ibid.

13. Ibid.

14. Many of the new practice leaders brought into IBM from other consulting firms believed IBMers could not consult, especially if they had a sales background.

15. "IBM Global Services: A Brief History," May 2002, IBM Corporate Archives, https://www.03 .ibm.com/ibm/history/documents/pdf/gservices.pdf.

16. The company set quantifiable annual targets for the reduction of field engineers and for increased quality performance of hardware.

17. International Business Machines Corporation, *Annual Reports,* 2002–2014.

18. Ibid.

19. Gerstner, *Who Says Elephants Can't Dance?,* 138.

20. Ibid., 140.

21. Doug Garr, *IBM Redux: Lou Gerstner and the Business Turnaround of the Decade* (New York: HarperBusiness, 1999), 218.

22. Ibid., 230.

23. It continued to also introduce PCs and, more important, laptops, but they were not essential to generating revenue.

24. For a popular IBM commercial about e-business, see https://www.youtube.com/watch?v =3LkQrtCIFA4.

25. Remember, however, that hundreds of millions of people knew about the IBM PC.

26. I sat in on presentations on this topic, some of which were attended by divisional and group executives. Management committee records for the period remain closed, and it is not certain that they even exist.

27. Lou Gerstner to Management Colleagues, September 18, 2001, copy in author's possession.

28. Robert A. Myers to Madison, Wisconsin, Employees, September 11, 2001, copy in author's possession.

29. E-mails in author's possession.

30. Maureen A. Power to James W. Cortada, September 12, 2001.

31. Gerstner, *Who Says Elephants Can't Dance?*, 280.

32. Manjeet Kripalani, "IBM's India Pep Rally," *BusinessWeek,* June 6, 2006.

33. Interview with Lee Conrad by James W. Cortada, November 18, 2016. Conrad had been a union organizer at IBM between 1983 and 2000 and subsequently a volunteer doing the same until 2016.

34. Quoted in Kevin Maney, Steve Hamm, and Jeffrey M. O'Brien, *Making the World Work Better: The Ideas That Shaped a Century and a Company* (Upper Saddle River, NJ: IBM Press, 2011), 212.

35. Ibid., 213.

36. Video of Sam Palmisano on the history of IBM, 2011, https://www.youtube.com/watch?v=0a6I JAZ3b9M. See also https://www.youtube.com/watch?v=HS40P7xxHkw.

37. International Business Machines Corporation, *2004 Annual Report,* 8.

38. International Business Machines Corporation, *2005 Annual Report.*

39. International Business Machines Corporation, *2006 Annual Report,* 6–7.

40. Ibid., 8.

41. International Business Machines Corporation, *2008 Annual Report,* 10–14.

42. International Business Machines Corporation, *2010 Annual Report.*

43. Edgar H. Schein, *Organizational Culture and Leadership* (San Francisco: Jossey-Bass and John Wiley and Sons, 2010), 293–294.

44. Interview with Lee Conrad by James W. Cortada, November 18, 2016.

45. Ibid.

46. These and thousands of other comments can be found at various organizing websites. See http://www.ibmemployee.com/; https://www.facebook.com/alliancemember/; http://endicottalliance.org/jobcutsreports.php.

47. E-mail, Lee Conrad to James W. Cortada, November 14, 2016.

48. IBM Employee News and Links, April 2, 2016, http://www.ibmemployee.com/.

49. Paul Hemp and Thomas A. Stewart, "Leading Change When Business Is Good," *Harvard Business Review* (December 2004), online edition.

50. Quoted in Maney, Hamm, and O'Brien, *Making the World Work Better,* 7.

51. Quoted from a *Bloomberg* report, October 26, 2011, in Ernest von Simson, *The Limits of Strategy: Lessons in Leadership from the Computer Industry* (Bloomington, IN: iUniverse, 2009), 393.

52. International Business Machines Corporation, "A Letter from the Chairman of the Board," *2011 Annual Report,* n.p.

CHAPTER 19: HARD TIMES, AGAIN, AND ANOTHER TRANSFORMATION

1. Glassdoor.com review of IBM, July 28, 2016. Of 8,000 individuals offering a rating of the CEO, 59 percent approved of her performance, and the company overall received a rating of 3.4 out of a possible 5. See https://www.glassdoor.com/Reviews/IBM-Reviews-E354.htm.

2. For an overview of the more traditional historiography, see Margaret B. W. Graham, "Technology and Innovation," in *The Oxford Handbook of Business History*, ed. Geoffrey Jones and Jonathan Zeitlin (New York: Oxford University Press, 2007), 347–373.

3. IBM's internal employee survey results made such comparisons about support possible.

4. In early 2017, Buffett reduced his ownership in IBM stock by a third, disappointed with the rate of its transformation and concerned about the steeply declining value of the stock.

5. Martin Campbell-Kelly and Daniel D. Garcia-Swartz, *From Mainframes to Smartphones: A History of the International Computer Industry* (Cambridge, MA: Harvard University Press, 2015), 208. For over a year, I struggled with whether, and how, to use their words "survive" and "thrive" as part of my book's title. In the end, either would have worked, for the reasons they explained in the quotation.

6. Steven Pinker, *Enlightenment Now: The Case for Reason, Science, Humanism, and Progress* (New York: Viking, 2018), 7.

7. Lillian Cunningham, "IBM Is Struggling. But Former CEO Sam Palmisano Says He Isn't Looking Back," *Washington Post*, June 26, 2015.

8. "Big Blue Yonder," *The Economist*, October 21, 2017, 63–64.

9. Jeff Matthews, "IBM: I've Been Manipulated," *NotMakingThisUp*, January 21, 2014, http://jeffmatthewsisnotmakingthisup.blogspot.com/2014/01/ibm-ive-been-manipulated.html.

10. Highly detailed financial analyses were prepared in the form of slide presentations made to investors to demonstrate how IBM would make it. See, for example, https://www.ibm.com/investor/events/investor0510/presentation/pres3.pdf.

11. International Business Machines Corporation, *2012 Annual Report*, 1.

12. Judith Hurwitz quoted in Cade Metz, "IBM Names Virginia Rometty as First Female CEO," *Wired*, October 25, 2011, https://www.wired.com/ibm/2011/10/virginia-rometty1.

13. International Business Machines Corporation, *2011 Annual Report*, 3.

14. Matthews, "IBM: I've Been Manipulated."

15. Interview with a GM who preferred to remain anonymous, October 30, 2016.

16. James Bandler and Doris Burke, "Dangerous Liaisons inside IBM: Inside the Biggest Hedge Fund Insider-Trading Ring," *Fortune*, July 26, 2010, http://fortune.com/2010/07/06/ibm-trading-scandal/.

17. Steve Lohr, "I.B.M. Names a New Chief Executive," *New York Times*, October 26, 2011, B1.

18. International Business Machines Corporation, "2012 Annual Meeting of Stockholders," press release, April 24, 2012.

19. Nick Summers, "The Trouble with IBM: Why Customers Are Breaking Up with IBM," *Bloomberg*, May 23, 2014, https://www.bloomberg.com/news/articles/2014-05-22/ibms-eps-target-unhelpful-amid-cloud-computing-challenges.

20. Steven Zolman, "Top 10 Reasons Why Ginni Rometty Will Fail as IBM's New CEO," *Net(net)*, undated (April 2014), http://www.netnetweb.com/blog/top-10-reasons-why-ginni-rometty-will-fail-ibm's-new-ceo.

21. Ibid.

22. Alex Barinka, "IBM's Sales Slump Turns Stock into Dow's Lone Loser of 2013," *Bloomberg*, December 31, 2013.

23. *The Motley Fool* defended IBM for years. For the situation facing IBM at that time, see, for example, Anders Bylund, "What Must IBM Do in 2014?," *The Motley Fool*, December 10, 2013, http://www.fool.com/investing/general/2014/01/02/2014-will-be-a-big-year-for-ibm.aspx#,Usbb Pv1gxz8.

24. Extending the essentially no raises strategy she had employed for years to bonuses, reducing them across the company.

25. Tiernan Ray, "IBM: $20/Sh. EPS Goal Increasingly Irrelevant, Says Bernstein, Why Stick to It?," *Barrons' Tech Trader Daily*, February 3, 2014.

26. Alternative measures can include cash earnings, earnings before interest, taxes, depreciation, and amortization (EBITDA).

27. Ray, "IBM: $20/Sh. EPS Goal Increasingly Irrelevant, Says Bernstein, Why Stick to It?" EPS means earnings per share. Buybacks of stock by IBM reduced the number of shares available on the market. EPS is determined by dividing the amount of net income earned by the number of outstanding shares. The fewer the number of outstanding shares, the higher the earnings per share made by the company. Investors aspire to higher EPS, and the only two ways to get that are by increasing income (which IBM was not able to do) or by reducing the number of available shares (which IBM was able to accomplish).

28. Ibid.

29. Tim Fernholz, "IBM Saved Its Earnings by Moving Almost Half Its Employees to the Netherlands," *QUARTZ*, February 4, 2014, http://www.qz.com/173735.

30. Quoted in Alex Konrad, "IBM Shares Dip As It Meets Q1 Earnings Expectations but Revenues Continue to Miss," *Forbes*, April 16, 2014.

31. Richard Saintvilus, "This Big IBM Bet Doesn't Deserve a Pass," *TheStreet*, March 11, 2014, https://www.thestreet.com/story/12524616/1/this-big-ibm-bet-doesnt-deserve-a-pass.html.

32. "IBM's Double Dilemma," *CNNMoney*, March 14, 2016, http://fortune.com/2014/03/14/ibms-double-dilemma/.

33. Adam Hartung, "Why You Don't Want to Own IBM," *Forbes*, May 16, 2014, https: www.forbescom/sites/adamhartung/2014/05/16/why-you-don't-want-to-own-ibm/.

34. Marie G. McIntyre, "Advice to IBM Management: Don't Be Jerks," CNBC, September 22, 2014.

35. *The Motley Fool*, July 16, 2014, http://www.fool.com/investing/general/2014/07/16/should-the-dow-jones-get-rid-of-international-busi.aspx.

36. Inside IBM, however, questions were raised about how the company could scale up across five initiatives, let alone on one or two. The answer was not obvious. Newly hired executives brought in to do just that did not know how IBM worked, such as how to obtain a budget, recruit personnel, and so forth. With so many initiatives, too many brands were competing

against each other for resources. Source: Anonymous executive in Corporate to author, January 24, 2017.

37. International Business Machines Corporation, "International Business Machines (IBM) CEO Ginni Rometty on Q3 2014 Results—Earnings Call Transcript," IBM Press Office, October 20, 2014. For a copy, see http://seekingalpha.com/article/2575975-international-business-machines-ibm-ceo-ginni-rometty-on-q3-2014-results-earnings-call-transcript.

38. Quoted in Julie Bort, "Mark Cuban Slams IBM: It's No Longer a Tech Company. They Have No Vision," *Business Insider,* October 22, 2014.

39. Ibid.

40. Andrew Ross Sorkin, "The Truth Hidden by IBM's Buybacks," *New York Times,* October 21, 2014, B1.

41. Quoted in ibid.

42. Ibid.

43. For a large collection of employee comments, see "IBM Employee News and Links," http://www.ibmemployee.com/.

44. Ibid.

45. International Business Machines Corporation, *2014 Annual Report.*

46. Nadia Damouni and Svea Herbst-Bayliss, "IBM Is Working on a Defense Plan against Activist Investors," *Business Insider* (Reuters), April 2, 2015; Amanda Schiavo, "Will IBM Stock Be Impacted Today after Hiring Advisors to Deal with Investors?," *Business Insider* (Reuters), April 6, 2015.

47. Alliance@IBM tracked IBM's population, and its numbers became the ones most frequently cited by the media after 2010. IBM's last stated number of U.S. employees came in 2009 at 105,000. The Alliance then estimated gradual declines of 4,000 in 2010, another 3,000 in 2011, 7,000 in 2012, 3,000 in 2013, 5,000 in 2014, and 5,000 in 2015, for a total of 27,000. There are no reliable figures on layoffs in other countries. For details, see http://www.allianceibm.org (last accessed March 15, 2015, but apparently no longer available), with data more readily available at http://www.ibmemployee.com/ and https://watchingibm.com/. For the demise of the employee organizing efforts, which included tracking layoffs, see Patrick Thibodeau, "IBM Union Calls It Quits," *Computerworld,* January 5, 2016, http://www.computerworld.com/article/3019552/it-industry/ibm-union-calls-it-quits.html.

48. Ibid.

49. Carol Quigley, "The Buyback of Things: IBM to Repurchase another $5 Billion in Stock in Next Two Quarters," *Zero Hedge,* October 28, 2014, http://carolquigley.tumblr.com/post/101183260401/the-buyback-of-things-ibm-to-repurchase-another.

50. International Business Machines Corporation, press release, January 19, 2017, and Form 8-K, January 19, 2017.

51. A purposeful action never done before at IBM. Employees suspected the company did not want the public or them to know how sharply IBM's U.S. employee population had dropped. Thus, all citations of employee populations by the start of the second decade of the twenty-first century are educated estimates.

52. From "Watching IBM," Facebook, https://www.facebook.com/alliancemember/.

53. Quoted in Rick Wartzman, *The End of Loyalty: The Rise and Fall of Good Jobs in America* (New York: Public Affairs Press, 2017), 320.

54. Quoted in ibid., 362.

55. International Business Machines Corporation, *2017 Annual Report*, 75.

56. Peter Gosselin and Ariana Tobin, "Cutting 'Old Heads' at IBM," *ProPublica*, March 22, 2018, https://features.propublica.org/ibm/ibm-age-discrimination-american-workers/.

57. To watch Rometty articulate her strategy, see the video "Behind Ginni Rometty's Plan to Reboot IBM," *Wall Street Journal*, April 20, 2016, http://www.wsj.com/articles/behind-ginni-romettys-plan-to-reboot-ibm-1429577076.

58. Named in honor of Thomas Watson Sr.

59. For a video of the competition, see https://www.youtube.com/watch?v=P0Obm0DBvwI.

60. John E. Kelly III and Steve Hamm, *Smart Machines: IBM's Watson and the Era of Cognitive Computing* (New York: Columbia University Press, 2013), 4.

61. Judith S. Hurwitz, Marcia Kaufman, and Adrian Bowles, *Cognitive Computing and Big Data Analytics* (Hoboken, NJ: John Wiley and Sons, 2015), 55.

62. Kevin Kelly, *The Inevitable: Understanding the 12 Technological Forces That Will Shape Our Future* (New York: Viking, 2016), 31.

63. IBM and Institute of Culinary Education, *Cognitive Cooking with Chef Watson: Recipes for Innovation from IBM & the Institute of Culinary Education* (Naperville, IL: Sourcebooks, 2015), 26–27.

64. Jon Brodkin, "IBM's Jeopardy-Playing Machine Can Now Beat Human Contestants," *Network World*, February 10, 2010, copy in author's possession.

65. Spencer E. Ante, "IBM Set to Expand Watson's Reach," *Wall Street Journal*, January 9, 2014.

66. Historians, economists, and business management scholars tend to use the term *innovation* to speak of similar themes. Historians and economists, in particular, have studied why and how large firms innovate. The IBM case mirrors their work, but I express the notion as "big bets," as that is a term frequently used by executives making such decisions in high-tech firms. For the ideas animating this chapter's discussion of "big bets," see William Lazonick, "The Innovative Firm," in *The Oxford Handbook of Innovation*, ed. Jan Fagerberg, David C. Mowery, and Richard R. Nelson (New York: Oxford University Press, 2005), 29–55.

67. Steve Lohr, "IBM, in It for the Long Haul, Is Betting Big on Watson," *New York Times*, October 17, 2016, B1.

68. Ibid.

69. Ibid.

70. International Business Machines Corporation, *2015 Annual Report*, first quotation at 3, second quotation at 5.

71. In June 2018, IBM laid off workers from its Watson Health unit, in some American cities by over 50 percent, an action suggesting that the company was having difficulty implementing its Watson aspiration. "IBM Confirms Layoffs Impacted Its Watson Health Division," June 4, 2018, *Health IT*, https://medcitynews.com/2018/06/ibm-layoffs/.

CHAPTER 20: THINK: IBM TODAY AND ITS LEGACY

1. "Quintessential Quotes," IBM Corporate Archives, http://www03.ibm.com/ibm/history/documents/pdf/quotes.pdf.

2. Ibid.

3. Steven Pinker, *Enlightenment Now: The Case for Reason, Science, Humanism, and Progress* (New York: Viking, 2018).

4. Peter Gosselin and Ariana Tobin, "Cutting 'Old Heads' At IBM," *ProPublica*, March 22, 2018, https://features.propublica.org/ibm/ibm-age-discrimination-american-workers/.

5. Robert X. Cringely, *The Decline and Fall of IBM: End of an American Icon?* (Lexington, KY: NeRDTV, 2014), xii.

6. Much of their complaining took place anonymously on websites, such as at "Watching IBM" on Facebook, https://www.facebook.com/alliancemember/, the sequel to an earlier, similar website hosted by Alliance@IBM. As of mid-2017, that organization's website appeared to have been taken down. I have kept nearly 1,000 pages of commentary from this organization dating from the early years postmillennium to 2015.

7. Peter E. Greulich, *THINK Again: IBM Can Maximize Shareholder Value* (No City: MBI Concepts Corporation, 2017), 1–5. Greulich worked at IBM between 1980 and 2011.

8. Since 2012, critics have argued that IBM needed "top line" revenue and should acquire firms that can provide it. IBM has chosen to value profits more than revenue, however. Its senior management has also argued that acquisitions were less about financial activities and more about acquiring firms that had products and patents in support of IBM's five initiatives, discussed later in this chapter.

9. Ibid.

10. Ibid.

11. The underlying problem is that IBM never took losses for businesses it acquired that failed to live up to expectations. Had it done so, write-offs would have run into the millions of dollars. The corporation did everything it could to report cash inflows but little of what it was required to do about expenses and charges.

12. Greulich, *THINK Again*.

13. For the report, see http://www.ibm.com/ibm/responsibility/report/2010/chairmans-letter/index.html?lnk=paper.

14. For an excellent example of this logic, see Crispus Nyaga, "IBM: Big Blue Is Fading," *Seeking Alpha*, May 23, 2017, https://seekingalpha.com/article/4075697-ibm-big-blue-fading.

15. Described in Kevin Maney, Steve Hamm, and Jeffrey M. O'Brien, *Making the World Work Better: The Ideas That Shaped a Century and a Company* (Upper Saddle River, NJ: IBM Press, 2011), 244–327.

16. In all periods of IBM's history, of course, there were exceptions, with individuals competing for promotions, particularly in the middle and upper ranks of the company.

17. https://finance.yahoo.com/quote/ibm/holders?ltr=1.

18. "International Business Machines (IBM) Management Presents at Credit Suisse Technology Brokers Conference (Transcript)," *SA Transcripts*, November 29, 2016.

19. Ibid.

20. Leo Sun, "International Business Machines Corp. in 6 Charts," *The Motley Fool,* August 30, 2016.

21. Ibid.

22. Robert X. Cringely, "A Glimmer of Hope for IBM," *Seeking Alpha,* October 31, 2016, https://seekingalpha.com/article/4017317-glimmer-hope-ibm.

23. James Beniger, *The Control Revolution: Technological and Economic Origins of the Information Society* (Cambridge, MA: Harvard University Press, 1986).

24. Richard Baldwin, *The Great Convergence: Information Technology and the New Globalization* (Cambridge, MA: Harvard University Press, 2016), 82.

25. James W. Cortada, *The Digital Hand,* 3 vols. (New York: Oxford University Press, 2004–2006).

26. Clayton M. Christensen, *The Innovator's Dilemma: When New Technologies Cause Great Firms to Fail* (Boston: Harvard Business Review Press, 1997).

27. For a useful discussion of his ideas and responses to them, see Bharat Anand, *The Content Trap: A Strategist's Guide to Digital Change* (New York: Random House, 2016), 330–333. On various theories of innovation familiar to IBM employees, see John F. Padgett and Walter W. Powell, "The Problem of Emergence," in *The Emergence of Organizations and Markets,* ed. John F. Padgett and Walter W. Powell (Princeton, NJ: Princeton University Press, 2012), 1–30.

28. For an early assessment of its cloud strategy, see Bob Evans, "Inside IBM's Stunning Transformation to the Cloud: 10 Key Insights," *Forbes,* June 15, 2017. For a recent example of the never-ending supply of media advice to IBM, see Steve Andriole, "Since IBM Never Called, Here's the Strategy Anyway," *Forbes,* June 6, 2017.

29. George Gilder, *Knowledge and Power: The Information Theory of Capitalism and How It Is Revolutionizing Our World* (Washington, DC: Regnery, 2013), 43–44, 47–56; Joseph E. Stiglitz and Bruce C. Greenwald, *Creating a Learning Society: A New Approach to Growth, Development, and Social Progress* (New York: Columbia University Press, 2014), 37–38.

30. Robert Fitzgerald, *The Rise of the Global Company: Multinationals and the Making of the Modern World* (Cambridge: Cambridge University Press, 2015), 503.

31. Ibid., 510.

32. Ibid., 500.

33. Jack Beach, *Leadership in My Rearview Mirror: Reflections from Vietnam, West Point and IBM* (Ketchum, ID: MC Press, 2012), 4.

34. Ibid., 5.

35. Richard Baldwin, *The Great Convergence: Information Technology and the New Globalization* (Cambridge, MA: Belknap Press of Harvard University Press, 2016), 109–110.

36. International Business Machines Corporation, SEC filing DEF14A, March 13, 2017, https://www.sec.gov/Archives/edgar/data/51143/000110465917016116/a17-2254_1def14a.htm.

37. Shareholders had no influence on such matters, despite growing discussions in recent years about whether they should. See Graeme Guthrie, *The Firm Divided: Manager-Shareholder Conflict and the Fight for Control of the Modern Corporation* (New York: Oxford University Press, 2017), 245–247.

38. Ibid., viii.

39. Interview with the author. The executive complaining about the board's age was himself 90 years old. Another retired executive, who also wished to withhold his name, made the same comment, and he was 101 years old, living in Texas.

40. The executive was Walter E. Burdick, and his comments came from his privately published memoirs intended largely for his family, Walter E. Burdick, *Family Values—Walter E. Burdick—An Autobiography* (No city, no publisher, circa 2000), 359.

41. Ernest von Simson, *The Limits of Strategy: Lessons in Leadership from the Computer Industry* (Bloomington, IN: iUniverse, 2009), 394–395.

42. Jacques Rojot, "Culture and Decision Making," in *The Oxford Handbook of Organizational Decision Making,* ed. Gerard P. Hodgkinson and William H. Starbuck (New York: Oxford University Press, 2008), 147.

43. All quotations are from Steven W. Usselman, "The Watson Dynasty: The Fiery Reign and Troubled Legacy of IBM's Founding Father and Son and The Maverick and His Machine: Thomas Watson, Sr. and the Making of IBM (review)," *Enterprise and Society* 6, no. 1 (March 2005): 189.

44. I was a salesman in that branch office and was at that meeting, witnessing what happened.

Bibliographic Essay

A LARGE NUMBER of books and scholarly articles have been published about IBM, and the company has received continuous extensive press coverage for decades. While a definitive bibliography of studies of the company would run to scores of book titles and even more articles, this bibliographic essay will point out key works. For a detailed bibliography, however, along with an account of many archival sources, consult Jeffrey R. Yost, ed., *The IBM Century: Creating the IT Revolution* (Los Alamitos, CA: IEEE Computer Society, 2011). It is also an anthology of articles written by IBM employees about the history of the firm. The endnotes in my history of IBM cite other sources, such as internal IBM publications, newspaper and magazine articles, and archival materials. IBM has a well-organized corporate archive, and the Charles Babbage Institute at the University of Minnesota has many business collections relevant to this company's history. Also not to be overlooked are the Watson Papers at New York University.

A few general histories of IBM exist, although all are out of date because they were published years ago and we know so much more today about all periods of the company's past. See Robert Sobel, *IBM, Colossus in Transition* (New York: Times Books, 1981); Saul Engelbourg, *International Business Machines: A Business History* (New York: Arno, 1976 reprint of 1954 dissertation); James W. Cortada, *Before the Computer: IBM, NCR, Burroughs, and Remington Rand and the Industry They Created, 1865–1956* (Princeton, NJ: Princeton University Press, 1993); and Emerson W. Pugh, *Building IBM: Shaping an Industry and Its Technology* (Cambridge, MA: MIT Press,

1995). Two more current accounts that discuss IBM as part of the computer industry are Jeffrey R. Yost, *The Computer Industry* (Westport, CT: Greenwood, 2005), and Martin Campbell-Kelly and Daniel D. Garcia-Swartz, *From Mainframes to Smartphones: A History of the International Computer Industry* (Cambridge, MA: Harvard University Press, 2015). IBM published a history on the occasion of its centennial celebration, Kevin Maney, Steve Hamm, and Jeffrey M. O'Brien, *Making the World Work Better: The Ideas That Shaped a Century and a Company* (Upper Saddle River, NJ: IBM Press, 2011).

On IBM's relations with the U.S. government and the computer industry, there are excellent studies. The most useful include D. M. Hart, "Red, White, and 'Big Blue': IBM and the Business-Government Interface in the United States, 1956–2000," *Enterprise and Society* 8, no. 1 (2007): 1–34, which includes a useful account of IBM's lobbying efforts; D. M. Hart, "IBM in American Politics, 1970–1999," *Business and Economic History* 28, no. 2 (Winter 1999): 49–59; Steven W. Usselman, "IBM and Its Imitators: Organizational Capabilities and the Emergence of the International Computer Industry," *Business and Economic History* 22, no. 2 (1993): 1–35; and Steven W. Usselman, "Unbundling IBM: Antitrust and the Incentives to Innovation in American Computing," in *The Challenge of Remaining Innovative: Insights from Twentieth-Century American Business,* ed. S. N. Clarke, N. Lamoreaux, and S. Usselman (Stanford, CA: Stanford Business School Books, 2009), 249–279, which provides an excellent analysis of IBM's antitrust problems. For contemporary comments regarding IBM, see International Data Corporation, *IBM and the Courts: A Six Year Journal* (Framingham, MA: IDC, 1975).

The most useful biography of Herman Hollerith is Geoffrey D. Austrian, *Herman Hollerith, Forgotten Giant of Information Processing* (New York: Columbia University Press, 1982). For more on his work and his tabulating machines, consult Lars Heide, *Punched-Card Systems and the Early Information Explosion, 1880–1945* (Baltimore: Johns Hopkins University Press, 2009). The two books should be consulted in tandem, along with Cortada, *Before the Computer.* On Thomas J. Watson Sr., the definitive biography is Kevin Maney, *The Maverick and His Machine:*

Thomas J. Watson, Sr. and the Making of IBM (Hoboken, NJ: John Wiley and Sons, 2003), but also see Richard S. Tedlow, *The Watson Dynasty: The Fiery Reign and Troubled Legacy of IBM's Founding Father and Son* (New York: HarperCollins, 2003), which includes discussion about the role of his son Thomas J. Watson Jr. One of the best business memoirs written by an American executive is by Tom Jr., covering the 1930s through the early 1970s. See Thomas J. Watson Jr. and Peter Petre, *Father, Son & Co.: My Life at IBM and Beyond* (New York: Bantam, 1990). Other personal accounts discuss IBM of the 1920s through the 1980s, such as for the 1920s to 1940s. See Walter D. Jones, "Watson and Me: Life at IBM," *IEEE Annals of the History of Computing* 24, no. 1 (2002): 4–18. On the 1930s to 1950s, see Ruth Leach Amonette, *Among Equals: A Memoir. The Rise of IBM's First Woman Corporate Vice President* (Berkeley, CA: Creative Arts Books, 1999). On IBM in Latin America, see Luis A. Lamassonne, *My Life with IBM* (Atlanta: Protea, 2000). On the 1950s to 1960s, see W. W. Simmons with R. B. Elsberry, *Inside IBM: The Watson Years, a Personal Memoir* (Pittsburgh: Dorrance, 1988). On the 1970s and 1980s, see James W. Cortada, "Carrying a Bag: Memoirs of an IBM Salesman, 1974–1981," *IEEE Annals of the History of Computing* 34, no. 4 (October–December 2013): 32–47. On the 1970s to 1980s, see Milton Drandell, *IBM: The Other Side. 101 Former Employees Look Back* (San Luis Obispo, CA: Quait, 1984); David Mercer, *The Global IBM: Leadership in Multinational Management* (New York: Dodd, Mead, 1988); and the most familiar to historians of IBM, Emerson W. Pugh, *Memories That Shaped an Industry: Decisions Leading to IBM System 360* (Cambridge, MA: MIT Press, 1984).

On IBM's technology, the key works on the earliest period are those by Austrian and Heide cited earlier. On mainframes, see Charles J. Bashe, Lyle R. Johnson, John H. Palmer, and Emerson W. Pugh, *IBM's Early Computers* (Cambridge, MA: MIT Press, 1986), and Emerson W. Pugh, Lyle R. Johnson, and John H. Palmer, *IBM's 360 and Early 370 Systems* (Cambridge, MA: MIT Press, 1991), both of which look at technological, institutional, and manufacturing aspects of technology development and production. To understand how IBM's machines fit into the broader history of computing, the essential study is Paul E. Ceruzzi, *A History of*

Modern Computing, 2nd ed. (Cambridge, MA: MIT Press, 2003). A major study about how to run computer projects based on IBM's experiences of the 1960s is Frederick P. Brooks Jr., *The Mythical Man-Month: Essays on Software Engineering* (Reading, MA: Addison-Wesley, 1975). On the role of IBM's AS/400 of the 1980s, see R. A. Bauer, E. Collar, V. Tang, J. Wind, and P. Houston, *The Silverlake Project: Transformation of IBM* (New York: Oxford University Press, 1992). Finally, on the role of services at IBM and other firms for most of the second half of the twentieth century, see Jeffrey R. Yost, *Making IT Work: A History of the Computer Services Industry* (Cambridge, MA: MIT Press, 2017).

In studies of the antitrust suit of the 1960s and 1970s, economics received considerable attention. In defense of IBM's market behavior, see Franklin M. Fisher, James W. McKie, and Richard B. Mancke, *IBM and the U.S. Data Processing Industry: An Economic History* (New York: Praeger, 1983); Franklin M. Fisher, John J. McGowan, and Joen E. Greenwood, *Folded, Spindled and Mutilated: Economic Analysis and U.S. vs. IBM* (Cambridge, MA: MIT Press, 1983). For a study critical of IBM, see Richard Thomas DeLamarter, *Big Blue: IBM's Use and Abuse of Power* (New York: Dodd, Mead, 1986). For a broader discussion of IBM's role as part of the U.S. government's promotion of the computer industry in the 1950s to 1970s, see Kenneth Flamm, *Creating the Computer: Government, Industry, and High Technology* (Washington, DC: Brookings Institution, 1988); Kenneth Flamm, *Targeting the Computer: Government Support and International Competition* (Washington, DC: Brookings Institution, 1987); and an often overlooked economic analysis of IBM's performance in the 1950s and 1960s, Alvin J. Harman, *The International Computer Industry: Innovation and Comparative Advantage* (Cambridge, MA: Harvard University Press, 1971).

There does not yet exist a full history of personal computers, although journalists have commented on IBM's PC and more broadly about the company in the 1980s and early 1990s, linking the company's woes of the period to its PC business. These include Paul Carroll, *Big Blues: The Unmaking of IBM* (New York: Crown, 1994), criticizing how IBM managed its PC business; Robert Heller, *The Fate of IBM* (Boston: Little, Brown,

1994), blaming IBM's troubles in the early 1990s on its mismanagement of the PC business; and Rex Malik, *And Tomorrow … The World? Inside IBM* (London: Millington, 1976), examining World Trade and centralized IBM management. For a forecast that IBM would go out of business, see Charles H. Fergusson and Charles R. Morris, *Computer Wars: How the West Can Win in a Post-IBM World* (New York: Times Books, 1993). For an in-depth study of the making of IBM's PC at the start of the 1980s, James Chposky and Ted Leonis, *Blue Magic: The People, Power, and Politics Behind the IBM Personal Computer* (New York: Facts on File, 1988), remains an excellent study. See also Jon Littman, *Once Upon a Time in Computerland* (Palo Alto, CA: HP Trade, 1987). A useful early study of PC computing is Paul Freiberger, *Fire in the Valley: The Making of the Personal Computer*, 2nd ed. (New York: McGraw-Hill, 1999). For a detailed study of IBM and its rivals, see Rod Canion, *Open: How Compaq Ended IBM's PC Domination and Helped Invent Modern Computing* (Dallas: BenBella, 2013).

On the broader theme of IBM's managerial practices, consult David B. Yoffie, *Strategic Management in Information Technology* (Englewood Cliffs, NJ: Prentice-Hall, 1994), 271–289. On the firm's business and product strategy, demonstrating how IBM surged in the 1950s to 1970s, see Alfred D. Chandler Jr., *Inventing the Electronic Century: The Epic Story of the Consumer Electronics and Computer Industries* (Cambridge, MA: Harvard University Press, 2005), 82–215. D. Quinn Mills and G. Bruce Friesen, *Broken Promises: An Unconventional View of What Went Wrong at IBM* (Boston: Harvard Business School Press, 1996), argues that IBM in the 1980s and 1990s got into trouble for reducing quality service to customers and for breaking its long-term full-employment practices, becoming arrogant and losing touch with its constituencies. Personnel practices have drawn attention from others, too, such as D. L. Stebenne, "IBM's 'New Deal': Employment Policies of the International Business Machines Corporation, 1933–1956," *Journal of the Historical Society* 5, no. 1 (Winter 2005): 47–77. For a study based on employee surveys done at IBM between 1967 and 1973, see Geert Hofstede, *Culture's Consequences: International Differences in Work-Related Values* (Beverly Hills, CA: Sage Publications, 1980). For a later study on related themes, see Leonard Greenhalgh, Robert B.

McKensie, and Rodrick Gilkey, *Rebalancing the Work Force at IBM: A Case Study of Redeployment and Revitalization* (Cambridge, MA: Sloan Management School, 1985). For a study by an anthropologist who examined IBM's role in Endicott, New York, see Peter C. Little, *Toxic Town: IBM, Pollution, and Industrial Risks* (New York: New York University Press, 2014). For a book on IBM's management practices covering the decades of the 1950s to 1980s and written by a company sales executive, see Buck Rodgers with Robert L. Shook, *The IBM Way: Insights into the World's Most Successful Marketing Organization* (New York: Harper and Row, 1986).

When historians discuss management practices of a corporation, they inevitably also deal with the issue of corporate culture. Useful for framing issues related to IBM are Kenneth Lipartito, "Business Culture," in *The Oxford Handbook of Business History,* ed. Geoffrey Jones and Jonathan Zeitlin (New York: Oxford University Press, 2007), 603–628, which also includes an excellent bibliography; Terrence E. Deal and Alan A. Kennedy, *Corporate Cultures: The Rites and Rituals of Corporate Life* (Reading, MA: Addison-Wesley, 1982); and Jacques Rojot, "Culture and Decision Making," in *The Oxford Handbook of Organizational Decision Making,* ed. Gerard P. Hodgkinson and William H. Starbuck (New York: Oxford University Press, 2008). Those studies should, however, be framed within the larger context of contemporary history. For my IBM history, I found the following useful: essays in Peter Hertner and Geoffrey Jones, eds., *Multinationals: Theory and History* (Aldershot: Gower, 1986); Glenn Porter, *The Rise of Big Business, 1860–1920* (Wheeling, IL: Harlan Davidson, 1992); Geoffrey Jones, *Multinationals and Global Capitalism: From the Nineteenth to the Twenty-First Century* (New York: Oxford University Press, 2005); Youssef Cassis, "Big Business," in *The Oxford Handbook of Business History,* ed. Geoffrey Jones and Jonathan Zeitlin (New York: Oxford University Press, 2007), and other essays in this volume. Alfred D. Chandler Jr., *The Visible Hand: The Managerial Revolution in American Business* (Cambridge, MA: Harvard University Press, 1977), remains essential reading.

On what it was like to work at IBM in the middle decades of the twentieth century, several memoirs are useful. These include Jacques Maisonrouge, *Inside IBM: A Personal Story* (New York: McGraw-Hill, 1988), written by a French IBMer who became CEO of World Trade. The original French edition, *Manager International* (Paris: Editions Robert Laffont, 1985), has slightly different content. Both laud the firm. For insights on engineering at IBM, see Garth Lambert, *Fifty Years in Information Systems* (No city: LuLu Press, 2005, 2006), covering the 1950s through the 1990s. On product development in the 1950s to 1970s, see George J. Laurer, *Engineering Was Fun! An Autobiography* (No city: LuLu Press, 2006, 2007), but it should be consulted in tandem with a similar memoir by Joseph C. Logue, "From Vacuum Tubes to Very Large Scale Integration: A Personal Memoir," *Annals of the History of Computing* 20, no. 3 (July–September 1998): 55–68.

The period of IBM's decline in the 1980s and early 1990s and revival in the later 1990s has been the subject of investigation by journalists and one IBMer. These include three well-informed studies: Robert X. Cringely (a journalist whose name is a pseudonym for Mark Stephens), *The Decline and Fall of IBM: End of an American Icon?* (Lexington, KY: NeRDTV, 2014), which, while negative, also offers suggestions on how the company can improve, largely by returning to its previous culture and behaviors; Peter E. Greulich (a retired IBM manager), *A View from Beneath the Dancing Elephant: Rediscovering IBM's Corporate Constitution* (Austin, TX: MBI Concepts, 2014); and Peter E. Greulich, *THINK Again!: IBM Can Maximize Shareholder Value* (Austin, TX: MBI Concepts, 2017), his most thorough analysis of the company's financial and business performance. IBM's CEO of the 1990s also published his memoirs of his time at IBM. See Louis V. Gerstner Jr., *Who Says Elephants Can't Dance?: Inside IBM's Historic Turnaround* (New York: HarperBusiness, 2002). Two studies by journalists review the Gerstner period. See Robert Slater, *Saving Big Blue: Leadership Lessons and Turnaround Tactics of IBM's Lou Gerstner* (New York: McGraw-Hill, 1999), and Doug Gaar, *IBM Redux: Lou Gerstner and the Business Turnaround of the Decade* (New York: HarperBusiness, 1999). Both are useful, detailed studies of IBM in the 1990s.

There is no full history of IBM World Trade, although it is discussed in bits and pieces in many of the sources cited earlier. On IBM in Europe and how it worked at its corporate headquarters in New York, there are the previously cited Maisonrouge memoirs, *Inside IBM*. The following excellent, although dated, study by a journalist remains an essential source: Nancy Foy, *The Sun Never Sets on IBM: The Culture and Folklore of IBM World Trade* (New York: William Morrow, 1975). On the 1950s to 1970s, see James W. Cortada, *The Digital Flood: The Diffusion of Information Technology across the U.S., Europe, and Asia* (New York: Oxford University Press, 2012). On IBM's relations with Hitler, there is the controversial book by Edwin Black, *IBM and the Holocaust: The Strategic Alliance between Nazi Germany and America's Most Powerful Corporation* (New York: Crown, 2001), and on IBM's post–World War II activities in Germany, see Corinna Schlombs, "The 'IBM Family': American Welfare Capitalism, Labor, and Gender in Postwar Germany," *IEEE Annals of the History of Computing* 39, no. 4 (October–December 2017): 12–26. A series of studies add to our understanding of IBM's role. See Steven W. Usselman, "Selecting Flexible Champions: Markets, Firms, and Public Policies in the Evolution of Computing in the U.S., U.K., and Japan," *Journal of Business Studies (Ryukoku University)* 35, no. 1 (June 1995): 27–43. On European debates, see Magnus Johansson, "Big Blue Gets Beaten: The Technological and Political Controversy of the First Large Swedish Computerization Project in a Rhetoric of Technology Perspective," *Annals of the History of Computing* 21, no. 2 (1999): 14–30; Corinna Schlombs, "Engineering International Expansion: IBM and Remington Rand in European Computer Markets," *IEEE Annals of the History of Computing* 30, no. 4 (October–December 2008): 42–58; Petri Paju, "National Projects and International Users: Finland and Early European Computerization," *IEEE Annals of the History of Computing* 30, no. 4 (October–December 2008): 77–91; Pierre E. Mounier-Kuhn, *L'Informatique de la seconde Guerre mondiale au Plan Calcul en France: L'émergence d'une science* (Paris: Presses de l'Université Paris-Sorbonne, 2010); Pierre E. Mounier-Kuhn, "Sur L'Histoire de L'Informatique en France," *Engineering Science and Education Journal* 3, no. 1 (February 1995): 37–40; Pierre E. Mounier-Kuhn, "Product Policies in Two French Computer Firms: SEA and Bull (1948–64)," in *Information Acumen: The Understanding and Use of Knowledge in Modern Business,* ed. Lisa Bu-Frierman (London: Routledge, 1994),

113–135; Alain Beltran, "Arrivée de l'informatique et organization des enterprises françaises (fin des années 1960–début des années 1980)," *Enterprises et histoire* 60 (September 2010): 122–137; François Hochereau, "Le movement de l'informatisation d'une grande entreprise. Les visions organisantes successives d'un processus d'activité stratégique," *Enterprises et histoire* 60 (September 2010): 138–157; Alfonso Molina, "The Nature of Failure in a Technological Initiative: The Case of the Europrocessor," *Technological Analysis and Strategic Management* 10, no. 1 (March 1998): 23–40. For issues central to the study of global diffusion of IT, see Cortada, *The Digital Flood*. Finally, a useful account, but nearly impossible to find copies of, is James Connolly, *History of Computing in Europe* (Paris: IBM World Trade Corporation, 1967). Another book written by an IBM employee that is worth consulting is David Mercer, *IBM: How the World's Most Successful Corporation Is Managed* (London: Kogan Page, 1987). On the early years of World Trade, not to be missed is Petri Paju and Thomas Haigh, "IBM Rebuilds Europe: The Curious Case of the Transnational Typewriter," *Enterprise and Society* 17, no. 2 (June 2016): 265–300. On IBM France, see *Chroniques de la Compaignie IBM France, 1914-1987* (Paris: IBM Corporation, 1988).

On the European "national champion" programs and how IBM was part of the topic, there is a large body of literature, including Margaret Sharp, ed., *Europe and the New Technologies: Six Case Studies in Innovation and Adjustment* (Ithaca, NY: Cornell University Press, 1986); ed. Richard O. Hundley,, *The Future of the Information Revolution in Europe: Proceedings of an International Conference* (Santa Monica, CA: RAND Corporation, 2001); Richard Coopey, "Empire and Technology: Information and Technology Policy in Postwar Britain and France," in *Information Technology Policy: An International Perspective,* ed. Richard Coopey (Oxford: Oxford University Press, 2004), 144–168; Eda Kranakis, "Politics, Business, and European Information Technology Policy: From the Treaty of Rome to Unidata, 1958–1975," in *Information Technology Policy: An International Perspective,* ed. Richard Coopey (Oxford: Oxford University Press, 2004), 209–246; Dimitris Assimakopoulos, Rebecca Marschan-Piekkari, and Stuart MacDonald, "ESPRIT: Europe's Response to US and Japanese Domination of Information Technology," in *Information Technology Policy: An International Perspective,* ed. Richard Coopey (Oxford: Oxford University Press, 2004), 247–263; James W. Cortada, "Public Policies and the Development of National Computer Industries in Britain, France, and the Soviet Union, 1940–80," *Journal of Contemporary History* 44, no. 3 (2009): 493–512; Pascal Griset, "Du 'temps réel' aux premiers réseaux: une entreprise rêvée, une informatique à l'épreuve du quotidian (des années 1970)," *Enterprises et Histoire* 60 (September 2010): 98–121; Gerard Alberts, "Appropriating America: Americanization in the History of European Computing," *IEEE Annals of the History of Computing* 32, no. 2 (April–June 2010): 4–5; Arthe Van Laer, "Developing an EC Computer Policy, 1965–1974," *IEEE Annals of the History of Computing* 32, no. 1 (January–March 2010): 44–59. Less consulted, but informed by economic and factual analysis, are Raimund Vollmer, *Mythos IBM: Aufbruch ins nächste Jahrtausend,* vol. 1, *Irrungen und Wirrungen* (Reutlingen: Verlag Blank-Vollmer, 1987), the earlier Henry Bakis, *I.B.M.: Une multinationale régionale de Grenoble* (Grenoble: Presses Universitaires de Grenoble, 1977), and contemporaneous and with a German perspective, Hermonn Relboldt and Raimund Vollmer, *Der Markt sind Wir: Die IBM und ihre Mitbewerber* (Stuttgart: Buchmagazin Verlag Computer-Buch-und Hobby GmbH, 1978). Also useful is William Rodgers, *THINK: A Biography of the Watsons and IBM* (New York: Stein and Day, 1972). On IBM's later role in Europe, see Roger Adraï, *IBM: L'Héritage dilapidé?* (Montrouge: Éditions John Libbey, 1994).

For a discussion of how many historians discussed IBM there is James W. Cortada, "Change and Continuity at IBM: Key Themes in Histories of IBM," *Business History Review* 92, no. 1 (2018): 117–148.

Index

Board of directors (cont.)
  during Great Depression, 97–98
  and IBM's decline, 440, 441, 460–461,
    463–466
  during IBM's early years, 5
  members of, 610–613, 674n39
  and Sam Palmisano, 524–526
  reporting to Thomas J. Watson Sr., 70
  and resistance to investing, 213
  and Ginni Rometty, 564
  secrecy of, 663n36
  transitions within, 533
Boca Raton (Florida), 385, 388, 392, 396,
  410–411, 416
Boeing, 162, 384
Bonuses
  and appraisal system, 568
  and banded employees, 662–663n19
  and corporate culture, 235
  and early retirement, 254–255
  and employee ranking, 444
  and growth strategy, 605
  and IBM benefits, 250
  and IBM sales culture, 49
  and layoffs, 542–543
  and PC sales, 417
  and poaching by rival firms, 262
  and quotas, 242, 245
  reduction of, 670n24
  and S/360, 224
  and shift away from leasing, 313
Boorstin, Daniel, 16
Booz Allen Hamilton, 512
Bork, Robert, 341
Braitmayer, Otto, 40, 69–70
Branch offices, 49f, 56f
  employees of, 244–245
  and engineering team, 79
  and excess employees, 255
  and Family Dinners, 117–118
  in former Iron Curtain countries, 374
  during Great Depression, 96

implementation of, 48
location of, 55
and market demand, 145
overseas during World War II, 142–143
and PC sales, 391
and reporting, 246
and sales reports, 51
and territory, 52
and Thomas J. Watson Sr., 628n41
Branding
  and "Baby Blues," 451
  and Louis V. Gerstner Jr., 474, 477
  and Internet adoption, 520–521
  and logos, 64–65
  and name recognition, 588–589
  of professions with IBM name, 84
Bribery, 248–249
Bricklin, Daniel, 383
British Empire, 88, 113
British Tabulating Machine Company (BTM),
  113, 196, 289
Brooks, Frederick P. Jr., 210–211, 220, 223,
  338, 638n52
Brown, Charlie, 457, 470
Brown University, 134
Bryce, James Wares, 69–70, 75, 76, 81, 130,
  155–156
Budgets, 241–243
Buffett, Warren, 549, 669n4
Bullen, Richard H. "Dick," 191
Bundles, 198, 259
Bundy, Harlow E., 12–13
Bundy, Willard H., 13
Bundy, Willard Legrand, 12–13
Bundy Manufacturing Company, 12–13,
  113–114
Bundy Time Recording Company, 13
Burdick, Walter E. "Walt," 255, 457, 468–469,
  675n40
Bureaucracy. *See also* micromanagement
  and antitrust cases, 350
  CEO struggles against, 467

Cloud computing
and Corporate financial objectives, 570–571
customers' shift to, 583, 604
and IBM competitors, 535–536, 558
IBM's slow shift to, 178, 547–548, 552, 584
and investors, 594
as IT outsourcing, 68
and outsourcing, 512
Sam Palmisano's nurturing of, 526
and Roadmap 2015, 554
and technology life cycles, 600–601
CMOS technology, 484
COBOL, 175, 364
Cocke, John, 403, 404
Codd, Edgar F. "Ted," 153–154
Cognitive Business Group, 576, 577, 633n33
Cognitive computing
in annual report, 627n26
and business strategy, 592
emergence of, 523
revenue from, 587
and Ginni Rometty, 560, 609–610
and software, 583
and technology life cycles, 600–601
and Watson computer, 573–577
Cohen, Stephen S., 385
Cold War
and computer technology, 353
end of, 373
and GPS, 515–516
and IBM R&D, 167–170
and IBM's Golden Age, 151–152
and military computing, 199
and Soviet Europe, 368–372
Collaboration. See teamwork
COLOSSUS, 131–132
Columbia University
and Wallace Eckert, 153, 154
and Herman Hollerith, 19
IBM ties with, 85, 127
and Moore School computing meeting,
summer 1946, 155

Commercial applications
of artificial intelligence, 575–576
of computers, 151, 161, 199
of data processing, 85
and System 360, 215
Commissions, 49, 52, 224, 242, 417,
662–663n19
Commodore Business Machines, 383, 414
Communications Workers of America, 540–541
Communist Europe, 360–361, 363, 369, 376.
See also Soviet Union
Compagnie Internacionale pour l'Informatique
(CII), 291
Compaq. See also Hewlett-Packard (H-P)
acquisition of by H-P, 586
as beneficiary of IBM eminence, 395
and Bill Gates, 397
as IBM competitor, 310, 311, 595
and IT ecosystem, 380
and open standards, 398
and PC business, 400–401, 411, 447, 457
and speed to market, 395, 406
Compatibility
and Cold War–era computing, 272
and IBM competitors, 225–227, 262–263,
293, 302, 304–305, 310–312, 326, 396,
399–400
and mainframes, 207–212
and PC business, 405–406
and PC Jr., 395
and Social Security, 101, 119
and Soviet computers, 362–365, 367
and System 360, 215, 217–218
and technology life cycles, 597
Competition
under John Akers's restructuring, 468–469
among IBM divisions, 192, 309
and antitrust cases, 105–106, 187, 351,
495–496
and Frank T. Cary, 304–306
and computer industry, 177–178
and C-T-R, 56

and software market, 457
and Windows, 402, 406–407
Middle East, 113, 292
Middleware, 519, 521
Military contracts, 122, 151
Military-industrial complex, 162
Mills, D. Quinn, 412–413, 428, 430
Mills, Steven A., 555
Minicomputers, 263–264, 310, 385, 414
Minorities, 250–251
MITI (Japan's Ministry of International Trade and Industry), 292–294, 326
Mizushina, Ko, 143
Mobile devices, 527
Mobile Machine Records Units (MRUs), 126–127
Mobile technologies, 570
Modularity, 217
Moerner, William E., 588
Moffat, Robert, 555, 603
Moneyweight Scale Company, 15
Monolithic chips, 259
Monopolies, 7, 8, 186–187. *See also* antitrust challenges
Moore, Gordon, 263–264
Moore School lectures, 155, 179
Moore's Law, 263, 395, 595
Morgan, J. P., 7
Morison, H. Graham, 186, 187–188
Mowery, David C., 548
Müller, Alex, 588
Munitions Manufacturing Corporation, 124
Mussolini, Benito, 116

Nashville (Tennessee), 55, 246
National Accounts Division (NAD), 245, 246, 312
National Bureau of Standards, 155
National Cash Register Company (NCR)
   and antitrust case, 32, 41
   and antitrust cases, 331, 335
   consolidation of, 10–11
   and cryptanalysis, 132
   and C-T-R, 23
   and C-T-R recruitment, 40
   demise of, 580
   during Great Depression, 97
   as IBM competitor, 67, 225–226, 262
   and IBM corporate culture, 37–38
   and IBM employees, 75
   and IBM sales culture, 50–51
   and sales culture, 28–29
   and Thomas J. Watson Sr., 30, 31
National Marketing Division (NMD), 245, 312
National Medal of Science, 403
National Medal of Technology, 403
National Recovery Act (NRA), 103
National Security Agency, 162
National Socialism. *See* Nazis
NATO (North Atlantic Treaty Organization), 272
Navigation systems, 266
Nazi Germany. *See also* Germany
   and Dehomag, 114, 634n31
   and Henry Ford, 116–117
   and Holocaust recordkeeping, 140–143
   and IBM, 122–123, 138–139, 603
   and Thomas J. Watson Sr., 113, 116
Nelson, Richard, 548
Nepotism, 184, 195, 200
Net earnings
   at C-T-R/IBM, 1914–1924, 57t
   at IBM, 1984–1990, 274t
Net profits, 241
   under Frank T. Cary, 307
   and global performance, 287–288
   and personnel practices, 249–250
   of World Trade, 1949–1990, 320–323, 321f
Netscape, 327
Networking
   and IBM's e-business, 521
   and killer apps, 383
   and open standards, 505